Market Risk Analysis
Volume IV

Value-at-Risk Models

Market Risk Analysis
Volume IV

Value-at-Risk Models

Carol Alexander

John Wiley & Sons, Ltd

Published in 2008 by   John Wiley & Sons Ltd, The Atrium, Southern Gate, Chichester,
West Sussex PO19 8SQ, England
Telephone   (+44) 1243 779777

Email (for orders and customer service enquiries): cs-books@wiley.co.uk

Visit our Home Page on www.wiley.com

Other Wiley Editorial Offices

John Wiley & Sons Inc., 111 River Street, Hoboken, NJ 07030, USA

Jossey-Bass, 989 Market Street, San Francisco, CA 94103-1741, USA

Wiley-VCH Verlag GmbH, Boschstr. 12, D-69469 Weinheim, Germany

John Wiley & Sons Australia Ltd, 42 McDougall Street, Milton, Queensland 4064, Australia

John Wiley & Sons (Asia) Pte Ltd, 2 Clementi Loop #02-01, Jin Xing Distripark, Singapore 129809

John Wiley & Sons Canada Ltd, 6045 Freemont Blvd, Mississauga, Ontario, Canada L5R 4J3

Wiley also publishes its books in a variety of electronic formats. Some content that appears in print may not be
available in electronic books

British Library Cataloguing in Publication Data

A catalogue record for this book is available from the British Library

ISBN 978-0-470-99788-8 (H/B)

Typeset in 10/12pt Times by Integra Software Services Pvt. Ltd, Pondicherry, India
Printed and bound by CPI Group (UK) Ltd, Croydon, CR0 4YY

C9780470997888_161222

To Boris and Helen

Contents

List of Figures

List of Tables

List of Examples

Foreword

How many children dream of one day becoming risk managers? I very much doubt little Carol Jenkins, as she was called then, did. She dreamt about being a wild white horse, or a mermaid swimming with dolphins, as any normal little girl does. As I start crunching into two kilos of Toblerone that Carol Alexander-Pézier gave me for Valentine's day (perhaps to coax me into writing this foreword), I see the distinctive silhouette of the Matterhorn on the yellow package and I am reminded of my own dreams of climbing mountains and travelling to distant planets. Yes, adventure and danger! That is the stuff of happiness, especially when you daydream as a child with a warm cup of cocoa in your hands.

As we grow up, dreams lose their naivety but not necessarily their power. Knowledge makes us discover new possibilities and raises new questions. We grow to understand better the consequences of our actions, yet the world remains full of surprises. We taste the sweetness of success and the bitterness of failure. We grow to be responsible members of society and to care for the welfare of others. We discover purpose, confidence and a role to fulfil; but we also find that we continuously have to deal with risks.

Leafing through the hundreds of pages of this four-volume series you will discover one of the goals that Carol gave herself in life: to set the standards for a new profession, that of market risk manager, and to provide the means of achieving those standards. Why is market risk management so important? Because in our modern economies, market prices balance the supply and demand of most goods and services that fulfil our needs and desires. We can hardly take a decision, such as buying a house or saving for a later day, without taking some market risks. Financial firms, be they in banking, insurance or asset management, manage these risks on a grand scale. Capital markets and derivative products offer endless ways to transfer these risks among economic agents.

But should market risk management be regarded as a professional activity? Sampling the material in these four volumes will convince you, if need be, of the vast amount of knowledge and skills required. A good market risk manager should master the basics of calculus, linear algebra, probability – including stochastic calculus – statistics and econometrics. He should be an astute student of the markets, familiar with the vast array of modern financial instruments and market mechanisms, and of the econometric properties of prices and returns in these markets. If he works in the financial industry, he should also be well versed in regulations and understand how they affect his firm. That sets the academic syllabus for the profession.

Carol takes the reader step by step through all these topics, from basic definitions and principles to advanced problems and solution methods. She uses a clear language, realistic illustrations with recent market data, consistent notation throughout all chapters, and provides a huge range of worked-out exercises on Excel spreadsheets, some of which demonstrate analytical tools only available in the best commercial software packages. Many chapters on advanced subjects such as GARCH models, copulas, quantile regressions, portfolio theory, options and volatility surfaces are as informative as and easier to understand than entire books devoted to these subjects. Indeed, this is the first series of books entirely dedicated to the discipline of market risk analysis written by one person, and a very good teacher at that.

A profession, however, is more than an academic discipline; it is an activity that fulfils some societal needs, that provides solutions in the face of evolving challenges, that calls for a special code of conduct; it is something one can aspire to. Does market risk management face such challenges? Can it achieve significant economic benefits?

As market economies grow, more ordinary people of all ages with different needs and risk appetites have financial assets to manage and borrowings to control. What kind of mortgages should they take? What provisions should they make for their pensions? The range of investment products offered to them has widened far beyond the traditional cash, bond and equity classes to include actively managed funds (traditional or hedge funds), private equity, real estate investment trusts, structured products and derivative products facilitating the trading of more exotic risks – commodities, credit risks, volatilities and correlations, weather, carbon emissions, etc. – and offering markedly different return characteristics from those of traditional asset classes. Managing personal finances is largely about managing market risks. How well educated are we to do that?

Corporates have also become more exposed to market risks. Beyond the traditional exposure to interest rate fluctuations, most corporates are now exposed to foreign exchange risks and commodity risks because of globalization. A company may produce and sell exclusively in its domestic market and yet be exposed to currency fluctuations because of foreign competition. Risks that can be hedged effectively by shareholders, if they wish, do not have to be hedged in-house. But hedging some risks in-house may bring benefits (e.g. reduction of tax burden, smoothing of returns, easier planning) that are not directly attainable by the shareholder.

Financial firms, of course, should be the experts at managing market risks; it is their métier. Indeed, over the last generation, there has been a marked increase in the size of market risks handled by banks in comparison to a reduction in the size of their credit risks. Since the 1980s, banks have provided products (e.g. interest rate swaps, currency protection, index linked loans, capital guaranteed investments) to facilitate the risk management of their customers. They have also built up arbitrage and proprietary trading books to profit from perceived market anomalies and take advantage of their market views. More recently, banks have started to manage credit risks actively by transferring them to the capital markets instead of warehousing them. Bonds are replacing loans, mortgages and other loans are securitized, and many of the remaining credit risks can now be covered with credit default swaps. Thus credit risks are being converted into market risks.

The rapid development of capital markets and, in particular, of derivative products bears witness to these changes. At the time of writing this foreword, the total notional size of all derivative products exceeds \$500 trillion whereas, in rough figures, the bond and money markets stand at about \$80 trillion, the equity markets half that and loans half that again. Credit derivatives by themselves are climbing through the \$30 trillion mark. These derivative markets are zero-sum games; they are all about market risk management – hedging, arbitrage and speculation.

This does not mean, however, that all market risk management problems have been resolved. We may have developed the means and the techniques, but we do not necessarily understand how to address the problems. Regulators and other experts setting standards and policies are particularly concerned with several fundamental issues. To name a few:

1. How do we decide what market risks should be assessed and over what time horizons? For example, should the loan books of banks or long-term liabilities of pension funds be marked to market, or should we not be concerned with pricing things that will not be traded in the near future? We think there is no general answer to this question about the most appropriate description of risks. The descriptions must be adapted to specific management problems.
2. In what contexts should market risks be assessed? Thus, what is more risky, fixed or floating rate financing? Answers to such questions are often dictated by accounting standards or other conventions that must be followed and therefore take on economic significance. But the adequacy of standards must be regularly reassessed. To wit, the development of International Accounting Standards favouring mark-to-market and hedge accounting where possible (whereby offsetting risks can be reported together).
3. To what extent should risk assessments be 'objective'? Modern regulations of financial firms (Basel II Amendment, 1996) have been a major driver in the development of risk assessment methods. Regulators naturally want a 'level playing field' and objective rules. This reinforces a natural tendency to assess risks purely on the basis of statistical evidence and to neglect personal, forward-looking views. Thus one speaks too often about risk 'measurements' as if risks were physical objects instead of risk 'assessments' indicating that risks are potentialities that can only be guessed by making a number of assumptions (i.e. by using models). Regulators try to compensate for this tendency by asking risk managers to draw scenarios and to stress-test their models.

There are many other fundamental issues to be debated, such as the natural tendency to focus on micro risk management – because it is easy – rather than to integrate all significant risks and to consider their global effect – because that is more difficult. In particular, the assessment and control of systemic risks by supervisory authorities is still in its infancy. But I would like to conclude by calling attention to a particular danger faced by a nascent market risk management profession, that of separating risks from returns and focusing on downside-risk limits.

It is central to the ethics of risk managers to be independent and to act with integrity. Thus risk managers should not be under the direct control of line managers of profit centres and they should be well remunerated independently of company results. But in some firms this is also understood as denying risk managers access to profit information. I remember a risk commission that had to approve or reject projects but, for internal political reasons, could not have any information about their expected profitability. For decades, credit officers in most banks operated under such constraints: they were supposed to accept or reject deals a priori, without knowledge of their pricing. Times have changed. We understand now, at least in principle, that the essence of risk management is not simply to reduce or control risks but to achieve an optimal balance between risks and returns.

Yet, whether for organizational reasons or out of ignorance, risk management is often confined to setting and enforcing risk limits. Most firms, especially financial firms, claim to have well-thought-out risk management policies, but few actually state trade-offs between risks and returns. Attention to risk limits may be unwittingly reinforced by regulators. Of course it is not the role of the supervisory authorities to suggest risk–return trade-offs; so supervisors impose risk limits, such as value at risk relative to capital, to ensure safety and fair competition in the financial industry. But a regulatory limit implies severe penalties if breached, and thus a probabilistic constraint acquires an economic value. Banks must therefore pay attention to the uncertainty in their value-at-risk estimates. The effect would be rather perverse if banks ended up paying more attention to the probability of a probability than to their entire return distribution.

With *Market Risk Analysis* readers will learn to understand these long-term problems in a realistic context. Carol is an academic with a strong applied interest. She has helped to design the curriculum for the Professional Risk Managers' International Association (PRMIA) qualifications, to set the standards for their professional qualifications, and she maintains numerous contacts with the financial industry through consulting and seminars. In *Market Risk Analysis* theoretical developments may be more rigorous and reach a more advanced level than in many other books, but they always lead to practical applications with numerous examples in interactive Excel spreadsheets. For example, unlike 90% of the finance literature on hedging that is of no use to practitioners, if not misleading at times, her concise expositions on this subject give solutions to real problems.

In summary, if there is any good reason for not treating market risk management as a separate discipline, it is that market risk management should be the business of *all* decision makers involved in finance, with primary responsibilities on the shoulders of the most senior managers and board members. However, there is so much to be learnt and so much to be further researched on this subject that it is proper for professional people to specialize in it. These four volumes will fulfil most of their needs. They only have to remember that, to be effective, they have to be good communicators and ensure that their assessments are properly integrated in their firm's decision-making process.

Jacques Pézier

Preface to Volume IV

Financial risk management is a relatively new discipline. It is driven internally by the need for optimal returns on risk-based capital and, ultimately, by the survival of the firm. External drivers include clients, who are typically risk averse, and industry regulators, whose objectives are to protect investors and to promote competition, although their ultimate concern is for financial stability in the global economy. In recent years market volatility has been rising as trading focuses on increasingly complex instruments whose risks are extremely difficult to assess. The origins of financial securities, futures and options go back several centuries, yet we are only just beginning to understand how to quantify the risks of complex financial products realistically, even though this makes all the difference between success and failure in the financial industry.

I liken the risk management profession as it stands today to that of medicine in the eighteenth century. Until this time general ill health in the population and continual outbreaks of uncontrolled diseases were met with ignorance, masked by mumbo-jumbo, in the medical profession. As a result average life expectancy was short and, for most, the quality of life was poor. But in the nineteenth century a number of comprehensive texts such as *Gray's Anatomy*[1] began to educate the medical profession. Such is the knowledge we have acquired during the past two centuries that nowadays even a general practitioner must spend many years in training. Modern medical training is very demanding, but as a result people live longer and healthier lives.

Turmoil in the banking industry following a collapse of credit markets began soon after I finished writing the *Market Risk Analysis* series. In September 2008 the Treasury-Eurodollar (TED) spread (which in normal markets is about 5–10 basis points) exceeded 300 basis points, and it remains above 200 basis points at the time of writing. The value of stocks around the entire globe has fallen drastically and rapidly, reminiscent of the world stock market crash of 1929. To give the reader some idea of the extent of the losses: between the end of August and mid November 1929 the benchmark Dow Jones Industrial Average Index of 30 US blue chip stocks lost almost 50% of its value; from the end of April 2008 until the end of October 2008 it had lost almost 40% of its value. The US markets are not falling as much as stock markets in most other countries and the dollar is stronger now than it has been for many years. Several exchanges have suspended trading on more than one occasion, and even then several markets have crashed by more than 10% in a single day. The currencies of some emerging

---

[1] See http://en.wikipedia.org/wiki/Gray's_Anatomy.

markets, such as the Korean wan, have plummeted in value against the US dollar. Markets in Europe have fallen more than 50% since the end of April, and some experts say further falls are imminent at the time of writing.

Why is this happening? And what is the likely effect on the financial system? These questions are not easy to answer, as the crisis is still ongoing at the time of writing. All the reasons for, and effects of, a catastrophe are usually revealed only after the event.

SUMMARY OF THE 2008 BANKING CRISIS

There is a trigger for all financial crises, and in this case the first crack appeared with the sub-prime mortgage crisis in the US. During the years 2004–2006 stock markets across the globe surged as the cost of credit reached all-time lows. New ways of securitizing loans meant that counterparty credit quality mattered little to the salesman on commission. European banks, and investors in countries where yields had been extremely low for years, flocked to buy collateralized debt obligations (CDO) and similar new products. The main sellers were the five largest investment banks: Goldman Sachs, Morgan Stanley, Merrill Lynch, Lehman Brothers and Bear Stearns. Even retail banks began to rely on securitizing their loans and short-term funding via the interbank market rather than on a deposit base.

Whenever there is uncertainty in a free market economy, this promotes a cycle in which optimism can lead to exuberance, followed by doubt and finally panic. The basic principle underlying the CDO is sound – after all, if the senior tranche of a mortgage-backed security corresponds to two-thirds of the whole and the recovery rate on defaulting mortgages is 50%, it would only be affected if more than two-thirds of the creditors defaulted! So we had reason to be optimistic in the mid 2000's and there was a strong market for these new yield-enhancement vehicles. A fundamental problem was that their pricing lacked transparency. Because of the very considerable pricing model risk – the mark-to-model prices being crucially dependent on the assumptions made – doubts began to infiltrate the exuberance. And, as doubt turned to panic, the market dried up, so market prices became even more unreliable than the model prices. Given the mark-to-market accounting framework used by banks, a huge liquidity risk appeared in the trading book, and this was not covered by the bank's regulatory capital.

As liquidity fell out of the CDO market, banks turned to the interbank market to fund their liquidity gap. Because cash-rich banks demanded such high levels of collateral guarantees, other banks – and hedge funds, some of which were very highly leveraged – had great difficulty rolling over credit lines. Hedge funds were hit particularly hard. As the bull market turned, the values of their investments began to fall, and they had less collateral than usual to meet these larger guarantees. They have been forced to liquidate investments to meet collateral calls, increasing the downward pressure on stocks. The result was a crash in market prices across the globe during October 2008, with emerging stock markets and currencies being the worst hit, as US and European hedge funds liquidated their holdings in emerging markets.

The full extent of the current financial crisis first began to unfold in September 2008, with the failure of three of the five largest investment banks and of the US insurance giant AIG which, like the huge financial conglomerates Fannie Mae and Freddie Mac a few months before, was bailed out by the US government. Speculative short selling on the last two major investment banks, Goldman Sachs and Morgan Stanley, spread to the many retail banks in various countries that had been actively operating in capital markets since the repeal of the Glass-Steagall agreement in 1999,[2] either buying CDOs or using proprietary trading in derivatives to boost profits. All three Icelandic banks defaulted, and with this some savers in other countries lost their capital. Then volatility in banking sector stocks spilled over into energy, commodities and related stocks, on fears of a falling demand for oil and raw materials with the onset of a global recession.

Eventually governments responded by increasing deposit protection, lowering interest rates and providing additional liquidity. As a last resort, schemes for partial nationalisation of banks have been proposed – schemes that include caps on the remuneration of executives and traders – along with bans on short selling to attempt to stem the slide in stock prices. Regulators disregarded anti-monopoly laws as distressed banks were taken over by large cash-rich retail banks. The banking sector has now moved towards oligopolistic competition, with a few huge conglomerates such as JP Morgan dominating the markets. Given the unthinkable threat of a collapse of the global banking system in which the general public lose their savings, most governments have now raised deposit insurance ceilings.

CAUSES AND EFFECTS OF THE CRISIS

A catalyst for this particular crisis was Alan Greenspan's policy of promoting US growth by keeping US interest rates low. After the Russian crisis in 1998 US treasury rates were also brought down, but as the market recovered interest rates were raised to prevent inflation increasing. During the technology crash in 2001 and 2002 US interest rates were brought down to about 1%, which encouraged increased consumption and promoted US exports, and thus revived the US economy. After the recovery started Greenspan did not raise interest rates quickly enough. There were no fears of inflation. Yet, every time interest rates are held too low for too long, it creates a bubble. This time the bubble was caused by an 'easy credit' environment, culminating in the 'credit crunch' which marked the beginning of the 2008 financial crisis.

The main factor underlying this financial crisis is the intrinsic instability in the banking system resulting from the lack of unified and intelligent principles for the accounting, regulation, and risk management of financial institutions. These principles have evolved separately in each framework, each without sufficient regard for the other two disciplines.

One of the major derivatives markets is driven by the different accounting frameworks used by banks and their clients. Differences between the principles of cost (or value) accounting used by non-financial companies on the one hand, and the mark-to-market (MtM) accounting used by banks in their trading books on the other hand, drives the market for interest rate swaps and their derivatives. Of course, companies will try to finance themselves by issuing bonds, but short term liquidity gaps are financed by taking loans from banks. Banks prefer to lend at a floating rate because this has very low risk in MtM accounting. On the other hand,

---

[2] The Glass-Steagall agreement of 1933 was named after the two US senators who proposed it in response to the 1929 stock market crash. Under this agreement *retail banks* and *commercial banks* were depository taking institutions, and only *investment banks* traded in capital markets, to create secondary markets for the bond issues they underwrote. The agreement was repealed in 1999, allowing retail and commercial banks to trade in capital markets, but investment banks were still not allowed to take deposits. The net effect of this asymmetry was that retail and commercial banks were better funded than investment banks. In September 2008 Goldman Sachs and Morgan Stanley were granted the status of 'bank holding companies', allowing them to take deposits. So, the distinction between retail and commercial banks on the one hand, and investment banks on the other, is disintegrating.

floating rate notes and bonds have high risk in cost accounting, so companies prefer to take loans at fixed rates, which have low risk in cost accounting. Thus, banks double their business, issuing low risk notes and then offering interest rate swaps for floating into fixed rates. And, since fixed rates have high risk in MtM accounting, they use derivatives on interest rate swaps to hedge.

In relation to the underlying securities markets and in relation to world gross domestic product (GDP) the volume of financial derivatives traded is huge. At the end of 2007 the total notional outstanding on bond issues was about \$80 trillion and the value of company stocks was about \$40 trillion. Relatively few stock and bond holders hedge their positions because securities are often held by investors that hope to make a profit over the long term. Thus the notional size of the derivatives market required for investors to hedge is a small fraction of \$120 trillion. Many companies involved with importing and exporting goods hedge their exposures to exchange rate fluctuations, and to rising interest rates. The size of these exposures is related to the value of all goods produced in the world economy. World GDP was about \$75 trillion in 2007, so corporate hedging activities should amount to some small fraction of this. Thus the two hedging activities should result in a derivatives market with notional size being just a small fraction of \$200 trillion. However, the total notional size of derivatives markets in 2007 was about \$600 trillion.

Before the crisis, the daily average trading volume (DATV) on derivatives exchanges was about \$2 trillion. Foreign exchange forward contracts had DATV of between \$2 and \$3 trillion, and other over-the-counter (OTC) derivatives trading amounted to about \$1 trillion per day. Most of these contracts had a very fast turnover rate – in fact, the vast majority of futures contracts are held for just a few days. Average daily production of goods and services, as measured by world GDP, was about \$0.3 trillion per day. So the DATV on derivatives was about *twenty times greater* than daily world GDP. Very approximately, about one-tenth of the volume traded is used for hedging. The remaining trades must be for speculative purposes.

Speculative traders include proprietary traders, hedge funds, companies making bets and day traders. They trade in capital markets for the purpose of making profits over a short-term horizon, which distinguishes them from investors, who buy-and-hold. Approximately half of the speculators in the derivatives markets are proprietary traders in banks.

When interest rates are cut banks turn to the capital markets to make profits by increasing the volume of their speculative trading. As a result, huge bonuses are often paid to successful proprietary traders and their managers. But why should banks bet with the money of their savers and their clients? Apart from the possibility that they may be better at speculation than ordinary investors, because of better information or cheaper access to markets,[3] banks need to create a liquid market in order to price derivatives. Their market makers provide OTC derivatives, making money on the bid-ask spread, quoting prices that are based on the cost of hedging. So they need a liquid market for their hedging instruments, which include futures and options. We absolutely need speculative trading in options, because the volume of trading creates a market where there is no reliable theoretical price. A case in point is the CDO market. But we do not necessarily need speculative trading on futures, because we know how to calculate the fair price of a futures contract. One reason why there was approximately \$25 trillion of speculative trades on futures last year is that senior managers and proprietary traders

---

[3] For instance, Salomon Brothers used to make the market for US junk bonds, so they could see the entire market and take positions accordingly.

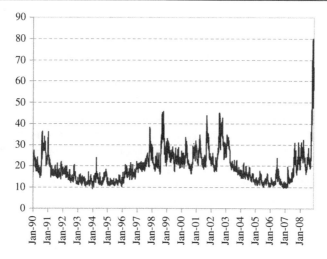

The Vix Volatility Index, January 1990 – October 2008

are being driven by greed to acquire huge bonuses. This is why the recent nationalisation deals for UK banks has included a clause for limiting remuneration.

Proprietary trading by banks increases liquidity, but it may also increase volatility. Traditionally, banks are short volatility because investors want to be long volatility – it is an excellent diversification instrument. If there is no liquid market for volatility, banks will simply overcharge on the spread, which is one of the reasons why implied volatility usually exceeds historical volatility. The markets for variance swaps on European and US stock indices have been surging, making pure volatility a new, liquid asset. However, the informed banks would have temporarily stopped writing variance swaps at the onset of the banking crisis in mid September 2008, leaving only those in ignorance of the huge sums that could be lost on these positions to take the knock. Near the end of October 2008 the Vix jumped up to almost 80%, its highs during previous crises rarely exceeding 40%, as shown in the figure above, so the banks that sold variance swaps in September 2008 could have lost millions of dollars.[4]

WHAT COULD (OR SHOULD) HAPPEN NOW?

As this book goes to press many large banks are cutting down on their proprietary trading businesses, reducing the number of employees and the bonuses that are paid. If banks and their employees no longer have the incentive to use proprietary trading to increase profits, or if their trading is curtailed by regulators or governments, the size of the current OTC derivatives markets will dramatically reduce. Yet banks will always seek new ways to increase their profits. So new, unregulated and (probably) misunderstood markets, like the CDO market, will still be created.

Very often, the demand for and supply of derivatives arises from differences in accounting rules. For instance, the swaps market, which is the largest of all derivatives markets, is driven

---

[4] Vix is the implied volatility index of the S&P 500 index.

by differences between cost and market-to-market accounting. As long as we have no unified accounting framework for all market participants, new derivatives markets will be created. However, given the time it has taken to agree on accounting standards in IAS39,[5] we should not expect much change in the near future.

This huge casino, in which many times world GDP is bet every year, has proved impossible to regulate. Regulators always respond to crises by tightening rules and increasing the minimum level of risk capital to be held by banks. But this exacerbates the problem, since the only way out of the current crisis is to create liquidity. Injecting taxpayers' money into the capital markets is only a temporary solution; what is needed now is a complete reform of financial regulations. This does not necessarily mean tighter control on market operations, or increases in the minimum level of risk capital held by banks. Indeed, there may be government pressure to loosen regulation in order to establish a leading financial centre.

The new Basel Accord, which took eleven years to develop, failed to control the systemic risk in financial markets. And the reason it has failed is that regulators are too fixed on detailed calculations of value at risk in their 'bottom-up' regulatory capital framework. That is, they have been focusing on micro-managing the banks in their jurisdiction, and not on *macro-financial* decision making under uncertainty. What may be needed now, in addition to curtailing the proprietary trading by banks, is a top-down, differential system of capital charges, with the major banks that pose the greatest systemic threat holding proportionally higher capital reserves than minor banks.

This last spectacular failure in financial markets calls for a revision of the global banking system. This does not necessarily mean the wholesale nationalisation of banks, or even a return to socialist principles. That would indeed be an admission of failure, especially for Russia and the Eastern European countries that have only recently embraced capitalism. Free capital markets are essential to globalisation, and globalisation is essential for the health of the world's economy. To prevent the next crisis being even more critical that this one, an urgent reform of the accounting, regulation and risk management principles that underpin financial markets is required.

After each market crash – e.g. following the burst of the technology bubble in the early part of this decade, and following the Russian debt default in 1998 – governments try to promote growth by cutting interest rates and by injecting capital into the financial system. And, to be effective, each time they have to inject *more* capital and introduce *more* drastic cuts in interest rates than before. This is because the banking system is unstable, and markets have recovered only by sowing even deeper seeds for the next crisis. Unless drastic reforms of the system are made in the near future, even more drastic action will be required to resolve the next crisis, when it comes.

And what about financial risk management, and market risk management in particular – what reforms are needed now? A fundamental distinction must be drawn between risk *managers* and risk *analysts*. A good risk manager should be adept at making decisions under uncertainty, and for this he needs to be well-informed about the basic *economic* principles that underpin price formation in capital markets. And risk managers, like all managers, should be held accountable for their actions. Unfortunately, the opposite is usually the case. If a bank encounters problems due to bad management, then senior executives and directors can leave to join another firm, often with guaranteed bonuses on top of a six-figure salary.

---

[5] These standards were developed by the International Accounting Standards Board. See http://www.iasb.org.

Risk analysts and financial engineers – for whom these books are designed – use *mathematical* models to measure risk, and to price illiquid products using arbitrage pricing theory. The assumptions made by these models need constant testing and refining, so that superior models can be developed. With greater confidence in mark to model prices, and in portfolio risk assessment, it may be easier to stem the panic when the next crisis comes. Clearly, better education in quantitative risk analysis is the key to developing effective risk models and accurate pricing models for financial institutions.

Each financial crisis has a disastrous effect on the global economy, so the lives of ordinary people are adversely affected. I believe these crises can and will be avoided, but only when financial risk managers acquire the knowledge, skills and framework they really need to operate effectively in their profession. The recent crisis has shown that there is an urgent need for growth and change in the entire financial industry and in the financial risk management profession in particular.

An important and fundamental change must be to start educating risk analysts properly, so that their managers really understand the risks that banks and other financial institutions are taking, as far as this is possible. Risk is a mathematical concept: it is a measure of uncertainty. So risk managers or, at least, their trusted analysts, need to understand mathematics first, before they can even begin to understand risk.

There are two international financial risk management associations, the *Professional Risk Managers' International Association* (PRMIA) and the *Global Association of Risk Professionals* (GARP).[6] These associations provide entry-level qualifications for financial risk management. The PRM qualification is at a higher level than the FRM or the Associate PRM, but even the four exams for the full PRM qualification can be passed with only one year of part-time study.

In the UK medical doctors must undergo a minimum of 5 years' full-time study, and to rise to senior positions they must take tough examinations every few years. Health risk management is so important to the economy that our National Health Service offers a regular programme of free vaccinations and free screenings for cancer, heart disease, and so forth. Why, then, have banks been treating financial risk management so casually, placing inappropriately qualified people in senior positions and taking less than adequate care over the education of their junior staff? Financial risk management is such a vast subject that to learn what we need to provide effective risk management in today's complex and volatile markets should take many years of full-time study, just as it does for medical doctors.

ABOUT THE MARKET RISK ANALYSIS SERIES

Sitting at my desk, writing this preface – the very last item on the agenda of the *Market Risk Analysis* series – I feel a huge sense of relief that the punishing work schedule I have been setting myself has nearly reached its conclusion. When I started out, five years ago, I did not intend to write four books. I just wanted to write one book: a book that describes all that a market risk analyst should know about building market value-at-risk (VaR) models; to explain everything in great detail so that readers came away with something they could actually use to educate themselves, without the need for formal courses. I also wanted to provide numerous practical examples, showing how to implement the theory that I cover in all types of financial

---

[6] See www.prmia.org and www.garp.com.

markets. That is why I put every idea that I possibly could into a simple, interactive Excel workbook, with real financial data on equities, currencies, interest rates and commodities; this way, readers experience the idea 'hands-on', right from the start, and I truly believe this is a fantastic learning tool for an intelligent, self-motivated reader.[7]

I soon realized that in rising to this challenge I had set myself a very considerable task. To fully understand all aspects of market VaR as it is (or should be) used by major financial institutions today, the analyst needs to understand a good deal of mathematics, especially statistics and financial econometrics, as well as knowing about financial markets, the type of instruments traded in these markets, how to price them, why we hedge them and how to hedge them properly. It is a huge agenda – and this is just for the *market* risk analyst! As a result, there are numerous references to the earlier volumes of *Market Risk Analysis* in this book.

Please do not buy these books if you think you can be a financial risk analyst without understanding much mathematics. It is important to distinguish between risk *management* and risk *analysis*. Whilst I very often refer to risk management, this book series is called Market Risk *Analysis*, because it focuses on the mathematical modelling of market risks. A financial risk manager requires the same skills as any business manager, including a capacity for leadership, some knowledge of economics and of psychology and a superficial, not necessarily detailed, understanding of the technical side of the business. By contrast, the financial risk analyst's profession requires a very broad and in-depth knowledge of financial markets, finance theory, mathematics, statistics and econometrics.

One of the first developments in the financial risk management profession was to categorize risks into three broad types, labelled market, credit and operational risk. This was convenient because quite different techniques are used to assess each type of risk. My definition of *market risk* is the risk resulting from adverse moves in prices of liquid financial instruments. Market risk therefore includes credit spread risk, just as it includes interest rate risk. The probability of default affects credit spreads, so credit risk affects spread risk. But the scope of these books does not extend to credit risk analysis, just as monetary policy affects base interest rates but the theory of economic policy decision making is not within the scope of these books.

This book series is not, at least primarily, about the risk management of financial markets; it is called *Market* Risk Analysis, because it deals with market risk in the narrow sense, defined above, and when risk management (as opposed to risk analysis) is discussed it is market risk management, not credit or operational risk management. In particular, *please do not buy these books* if you want to learn about credit risk analysis, or about credit risk management, or about collateralized debt obligations and counterparty default. Neither should you buy these books if you want everything in one volume. At this level of detail, such a book would be more than 1500 pages long, and not easy to carry around with you. Also, there are separate markets for the earlier volumes in the series; not *everyone* in the finance industry wants to learn how to assess risk in a VaR framework.

Why did I write this book? To answer this fully I should first explain why I changed my agenda and wrote the precursors, starting with Volume I: *Quantitative Methods in Finance*. I started teaching mathematics to non-mathematicians over 20 years ago, and have continued to develop materials that allow intelligent students with relatively little quantitative background to undertake a fast-track course in mathematics that is oriented towards their specialism. For the past five years I have been teaching a course in Quantitative Methods for

---

[7] I have constructed 140 Excel workbooks for the examples, figures, tables and case studies in this series. That is about 1500 spreadsheets in total. Phew!

Finance to master's degree students at the ICMA Centre. In 10 weeks I need to bring students up to scratch in Excel as well as equipping them with the basic knowledge of calculus, linear algebra, statistics, econometrics and numerical methods, and how these subjects are used for financial applications. So each year I teach finance through mathematical applications in a very pedagogical way, sometimes in a single class with over 200 students having disparate quantitative backgrounds. I decided to write the first volume with two purposes in mind – as a set text for my Quantitative Methods for Finance course and similar courses (there are plenty) and to provide a fast-track route to intelligent, independent readers who want a succinct, targeted and pedagogical exposition of the mathematical knowledge required by a market risk analyst.

What about Volume II: *Practical Financial Econometrics*? When I was young I trained as an algebraist, developed only a passing interest in game theory, unfortunately, and at the time that my work focused on econometrics (because I had to teach it) I was drawn into financial econometrics by consultancy work. Thus, during the 1990s and well before most real academic econometricians discovered this veritable motorway into finance, I was accidentally positioned as one of the better known financial econometricians in the industry. Then I wrote *Market Models* – but this book is now over seven years old – so why not write a more rigorous, complete and up-to-date financial econometrics text for the *Market Risk Analysis* series? Volume II is primarily aimed at market risk professionals working in portfolio management or for hedge funds, students on Finance master's courses, and academic researchers. But a secondary purpose is that Volume II is required knowledge for all serious market risk analysts, and most of the material covered is pre-requisite for readers of this book, at least if they want to gain an in-depth understanding of advanced VaR models.

During the past few years I have developed research interests in continuous time finance: in volatility theory and in option pricing and hedging in particular. Volatility theory is a complex subject, and there are only a few texts in this area that are accessible to non-specialists. Believing that I could write a comprehensive and clear exposition of volatility theory, option pricing and hedging, I decided to augment the text for Volume III: *Pricing, Hedging and Trading Financial Instruments* to include interest rate sensitive instruments, futures and forwards, describing the markets but with an emphasis on the efficient pricing and hedging of portfolios containing such instruments. The final chapter of Volume III draws the previous chapters together by describing the mapping of portfolios of different classes of financial instruments; this way, Volume III lays the essential finance theory foundations for the VaR models that are described in this book.

Although the four volumes of *Market Risk Analysis* are very much interlinked, each volume serves a different purpose. Volume IV: *Value-at-Risk Models* could be adopted as a stand-alone text for an advanced course in Market Risk, but only for students who have already gained a good knowledge of quantitative methods, financial econometrics, finance theory, financial markets and financial instruments. Readers would benefit by working through the previous volumes before reading this one, or they may use the numerous cross-references to earlier volumes that are provided in the text. This requires a considerable investment of time and money. Although I hope that many university courses will adopt these books as core texts, my main purpose is to provide a self-study programme for readers wishing to gain a proper foundation for the job of market risk analysis. Dedicated and intelligent readers should be able to understand the material in all four books with one or two years of full-time study.

The aim of *Market Risk Analysis* is to define a syllabus for education in market risk analysis, from the basics to the most advanced level of understanding we have today, to set standards for the profession of market risk analyst, and to provide the means whereby the required skills may be attained. When I have time, I hope to develop a professional Market Risk Analyst qualification, with four exams based on each of these books and of a level equivalent to a challenging master's degree course.

The target readership for *Market Risk Analysis*, Volume IV: *Value-at-Risk Models* includes risk analysts in banks and finance-related firms such as software companies, insurance firms, investment companies and hedge funds; academics researching into market risk and/or fore-casting with econometric models; and students on financial risk management master's courses. No other existing text on value at risk takes such a pedagogical and practical approach as this, at the same time as covering the theory both rigorously and comprehensively. Several theoretical results are new and each empirical application is unique.

Because I focus exclusively on market risk the most similar existing texts, at least in terms of broad content, are Dowd (2005) and Danielsson (2007). However, Dowd's book is mainly on the theory of market VaR, with relatively little on its practical implementation for realistic risk management problems, and Danielsson's book is shorter and far less detailed or compre-hensive. *Market Risk Analysis*, Volume IV: *Value-at-Risk Models* is written at a quantitative level that is similar to Dowd (2005), Danielsson (2007) and Christoffersen (2003), higher than that of Jorion (2006) and lower than that of McNeil et al. (2005). It is more advanced and com-prehensive, than Butler (1999). In so far as I place an equal emphasis on theory and practical implementation, this book could be compared with Holton (2003).

I would not be surprised if some readers react badly to the advanced level of understand-ing required for this book. The discipline of market risk analysis has existed for nearly two decades, but by publishing this book I am, in a sense, challenging the entire profession. In my view, a market risk analyst should be able to understand everything I have written, and more. If he cannot, he is simply not qualified for this seriously responsible job. On the other hand, an analyst who gains this understanding can look forward to a stimulating and rewarding career, as a return on the investment of substantial time and effort required to obtain a mastery of this material.

OUTLINE OF VOLUME IV

Chapter 1, *Value at Risk and Other Risk Metrics*, introduces the risk metrics that are com-monly used by fund managers, banks and corporations. A market risk metric is a single number that captures the uncertainty in a portfolio's P&L, or in its return, summarizing the portfolio's potential for deviations from a target or expected return. Whilst VaR has become a universal risk metric used by banks and by non-financial corporations, fund managers have traditionally used quite different metrics. As well as tracking error and its limitations for use in active fund management, lower partial moments and VaR-based downside risk metrics such as benchmark VaR and expected shortfall are introduced. But VaR has some undesirable prop-erties. It is not a coherent risk metric, unless we make some simplifying assumptions about the behaviour of the risk factors and the portfolio type. We explain why it is important to aggre-gate and disaggregate risks in the bottom-up risk assessment paradigm that is prevalent today, and introduce conditional, stand-alone, marginal and incremental VaR in a general mathemat-ical framework. Empirical examples focus on the distinction between measuring VaR at the portfolio level and at the risk factor level, and the reason why we obtain different results when the same historical data are used in the three fundamental types of VaR model, i.e. parametric linear, historical and Monte Carlo VaR models.

Chapter 2, *Parametric Linear VaR Models*, is the longest chapter in the book. It covers the theory of parametric VaR models for linear portfolios in a rigorous mathematical framework, introducing several new results. We provide formulae for both VaR and expected tail loss (ETL) – which is also sometimes called conditional VaR – based on the assumptions that risk factor returns have a multivariate normal distribution, a Student t distribution and or a mixture of normal and/or Student t distributions. We also show how to use exponentially weighted moving average covariance matrices and how to scale VaR over different risk horizons when portfolio returns are autocorrelated. Thirty examples and several long case studies cover the aggregation and disaggregation of stand-alone and marginal VaR for large hedged and unhedged international portfolios containing interest rate sensitive instruments, equities and commodities, and each is supported with its own interactive Excel spreadsheet, usually based on real financial data.

Chapter 3, *Historical Simulation*, provides a critical introduction to the standard approach to measuring historical VaR and ETL. We address the need to measure historical VaR initially at the daily risk horizon, and the challenging problem of scaling VaR to longer risk horizons. Empirical examples motivate the need for volatility adjustment, and its extension to filtered historical simulation based on a generalized autoregressive conditional heteroscedasticity (GARCH) model. Again, numerous examples and case studies based on real financial data cover the practical implementation of historical VaR and ETL estimation, and its aggregation and disaggregation for portfolios containing interest rate sensitive instruments, equities and commodities and with foreign currency exposures. We explain how to improve the precision of VaR and ETL estimates at extreme quantiles, comparing the pros and cons of kernel fitting, Cornish – Fisher expansion, extreme value theory and fitting a Johnson SU distribution. Throughout this chapter we deal with linear portfolios, leaving the far more complex problem of measuring historical VaR and ETL for option portfolios to Chapter 5.

Chapter 4, *Monte Carlo VaR*, begins by reviewing some basic concepts in Monte Carlo simulation from univariate and multivariate distributions, including the generation of random numbers and variance reduction. However, fewer than 20 pages are devoted to this, and readers should not expect to cover the material in as much depth as textbooks that are exclusively concerned with simulation. The main focus of this chapter is a subject that has hitherto received little attention in the VaR literature: the need to provide a proper specification of the risk factor returns model when measuring Monte Carlo VaR. First we focus on building realistic dynamic models of individual risk factor returns, including volatility clustering and regime switching, and then we cover multivariate models, from multivariate normal i.i.d. processes to models with general parametric marginals with dependency captured by copulas. We also explain how to reduce the number of risk factors using principal component analysis. All of the complex models introduced are implemented in interactive Excel spreadsheets for a variety of real portfolios.

Chapter 5, *Value at Risk for Option Portfolios*, opens with a summary of the Taylor expansions that are used to map option portfolios to their main risk factors, and explains the likely effect on VaR estimates due to the size and magnitude of the different Greeks of a portfolio: specifically, these are termed delta, gamma, vega and theta effects. We take care to explain why these effects can be very different depending on whether we are estimating static VaR, which assumes the portfolio is not traded during the risk horizon, and dynamic VaR, where the portfolio is rebalanced daily over the risk horizon to return the risk factor sensitivities to their original level. Static VaR is suitable for estimating the risk of a single structured product that is not intended to be dynamically rebalanced, and dynamic VaR is useful for assessing risk when traders are at their limits. The main focus of this chapter is the practical implementation of both historical and Monte Carlo VaR models for option portfolios, evaluated both exactly and with risk factor mapping. Starting with simple, unhedged positions, the practical examples become increasingly complex, including VaR estimates for option portfolios with several underlyings and path-dependent claims.

Chapter 6, *Risk Model Risk*, covers the reasons why different VaR methodologies give different results and the statistical methods used to assess the accuracy of VaR estimates. There are many sources of error in VaR and ETL estimates. In equity and option portfolios even the risk factor mapping can be a very significant source of model risk, and quite different VaR estimates can result when we change the risk factors, or the data used to estimate the risk factor sensitivities, or the statistical methodology used for factor sensitivity estimation. In all portfolios it is the specification of the risk factor returns model that is the most significant source of model risk, and many empirical examples are provided to support this. After deriving theoretical results on confidence intervals for VaR estimates, the main focus of this chapter is on the VaR and ETL backtesting methodology. Starting with the simple backtests suggested by banking regulators, we describe unconditional and conditional coverage tests, regression-based backtests, ETL backtests based on standardized exceedance residuals, bias statistics and distribution forecasts. Throughout this section of the chapter, we illustrate the practical implementation of all these backtests in Excel workbooks using two different VaR and ETL estimates for a simple position on the S&P 500 index.

Chapter 7, *Scenario Analysis and Stress Testing*, opens by challenging the validity of historical data for estimating VaR and ETL, except over very short risk horizons. We maintain that using historical data itself implies a subjective view (that history will repeat itself) and that other beliefs or personal subjective views of senior management and the board of directors can and should be used in a mathematically coherent model of risk. Beginning with a description of how different types of beliefs about future market behaviour can be incorporated into VaR and ETL estimation, we argue that the traditional stress-testing framework that aims to quantify a 'worst case' loss is totally meaningless. So, whilst the standard stress testing methods such as 'factor push' are both described and illustrated, we focus on a coherent stress testing framework based on what I call 'distribution scenarios'. The last section of the chapter focuses on the use of historical or hypothetical stressed covariance matrices, stress tests based on principal components and on GARCH volatility clustering, and endogenous and exogenous liquidity adjustments to VaR.

Chapter 8, *Capital Allocation*, covers the application of VaR and ETL to regulatory and economic capital allocation. Beginning with the basic differences between banking and trading book accounting, we cover the minimum market risk capital requirements for banks under the 1996 Amendment to the first Basel Accord, describing and illustrating both the internal models approach and the standardized rules. After the new Basel II Accord, in the wake of the credit crunch that began in 2007, the Basel Committee suggested a new incremental risk charge for credit spread and equity risks, applied to internal models that have specific risk recognition. We provide empirical examples to illustrate how banks might choose to calculate this new add-on to the capital charge. The second half of the chapter opens with a description of the measurement and applications of economic capital, having particular emphasis on aggregation risk. We then introduce the most common types of risk adjusted performance measures for economic capital allocation, and provide empirical examples in Excel on the optimal allocation of economic capital under various constraints.

ABOUT THE CD-ROM

This book emphasizes teaching through practical examples supported by transparent Excel spreadsheets. Whenever it is possible to illustrate a model or a formula using a practical example – however simple or complex – I do this using Excel. This volume alone contains 62 Excel workbooks (each with several spreadsheets, some of which are fairly complex) covering all the examples and figures in the text, and 16 case studies that implement VaR models in practice. These may be found on the accompanying CD-ROM. The data can be used by tutors or researchers since they were obtained from free internet sources, and references for updating are provided. Also the graphs and tables can be modified if required, and copied into lectures notes based on this book. Within these spreadsheets readers may change any parameters of the problem (the parameters are indicated in *red*) and see the new solution (the output is indicated in *blue*). Rather than using VBA code, which will be obscure to many students, I have encoded the formulae directly into the spreadsheet. Thus the reader need only click on a cell to read the formula. The interactive spreadsheets are designed to offer tutors the possibility to set, as exercises for their courses, an unlimited number of variations on the examples in the text.

I hope you will find these examples and case studies useful. A great variety of problems have been illustrated, from the simple estimation of VaR at the portfolio level using basic forms of each VaR model, to advanced methodologies such as filtered historical simulation with adjustments for volatility and correlation clustering, or Monte Carlo VaR using copulas and non-normal marginals, applied at the risk factor level and disaggregated into stand-alone and marginal VaR components due to different risk factor classes.

ACKNOWLEDGEMENTS

An unkind Amazon reviewer once suggested that I only write books to make money. This is absurd, not only because if I wanted to increase my income I could have accepted many financially attractive invitations during the last five years instead of devoting my time to these books. I write mainly because I enjoy it; and also because I imagine that I have something to offer. However, when all is said and done, if readers appreciate these books, that is all to the good; and if they do not, I would have written them anyway.

The *Market Risk Analysis* series would never have been completed if I had been unable to hold to a strong purpose, which is to do whatever I can to further the financial risk management profession. In this respect it has been a pleasure to work with individuals whose tireless efforts to raise standards and form a truly global financial risk management network I very much admire. Of these I would like to say a special thank-you to David Koenig, who set up the PRMIA organization in which I play an active role, and to Elizabeth Sheedy, my co-editor, co-author, co-researcher and close friend.

I would like to express my thanks to all the individuals who have helped in the production and marketing of this series: to Sam Whittaker for her unerring faith in my judgement when one book turned into four; to Caitlin Cornish for her solid editorial decisions and Aimee Dibbens for her efficient handling of numerous issues; to Louise Holden for her energetic marketing support and Lori Boulton for her tireless, ongoing attempts to manage Amazon sites; to Richard Leigh for his careful copy-editing; to Viv Wickham and her excellent team in production; and especially to Philippe Derome and Ronnie Barnes, who contacted me whilst reading the earlier volumes in this series and volunteered their meticulous proof reading *before* the publication of this one. I know from experience that I can rely on their knowledge and intelligent, careful reading to detect many errors and that the book will be much improved by their work.

But most of all, I would like to thank my family – and my children Boris and Helen, in particular – who are only 20 and 12 respectively at the time of writing. For five crucial years of their lives they have shared their mother with another purpose. Maybe this has not been easy for them, but their unerring love and understanding during these long years has been the most valuable support of all.

Discussion forums and other resources for the Market Risk Analysis series are available at **www.marketriskanalysis.com**.

IV.1

Value at Risk and Other Risk Metrics

IV.1.1 INTRODUCTION

A market *risk metric* is a measure of the uncertainty in the future value of a portfolio, i.e. a measure of uncertainty in the portfolio's return or profit and loss (P&L). Its fundamental purpose is to summarize the potential for deviations from a target or expected value. To determine the dispersion of a portfolio's return or P&L we need to know about the potential for individual asset prices to vary and about the dependency between movements of different asset prices. *Volatility* and *correlation* are portfolio risk metrics but they are only sufficient (in the sense that these metrics alone define the shape of a portfolio's return or P&L distribution) when asset or risk factor returns have a *multivariate normal* distribution. When these returns are not multivariate normal (or multivariate Student *t*) it is inappropriate and misleading to use volatility and correlation to summarize uncertainty in the future value of a portfolio.[1]

Statistical models of volatility and correlation, and more general models of statistical dependency called *copulas*, are thoroughly discussed in Volume II of *Market Risk Analysis*. The purpose of the present introductory chapter is to introduce other types of risk metric that are commonly used by banks, corporate treasuries, portfolio management firms and other financial practitioners.

Following the lead from both regulators and large international banks during the mid-1990s, almost all financial institutions now use some form of *value at risk* (VaR) as a risk metric. This almost universal adoption of VaR has sparked a rigorous debate. Many quants and academics argue against the metric because it is not necessarily sub-additive,[2] which contradicts the principal of diversification and hence also the foundations of modern portfolio theory. Moreover, there is a closely associated risk metric, the *conditional VaR*, or what I prefer to call the *expected tail loss* (ETL) because the terminology is more descriptive, that *is* sub-additive. And it is very simple to estimate ETL once the firm has developed a VaR model, so why not use ETL instead of VaR? Readers are recommended the book by Szegö (2004) to learn more about this debate.

The attractive features of VaR as a risk metric are as follows:

- It corresponds to an amount that could be lost with some chosen probability.
- It measures the risk of the risk factors as well as the risk factor sensitivities.
- It can be compared across different markets and different exposures.
- It is a universal metric that applies to all activities and to all types of risk.

---

[1] See the remarks on correlation in particular, in Section II.3.3.2.
[2] See Section IV.1.8.3.

- It can be measured at any level, from an individual trade or portfolio, up to a single *enterprise-wide VaR* measure covering all the risks in the firm as a whole.
- When aggregated (to find the total VaR of larger and larger portfolios) or disaggregated (to isolate component risks corresponding to different types of risk factor) it takes account of dependencies between the constituent assets or portfolios.

The purpose of this chapter is to introduce VaR in the context of other 'traditional' risk metrics that have been commonly used in the finance industry. The assessment of VaR is usually more complex than the assessment of these traditional risk metrics, because it depends on the multivariate risk factor return distribution and on the dynamics of this distribution, as well as on the risk factor mapping of the portfolio. We term the mathematical models that are used to derive the risk metric, the *risk model* and the mathematical technique that is applied to estimate the risk metrics from this model (e.g. using some type of simulation procedure) the *resolution method*.

Although VaR and its related measures such as ETL and *benchmark VaR* have recently been embraced almost universally, the evolution of risk assessment in the finance industry has drawn on various traditional risk metrics that continue to be used alongside VaR. Broadly speaking, some traditional risk metrics only measure sensitivity to a risk factor, ignoring the risk of the factor itself. For instance, the *beta* of a stock portfolio or the *delta* and *gamma* of an option portfolio are examples of *price sensitivities*. Other traditional risk metrics measure the risk relative to a benchmark, and we shall be introducing some of these metrics here, including the *omega* and *kappa indices* that are currently favoured by many fund managers.[3]

The outline of the chapter is as follows. Section IV.1.2 explains how and why risk assessment in banking has evolved separately from risk assessment in portfolio management. Section IV.1.3 introduces a number of *downside risk metrics* that are commonly used in portfolio management. These are so called because they focus only on the risk of underperforming a benchmark, ignoring the 'risk' of outperforming the benchmark.

The reminder of the chapter focuses on VaR and its associated risk metrics. We use the whole of Section IV.1.4 to provide a thorough definition of market VaR. For instance, when VaR is used to assess risks over a long horizon, as it often is in portfolio management, we should adjust the risk metric for any difference between the expected return and the risk free or benchmark return.[4] However, a non-zero expected excess return has negligible effect when the risk horizon for the VaR estimate is only a few days, as it usually is for banks, and so some texts simply ignore this effect.

Section IV.1.5 lays some essential foundations for the rest of this book by stating some of the basic principles of VaR measurement. These principles are illustrated with simple numerical examples where the only aim is to measure the VaR

- at the *portfolio level*,[5] and where
- the portfolio returns are *independent and identically distributed* (i.i.d.).

---

[3] Contrary to popular belief, the *tracking error* risk metric does not perform this role, except for passive (index tracking) portfolios. I have taken great care to clarify the reasons for this in Section II.1.6.

[4] This is because a risk metric is usually measured in present value terms – see Section IV.1.5.4 for further details.

[5] This means that we measure only one risk, for the portfolio as a whole, and we do not attribute the portfolio risk to different market factors.

Section IV.1.6 begins by stressing the importance of measuring VaR at the *risk factor* level: without this we could not quantify the main sources of risk. This section also includes two simple examples of measuring the *systematic VaR*, i.e. the VaR that is captured by the entire risk factor mapping.[6] We consider two examples: an equity portfolio that has been mapped to a broad market index and a cash-flow portfolio that has been mapped to zero-coupon interest rates at standard maturities.

Section IV.1.7 discusses the aggregation and disaggregation of VaR. One of the many advantages of VaR is that is can be aggregated to measure the total VaR of larger and larger portfolios, taking into account diversification effects arising from the imperfect dependency between movements in different risk factors. Or, starting with total risk factor VaR, i.e. systematic VaR, we can disaggregate this into *stand-alone VaR* components, each representing the risk arising from some specific risk factors.[7] Since we take account of risk factor dependence when we aggregate VaR, the total VaR is often less than the sum of the stand-alone VaRs. That is, VaR is often *sub-additive*. But it does not *have* to be so, and this is one of the main objections to using VaR as a risk metric. We conclude the section by introducing *marginal VaR* (a component VaR that is adjusted for diversification, so that the sum of the marginal VaRs is approximately equal to the total risk factor VaR) and *incremental VaR* (which is the VaR associated with a single new trade).

Section IV.1.8 introduces risk metrics that are associated with VaR, including the *conditional VaR* risk metric or expected tail loss. This is the average of the losses that exceed the VaR. Whilst VaR represents the loss that we are fairly confident will not be exceeded, ETL tells us how much we would expect to lose given that the VaR has been exceeded. We also introduce *benchmark VaR* and its associated conditional metric, *expected shortfall* (ES). The section concludes with a discussion on the properties of a *coherent risk metric*. ETL and ES are coherent risk metrics, but when VaR and benchmark VaR are estimated using simulation they are not coherent because they are not sub-additive.

Section IV.1.9 introduces the three fundamental types of resolution method that may be used to estimate VaR, applying each method in only its most basic form, and to only a very simple portfolio. After a brief overview of these approaches, which we call the *normal linear VaR, historical VaR* and *normal Monte Carlo VaR* models, we present a case study on measuring VaR for a simple position of $1000 per point on an equity index. Our purpose here is to illustrate the fundamental differences between the models and the reasons why our estimates of VaR can differ so much depending on the model used. Section IV.1.10 summarizes and concludes.

Volume IV of the *Market Risk Analysis* series builds on the three previous volumes, and even for this first chapter readers first require an understanding of:[8]

- quantiles and other basic concepts in statistics (Section I.3.2);
- the normal distribution family and the standard normal transformation (Section I.3.3.4);
- stochastic processes in discrete time (Section I.3.7.1);
- portfolio returns and log returns (Section I.1.4);
- aggregation of log returns and scaling of volatility under the i.i.d. assumption (Section II.3.2.1);

---

[6] So systematic VaR may also be called *total risk factor VaR*.

[7] As its name suggests, 'stand-alone equity VaR' does not take account of the diversification benefits between equities and bonds, for instance.

[8] The most important sections from other volumes of *Market Risk Analysis* are listed after each topic.

- the matrix representation of the expectation and variance of returns on a linear portfolio (Section I.2.4);
- univariate normal Monte Carlo simulation and how it is performed in Excel (Section I.5.7).
- risk factor mappings for portfolios of equities, bonds and options, i.e. the expression of the portfolio P&L or return as a function of market factors that are common to many portfolios (e.g. stock index returns, or changes in LIBOR rates) and which are called the *risk factors* of the portfolio (Section III.5).

There is a fundamental distinction between *linear* and *non-linear* portfolios. A linear portfolio is one whose return or P&L may be expressed as a linear function of the returns or P&L on its constituent assets or risk factors. All portfolios except those with options or option-like structures fall into the category of linear portfolios.

It is worth repeating here my usual message about the spreadsheets on the CD-ROM. Each chapter has a folder which contains the data, figures, case studies and examples given in the text. All the included data are freely downloadable from websites, to which references for updating are given in the text. The vast majority of examples are set up in an interactive fashion, so that the reader or tutor can change any parameter of the problem, shown in *red*, and then view the output in *blue*. If the Excel data analysis tools or Solver are required, then instructions are given in the text or the spreadsheet.

IV.1.2   AN OVERVIEW OF MARKET RISK ASSESSMENT

In general, the choice of risk metric, the relevant time horizon and the level of accuracy required by the analyst depend very much on the application:

- A typical trader requires a detailed modelling of short-term risks with a high level of accuracy.
- A risk manager working in a large organization will apply a risk factor mapping that allows total portfolio risk to be decomposed into components that are meaningful to senior management. Risk managers often require less detail in their risk models than traders do. On the other hand, risk managers often want a very high level of confidence in their results. This is particularly true when they want to demonstrate to a rating agency that the company deserves a good credit rating.
- Senior managers that report to the board are primarily concerned with the efficient allocation of capital on a global scale, so they will be looking at long-horizon risks, taking a broad-brush approach to encompass only the most important risks.

The metrics used to assess market risks have evolved quite separately in banking, portfolio management and large corporations. Since these professions have adopted different approaches to market risk assessment we shall divide our discussion into these three broad categories.

IV.1.2.1   Risk Measurement in Banks

The main business of banks is to accept risks (because they know, or should know, how to manage them) in return for a premium paid by the client. For retail and commercial banks and for many functions in an investment bank, this is, traditionally, their main source of profit. For instance, banks write options to make money on the premium and, when market making, to make profits from the bid–ask spread. It is not their business, at least not their core business, to seek profits through enhanced returns on investments: this is the role of portfolio management. The asset management business within a large investment bank seeks superior returns on investments, but the primary concern of banks is to manage their risks.

A very important decision about risk management for banks is whether to keep the risk or to hedge at least part of it. To inform this decision the risk manager must first be able to *measure* the risk. Often market risks are measured over the very short term, over which banks could hedge their risks if they chose to, and over a short horizon it is standard to assume the expected return on a financial asset is the risk free rate of return.[9] So modelling the expected return does not come into the picture at all. Rather, the risk is associated with the *unexpected return* – a phrase which here means the deviation of the return about its expected value – and the expected rate of return is usually assumed to be the risk free rate.

Rather than fully hedging all their risks, traders are usually required to manage their positions so that their total risk stays within a limit. This limit can vary over time. Setting appropriate *risk limits* for traders is an important aspect of risk control. When a market has been highly volatile the risk limits in that market should be raised. For instance, in equity markets rapid price falls would lead to high volatility and equity betas could become closer to 1 if the stock's market correlation increased. If a proprietary trader believes the market will now start to rise he may want to buy into that market so his risk limits, based on either volatility or portfolio beta, should be raised.[10]

Traditionally risk factor exposures were controlled by limiting risk factor sensitivities. For instance, equity traders were limited by portfolio beta, options traders operated under limits determined by the net value Greeks of their portfolio, and bond traders assessed and managed risk using duration or convexity.[11] However, two significant problems with this traditional approach have been recognized for some time.

The first problem is the inability to compare different types of risks. One of the reasons why sensitivities are usually represented in value terms is that value sensitivities can be summed across similar types of positions. For instance, a value delta for one option portfolio can be added to a value delta for another option portfolio;[12] likewise the value duration for one bond portfolio can be added to the value duration for another bond portfolio. But we cannot mix two different types of sensitivities. The sum of a value beta, a value gamma and a value convexity is some amount of money, but it does not correspond to anything meaningful. The risk factors for equities, options and bonds are different, so we cannot add their sensitivities. Thus, whilst value sensitivities allow risks to be aggregated *within* a given type of trading activity, they do not aggregate *across* different trading units. The traditional sensitivity-based approach to risk management is designed to work only within a single asset class.

The second problem with using risk factor sensitivities to set traders' limits is that they measure only part of the risk exposure. They ignore the risks due to the risk factors themselves.

---

[9] We shall show that a different assumption would normally have negligible effect on the result, provided the risk horizon is only a few days or weeks.

[10] In this case the trader's economic capital allocation should be increased, since it is based on a risk adjusted performance measure that takes account of this positive expected return. See Section IV.8.3.

[11] For more information on the options 'Greeks' see Section III.3.4, and for duration and convexity see Sections III.1.5.

[12] These value sensitivities are also sometimes called 'dollar' sensitivities, even though they are measured in any currency. See Chapter III.5 and Section III.5.5.2 in particular for further details.

Traders cannot influence the risk of a risk factor, but they can *monitor* the risk factor volatility and manage their systematic risk by adjusting their exposure to the risk factor.[13]

In view of these two substantial problems most large banks have replaced or augmented the traditional approach. Many major banks now manage traders' limits using VaR and its associated risk metrics.

New banking regulations for market risk introduced in 1996 heralded a more 'holistic' approach to risk management. Risk is assessed at every level of the organization using a universal risk metric, such as VaR, i.e. a metric that applies to *all* types of exposures in any activity; and it relates not only to market risks, but also to credit and operational risks. Market VaR includes the risk arising from the risk factors as well as the factor sensitivities; it can be aggregated across any exposures, taking account of the risk factor correlations (i.e. the diversification effects) to provide an enterprise-wide risk assessment; and it allows risks to be compared across different trading units.[14] As a result most major banks have adopted VaR, or a related measure such as conditional VaR, to assess the risks of their operations at every level, from the level of the trader to the entire bank.

Banking risks are commonly measured in a so-called 'bottom-up' framework. That is, risks are first identified at the individual position level; then, as positions are aggregated into portfolios, we obtain a measure of portfolio risk from the individual risks of the various positions. As portfolios are aggregated into larger and larger portfolios – first aggregating all the traders' portfolios in a particular trading unit, then aggregating across all trading units in a particular business line, then aggregating over all business lines in the bank – the risk manager in a bank will aggregate the portfolio's risks in a similar hierarchy. A further line of aggregation occurs for banks with offices in different geographical locations.

IV.1.2.2   Risk Measurement in Portfolio Management

One of the reasons why risk assessment in banking has developed so rapidly is the impetus provided by the new banking regulations during the 1990s. Banks are required by regulators to measure their risks as accurately as possible, every day, and to hold capital in proportion to these risks. But no such regulations have provided a catalyst for the development of good risk management practices in the fund management industry. The fund manager does have a responsibility to report risks accurately, but only to his clients. As a result, in the first few years of this century major misconceptions about the nature of risk relative to a benchmark still persisted amongst some major fund managers.

Until the 1990s most funds were 'passive', i.e. their remit was merely to track a benchmark. During this time an almost universal approach to measuring risk relative to a benchmark was adopted, and this was commonly called the *tracking error*. Most managers were not allowed to sell short,[15] for fear of incurring huge losses if one of the shares that was sold short dramatically rose in price; clients used to limit mutual fund managers to long-only positions on a relatively small investment universe.[16]

---

[13] So if a particular risk factor has an unusually high volatility then a trader can reduce his exposure to that risk factor and increase his exposure to a less volatile one.

[14] Other advantages of VaR were listed in Section IV.1.1.

[15] To sell short is to sell a stock that is not owned: shares are borrowed on the 'repurchase' (repo) market and returned when the short sale is closed out with a corresponding purchase.

[16] The *investment universe* is the set of all assets available to the fund manager.

Then, during the 1990s actively managed funds with mandates to *outperform* a benchmark became popular. So, unlike banking, in portfolio management risks are usually measured relative to a benchmark set by the client. However, as portfolio managers moved away from passive management towards the so-called *alpha strategies* that are commonly used today, problems arose because the traditional control ranges which limited the extent to which the portfolio could deviate from the benchmark were dropped and many large fund managers used the tracking error as a risk metric instead. But tracking error is not an appropriate risk metric for actively managed funds.[17]

Also, with the very rapid growth in hedge funds that employ diverse long-short strategies on all types of investment universe, the risks that investors face have become very complex because hedge fund portfolio returns are highly non-normal. Hence, more sophisticated risk measurement tools have recently been developed. Today there is no universal risk metric for the portfolio management industry but it is becoming more and more common to use benchmark VaR and its associated risk metrics such as expected shortfall.

In portfolio management the risk model is often based on the expected returns model, which itself can be highly developed. As a result the risk metrics and the performance metrics are inextricably linked. By contrast, in banks the expected return, after accounting for the normal cost of doing business, is most often set equal to the risk free rate.

Another major difference between risk assessment in banking and in portfolio management is the *risk horizon*, i.e. the time period over which the risk is being forecast. Market risk in banking is assessed, at least initially, over a very short horizon. Very often banking risks are forecast at a daily frequency. Indeed, this is the reason why statistical estimates and forecasts of volatilities, correlations and covariance matrices are usually constructed from daily data. Forecasts of risks over a longer horizon are also required (e.g. 1-year forecasts are needed for the computation of economic capital) but in banking these are often extrapolated from the short-term forecasts. But market risk in portfolio management is normally forecast over a much longer horizon, often 1 month or more. This is linked to the frequency of risk reports that clients require, to data availability and to the fact that the risk model is commonly tied to the returns model, which often forecasts asset returns over a 1-month horizon.

IV.1.2.3 Risk Measurement in Large Corporations

The motivation for good financial risk management practices in large corporations is the potential for an increase in the value of the firm and hence the enhancement of value for shareholders and bondholders. Also, large corporations have a credit rating that affects the public value of their shares and bonds, and the rating agency requires the risk management and capitalization of the firm to justify its credit rating. For these two reasons the boards and senior managements of large corporations have been relatively quick to adopt the high risk management standards that have been set by banks.

Unlike portfolio management, market risks for corporations are not usually measured relative to a benchmark. Instead, risks are decomposed into:

- *idiosyncratic* or *reducible risk* which could be diversified away by holding a sufficiently large and diversified portfolio; and

---

[17] A long discussion of this point is given in Section II.1.6.

- *undiversifiable, systematic* or *irreducible risk*, which is the risk that the firm is always exposed to by choosing to invest in a particular asset class or to operate in a particular market.

Like banks, the expected returns to various business lines in a major corporation are usually modelled separately from the risks. The expected return forecasts are typically based on economic models for P&L predictions based on macroeconomic variables such as inflation, interest rates and exchange rates. Like banks, corporations will account for the normal 'cost' of doing business, with any expected losses being provisioned for in the balance sheet. Hence, from the point of view of the risk manager in a corporate treasury, the expected returns are taken as exogenous to the risk model.

The financial risks taken by a large corporation are typically managed using *economic capital*. This is a risk adjusted performance measure which does not necessarily have anything to do with ordinary capital.[18] The risk part of the risk adjusted performance measure is very commonly measured using a quantile risk metric such as VaR, or conditional VaR, to assess the market, credit and 'other' risks of:

- individual positions;
- positions in a trading book;
- trading books in the 'desk';
- desks in a particular activity or 'business unit';
- business units in the firm.

That is, the risk assessment proceeds from the bottom up, just as it does in a bank. Risks (and returns) are first assessed at the most elemental level, often instrument by instrument, and according to risk type, i.e. separately for market, credit and other risks such as operational risks. Then, individual positions are progressively aggregated into portfolios of similar instruments or activities, these are aggregated up to the business units, and then these are aggregated across all business units in the firm. Then, usually only at the very end, VaR is aggregated across the major types of risks to obtain a global representation of risks at the company or group level.

Expected returns are also assessed at the business unit level, and often also at the level of different types of activities within the business unit. The economic capital can thus be calculated at a fairly disaggregated level, and used for *risk budgeting* of the corporation's activities. To provide maximum shareholder value, the firm will seek to leverage those activities with the best risk adjusted performance and decrease the real capital allocation to activities with the worst risk adjusted performance, all else being equal.

The rating agency will assess the capitalization of the entire corporation. To justify its credit rating the corporation must demonstrate that it has a suitably low probability of default during the next year. As shown in Section IV.8.3.1, this probability is related to the total VaR of the firm, i.e. the sum of the market, credit and operational VaR over all the firm's activities. For instance, the AA credit rating corresponds to a 0.03% default probability over a year. This means that to obtain this credit rating the corporation may need to hold sufficient capital to cover the 99.97% total VaR at a 1-year horizon.

---

[18] Except at the firm-wide level – see Section IV.8.3 for further details.

IV.1.3   DOWNSIDE AND QUANTILE RISK METRICS

In this section we introduce the downside risk metrics that are popular for portfolio management. A *downside risk metric* is one that only focuses on those returns that fall short of a *target* or *threshold* return. The target or threshold return can be the benchmark return (appropriate for a passive fund) or some percentage above the benchmark return (appropriate for an active fund). Downside risk metrics are now common in active risk management, and there are a large number of possible risk metrics to choose from which are described below.

IV.1.3.1   Semi-Standard Deviation and Second Order Lower Partial Moment

The semi-standard deviation is the square root of the *semi-variance*, a concept introduced by Markovitz (1959). Semi-variance is a measure of the dispersion of only those realizations on a continuous random variable X that are less than the expectation of X.[19] It is defined as

$$SV(X) = E\big(\min(X - E(X), 0)^2\big). \tag{IV.1.1}$$

But since $E(\min(X - E(X), 0)) \neq 0$,

$$E\big(\min(X - E(X), 0)^2\big) \neq V(\min(X - E(X), 0)).$$

Hence, the terms semi-*variance* and semi-*standard deviation* are misnomers, even though they are in common use.

The ex post semi-standard deviation that is estimated from a sample $\{R_1, \ldots, R_T\}$ of T returns is

$$\hat{\sigma}_{\text{semi}} = \sqrt{T^{-1} \sum_{t=1}^{T} \min(R_t - \overline{R}, 0)^2}, \tag{IV.1.2}$$

where $\overline{R}$ is the sample mean return. Like most risk metrics, including the other lower partial moment metrics that we define in the next section, this is normally quoted in annualized terms. A numerical example is provided below.

We can extend the operator (IV.1.1) to the case where a target or threshold return τ is used in place of the expected return. We call this the *lower partial moment* (LPM) of order 2, or *second order* lower partial moment, and denote it $LPM_{2,\tau}$. The following example illustrates how an ex post estimate may be calculated.

EXAMPLE IV.1.1: SEMI-STANDARD DEVIATION AND SECOND ORDER LPM

A historical sample of 36 active returns on a portfolio is shown in Table IV.1.1. Calculate (a) the semi-standard deviation and (b) the second order LPM relative to a threshold active return of 2% per annum.

---

[19] All lower partial moment metrics may also be defined for discrete random variables, but for our purpose X is regarded as continuous.

Table IV.1.1   Active returns

Month	Active return	Month	Active return
Jan-06	0.40%	Jul-07	−1.15%
Feb-06	0.25%	Aug-07	0.36%
Mar-06	0.27%	Sep-07	0.26%
Apr-06	0.11%	Oct-07	0.25%
May-06	−0.13%	Nov-07	−0.21%
Jun-06	0.12%	Dec-07	−0.27%
Jul-06	0.21%	Jan-08	0.04%
Aug-06	0.05%	Feb-08	−0.05%
Sep-06	−0.13%	Mar-08	0.00%
Oct-06	−0.29%	Apr-08	0.29%
Nov-06	−0.49%	May-08	0.30%
Dec-06	−0.32%	Jun-08	0.53%
Jan-07	0.07%	Jul-08	0.41%
Feb-07	−0.22%	Aug-08	−0.05%
Mar-07	−0.63%	Sep-08	0.49%
Apr-07	0.03%	Oct-08	0.41%
May-07	0.06%	Nov-08	0.34%
Jun-07	−0.24%	Dec-08	−3.00%

SOLUTION   The spreadsheet for this example includes a column headed $\min(AR_t - x, 0)$ where AR_t is the active return at time t and where

(a) x is the sample mean active return (-0.03%) for the semi-standard deviation, and
(b) $x = 0.165\%$ for the LPM. Remember the active returns are monthly, so the target active return of 2% per annum translates into a target of 0.165% per month.

Dividing the sum of the squared excess returns by 36, multiplying by 12 and taking the square root gives the value in annualized terms: 1.81% for the semi-standard deviation and 2.05% for the second order LPM.

IV.1.3.2   Other Lower Partial Moments

More generally LPMs of order k can be defined for any positive k. The LPM operator is:

$$\mathrm{LPM}_{k,\tau}(X) = E\left(|\min(X - \tau, 0)|^k\right)^{1/k} = E\left(\max(\tau - X, 0)^k\right)^{1/k}, \qquad (\mathrm{IV.1.3})$$

where τ is some target or threshold return and k is positive, but need not be a whole number.[20] For instance the LPM of order 1, which is also called the *regret*, is

$$\mathrm{LPM}_{1,\tau}(X) = E(\max(\tau - X, 0)). \qquad (\mathrm{IV.1.4})$$

It follows immediately from (IV.1.4) that the regret operator is the expected pay-off to a put option with strike equal to the target return τ. So, like any put option, it has the intuitive

---

[20] We prefer the second notation in (IV.1.3), using the maximum function, because, being non-negative, we always obtain a positive value in the calculations. Otherwise, we can use the minimum value as before, but we must take the absolute value of this before operating with k.

interpretation of an insurance cost.[21] It is the cost of insuring the downside risk of a portfolio. Like semi-standard deviation, regret is able to distinguish 'good risk' from 'bad risk'.

As k increases, the kth order LPM places more weight on extremely poor returns. An ex post estimate of an LPM based on a sample $\{R_1, \ldots, R_T\}$ of T returns is

$$est.\text{LPM}_{k,\tau} = \left(T^{-1} \sum_{t=1}^{T} \max(\tau - R_t, 0)^k \right)^{1/k}. \tag{IV.1.5}$$

Note that $\text{LPM}_{3,0}$ is sometimes called the *semi-skewness* and $\text{LPM}_{4,0}$ is sometimes called the *semi-kurtosis*.

EXAMPLE IV.1.2: LPM RISK METRICS

Calculate the kth order LPMs for $k = 1, 2, 3, 4, 5, 10$ and 20 based on the sample of active returns in Example IV.1.1 and using (a) a threshold active return of 0%; and (b) a threshold active return of 2% per annum.

SOLUTION The calculations are very similar to (b) in the previous example, except that this time we use a power k of the series on $\max(\tau - R_t, 0)$ and take the kth root of the result. By changing the threshold for different values of k in the spreadsheet the reader will see that increasing the threshold increases the LPM, and for thresholds of 0% and 2% we obtain the results shown in Table IV.1.2. For $k \geq 2$, LPM measures also increase with k. However, this is not a general rule, it is because of our particular sample: as the order increases the measures put progressively higher weights on the very extreme active return of -3% in December 2008, which increases the risk considerably. In general, the behaviour of the LPM metrics of various orders as the threshold changes depends on the specific characteristics of the sample.

Table IV.1.2 LPM of various orders relative to two different thresholds

k	Threshold	
	0%	2%
1	2.06%	3.11%
2	1.84%	2.05%
3	2.09%	2.23%
4	2.28%	2.41%
5	2.41%	2.54%
10	2.69%	2.84%
20	2.84%	3.00%

IV.1.3.3 Quantile Risk Metrics

For any α between 0 and 1 the α quantile of the distribution of a continuous random variable X is a real number x_α such that[22]

$$P(X < x_\alpha) = \alpha.$$

---

[21] Recall that buying an out-of-the money put option on a share that you hold is like an insurance, since if the price of the share falls the option allows you to sell the share at some guaranteed price (the strike).
[22] As $\alpha \to 0$, $x_\alpha \to -\infty$ and as $\alpha \to 1$, $x_\alpha \to \infty$. Quantiles were formally introduced in Chapter I.3. See Sections I.3.2.8 and I.3.5.1 in particular.

If we know the distribution function $F(x)$ of X then the quantile corresponding to any given value of α may be calculated as

$$x_\alpha = F^{-1}(\alpha).$$

When a target return is an α quantile of the return distribution the probability of underperforming the target is α. For instance, if the 5% quantile of a return distribution is -3% then we are 95% confident that the return will not be lower than -3%. So a quantile becomes a downside risk metric when α is small, and very often we use standard values such as 0.1%, 1%, 5% or 10% for α.

In market risk, X is usually a return or P&L on an investment, and α is often assumed to be small so that the α quantile corresponds to a loss that we are reasonably certain will not be exceeded. The time horizon over which the potential for underperformance is measured is implicit in the frequency of returns or P&L. For instance, it would be measured over a month if X were a monthly return.

The next example considers a return that is assumed to be i.i.d. and normally distributed, with mean μ and standard deviation σ. Then, for any $\alpha \in (0, 1)$ applying the standard normal transformation gives

$$P(X < x_\alpha) = P\left(\frac{X - \mu}{\sigma} < \frac{x_\alpha - \mu}{\sigma}\right) = P\left(Z < \frac{x_\alpha - \mu}{\sigma}\right) = \alpha,$$

where Z is a standard normal variable. For instance, if a return is normally distributed with mean 10% and standard deviation 25% then the probability of returning less than 5% is 42%, because

$$P(X < 0.05) = P\left(\frac{X - 0.1}{0.25} < \frac{0.05 - 0.1}{0.25}\right) = P(Z < -0.2) = 0.42,$$

using the fact that -0.2 is the 42% quantile of the standard normal distribution.[23]

EXAMPLE IV.1.3: PROBABILITY OF UNDERPERFORMING A BENCHMARK

Consider a fund whose future active returns are normally distributed, with an expected active return over the next year of 1% and a standard deviation about this expected active return (i.e. tracking error) of 3%. What is the probability of underperforming the benchmark by 2% or more over the next year?

SOLUTION   The density function for the active return is $X \sim N(0.01, 0.0009)$, as illustrated in Figure IV.1.1. We need to find $P(X < -0.02)$. This is[24]

$$P(X < -0.02) = P\left(\frac{X - 0.01}{0.03} < \frac{-0.02 - 0.01}{0.03}\right) = P(Z < -1) = 0.1587.$$

Hence, the probability that this fund underperforms the benchmark by 2% or more is 15.87%. This can be also seen in Figure IV.1.1, as the area under the active return density function to the left of the point -0.02.

---

[23] We can find this using the command NORMSDIST (-0.2) in Excel.
[24] In Excel, NORMSDIST $(-1) = 0.1587$.

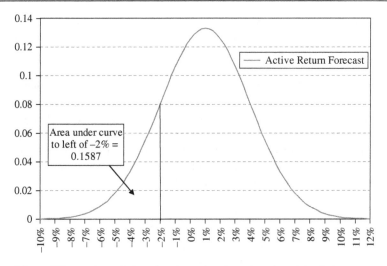

Figure IV.1.1 Probability of underperforming a benchmark by 2% or more

In the above example, we found the probability of underperforming the benchmark by knowing that -1 is the 15.87% quantile of the standard normal distribution. In the next section we shall show that the quantile of a distribution of a random variable X is a risk metric that is closely related to VaR. But, unlike LPMs, quantiles are *not* invariant to changes in the returns that are greater than the target or threshold return. That is, the quantile is affected by 'good returns' as well as 'bad returns'. This is not necessarily a desirable property for a risk metric.

On the other hand, quantiles are easy to work with mathematically. In particular, if $Y = h(X)$, where h is a continuous function that always increases then, for every α, the α quantile y_α of Y is just

$$y_\alpha = h(x_\alpha), \tag{IV.1.6}$$

where x_α is the α quantile of X. For instance, if $Y = \ln(X)$ and the 5% quantile of X is 1 then the 5% quantile of Y is 0, because $\ln(1) = 0$.

IV.1.4 DEFINING VALUE AT RISK

Value at risk is a loss that we are fairly sure will not be exceeded if the current portfolio is held over some period of time. In this section we shall assume that VaR is measured at the *portfolio level*, without considering the mapping of portfolios to their risk factors. More detailed calculations of VaR based on risk factor mappings are discussed later in this chapter and throughout the subsequent chapters.

IV.1.4.1 Confidence Level and Risk Horizon

VaR has two basic parameters:

- the *significance level* α (or *confidence level* $1 - \alpha$);
- the *risk horizon*, denoted h, which is the period of time, traditionally measured in trading days rather than calendar days, over which the VaR is measured.

Often the significance level is set by an external body, such as a banking regulator. Under the Basel II Accord, banks using internal VaR models to assess their market risk capital requirement should measure VaR at the 1% significance level, i.e. the 99% confidence level. A credit rating agency may set a more stringent significance level, i.e. a higher confidence level (e.g. the 0.03% significance or 99.97% confidence level). In the absence of regulations or external agencies, the significance/confidence level for the VaR will depend on the attitude to risk of the user. The more conservative the user, the lower the value of α, i.e. the higher the confidence level applied.

The risk horizon is the period over which we measure the potential loss. Different risks are naturally assessed over different time periods, according to their liquidity.[25] For instance, under the Basel banking regulations the risk horizon for the VaR is 10 days. In the absence of internal or external constraints (e.g. regulations) the risk horizon of VaR should refer to the time period over which we expect to be exposed to the position. An exposure to a liquid asset can usually be closed or fully hedged much faster than an exposure to an illiquid asset. And the time it takes to offload the risk depends on the size of the exposure as well as the market liquidity. Some of the most liquid positions are on major currencies and they can be closed or hedged extremely rapidly – usually within hours, even in a crisis. On the other hand private placements are highly illiquid:[26] there is no quotation in a market and the only way to sell the issue is to enter into private negotiations with another bank.

When the traders of liquid positions are operating under VaR limits they require real-time, intra-day VaR estimates to assess the effect of any proposed trade on their current level of VaR. The more liquid the risk, the shorter the time period over which the risk needs to be assessed, i.e. the shorter the risk horizon for the VaR model. Liquid risks tend to evolve rapidly and it would be difficult to represent the dynamics of these risks over the long term. Markets also tend to lose liquidity during stressful and volatile periods, when there can be sustained shortages of supply or demand for the financial instrument. Hence, the risk horizon should be increased when measuring VaR in stressful market circumstances.

At the desk level a risk manager often assesses only the liquid market risks, initially at least over a daily risk horizon. This will then be extended to a 10-day risk horizon when using an internal VaR model to assess minimum risk capital for regulatory purposes, and to a longer horizon (e.g. 1 year) for internal capital allocation purposes and for credit rating agencies.

The confidence level also depends on the application. For instance:

- VaR can be used to assess the probability of company insolvency, or the probability of default on its obligations. This depends on the capitalization of the company and the risks of all its positions over a horizon such as 6 months or 1 year. Credit rating agencies would only award a top rating to those companies that can demonstrate a very small probability of default, such as 0.03% over the next year for an AA rated company. So companies aiming for AA rating would apply a confidence level of 99.97% for enterprise-wide VaR over the next year.
- Regulators that review the regulatory capital of banks usually allow this capital to be assessed using an internal VaR model, provided they have approved the model and that certain qualitative requirements have also been met. In this case a 99% confidence level

---

[25] However, to assess capital adequacy regulators and credit rating agencies tend to set a single risk horizon, such as 1 year, for assessing all risks in the enterprise as a whole.

[26] A *private placement* is when an investment bank underwrites a company's bond issue and then buys the whole issue itself.

must be applied in the VaR model to assess potential losses over a 2-week risk horizon, i.e. a 1% 10-day VaR. This figure is then multiplied by a factor of between 3 and 4 to obtain the market risk capital requirement.[27]

- When setting trading limits based on VaR, risk managers may take a lower confidence level and a shorter risk horizon. For instance, the manager may allow traders to operate under a 5% 1-day VaR limit. In this case he is 95% confident that traders will not exceed the VaR overnight while their open positions are left unmanaged. By monitoring the traders' losses that exceed his VaR limit, further scrutiny could be given to traders who exceed their limit too often. A higher confidence level than 95% or a longer risk horizon than 1 day may give traders too much freedom.

IV.1.4.2   Discounted P&L

VaR assumes that current positions will remain static over the chosen risk horizon, and that we only assess the uncertainty about the value of these positions at the end of the risk horizon.[28] Assuming a portfolio remains static means that we are going to assess the uncertainty of the *unrealized* or *theoretical P&L*, i.e. the P&L based on a static portfolio. However, the *realized* or *actual P&L* accounts for the adjustment in positions as well as the costs of all the trades that are made in practice.

To have meaning today, any portfolio value that might be realized h trading days into the future requires discounting. That is, the P&L should be expressed in present value terms, discounting it using a risk free rate, such as the London Inter Bank Offered Rate (LIBOR).[29]

Hence, in the following when we refer to 'P&L' we mean the discounted theoretical h-day P&L, i.e. the P&L arising from the current portfolio, assumed to be static over the next h trading days, when expressed in present value terms.

Let P_t denote the value of the portfolio and let B_{ht} denote the price of a discount bond that matures in h trading days, both prices being at the time t when the VaR is measured. The value of the portfolio at some future time $t + h$, discounted to time t, is $B_{ht}P_{t+h}$ and the discounted theoretical P&L over a risk horizon of h trading days is therefore

$$\text{Discounted } h\text{-day P\&L} = B_{ht}P_{t+h} - P_t. \qquad (\text{IV.1.7})$$

Although we can observe the portfolio value and the value of the discount bond at time t, the portfolio value at time $t + h$ is uncertain, hence the discounted P&L (IV.1.7) is a random variable. Measuring the distribution of this random variable is the first step towards calculating the VaR of the portfolio.

IV.1.4.3   Mathematical Definition of VaR

We have given a verbal definition of VaR as the loss, in present value terms, due to market movements, that we are reasonably confident will not be exceeded if the portfolio is held static over a certain period of time. We cannot say anything for certain about a portfolio's P&L because it is a random variable, but we can associate a confidence level with any loss. For

---

[27] See Sections IV.6.4.2 and IV.8.2.4 for further details.
[28] See Section IV.1.5.2 for a full discussion of what is meant by a 'static' portfolio.
[29] LIBOR has become the standard reference rate for discounting short term future cash flows between banks to present value terms. See Section III.1.2.5 for further details.

instance, a 5% daily VaR, which corresponds to a 95% level of confidence, is a loss level that we anticipate experiencing with a frequency of 5%, when the current portfolio is held for 24 hours. Put another way, we are 95% confident that the VaR will not be exceeded when the portfolio is held static over 1 day. Put yet another way, we anticipate that this portfolio will lose the 5% VaR or more one day in every 20. Sometimes we quote results in terms of the confidence level $1 - \alpha$ instead of the significance level α. For instance, if

$$1\% \text{ 1-day VaR} = \$2 \text{ million,}$$

then we are 99% confident that we would lose no more than \$2 million from holding the portfolio for 1 day.

A loss is a negative return, in present value terms. In other words, a loss is a negative excess return. If the portfolio is expected to return the risk free discount rate, i.e. if the expected excess return is zero, then the $\alpha\%$ VaR is the α quantile of the discounted P&L distribution. For instance, the 1% VaR of a 1-day discounted P&L distribution is the loss, in present value terms that would only be equalled or exceeded one day in 100. Similarly, a 5% VaR of a weekly P&L distribution is the loss that would only be equalled or exceeded one week in 20.

Assuming the portfolio returns the risk free rate the discounted P&L has expectation zero. The two VaR estimates depicted in Figure IV.1.2 assume this, and also that discounted P&L is normally distributed. In the figure we assume daily P&L has a standard deviation of \$4 million and weekly P&L has a standard deviation of \$9 million.

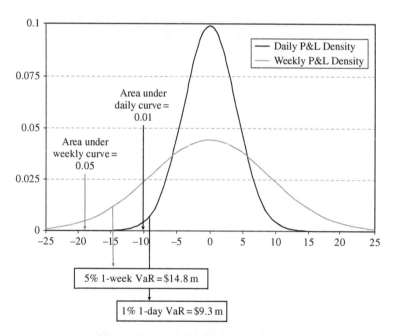

Figure IV.1.2   Illustration of the VaR metric

In mathematical terms the $100\alpha\%$ h-day VaR is the loss amount (in present value terms) that would be exceeded with only a small probability α when holding the portfolio static over the next h days. Hence, to estimate the VaR at time t we need to find the α quantile $x_{ht,\alpha}$ of the discounted h-day P&L distribution. That is, we must find $x_{ht,\alpha}$ such that

$$P(B_{ht}P_{t+h} - P_t < x_{ht,\alpha}) = \alpha, \qquad (IV.1.8)$$

and then set $\text{VaR}_{ht,\alpha} = -x_{ht,\alpha}$. We write $\text{VaR}_{ht,\alpha}$ when we want to emphasize the time t at which the VaR is estimated. However, in the following chapters we usually make explicit only the dependence of the risk metric on the two basic parameters, i.e. h (the risk horizon) and α (the significance level), and we drop the dependence on t.

When VaR is estimated from a P&L distribution it is expressed in value (e.g. dollar) terms. However, we often prefer to analyse the return distribution rather than the P&L distribution. P&L is measured in absolute terms, so if markets have been trending the P&Ls at different moments in time are not comparable. For instance, a loss of €10,000 when the portfolio has a value of €1 million has quite a different impact than a loss of €10,000 when the portfolio has a value of €10 million. We like to build mathematical models of returns because they are measured in relative terms and are therefore comparable over long periods of time, even when price levels have trended and/or varied considerably. But when the portfolio contains long and short positions, or when the risk factors themselves can take negative values, the concept of a return does not make sense, since the portfolio could have zero value. In that case VaR is measured directly from the distribution of P&L.

When VaR is estimated from a return distribution it is expressed as a percentage of the portfolio's current value. Since the current value of the portfolio is observable it is not a random variable. So we can perform calculations on the return distribution and express VaR as a percentage of the portfolio value and, if required, we can then convert the result to value terms by multiplying the percentage VaR by the current portfolio value.[30]

In summary, if we define the discounted h-day return on a portfolio as the random variable

$$X_{ht} = \frac{B_{ht}P_{t+h} - P_t}{P_t}, \qquad (IV.1.9)$$

then we can find $x_{ht,\alpha}$, the α quantile of its distribution, that is,

$$P(X_{ht} < x_{ht,\alpha}) = \alpha, \qquad (IV.1.10)$$

and our current estimate of the $100\alpha\%$ h-day VaR at time t is:

$$\text{VaR}_{ht,\alpha} = \begin{cases} -x_{ht,\alpha} & \text{as a percentage of the portfolio value } P_t, \\ -x_{ht,\alpha}P_t & \text{when expressed in value terms.} \end{cases} \qquad (IV.1.11)$$

IV.1.5 FOUNDATIONS OF VALUE-AT-RISK MEASUREMENT

In this section we derive a formula for VaR under the assumption that the returns on a linear portfolio are i.i.d. and normally distributed. After illustrating this formula with a numerical example we examine the assumption that the portfolio remains static over the risk horizon

---

[30] A VaR model is based on forward looking returns. So when we use a risk model to estimate h-day VaR we are producing a *forecast* of risk over the next h days. In much the same way as implied volatility is automatically defined as a forecast because it is based on option prices, VaR is automatically defined as a forecast: it summarizes the risk that the *future* return on a portfolio will be different from the risk free rate. But we shall refrain from using the terms 'VaR estimate' and 'VaR forecast' interchangeably, because we may want our risk model to really forecast VaR, i.e. to produce a forecast of what VaR will be some time in the future.

and show that this assumption determines the way we should scale the VaR over different risk horizons. Then we explain how the VaR formula should be adjusted when the expected excess return on the portfolio is non-zero. As the expected return deviates more from the risk free rate this adjustment has a greater effect, and the size of the adjustment also increases with the risk horizon. The adjustment can be important for risk horizons longer than a month or so. But when the risk horizon is relatively short, any assumption that returns are not expected to equal the risk free rate has only a very small impact on the VaR measure, and for this reason it is often ignored.

IV.1.5.1   Normal Linear VaR Formula: Portfolio Level

Suppose we only seek to measure the VaR of a portfolio without attributing the VaR to different risk factors. We also make the simplifying assumption that the portfolio's discounted h-day returns are i.i.d. and normally distributed. For simplicity of notation we shall, in this section, write the return as X, dropping the dependence on both time and risk horizon. Thus we assume

$$X \overset{i.i.d.}{\sim} N(\mu, \sigma^2). \tag{IV.1.12}$$

We will derive a formula for x_α, the α quantile return, i.e. the return such that $P(X < x_\alpha) = \alpha$. Then the $100\alpha\%$ VaR, expressed as a percentage of the portfolio value, is minus this α quantile. Using the standard normal transformation, we have

$$P(X < x_\alpha) = P\left(\frac{X - \mu}{\sigma} < \frac{x_\alpha - \mu}{\sigma} \right) = P\left(Z < \frac{x_\alpha - \mu}{\sigma} \right), \tag{IV.1.13}$$

where $Z \sim N(0, 1)$. So if $P(X < x_\alpha) = \alpha$, then

$$P\left(Z < \frac{x_\alpha - \mu}{\sigma} \right) = \alpha.$$

But by definition, $P(Z < \Phi^{-1}(\alpha)) = \alpha$, so

$$\frac{x_\alpha - \mu}{\sigma} = \Phi^{-1}(\alpha) \tag{IV.1.14}$$

where Φ is the standard normal distribution function. For instance, $\Phi^{-1}(0.01) = 2.3264$.

But $x_\alpha = -\text{VaR}_\alpha$ by definition, and $\Phi^{-1}(\alpha) = -\Phi^{-1}(1 - \alpha)$ by the symmetry of the standard normal distribution. Substituting these into (IV.1.14) yields an analytic formula for the VaR for a portfolio with an i.i.d. normal return, i.e.

$$\text{VaR}_\alpha = \Phi^{-1}(1 - \alpha)\sigma - \mu.$$

If we want to be more precise about the risk horizon of our VaR estimate, we may write

$$\text{VaR}_{h,\alpha} = \Phi^{-1}(1 - \alpha)\sigma_h - \mu_h. \tag{IV.1.15}$$

This is a simple formula for the $100\alpha\%$ h-day VaR, as a percentage of the portfolio value, when the portfolio's discounted returns are i.i.d. normally distributed with expectation μ_h and standard deviation σ_h.

To obtain the VaR in value terms, we simply multiply the percentage VaR by the current value of the portfolio:

$$\text{VaR}_{ht,\alpha} = (\Phi^{-1}(1-\alpha)\sigma_h - \mu_h)P_t, \tag{IV.1.16}$$

where P_t is the value of the portfolio at the time t when the VaR is measured. Note that when we express VaR in value terms, VaR *will* depend on time, even under the normal i.i.d. assumption using a constant mean and standard deviation for the portfolio return.

EXAMPLE IV.1.4: VAR WITH NORMALLY DISTRIBUTED RETURNS

What is the 10% VaR over a 1-year horizon of $2 million invested in a fund whose annual returns in excess of the risk free rate are assumed to be normally distributed with mean 5% and volatility 12%?

SOLUTION   Let the random variable X denote the annual returns in excess of the risk free rate, so we have

$$X \sim N(0.05, 0.12^2).$$

We must find the 10% quantile of the discounted return distribution, i.e. that x such that $P(X < x) = 0.1$. So we apply the standard normal transformation to X, and then find x such that

$$P\left(Z < \frac{x - 0.05}{0.12}\right) = 0.1.$$

From standard normal statistical tables or using NORMSINV(0.1) in Excel. We know that

$$P(Z < -1.2816) = 0.1.$$

Hence,

$$\frac{x - 0.05}{0.12} = -1.2816 \quad \text{or} \quad x = -1.2816 \times 0.12 + 0.05 = -0.1038.$$

Thus the 10% 1-year VaR is 10.38% of the portfolio value. With $2 million invested in the portfolio the VaR is $2m \times 0.1038 = \$207{,}572$. In other words, we are 90% confident that we will lose no more than $207,572 from investing in this fund over the next year.

Since we have assumed returns are i.i.d., the formula (IV.1.15) for the normal VaR, expressed as a percentage of the portfolio value, depends on the risk horizon h but it does not depend on time. That is, under the i.i.d. normal assumption VaR is a *constant* percentage of the portfolio value. However, to *estimate* VaR we need to use forecasts of σ_h and μ_h – forecasts that are based on an i.i.d. model for returns – and in practice these forecasts will change over time simply because the sample data change over time, or because our scenarios change over time. Hence, even though the model predicts that VaR is a constant percentage of the portfolio value, the estimated percentage will change over time, merely due to sample variations.

It is important to realize that all the problems with moving average models of volatility that we have discussed in Chapter II.3 will carry over to the normal linear VaR model. Since the returns are assumed to have a constant volatility, this should be estimated using an equally weighted moving average, which gives an unbiased estimator of the returns variance. But equally weighted average volatility estimates suffer from 'ghost features'. As a result, VaR will remain high for exactly T periods following one large extreme return, where T is the number of observations in the sample. Then it jumps down T periods later, even though nothing happened recently. See Section II.3.7 for further details.

In Section IV.3.3.1 we show that the choice of T has a very significant impact on an equally weighted VaR estimate – in fact, this choice has much more impact than the choice between using a normal linear (analytic) VaR estimate as above, and an estimate based on historical simulation. The larger T is, the less *risk sensitive* is the resulting VaR estimate, i.e. the less responsive is the VaR estimate to changing market conditions. For this reason many institutions use an exponentially weighted moving average (EWMA) methodology for VaR estimation, e.g. using EWMA to estimate volatility in the normal linear VaR formula. These estimates, if not the estimator, take account of volatility clustering so that EWMA VaR estimates are more risk sensitive than equally weighted VaR estimates. For example, the *RiskMetrics*™ methodology and supporting database allows analysts to choose between these two approaches. See Section II.3.8 for further details.

IV.1.5.2   Static Portfolios

Market VaR measures the risk of the current portfolio over the risk horizon, and in order to measure this we must hold the portfolio over the risk horizon. A portfolio may be specified at the asset level by stating the value of the *holdings* in each risky asset. If we know the value of the holdings then we can find the portfolio *value* and the *weights* on each asset. Alternatively, we can specify the portfolio weights on each asset and the total value of the portfolio. If we know these we can determine the holding in each asset.

Formally, consider a portfolio with (long or short) holdings $\{n_1, n_2, \ldots, n_k\}$ in k risky assets, so n_i is the number of units long ($n_i > 0$) or short ($n_i < 0$) in the ith asset, and denote the ith asset price at time t by p_{it}. Then the value of the holding in asset i at time t is is $n_i p_{it}$, and the portfolio value at time t is

$$P_t = \sum_{i=1}^{k} n_i p_{it}.$$

We can define the portfolio weight on the ith asset at time t as

$$w_{it} = \frac{n_i p_{it}}{P_t}.$$

In a long-only portfolio each $n_i > 0$ and so $P_t > 0$. In this case, the weights in a fully funded portfolio sum to one.

Note that even when the holdings are kept constant, i.e. the portfolio is not *rebalanced*, the value of the holding in asset i changes whenever the price of that asset changes, and the portfolio weight on every asset changes, whenever the price of one of the assets changes. So when we assume the portfolio is static, does this mean that the portfolio holdings are kept constant over the risk horizon, or that the portfolio weights are kept constant over the risk horizon? We cannot assume both. Instead we assume either

- *no rebalancing* – the portfolio holdings in each asset are kept constant, so each time the price of an asset changes, the value of our holding in that asset will change and hence all the portfolio weights will change; or

- *rebalancing to constant weights* – to keep the portfolio weights constant we must rebalance *all* the holdings whenever the price of just one asset changes.

Similar comments apply when a portfolio return (or P&L) is represented by a risk factor mapping. Most risk factor sensitivities depend on the price of the risk factor. For instance, the delta and the gamma of an option depend on the underlying price, and the PV01 of a cash flow depends on the level of the interest rate at that maturity. So when we say that a mapped portfolio is held constant, if this means that the risk factor sensitivities are held constant then we must rebalance the portfolio each time the price of a risk factor changes.

The risk analyst must specify his assumption about rebalancing the portfolio over the risk horizon. We shall distinguish between the two cases described above as follows:

- *Static VaR* assumes that no trading takes place during the risk horizon, so the holdings are kept constant, i.e. there is no rebalancing. Then the portfolio weights (or the risk factor sensitivities) will *not* be constant: they will change each time the price of an asset (or risk factor) changes. This assumption is used when we estimate VaR directly over the risk horizon, without scaling up an estimate corresponding to a short risk horizon to an estimate corresponding to a longer risk horizon. It does not lead to a tractable formula for the scaling of VaR to different risk horizons, as the next subsection demonstrates.
- *Dynamic VaR* assumes the portfolio is continually rebalanced so that the portfolio weights (or risk factor sensitivities, if VaR is estimated using a risk factor mapping) are held constant over the risk horizon. This assumption implies that the same risks are faced every trading day during the risk horizon, if we also assume that the asset (or risk factor) returns are i.i.d., and it leads to a simple scaling rule for VaR.

IV.1.5.3   Scaling VaR

Frequently market VaR is measured over a short-term risk horizon such as 1 day and then scaled up to represent VaR over a longer risk horizon. How should we scale a VaR that is estimated over one risk horizon to a VaR that is measured over a different risk horizon? And what assumptions need to be made for such a scaling?

The most tractable framework for scaling VaR is based on the assumption that the returns are i.i.d. normally distributed and that the portfolio is rebalanced daily to keep the portfolio *weights* constant. Similarly, if the VaR is based on a risk factor mapping, it is mathematically tractable to assume the *risk factor sensitivities* are constant over the risk horizon, and that the risk factor returns are i.i.d. and have a multivariate normal distribution. As a result the returns on a linear portfolio will be i.i.d. normally distributed.[31] So in the following we derive a formula for scaling VaR from a 1-day horizon to an h-day horizon under this assumption.

For simplicity of notation, from here onward we shall drop the t from the VaR notation, unless it is important to make explicit the time at which the VaR estimate is made. Also, in this section we do not include the discounting of the returns (or, equivalently, the expression of returns as excesses over the risk free rate) since this does not affect the scaling result, and it only makes the notation more cumbersome. Hence, to derive formulae (IV.1.18) and (IV.1.21) below we may, without loss of generality, assume the risk free rate is zero.

---

[31] Note that this assumption is very unrealistic, even for linear portfolios but especially for portfolios containing options. Since options prices are non-linear functions of the underlying price, if we assume the underlying returns are normally distributed (as is often assumed in option theory) then the returns on a portfolio containing options cannot be normally distributed.

Suppose we measure VaR over a 1-day horizon, and assume that the daily return is i.i.d. normal. Then we have proved above that the 1-day VaR is given by

$$\text{VaR}_{1,\alpha} = \Phi^{-1}(1 - \alpha)\,\sigma_1 - \mu_1 \tag{IV.1.17}$$

where μ_1 and σ_1 are the expectation and standard deviation of the normally distributed daily returns. We now use a log approximation to the daily discounted return. To be more specific, we let[32]

$$X_{1t} \approx \frac{P_{t+1} - P_t}{P_t} \approx \ln\left(\frac{P_{t+1}}{P_t}\right),$$

where P_t denotes the portfolio price at time t. We use this approximation because it is convenient, i.e. log returns are additive. That is, the h-day discounted log return is the sum of h consecutive daily discounted log returns. Since the sum of normal variables is another normal variable, the h-day discounted log returns are normally distributed with expectation $\mu_h = h\mu_1$ and standard deviation $\sigma_h = \sqrt{h}\sigma_1$, as proved in Section II.3.2.1.

We now approximate the h-day log return with the ordinary h-day return, and deduce that this is (approximately) normally distributed. Then the h-day VaR is given by the approximation

$$\text{VaR}_{h,\alpha} \approx \Phi^{-1}(1 - \alpha)\,\sqrt{h}\,\sigma_1 - h\,\mu_1. \tag{IV.1.18}$$

This approximation is reasonably good when h is small, but as h increases the approximation of the h-day log return with the ordinary h-day return becomes increasingly inaccurate.

What happens if we drop the assumption of independence but retain the assumption that the returns have identical normal distributions? In Section IV.2.2.2 we prove that if the daily log return follows a first order autoregressive process with autocorrelation ϱ then the expectation of the h-day log return is $\mu_h = h\mu_1$ (so autocorrelation does not affect the scaling of the mean) but the standard deviation of the h-day log return is

$$\sigma_h = \sqrt{\tilde{h}}\,\sigma_1, \tag{IV.1.19}$$

with

$$\tilde{h} = h + 2\varrho(1 - \varrho)^{-2}\left((h - 1)(1 - \varrho) - \varrho(1 - \varrho^{h-1})\right). \tag{IV.1.20}$$

Hence, in this case,

$$\text{VaR}_{h,\alpha} \approx \Phi^{-1}(1 - \alpha)\sqrt{\tilde{h}}\,\sigma_1 - h\,\mu_1, \tag{IV.1.21}$$

with $\tilde{h}$ defined by (IV.1.20).

EXAMPLE IV.1.5: SCALING NORMAL VAR WITH INDEPENDENT AND WITH AUTOCORRELATED RETURNS

A portfolio has daily returns, discounted to today, that are normally and identically distributed with expectation 0% and standard deviation 1.5%. Find the 1% 1-day VaR. Then find the 1% 10-day VaR under the assumption that the daily excess returns (a) are independent,

---

[32] Here we use the forward looking return because VaR measures risk over a future horizon, not over the past.

and (b) follow a first order autoregressive process with autocorrelation 0.25. Does positive autocorrelation increase or decrease the VaR?

SOLUTION   Using formula (IV.1.17), the 1% 1-day VaR is

$$\mathrm{VaR}_{1,0.01} = \Phi^{-1}(0.99) \times 0.015 = 0.034895,$$

i.e. 3.4895% of the portfolio value. Now we scale the VaR under the assumption of i.i.d. normal returns. By (IV.1.18) the 1% 10-day VaR is approximately $\sqrt{10}$ times the 1% 1-day VaR, because the discounted expected return is zero. So the 1% 10-day VaR is approximately

$$\mathrm{VaR}_{10,0.01} = \sqrt{10} \times 3.4895\% = 11.0348\%.$$

Finally, with $h = 10$ and $\varrho = 0.25$ the scaling factor (IV.1.20) is not 10, but 15.778. So under the assumption that returns have an autocorrelation of 0.25, the 1% 10-day VaR is approximately

$$\mathrm{VaR}_{10,0.01} = \sqrt{15.778} \times 3.4895\% = 13.8608\%.$$

A positive autocorrelation in daily returns increases the standard deviation of h-day returns, compared with that of independent returns. Hence, positive autocorrelation increases VaR, and the longer the risk horizon the more the VaR will increase. On the other hand, a negative autocorrelation in daily returns will decrease the VaR, especially over long time horizons. Readers may verify this by changing the parameters in the spreadsheet for this example.

Scaling VaR when returns are not normally distributed is a complex question to answer, so we shall address it later in this book. In particular, see Sections IV.2.8 and IV.3.2.3.

IV.1.5.4   Discounting and the Expected Return

We now examine the effect of discounting returns on VaR and ask two related questions:

- Over what time horizon does it become important to include any non-zero expected excess return in the VaR calculation?
- If we fail to discount P&L in the VaR formula, i.e. if we do not express returns as excess over the risk free rate, does this have a significant effect on the results?

Banking regulators often argue that the expected return on all portfolios should be equal to the risk free rate of return. In this case the discounted expected P&L will be zero or, put another way, the expected excess return will be zero. If we do assume that the expected excess return is zero the normal linear VaR formula becomes even simpler, because the second term is zero and the h-day VaR, expressed as a percentage of the current portfolio value, is just the standard deviation of the h-day return, multiplied by the standard normal critical value at the confidence level $1 - \alpha$.

The situation is different in portfolio management. When quoting risk adjusted performance measures to their clients, fund managers often believe that they can provide returns greater than the risk free rate by judicious asset allocation and stock selection. However, expectations are highly subjective and could even be a source of argument between a fund manager and his client, or between a bank and its regulator. Corporate treasurers, on the other hand, are free to assume any expected return they wish. They are not constrained by regulators or clients.

We now prove that when portfolios are expected to return a rate different from the risk free rate this should be included as an adjustment to the VaR. This is obvious in the normal i.i.d. framework described above, since the discounted mean return appears in the VaR formula. But it is also true in general. To see why, consider the distribution of P&L at time $t + h$, as seen from the current time t. This is the distribution of $P_{t+h} - E_t(P_{t+h})$ where $E_t(P_{t+h})$ is the conditional expectation seen from time t of the portfolio value at time $t + h$. That is, it is conditional on the information available up to time t.

Denote by $y_{ht,\alpha}$ the α quantile of this distribution, discounted to time t. That is,

$$P\big(B_{ht}(P_{t+h} - E_t(P_{t+h})) < y_{ht,\alpha}\big) = \alpha, \tag{IV.1.22}$$

where B_{ht} is the value at time t of a discount bond maturing in h trading days. Now (IV.1.22) may be rewritten as

$$P\big(B_{ht}P_{t+h} - P_t < y_{ht,\alpha} + (B_{ht}E_t(P_{t+h}) - P_t)\big) = \alpha,$$

or as

$$P\big(B_{ht}P_{t+h} - P_t < y_{ht,\alpha} - \varepsilon_{ht}\big) = \alpha, \tag{IV.1.23}$$

where $\varepsilon_{ht} = P_t - B_{ht}E_t(P_{t+h})$ is the difference between the current portfolio price and its expected future price, discounted at the risk free rate.[33]

Note that ε_{ht} is only zero if the portfolio is expected to return the risk free rate, i.e. if $E_t(P_{t+h}) = (B_{ht})^{-1}P_t$. Otherwise, comparing (IV.1.23) with (IV.1.8), we have

$$x_{ht,\alpha} = y_{ht,\alpha} - \varepsilon_{ht} \Rightarrow \text{VaR}_{ht,\alpha} = -y_{ht,\alpha} + \varepsilon_{ht}. \tag{IV.1.24}$$

Hence, the VaR is minus the α quantile of the discounted P&L distribution *plus* ε_{ht}, if this is not zero. When the expected return on the portfolio is greater than the risk free rate of return, ε_{ht} will be negative, resulting in a reduction in the portfolio VaR. The opposite is the case if the portfolio is expected to return less than the risk free rate, and in this case the VaR will increase.

The following example shows that this adjustment term ε_{ht}, which we call the *drift adjustment* to the VaR, can be substantial but only when VaR is measured over a risk horizon of several months or more.

EXAMPLE IV.1.6: ADJUSTING VAR FOR NON-ZERO EXPECTED EXCESS RETURNS

Suppose that a portfolio's return is normally distributed with mean 10% and standard deviation 20%, both expressed in annual terms. The risk free interest rate is 5% per annum. Calculate the 1% VaR as a percentage of the portfolio value when the risk horizon is 1 week, 2 weeks, 1 month, 6 months and 12 months.

SOLUTION   The calculations are set out in the spreadsheet and results are reported in Table IV.1.3 below. As anticipated, the reduction in VaR arising from the positive expected

---

[33] So if the portfolio price follows a martingale process, ε_{ht} is zero.

excess return increases with the risk horizon. Up to 1 month ahead, the effect of the expected excess return is very small: it is less than 0.5% of the portfolio value. However, with a risk horizon of one year (as may be used by hedge funds, for instance) the VaR can be reduced by almost 5% of the portfolio value if we take account of an expected excess return of 5%.

Table IV.1.3   Normal VaR with drift adjustment

Risk horizon (months)	0.25	0.5	1	3	6	12
Mean return	0.21%	0.42%	0.83%	2.50%	5%	10%
Volatility of return	3%	4%	6%	10%	14%	20%
Discount factor	0.99896	0.99792	0.99585	0.98765	0.97561	0.95238
Mean return*	0.10%	0.21%	0.41%	1.23%	2.44%	4.76%
Volatility of return*	2.88%	4.07%	5.75%	9.88%	13.80%	19.05%
Lower 1% quantile	−0.06605	−0.09270	−0.12961	−0.21742	−0.29658	−0.39549
1% VaR**	6.71%	9.48%	13.38%	22.98%	32.10%	44.31%
1% VaR	6.60%	9.27%	12.96%	21.74%	29.66%	39.55%
Difference	0.10%	0.21%	0.41%	1.23%	2.44%	4.76%

Note: * denotes that the quantities are discounted, and ** denotes that the VaR is based on a zero mean excess return.

Readers may use the spreadsheet to verify the following:

- Keep the mean return at 10% but change the volatility of the portfolio return. This has a great effect on the values of the VaR estimates but it has no influence on the difference shown in the last row; the only thing that affects the difference between the non-drift adjusted VaR and the drift adjusted VaR is the expected excess return (and the portfolio value, if the VaR is expressed in value terms).
- Keep the portfolio volatility at 20%, but change the expected return. This shows that when the portfolio is expected to return $x\%$ above the risk free rate, the reduction in VaR at the 1-year horizon is a little less than $x\%$ of the portfolio value.[34]

IV.1.6   RISK FACTOR VALUE AT RISK

In the previous section we described one simple model for measuring the VaR of a linear portfolio at the portfolio level. We also obtained just one figure, for the *total VaR* of the portfolio, but this is not where VaR measurement stops – if it were, this book would be considerably shorter than it is. In practice, VaR measures are based on a *risk factor mapping* of the portfolio, in which case the model provides an estimate of the *systematic VaR*, also called the *total risk factor VaR*. The systematic VaR may itself be decomposed into the VaR due to different types of risk factors. The *specific VaR*, also called *residual VaR*, measures the risk that is not captured by the mapping.

A risk factor mapping entails the construction of a model that relates the portfolio return, or P&L, to variations in its risk factors. For example, with an international equity portfolio

---

[34] It can be shown that the reduction in 1-year VaR when we take account of an expected return that is different from the risk free rate of return is approximately equal to $(E(R) - R_f) \times (1 - R_f)$, where $E(R)$ is the expected return on the portfolio and R_f is the risk free rate over the risk horizon of the VaR model.

having positions on cash equity and index futures we would typically consider variations in the following risk factors:

- major market spot equity indices (such as S&P 500, FTSE 100, CAC 40);
- spot foreign exchange (forex) rates (such as $/£, $/€);
- dividend yields in each major market;
- spot LIBOR rates of maturity equal to the maturity of the futures in the domestic and foreign currencies (such as USD, GBP and EUR).

In the factor model, the coefficient parameters on the risk factor variations are called the portfolio's *sensitivities* to variations in the risk factors. For instance, the international equity portfolio above has:

- a sensitivity that is called a *beta* with respect to each of the major stock indices;
- a sensitivity that is one with respect to each exchange rate;
- a sensitivity that is called a PV01 with respect to each interest rate, or each dividend yield.[35]

The whole of Chapter III.5 was devoted to describing risk factor mappings and risk factor sensitivities for different types of portfolios, and it is recommended that readers are familiar with this, or similar material.

IV.1.6.1 Motivation

The process of *risk attribution* is the mapping of total risk factor VaR to component VaRs corresponding to different types of risk factors. The reason why risk managers map portfolios to their risk factors is that the analysis of the components of risk corresponding to different risk factors provides an efficient framework for hedging these risks, and for capital allocation. Risk factors are often common to several portfolios, for instance:

- Foreign exchange rates are common to all international portfolios, whether they contain equities, commodities or bonds and other interest rate sensitive instruments. The enterprise-wide exposures to forex rates are often managed centrally, so that these risks can be netted across different portfolios. But a manager of an international equity or bond portfolio will still want to know his forex risk, as measured by his forex VaR. So will the risk manager and senior managers, since they need to know which activities are the main contributors to each type of risk.
- Zero-coupon yield curves are common to any portfolio containing futures or forwards, as well as to interest rate sensitive portfolios. And if the portfolio is international then yield curves in different currencies are risk factors. Interest rate risk is the uncertainty about the present value of future cash flows, and this changes as discount rates change from

---

[35] Note that the PV01 is measured in value (e.g. dollar) terms but the first two sensitivities are measured in percentage terms; to convert these into value terms we just multiply by the amount invested in each country, in domestic currency. Or, to convert the PV01 to percentage terms, divide it by the total amount invested in that portfolio which has exposure to that yield curve.

day to day. Except for portfolios consisting entirely of interest rate sensitive instruments, interest rate risk is often one of the smallest risks. The firm can use the VaR model to net these risks when aggregating interest rate VaR across different activities.

Another reason why we base VaR on a risk factor mapping is that typical portfolios are too large to measure VaR by mapping to all of its instruments. It is technically infeasible to analyse the risk of most portfolios without the aid of risk factor mapping. For example, measuring VaR at the level of each asset in a stock portfolio containing 1000 stocks requires modelling the multivariate distribution of 1000 stock returns. Usually we try to summarize this distribution using only the returns covariance matrix, but in this example we would still have to deal with an enormous matrix.

Only a few portfolios are so small that they do not require risk factor mapping. For instance, we do not really need to map a private investor's portfolio that has cash positions in only a few stocks, or any other small portfolio containing similar and straightforward positions. But small, cash portfolios are not the business of financial institutions. Typically, the institution will handle tens of thousands of complex positions with exposures to hundreds of different risk factors. Hence, even measuring VaR at the risk factor level is a formidable challenge.

Another advantage of risk factor mapping is that it provides a convenient framework for the daily work of a market risk manager. He requires many *stress tests* of current positions and an overall assessment of whether capital is available to cover these risks. Stress tests are usually conducted by changing risk factor values – firstly because this gives the risk manager further insight into his risk attribution, and secondly because it would be impossible to investigate different scenarios for each individual asset.

When we measure VaR on portfolios that are mapped to risk factors there are three important sources of *model risk* in the VaR estimate:

- The choice of risk factor mapping is subjective. A different risk manager might choose a different set of risk factors.
- The risk factor sensitivities may have estimation errors. For stock portfolios the risk factor sensitivities, which are called risk factor betas, depend on a model, and their estimation is subject to sampling error, as we have seen in Section II.1.2.
- The specific risk of the portfolio is ignored. By measuring VaR based on a risk factor mapping, all we capture is the systematic VaR.

There are many other sources of model risk in a VaR model and a full discussion of this is given in Chapter IV.6.

IV.1.6.2   Normal Linear Equity VaR

We now provide some very simple examples of the measurement of VaR based on a risk factor mapping. In this subsection we consider the case of a cash equity portfolio with excess return Y and we assume it has a single risk factor, such as a broad market index, with excess return X. Then the factor model may be written

$$Y_t = \tilde{\alpha} + \beta X_t + \varepsilon_t, \tag{IV.1.25}$$

where $\tilde{\alpha}$ and β are constant parameters and ε_t is the specific return.[36] We suppose the risk factor excess returns X are normally distributed, and that the expected excess return over the next h days is μ_h with a standard deviation of σ_h. Then the portfolio's excess returns due to the movements in the index will also be normally distributed, with expectation $\tilde{\alpha} + \beta\mu_h$ and standard deviation $\beta\sigma_h$.

Since the portfolio's alpha is idiosyncratic to the portfolio, it does not enter the systematic part of the risk; instead it enters the specific risk component of the VaR. Thus to measure the systematic VaR of the portfolio, which is here called the *equity* VaR since the only risk factor is an equity index, we assume the portfolio's excess return are normally distributed with expectation $\beta\mu_h$ and standard deviation $\beta\sigma_h$.

Now, using the same argument as in Section IV.1.5.1 when we derived the normal linear VaR formula at the portfolio level, the normal linear systematic VaR of the portfolio is

$$\text{Equity VaR}_{h,\alpha} = \beta\left(\Phi^{-1}(1-\alpha)\sigma_h - \mu_h\right). \tag{IV.1.26}$$

The following example illustrates a simple application of this formula for a two-stock portfolio with one risk factor.

EXAMPLE IV.1.7: EQUITY VAR

A portfolio contains cash positions on two stocks: $1 million is invested in a stock with a beta of 1.2 and $2 million is invested in a stock with a beta of 0.8 with respect to a broad market index. If the excess returns on the index are i.i.d. and normally distributed with expectation 5% and volatility 20% per annum, what is the 1% 10-day VaR of the portfolio?

SOLUTION   The net portfolio beta is measured in dollar terms as

$$\beta_\$ = \$1\text{m} \times 1.2 + \$2\text{m} \times 0.8 = \$2.8\text{m}.$$

Note that using the dollar beta in (IV.1.26) gives the equity VaR in dollar terms, not as a percentage of the portfolio value. The 10-day expected excess return on the risk factor is

$$\mu_{10} = 0.05 \times 10/250 = 0.2\%,$$

and the 10-day standard deviation of the excess returns on the market index is

$$\sigma_{10} = 0.2 \times (10/250)^{1/2} = 0.2/5 = 4\%.$$

Hence, the 1% 10-day equity VaR is

$$\text{Equity VaR}_{10,0.01} = \$2.8\text{m} \times (2.32635 \times 4\% - 0.2\%) = \$254,951.$$

---

[36] The only reason why we place a tilde '$\sim$' over α here is to avoid confusion with the α that denotes the significance level of the VaR estimate.

IV.1.6.3 Normal Linear Interest Rate VaR

This subsection introduces the interest rate VaR of bonds, swaps and loans portfolios that can be represented as a series of cash flows. In Section III.5.2.1 we explained how to represent an interest rate sensitive portfolio using an approximate linear risk factor model, called a *cash-flow map*, the salient details of which are summarized below for convenience.[37]

The discounted P&L on the portfolio is the net change in present value of the entire cash flow series, and the linear approximation derived in Section III.5.2.1 is

$$\Delta PV \approx -\sum_{i=1}^{n} PV01_i \times \Delta R_i.$$

Alternatively, using the matrix algebra that was introduced in Chapter I.2, this may be written in matrix form as

$$\Delta PV \approx -\boldsymbol{\theta}' \Delta \mathbf{r}, \qquad (IV.1.27)$$

where

- $\boldsymbol{\theta} = (PV01_1, \ldots, PV01_n)'$ is the vector of risk factor sensitivities, that is, $\boldsymbol{\theta}$ is a vector whose ith element is the PV01 of the cash flow that is mapped to the ith vertex;[38] and
- $\Delta \mathbf{r} = (\Delta R_1, \ldots, \Delta R_n)'$ is the vector of changes (measured in basis points) in interest rates at the standard maturities (which are also called the *vertices* of the risk factor mapping).

Since the PV01 is the *present value* of a basis point change, the change in the portfolio value given by the risk factor representation (IV.1.27) is already measured in present value terms.

Suppose that $\Delta \mathbf{r}$ has a multivariate normal distribution with mean $\boldsymbol{\mu}$ and covariance matrix $\boldsymbol{\Omega}$. Then, based on the linear mapping (IV.1.27), the discounted P&L also has a normal distribution with expectation $-\boldsymbol{\theta}' \boldsymbol{\mu}$ and variance $\boldsymbol{\theta}' \boldsymbol{\Omega} \boldsymbol{\theta}$. It is particularly important to understand the quadratic form $\boldsymbol{\theta}' \boldsymbol{\Omega} \boldsymbol{\theta}$ for the variance, since this will be used many times in Chapter IV.2.[39] The minus sign appears in the expectation because the PV01 measures the sensitivity to a one basis point *fall* in interest rates. Thus, applying the normal linear VaR formula (IV.1.15), the VaR of the cash flow is

$$VaR_\alpha = \Phi^{-1}(1 - \alpha)\sqrt{\boldsymbol{\theta}' \boldsymbol{\Omega} \boldsymbol{\theta}} + \boldsymbol{\theta}' \boldsymbol{\mu}.$$

We often assume that the same interest rate risk factors are used for discounting, in which case $\boldsymbol{\theta}' \boldsymbol{\mu}$, the expected change in portfolio value, is zero. We also measure the covariance matrix over a specific h-day period. Thus, denoting the h-day interest rate covariance matrix by $\boldsymbol{\Omega}_h$, the formula for the normal linear $100\alpha\%$ h-day VaR for a cash flow becomes

$$\text{Interest Rate } VaR_{h,\alpha} = \Phi^{-1}(1 - \alpha)\sqrt{\boldsymbol{\theta}' \boldsymbol{\Omega}_h \boldsymbol{\theta}}. \qquad (IV.1.28)$$

---

[37] The mapping procedure for creating the cash flows of different maturities to standard vertices is quite complex, and for this we refer readers to Section III.5.3. This is a long section that covers different cash-flow mappings in detail.

[38] See Section III.1.8 for the definition of PV01 and an approximation that is useful for calculating the PV01.

[39] Readers who are not entirely comfortable with this should consult Section I.2.4.2 for further information.

EXAMPLE IV.1.8: NORMAL VAR OF A SIMPLE CASH FLOW

Find the 1% 10-day VaR of a cash flow that is mapped to a 1-year and a 2-year vertex with PV01 of $50 and $75, respectively. Assume the absolute changes in 1-year and 2-year interest rates over the next 10 days have a multivariate normal distribution with expectation 0, correlation 0.9 and with annual volatilities of 100 basis points for the change in the 1-year rate and 80 basis points for the change in the 2-year rate.

SOLUTION   We use the formula (IV.1.28) with $h = 10$, $\alpha = 0.01$, $\boldsymbol{\theta} = (50,\ 75)'$ and where $\boldsymbol{\Omega}_{10}$ is the 10-day covariance matrix of the risk factor changes, expressed in basis points. We have the annual covariance matrix

$$\boldsymbol{\Omega} = \begin{pmatrix} 100^2 & 0.9 \times 100 \times 80 \\ 0.9 \times 100 \times 80 & 80^2 \end{pmatrix}.$$

So the 10-day matrix is

$$\boldsymbol{\Omega}_{10} = \frac{10}{250} \begin{pmatrix} 100^2 & 0.9 \times 100 \times 80 \\ 0.9 \times 100 \times 80 & 80^2 \end{pmatrix} = \begin{pmatrix} 400 & 288 \\ 288 & 256 \end{pmatrix}.$$

Hence,

$$\boldsymbol{\theta}'\boldsymbol{\Omega}_{10}\boldsymbol{\theta} = \begin{pmatrix} 50 & 75 \end{pmatrix} \begin{pmatrix} 400 & 288 \\ 288 & 256 \end{pmatrix} \begin{pmatrix} 50 \\ 75 \end{pmatrix} = 4,600,000$$

and

$$\sqrt{\boldsymbol{\theta}'\boldsymbol{\Omega}_{10}\boldsymbol{\theta}} = \$2144.76.$$

The 1% 10-day VaR is therefore $2.32635 \times \$2144.76 = \$4989$.

IV.1.7 DECOMPOSITION OF VALUE AT RISK

This section explains how to aggregate VaR over different activities and disaggregate it into components corresponding to different types of risk factors. The level of discussion is very general and we do not provide any examples. However, numerous numerical and empirical examples are given in later chapters as we investigate each of the three VaR models in greater depth.

The ability to aggregate and disaggregate VaR is an essential management tool. The aggregation of VaR allows total risk to be assigned to different activities. Indeed, this is the fundamental tool for the *risk budgeting* process, which is the allocation of economic capital to activities, the allocation of (VaR-based) limits for traders, and the estimation of the size of the regulatory capital requirement for market risk. Or they may call for further supervision of high risk activities. The disaggregation of VaR helps a risk analyst to understand the main sources of risk in a portfolio. Good risk managers use VaR decomposition to be better informed about the risks that need to be hedged, about the limits that traders should be set, and about the risks of potential trades or investments.

IV.1.7.1   Systematic and Specific VaR

The total risk of a portfolio may be decomposed into *systematic risk*, i.e. the risk that is captured by mapping the portfolio to risk factors, and *specific risk*, i.e. the risk that is not captured by the portfolio mapping. Some numerical and empirical illustrations of this type of VaR disaggregation are provided in Sections IV.2.5.2–IV.2.5.4.

For an example of specific risk, consider portfolios of commodity futures which use spot prices as risk factors. Here a specific risk arises due to fluctuations in carry costs, if these are not captured by the portfolio mapping. Another example is when a factor model is used to map an equity portfolio to its risk factors. Few factor models can provide perfect descriptions of portfolio returns. There will be a model residual that may have high volatility, especially when portfolios are not well diversified. In large diversified portfolios the specific returns on each stock that are left to the model's residuals tend to cancel each other out if the factor model is well specified. But if inappropriate (or too few) risk factors are used in the factor model, the specific risk of the portfolio can be large. In that case we can measure the specific risk by saving the factor model residuals and applying the VaR model directly to these.

The *total VaR* includes both the systematic and the specific VaR components. To calculate this directly we forget about the risk factor mapping and measure the VaR at the portfolio level, i.e. using a univariate series of portfolio returns or P&L. In the simple normal linear model this could be based on an assumed (or estimated) value for portfolio volatility; in the historical VaR model we build an empirical distribution using a time series for the portfolio returns or P&L; and in the Monte Carlo VaR model we simulate this distribution using a parametric model for the portfolio's P&L.

An alternative to the direct calculation of the total VaR is to assume the specific and systematic risks are approximately uncorrelated. Of course, this would only be the case when the factor model is capturing most of the variation in the portfolio. Then, in the normal linear model, the total VaR will be the square root of the sum of the systematic VaR squared and the specific VaR squared.[40] Just adding up the systematic and specific risks is not a good way to estimate the total risk, because this assumes the systematic and specific risks are perfectly correlated! Thus, the systematic risk should dominate the total risk, but this happens only if it is much larger than the specific risk of the portfolio. The regulatory requirements for specific risk are that a specific risk 'add-on' must be applied to the systematic risk to obtain the total risk, unless the risk model allows one to incorporate the specific risk into the total VaR estimate.[41]

IV.1.7.2   Stand-alone VaR

We may also decompose the systematic risk of a portfolio into 'stand-alone' components that correspond to fundamental risk factors. The aim is to disaggregate VaR into the risk associated with particular asset classes: *equity VaR, interest rate VaR, forex VaR* and *commodity VaR*.[42] This allows the forex and interest rate risks of all types of securities in international portfolios to be individually assessed, and then combined and managed by separate desks. The disaggregation of VaR into stand-alone components is important even for domestic portfolios.

---

[40] However, no such simple rules apply to the VaR models that are based on simulation.
[41] See Section IV.8.2.4 for further details.
[42] Gold is usually included in forex VaR rather than commodity VaR.

For instance, the systematic risk of commodity futures portfolios would be based on movements in spot commodity prices, if we used these as the risk factors, but under such a mapping portfolios also have interest rate and net carry cost VaR components.

The decomposition of systematic VaR into stand-alone components can be applied whatever the assumptions made about the evolution of risk factors, and for any type of portfolio. Stand-alone VaR is calculated by setting all the sensitivities to other risk factors to zero. The precise computation depends on the VaR model used and further details are given throughout the remaining chapters.[43]

Stand-alone VaR measures the risk of an asset class *in isolation*. It is stand-alone capital that should be used to compare the performance of different trading activities. Assuming the trading desks are managed separately, any diversification benefits should be excluded when assessing their risks. No single desk should be rewarded or penalized for diversification in the overall businesses. The correlation between different risk factors, e.g. the correlation between equity returns and changes in interest rates, is taken into account only when we aggregate stand-alone VaR estimates.

Stand-alone components of VaR do not 'add up', unless we assume that portfolios are linear and everything is perfectly correlated. In the normal linear VaR model the total risk factor VaR will be equal to the sum of the stand-alone component VaRs if *and only if* all the risk factors are perfectly correlated. Otherwise, the total VaR will be *less* than the sum of the stand-alone component VaRs, a property that is known as *sub-additivity*.[44] This is because the VaR is determined by the volatility of portfolio returns in the linear model, and variance (i.e. the square of the volatility) obeys nice mathematical rules.

More generally, we use some type of simulation to resolve the risk model. Then VaR is measured as a *quantile* and quantiles need not be sub-additive, as we shall demonstrate below. But if the sum of the stand-alone component VaRs does exceed the total VaR, then stand-alone capital is not appropriate for risk budgeting. Individual portfolios could be within their risk limits yet the business overall could be in breach of limits. The reason why many large economic capital driven organizations (mainly large banks and corporations) prefer to use conditional VaR (expected tail loss) instead of VaR for risk budgeting purposes is that conditional VaR is sub-additive, whatever the resolution method in the risk model.

IV.1.7.3 Marginal and Incremental VaR

An alternative way to disaggregate VaR is to decompose it into *marginal VaR* components. Marginal VaR assigns a *proportion* of the total risk to each component, and hence provides the risk manager with a description of the *relative* risk contributions from different factors to the systematic risk of a diversified portfolio. Unlike stand-alone VaR, marginal VaR is additive, by virtue of its definition as a proportion. In other words, the sum of the marginal VaR components is the systematic VaR. For this reason, marginal VaR can be used to allocate *real* capital which, being money, must add up.

---

[43] For specific examples of VaR decomposition in the parametric linear framework see Examples IV.2.5 and IV.2.6 for interest rate sensitive portfolios, Examples IV.2.14–IV.2.17 for equity portfolios and case study IV.2.7 for commodity portfolios. Historical VaR decomposition is also covered in a series of case studies: in Section IV.3.5.3 for equity and forex VaR, Section IV.3.5.4 for interest rate and forex VaR, and IV.3.5.5 for commodity VaR. We also derive the marginal VaR estimates in these examples and case studies.
[44] A formal definition of sub-additivity is given later in the chapter.

As its name suggests, marginal VaR is the sensitivity of VaR to the risk factor model parameters, i.e. the sensitivity of VaR to the risk factor sensitivities $\boldsymbol{\theta} = (\theta_1, \ldots, \theta_n)'$.[45] Note that $\boldsymbol{\theta}$ can usually be measured in either percentage or value terms, and this determines whether VaR itself is measured in percentage or value terms.

We now derive an expression for the marginal VaR, by writing VaR as a function of these parameters, and using some elementary calculus.[46] That is, we assume that

$$\text{VaR} = f(\boldsymbol{\theta})$$

for some unspecified but differentiable function f. The gradient vector of first partial derivatives is

$$\mathbf{g}(\boldsymbol{\theta}) = \big(f_1(\boldsymbol{\theta}), \ldots, f_n(\boldsymbol{\theta})\big)', \qquad\qquad\text{(IV.1.29)}$$

where

$$f_i(\boldsymbol{\theta}) = \frac{\partial f(\boldsymbol{\theta})}{\partial \theta_i} \quad \text{for } i = 1, \ldots, n.$$

Hence, a first order Taylor approximation to VaR is

$$f(\boldsymbol{\theta}) \approx \boldsymbol{\theta}'\mathbf{g}(\boldsymbol{\theta}) = \sum_{i=1}^{n} \theta_i f_i(\boldsymbol{\theta}). \qquad\qquad\text{(IV.1.30)}$$

Each term $\theta_i f_i(\boldsymbol{\theta})$ in the sum is called the ith marginal component VaR, or just the ith *marginal VaR* for short.

When the portfolio is linear and the VaR is estimated from the normal linear VaR model then the approximation in (IV.1.30) is exact. In this case the sum of the marginal VaRs is always equal to the total risk factor VaR. But for other portfolios, and also when VaR is estimated using simulation, the sum of the marginal VaRs is only approximately equal to the total risk factor VaR.

The gradient vector (IV.1.29) can also be used to approximate the VaR impact of a small trade. For instance, it can be used to assess the impact of a partial hedge on a trader's VaR limit. We use a first order Taylor approximation to the change in VaR for a small change in $\boldsymbol{\theta}$. Suppose $\boldsymbol{\theta}$ changes from $\boldsymbol{\theta}_0$ to $\boldsymbol{\theta}_1$. Then the associated change in VaR is

$$f(\boldsymbol{\theta}_1) - f(\boldsymbol{\theta}_0) \approx (\boldsymbol{\theta}_1 - \boldsymbol{\theta}_0)'\mathbf{g}(\boldsymbol{\theta}_0). \qquad\qquad\text{(IV.1.31)}$$

This change in VaR is called the *incremental VaR*.

IV.1.8 RISK METRICS ASSOCIATED WITH VALUE AT RISK

Active portfolio managers are usually required to benchmark their risk as well as their returns. During the last decade this task caused considerable confusion. Even the phrase 'the risk of returns relative to the benchmark' is ambiguous, as discussed in Section II.1.6. This section

---

[45] For portfolios that have not been mapped to risk factors, $\boldsymbol{\theta}$ can represent the portfolio weights (for VaR in percentage terms) or holdings (for VaR in nominal terms).

[46] Functions of several variables and their derivatives are covered in Section I.1.5 and Taylor expansion is introduced in Section I.1.6.

begins by introducing benchmark VaR, a metric that is suitable for measuring risk relative to a benchmark.

Unless VaR is measured using a simple model, such as the normal linear model, it is not sub-additive. That is, the sum of the stand-alone component VaRs may be greater than the total VaR. In this case the whole concept of risk budgeting flies out of the window. Traders could keep within risk limits for each portfolio but the total limit for the desk could be exceeded. Desk managers could adhere to strict limits, but the total risk budget for the organization as a whole could still be exceeded. Hence, for risk budgeting purposes most large economic capital driven organizations use a risk metric that is associated with VaR, and which is sub-additive. This is a *conditional* VaR metric that we call *expected tail loss* or, if measured relative to a benchmark, *expected shortfall*. Conditional VaR satisfies all the properties for being a *coherent* risk metric, in a sense that will presently be made precise.

IV.1.8.1   Benchmark VaR

When returns are measured relative to a benchmark we consider the *active return*, which we assume is the difference between the portfolio return and the benchmark return.[47] Then, expressing VaR in percentage terms, the *benchmark VaR* is the α quantile of the h-day active return distribution, discounted to today.

EXAMPLE IV.1.9: BENCHMARK VAR WITH NORMALLY DISTRIBUTED RETURNS

What is the 1% benchmark VaR over a 1-year horizon for $10 million invested in a fund with an expected active return equal to the risk free interest rate and a tracking error of 3%?[48]

SOLUTION   Since the expected active return is equal to the risk free rate, the discounted active return has expectation zero. The tracking error is the standard deviation of the active return. Hence, we apply the normal linear VaR formula (IV.1.15) with

$$h = 1\text{year}, \quad \alpha = 0.01, \quad \sigma_{1\text{year}} = 3\% \quad \text{and} \quad \mu_{1\text{year}} = 0.$$

The standard normal critical value is $\Phi^{-1}(0.99) = 2.3264$, hence the 1% 1-year benchmark VaR is

$$\text{VaR}_{1\text{year},0.01} = 2.3264 \times 0.03 = 6.98\%.$$

Multiplying this by the portfolio value of $10 million gives the 1% benchmark VaR of $697,904. Thus we are 99% confident that losses *relative to the benchmark* will not exceed $697,904 when holding this portfolio over the next year.

Compared with tracking error, benchmark VaR has two main advantages. Firstly, it measures the risk of underperforming the benchmark and not the 'risk' of outperforming it. Secondly, the expected active return *does* affect the benchmark VaR, whereas tracking error says nothing about the expected active return on the fund.[49]

---

[47] See Section II.1.6.2 for the formal mathematical definition of active return.

[48] The *tracking error* is the volatility of the active return.

[49] For instance, the fund could be underperforming the benchmark by 5% every year and still have a zero tracking error! See Section II.1.6 for an example.

The expected active return has a linear effect on the benchmark VaR, and we demonstrate this by reconsidering the previous example, this time allowing the expected active return to be different from zero. Figure IV.1.3 shows that, keeping the tracking error constant at 3%, the annual benchmark VaR decreases linearly as we increase the expected active return on the fund, shown on the horizontal axis. As we increase this from −5% up to 5%, the corresponding 1% 1-year benchmark VaR decreases from almost $1.2 million to only $200,000.[50]

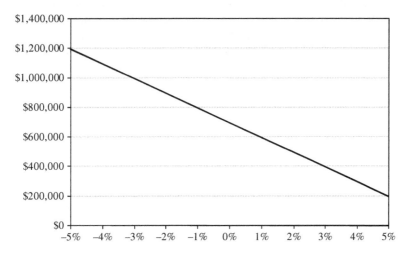

Figure IV.1.3   Effect of expected active return on benchmark VaR

In short, when a portfolio is expected to *outperform* a benchmark then the risk of the portfolio *reduces* if it is measured by benchmark VaR, but not if it is measured by the tracking error. Similarly, when a portfolio is expected to *underperform* a benchmark then the risk of the portfolio as measured by benchmark VaR *increases*. This is not a feature of the tracking error, because that metric only measures the risk relative to the expected active return and is not affected by the level of the expected active return.

IV.1.8.2   Conditional VaR: Expected Tail Loss and Expected Shortfall

VaR defines a level of loss that one is reasonably sure will not be exceeded. But VaR tells us nothing about the extent of the losses that could be incurred in the event that the VaR is exceeded. However, we obtain information about the *average* level of loss, given that the VaR is exceeded, from the conditional VaR.

There are two conditional VaR measures, depending on whether we are measuring the VaR relative to a benchmark or not. The $100\alpha\%$ h-day *expected tail loss* is the conditional VaR defined as

$$\text{ETL}_{h,\alpha} = -E(X_h|X_h < -\text{VaR}_{h,\alpha}) \times P, \tag{IV.1.32}$$

---

[50] This very noticeable effect is because the VaR is measured over a 1-year horizon. As we have seen in Section IV.1.5.2, over horizons of a month or less, the expected excess return has less effect on the VaR.

where X_h denotes the discounted h-day return on the portfolio, $\text{VaR}_{h,\alpha}$ is the $100\alpha\%$ h-day VaR expressed as a percentage of the portfolio's value and P is the current value of the portfolio.

The $100\alpha\%$ h-day *expected shortfall* is the conditional benchmark VaR defined as

$$\text{ES}_{h,\alpha} = -E\big(\tilde{X}_h \,|\, \tilde{X}_h < -\text{BVaR}_{h,\alpha}\big) \times P, \qquad\qquad \text{(IV.1.33)}$$

where $\tilde{X}_h$ denotes the discounted h-day active return on the portfolio and $\text{BVaR}_{h,\alpha}$ is the $100\alpha\%$ h-day benchmark VaR expressed as a percentage of the portfolio's value.

The distinction between VaR, benchmark VaR, ETL and ES can be illustrated by considering 1000 P&Ls for a portfolio and for its benchmark and looking at (a) the absolute losses on the portfolio, and (b) the relative losses, measured relative to a benchmark. Both losses are in present value terms. Then:

- the 1% VaR is the 10th largest absolute loss;
- the 1% ETL is the average of the 10 largest absolute losses;
- the 1% benchmark VaR is the 10th largest relative loss;
- the 1% ES is the average of the 10 largest relative losses.

Their difference is further illustrated by the following example, which is based on an empirical approach to VaR estimation which we shall later describe as *historical simulation*.

EXAMPLE IV.1.10: COMPARISON OF DIFFERENT VAR METRICS

The spreadsheet for this example contains a time series of daily values for the Dow Jones Industrial Average (DJIA) index and for a (hypothetical) portfolio of stocks that closely tracks the DJIA. The data in the spreadsheet are from 5 January 1998 to 31 December 2001 and at the end of this period the portfolio value was $1,007,580, which is similar to a $100 per point position on the DJIA index.

(a) Find the 1% 1-day VaR and the 1% 1-day ETL on the portfolio on 31 December 2001.
(b) Using the DJIA as benchmark, calculate the 1% 1-day benchmark VaR and expected shortfall for the portfolio on 31 December 2001.

SOLUTION   (a) There are exactly 1000 returns in the spreadsheet, so the 1% quantile is the tenth largest negative return. This is the return of -3.549% on 15 October 1999, as shown on the left-hand side of Table IV.1.4.[51] The 1% daily VaR is minus this return, multiplied by the current value of the portfolio and discounted by 1 day. But the risk free interest rate on 31 December 2001 was only approximately 4%, so the 1-day discount factor is almost one and we have set it to one.[52] Hence, we compute the portfolio VaR on 31 December 2001 as[53]

$$\text{VaR}_{1,0.01} = 3.549\% \times \$1,007,580 = \$35,764.$$

---

[51] Here we have listed the ten largest negative returns in decreasing order of magnitude, including the dates when they occurred, but the dates are just for interest.
[52] The discount factor is about $(1 - 0.04/365)^{-1} = 0.9998$. Discounting gives a 1% daily VaR $= \$35,761$, as opposed to $\$35,764$ without discounting.
[53] The spreadsheet shows that using the quantile function gives a different answer, not surprisingly given our observations about the Excel quantile function in Section I.3.2.8. In Excel the assumption is that, while the observations are discrete, the returns are a continuous random variable.

This tells us that we are 99% confident of not losing more than $35,764 between 31 December 2001 and 1 January 2002.

The ETL is the average of the ten largest negative returns that are shown in the first columns of Table IV.1.4, again multiplied by -1 and by the current portfolio value (ignoring the discounting as before). That is,

$$\text{ETL}_{1,0.01} = \text{Average } \{6.127\%, \ldots, 3.549\%\} \times \$1,007,580 = \$46,505.$$

This tells us that if we do exceed the VaR, which we expect to happen with a probability of 1%, on average we would lose $46,505 from our position. The conditional VaR is much greater than the ordinary VaR, as is often the case.[54]

Table IV.1.4   The tail of the return distribution and of the active return distribution

Date	Return	Date	Active Return
31-Aug-98	−6.127%	29-Sep-00	−1.564%
17-Sep-01	−6.033%	27-Feb-98	−1.548%
14-Apr-00	−5.690%	02-Aug-99	−1.514%
20-Sep-01	−5.233%	10-Jul-98	−1.508%
12-Oct-00	−4.241%	30-Dec-98	−1.505%
12-Mar-01	−3.891%	11-Sep-98	−1.491%
14-Jan-99	−3.864%	16-Jun-99	−1.485%
14-Mar-01	−3.801%	12-Jan-01	−1.483%
07-Mar-00	−3.727%	06-Apr-01	−1.472%
15-Oct-99	−3.549%	01-May-98	−1.445%

(b) The benchmark VaR and ES are calculated using a similar process to that in (a), but this time using the active returns relative to the DJIA benchmark rather than the returns on the portfolio itself. The tenth largest negative active return was -1.445% on 1 May 1998, and this and the other 9 largest negative active returns are shown on the right-hand side of Table IV.1.4. Recalling that the value of the portfolio on 31 December 2001 was $1,007,580, we calculate the benchmark VaR and the expected shortfall as:

$$\text{BVaR}_{1,0.01} = 1.445\% \times \$1,007,580 = \$14,557,$$

and

$$\text{ES}_{1,0.01} = \text{Average } \{1.564\%, \ldots., 1.445\%\} \times \$1,007,580 = \$15,129.$$

Hence, we are 99% confident of not losing more than $14,557 more than we would with a $100 per point position on the DJIA, over a 1-day period. And if we do exceed this figure then the expected loss, relative to the DJIA position, would be $15,129.

---

[54] By definition, the conditional VaR can never be less than the VaR. The difference between the conditional VaR and the corresponding VaR depends on the heaviness of the lower tail of the return distribution – the heavier this tail, the greater the difference.

IV.1.8.3   Coherent Risk Metrics

A risk metric is a single number that is used to summarize the uncertainty in a distribution. For instance, volatility is a risk metric that summarizes the dispersion over the whole range of a distribution. Other risk metrics, such as the downside risk metrics introduced in Section IV.1.3, only summarize the uncertainty over a restricted range for the random variable.

How do we choose an appropriate risk metric? In portfolio management we choose risk metrics that have an associated risk adjusted performance measure that ranks investments in accordance with a utility function – and hopefully, a utility function with desirable properties. But in banking we tend to choose risk metrics that have certain 'intuitive' properties. For instance, we prefer risk metrics that can aggregate risks in a way that accounts for the effects of diversification.

What other intuitive properties should a 'good' risk metric possess? In Section I.6.5.2 we introduce a property called *weak stochastic dominance*. Suppose one investment A dominates another investment B in the sense that the probability of the return exceeding any fixed value is never greater with investment B than it is with investment A. Any rational investor should rank A above B. Yet some basic risk adjusted performance measures such as the Sharpe ratio (see Sharpe, 1994) do not preserve this property, as have seen in Section I.6.5.2. We can construct two investments A and B where the Sharpe ratio of A is less than that of B even though A weakly stochastically dominates B.

Clearly, requiring a risk metric to preserve stochastic dominance is not a trivial property. We shall now phrase this property as the first of several 'axioms' that should be satisfied by a 'good' risk metric. In the following we use the notation ϱ to denote an arbitrary *risk metric*.[55]

Monotonicity

If A weakly stochastically dominates B then A should be judged as no more risky than B according to our risk metric. We write this property mathematically as

$$\varrho(A) \leq \varrho(B) \text{ if } A \text{ has weak stochastic dominance over } B. \qquad \text{(IV.1.34)}$$

Sub-additivity

Furthermore, as mentioned above, we would like the risk metric to aggregate risks in an intuitive way, accounting for the effects of diversification. We should ensure that the risk of a diversified portfolio is no greater than the corresponding weighted average of the risks of the constituents. For this we need

$$\varrho(A + B) \leq \varrho(A) + \varrho(B). \qquad \text{(IV.1.35)}$$

Without sub-additivity there would be no incentive to hold portfolios. For instance, we could find that the risk of holding two stocks with agent 1, who can then net the risk by taking into account the correlation between the stock returns, is *greater* than the risk of holding stock A with agent 1 and stock B with agent 2, with no netting of the two agents' positions. As remarked in the introduction to this section, without sub-additivity the risk metric cannot be used for risk budgeting.

---

[55] For instance, if ϱ is a variance and A is a return X, then $\varrho(A) = V(X)$.

Homogeneity

Note that a risk metric is simply a measure of uncertainty in a distribution; it says nothing at all about the risk attitude of an investor. It is not a risk premium. For this reason some authors believe that another intuitive axiom is that if we double our bet, then we double our risk. More generally, for any positive constant k the homogeneity axiom requires

$$\varrho(kA) = k\varrho(A). \qquad \text{(IV.1.36)}$$

This axiom states that risk preference has nothing to do with the risk metric, or at least if users are endowed with a utility function then they must be risk neutral. Risk aversion or risk loving behaviour is, rather, *inhomogeneity*, in that the marginal utility of wealth typically depends on the level of wealth. Of all the four axioms for a coherent risk metric, it is this axiom that states that a risk metric is a measure of *uncertainty*, rather than of an agent's perception of risk. For this reason, several authors find the homogeneity axiom rather contentious and prefer to use an axiom that can link the risk metric with risk attitude.

Risk free condition

Finally, we note that some risk metrics, such as VaR, may be measured in value terms (e.g. in dollars or euros). Others, such as volatility of returns, are measured on a relative scale. It is more convenient to represent risks on a value scale because then the capital that is at risk can be offset by capital held in cash or a risk free asset.

For example, suppose that risk is measured in US dollars and that we have capital of $1 million of which 90% is invested in a risky portfolio A and 10% is held in a risk free asset. Suppose further that the risk of our $0.9 million capital invested in A is $250,000 according to our risk metric ϱ. In other words, $\varrho(A) = \$250,000$. So we have capital at risk of $250,000 but risk free capital of $100,000. Then, according to the risk free axiom, the net capital at risk should be $150,000. The intuition behind this is that we could use the $100,000 of risk free capital to cover the risk on the risky asset.

More generally, suppose we divide our capital into an investment A and amount γ earning the risk free return. Then the net capital at risk is

$$\varrho(A + \gamma) = \varrho(A) - \gamma. \qquad \text{(IV.1.37)}$$

Artzner et al. (1999) introduced the label *coherent* for any risk metric that satisfies the four axioms above. They showed that lower partial moment risk metrics are coherent, and that conditional VaR, i.e. expected shortfall and expected tail loss, are also coherent risk metrics. But many common risk metrics are not coherent. For instance, any risk metric expressed in relative terms, like volatility or tracking error, will not satisfy the risk free condition.

VaR is measured in value terms, but it is only coherent under special assumptions about the distribution of returns. When returns are normally distributed VaR is a coherent risk metric, because it behaves like the volatility of returns (converted into value terms). But more generally, VaR is not coherent because quantiles, unlike the variance operator, do not obey simple rules such as sub-additivity unless the returns have an elliptical distribution. The next example constructs a portfolio containing only two instruments for which VaR is not sub-additive.

EXAMPLE IV.1.11: NON-SUB-ADDITIVITY OF VAR

Suppose we write the following two binary options: option A pays \$10,000 if the monthly return on the S&P 500 index is at least 20% and option B pays \$10,000 if the monthly return on gold is at least 20%. Both options are sold for \$1000. We assume that the returns on the S&P 500 and gold are independent and that each has a probability of 0.02532 of returning at least 20%.[56] Show that the sum of the 5% VaRs on each separate position is less than the 5% VaR when the two options are taken together in a portfolio.

SOLUTION   First consider each position separately: in each individual position there is only a 2.532% chance that we pay out \$10,000. Put another way, the P&L distribution is exactly

$$P(\text{P\&L} = -9000) = 2.532\% \quad \text{and} \quad P(\text{P\&L} \leq 1000) = 1.$$

This is depicted in Figure IV.1.4.

We cannot lose more than \$9000, so this is the 1% VaR, i.e. $P(\text{P\&L} \leq -\$9000) = 1\%$. And indeed, \$9000 is also the 2.5% VaR. But what is the 5% VaR, i.e. the amount X such that $P(\text{P\&L} \leq -X) = 5\%$? It is important to note that the P&L is truly discrete for this binary option, it is not just a discrete approximation to a continuous random variable. Either we make a profit of \$1000 or we lose \$9000. These are the only alternatives. It makes no sense to *interpolate* between these outcomes, as if we could obtain a P&L between them. We know the distribution function is exactly as shown Figure IV.1.4, so we can read off the 5% quantile: it is +\$1000. The sum of the two 5% VaRs is thus −\$2000.

Now consider a portfolio containing both the options. The most we can lose is \$18,000, if both options are called. By the independence assumption, this will happen with probability $0.02532^2 = 0.000642$. We could also lose exactly \$9000 if one option is called and the other is not. The probability of this happening is $2 \times 0.02532 \times (1 - 0.02532) = 0.049358$.

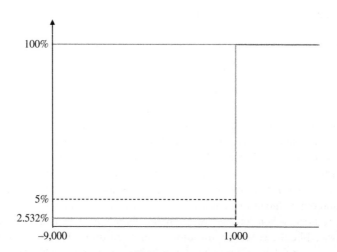

Figure IV.1.4   P&L distribution for one binary option

---

[56] Readers will see from the solution that the probability 0.02532 is chosen so that −\$9000, is the 5% quantile of the portfolio P&L.

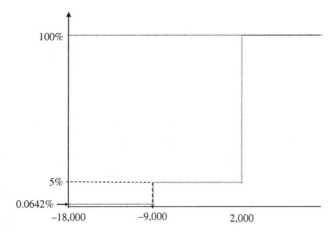

Figure IV.1.5   P&L distribution for a portfolio of two binary options

Hence, the probability that we lose $9000 or more is 4.9358% + 0.0642% = 5%. Hence, as depicted in Figure IV.1.5, the 5% VaR of the portfolio is $9000. This is *greater* than −$2000, i.e. the sum of the VaR on the two individual positions taken separately. Hence, the VaR is not sub-additive.

IV.1.9 INTRODUCTION TO VALUE-AT-RISK MODELS

The material presented in this section, which provides essential background reading for the remainder of the book, introduces the three basic types of VaR models:

- the normal linear VaR model, in which it is assumed that the distribution of risk factor returns is multivariate normal and the portfolio is required to be linear;
- the historical simulation model, which uses a large quantity of historical data to estimate VaR but makes minimal assumptions about the risk factor return distribution; and
- the Monte Carlo VaR model, which in its most basic form makes similar assumptions to the normal linear VaR model.

It is easy to estimate VaR once we have the discounted return distribution, but constructing this distribution can take considerable effort. The only differences between the three VaR models are due to the manner in which this distribution is constructed. All three approaches may be developed and generalized, as will be explained in the next three chapters. The Monte Carlo framework is the most flexible of all, and may be used with a great diversity of risk factor return distributions. And, like historical simulation, it also applies to option portfolios.

IV.1.9.1 Normal Linear VaR

A note on terminology is appropriate first. The risk factor (or asset) returns covariance matrix is central to this approach and for this reason some people call this approach the *covariance VaR* model. However, I find this terminology slightly ambiguous for two reasons. Firstly, in its most basic form the Monte Carlo VaR model *also* uses the risk factor returns covariance matrix. Secondly, a parametric linear VaR model need not summarize the risk factor dependency with a single covariance matrix. For instance, we could use several covariance matrices in the normal or Student t mixture linear VaR model, as we shall see in the next chapter.

In fact, the parametric linear VaR models have been given many different names by many different authors. Some refer to them as the *analytic VaR* models, but analytic expressions for VaR may also be derived for non-linear portfolios. Other authors call normal linear VaR the *delta–normal* VaR, but we do not actually need to assume that risk factors are normally distributed for this approach and the use of the term 'delta' gives the impression that it always refers to a linearization of the VaR for option portfolios.

The parametric linear VaR model is only applicable to a portfolio whose return or P&L is a linear function of its risk factor returns or its asset returns. The most basic assumption in the model is that risk factor returns are normally distributed, and that their joint distribution is multivariate normal, so the covariance matrix of risk factor returns is all that is required to capture the dependency between the risk factor returns. Under these assumptions it is possible to derive an explicit formula for the VaR, and we have already demonstrated this in Sections IV.1.5.1, IV.1.6.2 and IV.1.6.3.

VaR is usually measured over a short risk horizon, and we have shown in Section IV.1.5.2 that it is a reasonable approximation to assume that the excess return on the portfolio is zero over such an horizon. Then the normal linear VaR formula takes a very simple form. As a percentage of the portfolio value, the $100\alpha\%$ normal linear VaR is simply minus the standard normal α quantile, multiplied by the standard deviation of the portfolio returns over the risk horizon. In a linear portfolio, this standard deviation may be represented as the square root of a quadratic form that is based on the risk factor sensitivity vector and the risk factor covariance matrix over the risk horizon.[57]

The next chapter is a very long chapter, completely devoted to discussing the parametric linear VaR model. We shall see that it is not necessary to assume that risk factors returns have a multivariate normal distribution in order to derive a formula for the VaR. It is also possible to derive a formula when risk factor returns have a multivariate Student t distribution, or when they have a mixture of normal or Student t distributions. However, in the mixture case the formula gives VaR as an implicit rather than an explicit function, so a numerical method needs to be applied to solve for the VaR.

Furthermore, it is not necessary to assume that each risk factor return follows an i.i.d. process, although this is a standard assumption for scaling VaR over different risk horizons. It is possible to find a simple scaling rule for linear VaR when the risk factor returns are autocorrelated, provided there is no time-varying volatility.[58]

IV.1.9.2 Historical Simulation

The historical VaR model assumes that all possible future variations have been experienced in the past, and that the historically simulated distribution is identical to the returns distribution over the forward looking risk horizon. Again, a note on terminology is in order. Some authors call this model the *non-parametric* VaR model, but I do not like this nomenclature because parametric distributions can be a useful addition to this framework when estimating VaR at

---

[57] See Section I.2.4 for the derivation of this result.
[58] We have already stated this rule, in the context of the normal linear model, in Section IV.1.5.3. Further details are given in Section IV.2.2.2.

very high quantiles. Having said this, the term 'historical VaR' is a little unfortunate, since both of the other models can use historical data, if required. For instance, we may use a risk factor return covariance matrix forecast that is based on historical data for the risk factors.

Historical scenarios on contemporaneous movements in risk factors are used to simulate many possible portfolio values in *h* days' time. For this, we need to apply the risk factor mapping (e.g. the factor model for equities, the cash-flow map for interest rate sensitive portfolios, or the Taylor expansion for options) to each one of these contemporaneous simulated risk factor returns. We assume the risk factor sensitivities are held constant at their current levels, as discussed in Section IV.1.5.2. Then the risk factor mapping changes each set of correlated risk factor returns into one possible return for the portfolio over the risk horizon of the VaR model. This *h*-day return is discounted to today, if necessary, using the *h*-day discount rate.[59]

Taking all the simulated discounted portfolio returns together, we can build an empirical distribution of the *h*-day portfolio return or P&L. Then the 100α% *h*-day VaR is minus the α quantile of the historically simulated distribution. If the distribution is of portfolio returns then VaR is expressed as a percentage of the current portfolio value, and if the distribution is of portfolio P&L VaR is expressed in value terms.

One such simulated P&L density is depicted in Figure IV.1.6. The lower 1% quantile of the distribution is −0.04794 million dollars. This is calculated in the spreadsheet using linear interpolation. Hence the 1% VaR based on this set of simulations is $47,940.

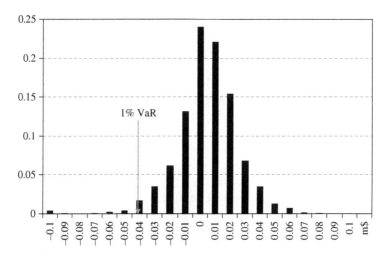

Figure IV.1.6 Simulated P&L density showing 1% VaR

The main limitations of historical VaR stem from the constraints imposed by the sample size. The number of data points used to construct the historical distribution is equal to the number of observations on each risk factor return in the simulation. This number should be as large as possible, otherwise there would be very few points in the lower tail of the distribution and the VaR, especially at high confidence levels, would be imprecise. The historical data should be sampled at the daily frequency and should span many years into the past. This is because we need very many data points to estimate the quantiles of an empirical

---

[59] But this is not necessary if the discounting is already accounted for in the risk factor sensitivity, as it is in PV01.

distribution, especially those quantiles in the extreme lower tail (which are required for VaR estimates at high confidence levels). Gathering such data can be a difficult and time-consuming task. We should try not to use overlapping h-day returns in the model, for reasons that will be clarified in Section IV.3.2.7. So even if we have many, many years of daily data on each risk factor we can initially measure VaR at the daily risk horizon only. If we require VaR over a longer horizon we need to scale up the daily VaR estimate somehow. The problem is that scaling historical VaR estimates is very tricky. This is fully discussed in Section IV.3.2.

On the other hand, one great advantage of historical VaR is that it makes few distributional assumptions. No assumption is made about the parametric form of the risk factor return distribution, least of all multivariate normality. For instance, we do not need to assume that the risk factor returns covariance matrix can capture all the complex dependencies between risk factors. The only distributional assumption is that the multivariate distribution of the risk factor returns over the risk horizon will be identical to the distribution in the past. Also, if we scale the historical VaR to a longer risk horizon, we need to assume the risk factor returns are i.i.d. They need not be normally distributed; as long as they have a 'stable distribution'[60] we can derive a scaling rule for historical VaR.

In summary, a major advantage of historical VaR is that it bases risk factor dependencies on experienced risk factor returns and comovements between these, rather than on a parametric model for their distribution. However, the model also suffers from a major drawback. Due to sample size constraints historical VaR needs to be assessed initially at the daily horizon, and then scaled up to longer horizons. The scaling of historical VaR from a daily to a longer risk horizon requires a detailed investigation of the nature of the empirical return distribution. Usually it is not appropriate to apply the square-root-of-time scaling rule, as we do for normal i.i.d. returns. Moreover, historical VaR has only limited applications to option portfolios because any type of scaling will distort their gamma effects, as we shall demonstrate in Section IV.5.4.

IV.1.9.3   Monte Carlo Simulation

In its most basic form the Monte Carlo VaR model uses the same assumptions as the normal linear VaR model, i.e. that the risk factor returns are i.i.d. with a multivariate normal distribution. In particular, it assumes that the covariance matrix is able to capture all possible dependency between the risk factor returns. However, the Monte Carlo VaR model is extremely flexible and many different assumptions about the multivariate distribution of risk factor returns can be accommodated. For instance, we could use a copula to model the dependence and specify any type of marginal risk factor return distributions that we like.[61]

In the i.i.d. multivariate normal Monte Carlo VaR model we simulate independent standard normal vectors and these are transformed to correlated multivariate normal vectors using the Cholesky decomposition of the risk factor returns covariance matrix.[62] Then the portfolio mapping is applied to each vector of simulated risk factor changes to obtain a simulated portfolio value at the end of the risk horizon, one for each simulated vector of correlated risk

---

[60] See Section I.3.3.11 for further details about stable distributions.

[61] Copulas are dependence models that allow one to build any number of multivariate distributions from a given set of marginal distributions. Chapter II.6 is completely devoted to introducing copulas, and provides many copulas, and copula simulations, in Excel.

[62] The Cholesky matrix is introduced in Section I.2.5 and its role in generating correlated simulations is described, with Excel examples, in Section I.5.7.

factor returns. To reduce the sampling error we generate a very large number of simulations and apply techniques to reduce the error variance.[63]

For example, if we use 100,000 simulations then we have 100,000 simulated portfolio values at the risk horizon in h days' time, and hence also 100,000 simulated returns on the portfolio. These are expressed in present value terms and then the $100\alpha\%$ h-day VaR is obtained as minus the lower α quantile of the discounted h-day portfolio return distribution.

Both the multivariate normality and the i.i.d. assumptions can be generalized, and we shall discuss how this is done in Sections IV.4.3 and IV.4.4. Another essential difference between the Monte Carlo VaR and parametric linear VaR models is that the Monte Carlo approach can be applied to non-linear portfolios, and to option portfolios in particular.

Clearly the normal linear VaR and the normal Monte Carlo VaR models are very similar because they make identical assumptions about risk factor distributions. The only difference between the two models is that the evolution of the risk factors is simulated in the Monte Carlo VaR model whereas it is obtained analytically in the normal linear VaR model. Thus the normal linear VaR is precise, albeit based on an assumption that is unlikely to hold, whilst the normal Monte Carlo VaR estimate is subject to simulation error. Thus, the normal Monte Carlo VaR estimate should be similar to the normal linear VaR estimate. If it is different, that can only be because an insufficient number of simulations were used. In fact, it is a waste of time to apply *normal* Monte Carlo VaR to a linear portfolio, because this merely introduces sampling errors that are not present in the normal linear VaR model. Nevertheless, there is still a good reason for applying Monte Carlo VaR to a linear portfolio, and this is that the Monte Carlo VaR can be based on virtually *any* multivariate distribution for risk factor returns, whereas closed-form solutions for parametric linear VaR only exist for a few select distributions.

IV.1.9.4   Case Study: VaR of the S&P 500 Index

The aim of this subsection is to illustrate the three standard VaR models, in their most basic form, by applying them to measure the VaR of a very simple portfolio with a position of $1000 per point on the S&P 500 index. We use the case study to illustrate the different ways in which the three models build the portfolio return distribution, and to give the reader some insight into the reasons why different VaR models give different results. A more thorough discussion of this topic is left until Chapter IV.6, after we have reviewed all three models in detail.

Daily historical data on the S&P 500 index from 3 January 2000 until 8 January 2008 are downloaded from Yahoo! Finance.[64] Using the same data set for each, we apply the three models to estimate the VaR of a position of $1000 per point on the index on 8 January 2008. Since the index closed at 1390.19 on that day, the nominal value of our position is $P = \$1,390,190$.

Normal Linear VaR

Here we assume a normal distribution for the portfolio's daily returns, and we use the log approximation since this is usually very accurate over a 1-day horizon. From the historical price series in the spreadsheet we compute the daily log returns over the whole sample,

---

[63] See Section IV.4.2.3 for an overview of these techniques.
[64] The symbol for the S&P 500 index is ^GSPC.

and hence estimate the standard deviation σ of these returns as $\hat{\sigma} = 1.116\%$.[65] Under the assumption that the log returns are i.i.d. we can use the square-root-of-time rule, setting the h-day standard deviation $\hat{\sigma}_h = \sqrt{h}\hat{\sigma}$. For example, $\hat{\sigma}_{10} = \sqrt{10} \times 1.116\% = 3.53\%$.

For simplicity, and because it will not detract from the illustration, we assume that the expected return on our position and the risk free rate are both zero, so that no discounting or drift adjustment needs to be made to the returns before calculating the VaR. Hence, we set

$$\text{Normal Linear VaR}_{h,\alpha} = \Phi^{-1}(1-\alpha)\hat{\sigma}_h P. \tag{IV.1.38}$$

For example,

$$\text{Normal Linear VaR}_{10,0.1} = 2.32635 \times 0.0353 \times \$1,390,190 = \$114,168.$$

Historical VaR

The historical VaR estimate uses exactly the same historical daily log returns as above, but now no parametric form is assumed for the log returns distribution. The α quantile is calculated on the actual daily (log) returns that were realized over the sample.[66] This is then multiplied by -1 and by the nominal value of the portfolio, to convert the quantile into a 1-day VaR in nominal terms. For comparison with the other models we also apply a square-root scaling law to the historical 1-day VaR to obtain the h-day historical VaR, even though there may be no theoretical justification for the use of this rule. Thus we multiply the 1-day historical VaR by $\sqrt{h}$ to obtain the h-day historical VaR.

For example, the 1% quantile of the empirical return distribution in our case study is -2.959%, so the 1% 10-day historical VaR estimate is

$$\text{Historical VaR}_{10,0.1} = \sqrt{10} \times 0.02959 \times \$1,390,190 = \$130,666.$$

Monte Carlo VaR

For the Monte Carlo VaR we take the same standard deviation estimate $\hat{\sigma}_h$ as that used in the normal linear VaR model. Using the Excel command $=\text{NORMSINV(RAND())}^*\hat{\sigma}_h$, as explained in Section I.5.7, we simulate a very large number of hypothetical h-day returns. Only 5000 are set into the spreadsheet, but readers may increase the number of simulations by filling down column D. Then we apply the Excel PERCENTILE function to find the α quantile of their distribution. This is multiplied by the nominal value of the portfolio to convert the quantile into a $100\alpha\%$ h-day VaR in nominal terms.

The Monte Carlo simulations are automatically repeated each time you change any data in the spreadsheet, unless you turn the automatic calculation option to manual. To repeat the simulations at any time just press F9. We use no variance reduction technique here, so unless a very large number of simulations are used the result can change considerably each time. Table IV.1.5 summarizes results for $\alpha = 1\%$ and 5% and for $h = 1$ and 10. Of course, in the spreadsheet readers will see a different value for Monte Carlo VaR than that shown in the

---

[65] The caret '^' above the symbol denotes the sample estimate.
[66] Using the Excel PERCENTILE function for expediency, if not accuracy! See Section I.3.2.8 for a critique of the Excel percentile function.

right-hand column of Table IV.1.5. Remember, the linear VaR gives the exact figure and the Monte Carlo VaR is subject to simulation errors, but the variance of this error decreases as we increase the number of simulations.[67]

Table IV.1.5 Comparison of estimates from different VaR models

	Normal linear	Historical	Normal Monte Carlo
5% 1-day VaR	$25,527	$25,579	$25,125
1% 1-day VaR	$36,103	$41,130	$36,160
5% 10-day VaR	$80,723	$80,887	$80,246
1% 10-day VaR	$114,168	$130,066	$113,248

The difference between the normal linear and the historical VaR estimates is more apparent at the 1% significance level. At the 5% level the two estimates are similar, but the historical return distribution is leptokurtic. That is, it has heavier tails than the normal distribution, so the VaR at extreme quantiles is greater when estimated using the historical simulation approach. The square-root scaling rule may not appropriate for historical VaR, but even without this potential error the 1% 1-day VaR estimates are already very different. The estimated VaR is about 14% greater when based on historical simulation. Relative to the portfolio value of $1,390,190, we have a 1% 1-day VaR of:

- $36,103/1,390,190 = 2.6\%$ according to the normal linear VaR model, but
- $41,130/1,390,190 = 2.96\%$ according to the historical VaR model.

The reason is that the normal linear VaR model assumes the returns have a normal distribution, whereas the sample excess kurtosis of the daily log returns is 2.538. Such a high positive excess kurtosis indicates that the empirical S&P 500 return distribution has heavy tails, so the assumption of normality that is made in the linear and Monte Carlo VaR models is not validated by the data.

IV.1.10 SUMMARY AND CONCLUSIONS

We opened this chapter by discussing the risk metrics that are commonly used by fund managers, banks and corporations. In the fund management industry risk is commonly measured in the context of a returns model, whereas in banking and corporate treasury the risk model is usually separate from the returns model. Hence, quite different risk metrics were traditionally used in these industries.

A market risk metric is a single number which measures the uncertainty in a portfolio's P&L, or in its return. Its fundamental purpose is to summarize the portfolio's potential for deviations from a target or expected return. A typical risk metric for *passive* fund management is *tracking error*, which is the volatility of the active return. Unfortunately tracking error has also been adopted by many *active* portfolio managers, even though it is not an appropriate risk metric for actively managed funds. One of the reasons for this is that tracking error is

---

[67] Further discussion of this point is given in Section IV.4.2.3.

not a *downside risk metric*. Many downside risk metrics have been developed for active fund managers and several of these have better properties than tracking error. Increasingly, portfolio managers are adopting VaR-based downside risk metrics, such as *benchmark VaR* and *expected shortfall*, because these metrics tell clients about the probability of losing money. Tracking error is more difficult for clients to understand, particularly when it is linked to the (possibly erroneous) assumption that the portfolio returns are normally distributed. VaR does not have to assume that returns are normally distributed.

VaR is a quantile risk metric. But when returns are normal every quantile is just a multiple of the standard deviation, so in this special case VaR obeys the same rules as a standard deviation. Otherwise, VaR does not obey nice rules and it may not even be sub-additive.

VaR and its associated risk metrics have become the universal risk metrics in banking and corporate treasury. The reason why large companies measure risks using a VaR model is that these firms often have a management structure that is based on economic capital allocation. Most major banks use VaR to measure both economic and regulatory capital. Economic capital affects the bank's credit rating, and is a primary tool for management. Regulatory capital is determined by either standardized rules or an internal VaR model. We shall return to this topic in the final chapter of this book.

There are many reasons why banks like to use VaR, which are listed in the introduction and explained in this chapter. But VaR has some undesirable properties. It is not a *coherent* risk metric, unless we make some simplifying assumptions about the behaviour of the risk factors and the portfolio is a linear portfolio. However, the *conditional VaR* metric is always coherent, so many banks use a conditional VaR such as *expected tail loss* in their internal economic capital calculations.

In the bottom-up risk assessment paradigm that is prevalent today, risks are assessed first at the individual position level, and then positions are progressively aggregated into larger and larger portfolios. A *portfolio* can contain anything from a single instrument to all the positions in the entire firm. At each stage of aggregation VaR is estimated and decomposed into the VaR due to different classes of risk factors. This decomposition allows the VaR due to risk factors in different asset classes to be identified, monitored and hedged efficiently. It also allows capital to be allocated in accordance with a universal risk metric, used for all the activities in the firm.

The disaggregation of VaR allows risk to be allocated to different activities and risk capital to be allocated accordingly. VaR can be decomposed into *systematic* and *specific* components, and systematic VaR can be further decomposed into *stand-alone* or *marginal* VaR components belonging to different types of risk factors. Thus, taking all the positions in the entire bank, we estimate stand-alone and/or marginal VaR for equity, interest rates, credit spreads, commodity groups, and forex. Stand-alone VaR is used in performance measures that determine the internal allocation of economic capital. It measures the risk of an activity (e.g. proprietary trading, or swaps) in isolation. It does not reduce the risk of any component by accounting for any diversification benefits (e.g. between equities and interest rates). Marginal VaR can be used to allocate real capital. It tells us the proportion of total risk stemming from different activities and it accounts for diversification benefits between the components. Marginal VaR can be extended to the concept of *incremental VaR*, i.e. the impact on the portfolio's VaR of adding a small new position to the portfolio.

Aggregation of VaR provides information about the total risk faced by a firm and the adequacy of its total capital to cover risky positions given an adverse market move. Marginal VaR is constructed in such as way that the sum of marginal VaRs is the total risk factor VaR.

But stand-alone VaR estimates do not sum to the total risk factor VaR. Since stand-alone VaR measures risk in isolation, the aggregation of stand-alone component VaRs takes no account of diversification.

We have defined several distinct steps to take when building a VaR model, and provided a preliminary discussion on the choice available at each step. The model building process may be summarized as follows:

1. *Define the portfolio and identify its risk factors.* Portfolios may be characterized by their asset holdings, and long-only portfolios may be characterized by the portfolio weights.
2. *Set the basic parameters for the model.* The basic parameters of a VaR model are the *confidence level* and the *risk horizon*, and a VaR estimate increases with both these parameters. The choice of these parameters depends on the end use of the model. For instance, trading limits may be set at 95% confidence and a horizon of 1 day, whereas economic capital estimates may be based on 99.9% confidence with a risk horizon of 1 year.
3. *Map the portfolio to its risk factors.* This entails building a model for the portfolio return, or P&L, as a function of the absolute or percentage returns to its risk factors. The risk factor mapping process greatly facilitates (a) the subsequent VaR computations, which indeed in many cases would be impossible without a risk factor mapping; and (b) the efficient firm-wide hedging of risks, as the fundamental risk factors can be isolated and the exposures netted centrally.
4. *Model the evolution of the risk factors over the risk horizon.* It is here that the three different VaR models adopt different approaches. Both the parametric linear VaR and Monte Carlo VaR models assume we know a functional form for the multivariate stochastic process generating the time series of risk factor returns. For instance, they could assume that an independent, normally distributed process generates each risk factor returns series. In that case the returns on each risk factor have no autocorrelation or time-varying volatility, but the risk factor returns at any particular point in time are assumed to be correlated with each other. The *historical VaR* model uses an empirical risk factor return distribution, without assuming it takes any specific parametric form. It is only based on the risk factor variations and dependencies that have been experienced in a historical sample. Importantly, it does not rely on a covariance matrix to capture all the risk factor variations and dependencies.
5. *Revalue the portfolio for each realization of the risk factors.* Here we typically assume the risk factor sensitivities are held constant over a risk horizon of *h* days. But these sensitivities depend on the risk factor values and the risk factor values change over the risk horizon. Hence, there is an implicit assumption that the portfolio is rebalanced to maintain constant risk factor sensitivities.
6. *Build a distribution for the portfolio return or P&L.* Which of these distributions is used will depend on the risk factor mapping. In some cases (e.g. interest rates or long-short portfolios) it is more natural to generate the P&L distribution, in others it is more natural to use the return distribution. The *h*-day portfolio return or P&L must also be expressed in *present value* terms. If the expected return on the portfolio is very different from the discount rate, then the return distribution should be modified to account for this. When VaR is measured over a long horizon such as a year, this adjustment may result in a significant reduction in VaR. This is particularly important when VaR is used to

assess the absolute risk of funds, which typically expect to return more than the risk free rate and have risks that are measured over long horizons. However, when the risk of funds is benchmarked, in which case the VaR is based on the *active returns* rather than the ordinary returns on the fund, there may be little justification to suppose that the expected active return will be any different from zero whatever the fund manager tells you.

7. *Calculate the VaR and ETL.* The 100α% h-day VaR is (minus) the α quantile of the discounted h-day distribution. If we build a P&L distribution, the VaR and ETL will be measured in value terms and if we build a return distribution they will be expressed as a percentage of the portfolio value. It is possible to obtain the quantiles using analytical methods in parametric linear VaR models. Otherwise, the returns or P&L distribution must be simulated, and the quantile is calculated using interpolation on the simulated distribution. Often we assume that an i.i.d. process generates each risk factor return; then we can measure the VaR initially over a 1-day horizon, and scale this up to a VaR estimate for a longer risk horizon. Under some conditions we can use a *square-root* scaling rule for VaR, for instance when the discounted portfolio returns are i.i.d. and normally distributed with mean zero.

For a linear portfolio with i.i.d. normally distributed returns, the normal linear VaR should be identical to the normal Monte Carlo VaR. But in the ensuing chapters we shall see that both the parametric linear VaR model and the Monte Carlo VaR model may be generalized to make other distributional assumptions. The Monte Carlo VaR model is particularly flexible in that the returns may be assumed to have *any* parametric distribution that we care to specify.

An obvious problem with the historical VaR model is the severe constraints that are imposed by sample size limitations. In their basic form the other two models only require a covariance matrix, and this can be based on only very recent historical data – or indeed, it can be set according to the personal views of the analyst, using no historical data at all. But in historical VaR one has to re-create an artificial history for the portfolio, holding its current weights, holdings or risk factor sensitivities constant over a very long historical period. Even when this is possible, it is not necessarily desirable because the market conditions in the recent past and the immediate future may have been very different from those experienced many years ago. As its name suggests, the historical model assumes that the distribution of the portfolio returns or P&L over the risk horizon is the same as the historical distribution. This makes it more difficult to perform scenario analysis in the historical model, although we shall demonstrate how to do this in Section IV.7.5.1.

A further distinguishing feature between the models is that a normal linear VaR estimate can only be applied when the portfolio return is a linear function of its risk factor returns. This restriction does not apply to the Monte Carlo VaR and historical VaR models, although the application of historical VaR to option portfolios is fairly limited, as explained in Section IV.5.4.

To summarize the main advantage of each approach:

- The normal linear VaR model is analytically tractable.
- Historical VaR makes no (possibly unrealistic) assumption about the parametric form of the distribution of the risk factors.

- The Monte Carlo VaR model is very flexible, and it can be applied to any type of position, including non-linear, path-dependent portfolios.

To summarize the main limitations of each approach:

- The normal linear VaR model is restricted to linear portfolios and it can only be generalized to a few simple parametric forms, such as a Student t or a mixture of normal or Student t distributions.
- Historical VaR assumes that all possible future variation has been experienced in the past. This imposes very stringent, often unrealistic, requirements on data.
- Monte Carlo VaR is computationally intensive and without sophisticated sampling methods, simulation errors can be considerable.

The chapter concluded with a case study that highlights the similarities and the differences between the three VaR models, using a simple position on the S&P 500 index as an illustration. We used an i.i.d. normal assumption in the linear and Monte Carlo VaR models, so the two VaR estimates should be identical for every significance level and risk horizon. However, even with many thousand simulations and a very simple portfolio, the simulation errors in Monte Carlo VaR were considerable. Also, there was a highly significant excess kurtosis in the S&P return distribution, and for this reason the normal linear and Monte Carlo VaR estimates were significantly lower than the historical VaR estimates at the 1% significance level. However, at the 5% significance level, all three models gave similar results.

Parametric Linear VaR Models

IV.2.1 INTRODUCTION

The parametric linear model calculates VaR and ETL using analytic formulae that are based on an assumed parametric distribution for the risk factor returns, when the portfolio value is a linear function of its underlying risk factors. Specifically, it applies to portfolios of cash, futures and/or forward positions on commodities, bonds, loans, swaps, equities and foreign exchange. The most basic assumption, discussed in the previous chapter, is that the returns on the portfolio are independent and identically distributed with a normal distribution. Now we extend this assumption so that we can decompose the portfolio VaR into VaR arising from different groups of risk factors, assuming that the risk factor returns have a *multivariate normal* distribution with a constant covariance matrix. We derive analytic formulae for the VaR and ETL of a linear portfolio under this assumption and also when risk factor returns are assumed to have a *Student t distribution*, or a *mixture* of normal or Student t distributions.

In bond portfolios, and indeed in any interest rate sensitive portfolio that is mapped to a cash flow, the risk factors are the *interest rates* of different maturities that are used to both determine and discount the cash flow. When discounting cash flows between banks we use a term structure of LIBOR rates as risk factors. Additional risk factors may be introduced when a counterparty has a credit rating below AA. For instance, the yield on a BBB-rated 10-year bond depends on the appropriate spread over LIBOR, so we need to add the 10-year BBB-rated credit spread to our risk factors. More generally, term structures of *credit spreads* of different ratings may also appear in the market risk factors: when portfolios contain trans-actions with several counterparties having different credit ratings, one credit spread term structure is required for each different rating.

There is a non-linear relationship between the value of a bond or swaps portfolio and interest rates. However, this non-linearity is already captured by the sensitivities to the risk factors, which are in *present value of basis point* (PV01) terms. Hence, we can apply the parametric linear VaR model by representing the portfolio as a cash flow, because the discount factor that appears in the PV01 is a non-linear function of the interest rate.

We may also base parametric linear VaR and ETL estimates on an equity factor model, provided it is linear, which is very often the case. Foreign exchange exposures are based on a simple linear proportionality, and commodity portfolios can be mapped as cash flows on term structures of constant maturity forwards or interest rates. Thus, the only portfolios to which the parametric linear VaR method does *not* apply are portfolios containing options, or portfolios containing instruments with option-like pay-offs. That is, whenever the portfolio's P&L function is a *non-linear* function of the risk factors, the model will not apply.

In the parametric linear VaR model, all co-dependencies between the risk factors are assumed to be represented by correlations. We represent these correlations, together with the variance of each risk factor over some future risk horizon h, in an h-day *covariance matrix*. It is this covariance matrix – and in mixture linear VaR models there may be more than one covariance matrix – that really drives the model. To estimate the covariance matrix we employ a *moving average model*.[1] These models assume the risk factors are i.i.d. From this it follows that the h-day covariance matrix is just h times the 1-day covariance matrix, a result that is commonly referred to as the *square-root-of-time rule*.[2]

In the standard parametric linear VaR model we cannot forecast the covariance matrix using a GARCH model.[3] When a return is modelled with a GARCH process it is not i.i.d.; instead it exhibits *volatility clustering*. As a result the square-root-of-time rule does not apply. However, this is not the reason why we cannot use a GARCH process in the parametric linear VaR model. The problem is that when a return follows a GARCH process we do not know the exact price distribution h days from now. We know this distribution when the returns are i.i.d., because it is the same as the distribution we have estimated over a historical sample. But the h-day log return in a GARCH model is the sum of h consecutive daily log returns and, due to the volatility clustering it is the sum of non-i.i.d. variables. Thus far, we only know the *moments* of the h-day log return distribution, albeit for a general GARCH process.[4]

The outline of this chapter is as follows. In Section IV.2.2 we introduce the basic concepts for parametric linear VaR. Starting with VaR estimation at the *portfolio level* (i.e. we consider the returns or P&L on a portfolio, without any risk factor mapping), we examine the properties of the i.i.d. normal linear VaR model and then extend this assumption to the case where returns are still normally distributed, but possibly autocorrelated. This assumption only affects the way that we scale VaR estimates over different risk horizons; the formula for 1-day VaR remains the same. An extension of the normal linear VaR formula for h-day VaR is derived for the case where daily returns are autocorrelated, and this is illustrated with a numerical example.

Then we consider the more general case, in which we assume the portfolio has been mapped to its risk factors using an appropriate mapping methodology.[5] We provide the mathematical definitions, in the general context of the normal linear VaR model, of the different components of the total VaR of a portfolio. The total VaR may be decomposed into *systematic* (or *total risk factor*) VaR and *specific* (or *residual*) VaR, where the systematic VaR is the VaR that is captured by the risk factor mapping. The systematic VaR may be further decomposed into *stand-alone* VaR or *marginal* VaR components, depending on our purpose:

- Stand-alone VaR estimates are useful for estimating the risk of a particular activity in isolation, without considering any netting or diversification effects that this activity may have with other activities in the firm. Diversification effects are accounted for when aggregating stand-alone VaRs to a total risk factor VaR. The ordinary sum of the stand-alone VaRs is usually greater than the total risk factor VaR, and in the normal linear VaR model it can never be less that the total risk factor VaR.

---

[1] Full details of the estimation of equally and exponentially weighted moving average covariance matrices are given in Chapter II.3.
[2] See Section II.3.2.1 for further details.
[3] For further details on GARCH models see Chapter II.4.
[4] Alexander et al. (2008) have derived analytic formulae for the first eight moments of the aggregated return distribution based on asymmetric GARCH with a general error distribution. By fitting a parametric form to these moments Alexander et al. (2009) derive a quasi-analytic VaR model.
[5] Portfolio mapping for all types of financial instruments is fully described in Chapter III.5.

- Marginal VaR estimates are useful for the allocation of real capital (as opposed to economic capital) because the sum of all the marginal VaR estimates is equal to the total risk factor VaR (and real capital must always add up).

The next five sections provide a large number of numerical and empirical examples, and two detailed case studies, on the application of the normal linear model to the estimation of total portfolio VaR. We focus on the decomposition of the systematic VaR into components corresponding to different types of risk factor. Each section provides a detailed analysis of a different type of asset class.

- Section IV.2.3 examines the VaR of interest rate sensitive portfolios. These portfolios are represented as a sequence of cash flows that are mapped to standard maturities along a term structure of interest rates. Their risk factors are the LIBOR curve and usually one or more term structures of credit spreads. The risk factor sensitivities are the PV01s of the mapped cash flows. Here we use numerical examples to show how to disaggregate the total VaR into *LIBOR* VaR and *credit spread* VaR components.
- Section IV.2.4 presents the first case study of this chapter, on the estimation of VaR for a portfolio of UK bonds. We demonstrate how to use *principal component analysis* to reduce the dimension of the risk factors from 60 to only 3, and describe some risk management applications of this technique.
- Section IV.2.5 examines the normal linear VaR for stock portfolios, from a small portfolio with just a few positions on selected stocks, to a large international portfolio that has been mapped to broad market risk factors. We focus on the decomposition of VaR into systematic and specific factors, and the moving average methods that are used to estimate the covariance matrix.
- Section IV.2.6 shows how to estimate the total VaR for an international stock portfolio, how to decompose this into specific and systematic VaR, and how to disaggregate total VaR into equity VaR, foreign exchange (forex) VaR and interest rate VaR components. We use numerical and empirical examples to calculate *stand-alone* and *marginal* VaR components for different types of risk factor, and to illustrate the *sub-additivity* property of normal linear VaR when component VaRs are aggregated.
- Section IV.2.7 presents a case study on the normal linear VaR of a commodity futures trading desk, using constant maturity futures as risk factors.

There are three other parametric linear VaR models that have analytic solutions for VaR. These are the *Student t*, the *normal mixture* and the *Student t mixture* models. They are introduced and illustrated in Sections IV.2.8 and IV.2.9. Of course, other parametric forms are possible for return distributions but these do not lead to a simple analytic solution and instead we must use Monte Carlo resolution methods. The formulae that we derive in Section IV.2.8 are based on the assumption that returns are i.i.d. We describe a simple technique to extend these formulae so that they assume autocorrelated returns. However, to include volatility clustering we would normally use Monte Carlo simulation for the resolution.[6]

---

[6] See Section IV.4.3 for further details.

Section IV.2.10 explains how *exponentially weighted moving averages* (EWMAs) are applied in the parametric linear VaR model, with a particular emphasis on the advantages and limitations of the *RiskMetrics*™ VaR methodology that was introduced by JP Morgan in the 1990s. Section IV.2.11 derives analytic formulae for the *expected tail loss* associated with different parametric linear VaR models. The formal derivation of each formula is then illustrated with numerical examples. Section IV.2.12 presents a case study on estimating the VaR and ETL for an exposure to the iTraxx Europe 5-year credit spread index. The distribution of daily changes in the iTraxx index has a significant negative skew and a very large excess kurtosis and, of the alternatives considered here, we demonstrate that its highly non-normal characteristics are best captured by a mixture linear VaR model. Section IV.2.13 concludes by summarizing the main results in this long chapter. As usual there are numerous interactive Excel spreadsheets on the CD-ROM to illustrate virtually all of the examples and all three case studies.

IV.2.2   FOUNDATIONS OF NORMAL LINEAR VALUE AT RISK

This section introduces the normal linear VaR formula, first when VaR is measured at the portfolio level and then when the systematic VaR is measured by mapping the portfolio to its risk factors. We also discuss the rules for scaling normal linear VaR under both i.i.d. and autocorrelated returns. Then we derive the risk factor VaR, and its disaggregation into stand-alone VaR components and into marginal VaR components. We focus on consequences of the normal linear model's assumptions for aggregating VaR. Finally, we derive the incremental VaR, i.e. the impact on VaR of a small trade, in a linear portfolio with i.i.d. normally distributed returns.

IV.2.2.1   Understanding the Normal Linear VaR Formula

The formal definition of VaR was given in Section IV.1.4, and we summarize it here for convenience. Let

$$X_{ht} = \frac{B_{ht}P_{t+h} - P_t}{P_t}$$

be the discounted h-day return on a portfolio. Here B_{ht} denotes the price of a discount bond maturing in h trading days and P_t denotes the value of the portfolio at time t. Then the $100\alpha\%$ h-day VaR estimated at time t is

$$\text{VaR}_{ht,\alpha} = \begin{cases} -x_{ht,\alpha} & \text{as a percentage of the portfolio value } P_t \\ -x_{ht,\alpha}P_t & \text{when expressed in value terms} \end{cases} \tag{IV.2.1}$$

where $x_{ht,\alpha}$ is the lower α quantile of the distribution of X_{ht}, i.e. $P(X_{ht} < x_{ht,\alpha}) = \alpha$.

Derivation of the Formula

The normal linear VaR formula was derived in Section IV.1.5.1. It is convenient to summarize that derivation here, but readers should return to Section IV.1.5 if the following is too concise. In the normal linear VaR model we assume the discounted h-day returns on the portfolio follow independent normal distributions, i.e. X_{ht} is i.i.d. and

$$X_{ht} \sim N(\mu_{ht}, \sigma_{ht}^2). \tag{IV.2.2}$$

The parameters μ_{ht} and σ_{ht} are the forecasts made at time t of the portfolio's expected return over the next h days, discounted to today, and its standard deviation. Amongst other things, these will depend on both the risk horizon and the point in time at which they are forecast.

Applying the standard normal transformation to (IV.2.2) gives[7]

$$P(X_{ht} < x_{ht,\alpha}) = P\left(\frac{X_{ht} - \mu_{ht}}{\sigma_{ht}} < \frac{x_{ht,\alpha} - \mu_{ht}}{\sigma_{ht}}\right) = P\left(Z < \frac{x_{ht,\alpha} - \mu_{ht}}{\sigma_{ht}}\right) = \alpha,$$

where Z is a standard normal variable. Thus

$$\frac{x_{ht,\alpha} - \mu_{ht}}{\sigma_{ht}} = \Phi^{-1}(\alpha), \tag{IV.2.3}$$

where $\Phi^{-1}(\alpha)$ is the standard normal α quantile value, such as

$$\Phi^{-1}(0.01) = -2.32635, \qquad \Phi^{-1}(0.025) = -1.95996,$$
$$\Phi^{-1}(0.05) = -1.64485, \qquad \Phi^{-1}(0.1) \quad = -1.28155. \tag{IV.2.4}$$

By the symmetry of the normal distribution function,

$$\Phi^{-1}(\alpha) = -\Phi^{-1}(1 - \alpha).$$

Hence, substituting the above and (IV.2.1) into (IV.2.3) gives the $100\alpha\%$ h-day parametric linear VaR at time t, expressed as a percentage of the portfolio value, as

$$\text{VaR}_{ht,\alpha} = \Phi^{-1}(1 - \alpha)\sigma_{ht} - \mu_{ht}. \tag{IV.2.5}$$

To estimate normal linear VaR we require forecasts of the h-day discounted mean and standard deviation of the portfolio return, and to obtain these forecasts we can make up scenarios for their values, scenarios that would normally be based on the portfolio's risk factor mapping, so that we can find separate scenario estimates for the different risk factor component VaRs. Alternatively, we can base the forecasts for the mean and standard deviation of the portfolio return on historical data for the assets or risk factors. This is useful, to compare with the results based on the historical simulation model using identical data.

When using historical data, for a long-only portfolio we would create a constant weighted historical return series based on the current allocations.[8] Then we base our (ex-ante) forecasts of the mean and standard deviation on the (ex-post) sample estimates of mean and variance.

For a long-short portfolio we use changes (P&L) on the risk factors and keep the *holdings* constant rather than the portfolio weights constant. For a cash-flow map, we keep the PV01 vector constant, and use absolute changes in interest rates and credit spreads. In both cases we produce a P&L series for the portfolio. Then the mean and standard deviation of the P&L distribution, and hence also the VaR, are estimated directly in value terms.

---

[7] We have applied the same transformation to both sides of the inequality in the square bracket, so the probability α remains unchanged.
[8] A justification of the constant weights assumption was given in Section IV.1.5.3.

Drift Adjustment

From the discussion in Section IV.1.5.2 we know that a non-zero discounted expected return μ_{ht} can be important. Fund managers, for instance, may sell their services on the basis of expecting returns in excess of the discount rate. Figure IV.2.1 illustrates how a positive mean discounted return will have the effect of reducing the VaR. We have drawn here a normally distributed h-day discounted returns density at time t, with positive mean μ_{ht} and where the area under the curve to the left of the point $\mu_{ht} - \Phi^{-1}(1 - \alpha)\sigma_{ht}$ is equal to α, by the definition of VaR.

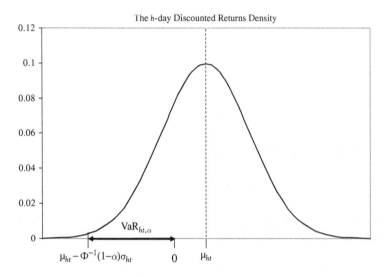

Figure IV.2.1   Illustration of normal linear VaR

In Section IV.1.5.2 we showed that it is only for long risk horizons and when a portfolio is expected to return substantially more than the discount rate that the drift adjustment to VaR, i.e. the second term in (IV.2.5), will have a significant effect on VaR. Hence, we often assume the portfolio is expected to return the risk free rate so that μ_{ht}, the present value of the expected return, is zero. We shall assume this in the following, unless explicitly stated otherwise.

Without the drift adjustment, the normal linear VaR formula is simply

$$\text{VaR}_{ht,\alpha} = \Phi^{-1}(1 - \alpha)\sigma_{ht}.$$

Henceforth in this chapter we shall also drop the implicit dependence of the VaR estimate on the time at which the estimate is made, and write simply

$$\text{VaR}_{h,\alpha} = \Phi^{-1}(1 - \alpha)\sigma_h \qquad (\text{IV.2.6})$$

for the $100\alpha\%$ h-day VaR estimate made at the current point in time, when the portfolio's expected return is the discount rate.

Scaling VaR to Different Risk Horizons

When normal linear VaR estimates are based on daily returns to the portfolio, we obtain a 1-day VaR estimate using the daily mean μ_1 and standard deviation σ_1 in the VaR formula. How can we scale this 1-day VaR estimate up to a 10-day VaR estimate, or more generally to an h-day VaR estimate?

The normal linear VaR estimate assumes that the daily returns are i.i.d. We have to approximate the returns by the *log* returns, as explained in Section IV.1.5.4, then

- the h-day mean is $h \times$ daily mean, $\mu_h = h\mu_1$;
- the h-day variance is $h \times$ daily variance, $\sigma_h^2 = h\sigma_1^2$.

In this case, it now follows directly from (IV.2.5) that

$$\text{VaR}_{h,\alpha} \approx \Phi^{-1}(1-\alpha)\sqrt{h}\sigma_1 - h\,\mu_1$$

So, under the assumption of i.i.d. returns, it is only when the portfolio is expected to return the discount rate, i.e. $\mu_1 = 0$, that

$$\text{VaR}_{h,\alpha} \approx \sqrt{h} \times \text{VaR}_{1,\alpha}. \tag{IV.2.7}$$

Note that the scaling argument above applies to any base frequency for the VaR. For instance, we could replace 'day' with 'month' above. Then the square-root-of-time scaling rule will apply to scaling the 1-month VaR to longer horizons, but only if we assume the monthly return on the portfolio is the risk free (discount) rate. For example, if this assumption holds and the 1-month VaR is 10% of the portfolio value, then the 6-month VaR will be $\sqrt{6} \times 10\% = 24.5\%$ of the portfolio value. When returns are normal and i.i.d. and the expected return on the portfolio is the risk free rate, we could also apply the square-root law for scaling from longer to shorter horizons. For example, annual VaR $= 25\% \Rightarrow$ monthly VaR $= 25\% \times 12^{-1/2} = 7.22\%$.

However, the square-root scaling rule should be applied with caution. Following our discussion in Section IV.1.5.4, we know that even when the returns are i.i.d. the square-root scaling rule is not very accurate, except for scaling over a few days, because we have to make a log approximation to returns and this approximation is only accurate when the return is very small.[9] Moreover, it does not usually make sense to scale 1-day VaR to risk horizons longer than a few days, because the risk horizon refers to the period over which we expect to be able to liquidate (or completely hedge) the exposure. Typically portfolios are rebalanced very frequently and the assumption that the portfolio weights or risk factor sensitivities remain unchanged over more than a few days is questionable. Hence, to extrapolate a 1-day VaR to, for instance, an annual VaR using a square-root scaling rule is meaningless.

How Large is VaR?

The assumption that portfolio returns are i.i.d. and normal is usually not justified in practice, so the normal linear VaR model gives only a very crude estimate for VaR. However, this is

---

[9] See Section I.1.4.4 for further explanation of this point.

still very useful as a benchmark. It provides a sort of 'plain vanilla' VaR estimate for a linear portfolio, against which to measure more sophisticated models.

Table IV.2.1 illustrates the normal linear VaR given by (IV.2.6) for different levels of volatility and some standard choices of significance level and risk horizon. All VaR estimates are expressed as a percentage of the portfolio value. Each row corresponds to a different volatility, and these volatilities range from 5% to 100%. We only include risk horizons of 1 day and 10 days in the table, since the VaR for other risk horizons can easily be derived from these. In fact, we only really need to display the 1-day VaR figures, because the corresponding 10-day VaR is just $\sqrt{10}$ times the 1-day VaR under the i.i.d. normal assumption.

Table IV.2.1 Normal linear VaR for different volatilities, significance levels and risk horizons

α	0.1%		1%		5%		10%	
h	10	1	10	1	10	1	10	1
5%	3.1%	1.0%	2.3%	0.7%	1.6%	0.5%	1.3%	0.4%
10%	6.2%	2.0%	4.7%	1.5%	3.3%	1.0%	2.6%	0.8%
15%	9.3%	2.9%	7.0%	2.2%	4.9%	1.6%	3.8%	1.2%
20%	12.4%	3.9%	9.3%	2.9%	6.6%	2.1%	5.1%	1.6%
25%	15.5%	4.9%	11.6%	3.7%	8.2%	2.6%	6.4%	2.0%
30%	18.5%	5.9%	14.0%	4.4%	9.9%	3.1%	7.7%	2.4%
40%	24.7%	7.8%	18.6%	5.9%	13.2%	4.2%	10.3%	3.2%
50%	30.9%	9.8%	23.3%	7.4%	16.4%	5.2%	12.8%	4.1%
75%	46.4%	14.7%	34.9%	11.0%	24.7%	7.8%	19.2%	6.1%
100%	61.8%	19.5%	46.5%	14.7%	32.9%	10.4%	25.6%	8.1%

In our empirical examples we shall very often calculate the 1% 10-day VaR, as this is the risk estimate that is used for market risk regulatory capital calculations. Hence, from the results in Table IV.2.1:

- in major *currency* portfolios that have recently had volatility in the region of 10%, we would expect the 1% 10-day VaR estimate to be about 5% of the portfolio value;
- *equity* portfolios, with volatilities running at 40–60% at the time of writing, could have 1% 10-day VaR of about 25% of the portfolio value;
- *credit spreads* have been extremely volatile recently and so interest rate VaR is unusually high at the moment, unless all counterparties have AA credit rating;
- *energy* portfolios, and many other *commodity* portfolios, tend to have the highest VaR. With oil prices being highly volatile at the time of writing, the 1% 10-day VaR for energy portfolios could be up to 40% of the portfolio value!

IV.2.2.2 Analytic Formula for Normal VaR when Returns are Autocorrelated

It is important to simplify models when they are applied to thousands of portfolios every day. A very common simplification is that returns are not only normally distributed but also generated by an i.i.d. process. But in most financial returns series this assumption is simply not justified. Many funds, and hedge funds in particular, smooth their reported results, and this introduces a positive autocorrelation in the reported returns. Even when returns are not autocorrelated, squared returns usually are, when they are measured at the daily or weekly frequency. This is because of the volatility clustering effects that we see in most markets.

There are no simple formulae for scaling VaR when returns have volatility clustering. Instead, we could apply a GARCH model to simulate daily returns over the risk horizon, as explained in Sections IV.3.3.4 and IV.4.3. In this section we derive a formula for scaling VaR under the assumption that the daily log returns r_t are not i.i.d. but instead they follow a *first order autoregressive* process where ϱ is the *autocorrelation*, i.e. the correlation between adjacent log returns.[10]

Write the h-period log return as the sum of h consecutive one-period log returns:

$$r_{ht} = \sum_{i=0}^{h-1} r_{t+i}.$$

Assuming the log returns are identically distributed, although no longer independent, we can set $\mu = E(r_{t+i})$ and $\sigma^2 = V(r_{t+i})$ for all i. Autocorrelation does not affect the scaling of the expected h-period log return, since $E(r_{ht}) = \sum_{i=0}^{h-1} E(r_{t+i}) = h\mu$. So the h-day expected log return is the same as it is when the returns are i.i.d.

But autocorrelation *does* affect the scaling standard deviation. Under the first order autoregressive model the variance of the h-period log return is

$$V(r_{ht}) = \sum_{i=0}^{h-1} V(r_{t+i}) + 2 \sum_{i \neq j} \text{Cov}(r_{t+i}, r_{t+j}) = \sigma^2 \left(h + 2 \sum_{i=1}^{h-1} (h-i)\varrho^i \right).$$

Now we use the identity

$$\sum_{i=1}^{n} (n-i+1)x^i = \frac{x}{(1-x)^2} [n(1-x) - x(1-x^n)], \quad |x| < 1. \tag{IV.2.8}$$

Setting $x = \varrho$ and $n = h - 1$ in (IV.2.8) gives

$$V(r_{ht}) = \sigma^2 \left(h + 2 \frac{\varrho}{(1-\varrho)^2} [(h-1)(1-\varrho) - \varrho(1-\varrho^{h-1})] \right). \tag{IV.2.9}$$

This proves that when returns are autocorrelated with first order autocorrelation coefficient ϱ then the scaling factor for standard deviation is not $\sqrt{h}$ but $\sqrt{\tilde{h}}$, where

$$\tilde{h} = h + 2 \frac{\varrho}{(1-\varrho)^2} [(h-1)(1-\varrho) - \varrho(1-\varrho^{h-1})]. \tag{IV.2.10}$$

Hence, we should scale normal linear VaR as

$$\text{VaR}_{h,\alpha} = \sqrt{\tilde{h}} \; \Phi^{-1}(1-\alpha)\sigma_1 - h\,\mu_1. \tag{IV.2.11}$$

---

[10] This representation for a time series is introduced in Section I.3.7.

Even a small autocorrelation has a considerable effect on the scaling of volatility and VaR. The following example shows that this effect is much more significant than the effect of a mean adjustment term when the portfolio is not expected to return the risk free rate. Thus for the application of parametric linear VaR to hedge funds, or any other fund that smoothes its returns, the autocorrelation adjustment is typically more important than an adjustment to the VaR that accounts for a positive expected excess return.

EXAMPLE IV.2.1: ADJUSTING NORMAL LINEAR VAR FOR AUTOCORRELATION

Suppose a portfolio's daily log returns are normally distributed with a standard deviation of 1% and a mean of 0.01% above the discount rate. Calculate (a) the portfolio volatility and (b) the 1% 10-day normal linear VaR of the portfolio under the assumption of i.i.d. daily log returns and under the assumption that daily log returns are autocorrelated with first order autocorrelation $\varrho = 0.2$.

SOLUTION   Under the i.i.d. assumption and assuming 250 trading days per year, the annual excess return is $0.01\% \times 250 = 2.5\%$ and the volatility is

$$1\% \times \sqrt{250} = 15.81\%.$$

The 1% 10-day VaR is

$$2.32635 \times 0.01 \times \sqrt{10} - 10 \times 0.0001 = 0.0726.$$

That is, the 1% 10-day VaR is 7.26% of the portfolio's value.

But under the assumption that daily log returns have an autocorrelation of 0.2, the volatility and the VaR will be greater. The adjustment factor, i.e. the second term on the right-hand side of (IV.2.10) is calculated in the spreadsheet. It is 124.375 for $h = 250$, and 4.375 for $h = 10$. Hence, the volatility is

$$1\% \times \sqrt{374.375} = 19.35\%,$$

and the 1% 10-day VaR is

$$2.32635 \times 0.01 \times \sqrt{14.375} - 10 \times 0.0001 = 0.0872.$$

That is, the 1% 10-day VaR is now 8.72% of the portfolio's value.

Following this example, some general remarks are appropriate.

- Even this relatively small autocorrelation of 0.2 increases the 1% 10-day VaR by about one-fifth, whereas the daily mean excess return of 0.01% (equivalent to an annual expected return of 2.5% above the discount rate) only decreases the 1% 10-day VaR by 0.1%.
- The higher the autocorrelation and the longer the risk horizon, the greater the effect that a positive autocorrelation has on increasing the VaR. For higher autocorrelation and longer risk horizons, the VaR could easily double when autocorrelation is taken into account. And of course, negative autocorrelation decreases the VaR in a similar fashion.

IV.2.2.3   Systematic Normal Linear VaR

For reasons that have been discussed in the previous chapter, it is almost always the case that the risk manager will map each portfolio to a few well-chosen risk factors.[11] The *systematic* return or P&L on a portfolio is the part of the return that is explained by variations in the risk factors. In a linear portfolio it may be represented as a weighted sum,

$$Y = \sum_{i=1}^{m} \theta_i X_i, \tag{IV.2.12}$$

where X_i denotes the return or P&L on the ith risk factor and the coefficients θ_i denote the portfolio's sensitivity to the ith risk factor.[12] If we use the risk factor returns on the right-hand side of (IV.2.12) rather than their P&L, and the sensitivities are measured in percentage terms, then Y is the systematic return; otherwise Y is the systematic P&L on the portfolio.[13]

To calculate the systematic normal linear VaR we need to know the expectation $E(Y_h)$ and variance $V(Y_h)$ of the portfolio's h-day systematic return or P&L. We can use the factor model (IV.2.12) to express these in terms of the expectations, variances and covariances of the risk factors. To see this, write the vector of expected excess returns on the risk factors as

$$\boldsymbol{\mu}_h = \big(E(X_{1h}), \ldots, E(X_{mh})\big)',$$

write the vector of current sensitivities to the m risk factors as $\boldsymbol{\theta} = (\theta_1, \ldots, \theta_m)'$ and denote the $m \times m$ covariance matrix of the h-day risk factor returns by $\boldsymbol{\Omega}_h$. Then the mean and variance of the portfolio's h-day systematic returns or P&L may be written in matrix form as[14]

$$E(Y_h) = \boldsymbol{\theta}'\boldsymbol{\mu}_h, \quad V(Y_h) = \boldsymbol{\theta}'\boldsymbol{\Omega}_h\boldsymbol{\theta}. \tag{IV.2.13}$$

The normal linear VaR model assumes that risk factors have a multivariate normal distribution; hence, the above mean and variance are all that is required to specify the entire distribution. Substituting (IV.2.13) into (IV.2.5) gives the following formula for the $100\alpha\%$ h-day systematic VaR:

$$\text{Systematic VaR}_{h,\alpha} = \Phi^{-1}(1-\alpha)\sqrt{\boldsymbol{\theta}'\boldsymbol{\Omega}_h\boldsymbol{\theta}} - \boldsymbol{\theta}'\boldsymbol{\mu}_h. \tag{IV.2.14}$$

In many cases we assume that the expected systematic return is equal to the discount rate, in which case the discounted mean P&L will be zero and (IV.2.14) takes a particularly simple form:

$$\text{Systematic VaR}_{h,\alpha} = \Phi^{-1}(1-\alpha)\sqrt{\boldsymbol{\theta}'\boldsymbol{\Omega}_h\boldsymbol{\theta}}. \tag{IV.2.15}$$

---

[11] Risk factor mapping models are specific to each asset class, and were explained in detail in Chapter III.5.
[12] If the mapping has a constant term we set $X_1 = 1$.
[13] If the risk factor sensitivities are also measured in present value terms (as is the PV01, for instance) then the above P&L is also in present value terms. Otherwise (IV.2.12) represents the undiscounted P&L. More specific details are given in Section III.5.2.7.
[14] See Sections I.2.4 and IV.1.6.3, where the same matrix forms were applied specifically to cash flow portfolios.

The above shows how the systematic normal linear VaR can be obtained straight from the risk factor mapping. We only need to know the current:

- estimate of the risk factor sensitivities $\boldsymbol{\theta}$;
- forecast of the h-day risk factor returns covariance matrix $\boldsymbol{\Omega}_h$.

Note that *both* these inputs can introduce significant errors into the VaR estimate, as will be discussed in detail in Chapter IV.6.

A common assumption is that each of the risk factors follows an i.i.d. normal process. In the absence of autocorrelation or conditional heteroscedasticity in the processes, the square-root-of-time rule applies. In this case,

$$\boldsymbol{\Omega}_h = h\boldsymbol{\Omega}_1. \tag{IV.2.16}$$

In other words, each element in the 1-day covariance matrix is multiplied by h. Thus, just as for the total VaR in (IV.2.7), the h-day systematic VaR (IV.2.15) can be scaled up from the 1-day systematic VaR using a square-root scaling rule:

$$\text{Systematic VaR}_{h,\alpha} = \sqrt{h} \times \text{Systematic VaR}_{1,\alpha}.$$

Two simple numerical examples of normal linear systematic VaR have already been given in Section IV.1.6. A large number of much more detailed examples and case studies on normal linear systematic VaR for cash flows, stock portfolios, currency portfolios and portfolios of commodities will be given in this chapter and later in the book.

IV.2.2.4   Stand-Alone Normal Linear VaR

In Section IV.1.7 we explained, in general non-technical terms, how systematic VaR may be disaggregated into components consisting of either stand-alone VaR or marginal VaR, due to different types of risk factor. The stand-alone VaR is the systematic VaR due to a specific type of risk factor. So, depending on the type of risk factor, stand-alone VaR may be called *equity* VaR, *forex* VaR, *interest rate* VaR, *credit spread* VaR or *commodity* VaR.

Due to the diversification effect between risk factor types, and using the summation rule for the variance operator, in the normal linear model the sum of the stand-alone VaRs is greater than or equal to the total systematic VaR, with equality only in the trivial case where all the risk factors are perfectly correlated. However, in the next subsection we show how to transform each stand-alone VaR into a corresponding *marginal VaR*, where the sum of the marginal VaRs *is* equal to the total risk factor VaR.

In this subsection we specify the general methodology for calculating stand-alone VaRs in the normal linear VaR model. Although the derivation of theoretical results is set in the context of the normal linear VaR model, it is important to note that similar aggregation and decomposition rules apply to the other parametric linear VaR models that we shall introduce later in this chapter.

For the disaggregation of systematic VaR into different components we need to partition the risk factor covariance matrix $\boldsymbol{\Omega}_h$ into sub-matrices corresponding to equity index, interest rate, credit spread, forex and commodity risk factors. In the following we illustrate the decomposition when there are just three risk factor types, and we shall assume these are the equity, interest rate and forex factors. Although we do not cover this explicitly here, other classes of risk factor may of course be included.

Let the risk factor sensitivity vector $\boldsymbol{\theta}$, estimated at the time that the VaR is measured, be partitioned as

$$\boldsymbol{\theta} = (\boldsymbol{\theta}'_E, \boldsymbol{\theta}'_R, \boldsymbol{\theta}'_X)', \qquad (IV.2.17)$$

where $\boldsymbol{\theta}_E$, $\boldsymbol{\theta}_R$ and $\boldsymbol{\theta}_X$ are column vectors of equity, interest rate and forex risk factor sensitivities. For simplicity we assume the interest rate exposure is to only one risk free yield curve, but numerical examples of interest rate VaR when there are several yield curve risk factors and the exposures are to lower credit grade entities are given in Section IV.2.3.

For ease of aggregation it is best if all three vectors $\boldsymbol{\theta}_E$, $\boldsymbol{\theta}_R$ and $\boldsymbol{\theta}_X$ are expressed in percentage terms, or all three are expressed in nominal terms. Table IV.2.2 explains how these vectors are measured, and here we assume the numbers of equity, interest rate and forex risk factors are n_E, n_R and n_X respectively. We also use the notation:

- P to denote the value of the portfolio in domestic currency at the time the VaR is measured;
- β_i to denote the portfolio's percentage beta with respect to the ith equity risk factor;
- $PV01_i$ to denote the portfolio's PV01 with respect to the ith interest rate risk factor;
- X_i to denote the portfolio's nominal exposure to the ith foreign currency in domestic terms.

Table IV.2.2   Risk factor sensitivities

	Percentage sensitivities	Nominal sensitivities
Equity	$\boldsymbol{\theta}_E = (\beta_1, \ldots, \beta_{n_E})'$	$\boldsymbol{\theta}_E = P(\beta_1, \ldots, \beta_{n_E})'$
Interest rate	$\boldsymbol{\theta}_R = P^{-1}(PV01_1, \ldots, PV01_{n_R})'$	$\boldsymbol{\theta}_R = (PV01_1, \ldots, PV01_{n_R})'$
Forex	$\boldsymbol{\theta}_X = (1, \ldots, 1)'$	$\boldsymbol{\theta}_X = (X_1, \ldots, X_{n_X})'$

Now we partition the h-day covariance matrix $\boldsymbol{\Omega}_h$ into sub-matrices of equity risk factor return covariances $\boldsymbol{\Omega}_{Eh}$, interest rate risk factor return covariances $\boldsymbol{\Omega}_{Rh}$ and forex risk factor return covariances $\boldsymbol{\Omega}_{Xh}$ and their cross-covariance matrices $\boldsymbol{\Omega}_{ERh}$, $\boldsymbol{\Omega}_{EXh}$ and $\boldsymbol{\Omega}_{RXh}$. Thus we write the risk factor covariance matrix in the form

$$\boldsymbol{\Omega}_h = \begin{pmatrix} \boldsymbol{\Omega}_{Eh} & \boldsymbol{\Omega}_{ERh} & \boldsymbol{\Omega}_{EXh} \\ \boldsymbol{\Omega}'_{ERh} & \boldsymbol{\Omega}_{Rh} & \boldsymbol{\Omega}_{RXh} \\ \boldsymbol{\Omega}'_{EXh} & \boldsymbol{\Omega}'_{RXh} & \boldsymbol{\Omega}_{Xh} \end{pmatrix}. \qquad (IV.2.18)$$

This partitioned matrix has off-diagonal blocks equal to the cross-covariances between different types of risk factors. For instance, if there are five equity risk factors and four foreign exchange risk factors, the 5×4 matrix $\boldsymbol{\Omega}_{EXh}$ contains the 20 pairwise h-day covariances between equity and foreign exchange factors, with i,jth element equal to the covariance between the ith equity risk factor and the jth forex risk factor.

Ignoring any mean adjustment, the systematic normal linear VaR is given by (IV.2.15) with $\boldsymbol{\theta}$ partitioned as in (IV.2.17) and with $\boldsymbol{\Omega}_h$ given by (IV.2.18). With this notation it is easy to isolate the different risk factor VaRs.

- *Equity VaR*, i.e. the risk due to equity risk factors alone:
  Set $\theta_R = \theta_X = 0$ and (IV.2.15) yields

$$\text{Equity VaR}_{h,\alpha} = \Phi^{-1}(1 - \alpha)\sqrt{\theta'_E \Omega_{Eh} \theta_E}. \tag{IV.2.19}$$

- *Interest rate VaR*, i.e. the risk due to interest rate risk factors alone:
  Set $\theta_E = \theta_X = 0$ and (IV.2.15) yields

$$\text{Interest rate VaR}_{h,\alpha} = \Phi^{-1}(1 - \alpha)\sqrt{\theta'_R \Omega_{Rh} \theta_R}. \tag{IV.2.20}$$

- *Forex VaR*, i.e. the risk due to forex risk factors alone:
  Set $\theta_E = \theta_R = 0$ and (IV.2.15) yields

$$\text{Forex VaR}_{h,\alpha} = \Phi^{-1}(1 - \alpha)\sqrt{\theta'_X \Omega_{Xh} \theta_X}. \tag{IV.2.21}$$

Even if the cross-covariance matrices are all zero the total VaR would not be equal to the sum of these three 'stand-alone' VaRs. The only aggregation rules we have are that the sum of the stand-alone components equals the total systematic VaR if and only if the risk factors are all perfectly correlated, and that the sum of the squared stand-alone VaRs is equal to the square of the total VaR if the cross correlations between risk factors are all zero.[15]

IV.2.2.5 Marginal and Incremental Normal Linear VaR

In Section IV.1.7.3 we showed that the total systematic VaR *is* equal to the sum of the *marginal* component VaRs, to a first order approximation. In the normal linear model the gradient vector (IV.1.29) is obtained by differentiating (IV.2.15) with respect to each component in θ.

Using our partition of the covariance matrix as in (IV.2.18) above, and the risk factor sensitivities vector θ partitioned as in (IV.2.17), the *equity marginal VaR* is given by the approximation (IV.1.30) with $\theta_R = \theta_X = 0$, and so forth for the other component VaRs. That is, we set the other risk factor sensitivities in θ to zero, compute the gradient vector and then approximate the marginal VaR as

$$\text{Marginal VaR} \approx \theta' \mathbf{g}(\theta). \tag{IV.2.22}$$

In Section IV.1.7.3 we also showed how to use the gradient vector to assess the VaR impact of a trade, i.e. to compute the incremental VaR. In the specific case of the normal linear VaR model the incremental VaR is, to a first order approximation, given by

$$\text{Incremental VaR} \approx \Delta\theta' \mathbf{g}(\theta), \tag{IV.2.23}$$

where θ is the original risk factor sensitivity vector and $\Delta\theta$ is the change in the risk factor sensitivity vector as a result of the trade. Note that this approximation can lead to significant errors if used on large trades. The approximation rests on a Taylor linearization of the parametric linear VaR, but the parametric linear VaR is actually a quadratic function of the sensitivity vector.

---

[15] This is a feature of parametric linear VaR and it would not be true if VaR was measured using simulation.

To apply the general formulae (IV.2.22) and (IV.2.23) we must derive the gradient vector $\mathbf{g}(\boldsymbol{\theta})$ under the normal linear VaR model assumptions. The $100\alpha\%$ h-day normal linear systematic VaR is given by (IV.2.25). Differentiating this, using the chain rule, gives the gradient vector of first partial derivatives, which in this case is

$$\mathbf{g}(\boldsymbol{\theta}) = \Phi^{-1}(1-\alpha)(\boldsymbol{\Omega}_h\boldsymbol{\theta})(\boldsymbol{\theta}'\boldsymbol{\Omega}_h\boldsymbol{\theta})^{-1/2}. \tag{IV.2.24}$$

The gradient vector, which Garman (1996) calls the *DelVaR* vector, has elements equal to the derivative of VaR with respect to each of the components in $\boldsymbol{\theta}$. Now using (IV.2.22) gives the marginal VaR. A numerical illustration of the formula is given in Example IV.2.5 below.

Specific examples of the decomposition of normal linear VaR into stand-alone and marginal VaR components, and of the calculation of incremental VaR, will be given below. For instance, see Examples IV.2.4–IV.2.6 for cash flows and Examples IV.2.14–IV.2.16 for international equity portfolios.

IV.2.3   NORMAL LINEAR VALUE AT RISK FOR CASH-FLOW MAPS

This section analyses the normal linear VaR of a portfolio of bonds, loans or swaps, each of which can be represented as a cash flow. The risk factors are one or more yield curves, i.e. sets of fixed maturity interest rates of a given credit rating. Later in this section we shall decompose each interest rate into a LIBOR rate plus a credit spread. In that case the risk factors are the LIBOR curves and possibly also one or more term structures of credit spreads with different credit ratings.

The excess return on the portfolio over the discount rate will be significantly different from zero only when the portfolio has many exposures to low credit quality counterparties and when the risk horizon is very long. Since the PV01 vector is expressed in present value terms, and since there is no constant term in the risk factor mapping of a cash flow, the discounted expected return on the portfolio is zero, so it is only the volatility of the portfolio P&L that determines the VaR.

In this section all cash flows are assumed to have been mapped to standard maturity interest rates in a present value and volatility invariant fashion. Since we have covered cash-flow mapping in considerable detail in Section III.5.3, and furnished several numerical examples there, we shall assume the reader is familiar with cash-flow mapping in the following. We characterize a portfolio by its mapped cash flow at standard vertices, or by its PV01 sensitivity vector directly.

IV.2.3.1   Normal Linear Interest Rate VaR

We begin by considering only the interest rate risk factors, without decomposing these into LIBOR and credit spread components. In Section IV.1.6.3 we derived a formula for normal linear interest rate VaR, repeated here for convenience:

$$\text{Interest rate VaR}_{h,\alpha} = \Phi^{-1}(1-\alpha)\sqrt{\boldsymbol{\theta}'\boldsymbol{\Omega}_h\boldsymbol{\theta}}, \tag{IV.2.25}$$

where $\boldsymbol{\theta} = (\text{PV01}_1, \ldots, \text{PV01}_n)'$ is the vector of PV01 sensitivities to the various interest rates that are chosen for the risk factors.

A simple example of normal linear VaR for a cash-flow portfolio was given in Section IV.1.6.3, and the first remark that we make here is that in that example the covariance matrix was expressed in *basis points*. The reason for this is that the PV01 vector contains the risk factor sensitivities to absolute, basis point changes in interest rates, and not to relative changes.

In highly developed markets, returns on fixed income portfolios are usually measured in terms of changes, rather than relative terms. This is natural because the change in the interest rate is the percentage return on the corresponding discount bond. Volatilities of changes in interest rates are often of the order of 100 basis points. But in some countries, such as Brazil or Turkey (at the time of writing), interest rates are extremely high and variable and their volatilities are so high that they are commonly quoted in percentage terms. In this case care should be taken to ensure that the PV01 sensitivities are also adjusted to relate to percentage changes in interest rates or, when PV01 sensitivities relate to changes, the covariance matrix of interest rates must be converted to basis point terms. The following example illustrates how to do this, assuming the returns are normal and i.i.d.

EXAMPLE IV.2.2: CONVERTING A COVARIANCE MATRIX TO BASIS POINTS

Suppose two interest rates have a correlation of 0.9, that one interest rate is at 10% with a volatility of 30% and the other is at 8% with a volatility of 25%. What is the daily covariance matrix in basis point terms?

SOLUTION   For the 10% rate with 30% volatility, the volatility is $0.1 \times 0.3 = 300$ basis points; for the 8% rate with 25% volatility, the volatility is $0.08 \times 0.25 = 200$ basis points. For the correlation of 0.9, the covariance is $0.9 \times 300 \times 200 = 54,000$ in basis points *squared*. Hence the annual covariance matrix is

$$\begin{pmatrix} 90,000 & 54,000 \\ 54,000 & 40,000 \end{pmatrix}$$

and, assuming 250 trading days per year, the daily covariance matrix is, in basis point terms

$$\begin{pmatrix} 360 & 216 \\ 216 & 160 \end{pmatrix}.$$

IV.2.3.2 Calculating PV01

Consider a cash flow C_T at some fixed maturity T, measured in years, which we assume for simplicity is an integer.[16] The present value of the cash flow based on a discretely compounded discount rate R_T, expressed in annual terms, is

$$PV(C_T, R_T) = C_T(1 + R_T)^{-T}. \tag{IV.2.26}$$

Then, by definition,

$$PV01_T = PV01(C_T, R_T) = PV(C_T, R_T - 0.01\%) - PV(C_T, R_T). \tag{IV.2.27}$$

---

[16] See Section III.1.2.2 for details on discounting cash flows for a non-integer number of years.

A useful and very accurate approximation to (IV.2.27) is derived in Section III.1.8.2. It is repeated here for convenience:

$$PV01_T \approx TC_T(1 + R_T)^{-(T+1)} \times 10^{-4}. \tag{IV.2.28}$$

Again, this is valid when T is an integer number of years. Otherwise a small adjustment should be made to the discount factor, as explained in Section III.1.8.2.

Because of the unwanted technical details when working with discretely compounded rates, practitioners usually convert discretely compounded rates into their continuously compounded equivalents for calculations. Using the continuously compounded rate r_T that gives the same present value as the discretely compounded rate, we have, for *any* maturity T, not necessarily an integral number of years,

$$PV(C_T, R_T) = C_T\exp(-r_T T). \tag{IV.2.29}$$

Thus the PV01 approximation for any T may be written

$$PV01_T \approx TC_T\exp(-r_T T) \times 10^{-4}. \tag{IV.2.30}$$

See Section III.1.8.2 for further details and numerical examples.

The examples in the remainder of this section assume that a cash flow has been previously mapped to the interest rate risk factors, and that the values of the mapped cash flows are *not* discounted to present value terms. This is because the PV01 vector θ of risk factor sensitivities themselves will convert the change in portfolio value at some time in the future into present value terms.

We now consolidate the application of the normal linear VaR model to cash-flow portfolios by considering a simple numerical example. We make the assumption that the interest rate risk factors are the same as those used for discounting, so there is no drift adjustment term in the VaR formula. We also assume that interest rate changes are generated by i.i.d. multivariate normal processes, so that we can scale the normal linear VaR using the square-root-of-time rule. In particular, the h-day covariance matrix is just h times the 1-day covariance matrix.

EXAMPLE IV.2.3: NORMAL LINEAR VAR FROM A MAPPED CASH FLOW

Consider a cash flow of $1 million in 1 year and of $1.5 million in 2 years' time. Calculate the volatility of the discounted P&L of the cash flows, given that:

- the 1-year interest rate is 4% and the 2-year interest rate is 5%;
- the volatility of the 1-year rate is 100 basis points, and the volatility of the 2-year rate is 75 basis points; and
- their correlation is 0.9.

Hence calculate the 5% 1-day and the 1% 10-day normal linear VaR.

SOLUTION   In the spreadsheet we use (IV.2.27) to calculate the PV01 vector as

$$\theta = (92.465, 259.188)'.$$

Then we calculate the covariance matrix in basis point terms from the volatilities and correlation, as described above, yielding

$$\Omega_{250} = \begin{pmatrix} 10,000 & 6,750 \\ 6,750 & 5,625 \end{pmatrix}.$$

Now the volatility of discounted P&L is

$$\sqrt{(92.456 \quad 259.188) \begin{pmatrix} 10,000 & 6,750 \\ 6,750 & 5,625 \end{pmatrix} \begin{pmatrix} 92.456 \\ 259.188 \end{pmatrix}} = \$28,052.$$

To convert this into a $100\alpha\%$ h-day VaR figure we use the relevant standard normal critical value from (IV.2.4) and the square-root-of-time rule. Assuming 250 risk days per year, the 5% 1-day VaR corresponding to the volatility of $28,052 is

$$1.64485 \times 28,052/\sqrt{250} = \$2918.$$

Similarly, assuming the number of 10-trading-day periods per year is 25, the 1% 10-day VaR is

$$2.32635 \times 28,052/\sqrt{25} = \$13,052.$$

IV.2.3.3   Approximating Marginal and Incremental VaR

The gradient vector (IV.2.24) allows us to express, to a first order approximation, the incremental effect on VaR resulting from *each* of the cash flows in a trade. Denote the change in the PV01 cash-flow sensitivity vector as a result of a small trade by $\Delta\theta$. Each incremental VaR corresponding to a cash flow at one specific maturity is an element of another vector $\Delta\theta \otimes g(\theta)$, where $\otimes$ denotes the column vector obtained as the element by element product of two column vectors. The net incremental VaR of the new trade is given by the sum of the separate components of this vector, i.e. by (IV.2.23). Using this in (IV.2.23) will give a first order approximation to the change in VaR when any of the PV01 cash-flow sensitivities change.

   The following example illustrates how we can approximate the effect of a new trade on the VaR by considering only the cash flow resulting from the proposed trade, thus avoiding the need to revalue the VaR for the entire portfolio each time a new trade is considered.

EXAMPLE IV.2.4: INCREMENTAL VAR FOR A CASH FLOW

Consider a cash-flow map with the following sensitivity vector:

Year:	1	2	3
PV01($):	1000	1500	2000

Suppose the interest rates at maturities 1, 2 and 3 years have volatilities of 75 basis points, 60 basis points and 50 basis points and correlations of 0.95 (1yr, 2yr), 0.9 (1yr, 3yr), and 0.975

(2yr, 3yr). Find the 1% 10-day normal linear VaR. Now assume that interest rates are 4%, 4.5% and 5% at the 1-year, 2-year and 3-year vertices and suppose that a trader considers entering into a swap with the following cash flow:

Year:	1	2	3
Cash flow ($m)	3	−3	−0.25

What is the incremental VaR of the trade?

SOLUTION The 1-day risk factor covariance matrix, in basis point terms, is

$$\Omega_1 = \begin{pmatrix} 22.5 & 17.1 & 13.5 \\ 17.1 & 14.4 & 11.7 \\ 13.5 & 11.7 & 10.0 \end{pmatrix}.$$

For instance, the top left element 22.5 for the 1-day variance of the 1-year rate is obtained as $75^2/250 = 22.5$. We are given

$$\theta = \begin{pmatrix} 1000 & 1500 & 2000 \end{pmatrix}'$$

and so

$$\theta'\Omega_1\theta = \begin{pmatrix} 1000 & 1500 & 2000 \end{pmatrix} \begin{pmatrix} 22.5 & 17.1 & 13.5 \\ 17.1 & 14.4 & 11.7 \\ 13.5 & 11.7 & 10.0 \end{pmatrix} \begin{pmatrix} 1000 \\ 1500 \\ 2000 \end{pmatrix} = 270.4 \times 10^6.$$

The square root of this, i.e. $16,443, is the 1-day standard deviation of the discounted P&L. The 10-day standard deviation is obtained, using the square-root-of-time rule, as

$$\sigma_{10} = \$16,443 \times \sqrt{10} = \$52,000.$$

Hence the 1% 10-day normal linear VaR is

$$2.32635 \times \$52,000 = \$120,970.$$

For a 10-day risk horizon,

$$\Omega_{10}\theta = 10 \times \begin{pmatrix} 22.5 & 17.1 & 13.5 \\ 17.1 & 14.4 & 11.7 \\ 13.5 & 11.7 & 10.0 \end{pmatrix} \begin{pmatrix} 1000 \\ 1500 \\ 2000 \end{pmatrix} = \begin{pmatrix} 751,500 \\ 621,000 \\ 510,500 \end{pmatrix}.$$

From above we have $\sqrt{\theta'\Omega_{10}\theta} = \$52,000$. Hence the DelVaR vector is

$$g(\theta) = \frac{2.32635}{52,000} \begin{pmatrix} 751,500 \\ 621,000 \\ 510,500 \end{pmatrix} = \begin{pmatrix} 33.6202 \\ 27.7820 \\ 22.8385 \end{pmatrix}.$$

Calculating the PV01 sensitivity vector of the swap's cash flows, using (IV.2.27) gives

$$\Delta\theta = \begin{pmatrix} 277.3935 \\ -525.8534 \\ -61.7144 \end{pmatrix}.$$

Hence, the components of the incremental VaR are

$$\Delta\theta \otimes g(\theta) = \begin{pmatrix} 277.3935 \\ -525.8534 \\ -61.7144 \end{pmatrix} \otimes \begin{pmatrix} 33.6202 \\ 27.7820 \\ 22.8385 \end{pmatrix} = \begin{pmatrix} 9,326 \\ -14,609 \\ -1,409 \end{pmatrix}.$$

This shows that the positive cash flow at 1 year increases the VaR by approximately $9326 but both of the negative cash flows on the swap will decrease the VaR, by approximately $14,609 and $1409 respectively. The total incremental VaR for the swap is the sum of these, i.e. approximately −$6693. Hence, adding the swap would reduce the VaR of the portfolio.

Incremental VaR is based on a linear approximation to the VaR, which is a non-linear function of the risk factor sensitivities, so it should only be applied to assess the effect of trades that are small relative to the overall size of the portfolio. Also, in order to properly compare the incremental VaR of several different trades, the cash flows from these trades need to be normalized. Obviously, if trade A has double the magnitude of the cash flows of trade B, the incremental VaR of trade A will be twice that of trade B. That is, we should normalize the trades, so that the incremental VaRs *per unit of cash flow* are compared. There are several ways of doing this. For instance, we could divide each PV01 by the sum of the absolute values of all PV01s in the sensitivity vector of the trade, or we could divide each PV01 by the square root of the sum of the squared PV01s. More details are given in Garman (1996).

IV.2.3.4 Disaggregating Normal Linear Interest Rate VaR

In this subsection we continue with simple numerical examples of normal linear interest rate VaR to examine the case of an exposure to two yield curves. Such an exposure arises in many circumstances: it can result from an international portfolio containing interest rate sensitive securities; or from any type of foreign investment in forwards and futures;[17] even in international commodity portfolios, where we may prefer to use constant maturity futures as risk factors, the forex risk is usually managed by hedging with forex forwards and these are mapped to the spot forex rate. A forex forward mapping thus gives rise to an exposure to the foreign LIBOR curve.

In equity and commodity portfolios the interest rate risk factors are usually much less important than the equity or commodity risk factors and, for international portfolios, the forex risk factors. Usually the equity, commodity, interest rate and forex risk exposures are managed by separate desks. Hence, in the examples in this section we keep things simple by considering only the interest rate part of the risk.

---

[17] Following our discussion in Section III.5.2, we normally map an investment in equity forwards or futures to the spot price, using the no arbitrage relationship between spot and futures, and thus the foreign discount curve becomes a set of risk factors.

EXAMPLE IV.2.5: NORMAL LINEAR VAR FOR AN EXPOSURE TO TWO YIELD CURVES

In Table IV.2.3 we display the PV01 vectors, both in US dollars, for a portfolio with exposures to the UK and US government yield curves. For simplicity we assume the portfolio has been mapped to only the 1-year, 2-year and 3-year interest rates in each county, and the basis point volatilities for these interest rates are given below each PV01. The correlation matrix of daily interest rates is given in Table IV.2.4. Calculate the 1% 10-day normal linear interest rate VaR, the stand-alone VaR due to the US and UK yield curve risk factors, and the marginal VaRs of these risk factors.

Table IV.2.3   PV01 of cash flows and volatilities of UK and US interest rates

Interest Rate	US			UK		
Maturity (years)	1	2	3	1	2	3
PV01($)	1000	−1500	2000	800	900	−750
Volatility (bps)	100	80	70	85	75	65

Table IV.2.4   Correlations between UK and US interest rates

		US			UK		
		1	2	3	1	2	3
US	1	1	0.95	0.90	0.70	0.67	0.62
	2	0.95	1	0.97	0.65	0.75	0.75
	3	0.90	0.97	1	0.60	0.79	0.80
UK	1	0.70	0.65	0.60	1	0.98	0.95
	2	0.67	0.75	0.79	0.98	1	0.99
	3	0.62	0.75	0.80	0.95	0.99	1

SOLUTION   Using the information given in Tables IV.2.3 and IV.2.4, the annual covariance matrix is written in partitioned form as

$$\Omega = \begin{pmatrix} \Omega_{US} & \Omega_{US\text{-}UK} \\ \Omega'_{US\text{-}UK} & \Omega_{UK} \end{pmatrix},$$

where

$$\Omega_{US} = \begin{pmatrix} 1000 & 7600 & 6300 \\ 7600 & 6400 & 5432 \\ 6300 & 5432 & 4900 \end{pmatrix},$$

$$\Omega_{UK} = \begin{pmatrix} 7225 & 6247.5 & 5248.75 \\ 6247.5 & 5625 & 4826.25 \\ 5248.75 & 4826.25 & 4225 \end{pmatrix},$$

$$\Omega_{US\text{-}UK} = \begin{pmatrix} 5950 & 5025 & 4030 \\ 4420 & 4500 & 3900 \\ 3570 & 4147.5 & 3640 \end{pmatrix}.$$

We also write the PV01 vector as

$$\boldsymbol{\theta}' = (\boldsymbol{\theta}'_{US}, \boldsymbol{\theta}'_{UK}),$$

where

$$\boldsymbol{\theta}'_{US} = (1000, -1500, 2000), \quad \boldsymbol{\theta}'_{UK} = (800, 900, -750).$$

Under the usual normal i.i.d. assumption, the 1% 10-day total risk factor VaR is then

$$\Phi^{-1}(0.99)\sqrt{\boldsymbol{\theta}'\boldsymbol{\Omega}\boldsymbol{\theta}} \times \sqrt{10/250} = 2.32635 \times 188,466 \times 0.2 = \$87,688.$$

For the stand-alone US interest rate VaR we simply use $\boldsymbol{\Omega}_{US}$ and $\boldsymbol{\theta}_{US}$ in place of $\boldsymbol{\Omega}$ and $\boldsymbol{\theta}$ (and similarly, we use $\boldsymbol{\Omega}_{UK}$ and $\boldsymbol{\theta}_{UK}$ for the UK interest rate VaR). The results, which are calculated in the spreadsheet for this example, are:

$$1\% \text{ 10-day US interest rate VaR} = \$54,673,$$

$$1\% \text{ 10-day UK interest rate VaR} = \$40,931.$$

So the sum of the stand-alone VaRs is \$95,604, which is considerably more than the total interest rate VaR.

However, the marginal VaRs do add up to the total interest rate VaR. To calculate these we first compute the DelVaR vector $\mathbf{g}(\boldsymbol{\theta})$ using (IV.2.24). Working at the annual level,[18] we have

$$\mathbf{g}(\boldsymbol{\theta}) = \begin{pmatrix} \mathbf{g}(\boldsymbol{\theta}_{US}) \\ \mathbf{g}(\boldsymbol{\theta}_{UK}) \end{pmatrix} = ((215.52, 166.95, 145.79)', (171.90, 160.60, 133.73)')'.$$

Now we can recover the 1% annual total interest rate VaR as $\boldsymbol{\theta}'\mathbf{g}(\boldsymbol{\theta})$ and the two 1% annual marginal VaRs as

$$1\% \text{ annual US marginal VaR} = \boldsymbol{\theta}'_{US}\mathbf{g}(\boldsymbol{\theta}_{US}) = \$256,673$$
$$\Rightarrow 1\% \text{ 10-day US marginal VaR} = \$256,673 \times 0.2 = \$51,335.$$

Similarly,

$$1\% \text{ annual UK marginal VaR} = \boldsymbol{\theta}'_{UK}\mathbf{g}(\boldsymbol{\theta}_{UK}) = \$181,763$$
$$\Rightarrow 1\% \text{ 10-day US marginal VaR} = \$181,763 \times 0.2 = \$36,353.$$

The sum of the marginal VaRs is \$87,688, which is identical to the total interest rate VaR.

---

[18] Note that in the last example we worked at the 1-day level, but in the linear VaR model the order of applying the square-root-of-time rule does not matter.

IV.2.3.5   Normal Linear Credit Spread VaR

An exposure to curves with different credit ratings arises from a portfolio with investments in company bonds, corporate loans or swaps, asset backed securities, collateralized debt obligations and non-bank loans such as mortgages. All exposures can be mapped as cash flows at standard vertices, and for each vertex we represent the risk factors as the LIBOR rate of that maturity and the various spreads over LIBOR for each credit rating.

We now explain how to decompose the linear VaR of an interest rate sensitive portfolio into LIBOR and spread components, using continuous compounding (because the mathematics is so much easier). In this case we may write an interest rate of a given credit rating as the sum of the continuously compounded LIBOR rate and the continuously compounded credit spread for that rating. That is, for maturity T and at time t,

$$r_q(t, T) = r(t, T) + s_q(t, T), \tag{IV.2.31}$$

where $r(t, T)$ denotes the spot LIBOR rate with maturity T at time t, and $r_q(t, T)$ and $s_q(t, T)$ respectively denote the interest rate and credit spread, both with credit rating q.

The VaR is calculated in exactly the same way as above, and the only difference is that the variance of the interest rate $r_q(t, T)$ can, if we wish, be decomposed into three terms: the variances of the LIBOR rate and the credit spread, and their covariance. This variance decomposition is obtained by applying the variance operator to (IV.2.31):

$$V(r_q(t, T)) = V(r(t, T)) + V(s_q(t, T)) + 2\mathrm{Cov}(r(t, T), s_q(t, T)). \tag{IV.2.32}$$

We now explain how to decompose the total interest rate VaR into LIBOR VaR and credit spread VaR, for a portfolio of a given credit rating, in the context of the normal linear model. Dropping the time and maturity dependence for simplicity, we denote the set of interest rates of credit rating q with different maturities by the vector $\mathbf{r}_q$, the LIBOR rates of these maturities by $\mathbf{r}$ and the corresponding credit spreads by $\mathbf{s}_q$.

We account for the correlations between interest rates using the yield curve covariance matrix, and now we partition this matrix into LIBOR and spread covariance matrices, and their cross-covariance matrix, as

$$V(\mathbf{r}_q) = \mathbf{\Omega} = \begin{pmatrix} \mathbf{\Omega}_R & \mathbf{\Omega}_{RS} \\ \mathbf{\Omega}'_{RS} & \mathbf{\Omega}_S \end{pmatrix}. \tag{IV.2.33}$$

If we want to make the risk horizon of the matrix explicit, then the covariance matrix corresponding to h-day changes in interest rates is written as

$$V(\mathbf{r}_{hq}) = \mathbf{\Omega}_h = \begin{pmatrix} \mathbf{\Omega}_{hR} & \mathbf{\Omega}_{hRS} \\ \mathbf{\Omega}'_{hRS} & \mathbf{\Omega}_{hS} \end{pmatrix}. \tag{IV.2.34}$$

Suppose there are n LIBOR rate and n credit spread risk factors at the same maturities. The four matrices in the partition on the right-hand side of (IV.2.34) are then $n \times n$ matrices and $\mathbf{\Omega}$ has dimension $2n \times 2n$. Now, what is the $2n \times 1$ risk factor sensitivity vector? The PV01 sensitivity to the change in interest rate of a given maturity is the change in the present value of the cash flow for a one basis point fall in that interest rate. But since the interest rate is the sum of the LIBOR rate and the credit spread, this one basis point fall could be in either the LIBOR rate or the credit spread of that maturity. Thus, assuming the vertices of the risk factor mapping are the same for LIBOR and credit spreads, the PV01 is same for both LIBOR and the credit spread. In other words, with the decomposition (IV.2.34) of the covariance matrix, the corresponding PV01 is the vector with the PV01s at the n vertices in the LIBOR rate risk factor set, and then these are repeated for the vertices in the credit spread risk factor set. Thus $\theta = (\theta'_R, \ \theta'_S)'$ where in this case

$$\theta_R = \theta_S = (PV01_1, \ldots, PV01_n)'. \tag{IV.2.35}$$

But due to the limitations of historical data, it usually the case that the maturities at which credit spreads are recorded are a proper subset of the maturities in the LIBOR rate risk factor set.[19] So in general, $\theta_R \neq \theta_S$ because they do not even have the same dimension.

Now the total VaR due to LIBOR and spread is given by the usual formula,

$$\text{Total systematic VaR}_{h,\alpha} = \Phi^{-1}(1-\alpha)\sqrt{\theta'\Omega_h\theta}.$$

Setting $\theta_R = 0$ gives the stand-alone credit spread VaR, and setting $\theta_S = 0$ gives the stand-alone LIBOR VaR. The marginal contributions to VaR and the incremental VaR of a new trade are all calculated using the gradient vector in the usual way.

The extension of this decomposition to a portfolio containing exposures with several credit ratings is straightforward. For example, with two credit ratings in the portfolio we decompose the covariance matrix thus:

$$\Omega_h = \begin{pmatrix} \Omega_{hR} & \Omega_{hRS_1} & \Omega_{hRS_2} \\ \Omega'_{hRS_1} & \Omega_{hS_1} & \Omega_{hS_1S_2} \\ \Omega'_{hRS_2} & \Omega'_{hS_1S_2} & \Omega_{hS_2} \end{pmatrix}. \tag{IV.2.36}$$

and the PV01 vector is written as the column vector

$$\theta = (\theta'_R, \theta'_{S_1}, \theta'_{S_2})',$$

where θ_R is the PV01 of the combined exposure to the two different credit ratings, θ_{S_1} is the PV01 of the exposure to the first credit rating, and θ_{S_2} is the PV01 of the exposure to the second credit rating.

The following example illustrates the decomposition of interest rate VaR for a portfolio with exposures to a single credit rating.

EXAMPLE IV.2.6: SPREAD AND LIBOR COMPONENTS OF NORMAL LINEAR VAR

A portfolio of A-rated corporate bonds and swaps has its cash flows mapped to vertices at 1 year, 2 years, 3 years, 4 years and 5 years. The volatilities of the LIBOR rates (in basis points per annum) and PV01 vector of the portfolio are shown in Table IV.2.5. The correlations of the LIBOR rates are shown in Table IV.2.6.

The 1-year and 5-year A-rated credit spreads are, like the LIBOR parameters, assumed to have been estimated from a historical sample. Suppose the 1-year spread has volatility 80

---

[19] In this case, there are three ways to approach the problem of disaggregating VaR into LIBOR and credit spread components. We can use a different number of vertices for the LIBOR and credit spread mappings, in other words the credit spread and LIBOR risk factors result from cash-flow mappings to vertices at different maturities, and consequently the PV01 vector for credit spreads will be different from the PV01 vector for LIBOR. Alternatively, we can interpolate the volatilities and correlation of the credit spreads to obtain volatilities and correlations at the same maturities for credit spreads as used for LIBOR, or we can reduce the LIBOR rate risk factors to be at the same maturities as the credit spread risk factors.

Table IV.2.5   PV01 of cash flows and volatilities of LIBOR rates

Maturity (years)	1	2	3	4	5
PV01 ($)	750	1000	500	250	500
Volatility (bps)	100	95	85	75	60

Table IV.2.6   Correlations between LIBOR rates

Correlations		LIBOR				
		1yr	2yr	3yr	4yr	5yr
LIBOR	1yr	1	0.95	0.92	0.9	0.88
	2yr	0.95	1	0.97	0.65	0.75
	3yr	0.92	0.97	1	0.6	0.79
	4yr	0.9	0.65	0.6	1	0.98
	5yr	0.88	0.75	0.79	0.98	1

basis points per annum and the 5-year spread has volatility 70 basis points per annum, and their correlation is 0.9. Suppose the cross correlations between these credit spreads and the LIBOR rates of different maturities are as shown in Table IV.2.7. Estimate the 1% 10-day total interest rate VaR and decompose the total VaR into the VaR due to LIBOR rate uncertainty, and the VaR due to credit spread uncertainty. Then estimate the marginal VaR of the LIBOR and credit spread components.

Table IV.2.7   Cross correlations between credit spreads and LIBOR rates

Correlations		LIBOR				
		1yr	2yr	3yr	4yr	5yr
Credit spread	1yr	−0.25	−0.20	−0.18	−0.15	−0.10
	5yr	−0.20	−0.21	−0.23	−0.24	−0.25

SOLUTION   We shall employ a simple linear interpolation between variances and between squared correlations to fill in the elements of the matrices Ω_S and Ω_{RS}.[20] The full matrix Ω is a 10×10 matrix, and the volatilities and correlations in this matrix are shown in Table IV.2.8. The PV01 vector is

$$\theta' = (\theta'_R, \theta'_S),$$

with

$$\theta'_R = \theta'_S = (750, 1000, 500, 250, 500)$$

This yields the 1% annual total risk factor VaR:

$$\Phi^{-1}(0.99)\sqrt{\theta'\Omega\theta} = 2.32635 \times \$296,363 = \$689,443.$$

---

[20] Linear interpolation between correlations would lead to a singular correlation matrix. The interpolation method is *ad hoc*, hence a (small) model risk is introduced with this approach.

Table IV.2.8   Volatilities and correlations of LIBOR and credit spreads

Volatilities			LIBOR					Credit spreads		
Maturity (years)	1	2	3	4	5	1	2	3	4	5
PV01 ($)	750	1000	500	250	500	750	1000	500	250	500
Volatility (bps)	100	95	85	75	60	80	77.62	75.17	72.63	70

Correlations		1	2	3	4	5	1	2	3	4	5
LIBOR	1	1	0.95	0.92	0.9	0.88	−0.25	−0.2385	−0.2264	−0.2136	−0.2
	2	0.95	1	0.97	0.65	0.75	−0.2000	−0.2025	−0.2051	−0.2075	−0.2100
	3	0.92	0.97	1	0.6	0.79	−0.1800	−0.1937	−0.2065	0.2186	−0.2300
	4	0.9	0.65	0.6	1	0.98	−0.1500	−0.1768	−0.2001	−0.2210	−0.2400
	5	0.88	0.75	0.79	0.98	1	−0.1	−0.1521	−0.1904	−0.2222	−0.25
Credit spreads	1	−0.25	−0.20	−0.18	−0.15	−0.10	1	0.9760	0.9513	0.9260	0.9
	2	−0.2385	−0.2025	−0.1937	−0.1768	−0.1521	0.9760	1	0.9760	0.9513	0.9260
	3	−0.2264	−0.2051	−0.2065	−0.2001	−0.1904	0.9513	0.9760	1	0.9760	0.9513
	4	−0.2136	−0.2075	−0.2186	−0.2210	−0.2222	0.9260	0.9513	0.9760	1	0.9760
	5	−0.20	−0.21	−0.23	−0.24	−0.25	0.9	0.9260	0.9513	0.9760	1

Multiplying this by $\sqrt{10/250} = 0.2$ gives the 1% 10-day total risk factor VaR as $137,889.

For the stand-alone LIBOR VaR we simply use $\boldsymbol{\Omega}_R$ and $\boldsymbol{\theta}_R$ in place of $\boldsymbol{\Omega}$ and $\boldsymbol{\theta}$ (and similarly, we use $\boldsymbol{\Omega}_S$ and $\boldsymbol{\theta}_S$ for the credit spread VaR). The results, which are calculated in the spreadsheet for this example, are:

$$1\%\ 10\text{-day LIBOR VaR} = \$115{,}943,$$

$$1\%\ 10\text{-day credit spread VaR} = \$104{,}301.$$

So the sum of the stand-alone VaRs is $220,224, which is much larger than the total VaR, due to the negative correlation between interest rates and credit spreads.

As usual, the marginal VaRs sum to the total VaR. To calculate these we first compute the annual gradient vector using the usual formula. This gives

$$\mathbf{g}(\boldsymbol{\theta}_R) = (152.85, 145.87, 128.76, 94.34, 85.46)', \quad \mathbf{g}(\boldsymbol{\theta}_S) = (105.88, 103.16, 98.38, 92.68, 86.61)'.$$

The 1% annual total VaR is $\boldsymbol{\theta}_R'\mathbf{g}(\boldsymbol{\theta}_R) + \boldsymbol{\theta}_S'\mathbf{g}(\boldsymbol{\theta}_S)$ and this has already been calculated as $689,443. The two 1% annual marginal VaRs are

$$1\% \text{ annual marginal LIBOR VaR} = \boldsymbol{\theta}_R'\mathbf{g}(\boldsymbol{\theta}_R) = \$391{,}211$$

$$\Rightarrow 1\% \text{ 10-day marginal LIBOR VaR} = \$391{,}211 \times 0.2 = \$78{,}242$$

and

$$1\% \text{ annual marginal credit VaR} = \boldsymbol{\theta}_S'\mathbf{g}(\boldsymbol{\theta}_S) = \$298{,}233$$

$$\Rightarrow 1\% \text{ 10-day marginal credit VaR} = \$298{,}233 \times 0.2 = \$59{,}647.$$

The sum of the marginal VaRs is identical to the total VaR.

IV.2.4   CASE STUDY: PC VALUE AT RISK OF A UK FIXED INCOME PORTFOLIO

The above example employed a cash-flow mapping to just five vertices, and included just one credit rating. But in practice there could be 50 or 60 vertices, and several credit ratings. With n vertices and k credit ratings there will be kn risk factors, so the risk factor correlation matrix could have a very large dimension indeed. However, the risk factors are very highly correlated and for this reason lend themselves to *dimension reduction* through the use of principal component analysis (PCA).[21] This section demonstrates how to apply PCA to reduce the dimension of the risk factor space when estimating the VaR of interest rate sensitive portfolios so that the new risk factors (i.e. the principal components) are uncorrelated variables that capture the most commonly experienced moves in interest rates.

We consider a portfolio of UK bonds (and/or swaps) on 31 December 2007. We ignore the credit spread risk and suppose that its cash flows have been mapped to the spot market rates at intervals of one month using the volatility, present value and duration invariant cash-flow map described in Section III.5.3. Then the PV01 of the mapped cash flow is computed as explained in Section III.1.8 and the resulting PV01 vector is depicted in Figure IV.2.2.

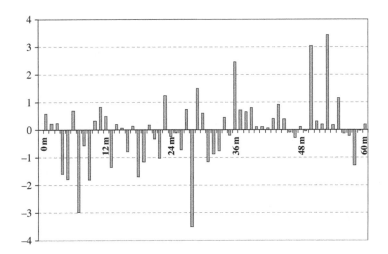

Figure IV.2.2   PV01 vector of a UK fixed income portfolio (£000)

Given the size of the PV01 sensitivities shown in Figure IV.2.2, with several exceeding $\pm£1000$, there must be cash flows of $\pm£5$ million or more at several maturities.[22] Hence, the portfolio could contain long positions on bonds with face value of around £1 billion, and short positions on bonds with face value of around £1 billion or more. The present value of the portfolio may be much less than £1 billion of course, because it has a rough balance of positive and negative cash flows.

---

[21] PCA is introduced in Section I.2.6 and fully discussed with numerous empirical examples in Chapter II.2.

[22] For a quick 'rule of thumb', a cash flow of N million at T years has a PV01 of a bit less than $N \times T \times 100$. So, for instance, the PV01 of £3000 at 4 years corresponds to a cash flow of approximately $0.3 \times 4 = £1.2$ million. But this is a very crude approximation. See Section IV.2.3.2 for a more precise approximation to the PV01.

IV.2.4.1   Calculating the Volatility and VaR of the Portfolio

This section contains two examples, the first showing how to use the cash-flow map and the second showing how to compute the volatility and VaR of the portfolio.

EXAMPLE IV.2.7: APPLYING A CASH-FLOW MAP TO INTEREST RATE SCENARIOS

Consider the portfolio of UK bonds and swaps with PV01 vector $\boldsymbol{\theta}$ shown in Figure IV.2.2. Find an approximation to the change in the portfolio's value given that UK interest rates change as follows:

(a) The UK yield curve moves upward with a parallel shift of 10 basis points at all maturities.
(b) There is a tilt in the UK yield curve where the 1-month rate increases by 35 basis points, the 2-month rate by 34 basis points, the 3-month rate by 33 basis points and so on up to the 59-month rate decreasing by 23 basis points and the 60-month rate decreasing by 24 basis points.

SOLUTION   In the spreadsheet for this example we apply the relationship (IV.1.25), i.e.

$$\Delta PV \approx -\boldsymbol{\theta}' \Delta \mathbf{r}, \qquad (IV.2.37)$$

with the basis point changes in interest rates specified in (a) and (b) above. Hence:

(a) $\Delta \mathbf{r} = (10, \ 10, \ \ldots, \ 10)'$ gives $\Delta PV = £9518$; and
(b) $\Delta \mathbf{r} = (35, \ 34, \ \ldots, \ -23, \ -24)'$ gives $\Delta PV = £396{,}478$.

Since the portfolio has a balance of long and short exposures, its present value does not change much when the yield curve shifts parallel, as is evident in case (a) above. But the portfolio is much more exposed to a change in slope of the yield curve; Figure IV.2.2 shows that the portfolio is predominately short in bonds with maturities up to 3 years but its positions on bonds with maturities between 3 and 5 years are predominately long. Hence, the portfolio will increase in value if the yield curve shifts up at the short end and down at the long end. Indeed, under the scenario for interest rates in (b) above, the portfolio would make a profit of £396,478.

In the next three examples, all of which are contained in the case study workbook, we use an equally weighted covariance matrix $\boldsymbol{\Omega}_1$ of the absolute daily changes in UK interest rates based on data from 2 January 2007 until 31 December 2007.[23] The covariance matrix has dimension 60×60, so we do not show it here, although it can be seen in the Excel spreadsheet accompanying the following example.

EXAMPLE IV.2.8: VAR OF UK FIXED INCOME PORTFOLIO

Use the 1-day covariance matrix $\boldsymbol{\Omega}_1$ given in the spreadsheet to find the volatility of the discounted P&L of the portfolio with PV01 vector $\boldsymbol{\theta}$ shown in Figure IV.2.2. Assuming that each interest rate change is i.i.d. normally distributed, calculate the 1% 10-day VaR on 31 December 2007.

---

[23] The data can be downloaded from the Bank of England website, http://www.bankofengland.co.uk/statistics/yieldcurve/index.htm.

SOLUTION   We first obtain the 1-day variance of the portfolio P&L as

$$\text{Daily P\&L variance} = \boldsymbol{\theta}'\boldsymbol{\Omega}_1\boldsymbol{\theta} = 575.945.$$

But $\boldsymbol{\theta}$ was given in units of £1000. Hence to convert this figure to the P&L volatility we must take the square root, multiply this by the square root of 250 (assuming there are 250 risk days per year) and then also multiply by £1000. The result is

$$\text{P\&L volatility} = £379,455.$$

Hence,

$$1\% \text{ 10-day VaR} = 2.32634 \times 379,455 \times 0.2 = £176,549.$$

IV.2.4.2   Combining Cash-Flow Mapping with PCA

Principal component analysis is a powerful tool for representing any highly correlated system. In Chapter II.2 we explained how to apply PCA to a set of interest rates, and in Section II.2.3 we used the UK bonds that we are considering in this case study as an example. In this section we shall combine a principal component representation with the PV01 vector shown in Figure IV.2.2. In this way we obtain a set of sensitivities to a new set of interest rate risk factors: the first three principal components of the UK yield curve.

The general expression for a principal component representation of the changes in interest rates $\Delta\mathbf{r}_t$ at time t is

$$\Delta\mathbf{r}_t \approx \mathbf{W}^*\mathbf{p}_t^*, \tag{IV.2.38}$$

where the *factor weights* matrix $\mathbf{W}^*$ is the $n \times k$ matrix whose columns are the first k eigenvectors of the covariance matrix of absolute changes in returns; n is the number of risk factors, i.e. the dimension of the covariance matrix; and $\mathbf{p}_t^*$ is the $k \times 1$ column vector of the first k principal components at time t.

We use (IV.2.38) to derive the representation of our UK bond portfolio P&L in terms of sensitivities $\boldsymbol{\beta}$ to just k orthogonal risk factors (i.e. the principal components) instead of sensitivities to n highly correlated risk factors. Combining (IV.2.37) with (IV.2.38) gives

$$\Delta\text{PV}_t \approx \boldsymbol{\beta}'\mathbf{p}_t^*, \quad \text{where} \quad \boldsymbol{\beta} = -\mathbf{W}^{*\prime}\boldsymbol{\theta}. \tag{IV.2.39}$$

Hence, the new factor sensitivity vector is the $k \times 1$ vector of constants obtained by taking (minus) the product of the transpose of the component factor weights matrix, $\mathbf{W}^{*\prime}$, which has dimension $k \times n$, and the $n \times 1$ PV01 vector $\boldsymbol{\theta}$. This way the number of risk factors has been reduced from n to k.

Now the interest rate VaR based on the principal component risk factors is

$$\text{PC VaR}_{h,\alpha} = \Phi^{-1}(1-\alpha)\sqrt{\boldsymbol{\beta}'\mathbf{D}\boldsymbol{\beta}} \tag{IV.2.40}$$

or, equivalently,

$$\text{PC VaR}_{h,\alpha} = \Phi^{-1}(1-\alpha)\sqrt{\boldsymbol{\theta}'\mathbf{W}^*\mathbf{D}\mathbf{W}^{*\prime}\boldsymbol{\theta}}, \tag{IV.2.41}$$

where $\mathbf{D} = \mathrm{diag}(\lambda_1, \ldots, \lambda_k)$ is the diagonal matrix of the first k eigenvalues of the h-day risk factor covariance matrix $\mathbf{\Omega}_h$. Note that if $n = k$ (i.e. we only make the risk factors uncorrelated and do not reduce the number of risk factors) then $\mathbf{W}^* = \mathbf{W}$, i.e. the matrix of all n eigenvectors, and $\mathbf{WDW}' = \mathbf{\Omega}_h$. So unless we use PCA to reduce dimensions, the PC VaR estimate is identical to the ordinary interest rate VaR estimate.

The approximation (IV.2.39) of portfolio P&L is now based on new risk factors, i.e. the first k principal components. These are uncorrelated, whereas interest rate risk factors themselves are highly correlated. Moreover, the new sensitivity vector β is just a $k \times 1$ vector, whereas the old PV01 sensitivity vector was an $n \times 1$ vector, where n is much larger than k. In practice it is typical for n to be around 50 or 60 and for k to be only 3 or 4. So there is a huge reduction in dimension from basing VaR measurement on (IV.2.39) rather than using the ordinary risk factor VaR. Yet, the loss of accuracy from using PC VaR as an approximation to the interest rate VaR is negligible, particularly when it is set in the context of all the other sources of model risk in the normal linear VaR model.

The next example shows how to derive the quantities in (IV.2.40) and applies this formula to measure the PC VaR of our UK bond portfolio.

EXAMPLE IV.2.9: USING PRINCIPAL COMPONENTS AS RISK FACTORS

Suppose that the cash-flow representation of the bond portfolio whose PV01 vector is shown in Figure IV.2.2 was taken on 31 December 2007. Also suppose that we base our daily interest rate covariance matrix $\mathbf{\Omega}_1$ on daily changes in the UK spot curve for maturities measured at monthly intervals up to 5 years, using the data period from 2 January to 31 December 2007.[24] Find a principal component representation based on $\mathbf{\Omega}_1$ with three principal components, and specify the diagonal matrix $\mathbf{D}$ that has their standard deviations along its diagonal. Then use this principal component representation to calculate the UK bond portfolio's sensitivities to the three principal component risk factors.

SOLUTION   A PCA on the 60×60 covariance matrix is given in the Excel workbook for this case study. The first three eigenvalues are shown in Table IV.2.9, and we see that together the first three components explain over 99% of the total variation in UK interest rates over the past year. The first component alone accounts for 93.41% of the variation, so the rates were extremely highly correlated along the yield curve during 2007.

Table IV.2.9   Eigenvalues of covariance matrix of UK spot rates – short end

	1	2	3
Eigenvalues	856.82	45.30	9.15
Percentage variation explained	93.41%	4.94%	1.00%
Cumulative variation explained	93.41%	98.35%	99.35%

The first three eigenvectors belonging to these eigenvalues are plotted, as a function of the maturity of the interest rate, in Figure IV.2.3. These have the usual 'trend–tilt–curvature'

---

[24] The Bank of England provides historical data on yield curves and many other financial variables such as exchange rates and option implied volatilities on http://www.bankofengland.co.uk/statistics/yieldcurve/index.htm. We have assumed the portfolio contains gilts and have therefore used the government liability curve in this case study, but the commercial liability curve is also available for download.

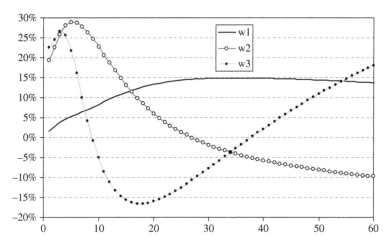

Figure IV.2.3 Eigenvectors of covariance matrix of UK spot rates – short end

interpretation that we are accustomed to when PCA is applied to a highly correlated yield curve, such as the Bank of England liability curves. However, as is usual for money market rates which are frequently affected by manipulation from the central bank, the very short term rates are less volatile than others, giving the eigenvectors a characteristic 'dip' at the short end. For instance, if the first principal component increases but the other components are unchanged, then the 1-month rate will hardly change, but the interest rates at maturities greater than 2 years will all change by a similar amount, i.e. by approximately 15% of the change in the first principal component.

The diagonal matrix of standard deviations of the principal components has elements equal to the square root of the eigenvalues in Table IV.2.9, i.e.

$$\mathbf{D} = \mathrm{diag}\left(\sqrt{856.82}, \sqrt{45.30}, \sqrt{9.15}\right). \tag{IV.2.42}$$

Since by definition the first principal component has much the largest standard deviation, this would be the main determinant of the VaR if the sensitivity to each PC were the same. We estimate the PC sensitivity vector β using (IV.2.39), i.e. multiplying the matrix $\mathbf{W}^*$ whose columns contain the first three eigenvectors by the 60×1 vector of PV01 sensitivities shown in Figure IV.2.2. In this way we obtain the new 3×1 sensitivity vector β for the principal component factors shown in Table IV.2.10. In fact, the sensitivity to the first PC is the smallest of the three.

Table IV.2.10 Net sensitivities on PC risk factors

Component	P1	P2	P3
Beta	£428	−£2975	£1041

Figure IV.2.4 shows the first principal component, which is obtained from the first eigenvector. Since it is based on a covariance matrix that is expressed in basis point terms, the

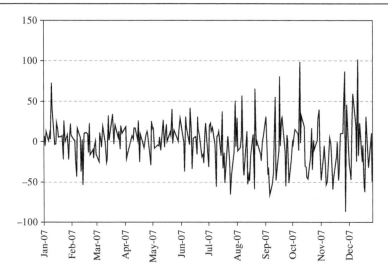

Figure IV.2.4   First principal component of the UK spot rates – short end

principal component is also measured in basis points. The coefficient of £428 on P1 means that a 100 basis point increase in the first principal component leads, approximately, to a £42,800 increase in the present value of the portfolio. From the first eigenvector in Figure IV.2.3 we see that a 100 basis point increase in the first component would be approximately equivalent to a yield curve movement that is up 15 basis points at maturities over 2 years, but up much less at shorter maturities. Our portfolio has some very large positive cash flows at maturities over 2 years so an upward shift of 15 basis points at the longer maturities, with less movement at the short end, will induce a much larger gain in the portfolio than a parallel shift of 15 basis points. The eigenvalues given in Table IV.2.1 tell us that the first principal component captured a very common type of movement in the yield curve. In fact, it accounts for 93.41% of the variation experienced in the UK government yield curve during 2007. By contrast, the exact parallel shift scenario that we used in Example IV.2.7 is not nearly as common.

EXAMPLE IV.2.10: COMPUTING THE PC VAR

Estimate the VaR of the portfolio based on the mapping to the first three principal components, i.e. based on (IV.2.40), and compare this with the full evaluation interest rate VaR from Example IV.2.8.

SOLUTION   The spreadsheet for this example first gives the result of estimating the P&L volatility using the β vector shown in Table IV.2.3 and the diagonal covariance matrix of the principal components given by (IV.2.42). This gives

$$\sqrt{\beta' \mathbf{D} \beta} = £377,109.$$

Then we compute the 1% 10-day VaR from this volatility, by multiplying it by the critical value $\Phi^{-1}(0.99) = 2.32635$ and by the scaling factor $\sqrt{10/250} = 0.2$, giving the 1% 10-day PC VaR as £175,457, compared with £176,549 under full evaluation. The PC approximation leads to only a very small error in VaR (of about 0.6%). The error is a result of taking only three principal components, but this ignores only a small fraction of the variation in the risk factors.

IV.2.4.3   Advantages of Using PC Factors for Interest Rate VaR

In addition to the advantage of dimension reduction, the principal component risk factors make it much easier to apply meaningful scenarios to interest rates. By changing just the first principal component, for instance, we obtain the change in our portfolio's value corresponding to the *most likely* shift in the yield curve, given the historical data used in the PCA. This is not usually a parallel shift in all yields, but it is approximately parallel at longer maturities, so for a portfolio with a high duration this scenario gives a portfolio·sensitivity that is similar to that obtained via the standard duration approximation. But, since interest rates do not normally shift exactly parallel all the time, using a change in the first principal component is more representative of historical movements in yields than a parallel shift.

Moreover, the representation (IV.2.39) provides a more detailed analysis of our portfolio's responses than duration–convexity analysis. In addition to a roughly parallel shift, by changing the second principal component we can find the change in portfolio value corresponding to a specific tilt in the yield curve, i.e. the tilt that is most likely to occur, based on the historical yield curve movements. On changing the third principal component we obtain our portfolio's response to a specific (most likely) change in the yield curve convexity, and so on if more than three principal components are used in (IV.2.39).

Covariance matrix scenarios, which form the basis of many stress tests, are also very easy to implement using PCA. For instance, suppose the original cash-flow mapping of the portfolio is to 50 different maturities of interest rates. Then their covariance matrix is very large, i.e. 50×50. Performing stress tests on this matrix will not be a simple task. However, when using the principal component representation (IV.2.39) of the portfolio's P&L, stress tests need only be performed on a $k \times k$ covariance matrix, where typically $k = 3$. PC-based stress tests also take on a meaningful interpretation, i.e. stressing the most common changes in trend, tilt and curvature of interest rates.

Finally, by choosing only the first few components in the representation we have cut down the 'noise' in the data that we would prefer not to contaminate our risk measures. In highly correlated yield movements there is very little 'noise' and for this reason a three-component representation captures over 99% of the variations in our example. But in less highly correlated yields, much of the idiosyncratic variation in yields may not be useful for risk analysis, especially over the longer term. We saw a small reduction in the PC VaR estimate, compared with the usual VaR estimate, and this is to be expected if some of the variation is ignored. But with the yield curves in major currencies this reduction will be very small indeed. However, other systems such as implied volatilities or equities have much more noise and in this case the use of principal components could reduce VaR more significantly.

IV.2.5   NORMAL LINEAR VALUE AT RISK FOR STOCK PORTFOLIOS

Starting with the simplest case of just a few cash stock positions, we shall consider many linear equity portfolios in this section, including cash and futures positions with and without foreign exchange risk. The systematic parametric linear VaR estimates of an equity portfolio are based on forecasts of expected returns and standard deviations of returns, taken in the context of an equity factor model. Hence, this section draws on the material presented in Chapter II.1, where we covered the different types of factor models that are used for mapping equity portfolios.

IV.2.5.1   Cash Positions on a Few Stocks

In Section I.2.4 we showed how to compute the volatility of portfolio P&L, when the portfolio is characterized by its holdings in each of n stocks and we are given the covariance matrix of the stocks returns. Denote the $n \times 1$ vector of portfolio weights on each stock by $\mathbf{w}$, where each element of $\mathbf{w}$ is the holding in that stock divided by the total amount invested, i.e. the current price of the portfolio P. Denote the $n \times n$ stock returns annual covariance matrix by $\mathbf{V}$.[25] Then the portfolio return volatility is $\sigma = \sqrt{\mathbf{w}'\mathbf{V}\mathbf{w}}$ and the P&L volatility is $P\sigma$.

In Section IV.2.2 we showed how to convert a portfolio volatility into a $100\alpha\%$ h-day normal linear VaR estimate, for an arbitrary portfolio, under the assumption that the risk factor returns are multivariate normal and i.i.d. with zero expected excess returns. We ignore the effect on VaR of an expected return that is different from the discount rate, since this is very small unless h is very large. Then, with h measured in days and assuming there are 250 trading days per year, we have

$$\mathrm{VaR}_{h,\alpha} = \Phi^{-1}(1-\alpha)\,\sigma\sqrt{h/250}\,P. \tag{IV.2.43}$$

More generally, and particularly when estimating the VaR for long term investments in equity funds, we may wish to include the possibility that the portfolio grows at a rate different from the discount rate over a long risk horizon. In this case we would include the drift adjustment to the VaR, as explained in Sections IV.1.5.1 and IV.2.2.

In the general case, to apply the normal linear VaR formula (IV.2.43) we need to forecast, over a risk horizon of h days, the standard deviation and mean of the portfolio returns. Let

- $\mathbf{w}$ denote the current vector of portfolio weights,
- $E(\mathbf{x}_h)$ be the $n \times 1$ vector of the stocks' expected excess h-day returns, and
- $\mathbf{V}_h$ be the h-day covariance matrix of stock returns.

Then the $100\alpha\%$ h-day normal linear VaR of the portfolio, under the assumption that the risk factor returns are multivariate normal and i.i.d. and expressed as a percentage of the portfolio value P is

$$\mathrm{VaR}_{h,\alpha} = \Phi^{-1}(1-\alpha)\sqrt{\mathbf{w}'\mathbf{V}_h\mathbf{w}} - \mathbf{w}'E(\mathbf{x}_h). \tag{IV.2.44}$$

The application of this formula is illustrated in the following example.

EXAMPLE IV.2.11: VaR FOR CASH EQUITY POSITIONS

Calculate the 1% 10-day parametric linear VaR for a portfolio that has the characteristics defined in Table IV.2.11, discounting using a risk free rate of 5%. How much is the VaR reduced by the mean adjustment? Repeat your calculations for a risk horizon of 1 year.

---

[25] Recall that we use the notation $\mathbf{V}$ for an *asset* covariance matrix and $\boldsymbol{\Omega}$ for a *risk factor* covariance matrix.

Table IV.2.11 Stock portfolio characteristics

	Position	Volatility	Expected return	Correlation	
Stock 1	€4m	20%	10%	Stock 1–Stock 2	0.8
Stock 2	−€5m	10%	2%	Stock 1–Stock 3	0.5
Stock 3	€1m	15%	5%	Stock 3–Stock 2	0.3

SOLUTION   The calculations are performed in the accompanying spreadsheet, using the 10-day expected returns and the covariance matrix of 10-day returns displayed in Table IV.2.12. This gives an expected P&L of €14,000, a P&L standard deviation of €117,898 and a 1% 10-day VaR of €259,765. But without the mean adjustment, i.e. without the second term on the right-hand side of (IV.2.44), the 1% 10-day VaR is €273,738. Hence, the mean adjustment reduces the VaR by about 5%. Over a 1-year risk horizon the 1% VaR is €1,384,864 without the mean adjustment and €1,051,530 with the mean adjustment. Hence, over 1 year the drift adjustment is very important, as it leads to a 24% reduction in VaR.

Table IV.2.12 Characteristics of 10-day returns

	10-day return	10-day covariance matrix		
Stock 1	0.004	0.0016	0.00064	0.0006
Stock 2	0.0008	0.00064	0.0004	0.00018
Stock 3	0.002	0.0006	0.00018	0.0009

Another way of looking at the results in the above example is to use Table IV.2.1, which tells us that the 1% 10-day VaR is very approximately about 10% of the portfolio value, depending of course on the portfolio volatility. So very approximately the VaR is about €100,000 per €1 million invested. In the above example the discount factor over 10 days corresponding to a 5% discount rate is 0.99805, and its effect is therefore about €(1 − 0.99805) million, i.e. approximately €195 per €1 million invested. This is negligible compared with the VaR. However, over a 1-year horizon the VaR is about 50% of the portfolio value, again depending on the portfolio volatility. And the discount factor over 1 year corresponding to a 5% discount rate is 0.95238. So its effect is about (1 − 0.95238) million euros, i.e. approximately €47,620 per €1 million invested, which is not insignificant compared with the VaR.

For simplicity, we shall often ignore discounting when VaR is measured over a short horizon such as 10 days, just as we shall often ignore the mean return. It is only when VaR is measured over a risk horizon of several weeks or months that the errors induced by ignoring the effects of discounting and of a non-zero discounted mean return really affect the accuracy of the VaR estimate. However, and we have stressed this before, such long term VaR estimates are only meaningful to investors who hold positions constant over a long term risk horizon without liquidating or hedging when market conditions are adverse.

IV.2.5.2 Systematic and Specific VaR for Domestic Stock Portfolios

In Section IV.1.7.1 we introduced, in general terms, the disaggregation of total VaR into systematic and specific components. Now we use the normal linear VaR model to provide some numerical examples that illustrate this decomposition for stock portfolios.

Portfolios that contain a large number of equities in the same currency are mapped to their risk factors via a factor model. The set of risk factors may include broad stock market indices, style indices such as value and growth indices of different capitalizations, or statistical factors such as those obtained using PCA. When portfolio returns are represented by a factor model, the systematic parametric linear VaR can be calculated using (IV.2.14) where:

- θ is the vector of stock betas with respect to each risk factor;[26]
- $E(\mathbf{x}_h)$ is the vector of the risk factors' expected h-day returns; and
- Ω_h is the h-day covariance matrix of the risk factor returns.

For risk assessment (rather than returns forecasting, which is another use of the factor model) the portfolio betas should be as *risk sensitive* as possible. Hence an exponentially weighted moving average (EWMA) on recent daily data maybe preferred to ordinary least squares (OLS) on weekly or monthly data over a long period. Note that if the betas are estimated using EWMAs, a time series of beta estimates is obtained over the sample period but it is only the last (today's) forecast that we use in the calculation.

EXAMPLE IV.2.12: SYSTEMATIC VAR BASED ON AN EQUITY FACTOR MODEL

A linear model with two risk factors indicates that a stock portfolio has net betas of 0.8 and 1.2 with respect to these factors. The factors have volatility 15% and 20% respectively, and a correlation of -0.5. If the portfolio is expected to return the risk free rate over the next month, calculate the 5% 1-month systematic VaR on an investment of \$20 million in the portfolio.

SOLUTION   The risk factors' monthly covariance matrix is

$$\Omega = \begin{pmatrix} 0.00188 & -0.0013 \\ -0.0013 & 0.00333 \end{pmatrix},$$

so the portfolio variance due to the risk factors is

$$\beta'\Omega\beta = \begin{pmatrix} 0.8 & 1.2 \end{pmatrix} \begin{pmatrix} 0.00188 & -0.0013 \\ -0.0013 & 0.00333 \end{pmatrix} \begin{pmatrix} 0.8 \\ 1.2 \end{pmatrix} = 0.0036.$$

Hence the monthly standard deviation is $\sqrt{0.0036} = 0.06$ and the systematic VaR is therefore

$$1.64485 \times 0.06 \times \$20m = \$1,973,824.$$

In Section II.1.2.5 we decomposed the total volatility of a stock portfolio into two portions, that due to the risk factors (the systematic risk) and that due to the idiosyncratic volatility (the specific or residual risk). Since the parametric linear VaR is a linear transformation of the portfolio volatility, this decomposition carries over into a decomposition of total VaR into systematic and specific VaR components.

---

[26] If we use net value betas here, i.e. the net percentage betas multiplied by the nominal value of the portfolio, then VaR is estimated in value terms; otherwise we estimate VaR as a percentage of the portfolio value.

The relationship between the total VaR, systematic VaR and specific VaR is easily explained using a simple factor model with only one risk factor, i.e. the market factor, as in Section II.1.2.5. Write the model as

$$Y_t = \alpha + \beta X_t + \varepsilon_t,$$

where Y_t is the return on the portfolio, X_t is the return on the market and ε_t is the specific return, all at time t. Taking variances gives

$$V(Y_t) = \beta^2 V(X_t) + V(\varepsilon_t) + 2\beta \text{Cov}(X_t, \varepsilon_t), \tag{IV.2.45}$$

or, in parameter notation,

$$\sigma_Y^2 = \beta^2 \sigma_X^2 + \sigma_\varepsilon^2 + 2\varrho\beta\sigma_X\sigma_\varepsilon,$$

where ϱ is the correlation between the market and the specific returns. This may be written in the alternative form

$$\sigma_Y^2 = (\beta\sigma_X + \sigma_\varepsilon)^2 - 2(1 - \varrho)\beta\sigma_X\sigma_\varepsilon. \tag{IV.2.46}$$

The market volatility, i.e. the volatility due to the market risk factor, is $\beta\sigma_X$, so (IV.2.46) may be expressed in words as

$$[\text{total volatility}]^2 = [\text{market volatility} + \text{specific volatility}]^2$$

$$- 2(1 - \varrho)[\text{market volatility}] \times [\text{specific volatility}].$$

But in the parametric linear VaR model, the VaR behaves just like volatility, assuming we ignore any adjustment for a non-zero discounted mean return. Hence, an expression similar to (IV.2.46) also holds with VaR in place of volatility:

$$[\text{total VaR}]^2 = [\text{systematic VaR} + \text{specific VaR}]^2$$

$$- 2(1 - \varrho)[\text{systematic VaR}] \times [\text{specific VaR}]. \tag{IV.2.47}$$

Hence, the total VaR is equal to the sum of the systematic VaR and the specific VaR if and only if ϱ, the correlation between the return explained by the risk factors and the specific return, is equal to 1. But, on the contrary, it is usually assumed that the factor model explains the portfolio return so well that $\varrho = 0$. Also, if the factor model is estimated by OLS, then $\varrho = 0$ by construction. Under this assumption the total VaR is the square root of the sum of the squared systematic VaR and the squared specific VaR.

In the more general case, when ϱ is not 0 but less than 1, the total VaR will be *less* than the sum of the systematic VaR and the specific VaR. This property, which is an example of the sub-additivity property of parametric linear VaR models, is a necessary property for the risk metric to be coherent. It implies that the risk of investing in a portfolio is no greater than the risk resulting from an equivalent sized investment in any single asset of that portfolio. It is related to the *portfolio diversification* effect that was introduced and discussed in Section I.6.3.1. There we showed that the volatility of a portfolio is never greater than the volatility of any of its constituent assets, and that the volatility of a fully funded long-only portfolio decreases with the asset returns correlations. Hence, to reduce risk (as measured by volatility), investors have the incentive to hold a diversified portfolio, i.e. a portfolio with investments distributed over many assets that have as low a correlation as possible.[27] The sub-additivity property of parametric linear VaR amounts to exactly the same thing as portfolio diversification, but now the portfolio risk is measured by its systematic and specific VaR and not its volatility.[28]

IV.2.5.3 Empirical Estimation of Specific VaR

The normal linear specific risk of an equity portfolio can be calculated in three different ways:

1. Save a time series of residuals from the factor model, and calculate the normal linear specific VaR directly from the residual variance.
2. First calculate the normal linear total VaR using the variance of the portfolio return.[29] Then calculate the systematic VaR using $\Phi^{-1}(1 - \alpha)\sqrt{\beta'\Omega\beta}$ and the specific VaR using (IV.2.47), under the assumption that $\varrho = 0$.
3. Use a *standardized rule*, such as setting specific risk = 8% of portfolio value (see Section IV.8.2.5).

An advanced risk assessment system should have a database of historical prices on all stocks and risk factors that enables the more precise estimation of specific VaR using method 1. Based on these data, the factor betas and the risk factor covariance matrix, and hence also the systematic VaR and (from the factor model residuals) the specific VaR, may all be estimated in-house. Holding the current portfolio weights constant, historical data on stock returns may be used to construct a current weighted returns series for the portfolio.[30] Then the total VaR may be estimated directly from the current weighted returns.[31] An empirical illustration, for a portfolio of stocks in the S&P 100 index, is provided in the next subsection.

However, method 2 is often used, even though it is based on the assumption that the specific returns and the systematic returns are uncorrelated, which may not be warranted. This would only be the case if the factor model were doing an excellent job of explaining the stock's returns, and the portfolio is well diversified, but often this is not the case.

EXAMPLE IV.2.13: DISAGGREGATION OF VaR INTO SYSTEMATIC VaR AND SPECIFIC VaR

Suppose the volatility of the portfolio returns in Example IV.2.12 is 25%. Find the 5% 10-day total VaR and the 5% 10-day specific VaR using the normal linear model, based on method 2 above.

SOLUTION   Since the portfolio volatility is 25%,

$$\text{Total VaR} = 1.64485 \times 0.25 \times (1/\sqrt{12}) \times \$20\text{m} = \$2,374,142.$$

The systematic VaR was found, in Example IV.2.12, to be \$1,973,824. Hence, assuming a zero correlation between the residual and the market returns, the specific VaR may be calculated

---

[27] Alternatively, the diversification could be achieved with long-short positions on highly correlated assets.
[28] However, it is important to note that only the parametric linear VaR model always has the sub-additivity property. When VaR is estimated using historical or Monte Carlo simulation, VaR need not be sub-additive. See Section IV.1.8.3 for further discussion and Example IV.1.11 for a numerical illustration.
[29] Also use the mean excess returns, if they are significantly different from zero and the risk horizon is longer than a few months.
[30] If the portfolio is long-short we keep the holding in each stock constant, rather than the portfolio weight, and use absolute rather than relative returns.
[31] This can be a time consuming and difficult exercise, e.g. when holding new issues.

as the square root of the difference between the square of the total VaR and the square of the systematic VaR, i.e.:

$$\text{Specific VaR} = \sqrt{2,374,142^2 - 1,973,824^2} = \$1,319,305.$$

Which of the three methods is used to estimate specific risk depends very much on the data available. If the risk factor betas are obtained directly from a data provider then method 1 cannot be used. If the risk factor returns covariance matrix $\mathbf{\Omega}$ is also obtained from a data provider, or provided in-house, then we can calculate the systematic VaR but not the total VaR, and in that case a standardized rule (see Section IV.8.2.5) must be applied to estimate the specific risk.

IV.2.5.4 EWMA Estimates of Specific VaR

When ordinary least squares is used to estimate both the factor model betas and the covariance matrix, on an identical sample, methods 1 and 2 above for estimating specific VaR will produce identical results.[32] However, OLS is not necessarily the best method to use. Indeed, OLS estimates merely represent an *average* value over the time period covered by the sample and will not reflect current market conditions. Risk managers often prefer to use more risk sensitive estimates of factor model betas and the covariance matrix, such as those obtained using the exponentially weighted moving average methodology. This approach for estimating risk sensitive betas was introduced and illustrated in Section II.1.2.3, and full details of the EWMA methodology were given in Section II.3.8.

We now show that when EWMA is applied to estimate portfolio betas we should use method 1 rather than method 2 (described in the previous subsection) to obtain the specific VaR. Using EWMA estimates instead of OLS, these two methods no longer yield identical results; in fact, method 2 could produce negative values for the specific VaR because the assumption that $\varrho = 0$ is not valid.

For simplicity we suppose the portfolio with returns Y has only one risk factor, with returns X. Then the EWMA beta is estimated by dividing the EWMA covariance by the EWMA variance with the same smoothing constant, i.e.

$$\hat{\beta}_{t,\lambda} = \frac{\text{Cov}_\lambda(X_t, Y_t)}{V_\lambda(X_t)}.$$

Having estimated beta, we obtain the residual returns series

$$\varepsilon_t = Y_t - \hat{\beta}_{t,\lambda} X_t.$$

Then, using method 1, the normal linear specific VaR is estimated from the EWMA standard deviation σ_t^ε of these residuals, using the usual formula, i.e.[33]

$$\text{Specific VaR}_{ht,\alpha} = \Phi^{-1}(1-\alpha)\sqrt{h}\,\sigma_t^\varepsilon. \tag{IV.2.48}$$

---

[32] This follows from the analysis of variance in a regression model (see Section I.4.2.4).
[33] This formula assumes the data are daily and that we ignore the discounted mean residuals, which anyway will be negligible unless h is very large.

This method will always gives a positive specific VaR that is less than the total VaR. To see this, substitute EWMA variances in (IV.2.45) and rearrange, yielding

$$V_\lambda(\varepsilon_t) = V_\lambda(Y_t) + \hat{\beta}_{t,\lambda}^2 V_\lambda(X_t) - 2\hat{\beta}_{t,\lambda} \mathrm{Cov}_\lambda(X_t, Y_t)$$

$$= V_\lambda(Y_t) + \hat{\beta}_{t,\lambda}\left(\hat{\beta}_{t,\lambda} V_\lambda(X_t) - 2\mathrm{Cov}_\lambda(X_t, Y_t)\right)$$

$$= V_\lambda(Y_t) - \hat{\beta}_{t,\lambda}(\mathrm{Cov}_\lambda(X_t, Y_t)).$$

But $\hat{\beta}_{t,\lambda}\mathrm{Cov}_\lambda(X_t, Y_t) > 0$ so the specific VaR is always less than the total VaR, and because it is a variance it is always positive.

Figure IV.2.5 illustrates the application of the EWMA methodology for estimating total, systematic and specific VaR to a portfolio of stocks in the S&P 100 index. The 1% 10-day VaR is here expressed as a percentage of the portfolio value and the smoothing constant used for the figure is $\lambda = 0.95$ (but this, as well as the portfolio weights and the VaR model parameters, may be changed by the reader in the spreadsheet). Although the portfolio is fairly highly correlated with the index most of the time, there are short intervals when the specific VaR is greater than the systematic VaR, but never greater than total VaR.

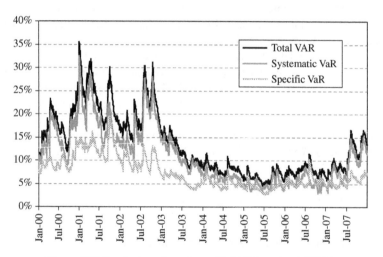

Figure IV.2.5   Systematic and specific VaR based on EWMA

In summary, both OLS and EWMA estimates for the factor model betas and the covariance matrix allow VaR decomposition into systematic and specific VaR, but the EWMA approach yields more risk sensitive estimates. It is inadvisable to mix methodologies, for instance, by using OLS for the covariance matrix and EWMA for the factor model betas, and when EWMA is used take care to follow the procedure outlined above. For consistency, all variances, covariances and betas should be estimated using the same smoothing constant in the EWMA.

IV.2.6 SYSTEMATIC VALUE-AT-RISK DECOMPOSITION FOR STOCK PORTFOLIOS

In Section IV.2.2 we explained how systematic VaR, i.e. total risk factor VaR, can be attributed to different risk factors under the normal linear VaR model. This section illustrates this VaR decomposition by considering several equity portfolios with different types of risk factor exposures, showing how to decompose the systematic VaR into stand-alone and marginal VaR components. Although we remain with the normal linear VaR model for our empirical examples, the decomposition method applies equally well to other types of parametric linear VaR model.

IV.2.6.1 Portfolios Exposed to One Foreign Currency

To purchase securities on foreign exchanges one has first to purchase the local currency. Hence, portfolios with international equities have forex rates as risk factors where the nominal factor sensitivity is equal to the amount invested in the currency. In this section we consider a stock portfolio with exposure to just one foreign currency, to illustrate the VaR decomposition into equity and forex components, assuming for simplicity that both domestic and foreign interest rates are zero. As usual, the discounted expected return on the portfolio is also assumed to be negligible over the risk horizon, so all we need to consider for the systematic VaR calculations is the covariance matrix of the risk factors.

We first prove that in the parametric linear VaR model the systematic VaR is sub-additive. That is, the total systematic VaR is never greater than the sum of the stand-alone component VaRs. To prove this we begin by noting that log returns are additive, so the log return in domestic currency on an exposure to a foreign equity market may be written as

$$R_h + X_h,$$

where R_h is the h-day log return on the portfolio in foreign currency and X_h is the h-day log return on the domestic/foreign exchange rate.

Now consider the factor model representation of the equity log return in foreign currency, i.e. set

$$R_h = \beta Y_h,$$

where Y_h is the h-day log return on the foreign risk factor (e.g. the foreign market index). Then the standard deviation σ_h of the h-day log return in domestic currency is the standard deviation of $\beta Y_h + X_h$. That is,

$$\sigma_h = \sqrt{\beta^2 \sigma_{Yh}^2 + \sigma_{Xh}^2 + 2\beta\varrho\sigma_{Yh}\sigma_{Xh}} = \sqrt{(\beta \ \ 1)\, \Omega_h \begin{pmatrix} \beta \\ 1 \end{pmatrix}}. \tag{IV.2.49}$$

In the above, ϱ denotes the *quanto correlation* between the foreign market index returns in foreign currency terms and the exchange rate returns, and

$$\Omega_h = \begin{pmatrix} \sigma_{Yh}^2 & \varrho\sigma_{Yh}\sigma_{Xh} \\ \varrho\sigma_{Yh}\sigma_{Xh} & \sigma_{Xh}^2 \end{pmatrix}$$

is the h-day covariance matrix of these returns.

Decomposition into stand-alone components

Knowing σ_h, we can compute

$$\text{Systematic VaR}_{h,\alpha} = \Phi^{-1}(1-\alpha)\sigma_h, \tag{IV.2.50}$$

expressed as a percentage of portfolio value. The equity and forex components of the systematic VaR are

$$\text{Equity VaR}_{h,\alpha} = \beta\Phi^{-1}(1-\alpha)\sigma_{Yh} \tag{IV.2.51}$$

and

$$\text{Forex VaR}_{h,\alpha} = \Phi^{-1}(1-\alpha)\sigma_{Xh}. \tag{IV.2.52}$$

Rewriting (IV.2.49) as

$$\sigma_h^2 = (\beta\sigma_{Yh} + \sigma_{Xh})^2 - 2\beta(1-\varrho)\sigma_{Yh}\sigma_{Xh}$$

and using the expressions for equity and forex VaR above gives an exact decomposition of systematic VaR as

$$[\text{Total systematic VaR}]^2 = [\text{Equity VaR}^2 + \text{Forex VaR}^2]$$
$$- 2(1-\varrho)[\text{Equity VaR}] \times [\text{Forex VaR}].$$

Hence,

$$\text{Total systematic VaR} \leq \text{Equity VaR} + \text{Forex VaR}, \tag{IV.2.53}$$

with equality if and only if $\varrho = 1$.

However, it is extremely unlikely that $\varrho = 1$. Indeed, since quanto correlations can be small and are often very difficult to forecast, the quanto correlation ϱ might be assumed to be zero. In that case the decomposition into stand-alone VaR components becomes

$$\text{Total systematic VaR} = \sqrt{\text{Equity VaR}^2 + \text{Forex VaR}^2}.$$

If the quanto correlation is large and negative it is possible that the systematic VaR is less than both the stand-alone equity VaR and the forex VaR, as illustrated in Example IV.2.14.

Decomposition into marginal components

For the decomposition of total systematic VaR into marginal components we use the approximation described in Section IV.2.2.4. In the case of the parametric linear VaR model the gradient vector is given by

$$\mathbf{g}(\boldsymbol{\theta}) = \frac{\Phi^{-1}(1-\alpha)\boldsymbol{\Omega}_h\boldsymbol{\theta}}{\sqrt{\boldsymbol{\theta}'\boldsymbol{\Omega}_h\boldsymbol{\theta}}}, \tag{IV.2.54}$$

where $\boldsymbol{\theta}$ is the vector of risk factor sensitivities.

Following our discussion in Section IV.2.2.3, the ith marginal component VaR is obtained by multiplying the ith component of the gradient vector by the ith nominal sensitivity. Note that

$$\boldsymbol{\theta}'\mathbf{g}(\boldsymbol{\theta}) = \Phi^{-1}(1-\alpha)\sqrt{\boldsymbol{\theta}'\boldsymbol{\Omega}_h\boldsymbol{\theta}}, \qquad \text{(IV.2.55)}$$

and so the total systematic VaR is the sum of the marginal VaR components. The next numerical example illustrates this construction.

EXAMPLE IV.2.14: EQUITY AND FOREX VaR

A US investor buys \$2 million of shares in a portfolio of UK (FTSE 100) stocks and the portfolio beta is 1.5. Suppose the FTSE 100 and \$/£ volatilities are 15% and 20% respectively, and their correlation is 0.3. What is the 1% 10-day systematic VaR in US dollars? Decompose the systematic VaR into (a) stand-alone and (b) marginal equity and forex components.

SOLUTION   Given the data, the 10-day risk factor covariance matrix has the following elements:

- FTSE 100 variance $0.0225/25 = 0.0009$;
- \$/£ variance $0.04/25 = 0.0016$;
- with a correlation of 0.3, the 10-day covariance is

$$(0.3 \times 0.15 \times 0.2)/25 = 0.00036.$$

The 10-day returns variance is thus

$$(1.5 \quad 1)\begin{pmatrix} 9 & 3.6 \\ 3.6 & 16 \end{pmatrix}\begin{pmatrix} 1.5 \\ 1 \end{pmatrix} \times 10^{-4} = 0.004705,$$

so the 10-day 1% systematic VaR is $2.32635 \times \sqrt{0.004705} = 15.9571\%$ of the portfolio value. Since the portfolio has \$2 million invested in it, its 1% 10-day systematic VaR is 15.9571% of \$2,000,000, i.e. \$319,142.

(a) Consider the stand-alone component VaRs:

$$\text{Equity VaR} = 2.32635 \times (0.15/5) \times 3,000,000 = 2.32635 \times 90,000$$
$$= \$209,371,$$
$$\text{Forex VaR} = 2.32635 \times (0.2/5) \times 2,000,000 = 2.32635 \times 80,000$$
$$= \$186,108.$$

Hence

$$\text{Equity VaR} + \text{Forex VaR} = \$395,479,$$

which is greater than the total systematic VaR.

(b) For the marginal VaRs we first compute the gradient vector. Since

$$\mathbf{\Omega}_{10}\mathbf{\theta} = \begin{pmatrix} 9 & 3.6 \\ 3.6 & 16 \end{pmatrix}\begin{pmatrix} 1.5 \\ 1 \end{pmatrix} \times 10^{-4} = \begin{pmatrix} 17.1 \\ 21.4 \end{pmatrix} \times 10^{-4},$$

the gradient vector is

$$\frac{\Phi^{-1}(0.99)\mathbf{\Omega}_{10}\mathbf{\theta}}{\sqrt{\mathbf{\theta}'\mathbf{\Omega}_{10}\mathbf{\theta}}} = \frac{2.32635}{\sqrt{0.004705}}\begin{pmatrix} 17.1 \\ 21.4 \end{pmatrix} \times 10^{-4} = \begin{pmatrix} 0.05800 \\ 0.07258 \end{pmatrix}.$$

Hence the marginal VaRs are:

$$\text{Equity marginal VaR} = 3{,}000{,}000 \times 0.05800 = \$173{,}985,$$
$$\text{Forex marginal VaR} = 2{,}000{,}000 \times 0.07258 = \$145{,}157.$$

and the sum of these is $319,142, which is equal to the total VaR.

When marginal VaRs are expressed as a percentage of the total VaR they tell the investor how much risk stems from each risk factor in a diversified portfolio. Hence

- $173,985/319,142 = 54.5\%$ of the risk is associated with the equity exposure, and
- $145,157/319,142 = 45.5\%$ of the risk is from the foreign exchange exposure.

When the quanto correlation is large and negative it may be that the total risk factor VaR is less than either the equity VaR or the forex VaR, and in fact it can be less than both of them. To illustrate this point we change the quanto correlation in the above example between -1 and $+1$, and this gives different figures for the total risk factor VaR shown by the grey line in Figure IV.2.6. We see that when the quanto correlation is less than about -0.6, the total

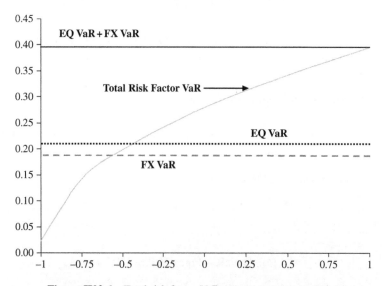

Figure IV.2.6   Total risk factor VaR versus quanto correlation

systematic VaR due to both equity and forex factors becomes less than both the equity VaR and the forex VaR.

The general point to take away from this section is that the total systematic VaR is always equal to the sum of the marginal VaRs, but it is almost always less than the sum of the stand-alone VaRs, because stand-alone VaR measures the risk due to a factor in isolation and does not account for any diversification effects. Indeed, the total systematic VaR could be less than either, or both, of the stand-alone VaRs. It would only be equal to the sum of the stand-alone VaRs if the risk factor correlations were all equal to 1, which is extremely unlikely.

IV.2.6.2 Portfolios Exposed to Several Foreign Currencies

We now consider stock portfolios with investments in several different countries, using a broad market index as the single equity risk factor in each country. Following our general discussion in Sections IV.2.2.3 and IV.2.2.4, it is convenient to partition the risk factors into equity and foreign exchange factors. For the moment we retain the assumptions that both domestic and foreign interest rates are zero (and that the discounted expected return on the portfolio is also zero) so there are no interest rate risk factors.

Denote by $\boldsymbol{\theta}_E$ and $\boldsymbol{\theta}_X$ the vectors of equity and forex rate risk factor sensitivities. The stand-alone VaR decomposition is based on the variance decomposition:

$$\boldsymbol{\theta}'\boldsymbol{\Omega}_h\boldsymbol{\theta} = \boldsymbol{\theta}'_E\boldsymbol{\Omega}_{Eh}\boldsymbol{\theta}_E + \boldsymbol{\theta}'_X\boldsymbol{\Omega}_{Xh}\boldsymbol{\theta}_X + 2\boldsymbol{\theta}'_E\boldsymbol{\Omega}_{EXh}\boldsymbol{\theta}_X, \tag{IV.2.56}$$

where $\boldsymbol{\theta} = (\boldsymbol{\theta}'_E, \boldsymbol{\theta}'_X)'$ and

$$\boldsymbol{\Omega}_h = \begin{pmatrix} \boldsymbol{\Omega}_{Eh} & \boldsymbol{\Omega}_{EXh} \\ \boldsymbol{\Omega}'_{EXh} & \boldsymbol{\Omega}_{Xh} \end{pmatrix} \tag{IV.2.57}$$

is the h-day risk factor covariance matrix, partitioned into equity and forex risk factors. Note that the quanto correlation between equity returns and forex returns is often negative. If it is both large and negative, the total systematic VaR can be less than either the equity VaR or the forex VaR, or both, as we have seen (for the single risk factor case) in Example IV.2.14 above.

EXAMPLE IV.2.15: VAR FOR INTERNATIONAL EQUITY EXPOSURES

Consider a US dollar investment in a large international stock portfolio with the characteristics shown in Table IV.2.13. Suppose that the correlation between all equity risk factors is 0.75, the correlation between the two forex risk factors is 0.5, and the quanto correlations are each 0.2.

Table IV.2.13 Characteristics of an international equity portfolio

Index	Local equity					Forex		
	Nominal	β	Return	Volatility	Net dollar β	Return	Volatility	Nominal
S&P 500	$2m	0.9	X_1	20%	$1.8m		N/A	
FTSE 100	$2m	1.1	X_2	22%	$2.2m	X_5 ($/£)	15%	$2m
CAC 40	$3m	1.2	X_3	25%	$3.6m	X_6 ($/€)	10%	$7m
DAX 30	$4m	1.3	X_4	27%	$5.2m			

Find the 1% 10-day systematic VaR of this portfolio and decompose this into (a) stand-alone and (b) marginal equity and forex components.

SOLUTION   In Table IV.2.13 the net dollar beta is the product of the percentage beta and the nominal dollar exposure to the index. With these dollar betas, and the notation defined in the table, we can write the systematic P&L, Y in US dollars as

$$Y = 1.8\,X_1 + 2.2\,X_2 + 3.6\,X_3 + 5.2\,X_4 + 2\,X_5 + 7\,X_6.$$

Given the data on risk factor volatilities and correlations, we construct the annual risk factor covariance matrix Ω shown in Table IV.2.14, with the partition drawn as in (IV.2.57).

Table IV.2.14   Annual covariance matrix Ω of equity and forex risk factor returns

0.04	0.033	0.0375	0.0405	0.006	0.004
0.033	0.0484	0.04125	0.04455	0.0066	0.0044
0.0375	0.04125	0.0625	0.050625	0.0075	0.005
0.0405	0.04455	0.050625	0.0729	0.0081	0.0054
0.006	0.0066	0.0075	0.0081	0.0225	0.0075
0.004	0.0044	0.005	0.0054	0.0075	0.01

The total P&L annual variance due to all risk factors is given by $\theta'\Omega\theta$, where Ω is as above and $\theta = (1.8,\ 2.2,\ 3.6,\ 5.2,\ 2,\ 7)'$. The value of $\theta'\Omega\theta$ is calculated in the Excel spreadsheet and the result is 10.2679. To find the systematic normal linear VaR of this portfolio, we simply take the square root of the P&L variance and use the square-root-of-time rule. Hence the 1% 10-day systematic VaR due to all risk factors is:

$$2.32635 \times \sqrt{10.2679} \times 0.2 = 2.32635 \times 3.2044 \times 0.2 = \$1.490889 \text{ million}.$$

(a) We use (IV.2.56) to decompose the total P&L variance due to all risk factors into

- the variance due to the equity factors,

$$(1.8\ \ 2.2\ \ 3.6\ \ 5.2)\begin{pmatrix} 0.04 & 0.033 & 0.0375 & 0.0405 \\ 0.033 & 0.0484 & 0.04125 & 0.04455 \\ 0.0375 & 0.04125 & 0.0625 & 0.05063 \\ 0.0405 & 0.04455 & 0.05063 & 0.0729 \end{pmatrix}\begin{pmatrix} 1.8 \\ 2.2 \\ 3.6 \\ 5.2 \end{pmatrix} = 8.2187;$$

- the variance due to the forex factors,

$$(2\ \ 7)\begin{pmatrix} 0.0225 & 0.0075 \\ 0.0075 & 0.01 \end{pmatrix}\begin{pmatrix} 2 \\ 7 \end{pmatrix} = 0.79;$$

- and the covariance due to the 'quanto' factors,

$$(1.8\ \ \ 2.2\ \ \ 3.6\ \ \ 5.2)\begin{pmatrix} 0.006 & 0.004 \\ 0.0066 & 0.0044 \\ 0.0075 & 0.005 \\ 0.0081 & 0.0054 \end{pmatrix}\begin{pmatrix} 2 \\ 7 \end{pmatrix} = 0.6296.$$

Taking the square root of the equity and forex variances, multiplying by the relevant critical value of the standard normal distribution and diving by 5 (to convert the annual VaRs into 10-day VaRs), the decomposition of the 1% 10-day total systematic VaR is summarized in Table IV.2.15.

Table IV.2.15 VaR decomposition for diversified international stock portfolio

Equity VaR	$1,333,847
FX VaR	$413,541
Sum of stand-alone VaRs	$1,747,388
Total systematic VaR	$1,490,889

(b) To estimate the marginal VaRs we first compute the gradient vector, in annual terms. Since

$$\Omega\,\theta = \left(\begin{pmatrix} 0.04 & 0.033 & 0.0375 & 0.0405 \\ 0.033 & 0.0484 & 0.04125 & 0.04455 \\ 0.0375 & 0.04125 & 0.0625 & 0.05063 \\ 0.0405 & 0.04455 & 0.05063 & 0.0729 \end{pmatrix} \begin{pmatrix} 0.006 & 0.004 \\ 0.0066 & 0.0044 \\ 0.0075 & 0.005 \\ 0.0081 & 0.0054 \end{pmatrix} \begin{pmatrix} 1.8 \\ 2.2 \\ 3.6 \\ 5.2 \\ 2 \\ 7 \end{pmatrix} \right) = \begin{pmatrix} 0.5302 \\ 0.5900 \\ 0.6965 \\ 0.7862 \\ 0.1919 \\ 0.1480 \end{pmatrix},$$

$$\begin{pmatrix} 0.006 & 0.0066 & 0.0075 & 0.0081 \\ 0.004 & 0.0044 & 0.005 & 0.0054 \end{pmatrix} \quad \begin{pmatrix} 0.0225 & 0.0075 \\ 0.0075 & 0.01 \end{pmatrix}$$

the annual gradient vector is

$$\frac{\Phi^{-1}(0.99)\Omega\theta}{\sqrt{\theta'\Omega\,\theta}} = \frac{2.32635}{\sqrt{10.2679}} \begin{pmatrix} 0.5302 \\ 0.5900 \\ 0.6965 \\ 0.7862 \\ 0.1919 \\ 0.1480 \end{pmatrix} = \begin{pmatrix} 0.3849 \\ 0.4284 \\ 0.5057 \\ 0.5708 \\ 0.1393 \\ 0.1074 \end{pmatrix}.$$

The marginal VaRs are, therefore,[34]

Equity marginal VaR $= \$(1.8 \times 0.3849 + 2.2 \times 0.4284 + 3.6 \times 0.5057 + 5.2 \times 0.5708) \times 0.2$
$$= \$1,284,765$$

and

Forex marginal VaR $= \$(2 \times 0.1394 + 7 \times 0.1074) \times 0.2 = \$206,125.$

As usual, the sum of these is equal to the total VaR. Hence, approximately

$$\frac{1,284,765}{1,490,889} = 86\%$$

---

[34] The marginal VaRs may be further decomposed into marginal components due to each specific risk factor, as shown in the spreadsheet for this example.

of the risk, on a diversified basis, stems from the equity exposure and only

$$\frac{206,125}{1,490,889} = 14\%$$

of the risk arises from the forex exposure. Notice that the marginal forex VaR is less than half of the stand-alone forex VaR; the forex exposure has this effect because the diversification benefit is significant, due to the low quanto correlation.

IV.2.6.3 Interest Rate VaR of Equity Portfolios

Exposures to interest rates arise in equity portfolios that are hedged with futures or when the foreign currency exposures that arise in international equity portfolios are transacted on the forward currency market.[35] Assuming that an investment of $N in a foreign equity index is financed by taking a foreign currency forward position, there are equal and opposite exposures of +$N and −$N to the foreign and domestic zero-coupon interest rates of maturity equal to the maturity of the currency forward.

EXAMPLE IV.2.16: INTEREST RATE VAR FROM FOREX EXPOSURE

A US investor buys $2 million of sterling 10 days forward, when the 10-day Treasury bill rate is 5% and the 10-day spot rate is 4.5% in the UK. If these interest rates have volatilities of 100 basis points for the Treasury bill and 80 basis points for the UK rate, and a correlation of 0.9, calculate the 1% 10-day interest rate VaR.

SOLUTION   The interest rate risk arises from the cash flows of $2 million on the UK interest rate and −$2 million on the US interest rate. The PV01 vector is calculated in the spreadsheet using the method described in Section III.1.8. First we compute the change in each discount factor for a one basis point decrease in the corresponding interest rate and then we multiply these changes by the exposures of $2 million and −$2 million, respectively. This gives the PV01 vector $\theta = (5.47, -5.46)'$ in US dollars. The annual covariance matrix of the interest rates, in basis points, is

$$\Omega = \begin{pmatrix} 6,400 & 7,200 \\ 7,200 & 10,000 \end{pmatrix}.$$

Now using the usual formula $(\theta'\Omega\theta)$ for the variance and calculating the 1% 10-day VaR in the usual way gives a grand total of $114 for the interest rate VaR.

This example shows that interest rate VaR on equity portfolios arising from foreign exchange forward positions is very small indeed. Unless there are large interest rate differentials between the domestic and foreign currencies and the forward date for the forex transaction is very distant, the interest rate risks arising from this type of transaction are negligible compared with the equity and forex risks.

---

[35] Hedging with futures introduces a dividend risk in addition to interest rate risk and we shall deal with this separately in the next section.

IV.2.6.4   Hedging the Risks of International Equity Portfolios

Foreign investors wishing to accept risks only on equity markets can hedge the forex risk by taking an equal and opposite position in the currency, so that the forex VaR is zero. For instance, in Example IV.2.15 where the US investor has a long sterling exposure of $2 million and a long exposure to the euro of $7 million, if the investor wants to hedge the forex risk he should take a short position of $2 million on sterling and a short position of $7 million on the euro. Then the net currency exposure is zero, so the forex VaR is zero. Thus the total systematic VaR is equal to the equity VaR.

The forex hedges introduce a new systematic VaR due to the interest rate risk factors, but we have seen from the previous example that the interest rate VaR is very small compared with the equity VaR, and compared with the specific VaR of a stock portfolio. Nevertheless, for the sake of completeness, the following example shows how to measure all the sources of risk for a typical, hedged stock portfolio.

EXAMPLE IV.2.17: VaR FOR A HEDGED INTERNATIONAL STOCK PORTFOLIO

A European investor has $5 million invested a portfolio of volatile S&P 500 stocks, with an S&P 500 market beta of 1.5. The volatilities of the S&P 500 and €/$ rate are 20% and 15% respectively, and their correlation is −0.5.

(a) Find the 1% 1-day total systematic VaR and the VaR due to each risk factor.
(b) He now hedges the portfolio's equity exposure by selling a 3-month future on the S&P 500 index and further hedges the currency exposure with a short position on US dollars, 3 months forward. The 3-month US dollar and euro interest rates are 4% and 3.5% respectively, and the dividend yield on the S&P 500 is 3%. The volatilities and correlations of these risk factors are summarized in Table IV.2.16. Find the 1% 1-day VaR due to each of the risk factors.
(c) If the portfolio volatility is 35%, calculate the hedged portfolio's 1% 1-day specific VaR.

Table IV.2.16   Volatilities and correlations of risk factors

Volatilities		Correlations	
US 3-month interest rate	80bps	US interest rate–euro interest rate	0.5
Euro 3-month interest rate	100bps	US interest rate–dividend yield	0.3
S&P 500 dividend yield	20bps	Euro interest rate–dividend yield	0

SOLUTION

(a) The initial VaR calculations, before hedging, are based on the same method as Example IV.2.14 and the results are shown in Table IV.2.17.

Table IV.2.17   VaR decomposition into equity and forex factors

Total systematic VaR	$191,129
Equity VaR	$220,697
Forex VaR	$110,348

(b) The equity and forex hedges introduce three new risk factors: the 3-month euro interest rate, with an exposure of $5 million because he has sold $5 million 3 months forward against the euro; the S&P 500 dividend yield, with an exposure of $7.5 million because, with a beta of 1.5, this is the amount he sells of the 3-month S&P 500 future for the equity hedge; and the 3-month US interest rate with an exposure of $-$5 million from the forex hedge and an additional $-$7.5 million from the equity hedge, making a total exposure of $-$12.5 million to the US interest rate.

We now calculate the sensitivities of these exposures. With a 4% (annual) 3-month interest rate, the discount factor is $(1.01)^{-1} = 0.9901$ and, as shown in the spreadsheet, the change in the discount factor for a one basis point decrease in the interest rate, i.e. the $\delta 01$, is

$$\delta 01_{3-\text{month}} = 0.245 \times 10^{-4}.$$

Similarly the euro interest rates and the US dividend yield have $\delta 01$s that are calculated in the spreadsheet to be 0.246×10^{-4}.

The exposure to the US interest rate, the euro interest rate and the dividend yield respectively is $\{-12.5, \ 5, \ 7.5\}$ in millions of dollars. Hence, the PV01 vector in dollars is[36]

$$\boldsymbol{\theta} = 100 \times (-12.5 \times 0.245, 5 \times 0.246, 7.5 \times 0.246)' = (-306.35, \ 122.84, \ 184.72)'.$$

Given the risk factor volatilities and correlations in Table IV.2.16, the 1-day covariance matrix of the risk factor returns is

$$\boldsymbol{\Omega}_1 = \begin{pmatrix} 25.6 & 16 & 1.92 \\ 16 & 40 & 0 \\ 1.92 & 0 & 1.6 \end{pmatrix}.$$

For instance, $25.6 = 80^2/250$, and so forth. Hence, the 1-day variance of the P&L is

$$\boldsymbol{\theta}' \boldsymbol{\Omega}_1 \boldsymbol{\theta} = 1,639,222.$$

So, after the hedges the 1% 1-day total systematic VaR is:

$$\text{Total systematic VaR}_{1,0.01} = 2.32635 \times \sqrt{1,639,222} = \$2978.$$

The 1% 1-day VaR due to each risk factor is

$$2.32635 \times |PV01_i| \times \sigma_{1,i},$$

where $\sigma_{1,i}$ is the 1-day standard deviation of the ith risk factor. Hence,

$$\text{US interest rate VaR}_{1,0.01} = 2.32635 \times 306.35 \times 80/\sqrt{250} = \$3606,$$

$$\text{Euro interest rate VaR}_{1,0.01} = 2.32635 \times 122.84 \times 100/\sqrt{250} = \$1807,$$

$$\text{US dividend yield VaR}_{1,0.01} = 2.32635 \times 184.72 \times 20/\sqrt{250} = \$544.$$

Note that the US interest rate VaR is larger than the total VaR, which is not unusual when we have opposite positions in positively correlated risk factors.

---

[36] The factor of 100 here arises because we multiply by $1,000,000 and by 1 basis point, i.e. 0.0001.

(c) By far the largest residual VaR after the equity and forex hedge is going to arise from the specific VaR, i.e. from the tracking error of this portfolio. This is because we are hedging a portfolio that has a market beta of 1.5 with an index futures contract. Assuming the residuals are uncorrelated with the futures, the specific variance, in annual terms, is

$$0.35^2 - 1.5^2 \times 0.2^2 = 0.0325.$$

Hence, the 1% 1-day specific VaR is

$$\text{Specific VaR}_{1,0.01} = 2.32635 \times \sqrt{\frac{0.0325}{250}} \times \$5,000,000 = \$132,622.$$

IV.2.7   CASE STUDY: NORMAL LINEAR VALUE AT RISK FOR COMMODITY FUTURES

In this section we calculate the normal linear VaR for two commodity futures trading desks, one trading natural gas futures and the other trading silver futures. We shall calculate the VaR for each desk, and then aggregate these into a total VaR covering both the desks. The data used in this study are NYMEX futures on natural gas and silver with maturities up to 6 months. Each natural gas futures contract is for 10,000 million British thermal units and each silver futures contract is for 5000 troy ounces.

The desks can take long or short positions on the futures according to their expectations and we assume the traders have mapped their positions to constant maturity futures at 1, 2, 3, 4 and 5 months using the commodity futures mapping described in Section III.5.4.2.

Applying linear interpolation to daily data on the NYMEX traded futures prices, we first construct a historical series of daily data on constant maturity futures from 3 January 2006 to 31 January 2007. We shall use these data to measure the VaR on 31 January 2007. The constant maturity futures on the two commodities over the sample period are shown in Figures IV.2.7 and IV.2.8.

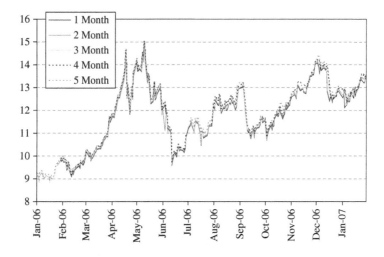

Figure IV.2.7   Constant maturity futures prices, silver

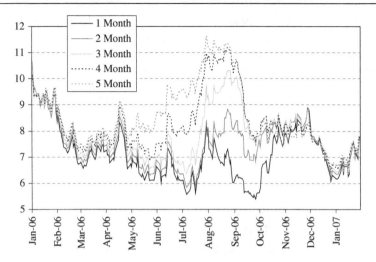

Figure IV.2.8   Constant maturity futures prices, natural gas

The natural gas futures prices have a very strong *contango* (upward sloping term structure) during the summer of 2006. Like the spot price, near term futures prices were rather low in the summer of 2006 because storage was almost full to capacity. The silver futures prices are much closer to each other than the natural gas futures prices. The silver term structure is very flat most of the time and there is no seasonality in the prices. Price jumps are quite common, due to speculation, because silver is an investment asset as well as being used in industrial processes.

Table IV.2.18 shows the volatilities and correlations of each set of constant maturity futures returns. These are calculated from the daily returns over the entire sample. Both are highly

Table IV.2.18   Volatilities and correlations of natural gas and silver futures

Gas

Correlations	1 month	2 month	3 month	4 month	5 month
1 month	1				
2 month	0.910	1			
3 month	0.914	0.9492	1		
4 month	0.912	0.9276	0.960	1	
5 month	0.888	0.9173	0.950	0.9639	1
Volatilities	58.70%	55.09%	49.82%	45.87%	41.85%

Silver

Correlations	1 month	2 month	3 month	4 month	5 month
1 month	1				
2 month	0.939	1			
3 month	0.942	0.918	1		
4 month	0.880	0.863	0.960	1	
5 month	0.799	0.840	0.892	0.935	1
Volatilities	44.13%	43.98%	42.78%	43.35%	40.46%

correlated along their own term structures and natural gas futures returns are more volatile than silver futures returns.

We now consider the positions taken on each trading desk on 31 January 2007. These are shown in Table IV.2.19. First we show the price and number of units of each futures contract, then the position values are calculated as the product of the number of contracts and the price of the contract, multiplied by either 10,000 (the trading unit for natural gas futures) or 5000 (the trading unit for silver futures).

Table IV.2.19   Commodities trading desk positions on natural gas and silver

	1 month	2 month	3 month	4 month	5 month
Price: gas futures	7.67	7.66	7.69	7.70	7.84
Price: silver futures	13.50	13.39	13.62	13.62	13.56
No contracts: gas	−75	−30	−10	15	25
No contracts: silver	100	50	20	−50	−100
Position values: gas	−$5,750,250	−$2,297,200	−$769,000	$1,155,000	$1,960,875
Position values: silver	$6,748,000	$3,347,150	$1,362,100	−$3,405,250	−$6,777,721

The commodities trading desks are betting on an imminent fall in price for natural gas, since it has short positions on the short maturities and long positions on longer maturities, and an imminent rise in price for silver, taking long positions in shorter maturities and short positions in longer maturities.

The 1% 10-day stand-alone VaR for each desk is calculated in the spreadsheet using the formula

$$\text{VaR}_{10,0.01} = \Phi^{-1}(0.99)\sqrt{\boldsymbol{\theta}'\boldsymbol{\Omega}_1\boldsymbol{\theta}} \times \sqrt{10},$$

where $\boldsymbol{\theta}$ is the position value vector given in the last rows of Table IV.2.19 and $\boldsymbol{\Omega}_1$ is the 5 × 5 1-day covariance matrix of the constant maturity gas or silver futures daily returns. A similar formula is applied to obtain the total VaR aggregated over both desks, now using the position value vector in the last two rows of Table IV.2.19 combined, and the 10 × 10 1-day covariance matrix of natural gas and silver futures daily returns. The marginal VaRs were calculated using the methodology described in Section IV.2.2.4.[37]

The results are shown in Table IV.2.20. The marginal VaRs tell us that trading on gas futures contributes 69% of the total risk and trading on silver futures contributes 31% of the total risk, after adjusting for the diversification effects from the two activities.[38]

The stand-alone VaRs measure risk without accounting for diversification. Hence, the sum of the two stand-alone VaRs is greater than the total VaR – this is because the natural gas and silver futures have less than perfect correlation. If the correlation between natural gas and

---

[37] We do not give full details of this calculation here, since several other numerical examples have already been provided and the calculation is performed in the spreadsheet for this case study.
[38] However, this does not imply that capital allocation should use these marginal VaRs in a risk adjusted performance measure. There is no reason why either trading desk should be advantaged (or disadvantaged) by the fact that diversification across trading activities reduces total risk. Indeed capital would normally be allocated using a risk adjusted performance measure based on the stand-alone VaR for each desk.

Table IV.2.20 1% 10-day VaR of commodity futures desks

VaR	Stand-alone	Marginal
Gas	$1,720,139	$1,394,727
Silver	$1,180,168	$614,955
Total	$2,009,682	

silver futures changed, all else remaining the same, this would not affect the stand-alone VaRs. But it would affect the total VaR and hence also the marginal VaRs.

IV.2.8   STUDENT *t* DISTRIBUTED LINEAR VALUE AT RISK

In this section we shall extend the analytic formula for normal linear VaR to the case where the portfolio returns and the risk factor returns are assumed to have a Student *t* distribution. First, to motivate this formula, Section IV.2.8.1 describes the effect that leptokurtosis has on a VaR estimate. Then Section IV.2.8.2 derives a parametric linear VaR formula for the case where the portfolio's returns are generated by a Student *t* distribution, and extends this to systematic VaR when the risk factor returns have a multivariate Student *t* distribution. Empirical examples are provided in Section IV.2.8.3.

IV.2.8.1   Effect of Leptokurtosis and Skewness on VaR

A *leptokurtic* distribution is one whose density function has a higher peak and greater mass in the tails than the normal density function of the same variance. In a symmetric unimodal distribution, i.e. one whose density function has only one peak, leptokurtosis is indicated by a positive excess kurtosis.[39]

Leptokurtosis is one of the basic 'stylized facts' emerging from examination of the empirical distributions of financial asset returns. Also apparent is the skewness of return densities, particularly for equity returns which often have a strong negative skew (heavier lower tail). With leptokurtosis and negative skewness in risk factor return distributions the normal linear VaR formula is likely to underestimate the VaR at high confidence levels. In commodity returns a positive skew (heavier upper tails) is often seen, but for companies that are short commodity futures, losses are made following price rises, and here the positive skewness effect compounds the leptokurtosis effect on VaR. Again, the normal linear VaR formula is likely to underestimate the VaR at high confidence levels.

Figure IV.2.9 illustrates the impact of leptokurtosis on the VaR estimate. Both of the density functions shown in the figure are symmetric, but the density depicted by the black line is leptokurtic, i.e. it has a higher peak and heavier tails than the 'equivalent' normal density (i.e. the normal density with the same variance) which is shown in grey. For each density the corresponding 1% and 5% VaR estimates are shown. We observe the following:

---

[39] For an introduction to skewness and kurtosis, see Section I.3.2.7.

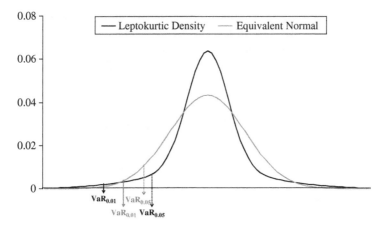

Figure IV.2.9   Comparison of normal VaR and leptokurtic VaR

- For low significance levels (e.g. 5%), the normal assumption can *overestimate* VaR if the return distribution is leptokurtic.
- For higher significance levels (e.g. 0.5%), the normal assumption can seriously *underestimate* VaR if the return distribution is leptokurtic.
- The significance level at which the VaR becomes greater under the leptokurtic distribution depends on the extent of the excess kurtosis. If the excess kurtosis is large, the leptokurtic VaR will exceed the normal VaR even at 10% significance levels. For an empirical illustration of this, see Example IV.2.20.

As the confidence level of the VaR estimate increases (i.e. α becomes smaller) there always comes a point at which the leptokurtic VaR exceeds the normal VaR. Referring to Figure IV.2.9, and noting the 'intermediate' region where the leptokurtic density curve lies below the equivalent normal density, the reason for this becomes clear. In the tails (and the centre) the leptokurtic density function lies above the equivalent normal density function; hence the leptokurtic VaR will be the greater figure for all significance levels above some threshold. But in the intermediate region, the ordering may be reversed.

We know from Section I.3.3.7 that Student t distributions are leptokurtic. When significant positive excess kurtosis is found in empirical financial return distributions, the Student t distribution is likely to produce VaR estimates that are more representative of historical behaviour than normal linear VaR. However, by the central limit theorem, the excess kurtosis in financial returns decreases as the sampling interval increases. Thus, whilst daily returns may have a large positive excess kurtosis, weekly returns have lower kurtosis and monthly returns may even have excess kurtosis that is close to zero.

IV.2.8.2   Student t Linear VaR Formula

In this subsection we derive an analytic formula for the Student t VaR.[40] It is useful when VaR is estimated over a short risk horizon, as positive excess kurtosis can be pronounced over a

---

[40] One of the first applications of the Student t distribution to VaR estimation was by Huisman et al. (1998).

period of a few days or even weeks. But for risk horizons of a month or more, returns are likely to be approximately normally distributed, by the central limit theorem.

The standard Student t distribution with ν degrees of freedom was introduced in Section I.3.3.7. If a random variable T has a Student t distribution with ν degrees of freedom we write $T \sim t_\nu$, and its density function is

$$f_\nu(t) = (\nu\pi)^{-1/2}\Gamma\left(\frac{\nu}{2}\right)^{-1}\Gamma\left(\frac{\nu+1}{2}\right)\left(1+\nu^{-1}t^2\right)^{-\left(\frac{\nu+1}{2}\right)}, \qquad (IV.2.58)$$

where the *gamma function* Γ is an extension of the factorial function to non-integer values.[41]

The distribution has zero expectation and zero skewness. For $\nu > 2$ the variance of a Student t distributed variable is *not* 1, but

$$V(T) = \nu(\nu - 2)^{-1}. \qquad (IV.2.59)$$

Its excess kurtosis $\varkappa$ is finite for $\nu > 4$, and is given by

$$\varkappa = 6(\nu - 4)^{-1}. \qquad (IV.2.60)$$

The Student t density has a lower peak than the standard normal density, and it converges to the standard normal density as $\nu \to \infty$. But the density is leptokurtic, since when we compare it with the equivalent normal density, i.e. the one having the *same* variance as (IV.2.59), the peak in the centre of the distribution is higher than the peak of the equivalent normal density, and the tails are heavier.

The α quantile of the standard Student t distribution is denoted by $t_\nu^{-1}(\alpha)$. Since quantiles translate under monotonic transformations,[42] the α quantile of the *standardized* Student t distribution with ν degrees of freedom, i.e. the Student t distribution with mean 0 and variance 1, is $\sqrt{\nu^{-1}(\nu-2)}t_\nu^{-1}(\alpha)$. Let X denote the daily return on a portfolio and suppose it has standard deviation σ and discounted mean μ. To apply a Student t linear VaR formula to the portfolio we need to use the quantiles from a *generalized* Student t distribution, i.e. the distribution of the random variable $X = \mu + \sigma T$, where T is a *standardized* Student t random variable.

Note that the ordinary Student t quantiles satisfy

$$-t_\nu^{-1}(\alpha) = t_\nu^{-1}(1 - \alpha), \qquad (IV.2.61)$$

because the distribution is symmetric about a mean of zero. So, using the same argument that we used in Section IV.2.2 to derive the normal linear VaR formula, it follows that

$$\text{Student } t \text{ VaR}_{\alpha,\nu} = \sqrt{\nu^{-1}(\nu - 2)}\, t_\nu^{-1}(1 - \alpha)\sigma - \mu. \qquad (IV.2.62)$$

---

[41] When x is an integer, $\Gamma(x) = (x-1)!$. See Section I.3.4.8 for further details about the gamma function.
[42] That is, if X has distribution $F(x)$ and $y = aX$, a being a constant, then Y has α quantile $y_\alpha = ax_\alpha = aF^{-1}(\alpha)$.

The Student t distribution is not a stable distribution,[43] so the sum of i.i.d. Student t variables is not another Student t variable. Indeed, by the central limit theorem the sum converges to a normal variable as the number of terms in the sum increases. When h is small, a very approximate formula for the $100\alpha\%h$-day VaR, as a percentage of the portfolio value, is

$$\text{Student } t \text{ VaR}_{h,\alpha,\nu} = \sqrt{\nu^{-1}(\nu - 2)h}\; t_\nu^{-1}(1 - \alpha)\sigma - h\mu. \tag{IV.2.63}$$

But when h is more than about 10 days (or even less, if ν is relatively large) the normal linear VaR formula should be sufficiently accurate.

The extension of (IV.2.63) to the systematic VaR for a linear portfolio that has been mapped to m risk factors with sensitivities $\boldsymbol{\theta} = (\theta_1, \ldots, \theta_m)'$ is, assuming the risk factors have a multivariate Student t distribution with ν degrees of freedom,

$$\text{Systematic Student } t \text{ VaR}_{h,\alpha} = \sqrt{\nu^{-1}(\nu - 2)}\; t_\nu^{-1}(1 - \alpha)\sqrt{\boldsymbol{\theta}'\boldsymbol{\Omega}_h\boldsymbol{\theta}} - \boldsymbol{\theta}'\boldsymbol{\mu}_h, \tag{IV.2.64}$$

where $\boldsymbol{\Omega}_h$ denotes the $m \times m$ covariance matrix of the risk factor returns and $\boldsymbol{\mu}_h$ denotes the $m \times 1$ vector of expected excess returns over the h-day risk horizon.

IV.2.8.3 Empirical Examples of Student t Linear VaR

The critical value $t_\nu^{-1}(1 - \alpha)$ can be found in statistical tables or using the Excel function TINV.[44] The degrees of freedom parameter ν is estimated by fitting the distribution using *maximum likelihood estimation* (MLE). Example I.3.17 and its accompanying spreadsheet explain how to do this in practice. Alternatively, a quick approximation to ν may be obtained using a simple 'moment matching' method called the *method of moments*, which entails equating the sample moments to population moments.[45] We shall compare both methods in the following example.

EXAMPLE IV.2.18: ESTIMATING STUDENT T LINEAR VAR AT THE PORTFOLIO LEVEL

Using the daily FTSE 100 data from 4 January 2005 to 7 April 2008 shown in Figure IV.2.10, estimate the degrees of freedom parameter for a generalized Student t distribution representation of the daily returns, using (a) the method of moments and (b) MLE.[46] Then compute the 1% 1-day Student t VaR, as a percentage of portfolio value, using both estimates for the degrees of freedom parameter.

SOLUTION   The method of moments gives an estimate $\hat{\nu} = 6.07$ for the degrees of freedom parameter, but MLE gives $\hat{\nu} = 4.14$.[47] The resulting estimates of 1% 1-day VaR are 2.81% for the method of moments estimate and 2.94% for the maximum likelihood estimate. Both estimates are ignoring the possibility of non-zero skewness, because the Student t distribution is symmetric. But in fact the sample skewness is -0.258. This is because of the large falls in the FTSE 100 index that are evident from Figure IV.2.10.

---

[43] See Section I.3.3.11.
[44] See Section IV.4.2.4 (or Excel help) for details on how to apply the TINV function.
[45] Note that the kurtosis is defined only for $\nu > 4$, so we must assume this, to apply the method of moments.
[46] Data were downloaded from Yahoo! Finance, symbol ^FTSE.
[47] Note that it is not necessary to use an integer value for the degrees of freedom in the Student t distribution.

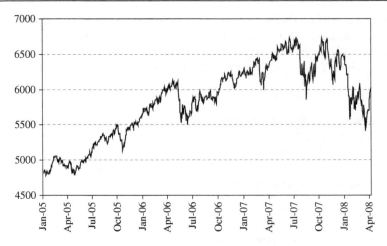

Figure IV.2.10   FTSE 100 index price

EXAMPLE IV.2.19: COMPARISON OF NORMAL AND STUDENT T LINEAR VAR

Using the maximum likelihood estimate of the degrees of freedom for the Student t representation of the FTSE 100 index returns from the previous example, compare the Student t linear VaR with the normal linear VaR over a 1-day horizon, at the 0.1%, 1% and 10% significance levels. Express your results as a percentage of the portfolio value.

SOLUTION   The spreadsheet for the previous example is extended to include the normal linear VaR, and using the three different significance levels. The results are displayed in Table IV.2.21.

Table IV.2.21   Normal and Student t linear VaR

Significance Level	0.1%	1%	10%
Student t VaR	5.64%	2.94%	1.20%
Normal VaR	3.39%	2.55%	1.41%

The 1-day Student t VaR is considerably greater than the normal VaR at the 0.1% significance level, it is a little greater than the normal VaR at the 1% level, and at the 10% significance level the normal VaR is greater than the Student t VaR. This is because the tails of the Student t density have greater mass and the peak at the centre is higher than the normal density with the same variance. Hence, for quantiles lying further toward the centre there may be less mass in the tail of the Student t density than in the tail of the normal density.

The above examples show that the model risk arising from the assumption that returns are normally distributed is very significant, especially when VaR is measured at high confidence levels such as 99.9%. The Student t VaR model provides a more accurate representation of most financial asset returns, but a potentially significant source of model risk arises from assuming the return distribution is symmetric. Although there are skewed versions of the Student t distribution (see McNeil et al. (2005) and references therein), the non-linear transformations that underpin these distributions remove the possibility of simple parametric linear VaR formulae. By far the easiest way to extend the parametric linear VaR model to accommodate the skewness that is so often evident in financial asset returns is to use the mixture linear VaR model, which is explained in the next section.

IV.2.9   LINEAR VALUE AT RISK WITH MIXTURE DISTRIBUTIONS

In this section we show how mixtures of normal or Student t distributions can be used to estimate VaR, capturing both leptokurtosis and skewness in return distributions. Section IV.2.9.1 provides a gentle introduction to the subject by summarizing the important features of simple mixtures of two distributions. Section IV.2.9.2 explains how to calculate VaR when the portfolio return distribution is assumed to be a normal mixture or a Student t mixture distribution. In this case the parametric linear VaR is given by an analytic formula that does not have an explicit solution, so we use numerical methods to find the mixture linear VaR. Section IV.2.9.3 explains how mixture distribution parameters are estimated from historical data and Section IV.2.9.4 provides empirical examples. Section IV.2.9.5 illustrates the potential for mixture VaR to be applied in a *scenario VaR* setting, when using little or no historical data on a portfolio's returns. Finally, Section IV.2.9.6 considers the case where the portfolio is mapped to risk factors whose returns are generated by correlated i.i.d. normal mixture processes with two multivariate normal components.

IV.2.9.1   Mixture Distributions

The mixture setting is designed to capture different *market regimes*. For instance, in a mixture of two normal distributions, there are two regimes for returns: one where the return has mean μ_1 and variance σ_1^2 and another where the return has mean μ_2 and variance σ_2^2. The other parameter of the mixture is the probability π with which the first regime occurs, so the second regime occurs with probability $1 - \pi$.

The distribution function of a mixture distribution is a probability-weighted sum of the component distribution functions. For instance, a mixture of just two normal distributions has distribution function defined by

$$G(x) = \pi \, F(x; \mu_1, \sigma_1^2) + (1 - \pi)F(x; \mu_2, \sigma_2^2), \quad 0 < \pi < 1, \tag{IV.2.65}$$

where $F(x; \mu_i, \sigma_i^2)$ denotes the normal distribution function with mean μ_i and variance σ_i^2, for $i = 1, 2$, and where π is the probability associated with the normal component with mean μ_1 and variance σ_1^2. Differentiating (IV.2.65) gives the corresponding normal mixture density function

$$g(x) = \pi \, f(x; \mu_1, \sigma_1^2) + (1 - \pi)f(x; \mu_2, \sigma_2^2), \quad 0 < \pi < 1, \tag{IV.2.66}$$

where $f(x; \mu_i, \sigma_i^2)$ denotes the normal density function with mean μ_i and variance σ_i^2, for $i = 1, 2$. Full details about normal mixture distributions are given in Section I.3.3.6.

We illustrate the basic properties of mixture distributions by considering a simple mixture of two zero-mean normal components, i.e. where $\mu_1 = \mu_2 = 0$. In this case the variance of the normal mixture distribution is

$$\sigma^2 = \pi\sigma_1^2 + (1-\pi)\sigma_2^2, \tag{IV.2.67}$$

The skewness is zero and the kurtosis is

$$\varkappa = 3\left(\frac{\pi\sigma_1^4 + (1-\pi)\sigma_2^4}{\left[\pi\sigma_1^2 + (1-\pi)\sigma_2^2\right]^2}\right). \tag{IV.2.68}$$

For instance, Figure IV.2.11 shows four densities:

- three zero-mean normal densities with volatility 5%, 10% (shown in grey) and 7.906% (shown as dotted line);
- a normal mixture density, shown in black, which is a mixture of the first two normal densities with probability weight of 0.5 on each of the grey normal densities, and which has volatility 7.906%.

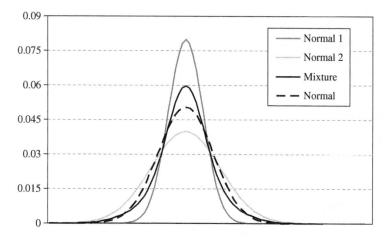

Figure IV.2.11   Comparison of a normal mixture with a normal density of the same variance

The variance of the mixture distribution is $0.5 \times 5^2 + 0.5 \times 10^2 = 62.5$. Since $7.906 = \sqrt{62.5}$, the mixture has the same variance as the dashed normal curve. However, it has a kurtosis of 4.87. In other words it has an excess kurtosis of 1.87, which is significantly greater than zero (zero being the excess kurtosis of the equivalent (dashed) normal density in the figure).

Normal mixture distributions provide a simple means of capturing the empirically observed skewness and excess kurtosis of financial asset returns. It is always the case that zero-mean normal mixture densities have zero skewness but positive excess kurtosis: they have higher peaks and heavier tails than normal densities with the same variance. Taking different means in the component normal densities gives a positive or negative skew. See Figure I.3.14 for an example.

IV.2.9.2   Mixture Linear VaR Formula

When the excess return X on a linear portfolio has a normal distribution, the analytic formula (IV.2.5) for normal linear VaR follows directly from the definition of VaR. But there is no explicit formula for estimating VaR under the assumption that portfolio returns follow a mixture density. However, using exactly the same type of argument as in Section IV.2.2.1, we can derive an implicit formula that we can solve using a numerical algorithm.

For instance, suppose there are only two components in a mixture density for the portfolio's returns, and write

$$G(x) = \pi\, F_1\big(x; \mu_1, \sigma_1^2\big) + (1 - \pi)F_2\big(x; \mu_2, \sigma_2^2\big), \quad 0 < \pi < 1, \tag{IV.2.69}$$

where $F_i(x; \mu_i,\ \sigma_i^2)$ denotes the distribution function with mean μ_i and variance σ_i^2, for $i = 1,\ 2$, and where π is the probability associated with the component with mean μ_1 and variance σ_1^2. Note that F_1 and F_2 need not be both normal; one or both of them could be a Student t distribution, in which case the degrees of freedom ν_i should be included in their list of parameters.

We have

$$P(X < x_\alpha) = G(x_\alpha) = \pi\, F_1\big(x_\alpha; \mu_1, \sigma_1^2\big) + (1 - \pi)F_2\big(x_\alpha; \mu_2, \sigma_2^2\big), \tag{IV.2.70}$$

and when $P(X < x_\alpha) = \alpha$, then x_α is the α quantile of the mixture distribution. Let X_i be the random variable with distribution function $F_i(x; \mu_i,\ \sigma_i^2)$. Then

$$F_i\big(x_\alpha; \mu_i, \sigma_i^2\big) = P(X_i < x_\alpha) = P\big(\sigma_i^{-1}(X_i - \mu_i) < \sigma_i^{-1}(x_\alpha - \mu_i)\big).$$

But

$$\sigma_i^{-1}(X_i - \mu_i) = Y_i = \begin{cases} Z, & \text{if } F_i \text{ is a normal distribution,} \\ T_i, & \text{if } F_i \text{ is a Student } t \text{ distribution,} \end{cases}$$

where Z is a standard normal variable and T_i is a standardized Student t variable with ν_i degrees of freedom. Hence,

$$\pi P\big(Y_1 < (x_\alpha - \mu_1)\sigma_1^{-1}\big) + (1 - \pi)P\big(Y_2 < (x_\alpha - \mu_2)\sigma_2^{-1}\big) = \alpha. \tag{IV.2.71}$$

But since Y_i is a standardized Student t or normal variable, we know its quantiles. That is, we know everything in the above identity except the mixture quantile, x_α. Hence, the mixture quantile can be 'backed out' from (IV.2.71) using an iterative approximation method such as the Excel Goal Seek or Solver algorithms (see Section I.5.2.2). Finally, we find the mixture VaR by setting $\mathrm{VaR}_\alpha = -x_\alpha$.

For greater flexibility to fit the empirical return distribution we may also include more than two component distributions in the mixture. The general formula for the mixture VaR, now making the risk horizon h over which the returns are measured explicit, is therefore

$$\sum_{i=1}^{n} \pi_i P\big(Y_i < (x_{h,\alpha} - \mu_{ih})\sigma_{ih}^{-1}\big) = \alpha. \tag{IV.2.72}$$

As before, backing out $x_{h,\alpha}$ from the above gives $\mathrm{VaR}_{h,\alpha} = -x_{h,\alpha}$.

IV.2.9.3   Mixture Parameter Estimation

The $100\alpha\%$ h-day mixture VaR that is implicit in (IV.2.72) will be expressed as a percentage of the portfolio value if μ_{ih} and σ_{ih} are the expectation and standard deviation of the component returns, and it will be expressed in nominal terms if μ_{ih} and σ_{ih} are the expectation and standard deviation of the component P&L. But how do we estimate these component means and variances?

The estimation of the mixture parameters from historical data is best performed using the *EM algorithm*, especially when the mixture is over more than two distributions. A description of this algorithm and a case study illustrating its application to financial data are given in Section I.5.4. Empirically, we often find that we can identify two significantly different regimes: a regime that occurs most of the time and governs ordinary market circumstances, and a second 'high volatility' regime that occurs with a low probability. In an equity portfolio the low probability, high volatility regime is usually captured by a component with a large and negative mean; in other words, this component usually corresponds to a *crash market regime*.

As the number of distributions in the mixture increases the probability weight on some of these components can become extremely small. However, in finance it is seldom necessary to use more than two or three components in the mixture, since financial asset return distributions are seldom so irregular as to have multiple modes. When there are only a few components the *method of moments* may be used estimate the parameters of a normal mixture distribution in Excel. In this approach we equate the first few sample moments (one moment for each parameter to be estimated) to the corresponding theoretical moments of the normal mixture distribution.

The theoretical moments for normal mixture distributions are now stated for the general case where there are m normal components with means and standard deviations μ_i and σ_i, for $i = 1, 2, \ldots, m$. The vector of probability weights, i.e. the *mixing law* for the normal mixture, is denoted by $\boldsymbol{\pi} = (\pi_1, \ldots, \pi_m)$ where $\sum_{i=1}^{m} \pi_i = 1$. The non-central moments are

$$M_1 = E[X] = \sum_{i=1}^{m} \pi_i \mu_i,$$

$$M_2 = E[X^2] = \sum_{i=1}^{m} \pi_i (\sigma_i^2 + \mu_i^2),$$

$$M_3 = E[X^3] = \sum_{i=1}^{m} \pi_i (3\mu_i \sigma_i^2 + \mu_i^3),$$

$$M_4 = E[X^4] = \sum_{i=1}^{m} \pi_i (3\sigma_i^4 + 6\mu_i^2 \sigma_i^2 + \mu_i^4),$$

(IV.2.73)

and the mean, variance, skewness and kurtosis are

$$\mu = E[X] = M_1,$$

$$\sigma^2 = E[(X - \mu)^2] = M_2 - M_1^2,$$

$$\tau = \sigma^{-3} E[(X - \mu)^3] = \sigma^{-3}(M_3 - 3M_1 M_2 + 2M_1^3),$$

$$\varkappa = \sigma^{-4} E[(X - \mu)^4] = \sigma^{-4}(M_4 - 4M_1 M_3 + 6M_1^2 M_2 - 3M_1^4).$$

(IV.2.74)

Hence, when the method of moments is applied to estimate the parameters of a normal mixture distribution, we equate (μ, σ, τ, $\varkappa$) to the first four sample moments ($\hat{\mu}$, $\hat{\sigma}$, $\hat{\tau}$, $\hat{\varkappa}$) by changing the parameters of the normal mixture distribution. An empirical example is given in the next subsection.

IV.2.9.4 Examples of Mixture Linear VaR

In a case study in Section I.5.4.4 we applied the EM algorithm to fit a mixture of two normal distributions to the daily returns on the FTSE 100 index, and likewise for the S&P 500 index and the \$/£ exchange rate. For convenience, Table IV.2.22 states the sample moments and Table IV.2.23 states the normal mixture parameter estimates for each of these variables, based on the EM algorithm. In both tables the means and standard deviations are quoted in annualized terms, assuming the returns are i.i.d.

Table IV.2.22 Moments of the FTSE 100 and S&P 500 indices and of the \$/£ forex rate

Variable	Annualized Mean	Volatility	Skewness	Excess Kurtosis
FTSE 100	4.62%	17.57%	0.0205	3.2570
S&P 500	7.35%	17.73%	−0.0803	1.0525
FX rate	2.04%	7.99%	−0.1514	2.6332

Table IV.2.23 Estimated parameters of normal mixture distributions (annualized)

Variable	π	μ_1	μ_2	σ_1	σ_2
FTSE 100	0.3622	−3.58%	9.28%	26.35%	5.48%
S&P 500	0.2752	−1.01%	10.52%	29.80%	7.84%
FX Rate	0.6150	1.94%	2.21%	9.68%	4.01%

In the next example we use these parameters to estimate the normal mixture VaR for a US investor in the FTSE 100 and S&P 500 indices.

EXAMPLE IV.2.20: ESTIMATING NORMAL MIXTURE VAR FOR EQUITY AND FOREX

Use the parameters in Table IV.2.23 to estimate the $100\alpha\%$ 10-day normal mixture VaR for a US investment in the FTSE 100 and S&P 500 indices. Report your results as a percentage of the local currency exposure to each risk factor and compare them with the normal estimate of VaR. Use significance levels of $\alpha = 10\%, 5\%, 1\%$ and 0.1%.

SOLUTION   For each of the three risk factors we use Solver or Goal Seek to back out the normal mixture VaR from the formula (IV.2.71).[48] The results are reported in Table IV.2.24, where they are compared with the equivalent normal VaR. Compared with the normal VaR, the normal mixture VaR is greater than the normal VaR at higher significance levels. As expected, the extent to which it exceeds the normal VaR increases as we move to a greater confidence

---

[48] The algorithm must be repeated whenever you change the significance level.

Table IV.2.24   Comparison of normal mixture and normal VaR

VaR Model	NM	Normal	NM	Normal	NM	Normal	NM	Normal
Significance	$\alpha = 0.1\%$		$\alpha = 1\%$		$\alpha = 5\%$		$\alpha = 10\%$	
FTSE 100 VaR	14.77%	10.67%	10.25%	7.99%	5.88%	5.60%	3.29%	4.32%
S&P 500 VaR	16.04%	10.66%	10.74%	7.96%	5.46%	5.54%	2.88%	4.25%
Forex VaR	5.62%	4.86%	4.06%	3.64%	2.63%	2.55%	1.86%	1.97%

level in the VaR estimate, and the difference is most pronounced in the S&P 500 since this has the largest negative skewness of all three risk factors. In both VaR models the forex risk is much the smallest, since the forex volatility is considerably lower than the volatility of the equity risk factors.

The next example further investigates the effect that a large negative skewness has on the normal mixture VaR estimate. It also illustrates the application of the method of moments to the estimation of the normal mixture parameters.

EXAMPLE IV.2.21: COMPARISON OF NORMAL MIXTURE AND STUDENT T LINEAR VAR

Using the daily FTSE 100 index data from 4 January 2005 to 7 April 2008 shown in Figure IV.2.10, apply the method of moments to estimate the parameters for a mixture of two normal distributions representation of the daily returns. Then, using both the maximum likelihood and the method of moments estimate of the degrees of freedom for the Student t density representation of the FTSE 100 index returns from Example IV.2.18, compare the Student t linear VaR with the normal mixture linear VaR over a 10-day horizon, at the 0.1%, 1% and 5% significance levels. Express your results as a percentage of the portfolio value.

SOLUTION   The sample moments that we want to match are shown in Table IV.2.25. The sample is of daily log returns between January 2006 and April 2008.

Table IV.2.25   Sample moments of daily returns on the FTSE 100 index

Moment	Estimate
Mean	0.012%
Standard deviation	1.097%
Skewness	−0.2577
Excess kurtosis	2.9049

The application of Solver to the problem of estimating the parameters of a mixture of two normal distributions is highly problematic. Firstly, with five parameters there would be no unique solution even if the system were linear – and the optimization problem here is highly non-linear. Secondly, we require a better optimization algorithm (such as the EM algorithm) than the simple Newton or conjugate gradient methods employed by Solver. So the user needs to 'nurse' the optimization through stages, trying to equate each moment in turn. Without going into details, I was able to match the sample and population moments to five decimal places and the resulting parameter estimates are shown in Table IV.2.26.[49]

Table IV.2.26   Normal mixture parameters for FTSE 100 returns

FTSE 100	π	μ_1	μ_2	σ_1	σ_2
Daily	0.34003	−0.124%	0.082%	1.675%	0.602%
Annual		−31.07%	20.52%	26.49%	9.52%

We now compare the results obtained using the normal mixture distribution with the Student t VaR results from Examples IV.2.18 and IV.2.19. The $100\alpha\%$ 10-day VaR estimates are displayed in Table IV.2.27, for different values of α. The Student t VaR estimates ignore the large negative skewness of the FTSE 100 returns, and as a result they tend to underestimate the VaR. The only Student t VaR estimate that exceeds the normal mixture VaR is the one based on the maximum likelihood estimate of the degrees of freedom, at the 0.1% significance level.

Table IV.2.27   Comparison of normal and Student t linear VaR

Significance level	0.1%	1%	5%
Normal mixture VaR	15.95%	11.40%	7.01%
Student t VaR (MLE)	17.76%	8.07%	5.71%
Student t VaR (MM)	14.67%	8.81%	5.40%

The final example in this section illustrates the application of a mixture of Student t distributions to the estimation of VaR, comparing the result with the normal mixture VaR. Note that we require the standardized t distribution in (IV.2.71), and Excel only has the ordinary Student t distribution function. Even this has some strange properties, so that in the example we must set[50]

$$\text{Standardized } t_\nu(x) = \begin{cases} \sqrt{\nu(\nu-2)^{-1}}\,\text{TDIST}(-x, \nu, 1), & \text{if } x \le 0, \\ 1 - \sqrt{\nu(\nu-2)^{-1}}\,\text{TDIST}(x, \nu, 1), & \text{if } x > 0. \end{cases}$$

EXAMPLE IV.2.22: COMPARISON OF NORMAL MIXTURE AND STUDENT T MIXTURE VAR

For $\alpha = 0.1\%$, 1%, 5% and 10%, compute the $100\alpha\%$ 10-day VaR of a mixture of two distributions, the first with mean 0 and volatility 20% and the second with (annualized) mean -10% and volatility 40%. The probability weight associated with the first distribution is 75% and the daily returns are assumed to be i.i.d. Compare two cases: in the first case the two component distributions are assumed to be normal, and in the second case the first component distribution is a Student t distribution with 10 degrees of freedom and the second is a Student t distribution with 5 degrees of freedom.

---

[49] These parameters differ from those shown in Table IV.2.23 not only because the estimation algorithm is different; the historical data period is also different. During the last six months of the data period for this example, the FTSE volatility increased as the index fell consistently during the credit crisis, and this period is not included in the data for the previous example.
[50] In general, if X has distribution $F(x)$ and $Y = aX$, a being a constant, then y has distribution function $a^{-1}F(x)$.

SOLUTION   In each case the implicit formula (IV.2.71) is implemented in the spreadsheet, based on the data in the question, and set up to back out the mixture VaR using Solver. Solver is reapplied to obtain both VaR estimates each time we change the significance level (or if we were to change any other parameter). The results, expressed as a percentage of the portfolio value, are summarized in Table IV.2.28. Predictably, the Student t mixture VaR is the greater at all significance levels, and the difference increases as we move to higher significance levels.

Table IV.2.28   Comparison of mixture VaR estimates

α	0.1%	1%	5%	10%
Normal mixture VaR	21.61%	14.45%	8.60%	6.33%
Student t mixture VaR	36.70%	19.73%	10.78%	7.70%

EXAMPLE IV.2.23: MIXTURE VAR IN THE PRESENCE OF AUTOCORRELATED RETURNS

Recalculate the normal mixture and Student t mixture 1% 10-day VaR estimates from the previous example when daily returns are assumed to have autocorrelation $+0.25$, and when the are assumed to have autocorrelation -0.25.

SOLUTION   The calculation proceeds as before, but instead of scaling daily returns by $\sqrt{10} = 3.1623$ for the 10-day standard deviation, we use the scale factor based on (IV.2.10). This is

$$\sqrt{10 + 2\frac{0.25}{0.75^2}[9 \times 0.75 - 0.25(1 - 0.25^9)]} = 3.97$$

when the autocorrelation is 0.25, and

$$\sqrt{10 - 2\frac{0.25}{1.25^2}[9 \times 1.25 + 0.25(1 - 0.25^9)]} = 2.51.$$

when the autocorrelation is -0.25. Using this scaling factor for the standard deviations in (IV.2.71), and then applying Solver to back out the VaR, we obtain the results for 1% 10-day VaR shown in Table IV.2.29.

Table IV.2.29   Effect of autocorrelation on mixture VaR

ϱ	−0.25	0	0.25
Normal mixture VaR	11.56%	14.45%	18.05%
Student t mixture VaR	15.76%	19.73%	24.68%

As when the distribution is normal, the effect of positive autocorrelation on non-normal parametric linear VaR will be to increase the VaR estimate, relative to the case where autocorrelation is assumed to be zero; and the opposite is the case when there is negative autocorrelation.

IV.2.9.5   Normal Mixture Risk Factor VaR

In applications of the parametric linear VaR model we use a cash-flow mapping to represent interest rate sensitive portfolios, equity portfolios are represented by a linear factor model and the log returns on commodity futures are a linear function of the log spot returns and the carry cost. Then the variance of the systematic return (i.e. the return that is explained by the risk factor mapping) is given by a quadratic form $\boldsymbol{\theta}'\boldsymbol{\Omega}\boldsymbol{\theta}$, where $\boldsymbol{\theta}$ denotes the vector of sensitivities to the risk factors and $\boldsymbol{\Omega}$ denotes the risk factor returns covariance matrix. There is only one covariance matrix and in the normal linear VaR model we assume that all risk factor returns are normally distributed.

We now extend the normal linear risk factor VaR model to the mixture framework, in the case where there are two risk factors and each marginal risk factor return distribution is a mixture of two normal components. In this case the risk factor covariance structure may be captured by four covariance matrices and the portfolio return distribution will be a mixture of four normal components.

To see why this is the case, suppose we have two risk factors X_1 and X_2 with return densities that have correlated normal mixture distributions. The marginal densities of the risk factors are

$$f_1(x_1) = \pi_1 f\left(x_1; \mu_{11}, \sigma_{11}^2\right) + (1 - \pi_1) f\left(x_1; \mu_{12}, \sigma_{12}^2\right),$$
$$f_2(x_2) = \pi_2 f\left(x_2; \mu_{21}, \sigma_{21}^2\right) + (1 - \pi_2) f\left(x_2; \mu_{22}, \sigma_{22}^2\right),$$

where $f\left(x; \mu, \sigma^2\right)$ denotes the normal density function for a random variable X with mean μ and variance σ^2. Thus, we may assume that so that each risk factor representation has

- a 'core' normal density with weight $1 - \pi_i$ in the mixture and with the lower volatility,
- a 'tail' normal density with weight π_i in the mixture and a higher volatility.

Since each risk factor return density has two normal components, their joint density is a bivariate normal mixture density of the form

$$f(x_1, x_2) = \pi_1 \pi_2 \mathbf{F}(x_1, x_2; \boldsymbol{\mu}_1, \boldsymbol{\Omega}_1) + (1 - \pi_1) \pi_2 \mathbf{F}(x_1, x_2; \boldsymbol{\mu}_2, \boldsymbol{\Omega}_2)$$
$$+ \pi_1 (1 - \pi_2) \mathbf{F}(x_1, x_2; \boldsymbol{\mu}_3, \boldsymbol{\Omega}_3) + (1 - \pi_1)(1 - \pi_2) \mathbf{F}(x_1, x_2; \boldsymbol{\mu}_4, \boldsymbol{\Omega}_4),$$

where $\mathbf{F}(x_1, x_2; \boldsymbol{\mu}, \boldsymbol{\Omega})$ is the bivariate normal density function with mean vector $\boldsymbol{\mu}$ and covariance matrix $\boldsymbol{\Omega}$ and

$$\boldsymbol{\mu}_1 = \begin{pmatrix} \mu_{11} \\ \mu_{21} \end{pmatrix}, \quad \boldsymbol{\mu}_2 = \begin{pmatrix} \mu_{12} \\ \mu_{21} \end{pmatrix}, \quad \boldsymbol{\mu}_3 = \begin{pmatrix} \mu_{11} \\ \mu_{22} \end{pmatrix}, \quad \boldsymbol{\mu}_4 = \begin{pmatrix} \mu_{12} \\ \mu_{22} \end{pmatrix},$$

$$\boldsymbol{\Omega}_1 = \begin{pmatrix} \sigma_{11}^2 & \varrho_1 \sigma_{11}\sigma_{21} \\ \varrho_1 \sigma_{11}\sigma_{21} & \sigma_{21}^2 \end{pmatrix}, \quad \boldsymbol{\Omega}_2 = \begin{pmatrix} \sigma_{12}^2 & \varrho_2 \sigma_{12}\sigma_{21} \\ \varrho_2 \sigma_{12}\sigma_{21} & \sigma_{21}^2 \end{pmatrix},$$

$$\boldsymbol{\Omega}_3 = \begin{pmatrix} \sigma_{11}^2 & \varrho_3 \sigma_{11}\sigma_{22} \\ \varrho_3 \sigma_{11}\sigma_{22} & \sigma_{22}^2 \end{pmatrix}, \quad \boldsymbol{\Omega}_4 = \begin{pmatrix} \sigma_{12}^2 & \varrho_4 \sigma_{12}\sigma_{22} \\ \varrho_4 \sigma_{12}\sigma_{22} & \sigma_{22}^2 \end{pmatrix}.$$

The covariance matrix $\boldsymbol{\Omega}_1$ represents the volatilities and correlation in the 'tails' of the two distributions and $\boldsymbol{\Omega}_4$ represents the volatilities and correlation in the 'core' of the two distributions. The other two matrices $\boldsymbol{\Omega}_2$ and $\boldsymbol{\Omega}_3$ represent the volatilities and correlation when one risk factor is in the 'core' of its distribution and the other is in the 'tail'.

Then the portfolio return will have a normal mixture distribution with four normal components and parameters given by the mixing law

$$\boldsymbol{\pi} = (\pi_1 \pi_2, (1 - \pi_1)\pi_2, \pi_1(1 - \pi_2), (1 - \pi_1)(1 - \pi_2))', \qquad \text{(IV.2.75)}$$

the component means

$$\left\{ \boldsymbol{\theta}'\boldsymbol{\mu}_1, \boldsymbol{\theta}'\boldsymbol{\mu}_2, \boldsymbol{\theta}'\boldsymbol{\mu}_3, \boldsymbol{\theta}'\boldsymbol{\mu}_4 \right\}, \qquad \text{(IV.2.76)}$$

and the component variances

$$\left\{ \boldsymbol{\theta}'\boldsymbol{\Omega}_1\boldsymbol{\theta}, \boldsymbol{\theta}'\boldsymbol{\Omega}_2\boldsymbol{\theta}, \boldsymbol{\theta}'\boldsymbol{\Omega}_3\boldsymbol{\theta}, \boldsymbol{\theta}'\boldsymbol{\Omega}_4\boldsymbol{\theta} \right\}, \qquad \text{(IV.2.77)}$$

where $\boldsymbol{\theta}$ is the vector of sensitivities of the portfolio to the two risk factors. Hence, to estimate the normal mixture VaR of the portfolio we apply Solver, or a similar numerical algorithm, to (IV.2.72) when the number of normal components is four and the mixing law, means and variances are given by (IV.2.75)–(IV.2.77).

As the number of risk factors increases, the number of components in the normal mixture distribution for the portfolio return increases. However, since the component means are different, the portfolio return may remain quite skewed and/or leptokurtic.

EXAMPLE IV.2.24: NORMAL MIXTURE VAR – RISK FACTOR LEVEL

A portfolio has two risk factors with percentage sensitivities to these risk factors of 0.8 and 1, respectively. The risk factor returns have a bivariate normal mixture distribution with the mean excess returns and volatilities shown in Table IV.2.30. Calculate the 1% 10-day VaR of the portfolio.

Table IV.2.30   Normal mixture parameters for risk factors

NM parameters	Risk factor 1	Risk factor 2	Correlations	
π	0.02	0.03		
Volatility 1	75%	65%	ϱ_1	0.3
Volatility 2	15%	18%	ϱ_2	0
Annual excess return 1	−300%	−200%	ϱ_3	0
Annual excess return 2	2%	2.5%	ϱ_4	0.8

SOLUTION   Using the data in Table IV.2.27 with the sensitivity vector $\boldsymbol{\theta} = (0.8, 1)'$ we calculate the means and variances of the four components in the normal mixture distribution of the portfolio return, using (IV.2.76) and (IV.2.77) above. Then the 1% 10-day VaR of the portfolio is calculated in the spreadsheet, using Excel Goal Seek (or Solver) to 'back out' the VaR from the formula (IV.2.72), just as in the previous examples. The result is a 1% 10-day normal mixture VaR that is 16.88% of the portfolio's value.

IV.2.10 EXPONENTIAL WEIGHTING WITH PARAMETRIC LINEAR VALUE AT RISK

Until now, when historical volatility estimates have been used they have been based on the the equally weighted unconditional variance estimate, which was introduced and illustrated in Section II.3.4. For instance, denoting the portfolio return at time t by r_t and assuming these returns are i.i.d. with zero mean, the equally weighted sample variance based on the most recent T returns is

$$\hat{\sigma}_t^2 = T^{-1} \sum_{k=1}^{T} r_{t-k}^2.$$

(IV.2.78)

If these returns are daily then our estimate at time t of the h-day standard deviation is $\hat{\sigma}_t \sqrt{h}$.[51] A formula similar to (IV.2.78) but based on cross products rather than squared returns, yields an equally weighted average covariance estimate. Dividing the covariance by the square root of the product of the two variances gives the equally weighted correlation. Since the variance and covariance of i.i.d. returns both scale with h, the correlation does not scale with the risk horizon of the returns.

Whilst equally weighted averages are useful for estimating VaR over a long term risk horizon, they have limited use for estimating VaR over a short term horizon. This is because they provide an estimate of the *unconditional* parameter, and the estimate represents only the average value of the corresponding conditional parameter over the historical sample of returns. For instance, if we use three years of data to estimate volatility, the equally weighted average represents the average sample volatility over the last three years. This may be fine for long-term VaR estimation, but short-term VaR estimates are supposed to reflect the *current* market conditions, and not the average conditions of the past three years. For this we need a forecast of the *conditional* volatility, which is time-varying, or at least we need a time-varying estimate of volatility.[52]

This section explains how the exponentially weighted moving average methodology may be used to provide more accurate short term VaR estimates than the standard equally weighted method for parameter estimation. Throughout this section all risk factors are assumed to have i.i.d. daily returns. Hence, in our empirical examples we use the square-root-of-time rule to scale VaR over different risk horizons.

IV.2.10.1 Exponentially Weighted Moving Averages

This section summarizes the EWMA statistical methodology as it is applied to estimating time series of volatilities and correlations. The EWMA methodology is described in full in Section II.3.8.1, to which readers are referred for further information.

The EWMA formula for the variance estimate at time t of a time series of returns $\{r_t\}$ is most easily expressed in a recursive form, as

$$\hat{\sigma}_t^2 = (1 - \lambda)r_{t-1}^2 + \lambda\hat{\sigma}_{t-1}^2, \quad t = 2, \ldots, T,$$

(IV.2.79)

---

[51] We often apply this square-root-of-time rule for scaling standard deviations of i.i.d. returns even when returns are not normally distributed – for instance in the Student t linear VaR model. But in that case, as we have already remarked in Section IV.2.8.1, it is only an approximation.

[52] GARCH models have time-varying conditional volatility. EWMA models give time-varying estimates of the unconditional volatility.

where λ denotes the smoothing constant, and $0 < \lambda < 1$.[53] The EWMA volatility is obtained by annualizing (IV.2.79) and taking the square root. For instance, if $\{r_t\}$ denotes a series of daily returns and there are 250 daily returns per year, then the EWMA volatility at time t is $\hat{\sigma}_t \sqrt{250}$, where $\hat{\sigma}_t^2$ is given by (IV.2.79).

Figure IV.2.12 depicts the EWMA volatility of the FTSE 100 index for two different values of the smoothing constant. This shows that the smoothing constant captures the persistence of variance from one time period to the next. The larger the value of λ, the smoother the resulting time series of variance estimates. The effect that a non-zero market return at time $t - 1$ has on the variance estimate at time t depends on $1 - \lambda$, and the lower the value of λ the more reactive the variance is to market events.

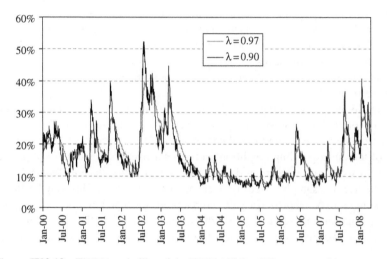

Figure IV.2.12   EWMA volatility of the FTSE 100 for different smoothing constants

Another way of viewing an EWMA estimate of volatility is as an *equally* weighted volatility estimate on *exponentially* weighted returns. That is, we multiply the return from n periods in the past by $\lambda^{(n-1)/2}$, for $n = 1, \ldots, T$ where T is the sample size. Then the EWMA variance estimate at time t is the equally weighted variance estimate based on the series $\lambda^{(n-1)/2} r_{t-n}$, $n = 1, \ldots, T$, but instead of dividing by T, we multiply by $1 - \lambda$.[54] Thus an alternative expression to (IV.2.79), valid only as $T \to \infty$, is

$$\hat{\sigma}_t^2 = (1 - \lambda)(r_{t-1}^2 + \lambda r_{t-2}^2 + \lambda^2 r_{t-3}^2 + \lambda^3 r_{t-4}^2 + \ldots). \qquad (\text{IV.2.80})$$

But since $0 < \lambda < 1$, $\lambda^k \to 0$ as $k \to \infty$, and so as returns move further into the past they will have less influence on the EWMA estimate (IV.2.80).

---

[53] The starting value σ_1^2 required for the recurrence may be set arbitrarily, or equal to r_1^2, or set to some unconditional variance for the returns.
[54] Because $1 + \lambda + \lambda^2 + \lambda^3 + \ldots = (1 - \lambda)^{-1}$.

The EWMA covariance of two contemporaneous time series of returns $\{r_{1t}\}$ and $\{r_{2t}\}$ may also be expressed in a recursive form, as

$$\hat{\sigma}_{12t} = (1 - \lambda)r_{1,t-1}r_{2,t-1} + \lambda\hat{\sigma}_{12,t-1}, \quad t = 2, \ldots, T. \tag{IV.2.81}$$

The EWMA correlation is obtained by computing three series based on the same value of the smoothing constant, two EWMA variances that are estimated using (IV.2.79) for each of the returns, and the EWMA covariance (IV.2.81). Then the covariance estimate at time t is divided by the square root of the product of the variance estimates at time t, and the result is the EWMA correlation estimate at time t.

As an example, we estimate the EWMA correlation between the NASDAQ 100 technology and S&P 500 indices, using daily log returns based on closing index prices.[55] The evolution of the two indices is depicted in Figure IV.2.13, where the effects on the NASDAQ 100 of the technology bubble at the turn of the century are clearly visible. Then, using daily log returns on the closing prices, the spreadsheet for Figure IV.2.14 computes the EWMA index volatilities for any value for the smoothing constant. For the graph shown here we have used the RiskMetrics™ daily smoothing constant of 0.94.

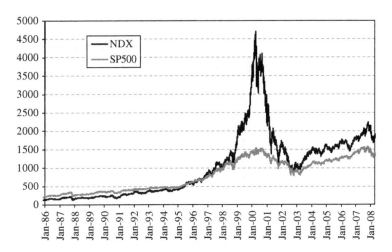

Figure IV.2.13   NASDAQ 100 and S&P 500 indices

Next we compute the daily EWMA covariance, using (IV.2.81) with the same value of λ, i.e. 0.94, for the two volatilities shown in Figures IV.2.14. Dividing this covariance by the square root of the product of the two daily variances gives the EWMA correlation. The resulting correlations are compared in Figure IV.2.15. In the spreadsheet for this figure readers may like to change the value of the smoothing constant and see the smoothing effect on the EWMA correlation as λ increases. Notice that, for any choice of λ, the average of the EWMA correlations over the sample is approximately 82%, i.e. the same as the equally weighted average correlation estimate over the entire sample.

---

[55] Data were downloaded from Yahoo! Finance, symbols ^GSPC and ^NDX.

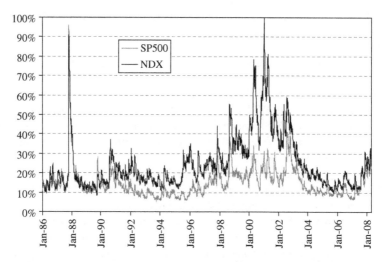

Figure IV.2.14   EWMA volatilities of NASDAQ and S&P 500 indices

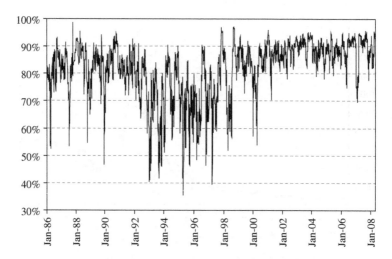

Figure IV.2.15   EWMA correlations of NASDAQ and S&P 500 indices

IV.2.10.2   EWMA VaR at the Portfolio Level

The previous subsection demonstrated that EWMA volatilities and correlations are more risk sensitive than equally weighted average estimates of the same parameters. That is, they respond more rapidly to changing market circumstances, particularly for low values of the smoothing constant λ. It is not easy to make equally weighted average parameter estimates risk sensitive, because as the sample size over which the average is taken decreases, the estimates become more seriously biased by *ghost features* of extreme market movements in the sample.[56]

---

[56] A full discussion of the reason for these ghost features, and the effects of these features on equally weighted moving average estimates, is given in Section II.3.7, and the interested reader is referred there for further information.

In this section we present some empirical examples to illustrate the effect of using EWMA on VaR estimation at the portfolio level, compared with VaR based on equally weighted estimates of the portfolio volatility. The i.i.d. normal assumption is retained, and the portfolio value is assumed to be a linear function of the prices of its assets or risk factors. Hence, the EWMA daily VaR estimate may be scaled to longer horizons using the square-root-of-time rule.[57]

Given an EWMA estimate $\hat{\sigma}_t$ of the daily standard deviation of the portfolio return or P&L at time t, when the VaR is measured, the normal linear EWMA estimate of the $100\alpha\%$ h-day VaR is[58]

$$\text{EWMA VAR}_{h,\alpha,t} = \Phi^{-1}(1-\alpha)\hat{\sigma}_t\sqrt{h}. \qquad (\text{IV.2.82})$$

We illustrate the application of this formula in the next example.

EXAMPLE IV.2.25: EWMA NORMAL LINEAR VaR FOR FTSE 100

Use an EWMA volatility series to estimate the $100\alpha\%$ 10-day normal linear VaR for a position on the FTSE 100 index on 18 April 2008. How does the choice of smoothing constant affect the result?

SOLUTION   We do not need a long period of historical data to compute the EWMA VaR. The spreadsheet for this example uses data from January 2006 until 18 April 2008, i.e. 580 daily returns.[59] The formula (IV.2.82) is implemented in the spreadsheet and the results are displayed in Table IV.2.31. In the last column we show the equally weighted VaR estimate over the whole sample of 580 observations, which is identical to the EWMA estimate with a smoothing constant of 1.

Table IV.2.31   EWMA VaR for the FTSE 100 on 18 April 2008

Significance level	Lambda			
	0.9	0.95	0.99	1
5%	7.42%	8.08%	7.81%	5.71%
1%	10.49%	11.43%	11.05%	8.07%
0.1%	13.93%	15.19%	14.86%	10.73%

As usual, all VaR estimates increase with the significance level. Also, at each significance level, each of the EWMA volatility estimates are greater than the equally weighted VaR estimate shown in the last column. This is because April 2008 was a fairly volatile period for the FTSE 100, as the effects of the credit crunch were still taking their toll on the financial sector of the UK economy. But the most interesting point to note about these results is that lower values of lambda do not necessarily give higher or lower VaR estimates, just because they use only very recent data. In fact, in our case the estimates based on $\lambda = 0.95$ are the greatest, at each significance level. This is because the FTSE 100 index was also very volatile during the

---

[57] However, we emphasize that it is not appropriate to scale an EWMA VaR to a time horizon longer than a month or so. The *raison d'être* for EWMA estimation of portfolio volatility is to capture the *current* market conditions, not a long term average.

[58] Since we do not apply EWMA VaR for long risk horizons, we can exclude the mean adjustment from the formula without much loss of accuracy.

[59] With $\lambda = 0.94$, the exponential weight on a return 580 days ago is $0.94^{290} = 0.000000016$ and even with $\lambda = 0.99$ the exponential weight on a return 580 days ago is only $0.99^{290} \approx 0.05$.

latter half of 2007, and not just in the first quarter of 2008. Of the three values used for λ, it seems that setting $\lambda = 0.95$ maximizes the total weight put on these more volatile data. Results for other values of λ and for different significance levels and risk horizons may be obtained by changing the parameters in the spreadsheet.

IV.2.10.3   RiskMetrics™ VaR Methodology

When the systematic VaR of a large portfolio is disaggregated into stand-alone or marginal component VaRs, we could base the systematic VaR on the normal linear VaR formula (IV.2.15). For a short-term VaR estimate to be more risk sensitive, the covariance matrix in this formula may be based on an EWMA covariance matrix, instead of using equally weighted averages of squared returns and their cross products. However, unless we apply the orthogonal EWMA methodology, which is described in Section II.3.8.7, the smoothing constant must be the *same* for the variance and covariance estimates in the matrix. Otherwise the matrix need not be positive semi-definite.[60]

The RiskMetrics group provides daily estimates of volatilities and correlations, summarized in three very large covariance matrices, with risk factors that include most commodities, government bonds, money markets, swaps, foreign exchange and equity indices for over 40 currencies. The three covariance matrices provided by the RiskMetrics group are as follows:[61]

1. *Regulatory matrix.* An equally weighted average matrix based on the last 250 days.
2. *Daily matrix.* An EWMA covariance matrix with $\lambda = 0.94$ for all elements.
3. *Monthly matrix.* An EWMA covariance matrix with $\lambda = 0.97$ for all elements and then multiplied by 25.[62]

In addition, the group provides VaR software based on these data and a number of documents, including a technical document, which describes its portfolio mapping procedures and the VaR methodology.

In the next example we use a portfolio of US stocks in the S&P 500 and NASDAQ 100 indices to illustrate the application of the RiskMetrics methodology and the decomposition of systematic VaR into stand-alone components.

EXAMPLE IV.2.26: COMPARISON OF RISKMETRICS™ REGULATORY AND EWMA VAR

Consider a large portfolio of US stocks having a percentage beta with respect to the S&P 500 index of 1.1 and a percentage beta with respect to the NASAQ 100 index of 0.85. Assume that $3 million is invested in the S&P 500 stocks and $1 million is invested in the NASDAQ 100 stocks. Compare the 1% 10-day normal VaR of this portfolio on 18 April 2008, based on the RiskMetrics regulatory matrix and based on the daily matrix, and in each case disaggregate the VaR into S&P 500 and NASDAQ 100 stand-alone VaR.

SOLUTION   We use the data shown in Figure IV.2.16, starting on 3 January 2006 and ending on 18 April 2008.[63] The NASDAQ 100 index is on the left-hand scale and the S&P index is on the right-hand scale.

---

[60] The reasons why correlation and covariance matrices must be positive definite are described in Section I.2.4.
[61] The methodology used to construct these matrices is described in full and illustrated in Section II.3.8.6.
[62] That is, using the square-root-of-time rule and assuming 25 days per month.
[63] Since 0.97^{250} is less than 0.0005, 500 data points are adequate, and we have 576 daily returns.

Figure IV.2.16   NASDAQ 100 and S&P 500 indices, 2006–2008

The EWMA variances and covariances are estimated as explained above, but we are not interested in a time series of variances and covariances, only in the covariance matrix on 18 April 2006, because we are only estimating VaR on this day. The volatilities and correlation estimated on 18 April 2006, based on an EWMA with $\lambda = 0.94$ and based on an equally weighted average of the last 250 returns, are shown in Table IV.2.32, and the resulting annual covariance matrices are shown in Table IV.2.33. Note that the US was still very much feeling the effects of the credit crisis in April 2008 and so, being based on more recent data, the EWMA volatilities and correlations are higher than the RiskMetrics regulatory estimates.

Table IV.2.32   Volatilities of and correlation between S&P 500 and NASAQ 100 indices

	S&P 500 volatility	NDX volatility	Correlation
EWMA	22.81%	28.03%	94.91%
Regulatory	19.63%	22.89%	89.88%

Table IV.2.33   Annual covariance matrix based on Table IV.2.32

	S&P 500	NDX
EWMA		
S&P 500	0.05205	0.06069
NDX	0.06069	0.07857
Regulatory		
S&P 500	0.03853	0.04038
NDX	0.04038	0.05239

The spreadsheet for this example implements the normal linear VaR formula (IV.2.15) where $\boldsymbol{\Omega}_h$ is the h-day matrix that is derived from the relevant annual matrix in Table IV.2.33, using the square-root-of-time rule, and $\boldsymbol{\theta}$ is the vector of nominal portfolio betas, that is,

($3.3m, $0.85m)'. We assume the excess return on each index is zero. Since θ is expressed in value terms, the VaR will also be expressed in value terms.

The stand-alone VaRs are estimated using the individual volatilities shown in Table IV.2.32, each scaled to a 10-day standard deviation using the square-root-of-time rule. Since both volatility estimates are lower when based on an equally weighted average over the last 250 days, we expect the stand-alone VaRs to be lower when they are based on the regulatory matrix. However, since the regulatory correlation estimate is also lower, the total systematic VaR could be greater than or less than the corresponding EWMA estimate, depending on the portfolio composition. The results for the portfolio given in the question are shown in Table IV.2.34.[64]

Table IV.2.34   RiskMetrics VaR for US stock portfolio

	Stand-alone VaR		Systematic VaR
	S&P 500	NDX	Total
EWMA	$350,284	$110,852	$456,833
Regulatory	$301,377	$90,522	$384,789

In both cases the sum of the stand-alone VaRs exceeds the total systematic VaR, due to the usual diversification effect in the total VaR. However, since the two risk factors have a high correlation, this diversification effect is small. Both stand-alone VaRs, and the total VaR estimate, are greater when based on the EWMA covariance matrix, because this captures the current, more volatile market circumstances, whereas the regulatory covariance matrix is based on an average over 1 year.

The Basel regulations that were introduced in 1996, specified that internal models which are used to calculate the market risk capital requirements must use at least 250 days of historical data. Hence the EWMA methodology, which effectively uses less than 250 days, due to the exponential weighting of returns, has been disallowed. However, following the credit crisis, in July 2008 the Basel Committee proposed extra capital charges for equity and credit spread risks, precisely because the use of 250 days or more of historical data is now thought to produce VaR estimates that are insufficiently risk sensitive. It is unfortunate that the Committee took so long to realise this fact. It is also unfortunate that the Committee believe that imposing additional capital charges is the appropriate response to the credit and banking crises.

IV.2.11   EXPECTED TAIL LOSS (CONDITIONAL VAR)

Section IV.1.8.2 introduced *expected tail loss*, also called *conditional VaR*. The ETL is defined by (IV.1.32) and its interpretation is the expected loss (in present value terms) given that the loss exceeds the VaR. The ETL risk metric is more informative than VaR, because VaR does not measure the extent of exceptional losses. VaR merely states a level of loss that we are reasonably sure will not be exceeded: it tells us nothing about how much could be lost if VaR is exceeded. However, ETL tells us how much we expect to lose, given than the VaR is exceeded. Clearly ETL gives a fuller description of the risks of a portfolio than just reporting the VaR

---

[64] Readers may change the portfolio composition in the spreadsheet and see the effect on the VaR.

alone. Since ETL is also a coherent risk metric (see Section IV.1.8.3) ETL is sub-additive even when VaR is not.[65] This means that ETL is a better risk metric to use for regulatory and economic capital allocation, a subject that we shall return to in Chapter 8.

We now present a mathematical description of ETL. Let X denote the discounted h-day return, and set

$$\mathrm{VaR}_{h,\alpha} = -x_\alpha,$$

where x_α denotes the α quantile of the distribution of X, i.e. $P(X < x_\alpha) = \alpha$. The definition of ETL, when it is expressed as a percentage of the portfolio value, is

$$\mathrm{ETL}_\alpha(X) = -E(X \mid X < x_\alpha).$$

Since the ETL is a conditional expectation, it is obtained by dividing the probability weighted average of the values of X that are less than x_α by $P(X < x_\alpha)$. But $P(X < x_\alpha) = \alpha$ so if X has density function $f(x)$ then

$$\mathrm{ETL}_\alpha(X) = -\alpha^{-1} \int_{-\infty}^{x_\alpha} x f(x)\, dx. \tag{IV.2.83}$$

In this section we derive formulae for ETL when VaR is estimated using the parametric linear model, beginning with the normal linear model and then extending this to Student t linear ETL, to normal mixture linear ETL and to Student t mixture ETL. We shall express the ETL as a percentage of portfolio value throughout.

IV.2.11.1 ETL in the Normal Linear VaR Model

Let the random variable X denote a portfolio's discounted h-day return. If $X \sim N(\mu_h, \sigma_h^2)$ then

$$\mathrm{ETL}_{h,\alpha}(X) = \alpha^{-1} \varphi\big(\Phi^{-1}(\alpha)\big)\, \sigma_h - \mu_h, \tag{IV.2.84}$$

where φ and Φ denote the standard normal density and distribution functions. Hence, $\Phi^{-1}(\alpha)$ is the α quantile of the standard normal distribution and $\varphi(\Phi^{-1}(\alpha))$ is the height of the standard normal density at this point.

To prove (IV.2.84) we first calculate the ETL of a standard normal variable Z. Since the standard normal density function is

$$\varphi(z) = \frac{1}{\sqrt{2\pi}} \exp\left(-\tfrac{1}{2}z^2\right),$$

we have

$$\mathrm{ETL}_\alpha(Z) = -\alpha^{-1} \int_{-\infty}^{\Phi^{-1}(\alpha)} z\varphi(z)dz = -\left(\sqrt{2\pi}\,\alpha\right)^{-1} \int_{-\infty}^{\Phi^{-1}(\alpha)} z \exp\left(-\tfrac{1}{2}z^2\right) dz$$

$$= \alpha^{-1} \left[\frac{1}{\sqrt{2\pi}} \exp\left(-\tfrac{1}{2}z^2\right)\right]_{-\infty}^{\Phi^{-1}(\alpha)} = \alpha^{-1} \varphi\big(\Phi^{-1}(\alpha)\big). \tag{IV.2.85}$$

---

[65] When VaR is estimated using historical or Monte Carlo simulation, it need not be sub-additive.

Now we use the standard normal transformation to write X in the form

$$X = Z\sigma_h + \mu_h, \quad Z \sim N(0, 1).$$

By the definition (IV.2.83) of ETL,[66]

$$ETL_{h,\alpha}(X) = ETL_\alpha(Z)\sigma_h - \mu_h$$

and this proves (IV.2.84).

EXAMPLE IV.2.27: NORMAL ETL

Suppose a portfolio is expected to return the risk free rate with a volatility of 30%. Assuming the returns are i.i.d., find the 1% 10-day parametric linear VaR and ETL as a percentage of the portfolio's value.

SOLUTION   The 10-day standard deviation is $0.3 \times \sqrt{10/250} = 0.3/5 = 0.06$. So the 1% 10-day normal ETL is

$$ETL_{10,0.01}(X_{10}) = 0.01^{-1}\varphi(Z_{0.01}) \times 0.06 = 0.06 \times \varphi(2.32635) = 15.99\%.$$

That is, the 1% 10-day normal ETL is about 16% of the portfolio's value. This should be compared with the 1% 10-day normal linear VaR, which is only 13.96% of the portfolio's value. By definition, the ETL is always at least as great as the corresponding VaR, and often it is much greater than the VaR.

IV.2.11.2   ETL in the Student t Linear VaR Model

Again let the random variable X denote a portfolio's discounted h-day return. In this section we show that if X has a Student t distribution with mean μ_h, standard deviation σ_h and ν degrees of freedom then

$$ETL_{h,\alpha,\nu}(X) = \alpha^{-1}(\nu - 1)^{-1}(\nu - 2 + x_\alpha(\nu)^2)f_\nu(x_\alpha(\nu))\sigma_h - \mu_h, \quad \text{(IV.2.86)}$$

where $x_\alpha(\nu)$ denotes the α quantile of the standardized Student t distribution (i.e. the one with zero mean and unit variance) having ν degrees of freedom, and $f_\nu(x_\alpha(\nu))$ is the value of its density function at that point. The standardized Student t density function is derived in Section I.3.3.7 as

$$f_\nu(x) = ((\nu - 2)\pi)^{-1/2}\Gamma\left(\frac{\nu}{2}\right)^{-1}\Gamma\left(\frac{\nu+1}{2}\right)\left(1 + (\nu - 2)^{-1}x^2\right)^{-(1+\nu)/2}. \quad \text{(IV.2.87)}$$

The result (IV.2.86) follows if we can prove that the ETL in a standardized Student t distribution with ν degrees of freedom is given by

$$ETL_{h,\alpha,\nu}(T) = \alpha^{-1}(\nu - 1)^{-1}(\nu - 2 + x_\alpha(\nu)^2)f_\nu(x_\alpha(\nu)), \quad \text{(IV.2.88)}$$

---

[66] Note that we subtract μ because of the minus sign in the definition of ETL.

where T denotes a standardized Student t variable with ν degrees of freedom. By the definition (IV.2.83) of ETL, we need to evaluate

$$\int\limits_{-\infty}^{x_\alpha(\nu)} x f_\nu(x)\, dx.$$

To shorten our notation, note that we may write (IV.2.87) more briefly as

$$f_\nu(x) = A\left(1 + ax^2\right)^b,$$

where

$$A = \left((\nu-2)\pi\right)^{-1/2}\Gamma(\nu/2)^{-1}\Gamma\left((\nu+1)/2\right), a = \left(\nu-2\right)^{-1} \text{ and } b = -(1+\nu)/2.$$

Then,

$$\int\limits_{-\infty}^{x_\alpha(\nu)} x f_\nu(x)\, dx = A\int\limits_{-\infty}^{x_\alpha(\nu)} x(1+ax^2)^b\, dx = \frac{A}{2a}\int\limits_{-\infty}^{B} y^b dy,$$

where we have set $y = 1 + ax^2$ and $B = 1 + (\nu-2)^{-1}x_\alpha(\nu)^2$. Then

$$\int\limits_{-\infty}^{B} y^b\, dy = \frac{B^{b+1}}{b+1} = \frac{2B^{(1-\nu)/2}}{1-\nu}$$

and

$$A = f_\nu\left(x_\alpha(\nu)\right)B^{(1+\nu)/2}.$$

So

$$\int\limits_{-\infty}^{x_\alpha(\nu)} x f_\nu(x)\, dx = \frac{f_\nu\left(x_\alpha(\nu)\right)B^{(1+\nu)/2}}{2(\nu-2)^{-1}} \times \frac{2B^{(1-\nu)/2}}{1-\nu} = -(\nu-1)^{-1}(\nu-2)Bf_\nu\left(x_\alpha(\nu)\right).$$

Now substituting in the above for B and using (IV.2.83) yields (IV.2.88).

EXAMPLE IV.2.28: STUDENT T DISTRIBUTED ETL

As in the previous example, suppose that a portfolio is expected to return the risk free rate with a volatility of 30%, but now suppose that its returns are i.i.d. with a Student t distribution with ν degrees of freedom. Find the 1% 10-day Student t VaR and ETL, as a percentage of the portfolio's value, for $\nu = 5, 10, 15, 20$ and 25.

SOLUTION   We base the calculations in the spreadsheet on (IV.2.63) for the VaR, and (IV.2.88) for the ETL. Thus we calculate the standardized t ETL, and transform the standardized t ETL to obtain the ETL for our return distribution using (IV.2.86). The results are summarized in Table IV.2.35 and, for comparison, the last column of this table reports the normal VaR and ETL for the same portfolio, with the results obtained from the previous example. For highly leptokurtic distributions (i.e. for low values for the degrees of freedom) the ETL is far greater than the VaR. For instance, the ETL is almost twice as large as the VaR

Table IV.2.35 VaR and ETL for Student t distributions

v	5	10	15	20	25	∞ (Normal)
VaR	15.64%	14.83%	14.54%	14.39%	14.30%	13.96%
ETL	20.69%	18.05%	17.30%	16.94%	16.74%	15.99%

under the t_5 distribution. But as the degrees of freedom increase, the Student t distribution converges to the normal distribution, so VaR and ETL converge toward to the normal VaR and ETL.

IV.2.11.3   ETL in the Normal Mixture Linear VaR Model

First suppose that a portfolio's discounted h-day return X has a normal mixture distribution G_0 with *zero* means in the components where

$$\boldsymbol{\pi} = (\pi_1, \ldots, \pi_n)$$

is the mixing law and the component variances are $\sigma_h^2 = (\sigma_{1h}^2, \ldots, \sigma_{nh}^2)$. We set

$$x_\alpha = G_0^{-1}(\alpha)$$

so that $-x_\alpha$ is the $100\alpha\%$ h-day VaR under the zero-mean normal mixture. Write the density function as $\sum_{i=1}^{n} \pi_i f_i(x)$, where each $f_i(x)$ is a zero-mean normal density with standard deviation σ_{ih}. Then, by extending the argument used in the normal case, we have

$$\text{ETL}_{h,\alpha}(X) = -\alpha^{-1} \sum_{i=1}^{n} \pi_i \int_{-\infty}^{x_\alpha} x f_i(x) dx.$$

Using an argument similar to that in (IV.2.85), it can be shown that

$$\int_{-\infty}^{x_\alpha} x f_i(x) \, dx = -\sigma_{ih} \varphi\left(\sigma_{ih}^{-1} x_\alpha\right),$$

where φ is the standard normal density function. Hence, we have

$$\text{ETL}_{h,\alpha}(X) = \alpha^{-1} \sum_{i=1}^{n} \left(\pi_i \sigma_{ih} \varphi(\sigma_{ih}^{-1} x_\alpha)\right).$$

Now suppose a portfolio's discounted h-day is expected to return are represented by a mixture of n normal distributions with distribution function G. That is, $X \sim \text{NM}(\boldsymbol{\pi}, \boldsymbol{\mu}_h, \sigma_h^2)$, where $\boldsymbol{\pi}$ and σ_h^2 are defined above and the component means are $\boldsymbol{\mu}_h = (\mu_{1h}, \ldots, \mu_{nh})$. Then the expected value of the normal mixture is $\sum_{i=1}^{n} \pi_i \mu_{ih}$ and, again by extending the argument used in the normal case, we have

$$\text{ETL}_{h,\alpha}(X) = \alpha^{-1} \sum_{i=1}^{n} (\pi_i \sigma_{ih} \varphi(\sigma_{ih}^{-1} x_\alpha)) - \sum_{i=1}^{n} \pi_i \mu_{ih}, \tag{IV.2.89}$$

where $-x_\alpha$ is the $100\alpha\%$ h-day VaR under the corresponding *zero-mean* normal mixture.

EXAMPLE IV.2.29: NORMAL MIXTURE ETL

As in Examples IV.2.27 and IV.2.28, suppose that a portfolio is expected to return the risk free rate with a volatility of 30%, but now suppose that its returns are i.i.d. with a normal mixture distribution with discounted mean returns of zero, but with two normal components having different volatilities: with probability 0.2 the volatility is 60% and with probability 0.8 the volatility is 15%. Find the 1% 10-day normal mixture VaR and ETL as a percentage of the portfolio's value.

SOLUTION   We remark that the volatility of the normal mixture is the same as that in the previous two examples, since

$$\sqrt{0.2 \times 0.6^2 + 0.8 \times 0.15^2} = 30\%.$$

Hence, we can compare the results with those in the previous examples for the normal and Student t ETL. First the spreadsheet uses Excel Solver or Goal Seek optimizer to back out the 1% 10-day normal mixture VaR using formula (IV.2.72). The normal mixture VaR is 19.74% of the portfolio's value. This is significantly greater than the normal VaR found in Example IV.2.27.

The normal mixture ETL is also much greater than the normal ETL derived in Example IV.2.27. A volatility of 60% corresponds to a 10-day standard deviation of 0.12 and a volatility of 15% corresponds to a 10-day standard deviation of 0.03. Thus, applying (IV.2.89), we have

$$\text{ETL}_\alpha(X) = 0.01^{-1}\left(0.2 \times \varphi\left(-\frac{0.1974}{0.12}\right) \times 0.12 + 0.8 \times \varphi\left(-\frac{0.1974}{0.03}\right) \times 0.03\right) = 24.75\%$$

So under the normal mixture distribution with an overall volatility of 30%, the 1% 10-day ETL is nearly 25% of the portfolio value, compared with approximately 16% if the distribution were normal with volatility 30%.

IV.2.11.4   ETL under a Mixture of Student t Distributions

It can be shown that when the return distribution is assumed to be a mixture of Student t distributions with different means, variances and degrees of freedom as in Section IV.5.2.7, then[67]

$$\text{ETL}_{h,\alpha,\mathbf{v}}(X) = \alpha^{-1}\sum_{i=1}^{n}\left(\pi_i(\nu_i - 1)^{-1}\left(\nu_i - 2 + t_{i\alpha}(\mathbf{v})^2\right)f_{\nu_i}(t_{i\alpha}(\mathbf{v}))\sigma_{ih}\right) - \sum_{i=1}^{n}\pi_i\mu_i, \qquad \text{(IV.2.90)}$$

where

$$t_{i\alpha}(\mathbf{v}) = x_\alpha(\mathbf{v})\nu_i^{-1}(\nu_i - 2)\sigma_{ih}^{-1}$$

and $x_\alpha(\mathbf{v})$ is minus the Student t mixture VaR. Here $\mathbf{v}$ denotes the vector of degrees of freedom for each component in the mixture. The next example illustrates the implementation of this formula, and compares the results with those in the previous examples.

---

[67] The details of this calculation are lengthy and are therefore omitted, but the arguments are similar to those used to derive the Student t ETL and the normal mixture ETL in the previous subsections.

EXAMPLE IV.2.30: STUDENT *T* MIXTURE ETL

As in Examples IV.2.27–IV.2.29, suppose that a portfolio is expected to return the risk free rate with a volatility of 30%, but now suppose that its is expected to return are i.i.d. with a Student *t* mixture distribution. Both Student *t* distributed components have a discounted mean return of zero, but the two components have different volatilities and degrees of freedom: with probability 0.2 the distribution has 5 degrees of freedom and a volatility of 45% and with probability 0.8 the distribution has 10 degrees of freedom and volatility of 25%.[68] Find the $100\alpha\%$ h-day VaR and ETL as a percentage of the portfolio's value for $\alpha = 0.1\%$ and 1% and $h = 1$ and 10. Compare your results with those obtained above, using a normal, normal mixture and individual Student *t* distributions.

SOLUTION   Table IV.2.36 compares the $100\alpha\%$ h-day VaR and ETL from all the distributions considered in these examples, for the different values of α and h.[69] The normal VaR and ETL are the smallest, which is as expected, due to the high significance level of the VaR and the leptokurtic nature of the other distributions. Comparing the normal mixture with the individual Student *t* estimates, the normal mixture VaR exceeds both the Student *t* VaR estimates, but the normal mixture ETL estimates lie between the two Student *t* ETL estimates. Although greater than the ETL estimates based on 10 degrees of freedom, the normal mixture ETL is substantially less than the Student *t* ETL with 5 degrees of freedom.[70] The Student *t* mixture VaR is less than the normal mixture VaR at the 1% level, but greater than the normal mixture VaR at the 0.1% level, and the Student *t* mixture ETL is greater than the normal mixture ETL at both the 1% and 0.1% levels.

Table IV.2.36   VaR and ETL for normal, Student *t* and mixture distributions

$h = 1$		Normal	t_{10}	t_5	NM	t Mixture
$\alpha = 1\%$	VaR	4.41%	4.69%	4.95%	6.24%	6.05%
	ETL	5.06%	6.33%	9.57%	7.83%	9.16%
$\alpha = 0.1\%$	VaR	5.86%	7.03%	8.66%	9.78%	11.51%
	ETL	6.39%	9.46%	17.48%	10.97%	23.92%
$h = 10$		Normal	t_{10}	t_5	NM	t Mixture
$\alpha = 1\%$	VaR	13.96%	14.83%	15.64%	19.74%	19.15%
	ETL	15.99%	20.00%	30.26%	24.75%	28.96%
$\alpha = 0.1\%$	VaR	18.54%	22.24%	27.39%	30.91%	36.39%
	ETL	20.20%	29.91%	55.28%	34.68%	75.62%

The above example shows that it is not only the excess kurtosis that determines the ETL: it is also very much influenced by the tail behaviour. The tails of a normal mixture distribution

---

[68] With this choice the square root of the probability weighted sum of the variances is 30%, so the overall volatility is similar to that in the previous examples. Readers may like to change the volatilities in the spreadsheet to 60% and 15%, to compare the result with the previous example (remembering to reapply Solver each time the parameters are changed). Clearly both VaR and ETL will be much greater than even the normal mixture VaR and ETL, due to the leptokurtosis of the component distributions.

[69] The results for the normal, individual Student *t* and normal mixtures are obtained using the spreadsheets from the previous examples, and for the individual Student *t* VaR estimates we assume the volatility is 30%.

[70] This happens even though the excess kurtosis in the Student *t* distribution with 5 degrees of freedom is 6, whereas that of the normal mixture is 6.75.

decline exponentially, but the tails of a Student t distribution decline more slowly than this. Hence, when the two distributions have similar excess kurtosis, the normal mixture ETL will be lower than the Student t ETL.

IV.2.12   CASE STUDY: CREDIT SPREAD PARAMETRIC LINEAR VALUE AT RISK AND ETL

We end the chapter with a short case study on estimating VaR and ETL for a highly non-normal and autocorrelated risk factor. The purpose of the study is to highlight the huge *model risk* that arises from the choice of VaR model. That is, we show that very different VaR estimates can be obtained even when we fix the same:

- broad methodology – i.e. the VaR estimates are based on different parametric linear VaR models;
- sample data – we shall use the same sample for all estimates;
- risk factor model – we consider the VaR and ETL from an exposure to a single credit spread risk factor.

IV.2.12.1   The iTraxx Europe Index

The risk factor we have chosen for this study is the iTraxx Europe 5-year index. In June 2004 the iBoxx and Trac-x *credit default swap* (CDS) indices merged to form the Dow Jones iTraxx index family, which consists of the most liquid single-name credit default swaps in the European and Asian markets. As well as representing an important risk factor for interest rate sensitive portfolios, the iTraxx indices for maturities of 3, 5, 7 and 10 years are traded over the counter (OTC), the 5- and 10-year maturities being the most liquid. Also, many major banks have been entering OTC trades on iTraxx options during the last few years. Their clients include hedge funds, proprietary trading desks, insurance companies, investment managers and index CDS traders who use options for the risk management of their positions. In March 2007 Eurex, the world's largest derivative exchange, launched exchange traded futures and will soon introduce other credit derivative products on iTraxx indices.

The main Europe index series, which is shown in Figure IV.2.17, is an equally weighted CDS spread, measured in basis points, and based on 125 single firm investment grade CDSs. Every six months a new series for each of the iTraxx indices is introduced in which defaulted, merged, sector changed or downgraded entities are replaced by the next most liquid ones. We splice the older series together with the most recent series to produce the data shown in the figure.

Figure IV.2.17 shows the iTraxx index's evolution, and its daily changes between 21 June 2004 and 10 April 2008.[71] The effects of the credit crunch that was precipitated by the sub-prime mortgage crisis in the US in the latter half of 2007 are clearly visible. In June 2007 credit spreads were at a historical low, having been trending down for several years. However, by mid-March 2008, with the onset of the crisis, the iTraxx Europe spread for investment

---

[71] The index itself is depicted by the black line and is measured on the right-hand scale, while the grey line, measured on the left-hand scale, represents the daily changes in the index. All units are basis points.

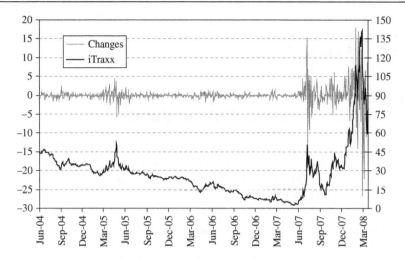

Figure IV.2.17   iTraxx Europe 5-year index

grade CDSs rose from less than 3 basis points to an unprecedented high of over 140 basis points. Then, by the beginning of April 2008, the index fell to less than 60 basis points.

Table IV.2.37 shows the sample statistics, with approximate standard errors, and the ratio of the statistic to its standard error, based on all 970 data points. All statistics except the mean appear to be highly significant, and in particular we have significant negative skewness, positive excess kurtosis and positive autocorrelation.

Table IV.2.37   Sample statistics for iTraxx Europe 5-year index

Sample statistics	Estimate	Standard error	Ratio
Mean	0.0242	0.0772	0.31
Standard deviation	2.4037	0.0012	1940
Skewness	−1.4356	0.1926	−7.45
Excess kurtosis	36.9630	0.7706	47.97
Autocorrelation	0.1079	0.03192	3.38

The annualized volatility of the index depends on the assumption made about the dynamics. Based on the i.i.d. assumption, it is

$$\sqrt{250} \times 2.4037 = 38 \text{ basis points per annum.}$$

But the autocorrelation of 0.1079 is positive and significant, and using the autocorrelation adjusted scaling factor (IV.2.10) we obtain a higher volatility, of

$$\sqrt{298} \times 2.4037 = 41.5 \text{ basis points per annum.}$$

Thus we expect that when the sample autocorrelation is taken into account the VaR and ETL estimates will be higher than when we assume the daily changes are i.i.d.

IV.2.12.2   VaR Estimates

We shall estimate the VaR and ETL for a simple linear exposure, with a PV01 of €1000, to the daily changes in the iTraxx Europe 5-year index. Using the PV01 approximation described in Section IV.2.3.2, we see that this represents a cash flow at 5 years of approximately €2.5 million.

Different VaR and ETL estimates will be based on the normal, Student t and normal mixture models that we have introduced in this chapter. Our focus is on the model risk arising from the choice of risk factor distribution, so we shall base all the estimates on the same, objective sample data. That is, we use all the data on iTraxx index changes shown in Figure IV.2.17. There are 970 daily changes, covering almost 4 years.

When estimating the 1% 10-day VaR and ETL, we consider two assumptions about the index dynamics: that daily changes are (a) i.i.d. and (b) autocorrelated. Thus, using exactly the same data in each case, we obtain six different estimates of the parametric linear VaR and six corresponding estimates of the ETL, over a risk horizon of 10 days and at the 99% confidence level.

The estimation of the model parameters is based on the method of moments. For the Student t degrees of freedom we follow Example IV.2.18, and for normal mixture parameters we use the same methodology as that described in Section IV.2.8.3 and applied in Example IV.2.21.[72] The method of moments estimate of the Student t degrees of freedom is 4.1623, which matches the sample excess kurtosis of 36.963. But note that the skewness is assumed to be zero under the Student t distribution.

The mixture distribution assumes only two components, one to represent the stable downward trending regime which prevailed most of the time prior to the credit crisis, and another to represent the volatile regime where credit spreads have the tendency to jump up rapidly and jump down even more rapidly. The estimated parameters, quoted in basis points per annum, are displayed in Table IV.2.38.[73]

Table IV.2.38   Normal mixture parameter estimates: iTraxx Europe 5-year index

π	μ_1	μ_2	σ_1	σ_2
0.06483	−308.92	27.86	142.47	10.36

The VaR and ETL estimates are obtained in the spreadsheet labelled 'VaR and ETL' in the case study workbook, using the methodology described in Sections IV.2.2 and IV.2.8, and the results are summarized in Table IV.2.39. The VaR estimates range from €17,683 for the normal i.i.d. VaR model, to €43,784 for the normal mixture model with the autocorrelation adjustment. Similarly, the ETL estimates range from €20,259 for the normal i.i.d. VaR model, to €48,556 for the Student t model with the autocorrelation adjustment.

All the estimates are based on exactly the same data, but the assumptions made by the normal i.i.d. model are clearly not justified for the daily changes in the iTraxx index. The normal i.i.d. VaR model ignores not only the autocorrelation, but also the large negative skewness

---

[72] We do not consider the Student t mixture since the parameters for this distribution need to be estimated by the *EM algorithm*, which is beyond the scope of Excel. See Section I.5.4.3 for further details.

[73] We have used square-root-of-time scaling to quote these parameters in annual terms in the table.

Table IV.2.39   VaR and ETL estimates for iTraxx Europe 5-year index

	VaR	ETL
Normal		
i.i.d.	€17,683	€20,259
Autocorrelation	€19,151	€21,941
Student t		
i.i.d.	€20,287	€44,814
Autocorrelation	€21,991	€48,556
Normal mixture		
i.i.d.	€41,375	€43,876
Autocorrelation	€43,784	€47,522

and the extremely high excess kurtosis (of almost 37 – see Table IV.2.37); instead both are assumed to be zero.

The Student t model has a high ETL, like the normal mixture model, but the VaR estimates based on the Student t distribution are much lower than those from the normal mixture. This is because the large negative skewness, which is ignored by the Student t model and is only captured by the normal mixture model, increases the VaR significantly.

The model that makes the most appropriate assumptions is the autocorrelated normal mixture model. This is able to capture all the features of the data, and in particular, it captures the two different regimes in credit spreads during the data period. Therefore the VaR and ETL estimates based on this model are, amongst all the estimates reported in Table IV.2.39, the most representative of the historical sample.

IV.2.13   SUMMARY AND CONCLUSIONS

The parametric linear VaR model is applicable to all portfolios except those containing options, or any other instruments with non-linear price functions. If we assume the portfolio returns have either a *normal distribution* or a *Student t distribution* it is possible to derive VaR as an explicit solution to an analytic formula. It is also possible to back out the VaR from a formula, using a simple numerical algorithm (such as Excel's Goal Seek or Solver) under the assumption that the portfolio return has a *mixture* of normal or Student t distributions. All these formulae, and the corresponding ETL formulae, have been derived in this chapter, and we have provided a very large number of numerical examples and empirical illustrations based on different types of linear portfolios.

The analytic VaR formulae hold for any confidence level and over any risk horizon. The general formulae contain an adjustment for the case where the portfolio is expected to grow at a rate different from the discount rate, but this adjustment is very small except for long risk horizons and when a portfolio has an expected return very different from the discount rate.

We do not need to assume the returns are i.i.d. It is also possible to adjust the general parametric linear VaR formula to account for *autocorrelation* in log returns. When the daily log returns are autocorrelated an adjustment needs to be made to the h-day standard deviation. No adjustment is required for the discounted expected return, if this is included in the VaR estimate. With positive or negative autocorrelation the h-day standard deviation is no longer $\sqrt{h}\,\sigma$, where σ is the standard deviation of daily log returns, but $\sqrt{\tilde{h}}\,\sigma$ where $\tilde{h} > h$ for positively autocorrelated daily log returns and $\tilde{h} < h$ for negatively autocorrelated daily log returns. Hence positive or negative autocorrelation can result in a significant increase or decrease in h-day VaR, even for short risk horizons.

When the portfolio has a discounted expected return of zero, parametric linear VaR behaves like volatility and so its aggregation rule can be derived from the rule for the variance of a sum. We first examined the disaggregation of the total VaR of a portfolio into a *systematic VaR* component that is explained by the mapping to risk factors, and a *specific VaR* or residual component. Our empirical examples here focused on the decomposition of the VaR for a stock portfolio into the systematic VaR due to the market risk factors, and a residual VaR.

Further, systematic VaR can be decomposed in two different ways. The first is the decomposition of systematic VaR into *stand-alone VaR* components that are due to each type of risk factor. Thus we have equity VaR, interest rate VaR, credit spread VaR, forex VaR, commodity VaR, and so forth. The stand-alone VaRs represent the risk taken by each individual trading activity without allowing for any diversification effects from other trading activities in the same firm. But when we measure VaR at an aggregate level, we take account of diversification. Hence, the sum of the stand-alone VaRs is not equal to the total systematic VaR. In fact, when VaR is measured by the parametric linear model, the sum of the stand-alone VaRs is always greater than or equal to the total systematic VaR. That is, parametric linear VaR is sub-additive. We have also shown how the total systematic VaR can be decomposed into *marginal VaR* components which are additive. Thus marginal VaRs are useful for the allocation of real capital which (unlike regulatory or economic capital) must be additive.

In the context of the normal linear VaR model we have derived simple formulae that may be applied to estimate the stand-alone and marginal VaR, and the corresponding ETL, for any given risk factor class. Another formula which, like marginal VaR, is based on the gradient vector, is derived for the *incremental VaR* that measures the impact of a small trade on the VaR of a given, large portfolio.

The normal linear VaR model can be extended to the case where the portfolio's returns, or the risk factor returns, have leptokurtic and skewed distributions. We have derived formulae for Student t distributed VaR, for normal mixture VaR and for Student t mixture distributed VaR. The mixture linear VaR models result in an implicit rather than an explicit formula for VaR. They provide an ideal framework for scenario VaR in the presence of two or more possible regimes, or states of the world. In Section IV.7.2 we shall illustrate this by considering the credit spread 1-year VaR of a BBB bond under three scenarios, i.e. that it is downgraded, upgraded, and that its rating remains the same by the end of the year.

The *expected tail loss* is the expected loss, in present value terms, given that VaR is exceeded. It is also called the *conditional VaR*. ETL is more informative than VaR because it provides information of the average or expected loss when the VaR is exceeded. We have derived general formulae for the ETL under the assumption that a portfolio's returns have normal, Student t and mixtures of these distributions. Empirical examples show that the normal mixture ETL and the Student t distributed ETL may be considerably greater than the normal ETL, when returns have leptokurtic and skewed distributions.

The examples in this chapter have focused on portfolios represented by cash flows, international equity portfolios and commodity futures portfolios. In each case we assumed the portfolio has been mapped to a set of standard risk factors following the techniques described in Chapter III.5. We have used these portfolios to:

- show that adjusting VaR and ETL for a non-zero discounted expected return only has a significant effect when the risk horizon is very long and the discounted expected return is very large;
- illustrate how to adjust VaR and ETL for autocorrelation in portfolio returns;
- estimate the systematic VaR and specific VaR for an equity portfolio using (a) equally and (b) exponentially weighted estimates for the portfolio volatility and its market beta;
- decompose total systematic VaR into different stand-alone and marginal VaR components, due to different classes of risk factors;
- aggregate stand-alone VaRs into the total risk factor VaR, in a sub-additive manner;
- measure the incremental VaR of adding a single swap to a large swaps portfolio;
- demonstrate how the different theoretical assumptions made by normal, Student t and mixture VaR models affect the VaR and ETL estimates; and
- explain how EWMA covariance matrices may be applied in the context of the parametric linear VaR model.

Our first case study was on a UK bond portfolio where the risk factors are fixed maturities along a zero coupon yield curve. We explained how to use principal component analysis to reduce the dimensions of the risk factor space: instead of 60 risk factors (constant maturity interest rates) we used only three risk factors (the first three principal components), and the approximation error was very small indeed. That is, the VaR was almost exactly the same whether we used 60 or three risk factors. It can also be argued that the VaR based on only three risk factors is the more accurate of the two, because the dimension reduction allows us to ignore extraneous 'noise' in the data that should not affect the VaR estimate.

The second case study examined the risks facing a commodity futures trading business with desks trading silver and natural gas. The study highlighted the very different characteristics of these two commodities and disaggregated the total VaR of the trading activities into the stand-alone and marginal VaRs due to trading in both natural gas and silver futures.

The last case study illustrated the application of different parametric linear models to estimate both the VaR and the ETL for an exposure to the iTraxx Europe 5-year credit spread index. The historical distribution of this risk factor is highly non-normal, with a large negative skewness and an extremely high excess kurtosis, and its daily changes have a significant positive autocorrelation. Hence, the normal i.i.d. model is totally inappropriate. The most representative parametric linear VaR model is the normal mixture VaR model with autocorrelated returns. This model provided 1% 10-day VaR and ETL estimates that are approximately 2.5 times the size of the normal i.i.d. VaR and ETL estimates! Clearly the use of a normal i.i.d. model would seriously underestimate the risk of such an exposure.

IV.3
Historical Simulation

IV.3.1 INTRODUCTION

Historical simulation as a method for estimating VaR was introduced in a series of papers by Boudoukh et al. (1998) and Barone-Adesi et al. (1998, 1999). A recent survey suggests that about three-quarters of banks prefer to use historical simulation rather the parametric linear or Monte Carlo VaR methodologies.[1] Why should this be so – what are the advantages of historical simulation over the other two approaches?

The main advantage is that historical VaR does not have to make an assumption about the parametric form of the distribution of the risk factor returns. Although the other models can include skewed and heavy tailed risk factor returns, they must still fit a parametric form for modelling the multivariate risk factor returns. And usually the dependencies between risk factors in this multivariate distribution are assumed to be much simpler than they are in reality.

For instance, the parametric linear model assumes that risk factor return dependencies are linear and are fully captured by one or more correlation matrices. This is also commonly assumed in Monte Carlo VaR, although here it is possible to assume more complex dependency structures as explained in the next chapter. Also, the parametric linear VaR model is a *one-step* model, based on the assumption that risk factor returns are i.i.d. There is no simple way that path-dependent behaviour such as *volatility clustering* can be accounted for in this framework. Monte Carlo VaR models can easily be adapted to include path dependency, as we shall see in the next chapter. But still, they have to assume some idealized form for the risk factor evolution. For instance, Monte Carlo VaR may assume that volatility and correlation clustering are captured by a GARCH model.

Historical VaR does not need to make any such parametric assumption, and instead the dynamic evolution and the dependencies of the risk factors are inferred directly from historical observations. This allows the model to assess the risk of complex path-dependent products or the risk of simple products, but still include the dynamic behaviour of risk factors in a natural and realistic manner.

Historical VaR is also not limited to linear portfolios, as the parametric linear VaR model is. So the advantages of historical simulation over the parametric linear model are very clear. However, both historical and Monte Carlo VaR may be applied to any type of portfolio. So, what are the advantages, if any, of the historical VAR model over Monte Carlo VaR? In fact, let us rephrase this question: 'Which model has the most substantial limitations?' The Monte Carlo VaR model suffers from the drawback of being highly dependent on finding a suitably realistic risk factor returns model. Likewise, in the course of this chapter

---

[1] In the research of Perignon and Smith (2006), of the 64.9% of firms that disclosed their methodology, 73% reported the use of historical simulation.

and Chapter IV.5 we shall show that if the historical VaR model is to be used then several challenges must be addressed.[2]

Firstly, it is difficult to apply historical VaR to risk assessments with a horizon longer than a few days. This is because data limitations are a major concern. To avoid unstable VaR estimates when the model is re-estimated day after day, we require a considerable amount of historical data. Even 4 years of daily historical data are insufficient for an acceptable degree of accuracy unless we augment the historical model in some way.[3] Overlapping data on h-day returns could be used, but we shall show in Section IV.3.2.7 that this can seriously distort the tail behaviour of the portfolio return distribution.

Hence, almost always, we base historical VaR estimation on the distribution of *daily* portfolio returns (or P&L) and then scale the 1-day VaR estimate to an h-day horizon. But finding an appropriate scaling rule for historical VaR is not easy, as we shall see in Section IV.3.2. Also, scaling up the VaR for option portfolios in this way assumes the portfolio is rebalanced daily over the risk horizon to return risk factor sensitivities to their value at the time the VaR is measured. That is, we can measure what I call the *dynamic* VaR of an option portfolio, but we shall see in Section IV.5.4 that the standard historical model is very difficult to apply to *static* VaR estimation, i.e. the VaR estimate based on no trading over the risk horizon.

We should recall that a vital assumption in all VaR models is that the portfolio remains the same over the risk horizon, in a sense that will be made more precise in Section IV.5.2.4. Since the historical simulation model forecasts future returns using a large sample of historical data, we have to recreate a historical 'current' returns series by holding the portfolio characteristics constant. For instance, in cash equity portfolios the current portfolio weights on each stock and the current stock betas are all held constant as we simulate 'current' portfolio returns for the entire historical data period. Hence, an implicit assumption of historical VaR is that the current portfolio, which is optimal now, would also have been the portfolio of choice during every day of the historical sample.[4] Thus a criticism of historical VaR that cannot always be levelled at the other two approaches is that it is unrealistic to assume that we would have held the current portfolio when market conditions were different from those prevalent today.

A difficulty that needs addressing when implementing the historical VaR model is that a long data history will typically encompass several *regimes* in which the market risk factors have different behaviour. For instance, during a market crash the equity risk factor volatilities and correlations are usually much higher than they are during a stable market. If all the historical data are treated equally, the VaR estimate will not reflect the market conditions that are currently prevailing. In Section IV.3.3 we shall recommend a parametric volatility adjustment to the data, to account for volatility clustering regimes in the framework of historical simulation.

Given the substantial limitations, it is difficult to understand why so many banks favour historical VaR over Monte Carlo VaR models. Maybe market risk analysts rely very heavily on historical data, because (usually) it is available, and they draw some confidence from a

---

[2] See also Pritsker (2006) for a critical review of the historical simulation approach to VaR estimation.

[3] Such as by fitting a Johnson distribution to the first four moments of the simulated portfolio returns, or using one of the other techniques described in Section IV.3.4.

[4] Of course the parametric linear and Monte Carlo VaR models also assume that the portfolio (as represented by its asset weights or risk factor sensitivities) is constant. But these models make no reference to a historical period. Both methods employ a covariance matrix of asset weights or risk factor returns over the risk horizon, but how we forecast this matrix is a *different* problem. Yes, we may use historical data to estimate the matrix, indeed this is the usual interpretation of the Basel Committee's recommendations for data. But we could base this matrix on just a year of daily data, or 'make up' a covariance matrix, i.e. use a subjective forecast for volatilities and correlations of the risk factor returns. See Section IV.7.2 for further information on scenario VaR in the parametric linear model.

belief that if a scenario has occurred in the past, it will reoccur within the risk horizon of the model. But in my view their reliance on historical data is misplaced. Too often, when a crisis occurs, it is a scenario that has not been experienced in the past.

In my view, the great advantage of Monte Carlo simulation is that is uses historical data more intelligently than standard historical simulation does. After fitting a parametric behavioural model (preferably with volatility clustering and non-normal conditional return distributions) to historical data, the analyst can simulate many thousands of possible scenarios that could occur with that model. They do not assume that the one, experienced scenario that led to that model will also be the one, of all the consistent scenarios, that is actually realized over the risk horizon. A distinct advantage of the *filtered historical simulation* approach (which is described in Section IV.3.3.4) over standard historical simulation is that it combines Monte Carlo simulation based on volatility clustering with the empirical non-normal return distributions that have occurred in the past.

The aim of the present chapter is to explain how to use historical VaR to obtain realistic VaR estimates. We focus on linear portfolios here, leaving the more complex (and thorny) problem of the application of historical VaR to option portfolios to Chapter IV.5. We shall propose the following, very general steps for the implementation of historical VaR for linear portfolios:

- Obtain a sufficiently long period of historical data.
- Adjust the simulated portfolio returns to reflect the current market conditions.
- Fit the empirical distribution of adjusted returns.
- Derive the VaR for the relevant significance level and risk horizon.

We now detail the structure of this chapter.

Section IV.3.2 focuses on the properties of standard historical VaR, focusing on the problems we encounter when scaling VaR from a 1-day to an h-day horizon. We describe how the *stable* distribution assumption provides a method for estimating a *scale exponent* and we explain how risk factor scale exponents can relate to a *power law* scaling of VaR for linear portfolios. Then we estimate this exponent for major equity, foreign exchange and interest rate risk factors. The case for non-linear portfolios is more difficult, because portfolio returns need not be stable even when the risk factor returns are stable; also, even if it was considered appropriate to scale equity, commodity, interest rate, and exchange rate risk factors with the square root of time, this is definitely *not* appropriate for scaling volatility.

Section IV.3.3 concerns the preparation of the historical data set. It is motivated by a case study which demonstrates that when VaR is estimated using equal weighing of historical returns it is the choice of data, rather than the modelling approach, that really determines the accuracy of a VaR estimate. We emphasize the need to adjust historical data so that they more accurately reflect current market conditions, and for short-term VaR estimation we recommend a volatility adjustment of historical returns. The section ends with a description and an illustration of filtered historical simulation, and a discussion of its advantages over standard historical simulation.

Section IV.3.4 provides advice on estimating historical VaR at extreme quantiles when only a few years of daily data are available. Non-parametric smoothing and parametric fitting of the empirical distribution of (adjusted) portfolio returns can improve the precision of historical VaR at the 99% and higher confidence levels. Non-parametric methods include the

Epanechnikov kernel and the *Gaussian kernel*, and we also discuss several parametric methods including the *Johnson SU distribution*, the *Cornish–Fisher expansion*, and the generalized Pareto and other *extreme value distributions*.

Up to this point we will have considered the measurement of VaR at the portfolio level. Now we consider the historical *systematic* VaR, which is based on the risk factor mapping of different linear portfolios. Section IV.3.5 describes the estimation of historical VaR when portfolio returns are a linear function of either asset or risk factor returns. Several case studies and examples of historical VaR modelling for cash flow, equity and commodity portfolios are presented, and we describe how systematic historical VaR may be disaggregated into stand-alone VaR and marginal VaR components.

Section IV.3.6 shows how to estimate the *conditional VaR* or *expected tail loss* in a historical VaR model. We give analytic formulae for computing ETL when the historical returns are fitted with a parametric form, and conclude with an example. The results confirm that fitting a Johnson distribution to the moments of the empirical returns can be a useful technique for estimating ETL (and VaR) at high levels of confidence. Section IV.3.7 summarizes and concludes.

IV.3.2   PROPERTIES OF HISTORICAL VALUE AT RISK

This section provides a formal definition of historical VaR and summarizes the approach for different types of portfolios. We then consider the constraints that this framework places on the historical data and justify our reasons for basing historical VaR estimation on daily returns. This leads to a discussion on a simple scaling rule for extending a 1-day historical VaR to a historical VaR at longer risk horizons.

IV.3.2.1   Definition of Historical VaR

The $100\alpha\%$ h-day historical VaR, in value terms, is the α quantile of an empirical h-day discounted P&L distribution. Or, when VaR is expressed as a percentage of the portfolio's value, the $100\alpha\%$ h-day historical VaR is the α quantile of an empirical h-day discounted return distribution. The percentage VaR can be converted to VaR in value terms: we just multiply it by the current portfolio value.

Historical VaR may be applied to both linear and non-linear portfolios. When a long-only (or short-only) linear portfolio is not mapped to risk factors, a historical series of returns on the portfolio is constructed by holding the current portfolio *weights* constant and applying these to the asset returns to reconstruct a constant weighted portfolio returns series. An example is given in Section IV.3.4.2.

But the concept of a 'return' does not apply to long-short portfolios, because they could have a value of zero (see Section I.1.4.4). So in this case we generate the portfolio's P&L distribution directly, by keeping the current portfolio *holdings* constant, and calculate the VaR in nominal terms at the outset. This approach is put into practice in the case study of Section IV.3.5.6.

When a portfolio is mapped to risk factors, the risk factor sensitivities are assumed constant at their current values and are applied to the historical risk factor returns to generate the portfolio return distribution. Case studies to illustrate this approach are provided in Sections IV.3.4.1 and IV.3.6.3.

IV.3.2.2   Sample Size and Data Frequency

For assessing the regulatory market risk capital requirement, the Basel Committee *recommends* that a period of between 3 and 5 years of daily data be used in the historical simulation model. But the *sample size* and the *data frequency* are not prescribed by any VaR model: essentially these are matters of subjective choice.

Sample Size

If VaR estimates are to reflect only the current market conditions rather than an average over a very long historical period, it seems natural to use only the most recent data. For instance, if markets have behaved unusually during the past year, we may consider using only data from the last 12 months. A relatively short data period may indeed be suitable for the linear and Monte Carlo VaR models. The covariance matrix will then represent only recent market circumstances. But the historical simulation VaR model requires much more than just estimating the parameters of a parametric return distribution. It requires one to actually build the distribution from historical data, and then to focus on the tail of this distribution. So, with historical simulation, the sample size has a considerable influence on the precision of the estimate.

Since VaR estimates at the 99% and higher confidence levels are the norm, it is important to use a large number of historical returns.[5] For a 1% VaR estimation, at least 2000 daily observations on all the assets or risk factors in the portfolio should be used, corresponding to at least 20 data points in the 1% tail. But even 2000 observations would not allow the 0.1% VaR to be estimated with acceptable accuracy. See Section IV.3.4 for a discussion on improving the precision of historical VaR at very high confidence levels.

However, there are several practical problems with using a very large sample. First, collection of a data on all the instruments in the portfolio can be a formidable challenge. Suppose the portfolio contains an asset that has only existed for one year: how does one obtain more than one year of historical prices? Second, in the historical model the portfolio weights, or the risk factor sensitivities if the model has a risk factor mapping, are assumed *constant* over the entire historical data period. The longer the sample period the more questionable this assumption becomes, because a long historical period is likely to cover several different market regimes in which the market behaviour would be very different from today.

Data Frequency

The choice of sample size is linked to the choice of data frequency. It is easier to obtain a large sample of high frequency data than of low frequency data. For instance, to obtain 500 observations on the empirical distribution we would require a 20-year sample if we used 10-day returns, a 10-year sample if we used weekly returns, a 2-year sample if we used daily returns, and a sample covering only the last month or so if we used hourly returns.

For computing VaR-based trading limits it would be ideal if the data warehouse captured intra-day prices on all the risk factors for all portfolios, but in most financial institutions today this is computationally impractical. Since it is not appropriate to hold the current portfolio

---

[5] For instance, if we were to base a 1% VaR on a sample size of 100, this is just the maximum loss over the sample. So it will remain constant day after day and then, when the date corresponding to the current maximum loss falls out of the sample, the VaR estimate will jump to another value.

weights and sensitivities constant over the past 10 years or more, and since also the use of such a long historical period is hardly likely to reflect the current circumstances, it is not appropriate to base historical VaR models on weekly or monthly data. There are also insufficient data to measure historical VaR at extreme quantiles using an empirical distribution based on weekly or monthly returns.

Hence, the historical h-day VaR is either scaled up from a 1-day VaR estimate based on historical data on the portfolio's daily returns or P&L, or we might consider using *multi-step* simulation. In the next subsection we consider the first of these solutions, leaving our discussion of multi-step simulation to Sections IV.3.2.7 and IV.3.3.4.

IV.3.2.3   Power Law Scale Exponents

In this subsection we discuss how to estimate the $100\alpha\%$ h-day historical VaR as some power of h times the $100\alpha\%$ 1-day historical VaR, assuming the $100\alpha\%$ 1-day historical VaR has been computed (as the α quantile of the daily returns or P&L distribution).

In Section IV.1.5.4 we showed that the assumption that returns are normal and i.i.d. led to a *square-root-of-time rule* for linear VaR estimates. For instance, to estimate the 10-day VaR we take the square root of 10 times the 1-day VaR. The square-root-of-time rule applies to linear VaR because it obeys the same rules as standard deviation, either approximately over short risk horizons or over all horizons when the expected return is equal to the discount rate. But in the historical model the VaR corresponds to a *quantile* of some unspecified empirical distribution and quantiles do *not* obey a square-root-of-time rule, except when the returns are i.i.d. and normally distributed.

Scaling rules for quantiles can only be derived by making certain assumptions about the distribution. Suppose we have an i.i.d. process for a random variable X, but that X is not necessarily normally distributed. Instead we just assume that X has a *stable distribution*.[6] When a distribution is ξ-stable then the whole distribution, including the quantiles, scales as $h^{1/\xi}$. For instance, in a normal distribution $\xi = 2$ and we say that its *scale exponent* is $\frac{1}{2}$. More generally, the scale exponent of a stable distribution is ξ^{-1}. This exponent is used to scale the whole distribution of returns, not just its standard deviation, and in VaR applications we use it to scale the quantiles of the distribution.

Let $x_{h,\alpha}$ denote the α quantile of the h-day discounted log returns. We seek ξ such that

$$x_{h,\alpha} = h^{1/\xi} x_{1,\alpha}. \tag{IV.3.1}$$

In other words, taking logs of the above,

$$\xi = \frac{\ln(h)}{\ln(x_{h,\alpha}) - \ln(x_{1,\alpha})}. \tag{IV.3.2}$$

Hence ξ can be estimated as the slope of graph with $\ln(x_{h,\alpha}) - \ln(x_{1,\alpha})$ on the horizontal axis and $\ln(h)$ on the vertical axis. If the distribution is stable the graph will be a straight line and ξ will not depend on the choice of α. Nor should it vary much when different samples are used, provided the sample contains sufficient data to estimate the quantiles accurately. When

---

[6] The concept of a stable distribution was introduced in Section I.3.3.11.

a constant scale exponent corresponding to (IV.3.1) exists, we say that the log return obeys a *power law* scaling rule with exponent ξ^{-1}.

IV.3.2.4   Case Study: Scale Exponents for Major Risk Factors

In this section we illustrate the estimation of (IV.3.2) for some major risk factors, and use the estimates for different values of α to investigate whether their log returns are stable. First we estimate the scale exponent using (IV.3.2), as a function of α, for the S&P 500 index. We base our results on daily data over a very long period from 3 January 1950 until 10 March 2007 and then ask how sensitive the estimated scale exponent is to (a) the choice of quantile α, and (b) the sample data.

The spreadsheet for Figure IV.3.1 aggregates daily log returns into h-day log returns for values of h from 2 to 20, and for a fixed α computes the quantile of the h-day log returns, $x_{h,\alpha}$. First ξ is estimated as the slope of the log-log plot of the holding period versus the quantile ratio, as explained above. Figure IV.3.1 illustrates the graph for $\alpha = 5\%$ where the quantiles are based on the entire sample period. The scale exponent ξ^{-1} is the reciprocal of the slope of the best fit line, which in Figure IV.3.1 is 0.50011. This indicates that a square-root scaling rule for 5% quantiles of the S&P 500 index is indeed appropriate.

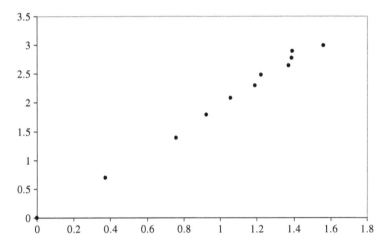

Figure IV.3.1   Log-log plot of holding period versus 5% quantile ratio: S&P 500 index

Table IV.3.1   Estimated values of scale exponent for S&P 500 index

α	0.1%	1%	5%	10%
1950–2007	0.4662	0.5186	0.5001	0.4853
1970–2007	0.5134	0.5074	0.4937	0.4639
1990–2007	0.4015	0.4596	0.4522	0.4268

However, there is some variation when different quantiles and different sample periods are chosen. Table IV.3.1 records the reciprocal of the slope of the log-log plot for different values of α and when the quantiles are based on three different sample periods: from the beginning of January 1950, 1970 and 1990 onward. Using data from 1990 onward the scale exponent for the 10% and 0.1% quantiles is less than 0.5, although it should be noted that with little more than 4000 data points, the 0.1% quantile may be measured imprecisely. Still, based on data since 1990 only, it appears that the scale exponent for the 1% quantile of the S&P 500 index is closer to 0.45 than to 0.5.

We also estimate the scale exponent for three other important risk factors, the $/£ exchange rate and two US Treasury interest rates at 3 months and 10 years, using daily data since January 1971. The relevant log-log plots are shown in Figures IV.3.2–IV.3.4, each time based on $\alpha = 5\%$ and the results for other quantiles are shown in Table IV.3.2.[7] The $/£ exchange rate has a lower estimated scale exponent than the interest rates and, again except for the 0.1% and 10% quantiles, appears to be close to 0.5. So, like the S&P 500 index, the $/£ exchange rate quantiles could be assumed to scale with the square root of time.

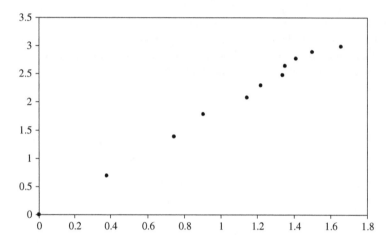

Figure IV.3.2   Log-log plot of holding period versus quantile ratio: $/£ forex rate

Table IV.3.2   Estimated scale exponents for $/£ forex rate and US interest rates

α	0.10%	1%	5%	10%
$/£	0.4543	0.4983	0.5298	0.5590
US 3m	0.5575	0.6065	0.5709	0.5795
US 10yr	0.5363	0.5651	0.5223	0.5591

The US interest rates show evidence of trending, since the estimated scale exponent is greater than 0.5. Thus if mean reversion occurs, it does so over long periods and with a scale exponent of 0.6, scaling the 1% 1-day VaR on the US 3-month Treasury bill rate over a 10-day period implies an increase over the 1-day VaR of $10^{0.6}$ rather than $10^{0.5}$. In other words, the 1-day VaR of $1 million becomes $3.98 million over 10 days, rather than $3.16 million under square-root scaling.

---

[7] For the interest rates we use daily changes, because these are the risk factors in the PV01 mapping, and for the exchange rate we use log returns.

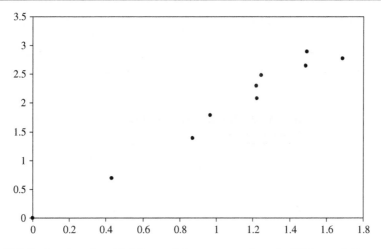

Figure IV.3.3   Log-log plot of holding period versus quantile ratio: US 3-month Treasury bills

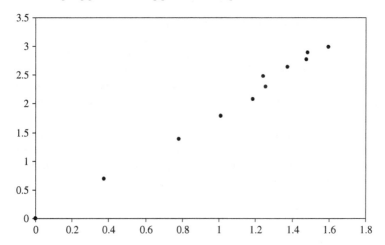

Figure IV.3.4   Log-log plot of holding period versus quantile ratio: US 10-year bond

In Tables IV.3.1 and IV.3.2 the estimated scale exponents were not identical when estimated at different quantiles. Either the variation is due to sampling error, or the distributions are not stable. In the next section we shall assume the variation is due to sampling error and use a scale exponent of 0.5 for the S&P 500 and the $/£ exchange rate,[8] 0.55 for the US 10-year bond and 0.575 for the US 3-month Treasury bill.

It is commonly assumed that volatility scales with the square root of time, but we now show that this assumption may not be appropriate. Indeed, due to the rapid mean reversion of volatility, we should apply a scale exponent that is significantly less than 0.5. Table IV.3.3 summarizes the scale exponent on the S&P 500 volatility index (Vix), the FTSE 100 volatility

---

[8] Note that the same scale exponent would apply to the £/$ exchange rate, since the log returns on one rate are minus the log returns on the other.

index (Vftse) and the DAX 30 volatility index (Vdax) estimated using data since 1992.[9] Scale exponent values estimated at an extreme quantile are very imprecise, but near-linear log-log plots are produced at the 5% quantile, and the spreadsheets accompanying this section imply that at this quantile the appropriate scale exponents are estimated at the values displayed in Table IV.3.3.

Table IV.3.3 Recommended scale exponents for volatility indices

Index	Scale exponent
Vix	0.355
Vftse	0.435
Vdax	0.425

IV.3.2.5 Scaling Historical VaR for Linear Portfolios

The returns on a linear portfolio are a weighted sum of returns on its assets or risk factors. If the returns on the assets or risk factors are stable, the portfolio returns will only be stable if all the assets or risk factors have the *same* scale exponents. In that case it makes no difference whether we scale the asset or risk factor returns before applying the portfolio mapping, or whether we apply the scaling to the portfolio returns directly. However, if the assets or risk factors have different scale exponents, which would normally be the case then the portfolio returns will not be stable.

To see this, consider the case of a portfolio, with weights $\mathbf{w} = (w_1, \ldots, w_n)'$ applied to n assets, and with daily log returns at time t denoted by $\mathbf{x}_t = (x_{1t}, \ldots, x_{nt})'$. The daily log return on the portfolio at time t is then $Y_{1t} = \mathbf{w}'\mathbf{x}_t$. Now suppose the ith asset return is stable and has scale exponent $\lambda_i = \xi_i^{-1}$. Then, the h-day log return on the portfolio is

$$Y_{ht} = \mathbf{w}'\mathbf{x}_t = \mathbf{w}'\left(h^{\lambda_1}x_{1t}, \ldots, h^{\lambda_n}x_{nt}\right) \neq h^\lambda Y_{1t}$$

unless $\lambda = \lambda_1 = \ldots = \lambda_n$.

For instance, consider a portfolio for a UK investor with 50% invested in the S&P 500 index and 50% invested in the notional US 10-year bond. The S&P 500 and £/$ exchange rate returns may scale with the square root of the holding period, but the scale exponent for the US 10-year bond is approximately 0.55. Hence, the portfolio returns will not scale with the square root of the holding period.

We could therefore consider using one of the following approximations for scaling historical VaR, for a linear portfolio:

- Assume the assets or risk factor daily returns are stable, estimate their scale exponents, take an average and use this to scale them to h-day returns. Then apply the portfolio mapping to obtain the h-day portfolio returns.
- Alternatively, compute the portfolio daily returns, assume these are stable and estimate the scale exponent, then scale the portfolio's daily returns to h-day returns.

---

[9] Unfortunately only a little volatility index data are currently available, the longest series being the Vix which starts in 1990.

The first approach is the more approximate of the two, but it has distinct practical advantages over the second approach. First, the analyst may store a set of estimated scale exponents for the major risk factors, in which case there is no need to re-estimate a scale exponent for each and every portfolio. Secondly, returns on major risk factors may be more likely to have stable distributions than arbitrary portfolios. The advantage of the second approach is that it should produce more accurate scaling rules, possibly with scale exponents depending on the significance levels for VaR, but its disadvantage is that a very large historical sample of portfolio returns is required if the scale exponents are to be measured accurately, particularly for extreme quantiles.

IV.3.2.6   Errors from Square-Root Scaling of Historical VaR

Any deviation from square-root scaling is of particular interest for economic capital allocation, where extreme quantiles such as 0.1% may be scaled over long horizons. Table IV.3.4 displays the h-day VaR that is scaled up from the 1-day VaR of $1 million, for different risk horizons h and for different values of the scale exponent. The square-root scaling rule gives the VaR estimates in the centre column (shown in bold). For instance, with square-root scaling a 1-day VaR of $1 million would scale to $10^{0.5}$ million, i.e. $3.16 million over 10 days. The other columns report the VaR based on other scale exponents, expressed as a percentage of this figure. For instance, if the scale exponent were 0.6 instead of 0.5, the 1-day VaR would scale to $1.259 \times$ $3.16 million, i.e. $3.978 million over 10 days.

Table IV.3.4   Scaling 1-day VaR for different risk horizons and scale exponents

Scale exponent Horizon (days)	0.3	0.35	0.4	0.45	0.5	0.55	0.6	0.65	0.7
2	87.1%	90.1%	93.3%	96.6%	**1.41**	103.5%	107.2%	111.0%	114.9%
5	72.5%	78.6%	85.1%	92.3%	**2.24**	108.4%	117.5%	127.3%	138.0%
10	63.1%	70.8%	79.4%	89.1%	**3.16**	112.2%	125.9%	141.3%	158.5%
30	50.6%	60.0%	71.2%	84.4%	**5.48**	118.5%	140.5%	166.6%	197.4%
100	39.8%	50.1%	63.1%	79.4%	**10.00**	125.9%	158.5%	199.5%	251.2%
250	33.1%	43.7%	57.6%	75.9%	**15.81**	131.8%	173.7%	228.9%	301.7%

If we applied a square-root scaling rule, when a power law scaling with a different exponent is in fact appropriate, the errors could be very large indeed. When the scale exponent is greater than 0.5 the square-root scaling law may substantially underestimate VaR and when it is greater than 0.5 the square-root scaling law may substantially overestimate VaR, especially for long term risk horizons. Given the scale exponents for major risk factors that were estimated in Section IV.3.2.4, using a square-root scaling rule is about right for the VaR on US equities and the £/$ exchange rate, but it would substantially underestimate the VaR on US interest rates. And when volatility is a risk factor, square-root scaling of a positive vega exposure would lead to a very considerable overestimation of VaR, because volatility mean-reverts rapidly.

IV.3.2.7   Overlapping Data and Multi-Step Historical Simulation

Historical scenarios capture the empirical dependencies between risk factors in a natural way, just by sampling contemporaneous historical returns on each risk factor. Multi-step historical scenarios can also capture the *dynamic* behaviour in each risk factor, such as volatility clustering, just by simulating *consecutive* returns in the order they occurred historically. For a linear portfolio, multi-step simulation consists of simulating an h-day log return by summing h consecutive daily log returns, and only then revaluing the portfolio. By contrast, for a portfolio of path-dependent products, we would need to evaluate the portfolio on every consecutive day over the risk horizon, which can be very time-consuming.

Unless we also apply a parametric model, as in the filtered historical simulation model described in Section IV.3.3.4, multi-step historical simulation presents a problem if we use *overlapping samples*, because this can distort the tail of the return distribution. To see why, suppose we observe 1000 daily P&Ls that are normal and i.i.d. with zero mean. Suppose that, by chance, these are all relatively small, i.e. of the order of a few thousand US dollars, except for one day when there was a very large negative P&L of $1 million. Then $1 million is the 0.1% daily VaR. However, the 1% daily VaR is much smaller. Let us assume it is $10,000, so that $VaR_{1,0.1\%}$ is 100 times larger than $VaR_{1,1\%}$. What can we say about the 10-day VaR at these significance levels?

Since the daily returns are normal and i.i.d. we may scale VaR using the square-root-of-time rule. Thus, $VaR_{10,0.1\%}$ will be 100 times larger than $VaR_{10,1\%}$. In other words, using the square-root-of-time rule, the loss that is experienced once every 40 years is 100 times the loss that is experienced once every 4 years.

Now consider the 10-day P&L on the same variable. When based on non-overlapping data there are 100 observations, only one of which will be about $1 million. So the 1% 10-day VaR is about $1 million, which is much larger than it would be using the square-root scaling rule. And the 0.1% 10-day VaR *cannot be measured* because there are not enough data. However, we might consider using *overlapping* 10-day P&Ls, so that we now have 1000 observations and 10 of these will be approximately $1 million. Then the 1% 10-day VaR is again about $1 million, and now we *can* measure the 0.1% 10-day VaR – and it will *also* be about $1 million! So, using overlapping data, the loss that is experienced once every 40 years is about the *same* as the loss that is experienced once every 4 years. That is, the 0.1% 10-day VaR is about the same as the 1% 10-day VaR. In short, using overlapping data in this way will distort the lower tail of the P&L distribution, creating a tail that is too 'blunt' below a certain quantile, i.e. the 1% quantile in this exercise.

Thus, to apply multi-step historical simulation for estimating h-day VaR without distorting the tails, one has to apply some type of filtering, such as method described in Section IV.3.3.4. However, we do not necessarily need to apply multi-step simulation. Under certain assumptions about risk factor returns and the portfolio's characteristics, we can scale up the daily VaR to obtain an h-day VaR estimate, as described in the previous subsections.

IV.3.3   IMPROVING THE ACCURACY OF HISTORICAL VALUE AT RISK

This section begins with a case study which demonstrates that the historical VaR based on an equally weighted return distribution depends critically on the choice of sample size. In fact, when data are *equally* weighted it is our choice of sample size, more than anything else, that influences the VaR estimate. By showing how close the normal linear VaR and historical VaR estimates are to each other, we show that the sample size is the most important determinant of the VaR estimate. The main learning point of this case study is that equal weighting of risk factor returns is not advisable for *any* VaR model.

In the linear and Monte Carlo VaR models the risk factor returns data are summarized in a covariance matrix, and instead of equally weighted returns this matrix can be constructed using an exponentially weighted moving average model. But, if not equal, what sort of weighting of the data should we use in historical VaR? After the case study we describe two different ways of weighting the risk factor returns data before the distribution of the portfolio returns is constructed: *exponential weighting of probabilities* and *volatility adjustment of returns*. Volatility adjustment motivates the use of filtered historical simulation, described in Section IV.3.3.4.

IV.3.3.1   Case Study: Equally Weighted Historical and Linear VaR

For a given portfolio the historical and normal linear VaR estimates based on the same sample are often much closer than two historical VaR estimates based on very different samples. We demonstrate this with a case study of VaR estimation for a simple position on the S&P 500 index. Figure IV.3.5 shows the daily historical prices of the S&P 500 index (in black) and its daily returns (in grey) between 31 December 1986 and 31 March 2008. The effects of the Black Monday stock market crash in October 1987, the Russian crisis in August 1998, the technology boom in the late 1990s and subsequent bubble burst in 2001 and 2002, and the US sub-prime mortgage crisis are all evident.

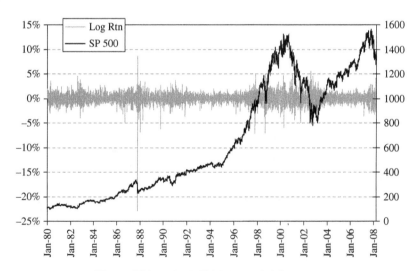

Figure IV.3.5   S&P 500 index and daily returns

In the case study we:

- apply both the normal linear and the historical VaR models to estimate VaR for a single position on the S&P 500 index, using an equally weighted standard deviation in the normal linear model and an equally weighted return distribution in the historical simulation model;

- compare time series of the two VaR estimates over a 1-day horizon at the 99% confidence level;[10]
- compare time series of VaR estimates over a rolling data window based on a sample of size $T = 500$ and of $T = 2000$ data points.

Hence, two time series of VaR estimates are computed, for each choice of T, using a quantile estimated from the histogram of returns for the historical simulation model and an equally weighted standard deviation for the normal linear VaR. All figures are expressed as a percentage of the portfolio value.

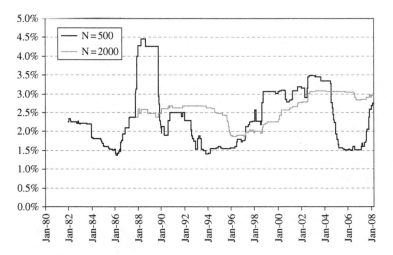

Figure IV.3.6 Time series of 1% historical VaR estimates, S&P 500

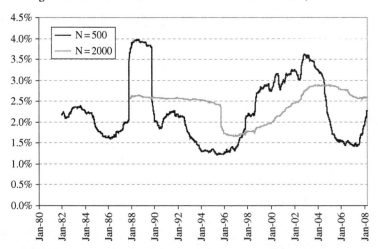

Figure IV.3.7 Time series of 1% normal linear VaR estimates, S&P 500

---

[10] The relevant graphs for other significance levels may be generated in the spreadsheet for this case study.

Figures IV.3.6 and IV.3.7 display the time series of 1-day 1% VaR estimates obtained from each model, starting in December 1981 for $T=500$ and starting in December 1987 for $T=2000$. For each estimate we use the T most recent daily returns. The VaR based on 500 observations is, of course, more variable over time than the VaR based on 2000 observations, since we are weighting all the data equally. The 'ghost effect' of the 1987 global crash is evident in both graphs, particularly so in the VaR based on 500 observations. Then, exactly 500 days after the crash – and even though nothing particular happened on that day – the VaR returned to more normal levels. Most of the time the historical VaR is dominated by a few extreme returns, even when the sample contains 2000 observations, and when one of these enters or leaves the data set the VaR can exhibit a discrete jump upward or downward.[11]

Notice that the two different historical VaR estimates based on N = 500 and N = 2000 differ by 1%–2% on average. The two normal linear VaR estimates have differences of a similar magnitude, though slightly smaller in general. In fact, there is more similarity between the normal and historical VaR estimates for a fixed sample size than there is between the historical VaR estimates for different sample sizes! Figure IV.3.8 shows that the historical VaR tends to be slightly greater than the normal linear VaR, and this is expected due to the excess kurtosis in the S&P 500 daily return distribution.[12] This figure shows that, on average, the historical VaR is about 0.2% (of the portfolio value) greater than the normal linear VaR.[13]

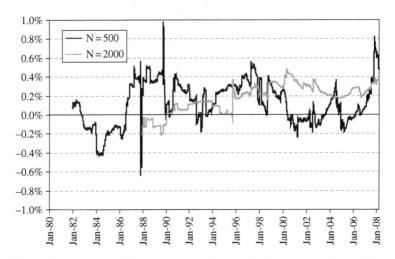

Figure IV.3.8   Time series of difference between historical VaR and normal linear VaR, S&P 500

---

[11] This is particularly evident for the 0.1% VaR, as the reader can verify by changing the significance level in the historical VaR spreadsheet of this case study workbook.

[12] The opposite is the case at the 10% significance level, as you can see in the spreadsheet. As we have seen in the previous chapter this is a feature of the leptokurtic nature of the returns.

[13] By contrast, and to back up our observation that the historical and linear VaR estimates based on the same sample size are much closer than two historical (or two linear) VaR estimates based on very different sample sizes, the average absolute difference between the two historical VaR estimates shown in Figure IV.3.6 is 0.74%, and the average absolute difference between the two normal linear VaR estimates shown in Figure IV.3.7 is 0.78%.

The global equity crash of 1987 is a major stress event in the sample: the S&P 500 fell by 23% in one day between 18 and 19 October 1987. This single return had a very significant impact on the normal linear VaR estimate because the equally weighted volatility estimate (based on the last 500 days) jumped up almost 7 percentage points, from 15.6% on 18 October to 22.5% on 19 October. However, this single initial return of the global equity crash had much less effect on the historical VaR: it was just another return in the lower tail and its huge magnitude was not taken into account. So on 19 October 1987, the normal linear VaR rose more than 1% overnight, whilst the historical VaR rose by only 0.03% of the portfolio value. It was not until we had experienced several days of large negative returns that the historical VaR 'caught up' with the normal linear VaR. Hence in Figure IV.3.8 we see a short period in October 1987 when the normal linear VaR was about 0.6% (of the portfolio value) above the historical VaR estimate. Then, exactly 500 days later, when the global crash data falls out of the sample, the normal linear VaR jumps down as abruptly as it jumped up, whilst the historical VaR takes a few days to decrease to normal levels. So in Figure IV.3.8, during October 1989, we see a short period where the historical VaR is much greater than the normal linear VaR.

We conclude that when returns data are equally weighted it is the sample size, rather than the VaR methodology, that has the most significant effect on the error in the VaR estimates. Clearly, equal weighting of returns data causes problems in *all* VaR models. Any extreme market movement will have the same effect on the VaR estimate, whether it happened years ago or yesterday, provided that it still occurs during the sample period. Consequently the VaR estimate will suffer from 'ghost features' in exactly the same way as equally weighted volatility or correlation estimates. Most importantly, when data are equally weighted, the VaR estimate will not be sufficiently *risk sensitive*, i.e it will not properly reflect the current market conditions. For this reason both the parametric linear and historical VaR models should apply some type of weighting to the returns data, after which ghost features are no longer so apparent in the VaR estimates.

IV.3.3.2 Exponential Weighting of Return Distributions

A major problem with all equally weighted VaR estimates is that extreme market events can influence the VaR estimate for a considerable period of time. In historical simulation, this happens even if the events occurred long ago. With equal weighting, the ordering of observations is irrelevant. In Chapter II.3 we showed how this feature also presents a substantial problem when equally weighted volatilities and correlations are used in short-term forecasts of portfolio risk, and that this problem can be mediated by weighting the returns so that their influence diminishes over time.

To this end, Section II.3.8 introduced the *exponentially weighted moving average* methodology. We applied EWMA covariance matrices in the normal linear VaR model in Section IV.2.10. In Section IV.2.10.1 we showed that a EWMA covariance matrix may be thought of as an equally weighted covariance matrix on exponentially weighted returns, where each return is multiplied by the square root of the smoothing constant λ raised to some power n, where n is the number of days since the observed return occurred. After weighting the returns in this way, we apply equal weighting to estimate the variances and covariances.

The historical VaR model can also be adapted so that it no longer weights data equally. But instead of *multiplying* the portfolio returns by the square root of the smoothing constant raised to some power, we *assign* an exponential weight to the probability of each return in its distribution.[14] Fix a smoothing constant, denoted λ as usual, between 0 and 1. Then assign the probability weight $1 - \lambda$ to the most recent observation on the return, the weight $\lambda(1 - \lambda)$ to the return preceding that, and then weights of $\lambda^2(1 - \lambda)$, $\lambda^3(1 - \lambda)$, $\lambda^4(1 - \lambda)$, ... as the observations move progressively further into the past. When the weights are assigned in this way, the sum of the weights is 1, i.e. they are *probability weights*.

Figure IV.3.9 shows the weights that would be assigned to the return on each day leading up to the time that the VaR is measured, for three different values of λ, i.e. 0.999, 0.99 and 0.9. The horizontal axis represents the number of days before the VaR is measured. The larger the value of λ, the lower the weight on recent returns and the higher the weight assigned to returns far in the past.

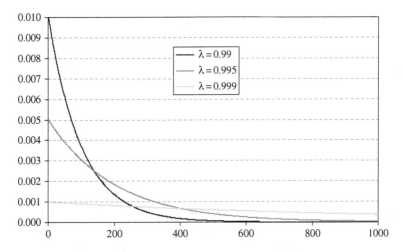

Figure IV.3.9   Exponential probability weights on returns

Then we use these probability weights to find the *cumulative probability* associated with the returns when they are put in increasing order of magnitude. That is, we order the returns, starting at the smallest (probably large and negative) return, and record its associated probability weight. To this we add the weight associated with the next smallest return, and so on until we reach a cumulative probability of $100\alpha\%$, the significance level for the VaR calculation. The $100\alpha\%$ historical VaR, as a percentage of the portfolio's value, is then equal to minus the last return that was taken into the sum. The risk horizon for the VaR (before scaling) is the holding period of the returns, i.e. usually 1 day.

Figure IV.3.10 shows the cumulative probability assigned to the S&P 500 empirical return distribution, based on the 1000 daily returns prior to 31 March 2008, the time when the VaR is measured. We use the same data as for the case study in the previous section, starting on 6 April 2004. For a given λ, start reading upward from the lowest daily return of -3.53% (which occurred on 27 February 2007) adding the exponentially weighted probability associated with each return as it is included. The α quantile return is the one that has a cumulative probability of α associated with it.

---

[14] The assigned weight is not the square root of the smoothing constant raised to some power. But we still call this approach 'exponential weighting' because the weights still decrease exponentially as the time since the return occurred increases.

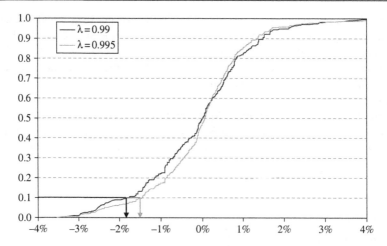

Figure IV.3.10   Exponentially weighted distribution functions, S&P 500 daily returns

The quantiles depend on the value chosen for the weighting constant λ. The 10% quantiles are indicated on Figure IV.3.10 for $\lambda = 0.99$ and 0.995.[15] From these we see immediately that the 10% VaR, which is minus the 10% quantile, is approximately 1.7% when $\lambda = 0.99$ and approximately 1.45% when $\lambda = 0.995$. But when $\lambda = 0.999$ the 10% VaR, not shown in Figure IV.3.10, is approximately 3%. Hence, the VaR does not necessarily increase or decrease with λ. It depends on *when* the largest returns occurred. If all the largest returns occurred a long time before the VaR is estimated, then higher values of lambda would give a larger VaR estimate. Otherwise, it is difficult to predict how the VaR at different quantiles will behave as λ varies. The problem with this methodology is that the choice of λ (which has a very significant effect on the VaR estimate) is entirely *ad hoc*.

IV.3.3.3   Volatility Adjustment

One problem with using data that span a very long historical period is that market circumstances change over time. Equity markets go through periods of relatively stable, upward-trending prices, periods of range bounded price behaviour, and periods where prices fall rapidly and (often) rebound. Commodity futures markets may be exposed to bubbles, seasonal price fluctuations and switching between backwardation and contango.[16] Currency market volatility comes in clusters and is influenced by government policy on intervention. Fiscal policy also varies over the business cycle, so the term structures of interest rates and the prices of interest rate sensitive instruments shift between different behavioural regimes. In short, regime specific economic and behavioural mechanisms are a general feature of financial markets.

Since historical simulation requires a very large sample, this section addresses the question of how best to employ data, possibility from a long time ago when the market was in a different

---

[15] Since the cumulative probability of 0.01 will almost certainly lie in between two observed returns, we can use linear interpolation to estimate the 1% quantile return, as explained in Section I.5.3.1.

[16] *Backwardation* is the term given to a downward sloping term structure of futures prices, and *contango* refers to an upward sloping term structure.

regime. As a simple example, consider an equity market that has been stable and trending for one or two years, but previously experienced a long period of high volatility. We have little option but to use a long historical sample period for the historical VaR estimate, but we would like to *adjust* the returns from the volatile regime so that their volatility is lower. Otherwise the current historical VaR estimate will be too high. Conversely, if markets are particularly volatile at the moment but were previously stable for many years, an unweighted historical estimate will tend to underestimate the current VaR, unless we scale up the volatility of the returns from the previous, tranquil period.

We now consider a *volatility weighting* method for historical VaR that was suggested by Duffie and Pan (1997) and Hull and White (1998). The methodology is designed to weight returns in such a way that we adjust their volatility to the current volatility. To do this we must obtain a time series of volatility estimates for the historical sample of portfolio returns. The best way to generate these would be to use an appropriate asymmetric GARCH model, as described in Section II.4.3, although a simple EWMA model may also be quite effective.[17]

Denote the time series of unadjusted historical portfolio returns by $\{r_t\}_{t=1}^{T}$ and denote the time series of the statistical (e.g. GARCH or EWMA) volatility of the returns by $\{\hat{\sigma}_t\}_{t=1}^{T}$, where T is the time at the end of the sample, when the VaR is estimated. Then the return at every time $t < T$ is multiplied by the volatility estimated at time T and divided by the volatility estimated at time t. That is, the volatility adjusted returns series is

$$\tilde{r}_{t,T} = \left(\frac{\hat{\sigma}_T}{\hat{\sigma}_t} \right) r_t, \tag{IV.3.3}$$

where T is fixed but t varies over the sample, i.e. $\{t = 1, \ldots, T\}$. A time-varying estimate of the volatility of the series (IV.3.3), based on the same model that was used to obtain $\hat{\sigma}_t$, should be *constant* and equal to $\hat{\sigma}_T$, i.e. the conditional volatility at the time the VaR is estimated.[18]

EXAMPLE IV.3.1: VOLATILITY ADJUSTED VAR FOR THE S&P 500 INDEX

Use daily log returns on the S&P 500 index from 2 January 1995 to 31 March 2008 to estimate symmetric and asymmetric GARCH volatilities. For each time series of volatility estimates, plot the volatility adjusted returns that are obtained using (IV.3.3), where the fixed time T is 31 March 2008, i.e. the date that the VaR is estimated. Then find the $100\alpha\%$ 1-day historical VaR estimate, as a percentage of the portfolio value, based on both of the volatility adjusted series. For $\alpha = 0.001, 0.01, 0.05$ and 0.1 compare the results with the unadjusted historical VaR.

---

[17] Many of our illustrative examples will keep the volatility model as simple as possible, and focus instead on the general features of historical VaR with and without any volatility adjustment. So we shall often use a simple EWMA volatility. However, EWMA introduces yet another subjective choice to the VaR model, i.e. the smoothing constant. See Section II.3.8 for further details. In practice readers should use GARCH volatility to adjust historical data because GARCH model parameters are estimated optimally from the sample (as explained in Section II.4.2.2).

[18] In the text we have called $\hat{\sigma}_t$ the 'volatility' at time t, but really it is the standard deviation. However, we divide one volatility by another in (IV.3.3). So the result is the same, whether or not we annualize the standard deviations to become volatilities. We do not have to use $\hat{\sigma}_T$ for the volatility that we are imposing on the transformed returns. For example, we could adjust the returns to have a long term average volatility or – in scenario analysis – a hypothetical value for volatility.

SOLUTION   The GARCH estimates are obtained using the Excel spreadsheet.[19] Table IV.3.5 displays the estimated parameters of the two GARCH models.[20]

Table IV.3.5   GARCH parameters for S&P 500 index

Parameter	GARCH	A-GARCH
ω	1.02638E-06	3.609464E-07
α	0.0676	0.0979
β	0.9225	0.8988
λ	–	0.0038
$\alpha + \beta$	0.9931	0.9967
Long term volatility	19.23%	36.47%
Log likelihood	13849.14	13887.96

There is a *leverage effect* in the A-GARCH model, which captures the asymmetric response of volatility to rises and falls in the index. The index has many significant falls during the sample period, each one precipitating a higher volatility than a rise in the index of the same magnitude. The symmetric GARCH volatility ignores this effect, and hence underestimates the long term average index volatility over the sample. This is about 20% according to the GARCH model, but over 36% according to the A-GARCH model.

Also, compared with the A-GARCH volatility the symmetric GARCH volatility shows less reaction to market events (because α is smaller) but greater persistence following a market shock (because β is greater). The log likelihood will always be higher in the asymmetric GARCH model, since it has one extra parameter. Nevertheless it is still clear that capturing an asymmetric volatility response greatly improves the fit to the sample data in this case.

The resulting GARCH volatility estimates are compared in Figure IV.3.11. This shows that the index volatility varied considerably over the sample period, reaching highs of over 45% during the Asian crisis in 1997, the Russian crisis in 1998 and after the burst of the technology bubble. The years 2003–2006 were very stable, with index volatility often as low as 10% and only occasionally exceeding 15%, but another period of market turbulence began in 2007, precipitated by the credit crisis.

We now calculate the volatility adjusted returns that form the basis of the empirical distribution from which the historical VaR is computed as a quantile. Figure IV.3.12 illustrates the A-GARCH volatility adjusted returns, and compares them with the unadjusted returns. Before adjustment, volatility clustering in returns is evident from the change in magnitude of the returns over the historical period. For instance, the returns during the years 2003–2006 were considerably smaller, on the whole, than the returns during 2002. But after adjustment the returns have a constant volatility equal to the estimated A-GARCH volatility at the end of the sample.

Now we estimate the 1% 1-day historical VaR for a position on the S&P 500 index on 31 March 2008, based on the unadjusted returns and based on the volatility adjusted

---

[19] See Examples II.4.1 and II.4.3 for further details. We emphasize again that the use of Excel to estimate GARCH parameters is not recommended and we only use it here for methodological transparency.

[20] I hope readers will not be confused by the use of α to denote both the significance level of the VaR estimate and the GARCH reaction parameter in this example. Unfortunately both notations are absolutely standard, and it should be clear from the context which α we are referring to. Note that the A-GARCH parameter λ is the *leverage coefficient*, and this is not the same as the EWMA parameter λ, which denotes the *smoothing constant*. We continue to use these notations since both are standard.

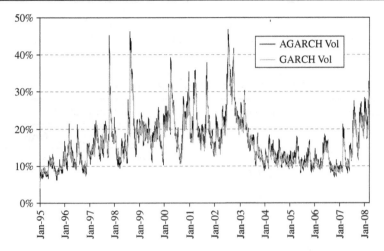

Figure IV.3.11   GARCH volatility estimates for the S&P 500 index

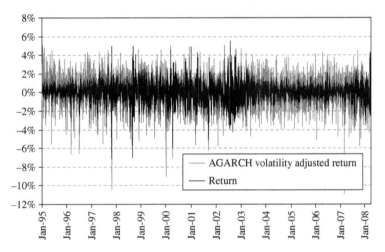

Figure IV.3.12   Returns and A-GARCH volatility adjusted returns

returns (IV.3.3) with both the symmetric and the asymmetric GARCH volatilities. The results, reported in Table IV.3.6, indicate a considerable underestimation of VaR when the returns are not adjusted.[21]

The above example demonstrates how volatility adjustment compares favourably with the exponential weighting method in the previous section. The main advantages of using a GARCH model for volatility adjustment are as follows:

- We do not have to make a subjective choice of an exponential smoothing constant λ. The parameters of the GARCH model may be estimated optimally from the sample data.

---

[21] But if we were to estimate the VaR during a particularly tranquil period, the VaR would be overestimated without the volatility adjustment.

- We are able to use a very large sample for the return distribution. In the above example we used 3355 returns, and an even larger sample would also be perfectly feasible.

Table IV.3.6   Historical VaR for S&P 500 on 31 March 2008

Quantile	Unadjusted	Volatility Adjusted	
		GARCH	A-GARCH
0.10%	4.84%	7.50%	7.04%
1%	2.83%	4.18%	4.28%
5%	1.78%	2.69%	2.79%
10%	1.27%	2.11%	2.11%

Hence this type of volatility adjustment allows the VaR at very high quantiles to be estimated reasonably accurately.

We end this subsection by investigating the effect of volatility adjustment on the scale exponent that we might use to transform a 1-day historical VaR estimate into an h-day historical VaR estimate. However, in the next subsection we shall describe a more sophisticated method for computing h-day historical VaR, which uses a dynamic model, such as the GARCH volatility adjustment models described above, and does not require the use of power law scaling.

Recall that to estimate the values of the scale exponent shown in Table IV.3.1, over 50 years of daily returns on the S&P 500 were used. We now scale these returns to have constant volatility, using (IV.3.3), this time using a simple EWMA volatility instead of a GARCH model. It does not matter which volatility level we scale the series to, the estimated scale exponent remains unchanged.[22] Table IV.3.7 reports the results, which are computed in an Excel workbook in the case study folder for this subsection. They are calculated in a similar way to the unadjusted scale exponents in Table IV.3.1, but now the results are presented using different values for the smoothing constant rather than different sample sizes.

Table IV.3.7   Estimated values of scale exponent for volatility adjusted S&P 500

Smoothing constant	Quantile			
λ	0.1%	1%	5%	10%
0.98	0.4848	0.5402	0.5368	0.5192
0.95	0.4527	0.5236	0.5366	0.5250
0.9	0.3972	0.5057	0.5334	0.5335

In this subsection we have considered volatility adjustment at the portfolio level. That is, we construct a returns series for the portfolio in the usual way, and then adjust this to have the

---

[22] In the spreadsheet the returns are scaled to have a volatility of 10%, but this can be changed and the user will see that it has no effect on the scale exponent.

required volatility. Later in this chapter, in Section IV.3.5.2, we show how to volatility-adjust individual risk factors for a portfolio, and we use a case study to compare the VaR based on volatility adjustment at the risk factor level with the VaR based on portfolio level volatility adjustment.

IV.3.3.4   Filtered Historical Simulation

Barone-Adesi et al. (1998, 1999) extend the idea of volatility adjustment to multi-step historical simulation, using overlapping data in a way that does not create blunt tails for the h-day portfolio return distribution. Their idea is to use a parametric dynamic model of returns volatility, such as one of the GARCH models that were used in the previous subsection, to simulate log returns on each day over the risk horizon.

For instance, suppose we have estimated a symmetric GARCH model on the historical log returns r_t, obtaining the estimated model

$$\hat{\sigma}_{t+1}^2 = \hat{\omega} + \hat{\alpha} r_t^2 + \hat{\beta} \hat{\sigma}_t^2. \qquad (IV.3.4)$$

The *filtered historical simulation* (FHS) model assumes that the GARCH innovations are drawn from the standardized empirical return distribution. That is, we assume the standardized innovations are

$$\varepsilon_t = \frac{r_t}{\hat{\sigma}_t}, \qquad (IV.3.5)$$

where r_t is the historical log return and $\hat{\sigma}_t$ is the estimated GARCH daily standard deviation at time t.

To start the multi-step simulation we set $\hat{\sigma}_0$ to be equal to the estimated daily GARCH standard deviation on the last day of the historical sample, when the VaR is estimated, and also set r_0 to be the log return on the portfolio from the previous day to that day. Then we compute the GARCH daily variance on day 1 of the risk horizon as

$$\hat{\sigma}_1^2 = \hat{\omega} + \hat{\alpha}\, \hat{r}_0^2 + \hat{\beta}\hat{\sigma}_0^2.$$

Now the simulated log return on the first day of the risk horizon is $\hat{r}_1 = \varepsilon_1 \hat{\sigma}_1$ where a value for ε_1 is simulated from our historical sample of standardized innovations (IV.3.5). This is achieved using the *statistical bootstrap*, which is described in Section I.5.7.2. Thereupon we iterate in the same way, on each day of the risk horizon setting

$$\hat{\sigma}_{t+1}^2 = \hat{\omega} + \hat{\alpha}\, \hat{r}_t^2 + \hat{\beta}\, \hat{\sigma}_t^2, \quad \text{with } \hat{r}_t = \varepsilon_t \hat{\sigma}_t \quad \text{for } t = 1, \ldots, h,$$

where ε_t is drawn independently of ε_{t-1} in the bootstrap. Then the simulated log return over a risk horizon of h days is the sum $\hat{r}_1 + \hat{r}_2 + \ldots + \hat{r}_h$. Repeating this for thousands of simulations produces a simulated return distribution, and the $100\alpha\%$ h-day FHS VaR is obtained as minus the α quantile of this distribution.

We do not need to use a symmetric GARCH model for the filtering. In fact, the next example illustrates the FHS method using the historical data and the estimated A-GARCH model from the previous example.

EXAMPLE IV.3.2: FILTERED HISTORICAL SIMULATION VAR FOR THE S&P 500 INDEX

Use daily log returns on the S&P 500 index from 2 January 1995 to 31 March 2008 to estimate the $100\alpha\%$ 10-day VaR using FHS based on an asymmetric GARCH model with the
parameters shown in Table IV.3.5. For $\alpha = 0.001, 0.01, 0.05$ and 0.1 compare the results with
the asymmetric GARCH volatility adjusted historical VaR that is obtained by scaling up the
daily VaR estimates using a square-root scaling rule.

SOLUTION   The starting values are taken from the results in Example IV.6.1: the A-GARCH
annual volatility on 31 March 2008, when the VaR is estimated, is 27.82% and the daily log
return on 31 March 2008 is 0.57%. Then each daily log return over the risk horizon is simulated by taking the current A-GARCH estimated standard deviation and multiplying this by
an independent random draw from the standardized empirical returns.[23] The results from one
set of 5000 simulations are shown in the second column of Table IV.3.8. The third column,
headed 'scaled volatility adjusted VaR', is obtained by multiplying the results in the last column of Table IV.3.6 by $\sqrt{10}$. The results vary depending on the simulation, but we almost
always find that the FHS 10-day VaR is just slightly lower than the volatility adjusted VaR
based on square-root scaling up of the daily VAR for every quantile shown.

Table IV.3.8   Scaling VaR versus filtered historical simulation

Quantile	Current volatility		10% volatility	
	FHS	Scaled volatility adjusted VaR	FHS	Scaled volatility adjusted VaR
0.10%	21.13%	22.25%	9.09%	8.00%
1%	12.79%	13.53%	5.44%	4.86%
5%	7.96%	8.84%	3.18%	3.18%
10%	5.70%	6.67%	2.29%	2.40%

Now suppose the current A-GARCH volatility were only 10% instead of 27.82%. Readers
can change the starting value in cell D3 of the spreadsheet to 0.6325%, i.e. the daily standard deviation corresponding to 10% volatility, and see the result. The results from one
set of 5000 filtered historical simulations are shown in the fourth column of Table IV.3.8
and the scaled up volatility adjusted VaR corresponding to 10% volatility is shown in the
last column. Now, more often than not, the FHS VaR is greater than the scaled volatility
adjusted daily VaR at the extreme quantiles but not, for instance, at the 10% quantile. Why is
this so?

Looking again at Figure IV.3.11, we can see that the average level of volatility over our
historical sample was below 20%. In fact, the average estimated A-GARCH volatility was
16.7% over the sample. So on 31 March 2008 the volatility was higher than average and in
the absence of an extreme return during the risk horizon it would revert toward the long term
average, as GARCH volatilities do, which in this case entails reverting downward. By contrast,
the 10% volatility is below average so it will start reverting upward toward 16.7% over the risk
horizon, in the absence of an extreme return during this period.

---

[23] As with the Monte Carlo VaR spreadsheets, we have reduced the number of simulations in the simulation spreadsheets so that they
fit on the CD-ROM. Copy the spreadsheet to your hard disk first, then fill down columns E to AH of the spreadsheet, so that thousands
of simulations are used to compute the results.

But there is no mean reversion in a square-root scaling of daily VaR. Indeed, this type of scaling is theoretically incorrect when we use a GARCH model for volatility adjustment.[24] It assumes the volatility remains constant over the risk horizon and does not mean-revert at all. Square-root scaling corresponds to an i.i.d. normal assumption for returns, which certainly does not hold in the FHS framework. Hence, when adjustment is made using a GARCH model, the scaled volatility adjusted VaR will overestimate VaR when the current volatility is higher than average, and underestimate VaR when volatility is lower than average.

IV.3.4 PRECISION OF HISTORICAL VALUE AT RISK AT EXTREME QUANTILES

When using very large samples and measuring quantiles no more extreme than 1%, the volatility adjustment and filtering described in the previous section are the only techniques required. For daily VaR you just need to estimate the required quantile from the distribution of the volatility adjusted daily portfolio returns, as described in Section IV.3.3.3. And when VaR is estimated over horizons longer than 1 day, apply the filtering according to your volatility adjustment model, as described in Section IV.3.3.4.

But it may be necessary to compute historical VaR at very extreme quantiles when it is impossible to obtain a very large sample of historical returns on all assets and risk factors. For instance, economic capitalization at the 99.97% confidence level is a target for most firms with a AA credit rating, but it is impossible to obtain reliable estimates of 0.03% VaR directly from a historical distribution, even with a very large sample indeed.

To assess historical VaR at very extreme quantiles – and also at the usual quantiles when the sample size is not very large – one needs to fit a *continuous* distribution to the empirical one, using a form that captures the right type of decay in the tails. This section begins by explaining how *kernel fitting* can be applied to the historical distribution without making any parametric assumption about tail behaviour. We then consider a variety of *parametric* or *semi-parametric* techniques that can be used to estimate historical VaR at extreme quantiles.

IV.3.4.1 Kernel Fitting

In Section I.3.3.12 we explained how to estimate a kernel to smooth an empirical distribution. Having chosen a form for the kernel function, the estimation algorithm fits the kernel by optimizing the bandwidth, which is like the cell width in a histogram. Fitting a kernel to the historical distribution of volatility adjusted returns allows even high quantiles to be estimated from relatively small samples. The choice of kernel is not really important, as shown by Silverman (1986), provided only that a reasonable one is chosen. For empirical applications of kernel fitting to VaR estimation see Sheather and Marron (1990), Butler and Schachter (1998) and Chen and Tang (2005).

To illustrate this we use Matlab to apply the Epanechnikov, Gaussian and lognormal kernels to a distribution of volatility adjusted returns shown in Figure IV.3.13. This series is of daily

---

[24] However, it is not necessarily theoretically incorrect when we use an EWMA model for volatility adjustment, because there is no mean reversion in EWMA volatility forecasts. If there is a power law for scaling, as discussed in Example IV.6.1, then we can use this law to scale up daily EWMA volatility adjusted VaR to longer horizons.

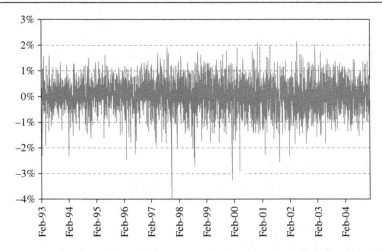

Figure IV.3.13   EWMA adjusted daily returns on S&P 500

returns on the S&P 500 index, and the volatility adjustment has been made using a EWMA volatility with smoothing constant 0.95. We fit a kernel to a sample size of 500, 1000, 2000 and 3000 returns. In each case the returns are standardized to have mean 0 and variance 1 before fitting the kernel. Figure IV.3.14 compares the three kernel densities with the standard normal density to give a visual representation of the skewness and excess kurtosis in the empirical densities. Whilst the Gaussian and Epanechnikov kernels are almost identical, the lognormal kernel fits the data very badly indeed.

Now without fitting a kernel, and for each fitted kernel, we estimate the 1-day VaR at 5%, 1%, 0.1% and 0.05% significance levels. The results are shown in Table IV.3.9 and, as usual, they are expressed as a percentage of the portfolio value. Note that there are two sets of results labelled 'No kernel': the first uses the Excel PERCENTILE function, which we know has some peculiarities;[25] and the second uses the Matlab quantile function which is more accurate than that of Excel.[26]

As remarked above, the lognormal kernel provides a poor fit and so the results should not be trusted. Whilst the VaR results for the Gaussian and Epanechnikov kernels are very similar (they are identical in exactly one-half of the cases) those for the lognormal kernel are very different and are very far from the quantiles that are calculated by Excel and Matlab. The Matlab quantiles estimate the VaR fairly accurately; in fact, the results are similar to those obtained using the Gaussian and Epanechnikov kernels. However, there is a marked difference between these and the quantiles estimated using the Excel function.

Another feature of the results in Table IV.3.9 is that the VaR estimates are sample-specific. The sample of the most recent 2000 returns clearly has heavier tails than the sample of the most recent 3000 returns or the sample of the most recent 1000 returns, since the VaR estimates are greatest when based on a sample size 2000.

---

[25] The problems associated with the Excel PERCENTILE function are described in Section I.3.2.8.
[26] Many thanks to my PhD student Joydeep Lahiri for providing the empirical results in this section.

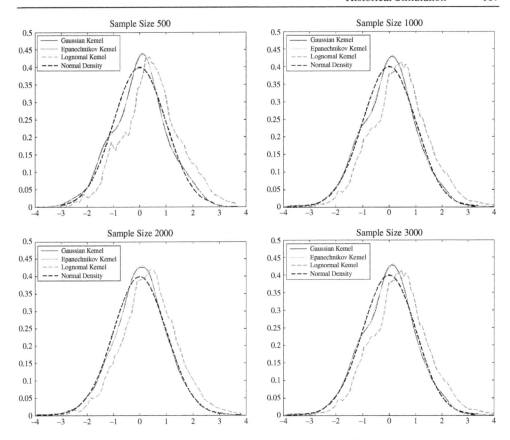

Figure IV.3.14   Kernels fitted to standardized historical returns

IV.3.4.2   Extreme Value Distributions

Kernel fitting is a way to smooth the empirical returns density whilst fitting the data as closely as possible. A potential drawback with this approach is that the particular sample used may not have tails as heavy as those of the population density. An alternative to kernel fitting is to select a parametric distribution function that is known to have heavy tails, such as one of the extreme value distributions. Then we fit this either to the entire return distribution or to only the observations in some pre-defined lower tail. A *generalized extreme value* (GEV) distribution can be fitted to the entire empirical portfolio return distribution, but the *generalized Pareto* distribution (GPD) applies to only those returns above some pre-defined threshold u.

Another potential drawback with kernel fitting is that it does not lend itself to scenario analysis in the same way as parametric distribution fitting. When a parametric form is fitted to the returns it is possible to apply scenarios to the estimated parameters to see the effect on VaR. For instance, having estimated the scale and tail index parameters of a GPD from the historical returns over some threshold, alternative VaR estimates could be obtained by changing the scale and tail index parameters.[27] For instance, we might fit the GPD to only

---

[27] This approach is advocated by Longin (2000, 2005), McNeil and Frey (2000), Aragones et al. (2001) and Gencay and Selcuk (2004).

Table IV.3.9   Historical VaR based on kernel fitting

		Significance Level			
		5%	1%	0.10%	0.05%
No kernel (Excel)					
Sample size	500	0.95%	1.35%	1.69%	1.75%
	1000	1.05%	1.52%	2.32%	2.43%
	2000	1.09%	1.72%	2.91%	3.26%
	3000	1.03%	1.66%	2.73%	3.08%
No kernel (Matlab)					
Sample size	500	1.03%	1.47%	1.88%	1.88%
	1000	1.04%	1.51%	2.42%	2.53%
	2000	1.10%	1.73%	3.09%	3.65%
	3000	1.03%	1.68%	2.82%	3.26%
Gaussian kernel					
Sample size	500	1.04%	1.48%	1.92%	2.00%
	1000	1.03%	1.58%	2.35%	2.46%
	2000	1.06%	1.61%	2.98%	3.53%
	3000	1.04%	1.59%	2.80%	3.21%
Epanechnikov kernel					
Sample size	500	1.04%	1.52%	1.92%	2.00%
	1000	1.09%	1.58%	2.40%	2.51%
	2000	1.12%	1.67%	3.05%	3.53%
	3000	1.04%	1.65%	2.80%	3.21%
Lognormal kernel					
Sample size	500	0.82%	1.29%	1.66%	1.75%
	1000	0.84%	1.30%	2.22%	2.33%
	2000	0.92%	1.48%	2.76%	3.19%
	3000	0.77%	1.46%	2.57%	2.99%

those returns in the lower 10% tail of the distribution. Provided that the historical sample is sufficiently large (at least 2000 observations), there will be enough returns in the 10% tail to obtain a reasonably accurate estimate of the GPD scale and tail index parameters, β and ξ.

It can be shown that when a GPD is fitted to losses in excess of a threshold u there is a simple analytic formula for the $100\alpha\%$ VaR,

$$\text{VaR}_\alpha = u + \frac{\beta}{\xi n^\xi}\left(\left(\frac{n_u}{1-\alpha}\right)^\xi - n^\xi\right), \tag{IV.3.6}$$

where n is the number of returns in the entire sample and n_u is the number of returns less than the threshold u. It is therefore simple to generate VaR estimates for different values of β and ξ.

EXAMPLE IV.3.3: USING THE GPD TO ESTIMATE VAR AT EXTREME QUANTILES

Estimate the parameters of a GPD for the EWMA volatility adjusted daily returns on the S&P 500 that were derived and analysed in Section IV.3.4.1. Base your results on the entire sample of 14,264 returns and also on a sample of the 5000 most recent returns. In each case set the volatility in the adjusted returns to be 10%.[28] Use only the returns that are sampled below a threshold of (a) 20%, (b) 10%, (c) 5% and (d) 1%. Hence, estimate the 1-day VaR using (IV.3.6) and compare the results with the historical VaR that is estimated without fitting a GPD. In each case use a risk horizon of 1 day and confidence levels of 99%, 99.9% and 99.95%, and express the VaR as a percentage of the portfolio value.

SOLUTION   The returns are first normalized by subtracting the sample mean and dividing by the standard deviation, so that they have mean 0 and variance 1. Then for each choice of threshold, the GPD parameters are estimated using maximum likelihood in Matlab.[29] The results are reported in the two columns headed 'GPD parameters' in Table IV.3.10.

Table IV.3.10   Estimates of GPD parameters (Matlab)

Sample size 14,264			GPD parameters		Confidence level for VaR		
Threshold	n_u	u	ξ	β	99%	99.9%	99.95%
1%	143	−2.5740	−0.3906	7.6815	1.69%	6.01%	7.27%
5%	713	−1.6097	−0.2425	4.4892	2.87%	6.43%	7.16%
10%	1426	−1.1960	−0.1870	3.3786	3.37%	6.10%	6.71%
20%	2853	−0.7203	−0.1289	2.2795	3.26%	5.30%	5.81%
Historical VaR (no GPD)					1.69%	3.00%	3.87%
Sample size 5000			GPD parameters		Confidence level for VaR		
Threshold	n_u	u	ξ	β	99%	99.9%	99.95%
1%	50	−2.5292	−0.4036	8.2127	1.67%	6.52%	7.83%
5%	250	−1.5360	−0.2305	4.4352	2.94%	6.59%	7.37%
10%	500	−1.1708	−0.1776	3.3405	3.42%	6.22%	6.86%
20%	1000	−0.6930	−0.1194	2.2280	3.27%	5.36%	5.89%
Historical VaR (no GPD)					1.67%	3.36%	4.86%

Since our GPD parameters were estimated on the normalized returns, after we compute the VaR using (IV.3.6) we must then de-normalize the VaR estimate, i.e. multiply it by the standard deviation and subtract the mean. This gives the results shown in Table IV.3.10 under the three columns headed 'Confidence level for VaR'. The GPD results should be compared to the historical VaR without fitting a GPD, i.e. the VaR that is estimated from a quantile of the volatility adjusted return distribution. This is shown in the last row of each half of the table.

---

[28] These data end on 31 December 2004, when the S&P500 index volatility was approximately 10%.

[29] Many thanks again to Joydeep Lahiri for providing these results.

The GPD VaR is greater than the volatility adjusted VaR that is obtained without the GPD fit, and substantially so for extreme quantiles. For instance, at the 0.05% quantile and based on the most recent 5000 returns, the GPD VaR based on a threshold of 10% is 6.86% of the portfolio value, whereas the historical VaR without fitting the GPD is estimated to be only 4.86% of the portfolio value.

Notice how the historical VaR that is obtained without fitting the GPD is greatly influenced by the sample size. Even after the volatility adjustment, 5000 returns are simply insufficient to estimate VaR at the 99.95% confidence level with accuracy. At this level of confidence we are looking for a loss event that has no more than 1 chance in 2000 of occurring.

The GPD VaR estimates are not greatly influenced by the sample size, but they are influenced by the choice of threshold. A threshold of 10% or 20% is adequate, but for thresholds of 5% and 1% there is insufficient data in the tail to fit the GPD parameters accurately starting with a sample size of 5000.[30]

An important point to learn from this example is that although the GPD VaR estimates are fairly robust to changes in sample size, they are not robust to the choice of threshold. This is one of the disadvantages of using the GPD to estimate VaR, since the choice of threshold is an important source of model risk. Advocates of GPD VaR argue that this technique allows suitably heavy tails to be fitted to the data, and so it is possible to estimate historical VaR at very high confidence levels such as 99.97%. Another convenient aspect of the approach is that the expected tail loss (also called the conditional VaR) has a simple analytic form, which we shall introduce in Section IV.3.7.2.

IV.3.4.3   Cornish–Fisher Approximation

The Cornish–Fisher expansion (Cornish and Fisher, 1937) is a semi-parametric technique that estimates quantiles of non-normal distributions as a function of standard normal quantiles and the sample skewness and excess kurtosis. In the context of historical VaR, this technique allows extreme quantiles to be estimated from standard normal quantiles at high significance levels, given only the first four moments of the portfolio return or P&L distribution.

The fourth order Cornish–Fisher approximation $\tilde{x}_\alpha$ to the α quantile of an empirical distribution with mean 0 and variance 1 is

$$\tilde{x}_\alpha \approx z_\alpha + \frac{\hat{\tau}}{6}\left(z_\alpha^2 - 1\right) + \frac{\hat{\varkappa}}{24}z_\alpha\left(z_\alpha^2 - 3\right) - \frac{\hat{\tau}^2}{36}z_\alpha\left(2z_\alpha^2 - 5\right), \tag{IV.3.7}$$

where $z_\alpha = \Phi^{-1}(\alpha)$ is the α quantile of a standard normal distribution, and $\hat{\tau}$ and $\hat{\varkappa}$ denote the skewness and excess kurtosis of the empirical distribution. Then, if $\hat{\mu}$ and $\hat{\sigma}$ denote the mean and standard deviation of the same empirical distribution, this distribution has approximate α quantile

$$x_\alpha = \tilde{x}_\alpha\hat{\sigma} + \hat{\mu}. \tag{IV.3.8}$$

---

[30] With a threshold of 1% and original sample size 5000, there are only 50 returns in the tail that we use to fit the GPD parameters. In fact, the Matlab optimizer did not converge properly, so the results in the penultimate row of Table IV.3.10 are unreliable.

EXAMPLE IV.3.4: CORNISH–FISHER APPROXIMATION

Find the Cornish–Fisher approximation to the 1% quantile of an empirical distribution with the sample statistics shown in Table IV.3.11. Then use this approximation to estimate the 1% 10-day VaR based on the empirical distribution, and compare this with the normal linear VaR.

Table IV.3.11   Sample statistics used for Cornish–Fisher approximation

Annualized mean	5%
Annualized standard deviation	10%
Skewness	−0.6
Excess kurtosis	3

SOLUTION   The normal linear VaR estimate is

$$\Phi^{-1}(0.99) \times 10\% \times \sqrt{10/250} = \Phi^{-1}(0.99) \times 2\% = 4.65\%.$$

To calculate the Cornish–Fisher VaR we first ignore the mean and standard deviation, and apply the expansion (IV.3.7) to approximate the 1% quantile of the normalized distribution having zero mean and unit variance.

Since $z_{0.01} = \Phi^{-1}(0.01) = -2.32635$ we have $z_{0.01}^2 = 5.4119$, so using (IV.3.7),[31]

$$\tilde{x}_{0.01} \approx -2.32635 - 0.1 \times 4.4119 - 0.125 \times 2.32635 \times 2.4119 + .01 \times 2.32635 \times 5.8238$$

$$= -3.3334.$$

The mean and variance over the risk horizon are 0.2% and 2%, so (IV.3.8) becomes

$$x_{0.01} = -3.3334 \times 0.02 + 0.002 = -0.0647.$$

Hence, based on the Cornish-Fisher expansion, the 1% 10-day VaR is 6.47% of the portfolio value, compared with 4.65% for the normal linear VaR.

Figure IV.3.15 illustrates the error arising from a Cornish–Fisher VaR approximation when the underlying return distribution is known to be a Student t distribution. We consider three different degrees of freedom, i.e. 6, 10 and 50 degrees of freedom, to see how the leptokurtosis in the population influences the fit of the Cornish–Fisher approximation to the true quantiles. The horizontal axis is the significance level of the VaR – in other words, the quantile that we are estimating with the Cornish–Fisher approximation.

The Student t VaR is given by (IV.2.62). This is the 'true' VaR because, for a given value of the degrees of freedom parameter, the quantiles along the horizontal axis are exactly equal to the Student t quantiles. Then, for each quantile, the error is defined as the difference between the Cornish–Fisher VaR and the Student t VaR, divided by the Student t VaR.

---

[31] Note that skewness and kurtosis are unaffected by the scaling and normalizing transforms.

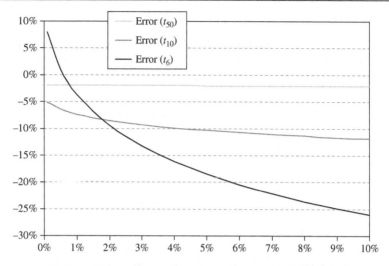

Figure IV.3.15   Error from Cornish–Fisher VaR approximation

With 50 degrees of freedom the population has very small excess kurtosis (of 0.13) and the Cornish–Fisher approximation to the VaR is very close. In fact, the Cornish–Fisher approximation underestimates the true VaR by only about 2%. When the population has a Student t VaR with 10 degrees of freedom, which has an excess kurtosis of 1, Cornish–Fisher also underestimates the VaR, this time by approximately 10%. But the errors that arise when the underlying distribution is very leptokurtic are huge. For instance, under the Student t distribution with 6 degrees of freedom, which has an excess kurtosis of 3, the Cornish–Fisher VaR considerably underestimates the VaR, except at extremely high confidence levels. We conclude that the Cornish–Fisher approximation is quick and easy but it is only accurate if the portfolio returns are not too highly skewed or leptokurtic.

IV.3.4.4   Johnson Distributions

A random variable X has a *Johnson SU distribution* if

$$\left(\frac{X - \xi}{\lambda}\right) = \sinh\left(\frac{Z - \gamma}{\delta}\right),$$ (IV.3.9)

where Z is a standard normal variable and sinh is the *hyperbolic sine function*.[32] The parameter ξ determines the location of the distribution, λ determines the scale, γ the skewness and δ the kurtosis. Having four parameters, this distribution is extremely flexible and is able to fit most empirical densities very well, provided they are leptokurtic.

It follows from (IV.3.9) that each α quantile of X is related to the corresponding standard normal quantile $z_\alpha = \Phi^{-1}(\alpha)$ as

$$x_\alpha = \lambda \sinh\left(\frac{z_\alpha - \gamma}{\delta}\right) + \xi.$$ (IV.3.10)

---

[32] This is one of three translations of normal distributions introduced by Johnson (1954).

Let X denote the h-day return on a portfolio. Then the $100\alpha\%$ h-day historical VaR of the portfolio, expressed as a percentage of the portfolio value, is $-x_\alpha$.[33] Hence, under the Johnson SU distribution

$$\text{VaR}_{h,\alpha} = -\lambda \sinh\left(\frac{z_\alpha - \gamma}{\delta}\right) - \xi. \tag{IV.3.11}$$

Thus, if we can fit a Johnson SU curve then we can use (IV.3.11) to estimate the VaR.

It is possible to fit the parameters of the Johnson SU distribution, knowing only the first four moments of the portfolio returns, using a simple moment matching procedure. For the examples in this chapter, this moment matching procedure has been implemented in Excel using the following algorithm, developed by Tuenter (2001):

1. Set $\omega = \exp(\delta^{-2})$.
2. Set

$$m = \left(4 + 2\left[\omega^2 - \left(\frac{\hat{\varkappa} + 6}{\omega^2 + 2\omega + 3}\right)\right]\right)^{1/2} - 2,$$

   where $\hat{\varkappa}$ is the sample excess kurtosis.
3. Calculate the upper bound for ω:

$$\omega^{\text{upper}} = \left(-1 + \left(2(\hat{\varkappa} + 2)\right)^{1/2}\right)^{1/2}.$$

4. Calculate the lower bound for ω:

$$\omega^{\text{lower}} = \max(\omega_1, \omega_2),$$

   where ω_1 is the unique positive root of $\omega^4 + 2\omega^3 + 3\omega^2 - \hat{\varkappa} - 6 = 0$, and ω_2 is the unique positive root of $(\omega - 1)(\omega + 2)^2 = \hat{\tau}^2$, where $\hat{\tau}$ is the sample skewness.
5. Find ω such that $\omega^{\text{lower}} < \omega \leq \omega^{\text{upper}}$ and

$$(\omega - 1 - m)\left(\omega + 2 + \frac{m}{2}\right)^2 = \hat{\tau}^2.$$

6. Now the parameter estimates are:

$$\hat{\delta} = (\ln \omega)^{-1/2},$$

$$\hat{\gamma} = \theta\,\hat{\delta}, \quad \text{where } \theta = -\text{sign}(\hat{\tau})\,\sinh^{-1}\left[\left(\frac{(\omega + 1)(\omega - 1 - m)}{2\omega m}\right)^{1/2}\right],$$

$$\hat{\lambda} = \left(\frac{2\hat{\sigma}^2}{(\omega - 1)(\omega \cosh 2\theta + 1)}\right)^{1/2},$$

$$\hat{\xi} = \hat{\mu} - \text{sign}(\hat{\tau})\frac{\hat{\sigma}(\omega - m - 1)^{1/2}}{(\omega - 1)},$$

   where $\hat{\mu}$ and $\hat{\sigma}$ are the mean and standard deviation of the portfolio returns.

---

[33] And, as usual, if X denotes the portfolio's P&L then $-x_\alpha$ is the VaR in nominal terms.

Note that there are three numerical optimizations involved: first in steps 3 and 4 of the algorithm we use Goal Seek twice to find the upper and lower bound for ω, and then in step 5 we apply Solver.[34]

EXAMPLE IV.3.5: JOHNSON SU VAR

Estimate the Johnson 1% 10-day VaR for a portfolio whose daily log returns are i.i.d. with skewness −0.2 and excess kurtosis 4, assuming that the mean excess return is 2% per annum and the portfolio's volatility is 25%.

SOLUTION   Figure IV.3.16 illustrates the spreadsheet that is used to implement Tuenter's algorithm. Hence, we calculate the 1% 10-day VaR of the portfolio as 13.68% of the portfolio's value, using a Johnson SU distribution to fit the sample moments. This should be

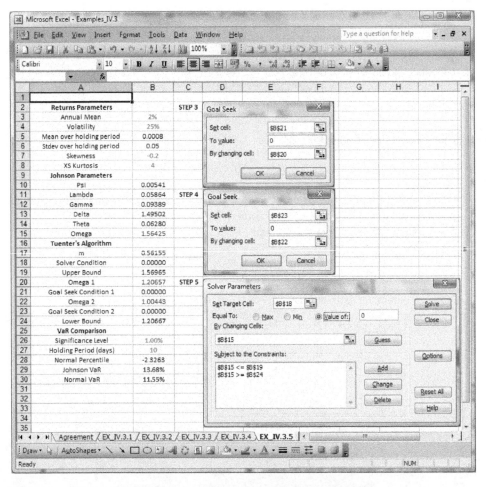

Figure IV.3.16   Tuenter's algorithm for Johnson VaR

---

[34] Note that the Solver constraints do not allow for strict inequality, hence we increase the lower bound and decrease the upper bound by a very small amount.

compared with 11.55% of the portfolio value, under the assumption that the portfolio returns are normally distributed.

We know from the previous subsection that Cornish–Fisher VaR is not a good approximation to VaR at extreme quantiles when the portfolio return distribution is very leptokurtic. Can Johnson's algorithm provide better approximations to the historical VaR at extreme quantiles than Cornish–Fisher VaR? Figure IV.3.17 demonstrates that the answer is most definitely yes. This figure shows the errors arising from the Johnson approximation to the same Student t populations as those used in Figure IV.3.15, and they are much lower than those arising from the Cornish–Fisher approximations in Figure IV.3.15.

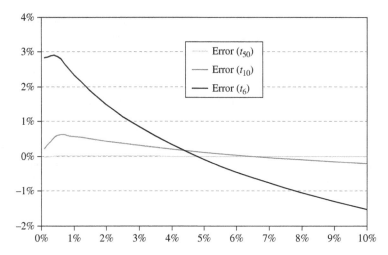

Figure IV.3.17   Error from Johnson VaR approximation

The error in the VaR estimate is virtually zero when the Johnson distribution is fitted to the Student t distribution with 50 degrees of freedom (excess kurtosis 0.13) and the error when it is fitted to the Student t VaR with 10 degrees of freedom is also negligible. Under the Student t distribution with 6 degrees of freedom (excess kurtosis 3), the Johnson VaR slightly underestimates the VaR at quantiles between 5% and 10% and slightly overestimates it at quantiles between 0.001% and 5%.

IV.3.5   HISTORICAL VALUE AT RISK FOR LINEAR PORTFOLIOS

Until now we have been focusing on the general features of historical VaR, and the ways in which the standard 'vanilla' historical simulation can be extended to improve the sample data (e.g. via volatility adjustment) and the accuracy of historical VaR at high levels of confidence. Throughout we have assumed that a risk factor mapping has already been applied to obtain a historical sample of returns for the portfolio. We shall now focus on the use of risk factor mapping in the context of historical VaR.

This section provides a sequence of five case studies that describe the estimation of historical VaR for different types of portfolio. We consider bonds, loans and swaps portfolios and any other interest rate sensitive portfolio that is represented by a sequence of cash flows, as well as stock and commodity portfolios. As in Chapter IV.2, we assume that readers are already familiar with the portfolio mapping methodologies for each type of portfolio.[35] Our main focus will be on the link between the asset class and the structure of the historical simulation model. For the sake of clarity, we shall not be as concerned with the precision of the estimate as we were in the previous section. We do not attempt to improve the accuracy of the VaR estimate by fitting a kernel or a parametric distribution, or by using Cornish–Fisher or Johnson approximations, and we shall only use the simple square-root-of-time scaling rule. However, in most of the case studies we shall examine the effects of a volatility adjustment. Even so, in order not to detract from our main focus, volatility adjustment is based on a simple EWMA model rather than a more sophisticated GARCH model.[36]

We begin in Section IV.3.5.1 with a case study that demonstrates how historical simulation is applied to an interest rate sensitive portfolio that is represented as a sequence of cash flows. We compare the historical VaR estimate to that obtained using a parametric linear VaR model on the same data. The case study in Section IV.3.5.2 considers a simple domestic stock portfolio, estimating the historical VaR first without and then with a risk factor mapping. We explain how to decompose the total historical VaR into systematic VaR due the risk factors and the residual or specific VaR. The case study in Section IV.3.5.3 examines a large international portfolio of stocks and bonds, and explains the decomposition of total systematic VaR into equity, interest rate and forex stand-alone VaRs, and into the corresponding marginal VaRs, all in the historical VaR framework. Section IV.3.5.4 estimates the interest rate, forex and total historical VaR of an international bond position and the final case study in Section IV.3.5.5 is on the decomposition of historical VaR for an energy trader in crack spreads.

IV.3.5.1 Historical VaR for Cash Flows

This case study uses historical simulation to estimate the VaR of the UK bond portfolio that was the subject of the case study in Section IV.2.4. As before, we assume that the cash flows on the portfolio have been mapped to a set of standard maturity interest rates, which are the UK spot interest rates at monthly maturities up to 5 years. So these are the portfolio's risk factors. The portfolio's PV01 vector on 31 December 2007 was depicted in Figure IV.2.2.

In this case study we shall estimate the historical VaR of the same portfolio, but now we need a very large sample of data on the risk factors. We shall use daily data starting on 4 January 2000 and ending at the time the VaR is estimated, i.e. on 31 December 2007. Thus we have 8 years of data on the interest rate risk factors, and these are illustrated in Figure IV.3.18. From the figure it is clear that UK interest rates passed through several different regimes during the sample period.

To find the historical VaR we must map the portfolio to its risk factors. Thus a historical series of daily P&L on the portfolio is constructed by holding the PV01 vector of the portfolio

---

[35] These are fully described in Chapter III.5.

[36] The RiskMetrics™ smoothing constant $\lambda = 0.94$ is used in the text, but readers may change this in the spreadsheets. From Section IV.3.3.4 we know that a univariate GARCH model is likely to lead to more accurate results, but since the volatility adjustment is not the focus of this section we use an EWMA volatility for simplicity.

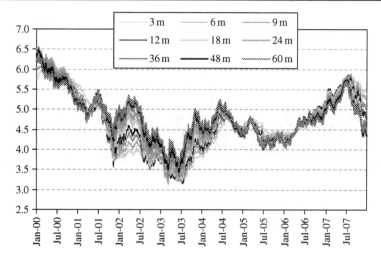

Figure IV.3.18   Bank of England short curve

constant.[37] We apply this to *each* of the daily returns over the sample period using the risk factor mapping

$$\Delta PV_t \approx -\sum_{i=1}^{60} PV01_i \times \Delta R_{it},$$ (IV.3.12)

which we already know may also be written in matrix form as

$$\Delta PV_t \approx -\mathbf{p}'\Delta \mathbf{r}_t$$ (IV.3.13)

where $\mathbf{p} = (PV01_1, \ PV01_2, \ldots, \ PV01_{60})'$ is the PV01 vector and $\Delta \mathbf{r}_t = (\Delta R_{1t}, \ \Delta R_{2t}, \ldots, \ \Delta R_{60t})'$ is the vector of daily interest rate changes at time t. The $100\alpha\%$ 1-day historical VaR is minus the α quantile of the P&L distribution. For longer holding periods the historical VaR is obtained using a square-root scaling rule.[38]

Such a large sample of daily data will allow the historical VaR to be estimated at fairly high confidence levels with reasonable accuracy. But if a long historical sample is used, we know from our discussions in Section IV.3.3.3 that a volatility adjustment should be applied to the daily changes in interest rates before estimating the VaR. A simple EWMA volatility estimate will be used, and the quickest and most effective way to do this is not on the risk factors, but on the P&L of the portfolio. The EWMA volatility of the portfolio's P&L is shown in Figure IV.3.19.[39]

First suppose that we are estimating VaR at the end of the sample, i.e. on 31 December 2007. At this time UK interest rate volatility was greater than it had been since January 2004, so a volatility adjustment will increase the dispersion of the return distribution. Figure IV.3.20

---

[37] The spreadsheet for this case study allows the reader to change the PV01 vector and the start and end dates that define the historical sample. The time of the VaR estimate refers to the end date and we assume the PV01 vector represents the portfolio at whichever time the VaR is measured.

[38] However, Table IV.3.2 suggests that a scale exponent slightly greater than 0.5 may be appropriate.

[39] The smoothing constant is assumed to be 0.9 for this figure, but this may be changed by the reader in the spreadsheet within the case study workbook. Recall that the choice of smoothing constant is entirely *ad hoc*.

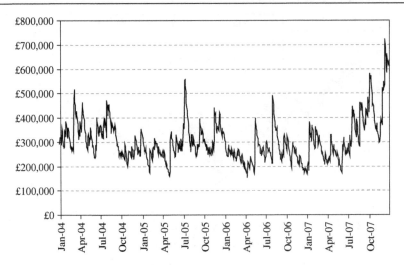

Figure IV.3.19   EWMA volatility of P&L on UK gilts portfolio

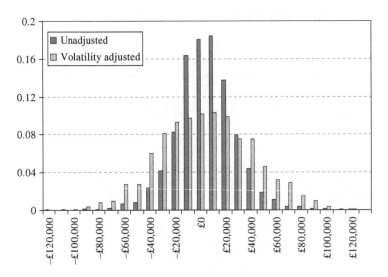

Figure IV.3.20   Empirical distribution of UK gilts portfolio P&L on 31 December 2007

depicts the portfolio's daily P&L distribution, before and after the volatility adjustment, based on the entire sample.

The excess kurtosis in the unadjusted P&L is huge – it is approximately 45 – but after volatility adjustment this is very significantly decreased. In fact, after volatility adjustment the excess kurtosis over the entire sample is −0.2267, so the adjusted P&L distribution is very slightly *mesokurtic* rather than leptokurtic. The volatility adjustment increases the small positive skewness from approximately 0.03 to approximately 0.07. Since negative excess kurtosis and positive skewness both serve to reduce the VaR relative to the normal VaR, after volatility adjustment we expect the historical VaR based on the entire sample to be very slightly less than the normal VaR.

Table IV.3.12 reports the 10-day historical VaR for the portfolio, with and without volatility adjustment, at the 1% and the 0.5% significance levels.[40] This is compared with the corresponding normal VaR, again with and without volatility adjustment.[41]

Table IV.3.12 Historical versus normal VaR for UK bond portfolio

	1%		0.5%	
	Unadjusted	Volatility adjusted	Unadjusted	Volatility adjusted
Historical VaR	£193,585	£259,231	£227,359	£283,567
Normal VaR	£198,579	£272,846	£219,651	£301,635

Table IV.3.12 is based on the entire sample from 5 January 2000 to 31 December 2007. But in the spreadsheet for this case study the reader may change the sample used to estimate the VaRs, including the time at which the VaR is measured, and by changing the PV01 vector the reader can also change the portfolio.

IV.3.5.2 Total, Systematic and Specific VaR of a Stock Portfolio

The case study in this section considers the historical VaR for a simple portfolio consisting of two stocks in the S&P 100 index, Apple Inc. and Citigroup Inc.[42] First we measure the total VaR using a long historical series of portfolio returns, based on a constant portfolio weights assumption. Then we decompose the total VaR into a systematic VaR component, due to movements in the S&P 100 index, and a specific VaR component, due to the idiosyncratic movements of each stock price.

The total historical VaR of an equity portfolio is calculated from a distribution of 'reconstructed' portfolio returns, in this case where the portfolio weights are held constant at their current values. Denote the date on which the VaR is calculated by T and the date of each set of returns on the stocks by t, for $t = 1, \ldots, T$. On each date t in the historical sample the portfolio return is calculated as

$$r_t = \mathbf{w}_T' \mathbf{x}_t, \quad t = 1, \ldots, T, \qquad (IV.3.14)$$

where $\mathbf{w}_T$ is the portfolio weights vector at time T (when the VaR is measured) and $\mathbf{x}_t$ is the vector of stock returns at time t.

Since the historical VaR will better reflect current market conditions when volatility adjusted stock returns are used, the next example compares the historical VaR estimates with and without volatility adjustment. However, the volatility adjustment may be computed in two different ways:

(i) adjust the volatility of each stock return and then apply the portfolio weights, or
(ii) apply the weights to obtain the portfolio returns r_t and then volatility-adjust these returns.

---

[40] However, even using the entire sample, only 10 or 12 observations lie in the 0.5% tail. Thus for the reasons explained in Section IV.3.4, the 0.5% VaR results should be treated with caution.
[41] In Section IV.2.4.1 we estimated the 1% 10-day normal linear VaR for this portfolio as £176,549, but this estimate was based only on daily data during 2007.
[42] Data were downloaded from Yahoo! Finance, symbols APPL and C.

The complication with (i) is that an individual volatility adjustment of each stock return would change their correlation, unless we apply the volatility adjustment in the context of a *multivariate* system. For this, following Duffie and Pan (1997) we use the *Cholesky matrix* of the covariance matrix of stock returns, in place of the square root of the variance of each stock return, in the volatility adjustment (IV.3.3).

To be more specific, suppose there are k stock returns and a total of T observations on each return in the historical sample. Denote the GARCH (or EWMA) covariance matrix of the stock returns at time t by $\mathbf{V}_t$ and denote the Cholesky matrix of $\mathbf{V}_t$ by $\mathbf{Q}_t$. In other words,

$$V_t(\mathbf{x}_t) = \mathbf{V}_t = \mathbf{Q}_t\mathbf{Q}'_t.$$

Now set

$$\tilde{\mathbf{x}}_t = \mathbf{Q}_T\mathbf{Q}_t^{-1}\mathbf{x}_t \quad t = 1, \dots, T. \tag{IV.3.15}$$

Then

$$V_t(\tilde{\mathbf{x}}_t) = V_t(\mathbf{Q}_T\mathbf{Q}_t^{-1}\mathbf{x}_t) = \mathbf{Q}_T\mathbf{Q}_t^{-1}V_t(\mathbf{x}_t)(\mathbf{Q}_T\mathbf{Q}_t^{-1})' = \mathbf{Q}_T(\mathbf{Q}_t^{-1}\mathbf{Q}_t)(\mathbf{Q}'_t\mathbf{Q}'^{-1}_t)\mathbf{Q}'_T = \mathbf{Q}_T\mathbf{Q}'_T = \mathbf{V}_T.$$

Thus $\tilde{\mathbf{x}}_t$ is a vector of stock returns at time t that is adjusted to have the constant covariance matrix $\mathbf{V}_T$, for all $t = 1, \dots, T$.

The following example demonstrates the differences that will arise, depending on the method of volatility adjustment.[43] As in the previous subsection, so as not to make the illustration too complex, instead of using a GARCH model we shall use a simple EWMA volatility adjustment for the daily VaR, with square-root scaling over a 10-day risk horizon.

EXAMPLE IV.3.6: VOLATILITY-ADJUSTING HISTORICAL VAR FOR A STOCK PORTFOLIO

You hold a portfolio on 21 April 2007 that has 30% invested in Citigroup Inc. stock and 70% invested in Apple Inc. stock. Assuming the returns are i.i.d., use daily returns data from 2 January 2001 to 21 April 2008 on the closing prices of these stocks to estimate the $100\alpha\%$ 10-day historical VaR, for $\alpha = 0.001, 0.01, 0.05$ and 0.1 and compare the results obtained before and after volatility adjustment.

SOLUTION   The evolution of the prices of the two stocks over the sample period is shown in Figure IV.3.21. The Citigroup price is on the left-hand scale and the Apple price is on the right-hand scale. Figure IV.3.22 shows the EWMA volatilities of each stock over the sample period. For the volatility adjustment in this case study we shall employ the same value for the smoothing constant in all the EWMA models that are applied, for both the estimation of portfolio betas and volatility adjustment of returns series. This is an *ad hoc* choice, so let us fix λ at the RiskMetrics™ value of 0.94.[44] Whilst both stock price volatilities displayed significant time variation over the sample period, and their volatility in April 2008 is high, both stocks

---

[43] The spreadsheets for this example and for Example IV.3.7 are in the case study workbook. Note that it is easier to use row vectors rather than column vectors for the stock returns, so in case (a) we apply (IV.3.15) in the form

$$\tilde{\mathbf{x}}'_t = \mathbf{x}'_t(\mathbf{Q}_T\mathbf{Q}_t^{-1})'.$$

[44] The reader can change the smoothing constant values in the workbook for this case study. The only way we can estimate an optimal value in an EWMA is to use maximum likelihood to estimate a normal symmetric integrated GARCH model, as explained in Section II.4.2.

Figure IV.3.21   Apple and Citigroup stock prices

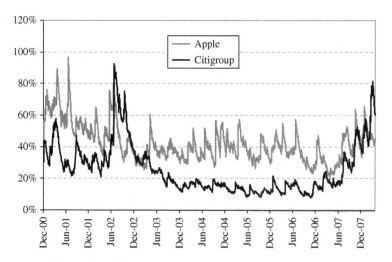

Figure IV.3.22   EWMA volatilities of Apple and Citigroup

also had high volatilities in the early part of the sample. Hence, it is unclear whether volatility adjustment would reduce or increase the historical VaR estimates.

The unadjusted historical VaR is calculated using the Excel PERCENTILE function on the portfolio returns series (IV.3.14), where $\mathbf{w}_T = (0.3, 0.7)'$ and the returns vector $\mathbf{x}_t$ is a 2×1 vector of the unadjusted daily returns on Citigroup and Apple stocks at time t. We shall consider three ways to obtain the volatility adjusted portfolio returns:

(a) Estimate the EWMA covariance matrix of the two stock returns. Then we can adjust each of the stock returns to have constant volatility using (IV.3.15), and then we compute (IV.3.14) using the adjusted returns for $\mathbf{x}_t$.

(b) Compute the portfolio's returns in the usual way, then adjust these to have constant volatility using (IV.3.3).

(c) Ignore the effect that volatility adjustment has on correlation and simply adjust each stock return to have constant volatility using (IV.3.3), and then compute (IV.3.14) using the volatility adjusted returns for $\mathbf{x}_t$.

Does the VaR change much, depending on the method used? Table IV.3.13 reports the results.

Table IV.3.13   Historical VaR with different volatility adjustments

Significance level	10%	5%	1%	0.1%
Unadjusted VaR	7.73%	10.47%	17.49%	29.26%
Method (a)	10.17%	13.41%	19.23%	25.55%
Method (b)	9.99%	13.11%	18.40%	25.43%
Method (c)	9.55%	12.29%	18.06%	25.21%

Clearly, some form of volatility adjustment is important. At low confidence levels (e.g. 90%) the unadjusted VaR is lower than the adjusted VaRs, and the opposite is the case for very high confidence levels (e.g. 99.9%). This implies that without the adjustment the historical return distribution is much more leptokurtic. But the method used to perform the volatility adjustment makes only a small difference to the result. At every confidence level the greatest VaR is obtained using method (a) and the lowest VaR is obtained using method (c), but the results are similar.

Should we adjust the stock returns before computing the portfolio's returns or adjust the portfolio returns? The answer depends on computation time, if this is a constraint. For instance, if we need to measure the VaR for many different portfolios in the same stock universe (or sharing the same risk factors) it may be more efficient to adjust each returns series before the portfolios returns are formed, and the correct method to use is (a). That is, we should use the entire covariance matrix to adjust the returns, rather than just the volatility of each return separately. However, method (c) is quicker and easier than (a) and, although it is approximate, the error it introduces is not large relative to the huge model risk that plagues many VaR models.

When a portfolio is mapped to its risk factors we can decompose the total VaR of the portfolio into the *systematic* VaR, due to changes in the risk factors, and the *specific* VaR which is not captured by the risk factor mapping. We have done this before in the context of normal linear VaR. In that model the square of the total VaR is equal to the sum of the square of the systematic VaR plus the square of the specific VaR. Unfortunately, there are no such simple aggregation rules between total VaR, systematic VaR and specific VaR in either the historical simulation or the Monte Carlo simulation VaR frameworks. Nevertheless we may still decompose total VaR into systematic and specific components.

We aim to estimate the systematic and specific VaR of the Apple and Citigroup portfolio, and to do this we must first estimate the portfolio betas with respect to an index; we choose the S&P 100 index for illustration.[45] To ensure that these are as risk sensitive as

---

[45] Data were downloaded from Yahoo! Finance, symbol ^OEX.

possible, we estimate the betas using EWMA instead of ordinary least squares regression. This method was described in full when we first introduced factor models for equity portfolios in Section II.1.2 and in Section II.3.8, so we merely provide a spreadsheet in the case study that illustrates the estimation of these betas, allowing the reader to change the smoothing constant. The S&P 100 betas corresponding to $\lambda = 0.94$ are shown in Figure IV.3.23.

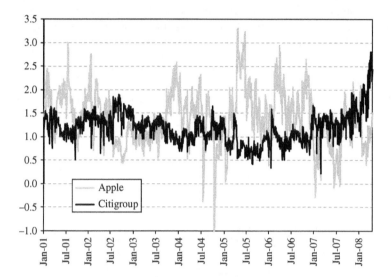

Figure IV.3.23   EWMA betas for Apple and Citigroup in S&P 100 index

The EWMA beta estimate varies over the sample period but it is only the *current* estimate of the beta (i.e. the estimate in the last sample period, at time T) that is used to construct the portfolio's systematic returns. With a smoothing constant of 0.94, we obtain

$$\beta_T = (1.5099, 2.4312)' \quad \text{when } T = 21 \text{ April } 2008,$$
$$\beta_T = (2.4256, 1.0831)' \quad \text{when } T = 30 \text{ October } 2006,$$

(IV.3.16)

where the first element is the beta for Apple and the second is for Citigroup.[46] Notice that the beta of Citigroup rose considerably during the credit crisis at the end of the period. The Citigroup beta was lower and less variable than the Apple beta in the earlier part of the sample, but since the credit crunch in 2007 it has become the more risky of the two stocks.

Fixing the stock betas at their current values, we now compute the systematic part of the portfolio return $\hat{Y}_t$ using

$$\hat{Y}_t = \left(\beta_T' \mathbf{w}_T\right) M_t, \quad t = 1, \dots, T,$$

(IV.3.17)

where $\mathbf{w}_T$ represents the weights and β_T is the beta vector at time T when the VaR is measured, and M_t is the index return at time t. In the next example we use the weights $\mathbf{w}_T = (0.3, 0.7)'$ as before, the market index is the S&P 100 and the betas are given by (IV.3.16).

---

[46] This is assuming $\lambda = 0.94$, but readers can see in the spreadsheet for this figure that higher values of λ give lower values for both betas.

EXAMPLE IV.3.7: SYSTEMATIC AND SPECIFIC COMPONENTS OF HISTORICAL VAR

As in Example IV.3.6, suppose you hold a portfolio that has 30% invested in Citigroup Inc. stock and 70% invested in Apple Inc. stock. Using the S&P 100 index as the risk factor, decompose the total 1% 10-day VaR of your portfolio, with and without a EWMA volatility adjustment, into systematic and specific components. Estimate the VaR on 21 April 2008 and compare your results with the VaR that is estimated on 30 October 2006 for the same portfolio, i.e. with 30% invested in Citigroup and 70% invested in Apple. In each case, use data starting on 2 January 2001 and express the VaR as a percentage of the portfolio value.

SOLUTION   We know from the previous example that our estimate of the total VaR of the portfolio depends on whether we apply volatility adjustment and, if so, how this is performed. The portfolio's systematic returns are obtained using (IV.3.17). Figure IV.3.24 shows the results before and after volatility adjustment. Figure IV.3.24(a) shows the returns adjusted

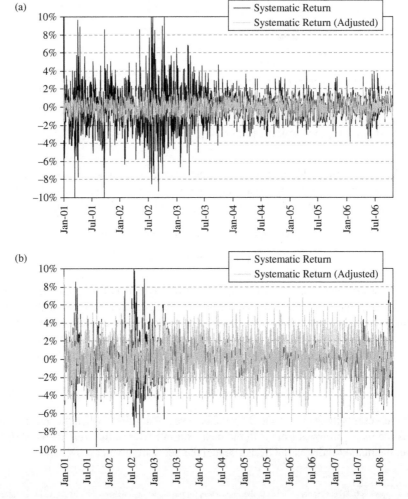

Figure IV.3.24   Systematic returns before and after volatility adjustment for the volatility on (a) 30 October 2006 and (b) 21 April 2008

for the relatively low volatility on 30 October 2006, and Figure IV.3.24(b) shows the returns adjusted for the relatively high volatility on 21 April 2008.

The specific returns, which are the portfolio returns minus the systematic returns, are also adjusted for volatility. Finally, we calculate the 1% 10-day historical VaR from the relevant quantile of each distribution, obtaining the results shown in Table IV.3.14. For comparison, we also include the normal linear VaR based on the same data. Results for other portfolio weights, data periods, significance levels and risk horizons can be generated by changing the dates and parameters in the spreadsheet for this example in the case study workbook.

Table IV.3.14   Total, systematic and specific VaR, US stock portfolio

30 October 2006	Historical		Normal	
	Unadjusted	Vol. adjusted	Unadjusted	Vol. adjusted
Total VaR	17.41%	5.84%	16.58%	6.32%
Systematic VaR	18.77%	5.98%	16.91%	6.34%
Specific VaR	15.11%	6.12%	14.17%	6.19%
21 April 2008	Unadjusted	Vol. adjusted	Unadjusted	Vol. adjusted
Total VaR	17.49%	17.06%	16.31%	18.06%
Systematic VaR	16.79%	17.70%	14.76%	18.13%
Specific VaR	13.31%	17.60%	13.07%	17.65%

On 30 October 2006 the 1% 10-day total VaR of the portfolio was 17.41% of the portfolio value before volatility adjustment but only 5.84% after adjusting for the low volatility leading up to this time. As Figure IV.3.24(a) shows, the extreme volatility of the portfolio during 2001–2003 means that the historical VaR will be much larger before the volatility adjustment. The systematic VaR is greater than the total VaR of the portfolio, and even the specific VaR is greater than the total VaR after the volatility adjustment.[47] It is again evident that the volatility adjustment decreases the excess kurtosis of the returns to such an extent that it becomes negative. We can see this from the fact that the normal linear VaR estimates are greater than the historical VaR estimates after the volatility adjustment, but not before.

A different picture emerges on 21 April 2008 (for which the systematic returns are shown in Figure IV.3.24(b)). The volatility at the time the VaR is measured was less than it was during 2001–2003 but higher than it was during 2004–2006, and so the volatility adjustment makes little difference to the VaR estimate based on the period 2001–2008. Still, the volatility adjustment alters the shape of the empirical distribution, slightly increasing the volatility but also decreasing the excess kurtosis. Thus the normal VaR estimates still increase after the volatility adjustment, and the historical systematic VaR, and the specific VaR again become greater than the total VaR after the volatility adjustment.

IV.3.5.3   Equity and Forex VaR of an International Stock Portfolio

Because historical VaR is calculated as a quantile it does not obey simple aggregation rules, such as the sub-additivity rule that applies to parametric linear VaR, whereby total linear VaR

---

[47] This is true even for the normal linear VaR model, because the correlation between the market return and the specific return is large and negative. When this correlation is negative it is quite possible for the total normal linear VaR to be less than both the systematic VaR and the specific VaR, as can be seen from the formula (IV. 2.47).

is never greater than the sum of the stand-alone linear VaRs. Normal and Student t VaR obeys the same rules as the variance operator, but historical VaR obeys the same rules as quantiles, and quantiles obey very few rules.

Quantiles translate under continuous monotonic increasing transformations. That is, if the variable X has α quantile x_α then, for any continuous monotonic increasing function f, $f(X)$ has α quantile $f(x_\alpha)$.[48] We call this the *monotonic property* of quantiles. *Time aggregation* of quantiles is also possible, but only under the assumption that portfolio returns are stable.[49]

However, aggregation of historical VaR *across positions* is not the same as monotonic transformation or time aggregation. No aggregation rules such as sub-additivity apply, but this does not imply that we cannot decompose and aggregate historical VaR. Indeed, dependencies between returns play a very important role in reducing risk via diversification, and an attractive feature of the historical model is that we do not capture any dependency using a correlation matrix; instead the dependencies are implicit in the historical data.

We now present a case study to illustrate the disaggregation of total systematic VaR into stand-alone and marginal VaR components, when the VaR model is based on historical simulation. Consider a UK investor holding a US and a UK stock portfolio on 21 April 2008. Suppose 70% of the total amount invested in pounds sterling is held in UK stocks and 30% is held in US stocks. The US portfolio has a beta of 1.8 relative to the S&P 500 index and the UK portfolio has a beta of 1.25 relative to the FTSE 100 index.

To assess the historical VaR for this portfolio we use daily log returns on the S&P 500 index, the FTSE 100 index and the £/$ exchange rate from 3 January 1996 to 21 April 2008.[50] The indices themselves are shown in Figure IV.3.25, with the S&P 500 measured on the right-hand scale and the FTSE 100 measured on the left-hand scale. The £/$ forex rate is shown in

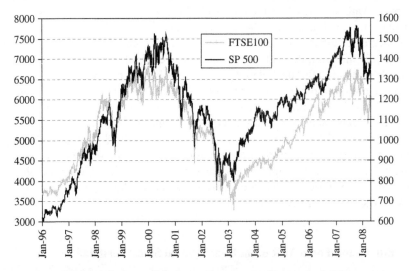

Figure IV.3.25   S&P 500 and FTSE 100 indices, 1996–2008

---

[48] To prove this, simply note that $\alpha = P(X < x_\alpha) = P(f(X) < f(x_\alpha))$.
[49] As shown in Section IV.3.2.
[50] Stock index data were downloaded from Yahoo! Finance, symbols ^GSPC and ^FTSE, and the exchange rate data were obtained from the Bank of England website, http://www.bankofengland.co.uk/statistics/about/index.htm.

Figure IV.3.26. This illustrates the fairly steady decline in the US dollar from January 2001 until the end of the sample. Hence, anything the investor has gained from his exposure to US stocks will be offset by losses on the currency position.

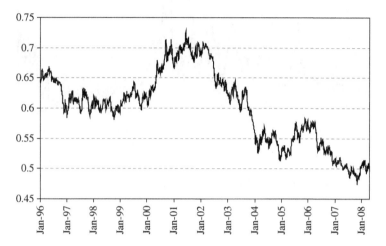

Figure IV.3.26   £/$ forex rate, 1996–2008

The VaR will be measured at an interesting time in equity markets. After several years of very low volatility stock markets in the US and the UK, volatility had risen following concerns about the Chinese and US economies and then in the aftermath of the sub-prime mortgage crisis, whose effects were still impacting stocks in the financial sector in April 2008. Since we use the entire sample with over 3000 observations, we shall estimate volatility adjusted historical VaR.[51] Based on EWMA with $\lambda = 0.94$, the volatilities of the FTSE 100 and S&P 500 index and of the forex rate are depicted in Figure IV.3.27. By the end of the sample equity volatilities had climbed to around 25%, but the £/$ exchange rate remained stable with a volatility of approximately 10%.

We now explain the methodology that underpins the VaR disaggregation into equity and forex components. The price in pounds sterling is the dollar price *multiplied* by the £/$ exchange rate; or, in symbols, $P_t^£ = P_t^\$ \times X_t^{£/\$}$. Hence, the log equity return and the log forex return are additive. In other words, the log return on the US stock portfolio in pounds sterling is the sum of the log return on the US stock portfolio in US dollars and the log return on the £/$ rate:

$$\ln\left(P_{t+1}^£/P_t^£\right) = \ln\left(P_{t+1}^\$/P_t^\$\right) + \ln\left(X_{t+1}^{£/\$}/X_t^{£/\$}\right).$$

Or, in alternative notation, $r_t^£ = r_t^\$ + r_t^{£/\$}$. Hence, the risk of a US stock portfolio to a UK investor has an equity component, which is based on the risk of the dollar returns on the portfolio, and a forex component, which is based on the risk of the £/$ forex rate.

---

[51] To keep the spreadsheet focused on VaR disaggregation rather than volatility adjustment, we use a simple approach where we adjust the volatility of the equity and forex parts of the portfolio returns individually, rather than using the full covariance matrix adjustment that was described in the previous subsection.

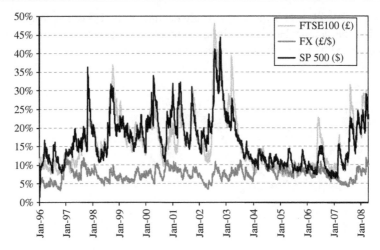

Figure IV.3.27   Volatilities of UK and US stock markets and the £/$ exchange rate

We have 70% of our capital invested in the UK portfolio, with sterling price at time t denoted by $P_{1t}^{£}$, and 30% of our capital is invested in the US portfolio, with sterling price $P_{2t}^{£}$. In other words, the total portfolio has a sterling price

$$P_t^{£} = \omega_1 P_{1t}^{£} + \omega_2 P_{2t}^{£}, \qquad (IV.3.18)$$

where $\omega_1 = 0.7$ and $\omega_2 = 0.3$. From (IV.3.18) is follows that now it is the percentage return, not the log return, that is additive. This means that to disaggregate the total VaR into equity and forex components we must assume the percentage return is approximately equal to the log return. We know from Section I.1.4 that this approximation is accurate only when the return is small, and this is another reason why it is standard to base historical VaR estimation on high frequency (e.g. daily) data.

Let β_1 denote the percentage beta of the UK portfolio with respect to the FTSE 100 at the time the VaR is measured and let ω_1 denote the proportion of total capital invested in the UK portfolio. Similarly, let β_2 denote the percentage beta of the US portfolio with respect to the S&P 500 at the time the VaR is measured and let ω_2 denote the proportion of total capital invested in the portfolio US. Thus $\omega_1 + \omega_2 = 1$. In local currency, the daily log returns on the UK and US portfolios are denoted by $r_{1t}^{£}$ and $r_{2t}^{£}$, and the daily log returns on the two equity indices are written $y_{1t}^{£}$ and $y_{2t}^{\$}$, so $r_{it}^{*} = \beta_i y_{it}^{*}$ for $i = 1$, 2 and $^* = £$ or $\$$. The £/$ forex log return is denoted by $r_t^{£/\$}$ as before.

Now, applying the log return approximation to the percentage return, we may write the sterling return on our combined portfolio of US and UK stocks as

$$
\begin{aligned}
r_t^{£} &\approx \omega_1 r_{1t}^{£} + \omega_2 r_{2t}^{£} \\
&= \omega_1 r_{1t}^{£} + \omega_2 \left(r_{2t}^{\$} + r_t^{£/\$} \right) \\
&= \left(\omega_1 \beta_1 y_{1t}^{£} + \omega_2 \beta_2 y_{2t}^{\$} \right) + \omega_2 r_t^{£/\$}.
\end{aligned} \qquad (IV.3.19)
$$

On the right-hand side above we have two components to the portfolio return:

1. the net equity return, $\omega_1\beta_1 y_{1t}^{\pounds} + \omega_2\beta_2 y_{2t}^{\$}$;
2. the forex return, $\omega_2 r_t^{\pounds/\$}$.

The return on the total portfolio is the sum of these.

Using historical data for each of the series of log returns (i.e. on the FTSE 100 index, the S&P 500 index and the £/$ exchange rate) we find the equity VaR and forex VaR from the quantiles of the corresponding empirical return distributions. Each time series runs from January 1996 until 21 April 2008. Adding the net equity return and forex return time series together gives a time series for the net portfolio return, and the total risk factor VaR is obtained from the quantile of this empirical distribution.

Table IV.3.15 presents the $100\alpha\%$ h-day risk factor VaR, disaggregated into equity and forex components. It is expressed as a percentage of the total sterling value of the US and UK portfolios and it is based on the entire sample of over 3000 observations.[52] The forex stand-alone VaR is relatively small and the total VaR is only slightly more than the equity stand-alone VaR. Total risk factor VaR is less than the sum of the equity VaR and the forex VaR, although this need not always be the case with historical VaR, since it is measured as a quantile rather than a volatility. Since the portfolio's volatility has previously been both higher and lower than the volatility at the time the VaR is measured, the volatility adjustment makes little difference to the VaR. However, by changing the start and end dates in the spreadsheet, readers can see that this is not always the case.

Table IV.3.15   Decomposition of systematic VaR into equity and forex stand-alone components

		$h=1$			$h=10$		
		Equity	Forex	Total	Equity	Forex	Total
Unadjusted	$\alpha = 1\%$	3.80%	0.37%	3.86%	12.03%	1.16%	12.22%
Volatility Adjusted		4.29%	0.44%	4.37%	13.55%	1.38%	13.83%
Unadjusted	$\alpha = 0.1\%$	6.15%	0.48%	6.34%	19.43%	1.52%	20.04%
Volatility Adjusted		5.46%	0.59%	5.48%	17.28%	1.87%	17.32%

We know from Section IV.1.7.3 that we measure the marginal VaR by estimating the gradient vector $\mathbf{g}(\boldsymbol{\theta})$ of first partial derivatives of VaR with respect to the risk factor sensitivities. In the parametric linear VaR framework there are analytic formulae that can be applied to obtain the gradient vector, as for instance in Section IV.2.2.5. But in the historical VaR model there are no such analytical formulae. So we estimate $\mathbf{g}(\boldsymbol{\theta})$ using a first order finite difference, as explained in Section I.5.5. That is, we make a small perturbation in each of the risk factor sensitivities in turn, and compute the first partial derivative of the total VaR with respect to that sensitivity by dividing the resulting change in the total VaR by the small perturbation.[53] The risk factor sensitivities, in percentage terms, are $\boldsymbol{\theta} = (1, \omega_2)'$ on the equity and forex returns respectively.

---

[52] Results for $\alpha = 1\%$ and 0.1% and for $h = 1$ and 10 days are shown here, but the reader may see other results by changing the values of the VaR parameters in the spreadsheet labelled 'VaR' in the case study workbook. You may also change the sample over which the VaR is measured, the relative weights on the UK and US portfolios and the portfolio betas.

[53] If the sensitivity increment is too large the finite difference approximation to the gradient vector will not be accurate. We have set a perturbation size of 0.1% for the results in Table IV.3.18.

Having estimated the gradient vector, we multiply each component in the vector by its risk factor sensitivity, before perturbation, to obtain the corresponding marginal VaR. For the portfolio in this case study the results are displayed in Table IV.3.16. Based on the unadjusted returns data from January 1996 to 21 April 2008, 92.29% of the total risk factor 1% 10-day VaR is due to equity risk and only 7.71% is due to forex risk. At the 0.1% significance level a slightly greater percentage of the VaR is due to equity risk. Note that when based on the volatility adjusted returns (which we know usually have less kurtosis than unadjusted returns) the contribution of forex risk to the total VaR is much smaller, and it can even be negative.

Table IV.3.16   Historical marginal VaR for international stock portfolio

Percentage contribution to total 10-day VaR		Equity	Forex
Unadjusted	$\alpha = 1\%$	92.29%	7.71%
Volatility adjusted		102.62%	−2.62%
Unadjusted	$\alpha = 0.1\%$	93.14%	6.86%
Volatility adjusted		99.68%	0.32%

IV.3.5.4   Interest Rate and Forex VaR of an International Bond Position

We now consider a case study where a UK bank buys £50 million nominal of an AA-rated 5-year US bond with an annual coupon of 4% on 21 April 2008. Since the bank needs to purchase £50 million in US dollars to finance the purchase, the total return will also have a currency component. So the risk factors are the US swap curve, which is AA-rated, and the sterling–dollar exchange rate. We shall decompose the historical VaR into interest rate and forex components.

Daily historical data on US swap rates from July 2000 until 21 April 2008 are shown in Figure IV.3.28.[54] The swap curve is upward sloping, except for two relatively flat periods during 2001 and during 2006–2007, and short term rates varied more than longer terms rates over the sample. The highest value for the 1-year swap rate was 7% at the beginning of the sample and its lowest value was about 1%, in June 2006.

The interest rate VaR is based on a P&L distribution that can be estimated in two approximately equivalent ways, either using the PV01 approximation to the bond P&L given by (IV.3.12) or by revaluing the bond directly. For the first approach the PV01 vector for the bond is calculated in the spreadsheet labelled VaR, using the approximation described in Section IV.2.3.2, and this is the PV01 vector reported in the last row of Table IV.3.17. This table also shows the price P of the bond per £100 nominal, and the number of units of £100 nominal that the bank purchases for £50 million cash, which is given by $N = 50 \times 10^6 \times P^{-1}$. Holding this PV01 vector constant, we apply (IV.3.12) with the historically observed time series of basis point changes to swap rates. This gives a time series of P&L on the bond that is shown in column H of the spreadsheet labelled 'VaR' in the case study workbook.

---

[54] The data on swap rates were downloaded from http://www.federalreserve.gov/releases/h15/data.htm, the exchanges rates were downloaded from http://www.bankofengland.co.uk/statistics/about/index.htm, and the S&P 500 index data were obtained from Yahoo! Finance, symbol ^GSPC.

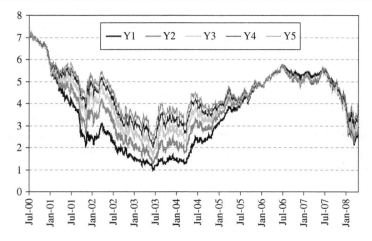

Figure IV.3.28   US swap rates

Table IV.3.17   Bond position

Bond characteristics		Maturity (years)	1	2	3	4	5
Cash (£m)	£50	Cash flow	4	4	4	4	104
Coupon	4%	Swap curve on 21/04/08	2.93%	3.09%	3.34%	3.58%	3.78%
P	101.1398	PV of cash flow	3.89	3.76	3.62	3.48	86.39
N	494,365	PV01 (£)	£187	£361	£520	£663	£20,576

Another way to derive a historical P&L distribution for a bond position is to apply the historical daily basis point changes to the current swap curve, and then to revalue our cash position keeping N constant. This gives the values in column I of the spreadsheet labelled VaR. Then the historical P&L is obtained by taking each simulated value and deducting the current value of £50 million. These P&L are shown in column J of the same spreadsheet. Note that the two approaches give almost identical results.[55]

The total VaR is based on the US dollar P&L distribution, and the dollar price at any point in time is the price in pounds multiplied by the $/£ exchange rate. The forex VaR is estimated from the historical distribution of daily log returns on the $/£ exchange rate, and the P&L distribution for the total VaR is obtained by converting the position value in column I into US dollars, and then recalculating the P&L. To find the relevant exchange rate to apply for each day, we apply the log return on the forex on that day to the current forex rate, i.e. the rate at the time the VaR is measured. The resulting P&L is shown in column L.

In each case the VaR is minus the α quantile of the daily P&L distribution, and the 1-day VaR estimates are multiplied by the square root of the risk horizon (in days) to estimate the corresponding h-day VaR.[56] The results for 1% 10-day VaR are given in the spreadsheet in both pounds sterling and US dollars, and the sterling figures are displayed in Table IV.3.18.

---

[55] For a simple bond such as this, both are fast and straightforward calculations, but the PV01 approximation would be preferable if full revaluation of the portfolio is computationally burdensome.

[56] We cannot calculate the total VaR using a PV01 approximation, e.g. by converting the PV01 vector into dollar terms. This is because that way the P&L would be zero whenever interest rates do not change, even though there could be a loss on the currency position.

Table IV.3.18   VaR decomposition for international bond position

Interest Rate VaR (PV01 approx.)	£1,381,833
Interest Rate VaR (direct valuation)	£1,374,072
Forex VaR	£2,042,953
Total VaR	£2,319,324

As already mentioned, it makes very little difference whether we estimate the interest rate VaR using the PV01 approximation or the bond evaluation method. The forex VaR is greater than the interest rate VaR, and the total VaR is less than the square root of the sum of the squared component VaRs, which indicates a small or negative dependency between the £/$ rate and the swap rates.

IV.3.5.5   Case Study: Historical VaR for a Crack Spread Trader

In this subsection we consider a trader in crack spread futures. There are two crack spreads, i.e. the difference between the heating oil futures price and the WTI crude oil futures price of the same maturity, and the difference between the gasoline futures price and the WTI crude oil futures price of the same maturity. NYMEX facilitates crack spread trading in its futures markets by treating both legs of the trade as a single transaction. Each futures contract is for 1000 barrels, priced in US dollars per barrel.

Because spreads can have negative values, it makes no sense to compute percentage returns on these risk factors, for the reasons explained in Section 1.5.5. Instead we compute the daily P&L on the crack spread futures and compute the VaR directly in nominal terms. We shall calculate the historical VaR of the entire portfolio, and then decompose the total VaR into the VaR due to the heating oil crack spread and the VaR due to the unleaded gasoline crack spread.

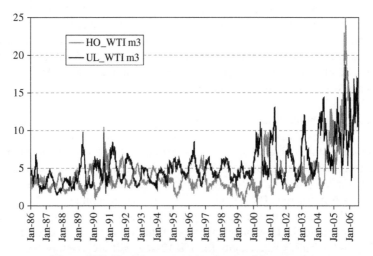

Figure IV.3.29   Three-month crack spread futures prices

Our risk factors are constant maturity futures on each spread for 1, 2, 3, 4, 5 and 6 months ahead.[57] The case study workbook contains over 20 years of daily data on these constant

---

[57] These were derived from the prices of traded futures using linear interpolation.

maturity futures, and the reader may use the spreadsheet labelled 'VaR' in this workbook to estimate the historical VaR, with and without volatility adjustment, using any start and end dates during this sample. The 3-month crack spread futures prices from 2 January 1996 to 1 August 2006, the day when the VaR is estimated, are shown in Figure IV.3.29. The trader's positions in crack spread futures, and their prices on 1 August 2006, are shown in Table IV.3.19.[58]

Table IV.3.19   Crack spread book, 1 August 2006

Prices	m1	m2	m3	m4	m5	m6
HO_WTI ($/barrel)	12.47	14.02	15.61	16.96	18.07	18.52
UL_WTI ($/barrel)	20.69	14.39	10.05	6.76	5.37	4.78
Positions	m1	m2	m3	m4	m5	m6
No. Contracts HO_WTI	100	50	50	0	0	−250
No. Contracts UL_WTI	−50	−100	0	0	150	100

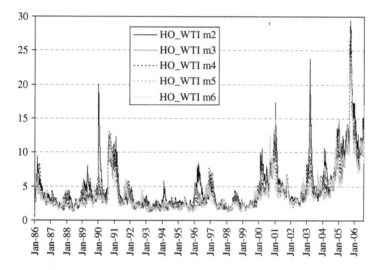

Figure IV.3.30   EWMA volatilities of heating oil crack spread futures P&L

Figures IV.3.30 and IV.3.31 show the volatilities of the crack spread futures P&L, calculated as an exponentially weighted moving average of squared daily changes in the futures price with a smoothing constant of 0.94.[59] These graphs display terrific variability in spread futures volatilities, so it is advisable to apply a volatility adjustment to the portfolio's P&L, and we shall use the EWMA volatilities shown in Figures IV.3.30 and IV.3.31 to derive a simple volatility adjustment, as described in Section IV.3.3.3. Since volatility was relatively high on

---

[58] Of course, there are no traded futures at exactly these maturities, but we assume the positions have been mapped to the standard maturities as explained in Section III.5.4.

[59] The volatilities of the 1-month crack spread futures are omitted because they are excessively volatile.

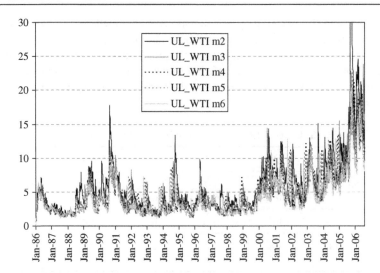

Figure IV.3.31   EWMA volatilities of gasoline crack spread futures P&L

1 August 2006, the volatility adjusted VaR on 1 August 2006 is likely to be much greater than the VaR based on unadjusted P&L.

In the case study workbook we hold the positions constant, at their values shown in Table IV.3.19, and simulate a historical series for the P&L on each futures position. The P&L series is simulated by multiplying the fixed number of contracts by the absolute change in the value of the spread on each day in the historical sample, after the volatility adjustment if this is used. Then we sum the P&L on each day due to (a) the six positions on heating oil crack spread futures of different maturities, and (b) the six positions on unleaded gasoline crack spread futures of different maturities, and (c) the 12 positions over all the futures. This gives three historical P&L series: one for the heating oil crack spread positions, another for the gasoline crack spread positions, and a third for the total positions. The historical VaR is calculated by finding the quantile of the simulated P&L distribution and then multiplying this quantile by -1000, since each futures contract is for 1000 barrels.

The reader may change the positions, the VaR parameters and the period over which the VaR is estimated in the spreadsheet labelled 'VaR'. The 1% 10-day VaR results for the positions in Table IV.3.19, with and without volatility adjustment, are given in Table IV.3.20. The volatility adjustment increases the VaR very considerably, since the spreads were unusually volatile at the time when the VaR is measured. The total VaR is much less than the sum of the two stand-alone VaRs, but still greater than the square root of the sum of the squared stand-alone VaRs, because there is a high positive correlation between the spreads.

Table IV.3.20   Total VaR and component VaRs for a crack spread trader

1% 10-day VaR	HO_WTI	UL_WTI	Total
VaR (Unadjusted) $	$661,578	$673,036	$1,246,270
VaR (Volatility adjusted) $	$1,666,862	$1,391,788	$2,577,317

IV.3.6   ESTIMATING EXPECTED TAIL LOSS IN THE HISTORICAL VALUE-AT-RISK MODEL

Section IV.2.11 derived analytic formulae for expected tail loss in parametric linear VaR models. This was possible because the model makes an assumption about the functional form of the return distribution. In the historical VaR model the ETL must be estimated directly, simply by taking the average of all the losses in the tail below the VaR. The exception is when a parametric distribution or approximation has been fitted to the historical distribution. In this case it is sometimes possible to derive an analytic formula for ETL.

In this section we first present some analytic formulae for the ETL when the historical distribution is fitted with a generalized Pareto distribution, a Johnson SU distribution and when the VaR is estimated using a Cornish–Fisher expansion. We end with a case study that compares the historical ETL estimates that are derived using these formulae with the historical ETL that is estimated directly, as the average of the losses that exceed the VaR.

IV.3.6.1   Parametric Historical ETL

From formula (I.3.68) derived in Section I.3.3.10 for the mean excess loss in the generalized Pareto distribution, it immediately follows that

$$\text{ETL}_\alpha = \text{VaR}_\alpha + \frac{\beta + \xi \text{VaR}_\alpha}{1 - \xi}, \tag{IV.3.20}$$

where the parameters β and ξ are estimated by fitting a GPD to excess losses and VaR_α is given by (IV.3.6).

The other two ETL formulae are derived from the transformation of the random variable into a standard normal variable. Using the fact that the standard normal $100\alpha\%$ ETL is $\alpha^{-1}\varphi(Z_\alpha)$,[60] for a Johnson SU distribution we have

$$\text{ETL}_\alpha = \hat{\lambda} \sinh\left(\frac{\alpha^{-1}\varphi(Z_\alpha) - \hat{\gamma}}{\hat{\delta}}\right) + \hat{\xi}. \tag{IV.3.21}$$

Finally, it follows from (IV.3.7) that the ETL under the Cornish–Fisher expansion is approximated by

$$\text{ETL}_\alpha = f\left(\alpha^{-1}\varphi(Z_\alpha)\right)\hat{\sigma} - \hat{\mu}, \tag{IV.3.22}$$

where

$$f(x) = x + \frac{\hat{\tau}}{6}\left(x^2 - 1\right) + \frac{\hat{\varkappa}}{24}x\left(x^2 - 3\right) - \frac{\hat{\tau}^2}{36}x\left(2x^2 - 5\right).$$

IV.3.6.2   Empirical Results on Historical ETL

We now present a case study that compares several estimates of the historical ETL. Using volatility adjusted log returns on the S&P 500 from 4 January 1950 until 9 March 2007, a GPD

---

[60] This is proved in Section IV.2.11.1.

has been fitted to the excess returns over a threshold u, and the Cornish–Fisher expansion and the Johnson SU distribution have been fitted to the first four moments of the empirical returns. We compare the results from applying (IV.3.20)–(IV.3.22) with the results from the empirical ETL, estimated as the average of the losses in excess of the VaR, and with the ETL under the assumption that the returns are normally distributed.

There are over 14,000 returns in the sample, which allows for a comparison of results at very high significance levels. Of course the Cornish–Fisher and Johnson ETL can be estimated from a very much smaller sample, because they require only the first four moments of the empirical return distribution. However, the GPD requires a considerable amount of data, since it is fitted only to the excess losses over a certain threshold.

We set significance levels 1%, 0.1% and 0.05%, corresponding to confidence levels of 99%, 99.9% and 99.95% respectively, and the results from estimating the daily VaR using the different models are displayed in Table IV.3.21. As usual the VaR estimates are reported as a percentage of the portfolio value at the time the VaR is estimated. The Johnson VaR estimates are generally closer to the GPD estimates but they do not suffer the disadvantage of the GPD VaR estimates, i.e. that they are sensitive to the choice of threshold. Moreover, as described in Section IV.3.4.4, estimation of Johnson SU parameters is straightforward, using the algorithm developed by Tuenter (2001). This algorithm is implemented in the spreadsheet for this case study.

Table IV.3.21   Estimates of GPD parameters and historical VaR estimates

	GPD parameter estimates				Significance level		
Threshold	n_u	u	ξ	β	1%	0.1%	0.05%
1%	143	−2.574	−0.3906	7.6815	1.69%	6.01%	7.27%
5%	713	−1.6097	−0.2425	4.4892	2.87%	6.43%	7.16%
10%	1426	−1.1960	−0.1870	3.3786	3.37%	6.10%	6.71%
20%	2853	−0.7203	−0.1289	2.2795	3.26%	5.30%	5.81%
Johnson VaR					3.57%	5.10%	5.60%
Cornish–Fisher VaR					2.48%	5.06%	5.96%
Empirical VaR					1.69%	3.00%	3.87%
Normal VaR					1.52%	2.03%	2.16%

Table IV.3.22 compares the daily historical ETL estimates based on a normal approximation to the return distribution, the empirical distribution. Notice that those based on the GPD, Johnson and Cornish–Fisher parametric fits. The empirical returns have an excess kurtosis of 4.93 and a very significant negative skewness. As a result the normal ETL estimates are far too low, and all the non-normal parametric ETL estimates exceed the empirical ETL. Even when the empirical ETL is based on 14,000 returns, the 0.1% ETL estimates are based on only 14 observations and the 0.05% ETL estimates are based on only 7 observations. Hence, they are likely to be imprecise.

Tables IV.3.21 and IV.3.22 indicate that there is a considerable degree of model risk associated with estimating VaR and ETL using historical simulation. There are very significant differences between the results that are obtained using different enhancements to the simulation model, particularly at very high confidence levels. So what advice, if any, can we glean from these diverse results?

Table IV.3.22 Comparison of ETL from parametric fits to historical return distribution

GPD (Threshold)	Significance level		
	1%	0.1%	0.05%
GPD (1%)	4.87%	7.98%	8.88%
GPD (5%)	4.70%	7.57%	8.16%
GPD (10%)	4.73%	7.02%	7.54%
GPD (20%)	4.22%	6.03%	6.48%
Johnson	3.47%	6.33%	7.31%
Cornish–Fisher	4.18%	5.81%	6.34%
Empirical	2.29%	4.48%	5.56%
Normal	1.74%	2.21%	2.33%

It is unlikely that risk analysts will be working with a sample having more than a few thousand observations, and the smaller the sample, the greater the model risk arising from the choice of parametric or semi-parametric method that is used to estimate the VaR and ETL. If the analyst does have a very large sample and therefore considers the use of the GPD, it seems better to use a relatively high threshold such as 20%, so that the tail contains a larger sample of returns.

IV.3.6.3   Disaggregation of Historical ETL

Historical ETL can be aggregated and disaggregated just like historical VaR, so we may compute stand-alone ETLs corresponding to different sub-portfolios. But, unlike historical VaR, the ETLs are always sub-additive. We now illustrate the disaggregation methodology with an extension of the case study in Section IV.3.5.3, where we disaggregated the total systematic VaR for an international equity portfolio consisting of US and UK stocks into equity and forex stand-alone components. In this case study we estimate the $100\alpha\%$ h-day historical ETL for the same portfolio.

The results for the 1% 10-day historical VaR and ETL estimated on 21 April 2008, using the same data as in Section IV.3.5.3, are displayed in Table IV.3.23. The upper part of the table shows the 1% 10-day historical VaR based on both unadjusted and EWMA volatility adjusted returns. These are identical to those reported in Table IV.3.15 for a significance level of 1% and $h = 10$. The lower part of the table displays the ETL estimates. These are estimated directly, by averaging the returns that exceed the VaR.

Table IV.3.23 Stand-alone equity and forex ETL for an international stock portfolio

VaR	Equity	Forex	Total
VaR (Unadjusted)	12.03%	1.16%	12.22%
VaR (Adjusted)	13.55%	1.38%	13.83%
ETL	**Equity**	**Forex**	**Total**
ETL (Unadjusted)	14.78%	1.33%	15.41%
ETL (Adjusted)	15.21%	1.57%	15.58%

In this case it happens that the volatility adjustment has as little effect on the ETL as it has on the VaR estimates. This is because the VaR is measured on 21 April 2008 at a time when the volatility was not far from its historical average. However, readers may generate other results by changing the start and end date for the calculations in the spreadsheet labelled 'ETL' in the case study workbook, as well as the VaR parameters and the EWMA smoothing constant for the volatility adjustment. When the end date is during one of the more volatile or tranquil years the volatility adjustment would have a more significant effect. For instance, when the VaR is measured on 21 April 2006, which was a particularly tranquil period for US and UK equities, the volatility adjusted ETL at any significance level is much lower than the unadjusted ETL. The effect of the volatility adjustment is also more pronounced at significance levels different from 1%. Since the volatility adjusted returns have a small but negative excess kurtosis in this case, the effect is to decrease the ETL at higher confidence levels (such as for $\alpha = 0.1\%$) and increase the ETL at lower confidence levels (such as for $\alpha = 10\%$).

IV.3.7 SUMMARY AND CONCLUSIONS

Historical simulation is a very popular approach to VaR estimation because it makes no parametric assumptions about the behaviour of risk factors. It only assumes that their future behaviour will be similar to their historical behaviour. Most importantly, it makes no assumption about the correlations, or more generally the dependencies, between the risk factors. Standard historical VaR estimates are based only upon the multivariate distributions of the assets or risk factors that are observed empirically, in a sample of historical returns. The historical distribution of portfolio returns or P&L is constructed by keeping the portfolio's holdings, weights or risk factor sensitivities constant at their current value. Then the historical VaR is calculated directly from the appropriate quantile of this distribution.

There are many challenges that must be overcome for a successful implementation of historical VaR. One of the main problems is that, on the one hand, a large sample is required to measure historical VaR at high confidence levels accurately, but on the other hand large samples are likely to cover long historical periods where markets have been through regimes that may be quite different from the current regime. In that case, the historical VaR estimate may not be representative of the portfolio's *current* market risk, unless the risk horizon is extremely long.

If historical VaR estimates are required for a long term risk horizon, then it would be entirely appropriate to use a long historical sample period covering many different regimes; it is an advantage to have data that cover many possible scenarios – who knows what could happen over the next year? However, unless funds are locked in (as is often the case for investing in hedge funds), market VaR is a risk metric that is only relevant for relatively short term risk horizons, because this horizon corresponds to the optimal liquidation or hedging period for the portfolio. Then the different market characteristics experienced five or ten years ago can bias the historical VaR estimate, so that it is not representative of the conditions that are likely to prevail in markets over the next few days or weeks.

For this reason we strongly recommend that the reconstructed portfolio returns be *adjusted* so that their conditional volatility is approximately constant over the entire sample period. That is, we remove the volatility clustering from the historical portfolio returns, and impose a constant volatility on the series, that is equal to the conditional volatility at the time that the VaR is estimated. In scenario analysis and stress testing, we could also adjust the constant volatility so that it is equal to any prescribed value.

We can either adjust the individual risk factor (or asset) returns to have constant volatility, provided we also change their conditional correlations, or adjust the reconstructed portfolio returns or P&L to have constant volatility. The latter is often simpler since then only *one* GARCH or EWMA model is required for volatility adjustment at the portfolio level. Volatility adjustment can be extended to *filtered historical simulation*, and this methodology allows the proper estimation of historical VaR over risk horizons that are longer than 1 day. That is, there is no scaling of daily VaR estimates, using a square root or some other power law exponent. Instead, we use multi-step simulation following a GARCH model.

A case study has demonstrated how critically important the sample size is to *all* VaR models, not only historical VaR. We showed that VaR estimates from the different models based on the same sample size and the same weighting of the data are relatively close, and much closer than the VaR estimates from any one of the models when we change the historical sample size by a considerable amount.

Volatility adjustment, and any subsequent filtering in multi-step simulations of returns over the risk horizon, allows very large historical samples to be used, yet these samples still represent current market conditions. It is important to use very large samples when estimating historical VaR and ETL at high levels of confidence, otherwise the quantile estimates will be imprecise. Volatility adjustment makes the sample closer to being i.i.d., so that VaR estimates become less sensitive to changes in sample size. So, at any level of confidence, the volatility adjusted historical VaR estimates should be more robust, i.e. they should be less variable from day to day, compared with unadjusted historical VaR estimates, especially those based on a short sample period.

At extreme quantiles it is still difficult to estimate historical VaR and ETL, even when we have several thousand observations in our sample. Certain non-parametric or parametric techniques may be applied to improve the precision of the quantile estimate. For a non-parametric fit we recommend the *Epanechnikov kernel*, although several other kernels would perform as well. For a parametric fit, the *Johnson SU distribution* appears to have some advantages over both the *generalized Pareto distribution* (GPD) and the *Cornish–Fisher expansion*. The GPD VaR estimates are sensitive to the choice of threshold and the Cornish–Fisher estimates will substantially overestimate VaR when data are very leptokurtic. However, the Johnson estimates are robust to strong deviations from normality and do not depend on an arbitrary choice of threshold.

When the historical distribution is fitted with a GPD or a Johnson SU distribution, or when the VaR is estimated using a Cornish–Fisher expansion, it is possible to derive analytic formulae for the *conditional VaR*, also called *expected tail loss*. The historical ETL estimates that are derived using these formulae have been compared empirically with the historical ETL that is estimated directly, as the average of the losses that exceed the VaR.

This chapter contains a large number of case studies on the estimation of historical VaR and ETL for specific portfolios, including interest rate sensitive, equity, and commodity portfolios. We have shown how to estimate the *systematic* VaR and *specific* VaR with historical simulation, illustrating this with a portfolio of US stocks. We have also disaggregated systematic historical VaR and ETL into *stand-alone* components. This is achieved by constructing sub-portfolios that are sensitive to a given subset of risk factors, and then estimating the stand-alone VaR from the quantiles of the return or P&L distribution of the relevant sub-portfolio. If required, the volatility of each sub-portfolio can be adjusted to be constant at its current level. In several case studies we also considered positions in foreign currencies, and isolated the *forex* VaR from the *equity* and *interest rate* VaR components.

Historical VaR may be disaggregated and aggregated, but it does not obey the same aggregation rules as linear VaR. In particular, historical VaR need not be sub-additive. That is, it is theoretically possible for the total systematic VaR to be greater than the sum of the stand-alone VaR components. We have also demonstrated, again in the context of a case study, how to estimate the historical *marginal* VaR. To calculate the marginal VaR, the gradient vector must be estimated using finite differences, since there is no simple analytic formula for the marginal VaR, as there is in the normal linear VAR model.

Time aggregation of historical VaR is also more complex than it is for normal linear VaR. The normal linear model assumes that risk factor returns are i.i.d. and normally distributed, and thus, under the assumption that the portfolio's risk factor sensitivities are constant over the next h days, we can scale a daily VaR estimate up to an h-day VaR estimate using a square-root scaling rule. We call this the dynamic VaR estimate, because this type of scaling implicitly assumes that the portfolio is dynamically rebalanced over the risk horizon, to maintain constant risk factor sensitivities. Then, it is theoretically correct to aggregate historical VaR in this framework, but only if we assume that the portfolio returns have a stable distribution.

However, the *scale exponent* for the aggregation need not be 0.5, as it is for the square-root-of-time scaling of i.i.d. normal random variables. We have explained how the scale exponent may be estimated from a large historical sample, if we assume it is drawn from a stable distribution, and we have estimated the scale exponents corresponding to several major risk factors, including equity indices, forex rates, interest rates and major volatility indices. Our analysis indicates that, whilst distributions of equity and currency returns may scale with the square root of time, distributions of interest rate changes are more 'trendy' and may require a scale exponent greater than 0.5. Volatility, on the other hand, is rapidly mean-reverting and hence should be scaled with an exponent less than 0.5. Since volatility is a main risk factor for option portfolios, the time aggregation of historical VaR for dynamically rebalanced option portfolios is quite complex, and we shall return to this in Section IV.5.4.

IV.4
Monte Carlo VaR

IV.4.1 INTRODUCTION

Monte Carlo simulation is an extremely flexible tool that has numerous applications to finance. It is often used as a method of 'last resort' when analytic solutions do not exist, or when other numerical methods fail. Its drawback has been the amount of time it takes to resolve a problem accurately using simulation, but as computers become more powerful this disadvantage becomes less relevant.

The purpose of this chapter is to provide a pedagogical introduction to Monte Carlo simulation with a specific focus on its applications to VaR estimation. There are two equally important design aspects of Monte Carlo VaR: the sampling algorithm and the model to which the algorithm is applied. Section IV.4.2 focuses on the first of these. It begins by explaining how *pseudo-random numbers* are generated. Then we introduce the sampling techniques that are based on *low discrepancy sequences*, which are commonly termed *quasi Monte Carlo* methods. The section then explains how to transform random numbers into simulations from a parametric distribution for risk factor returns, a process called *structured Monte Carlo*. Then we describe the technique of *multi-step Monte Carlo*, which is important for accounting for the dynamic properties of risk factor returns, such as volatility clustering.

The main aim of this chapter is to describe the different types of statistical models for risk factor returns that are used to underpin the simulation algorithm. A huge variety of static and dynamic models are available: static models are based on the assumption that each risk factor return is an *independent and identically distributed* process, in which case we only need to specify the multivariate *unconditional distribution* for the risk factor returns. But we can use a dynamic model to introduce time series effects such as volatility clustering and mean reversion. In this case we must specify how the multivariate *conditional distributions* for the risk factor returns evolve over time.

Section IV.4.3 focuses on describing various parametric static and dynamic models that are appropriate for different types of risk factor returns. As we know from previous chapters, volatility clustering can be a very important feature to capture in the VaR estimate. So here we apply exponentially weighted moving average and generalized autoregressive conditional heteroscedasticity processes to model *volatility clustering* in a single risk factor returns series. Later on, in Section IV.4.5.4, we give a practical example that illustrates the extension of this framework to a multivariate setting.

Section IV.4.4 focuses on modelling the interdependence between different types of risk factor returns. First we describe the standard multivariate normal and multivariate Student t distributions for i.i.d. returns. But Monte Carlo simulation is so flexible that we can very easily use copulas instead of correlation as the dependence metric. We end the section with a case study on the use of non-linear regression in the context of bivariate Monte Carlo simulation.

Section IV.4.5 builds on the three previous sections to demonstrate how Monte Carlo methods are used to estimate the VaR and expected tail loss of a portfolio, assuming it has a *linear mapping* to its risk factors (Monte Carlo VaR for option portfolios is dealt with in the next chapter). The section begins by outlining both static and dynamic (multi-step) algorithms for estimating Monte Carlo VaR and ETL for a linear portfolio, based on a generic model for the multivariate distribution of the risk factor returns.

Then we provide specific examples that are designed to emphasize different aspects of the Monte Carlo algorithm and different features of the returns model. We begin by considering *cash-flow* portfolios, firstly using different copulas to model credit spread changes and hence to estimate the credit spread VaR, and secondly using Monte Carlo simulation on *principal component risk factors* to estimate the interest rate VaR of a large portfolio of interest rate sensitive securities. In the interest rate VaR example we focus on the efficiency gains from dimension reduction and advanced sampling techniques, rather than on the specification of the multivariate return distribution.

The next example illustrates the use of Monte Carlo with a *multivariate normal mixture* distribution, using a stock portfolio to emphasize the advantages of this approach for scenario analysis. Finally, we extend the volatility clustering simulation model that was introduced earlier for a single risk factor, to a currency portfolio where forex log returns have a conditional multivariate Student t distribution and their dynamics are governed by a multivariate GARCH model. We use another empirical example to demonstrate that the VaR estimate is significantly affected by non-normality in conditional return distributions and by *volatility and correlation clustering* in risk factor returns, even over a relatively short risk horizon such as 10 days. Section IV.4.6 summarizes and concludes.

Besides the technical tools for modelling VaR with Monte Carlo simulation, the main message of this chapter is that we need to control two sources of *model risk* in Monte Carlo VaR models: that stemming from simulation errors and that resulting from inappropriate behavioural models for risk factor returns. There are many books about Monte Carlo techniques that focus on methods for reducing simulation error, most notably the comprehensive and classic text by Glasserman (2004). For this reason, I have provided only a short introduction to sampling methods and instead have devoted most of this chapter to the construction of a statistical model for risk factor returns that provides an appropriate basis for Monte Carlo VaR estimation.

There are many empirical examples for this chapter in Excel workbooks on the CD-ROM. To reduce file size each workbook is saved using only 100 or 1000 simulations. Before use, all the spreadsheets containing simulations and calculations on those simulations need to be extended by the reader after copying the workbooks onto their hard drive. Just take the last row of all the simulated vectors in each spreadsheet and fill down. I have turned the automatic calculation of results to manual so that new simulations are not repeated each time the spreadsheet is altered.[1] Due to the size constraints in Excel (especially before Excel 2007) many of our empirical results in the text are based on only 10,000 simulations. This is sufficient to illustrate the important points of each example, but without additional variance reduction there will be substantial sampling error in the results.

---

[1] This is an Excel option, found in the Tools menu of Excel 2003 or in Excel 2007 under Options | Formulas from the Excel Office button. Press F9 to repeat the calculations manually. Note that calculations are repeated on *all* open workbooks each time F9 is pressed.

IV.4.2   BASIC CONCEPTS

We begin this section by outlining some efficient algorithms for generating pseudo-random numbers. Section I.5.7 provided only a very brief and basic introduction to this vast subject, so this section develops the material in a little more depth. Then we move on to *advanced sampling techniques* for improving the efficiency of Monte Carlo simulation. We describe the use of *low discrepancy sequences* to cover the hypercube with the minimum number of simulations, and two simple *variance reduction* methods, i.e. *antithetic sampling* and *stratified sampling*.

By necessity, our treatment in these three subsections is extremely selective, and readers interested in commercial implementation of Monte Carlo VaR models are advised to consult texts that are specifically devoted to Monte Carlo algorithms and the control of simulation error. As mentioned in the previous section, I can particularly recommend the classic textbook written by Glasserman (2004).

It may be relatively straightforward, if time-consuming, to reduce sampling error, but it is not at all straightforward to select the appropriate behavioural model for risk factor returns in a Monte Carlo VaR framework.[2] So the next three sections will focus on the statistical aspects of a Monte Carlo VaR model. This section of the chapter gives an introduction to univariate and multivariate simulation and the subsequent estimation of Monte Carlo VaR, assuming that we already know the appropriate risk factor returns model.

IV.4.2.1   Pseudo-Random Number Generation

Random number generation is the first step in a Monte Carlo simulation algorithm. Its aim is to produce a sequence of numbers between 0 and 1 that are uniformly distributed, independent and non-periodic. That is, each number in the unit interval (0, 1) is equally likely to occur in the sequence, the ith number is independent of the jth number for all $i \neq j$, and the sequence does not repeat itself however long it becomes.

The only way to generate random numbers is to measure, without error, a physical phenomenon that is truly random. In practice computers generate *pseudo-random numbers*, which should be impossible to distinguish from a set of realizations of truly independent standard uniform random variables. These pseudo-random numbers are generated by an initial *seed*, such as the time of the computer's clock, and thereafter follow a deterministic sequence. In Excel, the function RAND ( ) produces a pseudo-random number.[3]

A simple but common type of generator is a *linear congruential generator*. This takes the form of an iteration that is based on the idea of *congruence*. For some fixed integer m, we say that two integers x and y are congruent modulo m, written

$$x \equiv y \bmod (m),$$

if m divides $x - y$.[4] To generate a linear congruential sequence we fix two positive integer values m and c greater than 1, start the sequence with a positive integer seed x_0 between 1 and $m - 1$ and perform the iteration

$$x_{i+1} \equiv c x_i \bmod (m), \tag{IV.4.1}$$

---

[2] Risk factor model selection requires very thorough backtesting, as described in Chapter IV.6, and this can entail months of research.
[3] See http://support.microsoft.com/kb/828795 for more details about their random number generator.
[4] For instance, $2 \equiv 5 \bmod(3)$.

each time choosing the unique integer value for x_{i+1} in $[1, m - 1]$. Then, for each i set $u_i = m^{-1}x_i$, and the resulting sequence $\{u_0, u_1, u_2, \ldots, u_N\}$ is our pseudo-random number sequence where N is the number of simulations. The following example shows that m should be a prime number.

EXAMPLE IV.4.1: LINEAR CONGRUENTIAL RANDOM NUMBER GENERATION

Generate a sequence of pseudo-random numbers using (IV.4.1) with $m = 13$, $c = 2$ and $x_0 = 1$. What happens if you use the same values of c and x_0 but set $m = 12$?

SOLUTION   With $m = 13$ the sequence for x is

$$\{1, 2, 4, 8, 3, 6, 12, 11, 9, 5, 10, 7, 1, 2, 4, 8, 3, 6, 12, 11, 9, 5, 10, 7, \ldots\},$$

where '...' here means that the sequence continues to cycle through the same sub-sequence $\{1, 2, 4, 8, 3, 6, 12, 11, 9, 5, 10, 7\}$. Dividing the numbers in this subsequence by 13 gives a sequence of 12 distinct pseudo-random numbers:

$$\{0.0769, 0.1538, 0.3077, 0.6154, 0.2308, 0.4615, 0.9231, 0.8462, 0.6923, 0.3846, 0.7692, 0.5385\}.$$

Now change the value of m from 13 to 12 in the spreadsheet for this example. The sequence of integers is $\{1, 2, 4, 8, 4, 8, 4, 8, \ldots\}$. Whereas the first sequence had full *periodicity*, i.e. the full set of integers between 1 and $m - 1$ are visited in the repeating subsequence, the second sequence has a periodicity of only 2. Hence setting $m = 12$, $c = 2$ is not a good choice for generating a sequence of pseudo-random numbers.

All random number generators have a periodicity, i.e. at some point in the sequence the numbers start repeating themselves. But one of the reasons why linear congruential generators are so popular is that they will have full periodicity if c is a *primitive root* of m.[5] In practice, m is chosen to be a very large prime number so that the sequence does not repeat itself too soon and very many distinct random numbers can be simulated in the cycle. That is, long sequences of pseudo-random numbers are easier to generate if we choose m to be a very large prime number.

A *Mersenne prime* is a prime number of the form $2^n - 1$, and many Mersenne primes are known for very large values of n.[6] For instance, one of the best generators, called the *Mersenne twister*, sets $m = 2^{19,937} - 1$. Since this m is prime, there will be $2^{19,937} - 1$ distinct pseudo-random numbers in the associated linear congruential generator.

IV.4.2.2   Low Discrepancy Sequences

Most portfolios have several risk factors, and simulations of a portfolio's P&L distribution are based on simulations of the returns on these risk factors. For this, we require a sequence of random numbers for each factor, and if there are k risk factors we need to generate k such

---

[5] We call c a 'primitive root' of m if $m - 1$ is the smallest positive integer value of n such that $c^n \equiv 1 \bmod (m)$. In our example therefore, $2^{12} \equiv 1 \bmod (13)$ and $n = 12$ is the lowest power n of 2 such that 13 divides $2^n - 1$.

[6] Marin Mersenne (1588–1648) was a French philosopher, mathematician and music theorist. For more details, see http://en.wikipedia.org/wiki/Mersenne.

sequences. We label these $\{u_{1i}, \ldots, u_{ki}\}_{i=1}^{N}$ where, typically, the number of simulations N in each sequence will be a very large number.[7]

For the ith simulation on the risk factor returns we start with a vector $(u_{1i}, \ldots, u_{ki})$ of numbers with each $u_{ji} \in (0, 1)$. For instance, if $k = 2$, the ith simulation could be based on a vector such as $(0.643278, 0.497123)$. This can be thought of as a point in the *unit square*, i.e. the square with sides along the two axes from 0 to 1. The two elements represent the coordinates of the point. If $k = 3$ the ith simulation is a point in the unit cube, and more generally the vector $(u_{1i}, \ldots, u_{ki})$ is a point in the k-dimensional unit *hypercube*.

We now motivate the concept of the *discrepancy* of a sequence with a simple numerical example.

EXAMPLE IV.4.2: DISCREPANCY OF LINEAR CONGRUENTIAL GENERATORS

Generate a sequence of pseudo-random numbers using the linear congruential generator (IV.4.1) with $m = 127$ and $c = 3$. Then plot the numbers (u_i, u_{i+1}), $i = 1, 2, \ldots$ on the two-dimensional unit cube.

SOLUTION   The spreadsheet for this example is similar to that for the previous example. The resulting plot of consecutive pseudo-random numbers, displayed in Figure IV.4.1, shows that the points are not uniformly covering the cube. Instead they lie along three distinct lines.

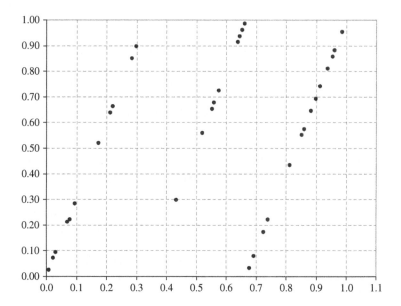

Figure IV.4.1   Consecutive pseudo-random numbers plotted as points in the unit cube

The feature illustrated in Figure IV.4.1 is not particular to our choice of $m = 127$ and $c = 3$, and nor is it particular to a plot of two consecutive points. The same features are apparent

---

[7] For instance, $N = 100,000$ or $1,000,000$. Smaller values for N are usually acceptable only if some *variance reduction* technique is applied, as we shall see presently.

in all linear congruential generators, and are evident in n-dimensional plots of n consecutive numbers for $n > 2$. That is, the points generated by such generators will lie in proper subspaces of the hypercube. This means that there can be large areas of the hypercube that contain no points. But if the hypercube is not covered uniformly the final result of the Monte Carlo simulation, which in our case is a VaR or ETL estimate, will not be robust. This is because we would cover different areas of the hypercube each time we perform another set of N simulations, starting with a different seed.

A low discrepancy sequence is a method for generating sequences of numbers that are not uniformly distributed random numbers at all; instead they are designed to cover the n-dimensional hypercube uniformly. The name *low discrepancy* means that the deviations from a uniform covering of the hypercube are minimal.[8] In other words, the purpose of a low discrepancy sequence is to cover the hypercube without gaps, using fewer simulations than are required from a pseudo-random generator, for the same uniformity of coverage.

After an initial seed, the remaining numbers in the sequence follow a deterministic path. Common examples of low discrepancy sequences are the *Faure* and *Sobol* sequences, both of which are based on *van der Corput* sequences. The technical details on generating these sequences are very well described in Glasserman (2004, Chapter 5).

IV.4.2.3 Variance Reduction

The computation time required for generating large numbers of pseudo- or quasi-random numbers is minimal. However, this is only the first step in Monte Carlo simulation. The computation time required by the application of the VaR model can be huge, for example if it requires complex models for repricing non-linear instruments on each set of simulations. For this reason we try to restrict the number of simulations to be as small as possible without sacrificing the accuracy of the resulting VaR or ETL estimate.

To assess the trade-off between speed and accuracy we need a measure of the extent to which the VaR or ETL estimates change each time the simulations are repeated. A common measure of this sampling uncertainty is the *variance of the simulation error*.

- When simulating a quantity such as an expected value or VaR, here simply denoted $\tilde{X}$, the *simulation error* is defined as $\hat{X}_N - \tilde{X}$, where $\hat{X}_N$ denotes the estimator of $\tilde{X}$ based on N simulations.
- If the estimator is *unbiased*, $E(\hat{X}_N - \tilde{X}) = 0$, in other words, $E(\hat{X}_N) = \tilde{X}$.
- Since $\tilde{X}$ is a constant, although it is unknown, the variance of the simulation error is equal to $V(\hat{X}_N)$.

If $\tilde{X}$ denotes an expected value, then $\hat{X}_N = \overline{X}$ is the sample mean based on N observations. Let μ and σ denote the mean and standard deviation of the distribution of the underlying random variable, X. By the central limit theorem, which is described in Section I.3.5.2, we know that the random variable

---

[8] Low discrepancy sequences are sometimes called *quasi-random numbers*. See Glasserman (2004, Section 5.1.1) for several formal definitions of discrepancy.

$$Y = \frac{\hat{X}_N - \mu}{\sigma/\sqrt{N}}$$

has a distribution that converges to a standard normal distribution as N increases. In other words, as N increases the distribution of $\hat{X}_N$ converges to a normal distribution with expectation μ and variance $N^{-1}\sigma^2$. Thus, the variance of the simulation error is approximately equal to $N^{-1}\sigma^2$ for large N.

Now suppose $\tilde{X}$ is an α quantile of an h-day portfolio return distribution. The asymptotic distribution for the number of returns $X(N, \alpha)$ that are less than the α quantile is described in Section II.8.4.1. From this we know that as N increases, the distribution of the proportion of returns that are less than the α quantile, i.e. $\hat{X}_N = N^{-1}X(N, \alpha)$, converges to a binomial distribution with expectation α and variance $N^{-1}\alpha(1 - \alpha)$. Hence the variable

$$Y = \frac{\hat{X}_N - \alpha}{\sqrt{N^{-1}\alpha(1 - \alpha)}}$$

has a distribution that converges to a standard normal distribution as N increases. In other words, the variance of the simulation error is approximately equal to $N^{-1}\alpha(1 - \alpha)$ for large N.

In both the cases above, the variance of the estimator decreases with N, that is, the accuracy in our simulations increases as N increases. In other words, we should use as many simulations as possible. But, as mentioned above, computation time can be a substantial constraint on the size of N.

We now describe two sampling techniques that have the effect of decreasing the variance of an estimator based on a given number of simulations. The simplest of these techniques, based on *antithetic variables*, is illustrated in the next example.

EXAMPLE IV.4.3: ANTITHETIC VARIANCE REDUCTION

Suppose we wish to estimate the expected value of a standard uniform variable using just 20 simulations.

(a) Use the Excel random number generator to simulate 20 realizations $\{u_1, \ldots, u_{20}\}$ on independent standard uniform variables and repeat the simulations 10 times, each time estimating the sample mean. Compute the sample standard deviation of the sample means obtained from the 10 different simulations.

(b) Now repeat this process, but this time use the Excel random number generator to simulate only the first 12 random numbers $\{u_1, \ldots, u_{12}\}$. For the next 8 numbers simply take 1 minus the first 8 of these 12 numbers. More generally, base your sample mean estimates on the sample $\{\tilde{u}_1, \ldots, \tilde{u}_{20}\}$ where, for some n such that $10 \leq n < 20$, we set $\tilde{u}_i = u_i$ for $i = 1, \ldots, n$, and $\tilde{u}_i = 1 - u_{i-n}$ for $i = n + 1, \ldots, 20$.

For different values of n, compare the sample standard deviations obtained in case (a) and case (b), and comment on your results.

SOLUTION   In the spreadsheet for this example we use the Excel RAND( ) function to generate 20 pseudo-random numbers for part (a). Then, in each set of simulations, the first 12 realizations $\{u_1, \ldots, u_{12}\}$ for (b) are identical to those in (a), but for the last 8 realizations they are $\{1 - u_1, \ldots, 1 - u_8\}$. Note that the last 8 realizations are still drawn from a standard uniform distribution, but they are no longer independent of the first 8 realizations.

With a sample size of only 20 the sampling variation over the 10 sets of simulations is very large in both cases. Nevertheless, the standard deviation of the means in (b) is virtually always *considerably* less than the standard deviation of the means (a). Readers can verify this by pressing F9 to repeat the simulations many times.

More generally, the value for n can be anywhere between 10 and 20. If $n = 10$ we obtain the maximum possible variance reduction, in fact in this case the sample mean estimates are all identical, so their variance is zero. Thus the variance reduction decreases as n increases until, when $n = 20$, there is no variance reduction at all.

We now provide a slightly more formal introduction to the concept of *antithetic sampling* of standard uniform random variables, and explain why this technique can reduce the variance of estimators when estimates are based on simulated samples. We shall again use an estimator of a sample mean for illustration.

Denote by $\{X_1, \ldots, X_N\}$ a sample of N i.i.d. random variables having distribution function F. Now let $\{X_1^*, \ldots, X_N^*\}$ denote another sample of N i.i.d. random variables, with the same distribution function F, and having a constant correlation with the first sample:

$$\mathrm{Corr}(X_i, X_i^*) = \varrho, \text{ for } i = 1, \ldots, N.$$

Finally, denote by $\{X_1, \ldots, X_{2N}\}$ a set of $2N$ i.i.d. random variables with distribution function F.

Consider the estimators of the sample mean based on a sample of size $2N$ using realizations from (a) $\{X_1, \ldots, X_{2N}\}$, and (b) $\{X_1, \ldots, X_N, X_1^*, \ldots, X_N^*\}$. These are:

(a) $\hat{X}_{2N} = \dfrac{1}{2N}\left(\displaystyle\sum_{i=1}^{2N} X_i\right)$, and

(b) $\hat{X}_{2N}^* = \dfrac{1}{2N}\left(\displaystyle\sum_{i=1}^{N} X_i + \sum_{i=1}^{N} X_i^*\right) = \dfrac{1}{N}\sum_{i=1}^{N} Y_i$ where $Y_i = \dfrac{X_i + X_i^*}{2}$.

What is the variance of the estimator in each case? Suppose the distribution F has variance σ^2. Then in case (a),

$$V(\hat{X}_{2N}) = \frac{2N\sigma^2}{4N^2} = \frac{\sigma^2}{2N}, \tag{IV.4.2}$$

since the variables are independent. However, although the variables $Y_i, i = 1, \ldots, N$ are independent their variance is not σ^2, but

$$V(Y_i) = \frac{V(X_i + X_i^*)}{4} = \frac{2\sigma^2 + 2\sigma^2\varrho}{4} = \frac{\sigma^2(1 + \varrho)}{2}.$$

Hence, in case (b),

$$V(\hat{X}_{2N}^*) = \frac{\sigma^2(1 + \varrho)}{2N}. \tag{IV.4.3}$$

So the variance of the estimator in case (b) will be less than the variance of the estimator in case (a) if and only if

$$\frac{\sigma^2(1+\varrho)}{2N} < \frac{\sigma^2}{2N},$$

that is, if and only if $\varrho < 0$.

This shows that a necessary and sufficient condition for antithetic sampling to reduce the variance of the estimator of a sample mean is that the antithetic variables have *negative correlation* with the original variables. The antithetic pairs in Example IV.4.3 were chosen to have correlation -1.[9] Then, by (IV.4.3), the variance of the sample mean estimator is zero when we use the same number of realizations on the antithetic variables as on the original variables.[10] This is true for any linear estimator, not just for the sample mean.[11]

In Monte Carlo simulation we often require a non-linear estimator; for instance, we shall be focusing on an estimator of a quantile. Nevertheless, there is considerable potential for the use of antithetic pairs to reduce the variance of a Monte Carlo VaR estimate as well.

We now introduce an alternative method for variance reduction, which may be applied in conjunction with antithetic sampling. The next example provides a simple illustration of the principle of *stratified sampling* on the *unit interval*, after which we generalize this concept to stratified sampling on the *hypercube*.

EXAMPLE IV.4.4: STRATIFIED SAMPLING FROM STANDARD UNIFORM DISTRIBUTIONS

Repeat the exercise from Example IV.4.3, but this time in case (b) set:

$$\begin{aligned} \tilde{u}_i &= u_i/4, & i &= 1, \ldots, 5; \\ \tilde{u}_i &= (u_i + 1)/4, & i &= 6, \ldots, 10; \\ \tilde{u}_i &= (u_i + 2)/4, & i &= 11, \ldots, 15; \text{ and} \\ \tilde{u}_i &= (u_i + 3)/4, & i &= 16, \ldots, 20. \end{aligned}$$

SOLUTION   The solution is implemented in the spreadsheet. Note that our construction for case (b) now generates random numbers in the intervals (0,0.25], (0.25,0.5], (0.5,0.75] and (0.75,1) respectively. The reader can verify that the standard deviation of the sample means is exactly $\frac{1}{4}$ of the standard deviation of the mean in case (a).

The above example illustrates that by stratifying the sample space $(0, 1)$ into n non-overlapping subspaces of equal size, the standard deviation of a linear estimator becomes n^{-1} times the standard deviation of the estimator based on a non-stratified sample. Another advantage is that when n is large, stratified sampling can provide a more uniform coverage of the unit interval than a standard unstratified sampling method.

---

[9] In Section IV.4.2.5 we see that the antithetic sampling realization $(u, 1-u)$ on a standard uniform variable translates into a realization $\left(F^{-1}(u), F^{-1}(1-u)\right)$ where F is the distribution function for our risk factor. But if F is symmetric then $F^{-1}(1-u) = -F^{-1}(u)$, so we have a set of antithetic pairs $\left\{F^{-1}(u_i), -F^{-1}(u_i)\right\}_{i=1}^{N}$ that still have correlation -1.

[10] This is why when we take $n=10$ in Example IV.4.3, each set of simulations has a sample mean of exactly 0.5 and the standard deviation of the sample means is zero.

[11] A *linear estimator* is an estimator that is a linear function of the random variables.

A simple way to generalize this concept to multiple dimensions is to use *Latin hypercube* sampling. For instance, to generate a stratified sample on the two-dimensional unit cube (i.e. the unit square) we can create nm simulations on pairs (u_1, u_2) in the unit square by:

   (i) taking two independent stratified samples on $(0, 1)$, in each case dividing the interval into n non-overlapping equal length sub-intervals and taking a random sample size m from each sub-interval; and

  (ii) randomly permuting the first column and, independently, randomly permuting the second column – i.e. we 'shuffle up' each sample of m random numbers separately.

EXAMPLE IV.4.5: LATIN HYPERCUBE SAMPLING

Generate two independent stratified samples of the unit interval with $n = 6$, and take a random sample size $m = 5$ from each sub-interval. Plot the 30 points that are generated in this way in the unit square. Now 'shuffle' each sample of 30 observations independently, and again plot the 30 points.

SOLUTION   In Figure IV.4.2 the 'unshuffled' stratified sample is plotted on the left and the 'shuffled' sample is plotted on the right. Clearly, step (ii) above is necessary otherwise all the points would lie along the diagonal blocks within the unit square, as seen in the left-hand figure. However, after shuffling the sample is uniformly distributed over the unit square.

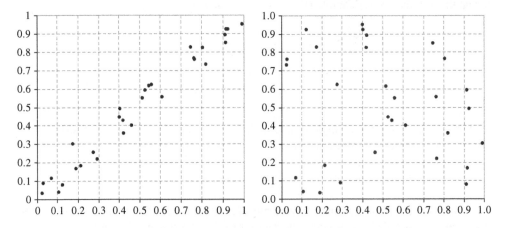

Figure IV.4.2   Effect of independently permuting stratified samples

Stratified sampling is a useful technique for generating *initial* values of a simulated process. For instance, it can be used in one-step Monte Carlo for an h-day VaR, when we are simulating the h-day risk factor returns directly. But it cannot be used to generate consecutive values along a simulated path of an i.i.d. process, because the stratification introduces dependence into the process.[12] Hence, it should not be applied to each step in a multi-step Monte Carlo VaR model.

---

[12] For instance, in the above example the first five simulations were all taken from the interval $(0, 1/6]$.

IV.4.2.4   Sampling from Univariate Distributions

Until this point we have focused on efficient methods for constructing random samples on standard uniform distributions. Now we show how to transform a random sample from a single standard uniform variable U into a random sample from a distribution of a random variable X with a given continuous distribution function, F. Since the values of F lie between 0 and 1, given a random number u in (0, 1) we obtain the corresponding value of x by setting

$$x = F^{-1}(u). \tag{IV.4.4}$$

In other words, given a random number u, the corresponding simulation for X is the u quantile of its distribution.

For example, Figure IV.4.3 illustrates this transformation in the case of a standard normal distribution when the random number generated is 0.3.[13] Note that given the sigmoid shape of the distribution function a uniform series of random numbers will be converted into simulations where more observations occur around the expected value than in the tails of the distribution.

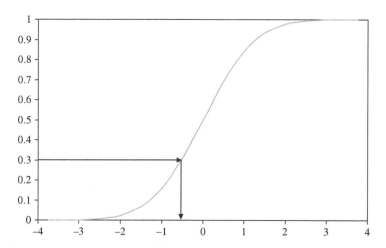

Figure IV.4.3   Simulating from a standard normal distribution

A sample from a standard normal distribution can be translated into a sample from any other normal distribution using the inverse of the standard normal transformation.[14] That is, we obtain a simulation on a normal variable with mean μ and standard deviation σ using

$$x = \Phi^{-1}(u)\sigma + \mu. \tag{IV.4.5}$$

More generally, we can use the inverse distribution of any univariate distribution in the transformation. For instance, in Excel we transform a standard uniform simulation u

---

[13] In Excel, RAND( ) generates a standard uniform simulation and, for instance, NORMSINV(RAND( )) generates a simulation $\Phi^{-1}(u)$ from a standard normal variable.
[14] See Section I.3.3.4 for the specification of the standard normal distribution.

into a simulation on a standard Student t variable with ν degrees of freedom using the command

$$t_\nu^{-1}(u) = \begin{cases} -\text{TINV}(2u, \nu), & \text{if } u \le \frac{1}{2} \\ \text{TINV}(2(1-u), \nu), & \text{if } u > \frac{1}{2}. \end{cases} \qquad (IV.4.6)$$

Note that the standard Student t distribution has mean zero and variance $\nu(\nu-2)^{-1}$, so to transform the simulations $t_\nu^{-1}(u)$ to simulations from a general Student t distribution with mean μ and standard deviation σ, we use the transformation

$$x = \sqrt{\nu^{-1}(\nu-2)}t^{-1}(u)\sigma + \mu. \qquad (IV.4.7)$$

Excel also provides inverse distribution functions for several other distributions. Table IV.4.1 shows the command for generating simulations from each, where $u = \text{RAND}()$.

Table IV.4.1   Excel commands for simulations

Distribution	Command	Parameters
Normal	NORMINV(u, μ, σ)	(μ, σ) mean and standard deviation parameters
Lognormal	LOGINV(u, μ, σ)	(μ, σ) parameters of normal distribution
Chi-squared	CHIINV(u, ν)	ν, degrees of freedom
F	FINV(u, ν_1, ν_2)	ν_1, ν_2 degrees of freedom
Gamma	GAMMAINV(u, α, β)	α and β shape and (inverse) scale parameters[a]
Beta	BETAINV(u, α, β)	α and β both shape parameters[b]

[a]The gamma density function is $f(x; \alpha, \beta) = x^{\alpha-1}\Gamma(\alpha)^{-1}\beta^\alpha e^{-\beta x}, x > 0$, where $\Gamma(\alpha)$ is the gamma function.
[b]The beta density function is $f(x; \alpha, \beta) = B(\alpha, \beta)^{-1}x^{\alpha-1}(1-x)^{\beta-1}, 0 < x < 1$, where $B(\alpha, \beta)$ is the beta function.

The *variance reduction* techniques that were described in the previous section can be translated into variance reduction for simulations based on other univariate distributions. For instance, if X has a normal, Student t, or any other symmetric distribution F then

$$x = F^{-1}(u) \Leftrightarrow -x = F^{-1}(1-u). \qquad (IV.4.8)$$

Hence antithetic sampling from a uniform distribution is equivalent to antithetic sampling from any symmetric distribution.

Stratified samples on a standard uniform distribution also correspond to stratified samples on any other distribution, because a distribution function is monotonic increasing. If the sub-intervals used for the stratification have equal probabilities under the standard uniform distribution, they will also have equal probabilities under a non-uniform distribution. For example, if the equiprobable sub-intervals for uniform stratification are

$$(0, \ 0.25], (0.25, \ 0.5], (0.5, \ 0.75] \text{ and } (0.75, \ 1)$$

then the equiprobable sub-intervals for *standard normal stratification* are

$$\left(-\infty, \Phi^{-1}(0.25)\right], \left(\Phi^{-1}(0.25), \Phi^{-1}(0.5)\right], \left(\Phi^{-1}(0.5), \Phi^{-1}(0.75)\right], \text{ and } \left(\Phi^{-1}(0.75), \infty\right).$$

However, the sub-intervals no longer have equal length.

Figure IV.4.4 compares the histogram of a stratified sample from a lognormal distribution with that based on an unstratified sample. The two empirical densities are based on the same sample of 500 random numbers, but the density shown in black is based on a stratified sample with 50 observations taken from 10 equiprobable sub-intervals of (0, 1). The mean and the standard deviation of the lognormal variable were both set equal to 1. The density based on the stratified sample should be closer to the theoretical distribution.

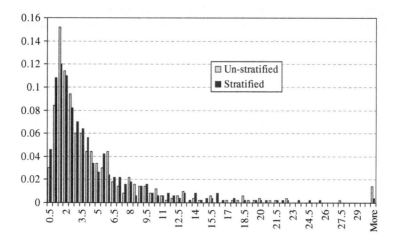

Figure IV.4.4   Densities based on stratified and unstratified samples

IV.4.2.5   Sampling from Multivariate Distributions

Several chapters in Volumes I and II of the *Market Risk Analysis* series have explained how to transform a random sample on several independent standard uniform variables $U_1, \ldots, U_k$ into a random sample from a multivariate distribution of several, non-independent and non-uniform random variables $X_1, \ldots, X_k$.[15] First we generate independent simulations on each marginal distribution, then we impose the dependence structure using *either* the Cholesky matrix of the correlation matrix,[16] *or* for more general distributions, the copula. We shall not repeat the theory here. The main focus of this chapter is to provide empirical examples and case studies of Monte Carlo VaR where simulations are based on realistic risk factor returns models.

IV.4.2.6   Introduction to Monte Carlo VaR

We know how to obtain variance reduced simulations on the returns to the risk factors of a portfolio, or indeed on the returns to any dependent set of asset prices. But how do we

---

[15] For instance, refer to Section I.5.7.5 for details on generating simulations from correlated normal or Student *t* distributed variables and to Section II.6.7 for simulations on a multivariate distribution, with marginal distributions that may have different parametric forms and where the dependence structure is represented by a *copula*.

[16] In the case of the multivariate normal or Student *t* distributions, we could simulate realizations of standardized normal or *t* variables, and then impose the variance as well as the correlation using the Cholesky matrix of the covariance matrix.

compute the portfolio's VaR and ETL?[17] The process is completely analogous to the estimation of VaR and ETL using historical simulation, only now we use Monte Carlo simulations instead of historical simulations. That is, we simulate a distribution for the portfolio's h-day returns, or for its h-day P&L, and the $100\alpha\%$ h-day VaR estimate is estimated empirically as -1 times the α quantile of this distribution.[18] The ETL is estimated empirically, by taking -1 times the average of the returns that are less than the VaR (or the losses that exceed the VaR).

When we base the portfolio's returns or P&L distribution on a portfolio mapping, each vector of simulations on the risk factor returns is input to this mapping to obtain one simulated portfolio return. Using a very large number N of simulated vectors on the risk factor returns gives N simulated portfolio returns, from which we derive their distribution. On the other hand, if we price the portfolio exactly, each vector of simulations on the risk factor or asset returns is used to derive values for the risk factors themselves, and these are used in the appropriate pricing model. Then the simulation of the portfolio's P&L is the difference between the simulated portfolio price and the current price of the portfolio.[19] Again, N simulations on vectors of risk factor returns give N points upon which to base the portfolio P&L distribution.

In the next chapter we shall make a strong case that Monte Carlo simulation is the most reliable method for estimating the VaR for option portfolios. Historical simulation is good when the risk horizon is 1 day and the confidence level is not too high, but it is very difficult to extend the model to longer risk horizons or higher confidence levels without introducing model risk in some form or another. And analytic approximations to the VaR for an option portfolio are usually too inaccurate to be of much use.

Monte Carlo simulation may also be applied to the VaR estimation of *linear* portfolios. Here the main advantage of Monte Carlo over historical simulation is the absence of restrictions on historical sample size. The calibration of the parametric distributions for risk factor or asset returns can be based on very little historical data, indeed we could just use scenario values for the parameters of the distributions. And if the parameters are calibrated on only very recent history, the Monte Carlo VaR estimates will naturally reflect these market circumstances.

The advantage of Monte Carlo VaR compared with parametric VaR estimates for linear portfolios is the large number of alternative risk factor return distributions that can be assumed. However, readers are warned that, if insufficient thought and effort have been invested in choosing and developing the statistical model of risk factor returns, this can be the major *drawback* of using Monte Carlo simulation to estimate VaR. It is important to apply simulations to a dynamic model of risk factor returns that captures path-dependent behaviour, such as volatility clustering, as well as the essential non-normal features of their multivariate conditional distributions. Without such a model, volatility adjusted historical simulation may be the better alternative, except for static option portfolios.

The next two sections of this chapter develop the risk factor returns models that underpin the Monte Carlo VaR estimate. Then, in Section IV.4.5 we illustrate these models with empirical examples for different types of linear portfolios. Linear portfolios of interest rate sensitive

---

[17] When these estimates are based on Monte Carlo simulations we call them 'Monte Carlo VaR' and 'Monte Carlo ETL' for short.

[18] As usual, if the α quantile is of the return distribution, the VaR is expressed as a percentage of the portfolio's value, and if the α quantile is of the P&L distribution, the VaR is expressed in value terms.

[19] This is for a long exposure to the portfolio – and for a short portfolio the simulated P&L is the current price minus the simulated price.

instruments, cash or futures positions on equities, currency forwards, and commodities are all treated in slightly different ways. First, if risk factor sensitivities are in value rather than percentage terms (e.g. for interest rate sensitive portfolios) we require absolute changes rather than returns in the risk factor mapping. Second, the essential features of the risk factor returns model differ according to the portfolio. For example, volatility clustering is more important in credit spreads than in interest rates, and asymmetry is more important in equities than in currencies.

IV.4.3 MODELLING DYNAMIC PROPERTIES IN RISK FACTOR RETURNS

This section describes the empirical characteristics of a single time series for a financial asset or risk factor and summarizes the econometric models that are commonly used to capture these characteristics. Since this is a vast subject we assume the reader is already armed with the relevant background knowledge. This can be found in *Market Risk Analysis* Volume II, the most important parts being:

- EWMA and GARCH models and their application to Monte Carlo simulation (see Chapters II.3 and II.4, and Section II.4.7 in particular);
- univariate time series models of stationary processes (see Chapter II.5, and Section II.5.2 in particular); and
- advanced econometric models (see Chapter II.7, and Section II.7.5 in particular).

When risk factor returns are assumed to be i.i.d., we simulate h-day returns on each risk factor, and hence estimate VaR and ETL in one step. However, when the risk factors have dynamic properties such as autocorrelation and volatility clustering, these properties will influence the Monte Carlo VaR estimate. Hence we must consider simulations of *time series* on risk factor returns, over the risk horizon. We begin with a general description of the multi-step framework for simulating time series that capture the dynamic behaviour of financial returns. We then introduce the concept of *importance sampling* as a useful means of decreasing computation time without sacrificing too much accuracy. If there is one overriding feature of financial returns that a dynamic model should necessarily capture, it is volatility clustering. To do this properly requires a technical background in statistical models for time varying volatility, but the exposition below is presented at a relatively low technical level. For equity, forex and currency exposures the major market risk factors are prices, and mean reversion in prices is weak, if it exists at all, at the daily level. But volatility is usually a rapidly mean-reverting time series so we should try to include this feature in a multi-step Monte Carlo framework for option portfolios. The last part of this section provides a gentle introduction to the inclusion of volatility regime-switching behaviour in Monte Carlo models for long term VaR estimation.

IV.4.3.1 Multi-Step Monte Carlo

The previous section focused on efficient algorithms for generating a very large number N of simulations on k variables. In the context of Monte Carlo VaR, these variables could represent the h-day returns on the k risk factors for a portfolio. Each row vector of simulations on the risk factors gives one simulated value for the portfolio, via the portfolio mapping.[20] Hence, we obtain N simulated portfolio values.

Commonly we would use one-step Monte Carlo to simulate h-day risk factor returns directly. But in many cases – such as estimating the VaR for a path-dependent option, or for estimating the VaR of a linear portfolio without ignoring the dynamic features of daily returns – it can be very important to capture the characteristics of *daily* returns in the simulation model. For this we need to use a multi-step Monte Carlo framework. For a linear portfolio, with simulations at the daily frequency, this consists of simulating an h-day log return by summing h consecutive daily log returns, and then just evaluating the portfolio once, h days ahead. But for an option portfolio, and particularly one with path-dependent products, we would evaluate the portfolio value on every consecutive day over the risk horizon.[21]

Multi-step Monte Carlo for a single risk factor is illustrated in Figure IV.4.5. Here we assume that the number of risk factors $k = 1$ and the risk horizon is $h = 10$ days, and we perform $N = 5$ simulations based on the assumption of i.i.d. lognormally distributed returns. We use log returns to simulate the price of our portfolio on each day over the risk horizon, starting from the current price, which we assume is 100, and ending in 10 days' time with five simulated prices. Hence, we simulate five *paths* for the daily log returns over the next 10 days. This means that, when we are estimating the risk of an option portfolio, the simulated daily log returns can be used to calculate the price tomorrow, the price in 2 days' time, and so on up to the risk horizon (of 10 days, in this case). It is these price paths that we depict in the figure.

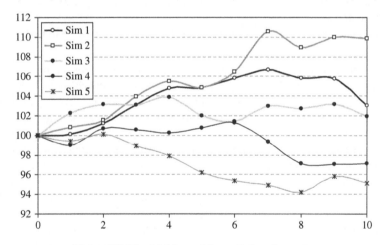

Figure IV.4.5   Multi-step Monte Carlo price paths

If the current price is 100, the simulated price in 10 days' time based on one-step Monte Carlo is $100\exp(r_{10})$, where r_{10} is a simulated 10-day log return. To take path dependence such as volatility clustering into account, we should use multi-step Monte Carlo to simulate each r_{10} as the sum of 10 consecutive daily log returns. If the log returns are i.i.d. this would be a waste of time, unless we are pricing a path-dependent product. When returns are i.i.d. the sum of 10 consecutive daily log returns should be the 10-day log return, so the result is

---

[20] Or, if the simulations are on the asset returns, we obtain the portfolio return using constant portfolio weights.
[21] Indeed, for path-dependent products we may also wish to simulate portfolio values at a higher frequency than daily.

theoretically the same whether we use 50 simulations for five 10-step paths, or use just five simulations on 10-day returns.[22] And the latter is 10 times quicker. However, if returns are not i.i.d. then multi-step Monte Carlo over h consecutive days will *not* give the same theoretical results as one-step h-day Monte Carlo, even for linear portfolios.

Multi-step Monte Carlo requires considerable effort compared with the one-step case. For instance, in Figure IV.4.5 we generated only five prices at the 10-day horizon but we needed 50 random numbers. In general, multi-step methods at the daily frequency over an h-day risk horizon require h times more simulations than one-step methods. And it is not just the extra simulations that take time: path-dependent products often require complex pricing models, and these have to be implemented at each step along the path.

Importance sampling is a technique for focusing simulations on the most important path. For instance, suppose we are using multi-step Monte Carlo to estimate the 10-day VaR of an up-and-out call option where the underlying asset price has a strong positive trend and the current price is not very far below its barrier. Then there is a reasonably high chance that within 10 days the underlying price will hit the barrier and knock out the option. If we simulated 50,000 10-day paths for this option – requiring 500,000 random numbers to be generated and 500,000 associated pricings for the barrier option – then perhaps about 20,000 of these paths could result in a zero price for the option. In other words, we would have wasted about 40% of the simulation time in generating paths for the underlying price that all lead to the same price for the option, i.e. zero.

Suppose the underlying asset price has a strong negative trend, instead of a strong upward trend, although the volatility remains unchanged.[23] Then relatively few of the price paths would result in a zero price for the up-and-out barrier option. As a result, our option price, which is computed as the average over all simulated discounted pay-offs, would be more accurate based on the same number of simulations. However, without modifying this price in some way, it would also be wrong, because it is based on the wrong drift for the process.

Importance sampling makes an artificial change to the drift in the price process, in order to shift the price density to one where more of the paths lead to informative simulated prices for the option. The only problem is that the average of such prices is not the option price we want. It is a price that has been simulated in the wrong *measure*.[24] However, we can derive the option price in the original measure from the price that we have simulated under the new measure. We just multiply each simulated option price by the ratio of the original underlying price density to the 'shifted' underlying price density, both evaluated at the simulated underlying price, before taking the average.[25]

In so far as it helps to price complex products, importance sampling based on a change of measure is a very useful technique for simulating VaR for large portfolios with exotic, path-dependent options. However, VaR is related to a quantile, not an expected value, so different

---

[22] However, due to sampling variation, the two results are not the same, as demonstrated in the spreadsheet for Figure IV.4.5.

[23] Thus the underlying price density is the same shape as before, but it has been shifted to the left because the drift has been reduced.

[24] This is because a change of drift in the price process is a change in the measure. An option price is a discounted expectation (which is why we can obtain the simulated price as an average) and we use the subscript on the expectation operator to denote the measure under which the expectation is taken. In this case we have two measures, the original price distribution P and the price distribution Q which is used to estimate the price after changing the drift so that more of the paths avoid the barrier. See Section III.3.2.3 for further details.

[25] This ratio is called the *likelihood ratio*, or the *Radon–Nykodym* derivative of the two measures. Further details are given in Section III.3.2.3.

techniques are required for the application of importance sampling to VaR estimation. For instance, Glasserman et al. (2000) apply importance sampling via an *exponential twisting* technique to the delta – gamma representation of the P&L of an option portfolio.

IV.4.3.2 Volatility Clustering and Mean Reversion

One of the most important features of high frequency returns on equity, currency and commodity portfolios is that volatility tends to come in clusters. Certainly at the daily frequency, but also when returns are sampled weekly if not monthly, large returns tend to follow large returns of either sign. Whilst returns themselves may show little or no autocorrelation, there is a strong positive autocorrelation in squared returns. We refer to this feature as *generalized autoregressive conditional heteroscedasticity* because the conditional volatility varies over time, as markets pass through periods with low and high volatility.

Chapter II.4 provided a comprehensive introduction to GARCH modelling, and to understand the current subsection readers are also referred to Sections II.3.8, which introduced *exponentially weighted moving averages*, a simple method for generating time varying estimates of volatility. It is not easy to estimate GARCH models in Excel without special add-ins. Nevertheless a number of spreadsheets that illustrated the use of Excel Solver to estimate GARCH parameters were provided with Chapter II.4. So as not to obscure the important learning points here, the examples in this subsection will be illustrated with user-defined GARCH parameters, or using a simple EWMA model. First, we illustrate the effect of volatility clustering on Monte Carlo VaR estimates using the simplest possible example, with EWMA volatility at the portfolio level.

When based on multi-step Monte Carlo simulations, the EWMA variance estimate $\hat{\sigma}_t^2$ at time t is computed using the recurrence

$$\hat{\sigma}_t^2 = (1 - \lambda)r_{t-1}^2 + \lambda\hat{\sigma}_{t-1}^2, \tag{IV.4.9}$$

where λ is a constant called the *smoothing constant*, and r_{t-1} is the simulated log return in the previous simulation. In the normal EWMA model for simulating log returns we set $r_t = \hat{\sigma}_t z_t$ where z_t is a simulation from a standard normal variable and $\hat{\sigma}_t$ is computed using (IV.4.9).

The next example shows that when EWMA is used to capture volatility clustering, the h-day Monte Carlo VaR estimates can be considerably greater than the equivalent constant volatility VaR estimates (even over short risk horizons) if the current return is relatively large.

EXAMPLE IV.4.6: MULTI-STEP MONTE CARLO WITH EWMA VOLATILITY

Compare the 10-day log returns that are obtained using multi-step Monte Carlo based on

(a) independent zero-mean normal log returns with a constant conditional volatility of 20%, and
(b) independent zero-mean normal log returns with a time-varying volatility estimate given by a EWMA model. Assume that the current conditional volatility is 25%, the current daily return is 1% and thereafter conditional volatilities are generated using EWMA with daily smoothing constant 0.9.

How do the 10-day VaR estimates that are based on the two return distributions compare? What happens if the current daily log return is 10%?

SOLUTION   We compute the 10-day log returns under each model using the same random numbers. The 10 standard normal realizations used for daily log returns are shown in columns B to K of the spreadsheet for this example. The log returns under the constant volatility model (a) are simulated by multiplying each standard normal realization z_i ($i = 1, \ldots, 10$) by the daily standard deviation, then these are summed to obtain the simulated 10-day log return shown in column V.

The log returns under the EWMA model (b) are based on the model (IV.4.9) with $\lambda = 0.9$. These are constructed in two interconnected parts. First we simulate the EWMA variance $\hat{\sigma}_1^2$, using the model (IV.4.9) with $r_0 = 0.01$ and $\hat{\sigma}_0 = 0.25/\sqrt{250}$. Then we multiply the same standard normal realization z_1 that was used to simulate the 1-day-ahead daily log return in model (a) by $\hat{\sigma}_1$, to obtain r_1, the 1-day-ahead daily log return in model (b). Then we use r_1^2 and $\hat{\sigma}_1^2$ in (IV.4.9) to obtain $\hat{\sigma}_2^2$, and multiply the same standard normal realization z_2 that was used to simulate the 2-day-ahead daily log return in model (a) by $\hat{\sigma}_2$, to obtain r_2, the 2-day-ahead daily log return in model (b). This process is repeated up to the 10-day-ahead daily log return and then the 10 log returns are summed to obtain the simulated 10-day log return shown in column AQ.

Table IV.4.2 compares 10 simulated 10-day log returns that are generated using each model. The first two columns are returns that are simulated using the current daily log return $r_0 = 1\%$, and these show that the return with EWMA volatility may be greater than or less than the constant volatility return, depending on the simulation. The second two columns of simulations set $r_0 = 10\%$, and with such a large daily shock, almost all the returns have greater magnitude, whether positive or negative, when based on the volatility clustering model.

Table IV.4.2   Simulated returns based on constant and EWMA volatilities

Shock	$r_0 = 1\%$		$r_0 = 10\%$	
Simulation	Constant volatility	EWMA volatility	Constant volatility	EWMA volatility
1	0.0820	0.0743	0.0441	0.1110
2	−0.0257	−0.0249	−0.0422	−0.1004
3	0.0117	0.0070	−0.0130	−0.0033
4	−0.1089	−0.1085	−0.0231	−0.0477
5	−0.0149	−0.0089	−0.1405	−0.3290
6	−0.0093	−0.0130	0.0332	0.0726
7	−0.0180	−0.0154	0.0312	0.0673
8	0.0146	0.0149	0.0200	0.0474
9	−0.0263	−0.0211	0.0993	0.2326
10	0.0008	−0.0124	0.0450	0.0968

After extending the simulations to a sufficiently large number, readers can use the spreadsheet for this example to compare the 10-day VaR estimates that are based on the 10-day return distributions generated by the two different volatility models. The first two rows of Table IV.4.3 report the results for 0.1%, 1%, 5% and 10% VaR estimates, expressed as a percentage of the portfolio value, based on the same set of 10,000 random numbers. Repeating the simulations shows that the P&L distribution becomes more leptokurtic when the simulations include volatility clustering. The second two rows of the table report the results from the same set of 10,000 random numbers – note these are different simulations from those used in the top part of the table – when the current daily log return is 10%. Notice that the constant volatility model is not influenced by the size of the shock.[26] But when volatility clustering is included in the returns model, all the VaR estimates are considerably greater following a shock of 10% than of 1%.

Table IV.4.3   Multi-step Monte Carlo VaR based on constant and EWMA volatilities

Shock	Significance level	0.1%	1%	5%	10%
$r_0 = 1\%$	Constant volatility	15.39%	15.30%	9.79%	7.25%
	EWMA volatility	18.57%	15.11%	9.58%	7.57%
$r_0 = 10\%$	Constant volatility	12.66%	11.55%	7.05%	5.99%
	EWMA volatility	26.98%	26.63%	17.91%	12.56%

The above example demonstrates that introducing volatility clustering in the dynamic model of portfolio returns produces heavier tails in the 10-day return distribution, and to capture this effect we need to use multi-step Monte Carlo simulation.

However, the EWMA model takes no account of the asymmetric relationship between returns and volatility. That is, the results in Example IV.4.5 would be similar to those presented here if the current daily returns were -1% and -10% respectively. EWMA ignores the fact that the volatility of equity portfolio returns increases considerably following a large negative return, but increases little, if at all, following a positive return of the same magnitude. That is, there is no asymmetric volatility clustering in EWMA. It also assumes there is no mean reversion in volatility.

To capture asymmetric volatility clustering and mean reversion in volatility following a shock, we can use an asymmetric GARCH model. The following example uses a similar methodology to that explained in the previous example, but now the EWMA model (IV.4.9) for the conditional variance of the returns is replaced by an A-GARCH model. This model takes the form[27]

$$\sigma_t^2 = \omega + \alpha(\varepsilon_{t-1} - \lambda)^2 + \beta\sigma_{t-1}^2, \qquad (IV.4.10)$$

where the parameter λ will be positive if the volatility increases more following a negative return than it does following a positive return of the same magnitude.[28] Here ε_t denotes the *unexpected return*, which is commonly set equal to its deviation from a constant mean. The EWMA model assumes this mean is zero, and we shall also assume this in the following example, hence we assume $\varepsilon_t = r_t$ for all t.

---

[26] In fact, because we used different simulations, and not nearly enough of them for good levels of accuracy, the constant volatility model actually has a lower VaR estimate in the second part of the table.

[27] Note that we do not use the caret '^' for the variance here, because the *model* conditional variances are time-varying in the GARCH framework. In the EWMA framework the true conditional variance is constant, with only its estimates varying over time.

[28] Not to be confused with the EWMA λ, which measures the persistence of volatility following a market shock (the GARCH parameter β plays this role); in the EWMA model $1 - \lambda$ captures the reaction of volatility to a market shock (the GARCH parameter α plays this role). The GARCH parameter ω affects the unconditional (i.e. long term average) volatility of the GARCH model. Readers should consult Section II.4.2.6 if they require further information on the association between GARCH and EWMA volatility models.

EXAMPLE IV.4.7: MULTI-STEP MONTE CARLO WITH ASYMMETRIC
GARCH VOLATILITY

Compare the multi-step VaR estimates that are obtained using

(a) a constant volatility model with volatility 25%, and
(b) an A-GARCH model (IV.4.10) with the parameters shown in Table IV.4.4 (note that the unconditional volatility of this model is 25%).[29]

Table IV.4.4   A-GARCH model parameters

Parameter	Value
ω	4×10^{-6}
α	0.06
λ	0.01
β	0.9

Estimate the 10-day VaR at the 0.1%, 1%, 5% and 10% significance levels, following a positive return of 10% and following a negative return of 10%. Use the same set of standard normal realizations to drive each model.

SOLUTION   The spreadsheet for this example is very similar to the spreadsheet for the previous example, the only difference being that we use an A-GARCH model instead of EWMA. The 10-day VaR estimates based on one set of 10,000 simulations are displayed in Table IV.4.5. The simulations for the constant volatility model are based on the same random numbers as those used in Example IV.4.6.

Table IV.4.5   Multi-step Monte Carlo A-GARCH VaR with positive and negative shocks

Significance level	0.1%	1%	5%	10%
Constant volatility	12.66%	11.55%	7.05%	5.99%
A-GARCH (+ve shock)	20.90%	19.65%	12.68%	9.26%
A-GARCH (−ve shock)	21.57%	19.88%	13.12%	9.14%

The VaR estimates based on constant volatility are identical those shown in Table IV.4.3, since the same 10,000 standard normal simulations were used. But the A-GARCH VaR estimates are considerably lower than the EWMA estimates in Table IV.4.3. This is because the volatility should revert quite rapidly following such a large shock, and this does not happen in the EWMA model. Instead, the EWMA model is highly reactive to the market because it has a reaction coefficient of 0.1. By comparison the GARCH model has a reaction coefficient of 0.06.

The asymmetric volatility response to positive and negative shocks is evident on comparing the last two rows in Table IV.4.5. At high levels of confidence the A-GARCH VaR based on

---

[29] The unconditional volatility is derived using the formula for the long term variance given in Section II.4.3.1.

a negative shock is greater than the VaR based on the same model, but following a positive shock of the same size. This asymmetric clustering effect is controlled by the λ parameter. When it is zero there is no differential effect, and when it is negative the A-GARCH VaR following a positive shock would be the greater. However, the asymmetric clustering effect is minor compared with the volatility mean reversion effect that all GARCH models capture.

To see this mean reversion in action, Figure IV.4.6 shows two simulations of daily returns over 10 days based on the same random numbers but using the EWMA (in grey) and the A-GARCH model (in black).[30] The asymmetric effect in the GARCH model is very small, in fact in these simulations, noting the scale of the returns, the volatility is greater following a very small positive first return (above) than following a large negative return (below). Both graphs illustrate the pronounced mean reversion in the A-GARCH volatility model. The

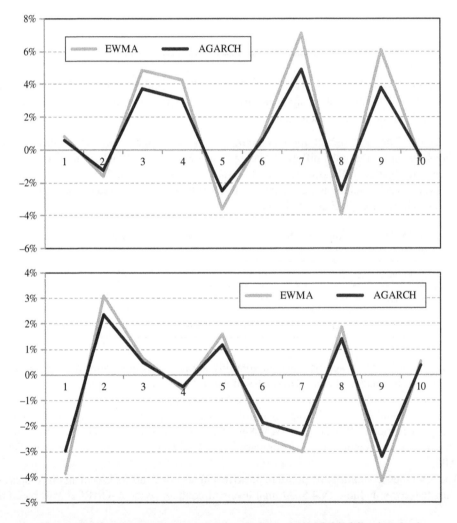

Figure IV.4.6   Simulated returns based on EWMA and GARCH following shock

---

[30] For this model set the A-GARCH parameter λ to zero.

EWMA model has volatility that remains higher for longer, because of the EWMA model's higher reaction coefficient.

I am often asked why we cannot use *analytic* volatility term structure forecasts, such as those derived for various asymmetric GARCH models in Section II.4.3, to estimate VaR with volatility clustering. That is, why can we not take the h-day GARCH volatility for the portfolio, for which there is an analytic formula, and multiply this by the standard normal critical value, just as we would to estimate VaR under the assumption of i.i.d. returns? There are two reasons. First, the h-day returns are not normal or i.i.d., because their volatility is time varying. Secondly, whilst these analytic formulae give us forecasts of h-day GARCH volatility, a forecast is only an expected value. Analytic GARCH volatility forecasts are based on the assumption that the squared return on every day between now and the risk horizon is equal to its expected value. The use of analytic forecasts therefore ignores a very considerable source of uncertainty in the 10-day log return distribution.[31] But the risk of the portfolio as measured by the 10-day VaR – or indeed as measured by the standard deviation or any other dispersion metric for 10-day returns – is a measure of the uncertainty of these returns. Therefore, the use of analytic formulae for GARCH volatility term structures, which ignores the most important part of this uncertainty, will tend to underestimate the VaR substantially.

To summarize, the advantage of using GARCH models in VaR estimates based on multi-step Monte Carlo is that these models include a mean reversion effect in volatility. That is, if the returns over the risk horizon were all equal to their expected value (which was assumed to be zero above) then the volatility would converge to its long term average value. Whenever a return is different from its expected value, GARCH volatility will react, but will also display mean reversion. Mean reversion in equity prices or in forex rates is negligible, in commodity prices it is questionable, and even in interest rates mean reversion tends to occur over a very long cycle.[32] But volatility is known to mean-revert relatively rapidly. Hence, volatility is a risk factor for which a mean reversion effect is important when designing dynamic models of market returns.

There are several papers on the ability of GARCH models to capture volatility clustering in the VaR estimation literature. Mittnik and Paolella (2000) and Giot and Laurent (2003) employ an asymmetric generalized t conditional distribution in the GARCH model; Venter and de Jongh (2002) use the normal inverse Gaussian distribution and Angelidis et al. (2004) apply the Student t EGARCH model. Both So and Yu (2006) and Alexander and Sheedy (2008) find that the Student t GARCH model performs well in VaR estimation for major currency returns. GARCH Monte Carlo VaR models also have important applications to stress testing portfolios, as we shall see in Chapter IV.7.

IV.4.3.3   Regime Switching Models

Our discussion of Monte Carlo simulation with GARCH models in Section II.4.7 made the case that Markov switching GARCH is the only model that properly captures the type of volatility clustering behaviour that we observe in most financial markets. In this section we explain how this model provides a useful framework for deriving VaR estimates over a long risk horizon, during which it is possible that volatility passes through different regimes. We

---

[31] However, see Alexander et al. (2009) for a quasi-analytic form for the distribution of returns under GARCH processes. Having derived analytic formulae for the first eight moments of the aggregated returns from a very general asymmetric GARCH process, we fit a distribution to h-day returns. The resulting VaR estimates, which are very quick to compute, are very close to those based on simulation.

[32] See Section III.1.4.4 for further details and an empirical study.

use a risk horizon of 250 days, although such long risk horizons are rare when we assess market risks.

Figure IV.4.7 is based on the same Markov switching GARCH model as was used in Section II.4.7.2. Each graph is generated from a different series of 250 simulated realizations of a returns process with a regime switching volatility. Notice how different the two simulations are, even though they are based on the *same* GARCH model. The sum of the 250 consecutive log returns is 29.23% for the upper graph but −26.29% for the lower graph in Figure IV.4.7. Also note that the initial return in the upper graph is quite large, and hence a high volatility cluster appears immediately, whereas the initial return in the lower graph is small and so the initial regime is one of low volatility. However, in this particular case it is the path in the lower graph that experiences the most volatility, especially between days 50 and

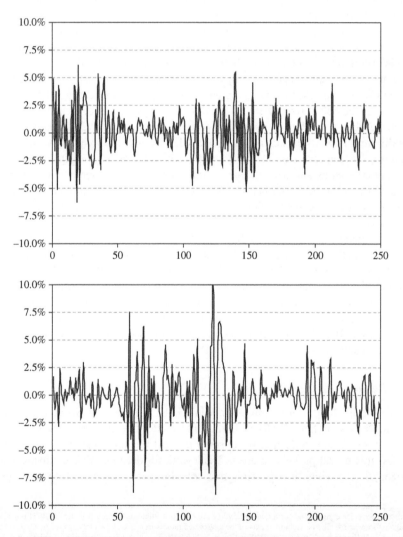

Figure IV.4.7   Log returns simulated under Markov switching GARCH

150. The path in the upper graph has smaller bursts of volatility that are less extreme than in the lower graph.

Each time we repeat the simulations the sum of the log returns can change considerably, even though we do not change the model parameters. For example, I have repeated the simulations ten times and obtained the following simulated values for the sum of the log returns:

10.91%, 18.93%, −1.55%, 42.65%, −54.60%, 32.67%, −35.68%, 28.45%, 5.08%, −14.46%.

We conclude that volatility clustering regimes introduce an additional source of uncertainty into long term return distributions. This could significantly increase the long term VaR estimate, depending on the volatility at the time is VaR is measured, compared with a constant volatility VaR estimate. For instance, the VaR could be measured at a time when the market was relatively tranquil, but there may still be a prolonged period of high volatility over the risk horizon, as in the lower graph in Figure IV.4.7.

Unfortunately, without VBA code it is beyond the scope of Excel to simulate many thousands of such annual returns, in order to estimate the Markov switching GARCH annual VaR. And so we end the illustration here, leaving the development of the spreadsheet for Figure IV.4.7 into a Markov switching GARCH model for long term VaR as an exercise for the reader.

IV.4.4   MODELLING RISK FACTOR DEPENDENCE

The primary purpose of a risk model is to disaggregate portfolio risk into components corresponding to different types of risk factors. That is why we use a portfolio mapping to derive the portfolio returns or P&L, rather than modelling the returns or P&L distribution directly at the portfolio level. All risk metrics, including VaR, should take account of portfolio diversification effects when aggregating risks across different types of risk factors.

In the traditional view of portfolio theory, diversification effects arise when there is less than perfect correlation between the assets or risk factors for a portfolio. More recently, we have widened this to include any type of less-than-perfect *dependence* between risk factors, where dependence in general is captured using a copula. In the elliptical copulas (i.e. normal and Student t copulas) dependence is captured by a correlation matrix. But in other copulas, different parameters govern dependence.

In this section we summarize the relevant material from Volumes I and II on statistical models for dependence between risk factors and explain how they are implemented in a Monte Carlo framework to simulate dependent vectors of risk factor returns. Several numerical examples are provided, for which you will need to install the Matrix.xla Excel add-in.[33]

---

[33] We use version 2.3 of this add-in, which is kindly provided free from http://digilander.libero.it/foxes by Leonardo Volpi of Foxes team, Italy. To install this add-in to Excel 2003, in the Tools menu of Excel click 'Add-ins' then 'Browse'. Find the location of Matrix.xla on your machine, highlight the icon and click OK. Once added in, it remains on your menu of possible add-ins, and unless you deselect it, it will be automatically loaded when you start Excel just like any other add-in. In Excel 2007 use the Excel Office button to find the Excel options, and then browse the add-ins. Note that the software is not supported and, for Vista users, the Help file requires the Windows Help program (WinHlp32.exe) for Windows Vista (as do all help files from earlier Microsoft operating systems!).

IV.4.4.1   Multivariate Distributions for i.i.d. Returns

Useful background reading for this section is the brief introduction to Monte Carlo simulation of correlated variables in Section I.5.7, the material on multivariate elliptical distributions in Section I.3.4, and Section II.6.7 on simulation with copulas.

We shall describe the process for estimating Monte Carlo VaR based on risk factor mapping, but a similar algorithm applies to estimate Monte Carlo VaR using asset returns rather than risk factor returns in the simulations. The only difference is that instead of applying the risk factor sensitivities in the portfolio mapping to compute the portfolio return, we use the portfolio weights.

We shall also assume that the portfolio mapping is based on returns rather than on changes in the equity, currency and commodity risk factors, so that the mapping yields a portfolio return. Hence, the VaR will be measured as a percentage of the portfolio value. But for interest rate sensitive portfolios the risk factor mapping is normally based on changes in interest rates, with the PV01 vector of sensitivities to these changes. Then the portfolio mapping gives the portfolio P&L, not the portfolio return, corresponding to each vector of interest rates changes.[34]

Multivariate Normal

The most basic algorithm for generating correlated simulations on k risk factor returns is based on a k-dimensional, i.i.d. normal process. So the marginal distribution of the ith risk factor's return is $N(\mu_i, \sigma_i^2)$, for $i = 1, \ldots, k$, and the risk factor correlations are represented in a $k \times k$ matrix C. The algorithm begins with k independent simulations on standard uniform variables, transforms these into independent standard normal simulations, and then uses the Cholesky matrix of the risk factor returns covariance matrix to transform these into correlated zero-mean simulations with the appropriate variance. Then the mean excess return is added to each variable.

With the above notation the risk factor excess returns covariance matrix Ω may be written

$$\Omega = DCD, \tag{IV.4.11}$$

where $D = \text{diag}(\sigma_1, \ldots, \sigma_k)$. Its *Cholesky matrix* is a lower triangular $k \times k$ matrix Q such that $\Omega = QQ'$. We also write the expected returns in a vector, as $\mu = (\mu_1, \ldots, \mu_k)'$. Then the $k \times 1$ multivariate normal vectors x are generated by simulating a $k \times 1$ independent standard normal vector z, and setting $x = Qz + \mu$.

We simulate a very large number N of such vectors x and apply the portfolio mapping to each simulation, thus producing N simulations on the portfolio returns. When the returns are i.i.d. we use one-step rather than multi-step Monte Carlo, so the expectations vector μ and standard deviation matrix D of the risk factor returns are h-day expected excess returns and standard deviations. Then we simulate N h-day portfolio excess returns, find their empirical distribution, find the α quantile of this distribution, multiply this by -1 and that is the h-day VaR estimate. And the corresponding ETL is -1 times the average of the returns below the α quantile.

---

[34] The differences between portfolio mappings for different types of risk factors were discussed in detail in Chapter III.5 and, if not already clear, this will be clarified in Section IV.4.5 when we provide specific examples for each different type of portfolio.

EXAMPLE IV.4.8: MULTIVARIATE NORMAL MONTE CARLO VAR

A linear portfolio has five correlated risk factors, labelled A–E, which we assume have i.i.d. normal returns. The annual expected excess returns on each risk factor, the risk factor volatilities and the current risk factor sensitivities are displayed in Table IV.4.6. Below these the table displays the risk factor returns correlation matrix. Use Monte Carlo simulation to estimate the 1% 10-day VaR of the portfolio.

Table IV.4.6 Risk factor returns, volatilities, sensitivities and correlations

Factor:	A	B	C	D	E
Expected excess return	4.0%	5.0%	2.0%	0.0%	−1.0%
Risk factor volatilities	20.0%	30.0%	15.0%	10.0%	40.0%
Risk factor sensitivities	0.75	0.5	0.25	0.1	−0.05
Correlation matrix	A	B	C	D	E
A	1	0.75	0.5	−0.25	−0.05
B	0.75	1	0.25	0.35	−0.25
C	0.5	0.25	1	0.5	−0.5
D	−0.25	0.35	0.5	1	0.05
E	−0.05	−0.25	−0.5	0.05	1

SOLUTION   Note that it is easier to represent the simulated vectors in the spreadsheet as row vectors, although we used columns vectors (as usual) in the mathematical description of the algorithm above. First the 10-day Cholesky matrix $\mathbf{Q}_{10}$ is calculated, and this is shown in cells B17:F21 of the spreadsheet. Then we simulate five independent standard normal realizations as a row vector $\mathbf{z}'$, post-multiply this by the transpose of the 10-day Cholesky matrix and add on the 10-day mean vector $\boldsymbol{\mu}'_{10}$. This gives $\mathbf{x}'_{10} = \mathbf{z}'\mathbf{Q}'_{10} + \boldsymbol{\mu}'_{10}$, i.e. one simulation of a row vector of correlated risk factor returns. Having simulated N such row vectors, we apply the linear risk factor mapping to each one of these, using the sensitivities shown in Table IV.4.6, to obtain N simulated portfolio 10-day returns. Finally, the 1% VaR is -1 times the 1% quantile of the distribution of these returns, and with $N = 10,000$ simulations we obtain a Monte Carlo VaR estimate of approximately 14% of the portfolio value.

Multivariate Student t

The above example illustrated the most basic risk factor mapping, i.e. a simple linear function, and the most basic risk factor returns model, i.e. where the multivariate distribution is normal and the risk factor returns are i.i.d. However, risk factor returns at the daily or weekly frequency rarely have normal distributions. In particular, for estimating Monte Carlo VaR over short risk horizons of up to a few weeks it is important to include leptokurtosis in the risk factor return distributions. The easiest way to do this is to use a multivariate Student t distribution, which has the distribution function specified in Section I.3.4.8. Note that there is only *one* degrees of freedom parameter ν in this distribution, so the marginal distributions of all risk factor returns are assumed to have the same excess kurtosis. But in the next subsection, when we introduce copulas, we show how this assumption may be relaxed.

The Monte Carlo VaR algorithm for i.i.d. multivariate Student t distributed risk factor returns is very similar to the multivariate i.i.d. normal algorithm. The only difference is that the vector $\mathbf{z}$ is replaced by a vector $\mathbf{t}$ containing simulations from a standardized multivariate Student t distribution, i.e. the distribution with zero mean, unit variance marginals. Since a Student t distributed variable with ν degrees of freedom parameter has mean zero but variance $\nu(\nu - 2)^{-1}$, we obtain $\mathbf{t}$ by multiplying independent standard Student t simulations by $\sqrt{\nu^{-1}(\nu - 2)}$.

EXAMPLE IV.4.9: MULTIVARIATE STUDENT T MONTE CARLO VAR

Suppose the risk factors in the previous example have a multivariate Student t distribution with 6 degrees of freedom, but otherwise the portfolio and the risk factors have the same characteristics as those displayed in Table IV.4.6. Re-estimate the 1% 10-day VaR based on this assumption.

SOLUTION   The spreadsheet for this example is similar to that for Example IV.4.8, except that now we use an extra set of five columns to produce the standardized uncorrelated simulations, one set to simulate standard Student t distributed returns with 6 degrees of freedom,[35] and a second set which transforms these to have unit variance. Otherwise the spreadsheet is unchanged from the previous example. With 10,000 simulations we obtain a 1% 10-day Monte Carlo VaR that is approximately 15% of the portfolio value.

Due to the leptokurtosis in the Student t distribution this is greater than the VaR estimate based on normally distributed risk factor returns.[36] The difference between the two VaR estimates becomes more pronounced at more extreme quantiles, but at the 5% quantile there may be little difference between the estimates, and at 10% the Student t VaR estimate may be less than the normal VaR estimate.

Multivariate Normal Mixture

It is possible to apply Monte Carlo to many distributions – indeed, this is one of the main advantages of Monte Carlo methods VaR. We now explain how to use Monte Carlo methods when risk factor returns have a multivariate normal mixture distribution, i.e. each multivariate normal in the mixture distribution has its own mean vector and covariance matrix. This is a simple way to capture non-zero skewness as well as leptokurtosis in the risk factor returns.

By way of illustration, let us suppose we have only two multivariate normal distributions in the mixture. In fact, this is often sufficient to capture the leptokurtosis and/or skewness that we often observe in risk factor returns. Suppose one multivariate normal occurs with a low probability π, has mean vector $\boldsymbol{\mu}_1$ and covariance matrix $\boldsymbol{\Omega}_1$ and reflects 'market crash' conditions, and the other, which occurs with probability $1 - \pi$, has mean vector $\boldsymbol{\mu}_2$ and covariance matrix $\boldsymbol{\Omega}_2$ and reflects ordinary market circumstances. The normal mixture distribution function on n random variables $\mathbf{x} = (x_1, \ldots, x_n)'$ may then be written

$$F(\mathbf{x}) = \pi\boldsymbol{\Phi}(\mathbf{x}; \boldsymbol{\mu}_1, \boldsymbol{\Omega}_1) + (1 - \pi)\boldsymbol{\Phi}(\mathbf{x}; \boldsymbol{\mu}_2, \boldsymbol{\Omega}_2), \tag{IV.4.12}$$

where $\boldsymbol{\Phi}$ is the multivariate normal distribution function.

---

[35] Note that the cumbersome form of the TINV function in Excel requires a conditional statement in these simulations. See Section I.3.5.3 for further details.
[36] The excess kurtosis of each marginal is $6/(\nu - 4) = 3$ when $\nu = 6$.

Monte Carlo simulation on (IV.4.12) is performed in two stages. First we take a random draw on a Bernoulli variable with success probability π. Then we sample from the first multivariate normal if the result is a 'success' and otherwise we sample from the second multivariate normal. Equivalently, when we perform a very large number N of simulations, we apply μ_1 and Ω_1 to πN of the independent standard normal simulations and μ_2 and Ω_2 to $(1 - \pi)N$ of them. An empirical illustration of normal mixture Monte Carlo is given in Example IV.4.13 below.

Copulas

In the examples considered so far all the risk factor returns were assumed to have identical marginal distributions. To allow for heterogeneous risk factor return distributions we must model dependence using a *copula* distribution. Copulas are multivariate distributions with uniform marginals that may be used to construct a huge variety of risk factor return distributions. The copula only models dependence; the marginal distribution of each of the risk factor returns may be anything we like. For instance, one risk factor could have a Student t return distribution with 6 degrees of freedom, another could have a normal return distribution, another could have a gamma distribution, and so on.

Normal (also called Gaussian) and Student t copulas capture dependency through a correlation matrix, which is a limited measure of only linear association. But there are many other copulas that capture more general dependency. One very attractive class of copulas, which have very parsimonious parameterizations, are the *Archimedean copulas*. See Sections II.6.4.4, II.6.5.4 and II.6.7.4 for further details.

Suppose the risk factor returns have some assumed marginal distributions, which need not be identical, and that their dependency is modelled with a copula. The simulation algorithm begins with simulations on independent uniform random variables. Then the *inverse conditional copula* functions are applied to obtain realizations of dependent uniform variables. Finally, the dependent uniform realizations are translated into simulations on the risk factor returns by applying the relevant *inverse marginal distribution function* to each realization.

The *elliptical copulas* (i.e. normal and Student t copulas) have dependency structure that is captured by a correlation matrix, and this makes simulation based on these copulas very easy, with risk factors that may have a variety of marginal distributions. In the next example we show how to estimate VaR based on simulated returns to five risk factors, each having different Student t marginal distributions, but with a normal copula. Because the marginals already have a variance different from one, for a normal or Student t copula we use the Cholesky matrix of the correlation matrix, not of the covariance matrix, to impose the dependency structure.

EXAMPLE IV.4.10: MONTE CARLO VAR BASED ON COPULAS

Suppose the risk factors have the same expected excess returns and volatilities as in the two previous examples and that their dependency is described by a normal copula with the same correlation matrix. The portfolio's risk factor sensitivities are also assumed to be the same as in the previous examples. However, now suppose that each risk factor return has a different univariate Student t marginal distribution. The degrees of freedom, in order of the five risk factors are: 5, 4, 6, 10, and 5. Re-estimate the 1% 10-day VaR based on this assumption.

SOLUTION   The result is only marginally less than that in the previous example: based on 10,000 simulations, the 1% 10-day VaR is approximately 14.75% of the portfolio value. The use of a normal copula rather than a Student t copula tends to decrease the VaR, but some of the marginals have more leptokurtosis than in the previous example, which tends to increase the VaR.

The purpose of the above example is not to discuss how the VaR behaves under different behavioural assumptions for the risk factors; it is merely to illustrate the algorithm for estimating VaR based on simulation from a normal copula with different marginals. The steps are as follows:

1. Simulate independent standard uniform observations, one column for each risk factor.
2. Transform these into independent standard normal observations, using the inverse standard normal distribution function.
3. Transform the independent standard normal observations into correlated multivariate standard normal observations, using the Cholesky matrix of the correlation matrix.
4. Transform the correlated multivariate standard normal observations into simulations from a normal copula, by applying the standard normal distribution function.
5. Transform the simulations from a normal copula into standard Student t observations with normal copula, using the inverse distribution function for the Student t with the required degrees of freedom. Note that the degrees of freedom can be different for each marginal. Indeed, the marginals do not have to have Student t distributions, we have just used these for illustration.
6. Use the required h-day mean and h-day standard deviation to transform the standard Student t observations with normal copula into simulations on h-day risk factor returns, with *general* Student t marginals, but still with dependency captured by a normal copula.
7. Apply the risk factor mapping and hence obtain simulated portfolio returns.
8. Estimate the α quantile of the simulated portfolio return distribution, and multiply this by -1 to obtain the $100\alpha\%$ VaR. If required, estimate the $100\alpha\%$ ETL as -1 times the average of the returns less than the α quantile.

Algorithms for simulation from bivariate distributions using various copulas are illustrated in the workbook 'Copula_Simulations_II.6.7.xls' that accompanies Volume II. Also in that workbook is an example on VaR estimation under various copulas, described in Section II.6.8.1. Readers may wish to study that workbook and then change the spreadsheet for the above example so that it uses a different copula and/or different marginals. For example, with a Student t copula with ν degrees of freedom, the transformation at step 2 is performed using the inverse Student t distribution with ν degrees of freedom, and then its distribution function is applied at step 4. But for other copulas we would not use a correlation matrix at all. For instance, for simulations under a Clayton copula the risk factor dependency is described by a single parameter.

IV.4.4.2 Principal Component Analysis

Principal component analysis is a standard statistical tool for *orthogonalizing* risk factors and for *reducing dimensions* of the risk factors. In other words, PCA is a technique for extracting a few key, uncorrelated risk factors – which are called the *principal components* – from a larger set of correlated risk factors. It works best when the original risk factors are highly correlated, since then we need only a few principal components to represent the system. The first component will be the most important, and in a highly correlated system it usually represents a *common trend*.

PCA works especially well when the risk factors are a highly correlated, *ordered* system since then *all* the principal components and not just the first one will have an intuitive financial meaning. This is why much of Chapter II.2 dealt with the principal component factor models for *term structures* of interest rates, credit spreads, futures, forwards or volatilities. The input to a PCA is either a *covariance* matrix or a *correlation* matrix. Then the principal components are derived from the eigenvectors of this matrix, which are ordered so that the first eigenvector belongs to the largest eigenvalue, and therefore the first component explains the most variation in the system. In very highly correlated systems this component captures an almost parallel shift in all variables, and more generally it is labelled the *common trend* component, because it captures the most often experienced type of common movement in all risk factors. The second eigenvector belongs to the second largest eigenvalue, and therefore the second component explains the second most variation in the system. In ordered and highly correlated systems such as a term structure this eigenvector captures an almost linear tilt in the variables, so it is commonly labelled the *tilt* component. The third most important component usually comes from an eigenvector that is an approximate quadratic function of the ordered variables, so it has the interpretation of *convexity* or *curvature*. Similarly, higher order principal components in ordered, highly correlated systems capture changes in risk factors that are cubic, quartic, quintic and so forth.

The ability of PCA to reduce dimensions, combined with the use of orthogonal variables for risk factors, makes this technique an extremely attractive option for Monte Carlo simulation. In highly correlated term structures of interest rates, credit spreads and volatilities the replacement of the original risk factors by just a few orthogonal risk factors introduces very little error into the simulations, and increases the efficiency of the simulations enormously, because it reduces the number of risk factors.

However, the application of PCA to Monte Carlo simulations of equity and currency risk factors, or to portfolios with different types of commodity futures, is limited. Typically, these systems are neither very highly correlated nor ordered. So a large number of principal components would usually be required in the representation, to avoid introducing a substantial risk model error. This means that there is less scope for computational efficiency gains.

Each volume of *Market Risk Analysis* has contained numerous empirical examples and case studies on the application of PCA to different types of risk factors. Here are some references to just a selection of these:

- equity indices – Section I.2.6.3;
- individual stocks – Section II.2.5.3;
- interest rate term structures – Section II.2.3;
- forward currency exposures – Section II.2.4.2;
- energy futures – III.2.6.3;
- implied volatility smiles – Section III.4.4.2;
- volatility term structures – Section III.5.7.

In this chapter we provide yet another illustration of the power of this technique. Example IV.4.12 in Section IV.4.5.2 presents an empirical example on Monte Carlo interest rate VaR based on principal component risk factors.

IV.4.4.3   Behavioural Models

One of the reasons why copulas are used in multivariate simulations is that the dependency between risk factor returns is not necessarily linear. When there are only a few risk factors, an alternative to copulas is to model the risk factor returns relationship using non-linear regression. For example, suppose there are two risk factors whose returns X and Y have a quadratic rather than a linear relationship, i.e.

$$Y = \alpha + \beta_1 X + \beta_2 X^2. \tag{IV.4.13}$$

Since X and Y are stochastic the relationship will not be exact, so we add an error term on the right-hand side of (IV.4.13). The error has zero mean and often we assume it is *homoscedastic* (i.e. has constant standard deviation, which we denote σ) and normally distributed. These are the standard assumptions for ordinary least squares regression (OLS).[37] Then we use T historical observations on the returns X and Y to estimate the model parameters α, β_1, β_2 and σ using OLS on the regression:

$$Y_t = \alpha + \beta_1 X_t + \beta_2 X_t^2 + \varepsilon_t, \quad t = 1, \ldots, T, \quad \varepsilon_t \sim N(0, \sigma^2). \tag{IV.4.14}$$

Other non-linear models are usually easy to estimate provided the right-hand side is only a non-linear function of the variables and not of the parameters. For instance, we may hypothesize a relationship of the form

$$Y = \alpha + \beta_1 X + \beta_2 X^{-1} + \beta_3 \ln X. \tag{IV.4.15}$$

Again the parameters may be estimated using OLS multiple regression, provided we make the standard assumption about homoscedasticity of the error term. Or, if the risk factor return Y is thought to be non-linearly related to two other risk factor returns, X_1 and X_2, their relationship could be of the form

$$Y = \alpha + \beta_1 X_1^2 + \beta_2 \ln X_2, \tag{IV.4.16}$$

for example. Since this is linear in the parameters, we may estimate them using OLS.[38]

IV.4.4.4   Case Study: Modelling the Price – Volatility Relationship

Consider Figure IV.4.8, which depicts a scatter plot of the daily log returns on the S&P 500 index (horizontal scale) and Vix index (vertical scale). The negative dependence and leptokurtosis are apparent and the grey curve is drawn through the scatter plot to highlight their non-linear relationship. We shall capture the relationship between implied volatility and the underlying price using a simple quadratic regression of daily log returns to the Vix index on the S&P 500 log returns over the same sample period.

---

[37] Since the model is linear in the parameters it may be regarded as a special case of multivariate regression. See Section I.4.4 for an introduction. Note that the normality assumption is not required to use OLS, but it *is* necessary to make inference on the model, for instance about the importance of each explanatory variable as given by the t-ratio. See Section I.4.2 for further details.

[38] See Section II.7.4.1 for a numerical method for deriving least squares estimates when the model is a non-linear function of the parameters, such as

$$Y = \alpha + \beta X_1^2 + \beta^2 \ln X_2.$$

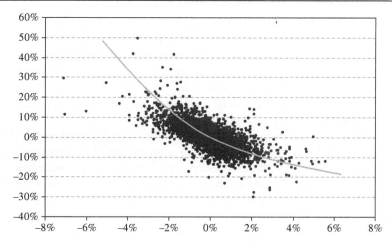

Figure IV.4.8   Scatter plot of S&P 500 and Vix daily log returns

In the case study workbook we estimate a quadratic regression via the data analysis tools in Excel. Using daily data from 2 January 2000 until 25 April 2008, the result is the estimated model

$$Y_t = -\underset{(-2.738)}{0.025}\,\% - \underset{(-52.252)}{3.814}\,X_t + \underset{(5.918)}{18.201}\,X_t^2 + \varepsilon_t, \qquad (IV.4.17)$$

where Y denotes the log return on the Vix, X denotes the log return on the S&P 500 index and the error term has standard deviation equal to the standard error of the regression, which is estimated to be 3.77%. The figures in parentheses denote the t statistics of the coefficients above them, so both the S&P 500 returns and the squared returns are very highly significant. This is to be expected, given the evident non-linearity in the scatter plot above.

However, no significant non-linearity is apparent in the weekly returns relationship. Using weekly data from 2 January 2000 until 28 April 2008, the result is the estimated model

$$Y_t = -\underset{(-0.092)}{0.036}\,\% - \underset{(-22.260)}{3.611}\,X_t - \underset{(-0.088)}{0.274}\,X_t^2 + \varepsilon_t, \qquad (IV.4.18)$$

where the estimated standard error of the regression is 7.54%. The quadratic term is no longer significant, and so we conclude that non-linearities in the S&P500 – Vix relationship are only important when simulations are at the daily frequency.

We can use the estimated model (IV.4.17) to simulate a daily log return Y on the Vix for any simulated daily log return X on the S&P 500. Because of their non-linear relationship, this is better than using a covariance matrix to capture their dependence. We shall return to this model in Section IV.5.5.3, where we use it to estimate the VaR for an option portfolio.

IV.4.5   MONTE CARLO VALUE AT RISK FOR LINEAR PORTFOLIOS

In Chapter IV.2 we showed how to extend the normal linear VaR formula to Student t and normal mixture VaR, and how to use a scaling constant that reflects autocorrelation in returns.

If we use one these models for the returns on the risk factors of a linear portfolio then there is no point in applying Monte Carlo to estimate the VaR.[39] The only difference between the Monte Carlo and the parametric linear VaR estimates would be due to simulation error, and it is the analytic formula that gives the correct result. The more simulations used, the more accurate the Monte Carlo VaR estimate, and as the number of simulations used increases the Monte Carlo VaR estimate converges to the parametric linear VaR estimate that is based on the same distributional model for returns.

So what is the advantage of using Monte Carlo to estimate VaR for a linear portfolio, compared with parametric linear VaR? The advantage is that the risk factor returns model is not limited to the simple models that we considered in Chapter IV.2, i.e. multivariate normal, Student t or mixture returns that are either i.i.d. or have a simple first order autoregressive structure. As we have seen in the previous two sections, a great variety of conditional multivariate distributions may be used as a basis for simulation. We may also want to use multi-step Monte Carlo simulations to introduce path dependence, either in an option's pay-off or in the volatility clustering behaviour of risk factor returns.

Compared with historical simulation, the advantage of using Monte Carlo to estimate VaR for a linear portfolio is that we can generate as many h-day returns as we like.[40] Whilst historical VaR is a natural way to capture the complex behaviour in and between risk factor returns it is, at least initially, limited to the 1-day horizon. This is because we simply do not have enough relevant historical data to use non-overlapping h-day returns.[41] But we can extend the standard historical simulation model to filtered historical simulation (FHS) which applies a statistical bootstrap on a parametric, dynamic model for return distributions, such as a GARCH model. This filtering allows h-day return distributions to be generated from overlapping samples and we can also increase the number of observations used for building the h-day portfolio return distribution through the use of the bootstrap. But FHS is in fact a hybrid method combining some attractive features of both historical and Monte Carlo VaR models.[42]

What is the effect on VaR of using parametric but non-normal distributions for the risk factors returns? We can use Monte Carlo VaR to answer this question, by comparing the Monte Carlo VaR estimates based on simple risk factor returns models with those based on more complex distributions. The result will depend on both the risk horizon and the type of portfolio. For instance, one might expect the i.i.d. multivariate normal or Student t distribution to be less appropriate for daily changes in credit spreads than it is for daily changes interest rates. But over a monthly risk horizon many risk factors might well be assumed to have i.i.d. multivariate normal or Student t distributions.

The purpose of this section is to illustrate the application of the risk factor returns models that we introduced in Sections IV.4.3 and IV.4.4 to the estimation of Monte Carlo VaR and ETL. We shall apply a different returns model to four different types of portfolios:

---

[39] By contrast, Monte Carlo simulation is the only reliable method for estimating the VaR for an option portfolio over a risk horizon of more than 1 day, as we demonstrate in the next chapter.

[40] Computation time is not an issue with linear VaR in practice, since the linear mapping can be performed in a few microseconds.

[41] We can try to scale a 1-day VaR using an approximate scale exponent, but this scaling can be a great source of model risk in historical VaR estimates, especially in option portfolios. If we use overlapping h-day returns on the risk factors, this will distort the tail behaviour of the return distributions, leading to significant error in the VaR estimates at extreme quantiles.

[42] See Sections IV.3.2.3, IV.3.2.4 and IV.5.4 for further details about these three approaches to estimating h-day historical VaR.

- elliptical copulas for credit spreads;
- principal component analysis for interest rates;
- multivariate normal mixture distributions for equities;
- volatility clustering for currencies.

Although we apply these different assumptions for Monte Carlo VaR in the framework of a particular type of portfolio, this is primarily for the purpose of illustrating each technique rather than a practical recommendation. For example, equity portfolios could benefit from modelling volatility clustering, as well as capturing the asymmetry and leptokurtosis in the conditional return distributions using multivariate normal mixture distributions.[43]

IV.4.5.1   Algorithms for VaR and ETL

The following summarizes the general one-step algorithm for estimating VaR and ETL when the risk factor mapping expresses the portfolio return as a linear combination of risk factor returns:

1. Simulate N independent $1 \times k$ vectors of standard uniform observations, where k is the number of risk factors and N is the number of simulations.
2. Use the i.i.d. risk factor returns model to transform these standard uniform observations into simulations on h-day risk factor returns, as described in Section IV.4.4.
3. Apply the risk factor mapping to the simulations on h-day risk factor returns to produce N simulated h-day returns on the portfolio, and discount these to today.
4. As a percentage of the portfolio value, the $100\alpha\%$ h-day VaR is -1 times the α quantile of the h-day return distribution and the $100\alpha\%$ h-day ETL is -1 times the average of all the h-day returns that are less than the α quantile. Multiplying these by the portfolio value today gives the VaR and ETL in value terms.

Depending on the type of portfolio, we may simulate h-day changes in risk factor values at step 2 instead of h-day returns. That is, we may take the simulated value of a risk factor in h days' time minus value of this risk factor today (i.e. the time when the VaR is measured).[44] In addition, or alternatively, the risk factor mapping may produce N simulated h-day P&Ls on the portfolio, discounted to today.[45] In that case the VaR and ETL estimated at step 4 will already be expressed in value terms.

To account for path dependence such as volatility clustering in risk factor returns, the general algorithm above is modified for multi-step Monte Carlo as follows:

1. Simulate N independent $1 \times k$ vectors of standard uniform observations, where k is the number of risk factors and N is the number of simulations.
2. Use the conditional 1-day risk factor log returns model to transform these standard uniform observations into simulations on 1-day risk factor log returns.

---

[43] We do not provide an example on commodity portfolios in this section, but these would benefit from all the techniques that we illustrate here. The construction of a non-normal conditional model with GARCH volatility clustering and principal component risk factors, if the portfolio contains commodity forwards or futures of different maturities, is left as an exercise for experienced readers.

[44] Or, if we are short the portfolio, the current value minus simulated value represents the P&L.

[45] This is the case when the risk factor sensitivities are expressed in value rather than percentage terms.

3. Return to step 1 and repeat h times, using the dynamic returns model to simulate each subsequent risk factor log return, as described in Section IV.4.3.
4. For each risk factor and for each of the N simulated paths, sum the log returns to obtain N simulated h-day log returns on each risk factor.
5. Apply the risk factor mapping to produce N simulated h-day returns on the portfolio, and discount these to today.
6. As a percentage of the portfolio value, the $100\alpha\%$ h-day VaR is -1 times the α quantile of the h-day return distribution and the $100\alpha\%$ h-day ETL is -1 times the average of all the h-day returns that are less than the α quantile. Multiplying these by the portfolio value today gives the VaR and ETL in value terms.

We now present some empirical implementations of these algorithms in the context of cash flow, equity and currency portfolios.

IV.4.5.2   Cash-Flow Portfolios: Copula VaR and PC VaR

A cash flow is mapped to a vector of default-free interest rates $\mathbf{r}$ at fixed maturities, and to a vector of credit spreads $\mathbf{s}$, also at fixed maturities. As explained in Section IV.2.3, the risk factor sensitivities are the PV01 of the mapped cash flows at each vertex, and the risk factors are the absolute changes in these interest rates and credit spreads, expressed in basis point terms. When an interest rate sensitive portfolio is represented as a cash flow the risk factor mapping therefore takes the form

$$\Delta PV \approx -(\boldsymbol{\theta}_r' \Delta \mathbf{r} + \boldsymbol{\theta}_s' \Delta \mathbf{s}), \qquad\qquad (IV.4.19)$$

where $\boldsymbol{\theta}_r$ and $\boldsymbol{\theta}_s$ are the PV01 vectors with respect to the interest rate and credit spread risk factors, and $\Delta \mathbf{r}$ and $\Delta \mathbf{s}$ are the basis point changes in these risk factors.[46] Since the PV01 is already in present value terms the algorithms described in the previous subsection provide N simulated values for the discounted P&L, from which we estimate the VaR and ETL.

The next example illustrates the estimation of Monte Carlo credit spread VaR based on elliptical copulas with different elliptical marginals. The parameters in the spreadsheet can be changed to reflect suitable distributions for any type of risk factors, such as interest rates, currencies, commodities or equities if so desired.

EXAMPLE IV.4.11: MONTE CARLO CREDIT SPREAD VAR

A portfolio of BBB-rated corporate bonds and swaps is mapped to vertices at 1 year, 2 years, 3 years, 4 years and 5 years. Table IV.4.7 shows the PV01 vector, along with the annual volatilities and correlations of the credit spread risk factors.[47] Compare the 10-day Monte Carlo VaR of this portfolio at different significance levels based on the assumption that changes in credit spreads have:

---

[46] Recall that for cash-flow portfolios the non-linearity of the portfolio P&L is captured by the PV01 sensitivities, so the risk factor mapping is a linear map with respect to interest rates and credit spreads.
[47] The PV01 vector is based on an exposure of $1 million at each maturity.

(a) a multivariate normal distribution;
(b) a normal copula and marginal Student t distributions having 5 degrees of freedom, and
(c) a multivariate Student t distribution with 5 degrees of freedom.

In case (b), readers may change the degrees of freedom to be different for each credit spread in the spreadsheet.

Table IV.4.7   Volatilities and correlations of LIBOR and credit spreads

Maturity (years)		Credit spreads				
		1	2	3	4	5
PV01 ($)		$951	$1,810	$2,582	$3,275	$3,894
Volatility (bps)		100	90	80	70	60
Correlations		1	2	3	4	5
	1	1	0.75	0.65	0.55	0.5
	2	0.75	1	0.85	0.8	0.7
	3	0.65	0.85	1	0.9	0.85
	4	0.55	0.8	0.9	1	0.95
	5	0.5	0.7	0.85	0.95	1

SOLUTION   We adapt the spreadsheets for Examples IV.4.8, IV.4.9 and IV.4.10 for parts (a), (b) and (c), respectively. We use the same 10,000 standard uniform simulations for each distribution, and the results for one set of 10,000 simulations are shown in Table IV.4.8.

Table IV.4.8   Comparison of Monte Carlo VaR estimates for credit spreads

Significance level	0.1%	1.0%	5.0%	10.0%
(a) Normal	$550,564	$505,273	$393,579	$279,299
(b) Normal copula, Student t marginals	$775,170	$688,562	$437,189	$264,868
(c) Student t	$990,768	$839,513	$584,871	$415,958

The results for (a) and (b) are similar at the 10% significance level, but as the confidence level of the VaR increases the difference between the normal copula VaR with Student t marginals and the normal VaR increases. This is due to the leptokurtosis in the Student t marginal distributions. The multivariate Student t VaR estimates (c) are greater than those in (b), readers may change the degrees of freedom to be different for each credit spread in the spreadsheet, because they are based on the same Student t marginals but have a Student t copula dependence, and the Student t copula has a greater tail dependency than the normal copula.

In practice cash flows are mapped to a very large number of fixed maturity interest rates and credit spreads. But interest rate risk factors are very highly correlated and so PCA can be applied to reduce the dimension of the risk factor space. Moreover, the construction of the principal components guarantees that they are uncorrelated, because they are generated by orthogonal eigenvectors. Thus, their correlation matrix is diagonal, and its Cholesky decomposition is also diagonal. The combination of dimension reduction and zero correlation reduces the complexity of the simulation algorithm considerably. Thus, using principal component risk factors will speed up the calculation of Monte Carlo VaR, with little loss of accuracy.

For instance, in Examples IV.2.8 and IV.2.10 we estimated the normal linear VaR of a cash flow characterized by the PV01 vector shown in Figure IV.2.2. We found that the 1% 10-day principal component VaR was £175,457, compared with £176,549 when calculated on the interest rates directly. Hence, interest rate VaR based on PCA tends to be very accurate, provided the interest rates of different maturities are highly correlated.[48]

When using principal components as risk factors, the mechanics of Monte Carlo VaR computation are basically identical to those outlined in the previous section. The dimension of the risk factor space is considerably reduced, which speeds up the computation. Also, with multivariate normal or Student t VaR, the steps are computationally simpler and therefore faster to execute, because the covariance matrix of the risk factors is diagonal.[49] In fact, the Cholesky matrix is already known from the PCA. Because the variance of the ith component is the ith eigenvalue, the Cholesky matrix is just a diagonal matrix with ith diagonal element equal to the square root of the ith largest eigenvalue.

The next example demonstrates how to perform simulations on the first few principal components alone, and then uses the results of each simulation in the PCA risk factor mapping (IV.2.39) to compute the associated discounted P&L of the portfolio.

EXAMPLE IV.4.12: MONTE CARLO INTEREST RATE VAR WITH PCA

Recall the case study on estimating VaR for a UK bond portfolio, presented in Section IV.2.4. In Example IV.2.10 the 1% 10-day normal linear VaR based on a three principal component representation was estimated as £175,457. Now estimate the VaR based on this same PCA representation, but use Monte Carlo simulation on the principal components. What is the effect on the PC VaR of assuming that the principal components have a multivariate Student t distribution with 6 degrees of freedom?

SOLUTION   The first three eigenvalues of the daily covariance matrix were found in the case study of Section IV.2.4 to be 856.82, 45.30 and 9.15. Hence the 10-day Cholesky matrix has diagonal elements

$$\sqrt{856.82 \times 10} = 92.56, \ \sqrt{45.30 \times 10} = 21.28 \text{ and } \sqrt{9.15 \times 10} = 9.57,$$

as shown in Table IV.4.9. In the first row of this table we show the net PC sensitivities of the bond portfolio. These were already calculated in the case study of Section IV.2.4, and they are obtained by multiplying each PV01 by the corresponding element of the eigenvector that defines the principal component.

The normal VaR spreadsheet in the workbook for this example estimates the multivariate normal linear VaR using Monte Carlo simulation. Without simulation error, this should be £175,457, i.e. the PC VaR based on the exact analytic solution.[50] The t VaR spreadsheet estimates the multivariate Student t linear VaR using Monte Carlo simulation. Based on 10,000 simulations this is approximately £185,000. Predictably, it is greater than the normal VaR, since the Student t distribution with 6 degrees of freedom has an excess kurtosis of 3.

---

[48] The number of principal components used will depend on the required degree of accuracy. For well-behaved yield curves three components are often sufficient to capture 95% of the historical variations in interest rates, but the less well-behaved the yield curve, the more components will be required.

[49] Because the risk factors are the principal components and these are uncorrelated.

[50] But since we have used only 10,000 unstructured simulations in this example, the result can vary considerably each time the simulations are repeated.

Table IV.4.9   PC sensitivities and the PC Cholesky matrix

PC sensitivities	PC 1	PC 2	PC 3
	£428.15	−£2,974.59	£1,041.21
	92.56	0	0
Cholesky matrix	0	21.28	0
	0	0	9.57

This illustrates the basic framework for Monte Carlo VaR calculations when the dimension of the risk factor space is reduced by using principal components. For clarity, the above example used only a simple i.i.d. model for the principal component factors, but it could easily be extended, to include volatility clustering for the principal components. The point to note is that it would take much longer to perform the simulations if we applied 100,000 or more simulations to 60 highly correlated interest rates, instead of to three uncorrelated principal components. And the error introduced by using principal component risk factors instead of the interest rates themselves will still be very small compared with the simulation error.

IV.4.5.3   Equity Portfolios: 'Crash' Scenario VaR

In the following we use $\mathbf{x} = (X_1, \ldots, X_k)'$ to denote a set of asset or risk factor returns for an equity portfolio. When a long-only stock portfolio is not mapped to broad market indices or other risk factors, the portfolio return Y may be written

$$Y = \mathbf{w}'\mathbf{x}, \tag{IV.4.20}$$

where $\mathbf{w}$ is the vector of portfolio weights and here $\mathbf{x}$ denotes a vector of stock returns. If the portfolio is mapped to a set of risk factors then the portfolio return may be written

$$Y = \boldsymbol{\beta}'\mathbf{x}, \tag{IV.4.21}$$

where $\boldsymbol{\beta}$ is the vector of net risk factor betas, expressed as a percentage of the portfolio value and here $\mathbf{x}$ denotes the risk factor returns.[51]

Now Monte Carlo VaR is based on the usual algorithm, using simulations of $\mathbf{x}$. We shall assume the portfolio is characterized by its current weights or betas, and that these are constant over the risk horizon. This assumption implies that the portfolio is rebalanced each time a stock price or risk factor changes. However, a long-short portfolio may have price zero, so returns are difficult to define. In this case it is standard to represent the P&L, not the return, as a linear sum. Here the coefficients will be the portfolio holdings and the risk factors are the P&L on each stock, and we assume the holdings are kept constant over the risk horizon, i.e. that the portfolio is not rebalanced.

This section demonstrates the flexibility of Monte Carlo simulation by applying it to the measurement of scenario VaR for a simple equity portfolio. Of course, volatility clustering is also an important feature of equity portfolios, and could easily be added by using EWMA or GARCH covariance matrices in a multi-step simulation framework, as will be demonstrated

---

[51] However, if $\boldsymbol{\beta}$ is expressed in value terms then $\boldsymbol{\beta}'\mathbf{x}$ is the portfolio P&L.

for currency portfolios in Example IV.4.14. However, here we want to focus on applying the unconditional normal mixture returns model that was described in Section IV.4.4. This framework is very useful for equity portfolios, because a mixture of two multivariate normal distributions can capture the leptokurtosis and asymmetry that characterize equity markets. We could use a mixture of three or more multivariate normal distributions, but two is often sufficient.

The analyst is required to assign, subjectively, a probability π to a market crash during the risk horizon. During such a crash he has a scenario for a negative excess return on each stock in the portfolio, and we denote these returns by the vector μ_1. The stock returns also become much more volatile and highly correlated, and the analyst summarizes this by assuming some covariance matrix Ω_1 that he believes best reflects 'market crash' conditions. But with probability $1 - \pi$ 'ordinary' market conditions will prevail throughout the risk horizon, and these conditions are captured by the expected excess return vector μ_2 and covariance matrix Ω_2. Any of these parameters may, if the analyst wishes, be estimated using historical data.

We know from Section IV.4.4.1 that the risk factor return distribution will take the form

$$F(\mathbf{x}) = \pi \Phi(\mathbf{x}; \mu_1, \Omega_1) + (1 - \pi) \Phi(\mathbf{x}; \mu_2, \Omega_2).$$

Now given N independent standard normal simulations, we apply μ_1 and Ω_1 to πN of the simulations and μ_2 and Ω_2 to the remaining $(1 - \pi)N$ simulations. Hence, we obtain simulations for the stock returns, or the risk factor returns, that are used in the estimation of Monte Carlo VaR. This approach is illustrated in the next example.

EXAMPLE IV.4.13: MONTE CARLO VAR WITH NORMAL MIXTURE DISTRIBUTIONS

Suppose an equally weighted portfolio contains three stocks having the regime dependent returns parameters shown in Table IV.4.10. Based on a normal mixture distribution for the stocks' returns with these parameters, compute the $100\alpha\%$ 10-day Monte Carlo VaR for $\alpha = 5\%$, 1% and 0.1%. Compare these results with the multivariate normal Monte Carlo VaR when the stocks have expected returns, volatilities and correlations equal to their expected values under the two-regime distribution.

Table IV.4.10   Parameters of normal mixture distribution for three stocks

	Crash market			Ordinary market		
	Stock 1	Stock 2	Stock 3	Stock 1	Stock 2	Stock 3
Expected returns	−100%	−150%	−200%	7%	12%	10%
Volatilities	90%	100%	125%	20%	30%	25%
	1	0.95	0.93	1	0.5	0.75
Correlation matrix	0.95	1	0.98	0.5	1	0.25
	0.93	0.98	1	0.75	0.25	1
Regime probability		0.01			0.99	

SOLUTION   We perform the Monte Carlo simulation in two stages. First we take a random draw on a Bernoulli variable with success probability 1%. Then we sample from the first multivariate normal, representing the crash regime, if the result is a 'success' and otherwise we sample from the 'ordinary' multivariate normal. For the comparison with a straightforward multivariate normal VaR, we use the parameters shown in Table IV.4.11, i.e. the expected values of the parameters under the regime distribution.

Table IV.4.11 Parameters of normal distribution for three stocks

	Stock 1	Stock 2	Stock 3
Expected returns	5.93%	10.38%	0.97%
Volatilities	24.30%	35.37%	34.39%
Correlation matrix	1	0.5045	0.7518
	0.5045	1	0.2573
	0.7518	0.2573	1

Monte Carlo VaR estimates, expressed as a percentage of the portfolio value and based on one set of 10,000 simulations, are displayed in Table IV.4.12. As expected, the higher the confidence levels, the greater the difference between the normal mixture VaR and the VaR based on a normal distribution, because the normal mixture VaR is based on a negatively skewed and leptokurtic distribution. Because the probability of a crash is very small the normal mixture distribution has extremely long thin tails. The effect is to reduce the VaR, compared with the normal VaR, at the 5% and 1% quantiles but to increase it tremendously at the 0.1% quantile.

Table IV.4.12 Comparison of normal and normal mixture Monte Carlo scenario VaR

α	Normal	Mixture
5%	7.07%	1.00%
1%	10.61%	3.28%
0.1%	14.73%	55.98%

Since the VaR at extreme quantiles is significantly influenced by a very small probability of a crash, the above example suggests that normal mixtures could be applied to stress testing portfolios in a VaR framework. In fact, this is only one of many ways that VaR models can be used for scenario analysis, as we shall see in Section IV.7.3.2.

IV.4.5.4 Currency Portfolios: VaR with Volatility Clustering

Currency portfolios have the simplest possible risk factor mapping. Given nominal exposures $\mathbf{n} = (N_1, \ldots, N_k)'$ to k foreign exchange rates with returns $\mathbf{x} = (X_1, \ldots, X_k)'$, the portfolio P&L is just $\mathbf{n'x}$.[52]

Before implementing this risk factor mapping in the next example, we ask: what are the important features to capture in multivariate forex return distributions? The *unconditional*

---

[52] For instance, if $k = 2$, $\mathbf{n} = (\$1m, \$2m)'$ and we simulate $\mathbf{x} = (5\%, 1\%)'$ then the simulated P&L is $\$50,000 + \$20,000 = \$70,000$.

marginal distributions may be more symmetric than the return distributions for most other financial assets, but they still have a high leptokurtosis. What features should we include in the *conditional* marginals, and how should we model conditional and unconditional dependence between forex returns?

In every financial market skewness and leptokurtosis in unconditional return distributions have two main sources: they stem from occasional large jumps in prices, and from volatility clustering. Large price jumps introduce skewness and leptokurtosis into the conditional distributions. But even when the conditional distributions are fairly close to normality, if they have pronounced asymmetric volatility clustering, the unconditional distributions will still be skewed and leptokurtic. The dependency between two financial asset returns also has conditional and unconditional features. Asymmetric dependence may be captured using a copula. But even when the dependency is symmetric and is captured by a correlation matrix, we should still ensure that this is time-varying, so that correlation clustering can be modelled.

In the next example we show how to estimate Monte Carlo VaR for a portfolio of two US dollar exchange rates. We shall capture *both* sources of leptokurtosis, by using multivariate Student t conditional distributions and a symmetric multivariate GARCH model to capture volatility and correlation clustering. This model entails a multi-step framework for the simulations, as described in Section IV.4.3. To estimate VaR with volatility clustering we must set a value for the current return on each forex rate, at the time that the VaR is measured. We shall call this return the 'shock' for short.

Asymmetric GARCH models and skewed multivariate conditional distributions may be appropriate, especially in equity markets, but our example examines forex portfolios, which have less asymmetry than equity portfolios. Besides, we prefer to use a relatively simple specification for the risk factor returns model because our main purpose is to illustrate the framework as clearly as possible, without too many technicalities.

EXAMPLE IV.4.14: VAR WITH VOLATILITY AND CORRELATION CLUSTERING

A bank has $15 million exposure to forex 1 and $10 million exposure to forex 2. A simple symmetric bivariate GARCH model of the daily log returns on the two forex rates is estimated and the parameters are shown in Table IV.4.13. Use a multi-step Monte Carlo framework, with volatility and correlation clustering based on this bivariate GARCH model, to estimate the 1% 10-day VaR of the portfolio following shocks of 1%, 3% and 5%, assuming there is the same shock to each forex rate. In each case compare the results obtained when we assume the conditional distributions are bivariate normal, with those obtained under the assumption that the conditional distributions are bivariate Student t with 6 degrees of freedom. Also, use the model with constant volatility and correlation as a benchmark for your results.

Table IV.4.13   Bivariate GARCH model parameters

GARCH parameters	Variance 1	Variance 2	Covariance
ω	5.0E-07	7.0E-07	1.0E-05
α	0.085	0.05	0.06
β	0.905	0.94	0.7
Unconditional standard deviation (covariance in last column)	0.71%	0.84%	4.2E-05
Unconditional volatility (correlation in last column)	11.18%	13.23%	0.7043

SOLUTION   To fully understand the rather complex spreadsheet for this problem, readers are advised to familiarize themselves with some other spreadsheets first: the multi-step simulation model of Example IV.4.6, the correlated normal and Student t simulations of Examples IV.4.8 and IV.4.9, and the 'Diag Vech' spreadsheet in the GARCH_Simulations_II.4.xls workbook.

For each shock we shall compare results based on the same set of 10,000 standard uniform simulations over 10 consecutive days. These simulations, one for each forex return, are shown in the spreadsheet labelled 'VaR' in the workbook for this example. Then two further spreadsheets have an identical structure, except for two sets of ten columns which contain standard normal simulations in one spreadsheet and standardized Student t simulations in the other. The algorithm in each spreadsheet is as follows:

1. Generate independent standard normal (or standardized Student t) returns for each day and for each forex rate. (The simulations on the second forex rate will subsequently be adjusted, as explained in step 4, to capture the conditional dependency.)
2. Use the GARCH parameters to simulate a path for each GARCH variance over the 10-day period, following the shock that we have assumed.
3. Also simulate the GARCH covariance over the 10-day period, and on each day divide this by square root of the product of the GARCH variances to obtain the GARCH correlation simulated on each day.
4. Use the GARCH correlation to adjust the return on forex 2 that was simulated at step 1, changing it so that instead of being independent of the simulation for forex 1, they are correlated with the GARCH correlation. That is, if from step 1 we have independent returns f_{1t} and f_{2t} simulated at time t, and if ϱ_t is the GARCH correlation simulated at time t, then set

$$\tilde{f}_{2t} = f_{2t}\sqrt{1 - \varrho_t^2} + \varrho_t f_{1t}. \qquad (\text{IV.4.22})$$

Now f_{1t} and $\tilde{f}_{2t}$ will have correlation ϱ_t.
5. Next, multiply f_{1t} by the square root of the GARCH variance for forex 1 at time t, and multiply $\tilde{f}_{2t}$ by the square root of the GARCH variance for forex 2 at time t. This gives two paths for log returns over 10 days, one for each forex rate, which display both volatility and correlation clustering.
6. Sum the log returns over each path to obtain a 10-day log return on each forex rate, and then use the risk factor mapping described at the beginning of this section to obtain one simulated 10-day P&L for the portfolio.
7. Repeat N times, and then the $100\alpha\%$ 10-day VaR estimate is -1 times the $100\alpha\%$ quantile of the distribution based on the N simulated 10-day P&Ls.

We also simulate paths under the assumption that parameters are constant, at the unconditional values shown in Table IV.4.13. As we have shown in Section IV.4.3, multi-step methods are unnecessary in this case. However, we do this to provide a benchmark against which to interpret our results, which for comparison are based on the same standard uniform simulations as those used in the conditional model.

In the first row of Table IV.4.14 we show the results based on constant volatility and correlation, and in the second row the results are based on the volatility and correlation clustering that is defined by the bivariate GARCH model. For each shock (1%, 3% and 5%) we display the result based on both normal and Student t marginal distributions for the forex returns, the Student t distributions each having 6 degrees of freedom.

Table IV.4.14   Comparison of normal GARCH and Student t GARCH VaR

Shock	1%		3%		5%	
Distribution	Normal	Student t	Normal	Student t	Normal	Student t
Constant	$1,306,577	$1,990,911	$1,354,720	$2,025,632	$1,311,185	$1,998,550
GARCH	$1,359,349	$2,173,931	$1,648,965	$2,699,410	$2,062,642	$3,349,197

The GARCH VaR estimates are always greater than the estimates based on our benchmark model with no volatility and correlation clustering. The bigger the shock, the greater the difference between the GARCH and the constant parameter VaR estimates. The difference is also more pronounced when we assume the return distributions are Student t with 6 degrees of freedom. We see that the VaR estimate could easily be doubled or halved, simply by changing our assumptions about the risk factor returns model.

These conclusions are fairly obvious. We do not need to build a complex Excel workbook to demonstrate them. But the aim of this above example, as with every example in this chapter, is to provide readers with an Excel template for building advanced Monte Carlo VaR models. Simple Monte Carlo models, such as those based on i.i.d. normal risk factor returns, are not usually justified, at least for short term risk horizons. Mixture, Student t or copula models with volatility clustering effects are generally thought to be more appropriate for short term VaR estimation.

IV.4.6   SUMMARY AND CONCLUSIONS

The parametric linear VaR model is used when returns are assumed to have a multivariate normal, Student t or normal mixture distribution. So why should we use Monte Carlo VaR for a linear portfolio? The reason is that Monte Carlo VaR is much more flexible than linear VaR. It can be applied with *any* assumed distribution for risk factor returns. We can also use *multi-step Monte Carlo* to simulate time-varying risk factor volatilities and correlations, or to account for path-dependent behaviour in options or in contingent cash flows.

Historical VaR has the distinct advantage that it does not need to impose a parametric model on risk factor return distributions. Instead the empirical risk factor return distribution is naturally embedded in the VaR estimate. In the next chapter we shall demonstrate that standard historical simulations have limited application to estimating VaR for option portfolios, but why should we use Monte Carlo VaR in preference to historical VaR for *linear* portfolios? The reason is that, whatever the portfolio, the limited size of a historical sample places a severe constraint on the accuracy of historical VaR estimates. Standard historical simulation cannot be based on overlapping h-day returns, because this truncates the tail of the P&L distribution. For this reason many practitioners scale up the 1-day historical VaR to an h-day VaR estimate, but this introduces a major model risk in VaR calculations, even for linear portfolios. We can only increase the number of simulations by using a parametric statistical bootstrap, as in *filtered* historical simulation. However, this is really a hybrid approach, a mixture between historical and Monte Carlo simulation, because it is based on simulations from a parametric, dynamic model for the returns process such as GARCH.

The great advantage of Monte Carlo VaR is that historical data place no restrictions on simulations. We can simulate as much data on risk factor returns as we like (and the more simulations used the more accurate the VaR estimate) since there are relatively few computational time constraints with the powerful computers used today. With Monte Carlo methods, the simulations do not necessarily have *any* basis in historical data. For instance, in scenario VaR calculations the analyst could use his own personal views about the values of the parameters of the risk factor returns model.

The first part of this chapter gave a brief survey of the sampling methods that form the basis of a Monte Carlo VaR estimate. We provided examples of pseudo-random number generation using *linear congruential generators* and introduced some basic *advanced sampling* methods and *variance reduction* techniques, again with numerical examples in Excel. Because sampling error can be controlled, the main source of model risk in Monte Carlo VaR models lies with the specification of the statistical model for the risk factor returns. These models are used to translate standard uniform simulations into risk factor returns simulations, and then the risk factor mapping is used to translate these into simulations on the portfolio returns or P&L. Finally, we derive the Monte Carlo VaR from a quantile of the simulated portfolio returns or P&L distribution.

Much of this chapter is devoted to developing adequate statistical models for static and dynamic risk factor returns, because this is a major source of model risk in Monte Carlo VaR estimates. Yet it requires considerable skill to develop a suitable risk factor returns model, even for a linear portfolio where we might feasibly assume that risk factor returns have i.i.d. multivariate normal or i.i.d. multivariate Student t distributions. In that case we can use an h-day covariance matrix to transform independent draws from a standard normal or standardized Student t distribution into correlated h-day returns on the risk factors. We have also shown how more complex returns models can be used to estimate Monte Carlo VaR. For instance, the risk factors may have different marginal distributions and their dependency may be captured by a copula.[53] We also explained how to design multi-step Monte Carlo for linear portfolios with risk factors that exhibit volatility and correlation clustering. All these features have been illustrated, for teaching purposes, using Excel workbooks.

---

[53] Experienced readers requiring further details are recommended to consult the path-breaking work of Patton (2008) in this area. Note that Matlab code is available from Andrew Patton's website. (http://www.economics.ox.ac.uk/members/andrew.patton/), and see the copula toolbox in particular.

IV.5
Value at Risk for Option Portfolios

IV.5.1 INTRODUCTION

The previous chapters in this book have focused on two aspects of VaR modelling: the risk characteristics of portfolios with different types of risk factors, and the modelling of the risk factors. Until now we have only applied the models that we have developed to simple portfolios where the portfolio mapping is a linear function of their risk factors. Now we extend the analysis to discuss how to estimate VaR and expected tail loss for option portfolios.

The most important risk factors for an option are the change in price of the underlying asset, the square of this price change and the change in the implied volatility. The squared price change is necessary because an option price is non-linearly related to the underlying price. This introduces an extra degree of complexity into the construction of a VaR model for an option portfolio.

When VaR estimates for option portfolios are scaled over different risk horizons we are making an implicit assumption that the portfolio is being dynamically rebalanced at the end of each day, to keep its risk factor sensitivities constant. For this reason, we call such a VaR estimate a *dynamic* VaR estimate. Then, even though the portfolio returns cannot be normal and i.i.d., it is common practice to scale the daily VaR to longer risk horizons using a square-root scaling rule. Indeed, it is admissible under banking regulations, although the Basel Committee indicates that this practice may ultimately be disallowed.[1] Dynamic VaR estimates are suitable for actively traded portfolios, in particular for assessing the risk of a portfolio that is always delta–gamma–vega neutral and for assessing the VaR when the portfolio is held at its risk limits, if these limits are defined in terms of risk factor sensitivities. However the use of a square-root scaling rule can be a significant source of model risk.

The alternative is to measure the VaR directly from the *h*-day P&L, without scaling up a 1-day VaR estimate to a longer risk horizon. In this case we are assuming the portfolio is not traded during the risk horizon, and so we call such a VaR estimate a *static* VaR estimate. Static VaR is suitable for estimating the risk of a single structured product that is not intended to be dynamically rebalanced. In practice, assuming no rebalancing over the risk horizon is not realistic for option portfolios. Option traders write options because they think they know how to hedge their risks, and they believe they can make a profit after accounting for their hedging costs, often rebalancing their hedged portfolio several times per day.

If the risk factor returns are normal and i.i.d. it makes no difference to a *linear* portfolio whether we scale the daily VaR to longer risk horizons using the square-root scaling rule, or measure the VaR directly from the *h*-day return or P&L distribution. That is, the static and dynamic VaR estimates are the same. But this is not the case for option portfolios. Static VaR

---

[1] BCBS (2006, p. 196) states that 'Banks are expected to ultimately move towards the application of a full 10-day price shock to options positions or positions that display option-like characteristics.'

estimates have gamma, vega and theta effects that are much more pronounced than they are in dynamic VaR, with the gamma effect being the greatest.

Our focus in this chapter will be on modelling the non-linear characteristics of portfolios, rather than on the precision of the VaR methodology. Nevertheless, from the many empirical examples given in this chapter we are able to draw some strong general conclusions about the appropriate type of VaR model to apply to option portfolios.

Whilst analytic approximations to options VaR based on delta–gamma mapping may seem attractive, the option portfolio P&L resulting from this approximation is highly skewed and bimodal so it is very difficult capture with a parametric model. Moreover, accurate VaR estimation requires a precise fit in the tails of this distribution, and even small discrepancies between the parametric form and the empirical distribution can lead to large errors in the analytic approximation to VaR.

We shall show that standard historical simulation is suitable for dynamic VaR estimation, but there are problems with trying to use a non-parametric model for static VaR estimation. Typically, the precision of a standard historical VaR estimate relies on using daily risk factor returns in a very large number of simulations. From these we could estimate a 1-day VaR non-parametrically and scale up this estimate to longer risk horizons, under the assumption that the option portfolio has stable, i.i.d. returns. But this approach assumes that the portfolio is rebalanced daily to return the risk factor sensitivities to their values at the time the VaR is estimated, so it gives an estimate of dynamic VaR, not static VaR. For a static portfolio that is not traded over the risk horizon we need to estimate the h-day VaR as a quantile of the h-day P&L distribution. Standard historical simulation based on overlapping data will distort the tail behaviour of the P&L distribution in such as way that VaR estimates at extreme quantiles can be seriously underestimated. In fact, the only way that we can estimate the static h-day VaR in the context of historical simulation is by introducing a parametric model for the conditional distributions of the portfolio returns, such as a GARCH model.[2]

A strong conclusion that is drawn from this chapter is that the only viable method for estimating the static VaR for option portfolios is *parametric* simulation, using either Monte Carlo or the filtered historical simulation method of Barone-Adesi et al. (1998, 1999). Either way, option portfolio VaR estimates must be based on a suitable risk factor returns model, not only a non-normal multivariate distribution for risk factor returns but also a model that captures the dynamic properties of risk factor returns. Our empirical examples demonstrate how important it is to include volatility clustering effects in price risk factors. Mean reversion in volatility risk factors is also of some importance, except over very short risk horizons.

Even if efficient Monte Carlo simulation algorithms are based on an appropriate model for risk factor returns, there is another important source of error in VaR for an option portfolio. This is the risk factor mapping. For a portfolio of options it is standard to base the risk factor mapping on a Taylor expansion, where the risk factor sensitivities are given by the portfolio Greeks. But a Taylor expansion is only a local approximation, meaning that it is only accurate for *small* changes in risk factors. However, because VaR is a loss that we are fairly confident will *not* occur, to assess VaR we need to consider *large* movements in risk factors. Thus the Greeks approximations only give a crude approximation to the VaR. In particular, these approximations are of limited use when stress testing a portfolio because, in stress testing, risk factors are set to very extreme values.

---

[2] Section IV.3.3.4 explains how filtered historical simulation applies the statistical bootstrap to combine a parametric dynamic model for portfolio returns with standard historical simulation.

On the other hand, to estimate VaR for a large complex option portfolio without using a risk factor mapping may take a considerable amount of time. The Greeks approximations have the major advantage that they facilitate *real-time* VaR calculations, and these are necessary when traders are operating under VaR limits. Typically, limits might be set at the 95% confidence level, over a daily risk horizon. Real time VaR calculations could then be based on delta–gamma–vega approximation in a Monte Carlo or historical dynamic VaR model.

The outline of this chapter is as follows. Section IV.5.2 discusses the characteristics that differentiate option portfolios from linear portfolios, for the purposes of VaR measurement. We briefly summarize the risk factor mappings for option portfolios and then provide a critical review of the practice of scaling VaR for option portfolios from a daily risk horizon to longer risk horizons.

Section IV.5.3 describes some simple analytic approximations to VaR estimates for option portfolios. We focus on a large complex portfolio where exact evaluation is impractical, so that a risk factor mapping must be applied. First we derive a simple *delta–normal* VaR approximation that treats an option portfolio as if it were linear. Then a quasi-analytical method for calculating the VaR, based on a delta–gamma mapping, is explained. The method relies on fitting quantiles, or better still the whole P&L distribution, to the moments of a multi-factor delta–gamma representation.

In Section IV.5.4 we explain how historical simulation could be applied to options and option portfolios. The section begins with empirical examples of VaR when options are revalued exactly, using the pricing model, starting with a standard European option but also including an example based on an analytic approximation to the price of an option with a path-dependent pay-off. Then we move on to option portfolios, first with exact repricing of the options at the risk horizon and then when the portfolio P&L is mapped to risk factors. Of particular interest is the study of historical VaR for a delta–gamma-hedged option portfolio. Such a portfolio has minimal price risk only if it is continually rebalanced to maintain delta–gamma neutrality. This section concludes with a case study on measuring the historical dynamic VaR of a hedged energy options trading book.

Section IV.5.5 describes the application of Monte Carlo VaR to options and option portfolios. The basic steps of Monte Carlo VaR for options are understood in the context of a simple application: measuring the VaR and ETL of a standard European index option.[3] The core of the model is the simulation of two negatively correlated risk factors, i.e. the underlying equity index price and its implied volatility. We use this example to demonstrate the difference between static and dynamic VaR. That is, we measure the h-day VaR directly from an h-day P&L distribution, which is the correct way to estimate the VaR of a static portfolio such as a simple European option, and then we measure it from the simulated daily P&L distribution and then scaling by the square root of h. The second method makes some strong assumptions about portfolio rebalancing over the risk horizon, which are not appropriate for a fixed position in a single option, and hence it ignores the crucial gamma, vega and theta effects that are very important to capture in a VaR estimate for an option.

Thereafter Section IV.5.5 considers Monte Carlo VaR based on risk factor mapping of an option portfolio. We explain how delta–gamma–vega mapping is used to revalue the option at the risk horizon and then examine the Monte Carlo VaR model for portfolios of options on several underlyings, applying a multivariate Taylor expansion for the mapping to risk factors.

---

[3] This is the only subsection where we consider the ETL of an option portfolio. Once VaR has been estimated, obtaining the ETL estimate is straightforward. See Sections IV.2.10 and IV.3.6 for further details.

We conclude with a case study on the development of an appropriate risk factor returns model for a large portfolio of energy options. Section IV.5.6 summarizes and concludes.

The material in this chapter assumes knowledge of the analytic, historical and Monte Carlo VaR models described in previous chapters of this volume. Readers should also be familiar with the option theory in Chapter III.3 and the option portfolio mapping methodologies described in detail in Sections III.5.5 and III.5.6.

IV.5.2   RISK CHARACTERISTICS OF OPTION PORTFOLIOS

The value of an option is a non-linear function of its risk factors. Even if we ignore volatility and other less important risk factors, the price of an option is always a non-linear function of the underlying asset price S. This section begins by reviewing the essential details about mapping option portfolios, then we discuss the implications of non-linear risk factor mapping for VaR assessment.

IV.5.2.1   Gamma Effects

In Section III.5.5 we developed the simplest possible mapping of a single option to its price risk factor, the *delta–gamma approximation*. This may be written:

$$P\&L \approx \delta^\$ R + \tfrac{1}{2}\, \gamma^\$ R^2, \tag{IV.5.1}$$

where $R = \Delta S/S$ is the return on the underlying asset and $\delta^\$$ and $\gamma^\$$ denote the *value delta* and *value gamma* of the option.[4] More precisely,

$$\delta^\$ = \delta \times N \times S \times pv, \tag{IV.5.2}$$

$$\gamma^\$ = \gamma \times N \times S^2 \times pv, \tag{IV.5.3}$$

where N is the number of units of the underlying that the option contracts to trade and pv is the point value of the option.

The P&L of a portfolio of options on the *same* underlying may also be represented by (IV.5.1), but now $\delta^\$$ and $\gamma^\$$ denote the *net* value delta and value gamma of the portfolio. For all options on the same underlying we can simply add up the value deltas to find the net value delta, and similarly the net value gamma is just the sum of the individual gammas.

When an option portfolio has *several* underlying price risk factors there are two alternative approaches to price risk factor mapping. Either we use a simple approximation like (IV.5.1) based on *price beta mapping* or we use a *multivariate delta–gamma approximation*. It is also possible to combine both approaches. Below we extract the relevant formulae from Section III.5.5 to summarize the possibilities.

The price beta mapping approach is described in Section III.5.5.5. It depends on representing each underlying price risk factor return R_i in terms of a single index risk factor return R. From the model derivation we know that formula (IV.5.1) still applies, but now

---

[4] These are also called *dollar delta* and *dollar gamma* by some authors. We use the value delta and value gamma because they are additive across different options. Position Greeks are only additive when the portfolio contains options on only one underlying, but value Greeks are additive for any option portfolio. For VaR assessment, we assume the returns are discounted, so that (IV.5.1) represented the discounted P&L.

$$\delta^\$ = \sum_{i=1}^{n} \delta_i^\$ \beta_i \text{ and } \gamma^\$ = \sum_{i=1}^{n} \gamma_i^\$ \beta_i^2, \qquad \text{(IV.5.4)}$$

where $\delta_i^\$$ and $\gamma_i^\$$ are the net value delta and gamma for each price risk factor and

$$\beta_i = \frac{\text{Cov}(R_i, R)}{V(R)}. \qquad \text{(IV.5.5)}$$

Thus we perform a regression of each underlying return on an index return and use the regression betas in (IV.5.4) to estimate the value delta and gamma.

In Section III.5.5.6 we developed an alternative mapping for portfolios with several underlying price risk factors. This is the *multivariate delta–gamma approximation*, which takes the form

$$P\&L \approx \delta_\$' R + \tfrac{1}{2} R' \Gamma_\$ R. \qquad \text{(IV.5.6)}$$

Here $R = (R_1, \ldots, R_n)'$ is the vector of the underlying assets' discounted returns,

$$\delta_\$ = (\delta_1^\$, \ldots, \delta_n^\$)', \quad \Gamma_\$ = (\gamma_{ij}^\$), \qquad \text{(IV.5.7)}$$

$$\delta_i^\$ = P_{S_i} \times S_i \times pv_i, \qquad \text{(IV.5.8)}$$

$$\gamma_{ij}^\$ = P_{S_i S_j} \times S_i \times S_j \times \sqrt{pv_i pv_j} \qquad \text{(IV.5.9)}$$

and

$$P_{S_i} = \frac{\partial P}{\partial S_i} \text{ and } P_{S_i S_j} = \frac{\partial^2 P}{\partial S_i \partial S_j}, \qquad \text{(IV.5.10)}$$

where P is the price of the portfolio. The multivariate mapping is more complex but more accurate than the price beta mapping approach. It is also possible to combine the two approaches using more than one index risk factor in the beta mapping, thus reducing dimensions of the multivariate delta–gamma approximation.

From our discussion in Section III.5.5.4 we know that a position with positive gamma (e.g. a long position on a standard call or put) has a convex pay-off, so that losses are less and profits are more than they would be under a corresponding linear position; and a position with negative gamma (e.g. a short position on a standard call or put) has a concave pay-off, so that losses are greater and profits are less than they would be under a corresponding linear position. An option portfolio with positive delta and gamma (e.g. a long call) gains more from an upward price move and loses less from a downward price move than a linear portfolio with the same delta. But an option portfolio with positive delta and negative gamma (e.g. a short put) will gain less from an upward price move and lose more from a downward price move than a linear portfolio with the same delta.[5] Thus positive gamma reduces the risk and negative gamma increases the risk of an option portfolio, relative to the delta-equivalent exposure. This is termed the *gamma effect* on the risk of an option portfolio.

---

[5] Similarly, an option portfolio with negative delta and positive gamma (e.g. a long put) gains more from a downward price move and loses less from an upward price move than a linear portfolio with the same delta. But an option portfolio with negative delta and negative gamma (e.g. a short call) will gain less from a downward price move and lose more from an upward price move than a linear portfolio with the same delta.

IV.5.2.2   Delta and Vega Effects

The general expression for the *delta–gamma–vega approximation* to the P&L of a portfolio of options, possibly on different underlyings, is

$$P\&L \approx \boldsymbol{\delta}'_\$\mathbf{R} + \tfrac{1}{2}\mathbf{R}'\boldsymbol{\Gamma}_\$\mathbf{R} + \mathbf{v}'_\$\Delta\boldsymbol{\sigma}. \tag{IV.5.11}$$

where $\Delta\boldsymbol{\sigma}$ is a vector of changes in implied volatilities, and the value delta and gamma are defined in (IV.5.7), but how is the *value vega* vector $\mathbf{v}_\$$ calculated? Each option in the portfolio has its own implied volatility as a risk factor. So in large portfolios it is necessary to reduce the number of volatility risk factors. Typically this will be achieved by either *vega bucketing* or *volatility beta mapping*.

Under volatility beta mapping, Section III.5.6.4 explains how to calculate the portfolio's position vega, v^P, with respect to a *reference volatility* such as the 3-month at-the-money (ATM) volatility or a volatility index. We use the formula

$$v^P = \sum_{i=1}^{n} v_i \times \beta_i^v \times N_i, \tag{IV.5.12}$$

where N_i denotes the number of units of the underlying that the ith option contracts to buy or sell, v_i denotes the vega of the ith option and β_i^v is the volatility beta of the ith option. This volatility beta may be estimated by regressing the ith option implied volatilities on the reference volatility. Then, the portfolio's value vega with respect to this reference volatility is the sum of the position vegas multiplied by the point values of the options.

If the underlying price and volatility are negatively and symmetrically related, then the *vega effect* reinforces the delta effect for a put and offsets the delta effect for a call. To see this, first suppose the price falls dramatically, and so the volatility jumps up. Now consider these positions:

- *long call* – the call price decreases due to the underlying price fall, but increases due to volatility increasing, thus compensating the loss on the long position;
- *short put* – the put price increases due to the underlying price fall, so you make a loss on the short position, and the put price increases due to volatility increasing and this compounds the loss.

Now suppose the price increases, so the volatility decreases, and consider these positions:

- *short call* – the call price increases due to the underlying price increase, but the loss on the short position is offset by a compensatory decrease in the call price due to volatility decreasing;
- *long put* – the put price decreases due to the underlying price increase, and the loss on the long position is compounded by a decrease in the put price due to volatility decreasing.

The situation is summarized in Table IV.5.1, which shows that the delta–vega effects are most prominent in put options.

However, in stock and equity index option portfolios, there is an *asymmetric* negative price–volatility relationship. That is, volatility tends to increase considerably when there is a large fall in the underlying price, but following a large rise in the underlying price of the same

Table IV.5.1 Delta and vega effects (symmetric negative price–volatility relationship)

	Call	Put
Long	$S\downarrow, \delta > 0 \Rightarrow P\downarrow$ $\sigma\uparrow, v > 0 \Rightarrow P\uparrow$	$S\uparrow, \delta < 0 \Rightarrow P\downarrow$ $\sigma\downarrow, v > 0 \Rightarrow P\downarrow$
Short	$S\uparrow, \delta < 0 \Rightarrow P\downarrow$ $\sigma\downarrow, v < 0 \Rightarrow P\uparrow$	$S\downarrow, \delta > 0 \Rightarrow P\downarrow$ $\sigma\uparrow, v < 0 \Rightarrow P\downarrow$

magnitude volatility tends to decrease only a little, if at all. Thus the vega effect on a long put or short call is negligible. Therefore the most important vega effect to account for in VaR estimation is on a short put, since here it augments the delta effect. By contrast, the vega effect on a long call offsets the delta effect. The situation is summarized in Table IV.5.2, where we see that short put positions have the most pronounced delta–vega effects.

Table IV.5.2 Delta and vega effects (asymmetric negative price–volatility relationship)

	Call	Put
Long	$S\downarrow, \delta > 0 \Rightarrow P\downarrow$ $\sigma\uparrow, v > 0 \Rightarrow P\uparrow$	$S\uparrow, \delta < 0 \Rightarrow P\downarrow$ σ approx. flat
Short	$S\uparrow, \delta < 0 \Rightarrow P\downarrow$ σ approx. flat	$S\downarrow, \delta > 0 \Rightarrow P\downarrow$ $\sigma\uparrow, v < 0 \Rightarrow P\downarrow$

Finally, suppose the underlying price and volatility are asymmetrically and *positively* related, as they often are for commodity options. That is, volatility increases considerably following a price rise, but does not decrease very much following a price fall of the same magnitude. Then the vega effect reinforces the delta effect on a long put, offsets the delta effect on a short call and is negligible for a long call or a short put. The situation is summarized in Table IV.5.3, where it is now the long put positions that have the most pronounced delta–vega effects.

Table IV.5.3 Delta and vega effects (asymmetric positive price–volatility relationship)

	Call	Put
Long	$S\downarrow, \delta > 0 \Rightarrow P\downarrow$ σ approx. flat	$S\uparrow, \delta < 0 \Rightarrow P\downarrow$ $\sigma\uparrow, v > 0 \Rightarrow P\downarrow$
Short	$S\uparrow, \delta < 0 \Rightarrow P\downarrow$ $\sigma\uparrow, v < 0 \Rightarrow P\uparrow$	$S\downarrow, \delta > 0 \Rightarrow P\downarrow$ σ approx. flat

IV.5.2.3 Theta and Rho Effects

Here we summarize the Taylor expansions that approximate the P&L of an option portfolio when interest rate and time risk factors are included in the mapping.[6] Later in this chapter we shall use these approximations to estimate the VaR of option portfolios.

---

[6] Again the material here is drawn from Chapter III.5 to which readers are referred for further explanation.

The general expression for the *delta–gamma–vega–theta–rho approximation* to the P&L of a portfolio of options, possibly on different underlyings, is

$$\text{P\&L} \approx \theta^{\$} \Delta t + \delta_{\$}' \mathbf{R} + \tfrac{1}{2}\mathbf{R}' \boldsymbol{\Gamma}_{\$}\mathbf{R} + \pi_{\$}' \Delta \mathbf{r} + \mathbf{v}_{\$}' \Delta \sigma, \qquad (\text{IV.5.13})$$

where the value delta and gamma are defined in (IV.5.7).[7] The *value theta* $\theta^{\$}$ is the sum of each position theta multiplied by the point value of the option. Since option prices generally decrease as they approach expiry, the *maturity* or *theta effect* is to increase the risk of long positions, and decrease the risk of short positions.

The *value rho* vector $\pi_{\$}$ is calculated as the sum of each position rho multiplied by the point value of the option. Note that there is a *curve* of interest rate risk factors $\mathbf{r}$ unless all the options in the portfolio have the same maturity. But unless the underlying of the option is an interest rate or bond, changes in interest rates only affect the discounting of future expected pay-offs. Hence, the *rho effect* on portfolio risk that stems from changes in interest rates is typically very small.

IV.5.2.4 Static and Dynamic VaR Estimates

Static VaR is calculated over an h-day risk horizon on the assumption that the current portfolio is held over the next h days. Of course, when no trading takes place the risk factor sensitivities are *not* constant during the risk horizon. In dynamic VaR we assume the risk factor sensitivities are constant over the risk horizon. Then the portfolio must be rebalanced each time a risk factor changes.

For portfolios containing very long-dated options, and a risk horizon of only a few days, a constant risk factor sensitivities assumption is feasible even without rebalancing. Otherwise the use of constant risk factor sensitivities over the risk horizon assumes that the portfolio is rebalanced at the end of each day to return risk factor sensitivities to their values at the beginning of the day. For instance, the portfolio may be rebalanced daily to be delta–gamma neutral, or to keep the position Greeks at their limit values. When a trader operates under limits on his net value delta, gamma, vega and possibly other Greeks, it is very informative to estimate the VaR assuming the trader is at his limits.

The assumption we make about rebalancing affects the way we compute an h-day VaR, for $h > 1$. We shall now explain exactly how our rebalancing assumption affects the option's VaR estimate, in the theoretical context of the delta–gamma approximation (IV.5.1) of the portfolio's P&L where the underlying log returns are assumed to be normal and i.i.d. The delta–gamma mapping gives an approximate change in the portfolio value as a quadratic function of the underlying return, with coefficients determined by the value delta and value gamma of the portfolio. Our assumption that the log returns on the underlying are normal and i.i.d. implies that they scale in distribution with the square root of time. We now consider two cases.

Static VaR

Denote by R the daily log return on the underlying price risk factor. Assuming this is i.i.d. and normal, the h-day log return on the underlying price has the same distribution as the

---

[7] Higher order Taylor approximations for the volatility risk may be used, such as the delta–gamma–vega–vanna–volga approximation. However, this commonly has little effect on the VaR of the portfolio. See Example IV.5.5 for an empirical illustration.

random variable $h^{1/2}R$.[8] Hence, the h-day P&L on the option portfolio, as represented by the delta–gamma mapping, may be written

$$P\&L_h \approx \delta^\$ h^{1/2}R + \tfrac{1}{2}\gamma^\$ hR^2, \tag{IV.5.14}$$

where $\delta^\$$ and $\gamma^\$$ are the value delta and value gamma at the time that the VaR is measured.

Note that the presence of the gamma term in (IV.5.14) implies that the P&L will *not* scale with the square root of h, hence

$$P\&L_h \neq h^{1/2}P\&L_1 \quad \text{and} \quad \text{VaR}_{h,\alpha} \neq h^{1/2}\text{VaR}_{1,\alpha}. \tag{IV.5.15}$$

We conclude that under the no rebalancing assumption it is *not correct* to compute the 1-day portfolio VaR of an option portfolio and simply scale this to an h-day horizon, using a square-root law or any other power scaling law. The correct procedure is to use the h-day risk factor returns to derive the portfolio's P&L distribution, and then derive the VaR.

The no rebalancing assumption has the advantage that the proper *theta effect* and *gamma effect* are captured by the VaR estimate if the position is not traded during the risk horizon. When revaluing the portfolio h days ahead, the time to expiry of each option is decreased by h days. Option prices generally decrease as they approach expiry, so the theta effect is to increase the VaR for long positions, and decrease the VaR for short positions. By contrast, the gamma effect decreases the VaR for long positions, and increases the VaR for short positions on standard options, as explained in Section IV.5.2.1.

It is easy to estimate static VaR using Monte Carlo simulations. This is because Monte Carlo VaR models are flexible enough to generate h-day log returns R_h directly. One simply obtains the structured Monte Carlo simulations using the assumed statistical model for h-day risk factor returns. The $100\alpha\%$ h-day delta–gamma VaR, based on the Monte Carlo approach then uses the approximation

$$P\&L_h \approx \delta^\$ R_h + \tfrac{1}{2}\gamma^\$ R_h^2. \tag{IV.5.16}$$

However, there are two problems here. First, the Taylor approximation is only valid for small changes in the underlying returns, and the potential size of these returns increases with h. So is it inadvisable to apply Taylor expansion to estimate static VaR over long risk horizons. A second problem is that to adopt the assumption of no rebalancing with standard historical VaR calculations,[9] we can only use overlapping data on the h-day risk factor returns, since non-overlapping data of frequency equal to the risk horizon are not usually available in sufficient quantity to estimate VaR accurately. But the use of overlapping data on risk factor returns will truncate the tails of the P&L distributions, as discussed in Section IV.3.2.7. This will be illustrated empirically in Section IV.5.4.

Dynamic VaR

Dynamic VaR assumes that the portfolio is rebalanced during the risk horizon to maintain constant risk factor sensitivities. If simulations are at the daily frequency, it must be assumed that the portfolio is rebalanced once a day over a period of h days, each time returning $\delta^\$$ and $\gamma^\$$ to the value delta and value gamma at the time that the VaR is estimated. This type of VaR

---

[8] See Section I.3.3.11 for further details.
[9] That is, in the absence of some parametric filtering based on a dynamic model for portfolio returns.

estimate is used to estimate the VaR of a dynamically hedged portfolio, or to estimate the VaR at a trader's sensitivity-based limits.

Assume that the daily log returns on the risk factors are i.i.d. Then, under the constant risk factor sensitivity assumption, the trader faces the *same* risk at the beginning of each day during the risk horizon. In this case, the h-day P&L for the option portfolio is just the sum of h independent and identical 1-day P&Ls. However, although i.i.d., the portfolio P&L distribution will not be normal even if the risk factor returns are, because the portfolio mapping is a quadratic and not a linear transformation of a normal variable. Hence, it may not be very accurate to scale the 1-day VaR to longer risk horizons using a square-root scaling rule. If the P&L distribution is stable then a different power law scaling rule may be applied (see Section IV.3.2) and then $\text{VaR}_{h,\alpha} = h^{1/\xi}\text{VaR}_{1,\alpha}$ for some constant ξ, not necessarily equal to 2.

Although the P&L of an option portfolio is definitely not normally distributed, it is sometimes assumed nevertheless that $\xi = 2$, and hence that

$$\text{VaR}_{h,\alpha} = \sqrt{h}\ \text{VaR}_{1,\alpha}. \tag{IV.5.17}$$

But this assumes the gamma, vega and theta effects on h-day P&L also scale with $\sqrt{h}$, which is not the case. The theta effect is captured by the term $\theta \Delta t$ in the Greeks approximation, so when a 1-day horizon is scaled up to 10 days using (IV.5.17) the effect is $\sqrt{10}\ \theta/365$, whereas based on a 10-day P&L it should be $10\ \theta/365$. And even if the delta effect scales with $\sqrt{h}$, the gamma effect should scale with h. The vega effect is more complex: if there is asymmetry in the price–volatility relationship this is only likely to be apparent at the daily frequency, so scaling up 1-day VaR by the square root of time could be augmenting or diminishing the VaR, depending on the market, the type of option and the sign of our position.

The daily rebalancing assumption is approximate for two main reasons. First, the square-root scaling rule may not be appropriate, if it is used. Whilst the P&L of an option might conceivably have a stable distribution, it highly unlikely to be normal. Secondly, the daily P&L distribution is estimated by decreasing the maturity of each option by only 1 day and discounting the portfolio price by only 1 day, so scaling up a VaR that is estimated this way diminishes the *theta effect*, i.e. that option prices tend to decrease as they approach expiry. Daily rebalancing also diminishes the *gamma effect*, which can be considerable for short dated options;[10] and it distorts the *vega effect*, which can be considerable for long dated options.

Over one day the underlying price and volatility tend to move much less than they would over a 10-day or longer risk horizon. Hence, when VaR is estimated over one day, and then scaled up, the gamma, vega and theta effects will be too small. As a result, we expect the VaR estimate for positive gamma positions (e.g. a long call or put option) to be greater when based on daily rebalancing than it is when we estimate VaR from a directly computed h-day P&L distribution. And the opposite is the case for positions with negative gamma.

We shall be comparing the static and dynamic VaR estimates in several empirical examples and case studies in this chapter, to highlight the effect that the assumption we make about rebalancing will have on the VaR estimate. And we shall specifically focus on this issue in Examples IV.5.3 and IV.5.7, in the context of the historical VaR model. As explained above the static VaR is more sensitive to the portfolio gamma, vega and theta than dynamic VaR.

---

[10] For large price moves VaR tends to decrease for positions with positive gamma but increase for positions with negative gamma. However, daily price variations are smaller than h-day price variations for $h > 1$, hence the gamma effect is diminished by the use of dynamic VaR.

Although they are the same at the daily horizon, the two assumptions can lead to totally different VaR estimates when the risk horizon is more than a few days, and so it is important to choose the assumption that is closest to the trading practice of the particular portfolio.

IV.5.3 ANALYTIC VALUE-AT-RISK APPROXIMATIONS

This section begins with a description of the mapping of option portfolios to the underlying prices, interest rates, time – and indeed any risk factor except volatility. Mapping to volatility risk factors is quite a challenge, and is covered in the next section. We then describe how these mappings allow an *analytic approximation* to the VaR of an option portfolio. However, for more complex risk factor mappings, and in particular those that include volatility as a risk factor, we must estimate VaR using simulation.

IV.5.3.1 Delta Approximation and Delta–Normal VaR

For a portfolio of options on a single underlying the first order Taylor approximation to the portfolio's discounted P&L is

$$\text{P\&L} \approx \delta^{\$}R, \tag{IV.5.18}$$

where $\delta^{\$}$ is the value delta of the portfolio and R is the discounted return on the underlying.

Since (IV.5.18) is a simple linear transformation the VaR based on (IV.5.18) is very easy to calculate. For instance, suppose the discounted h-day returns on the underlying asset are normally distributed with mean and standard deviation μ_h and σ_h. Thus

$$R_h \sim N(\mu_h, \sigma_h^2), \tag{IV.5.19}$$

where R_h denotes the discounted h-day return on the underlying. By (IV.5.18) the approximate distribution of the h-day P&L on the portfolio is

$$\text{P\&L}_h \sim N\big(\delta^{\$}\mu_h, (\delta^{\$}\sigma_h)^2\big). \tag{IV.5.20}$$

Option pricing theory is based on the assumption that the expected return on the underlying asset is the risk free discount rate. To be consistent with this assumption we set $\mu_h = 0$. Now, from (IV.5.20) it follows that we can apply the normal linear VaR formula given in Section IV.2.2.1 to approximate the $100\alpha\%$ h-day VaR of the option portfolio as

$$\text{VaR}_{h,\alpha} \approx \delta^{\$} \times \Phi^{-1}(1-\alpha)\sigma_h, \tag{IV.5.21}$$

where $\Phi^{-1}(1-\alpha)$ is the $1-\alpha$ quantile of the standard normal distribution. In other words, the portfolio has a VaR that is approximately $\delta^{\$}$ times the VaR of the underlying asset.

More generally, we can apply a delta mapping to portfolios of options on several underlyings. The mapping is

$$\Delta P \approx \sum_{i=1}^{n} \delta_i^P \Delta S_i = \boldsymbol{\delta}_P' \Delta \mathbf{S}, \tag{IV.5.22}$$

where P is the portfolio price, $\boldsymbol{\delta}_P = (\delta_1^P, \ldots, \delta_n^P)'$ is the vector of net position deltas and $\Delta \mathbf{S} = (\Delta S_1, \ldots, \Delta S_n)'$ is the vector of changes in the underlying prices. Equivalently,

$$\text{P\&L} \approx \sum_{i=1}^{n} \delta_i^\$ R_i = \boldsymbol{\delta}_\$' \mathbf{r}, \tag{IV.5.23}$$

where $\boldsymbol{\delta}_\$ = (\delta_1^\$, \ldots, \delta_n^\$)'$ is the vector of value deltas and $\mathbf{r} = (R_1, \ldots, R_n)'$ is the vector of returns on the underlying prices.

This is just a linear mapping based on risk factor returns that we might assume to have a multivariate normal distribution. So, following the usual reasoning (see Section IV.1.6.3, for instance) we have

$$\text{VaR}_{h,\alpha} \approx \Phi^{-1}(1-\alpha)\sqrt{\boldsymbol{\delta}_\$' \boldsymbol{\Omega}_h \boldsymbol{\delta}_\$}, \tag{IV.5.24}$$

where $\boldsymbol{\Omega}_h$ is the h-day covariance matrix of the discounted returns on the underlying asset. We might also assume they have a multivariate Student t distribution, as explained in Section IV.2.8, in which case (IV.5.24) would be modified to

$$\text{VaR}_{h,\alpha} \approx t^{-1}(1-\alpha)\sqrt{\nu^{-1}(\nu-2)}\sqrt{\boldsymbol{\delta}_\$' \boldsymbol{\Omega}_h \boldsymbol{\delta}_\$} \tag{IV.5.25}$$

EXAMPLE IV.5.1: DELTA–NORMAL VAR

A portfolio of options on the FTSE 100, S&P 500 and DJ Eurostoxx 50 indices has the characteristics shown in Table IV.5.4. The options are for £10 per point on the FTSE 100, $100 per point on the S&P 500 and €10 per point on the DJ Eurostoxx. Calculate the value deltas in sterling terms and hence compute the delta–normal approximation to the 1% 10-day VaR for a UK investor, under the assumption that exchange rates are constant.

Table IV.5.4   Characteristics of equity indices and their options

	FTSE 100	S&P 500	DJ Eurostoxx 50
Net position delta	0.5	−0.2	0.6
Current index value	6000	1000	4000
GBP exchange rate	1	2	1.5
Volatility	15%	12%	18%
Correlations	FTSE–S&P: 0.7	Stoxx–S&P: 0.5	Stoxx–FTSE: 0.6

SOLUTION   The net value deltas in sterling terms are as follows:

$$\text{FTSE 100: } 0.5 \times 10 \times 6000 = \pounds 30{,}000;$$

$$\text{S\&P 500: } -0.2 \times 100/2 \times 1000 = -\pounds 10{,}000;$$

$$\text{Eurostoxx: } 0.6 \times 10/1.5 \times 4000 = \pounds 16{,}000.$$

The 10-day covariance matrix of the daily risk factor returns is

$$\Omega_{10} = \frac{10}{250} \begin{pmatrix} 0.15^2 & 0.15 \times 0.12 \times 0.7 & 0.15 \times 0.18 \times 0.6 \\ 0.15 \times 0.12 \times 0.7 & 0.12^2 & 0.12 \times 0.18 \times 0.5 \\ 0.15 \times 0.18 \times 0.6 & 0.12 \times 0.18 \times 0.5 & 0.18^2 \end{pmatrix}$$

$$= \begin{pmatrix} 0.9 & 0.504 & 0.648 \\ 0.504 & 0.576 & 0.432 \\ 0.648 & 0.432 & 1.296 \end{pmatrix} \times 10^{-3},$$

and so the 10-day variance of the portfolio P&L is

$$\begin{pmatrix} 30 & -10 & 16 \end{pmatrix} \begin{pmatrix} 0.9 & 0.504 & 0.648 \\ 0.504 & 0.576 & 0.432 \\ 0.648 & 0.432 & 1.296 \end{pmatrix} \begin{pmatrix} 30 \\ -10 \\ 16 \end{pmatrix} \times 10^3 = 1,380,816.$$

Using (IV.5.24) this gives a 1% 10-day VaR of $2.32635 \times \sqrt{1,380,816} = £2734$.

Because the portfolio is assumed to be linear in the above example, we get the same answer from static and dynamic VaR estimation. That is, we get the same answer whether we assume that the portfolio is:

- rebalanced daily to maintain the current values of the net position deltas, in which case we can multiply the 1-day VaR by $\sqrt{10}$ to get the 10-day VaR; or
- not traded during the 10-day period, in which case we base the VaR on the 10-day covariance matrix.

This is true for a linear portfolio with i.i.d. normal returns, but when we include gamma effects we obtain different results depending on the assumption about rebalancing.

Several extensions to the normal linear VaR have been described in Chapter IV.2 of this volume. We can measure the VaR and the ETL of any portfolio with a linear risk factor mapping using a Student t distribution or a normal mixture distribution, for instance. All these generalizations can be carried over to option portfolios when their risk factor mapping is the basic delta map given by (IV.5.22). However, a linear risk factor mapping such as (IV.5.22) is extremely inaccurate as an approximation for the P&L for an option portfolio. The values of most option portfolios will be a highly non-linear function of the underlying asset prices. As a result, the delta–normal VaR model should not be used, even for simple option portfolios.

IV.5.3.2   P&L Distributions for Option Portfolios

Figure IV.5.1 illustrates how the delta–gamma approximation translates the distribution of risk factor changes into a distribution of price changes for the option portfolio. We assume there is a single risk factor with return R. The distribution of R is assumed to be normal and its density is shown by the black curve. The vertical axis represents the option portfolio P&L given by the delta–gamma approximation (IV.5.1). The delta–gamma approximation is a quadratic function of R that is indicated by the dashed curve, and the option portfolio P&L density that is derived by applying this approximation to each value of R is shown by the grey curve drawn relative to the vertical axis.

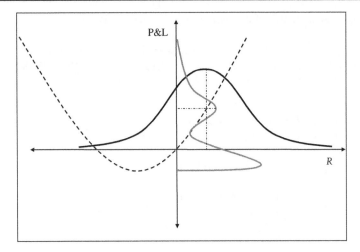

Figure IV.5.1   The P&L distribution resulting from delta–gamma approximation

On the figure we have indicated the mean return, assumed positive, using a dot-dashed vertical line. We also indicate, using a horizontal dot-dashed line, that the delta–gamma approximation translates the mean return into a *local maximum* of the P&L density. Another local maximum is obtained when the return is negative, and this time the maximum occurs at a negative value for P&L.

The figure shows that even when we use a simple delta–gamma approximation to the portfolio P&L, its distribution is highly non-normal. This is because the delta–gamma approximation gives the P&L as a weighted sum of the return and the *squared* return, and if the returns are normally distributed the squared returns have a chi-squared distribution. Also, the expectation of the squared return is not zero. Hence, the expected P&L is *not* zero even when the expected return on the underlying is zero.[11] The P&L distribution induced by the delta–gamma approximation is therefore positively skewed, bimodal and may also be highly leptokurtic.

IV.5.3.3   Delta–Gamma VaR

We now derive an analytic approximation to the VaR of a portfolio of options on several underlyings. To do this we need to fit a distribution with density function such as that shown by the grey, skewed, bimodal curve in Figure IV.5.1.

Consider the h-day P&L given by the delta–gamma representation (IV.5.6), where the returns on the underlying assets have a multivariate normal distribution with covariance matrix Ω_h. Of course the option portfolio P&L will not have a normal distribution, since it includes sums of squared normal variables. But we can use (IV.5.6) to estimate the mean, variance, skewness and kurtosis of the P&L distribution, assuming the approximation (IV.5.6) is reasonably accurate.

The expectation of the right-hand side of (IV.5.6) is given by[12]

---

[11] Since we have omitted the theta effect, a zero realized return would lead to a zero realized P&L; but a zero expected return does not give a zero expected P&L.

[12] Note that option pricing usually assumes each underlying assset is expected to return the risk free rate, i.e. that the expectation of the discounted return is zero. Hence $E(\mathbf{R}) = \mathbf{0}$. Also note that the gamma matrix is symmetric, so that it is equal to its transpose. If a delta–gamma–theta approximation is used the theta term should be added to the trace here.

$$E(P\&L) = \mu = \tfrac{1}{2}\,\text{tr}(\mathbf{\Gamma}_\$\mathbf{\Omega}_h), \tag{IV.5.26}$$

where tr is the trace of a matrix, i.e. the sum of its diagonal elements. After some calculations, we derive the following expressions for the higher moments of the distribution of the discounted P&L:

$$V(P\&L) = \sigma^2 = \tfrac{1}{2}\text{tr}\left[(\mathbf{\Gamma}_\$\mathbf{\Omega}_h)^2\right] + \boldsymbol{\delta}_\$'\mathbf{\Omega}_h\boldsymbol{\delta}_\$, \tag{IV.5.27}$$

$$E\left[(P\&L - \mu)^3\right] = \mu_3 = \text{tr}\left[(\mathbf{\Gamma}_\$\mathbf{\Omega}_h)^3\right] + 3\boldsymbol{\delta}_\$'\mathbf{\Gamma}_\$\mathbf{\Omega}_h\mathbf{\Gamma}_\$\boldsymbol{\delta}_\$, \tag{IV.5.28}$$

$$E\left[(P\&L - \mu)^4\right] = \mu_4 = 3\,\text{tr}\left[(\mathbf{\Gamma}_\$\mathbf{\Omega}_h)^4\right] + 12\boldsymbol{\delta}_\$'\mathbf{\Gamma}_\$(\mathbf{\Omega}_h\mathbf{\Gamma}_\$)^2\boldsymbol{\delta}_\$ + 3\sigma^2. \tag{IV.5.29}$$

Hence, the skewness and kurtosis of the delta–gamma representation are

$$\tau = \frac{\text{tr}\left[(\mathbf{\Gamma}_\$\mathbf{\Omega}_h)^3\right] + 3\boldsymbol{\delta}_\$'\mathbf{\Gamma}_\$\mathbf{\Omega}_h\mathbf{\Gamma}_\$\boldsymbol{\delta}_\$}{(\tfrac{1}{2}\,\text{tr}\left[(\mathbf{\Gamma}_\$\mathbf{\Omega}_h)^2\right] + \boldsymbol{\delta}_\$'\mathbf{\Omega}_h\boldsymbol{\delta}_\$)^{3/2}}, \tag{IV.5.30}$$

$$\varkappa = \frac{3\,\text{tr}\left[(\mathbf{\Gamma}_\$\mathbf{\Omega}_h)^4\right] + 12\boldsymbol{\delta}_\$'\mathbf{\Gamma}_\$(\mathbf{\Omega}_h\mathbf{\Gamma}_\$)^2\boldsymbol{\delta}_\$ + 3\sigma^2}{(\tfrac{1}{2}\,\text{tr}\left[(\mathbf{\Gamma}_\$\mathbf{\Omega}_h)^2\right] + \boldsymbol{\delta}_\$'\mathbf{\Omega}_h\boldsymbol{\delta}_\$)^2}. \tag{IV.5.31}$$

Although the above expressions look complicated, they allow one to calculate the mean, variance, skewness and kurtosis of the delta–gamma P&L distribution (IV.5.6) for an option portfolio with many underlyings. If we know the price risk factor sensitivities $\boldsymbol{\delta}_\$$ and $\mathbf{\Gamma}_\$$ that characterize the portfolio, and the covariance matrix $\mathbf{\Omega}_h$ of h-day returns on the underlying prices, then we can derive the moments of the P&L distribution.

Now suppose we have calculated the first four moments as explained above. How do we estimate the VaR? One possibility is to apply a *Cornish–Fisher expansion* to approximate a quantile from these moments using the methodology explained in Section IV.3.4.3. However, we know from our empirical studies in Section IV.3.4 that for highly leptokurtic distributions this is will not provide results that are as accurate as those derived by fitting a *Johnson SU distribution* to the moments. The method is illustrated in the next example. It uses *Tuenter's algorithm* for fitting the Johnson SU distribution, as explained in Section IV.3.4.4.[13]

EXAMPLE IV.5.2: DELTA–GAMMA VAR WITH JOHNSON DISTRIBUTION

Consider a portfolio of options on bonds and on equities with a P&L that has the delta–gamma approximation

$$P\&L \approx (1 \quad 5)\begin{pmatrix} R_E \\ R_B \end{pmatrix} + \tfrac{1}{2}(R_E \quad R_B)\begin{pmatrix} 25 & -7.5 \\ -7.5 & 125 \end{pmatrix}\begin{pmatrix} R_E \\ R_B \end{pmatrix}.$$

The units of measurement are millions of US dollars. Thus the net value delta is $1 million with respect to the bond index and $5 million with respect to the equity index. The value gamma matrix is also measured in millions of dollars. Suppose that the returns on the bond and equity indices are normally distributed with volatilities of 30% and 20% and a correlation

---

[13] The P&L, X, of an option portfolio when approximated with a delta–gamma representation often has a positive skewness as well as a positive excess kurtosis. In this case, we fit a Johnson SU distribution to $-X$ and compute the VaR from the upper tail of the fitted distribution. Note that if the excess kurtosis is negative we cannot use the Johnson SU distribution, but other types of Johnson distribution are available. See Mina and Ulmer (1999).

of -0.25. Fit a Johnson distribution to the distribution of the portfolio P&L. Hence, estimate the 1% 10-day VaR of the portfolio and compare your result with the delta–normal VaR based on (IV.5.25).

SOLUTION   We have

$$\delta_\$ = \begin{pmatrix} 1 \\ 5 \end{pmatrix} \text{ and } \Gamma_\$ = \begin{pmatrix} 25 & -7.5 \\ -7.5 & 125 \end{pmatrix}$$

The 10-day covariance matrix of the risk factor returns is

$$\Omega_h = \frac{10}{250} \begin{pmatrix} 0.09 & -0.015 \\ -0.015 & 0.04 \end{pmatrix} = \begin{pmatrix} 36 & -6 \\ -6 & 16 \end{pmatrix} \times 10^{-4}.$$

In the spreadsheet for this example we calculate the moments of the 10-day P&L distribution based on (IV.5.26)–(IV.5.31) and the results are: mean $0.150 million, standard deviation $0.256 million, skewness 1.1913, and excess kurtosis 47.153. Since the excess kurtosis is positive, we can fit a Johnson SU distribution to these parameters using Tuenter's algorithm.[14] The result is a delta–gamma 1% 10-day VaR of $261,024. The corresponding delta–normal VaR is $451,096. Clearly, ignoring the gamma effect leads to considerable error when computing VaR. The portfolio has a positive gamma, so we know from our discussion in Section IV.5.2.3 that the VaR will be considerably reduced when we take the gamma effect into account.

Because it is not bimodal the Johnson distribution that was applied in the above example is not the best way to fit the first four moments of the option portfolio P&L distribution. We have used it because it is practical, and because Section IV.3.4 demonstrated that if the P&L distribution is very leptokurtic, as it is in the example, it is better than using a four moment Cornish–Fisher expansion.[15] However, the P&L distribution is bimodal and highly skewed as well. The VaR at extreme quantiles is heavily influenced by the tail behaviour of the P&L distribution, and it is difficult to capture this well with *any* analytic approximation.

IV.5.4   HISTORICAL VALUE AT RISK FOR OPTION PORTFOLIOS

This section presents several empirical examples on the computation of historical VaR for option portfolios. We begin by studying the simplest possible portfolio: a position on a standard European option on the S&P 500 index. The position requires revaluing for every historical scenario of underlying price and volatility risk factor changes. This is easy when we just apply the Black–Scholes–Merton formula to revalue the portfolio at the risk horizon, but the portfolio revaluation can take considerable time for portfolios of exotic, path-dependent options.

We shall also discuss how to apply historical VaR to the risk assessment of path-dependent options, but since our focus is on the methodology rather than computational details, the position considered will be a simple European look-back option. Although its pay-off is path-dependent, under the constant volatility assumption we still have an analytic formula for its

---

[14] But since the skewness is positive we fit the Johnson distribution to the distribution with a mean of $-$0.150 million and a skewness of -1.913 and estimate the VaR from the upper tail of this distribution.

[15] A six-moment Cornish–Fisher expansion has been considered by some authors, but the tail behaviour of the distribution is still unlikely to be well represented.

price.[16] If numerical methods have to be applied to price a large complex option portfolio this will be very time-consuming. VaR with exact revaluation can usually be estimated overnight, but for high frequency risk assessment purposes such portfolios are often better represented by a risk factor mapping. Hence, another empirical example in this section illustrates the historical VaR approach for a portfolio of options that have been mapped to their risk factors, where all the options are on a single underlying. We then extend this to portfolios of options on several underlyings and end the section with a case study on the historical VaR for a trading book of energy options.

Various enhancements of standard historical simulation (e.g. to account for volatility adjustment, or to apply parametric filtering based on a GARCH model) that improve its accuracy have been described in Section IV.3.3. However, to include these in the empirical examples of this section – which already require quite complex Excel workbooks – would obscure the main purpose of this section. We therefore examine the application of standard historical simulation only, showing that it can usefully be applied to estimate the dynamic VaR of an option portfolio, but it is not the best VaR model to use for static options positions, except when the risk horizon is short.[17]

IV.5.4.1   VaR and ETL with Exact Revaluation

How does one calculate the historical VaR and ETL of an option that can be priced analytically? In this section we consider a very simple portfolio, i.e. a short position on a 30-day European put on the S&P 500 index. These options are very actively traded on the CME. Each option is for $250 per index point, i.e. the pay-off function is

$$\$250 \times \max\big(\omega(S - K), 0\big),$$

where ω is 1 for a call and -1 for a put and the strike K and S&P 500 index futures price S are measured in index points.[18]

Data

The risk factors of this portfolio are the S&P 500 futures price, the option's implied volatility, and the 30-day US LIBOR rate. For convenience, and specifically to avoid concatenating a very long series of 30-day index futures prices, we apply variations in the spot index price to the current index futures price. This only induces a very tiny error in our calculations because the basis risk between the S&P 500 spot index and its futures contract is negligible.[19] Similarly, we shall apply variations in the S&P 500 volatility index, i.e. the Vix index, to the current implied volatility of the option. This assumes the option has a volatility beta of 1 with respect to the Vix index.[20] Finally, for the interest rate we use the 1-month LIBOR rate.[21]

---

[16] Many exotic options such as Asians and barrier options also have analytic price approximations. See Section III.3.9.9 for the look-back option pricing formula.

[17] As already stated, this is because simulations cannot be based on overlapping h-day risk factor returns because the tail of the portfolio return distribution will be truncated, leading to imprecision of VaR estimates at high levels of confidence.

[18] The CBOE S&P 500 index options contract is for $100 per index point, but trading volume on this contract is minor compared to the trading volume on the CME contract. European and American index options are priced on the index futures contract with the same maturity as the option. See Section III.3.6 for further details.

[19] See Alexander and Barbosa (2007).

[20] Both index and index volatility data may be downloaded from Yahoo! Finance: symbols ^GSPC and ^VIX.

[21] These data may be downloaded from the British Bankers' Association website. See www.bba.org.uk.

Daily data on these risk factors from 3 January 1990 until 25 April 2008 are displayed in Figure IV.5.2. The Vix and LIBOR are measured on the left hand scale and the index is measured on the right hand scale. The VaR will be measured on 25 April 2008, when the index futures price stood at almost 1400 and the Vix was at almost 20%. The main influence on the markets at this time, not just in the US but also in Europe and Asia, was the credit crunch that was precipitated by the sub-prime mortgage crisis in the US during 2007. To ease the credit squeeze, US interest rates had been cut considerably so that the 1-month LIBOR rate stood at only 2.86% at this time.

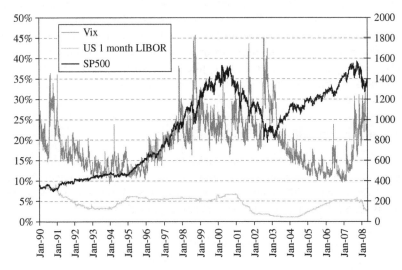

Figure IV.5.2   S&P 500 index price, Vix and 1-month US LIBOR, 1990–2008

Simulating Risk Factor Values

How should we simulate the risk factor values in the historical model? We know from our discussion in Section IV.3.2 that we need to use daily or even higher frequency returns on the risk factors so that we have enough data to measure VaR at the 99% or higher confidence level. This means that for $h > 1$ we have a choice between the following approaches, each having its own advantages and limitations.

 (i) Estimate the VaR for a dynamically rebalanced position, and scale up the 1-day VaR estimate. This assumes that we rebalance the position each day to keep the Greeks constant.
 (ii) Estimate the VaR for a static position using h-day simulations based on overlapping samples.
(iii) First estimate a parametric model for the conditional distributions of the returns in multi-step simulation, and then employ this model in the filtered historical simulation model of Barone-Adesi et al. (1998, 1999).[22]

---

[22] This approach is described in Section IV.3.3.4.

The first two approaches have the advantage of simplicity but the disadvantage of inaccuracy. In case (i) the error stems from an assumption that the position has stable, i.i.d. returns and that we know the appropriate power law for scaling,[23] and in case (ii) the error arises from the distortion of the tail behaviour of the portfolio return distribution.[24] The third approach is more complex than the others, requiring the estimation of a GARCH model on the position's daily log returns and the application of the statistical bootstrap for simulation over the risk horizon.

We now ask how we should model the evolution of an option's risk factor returns in the framework of standard historical simulation. We shall answer this question in the context of a 1-day VaR estimate. Given T historical daily returns (or changes) on a risk factor, the first step in historical simulation is to derive the set,

$$\left\{ \widetilde{X}_{1t}, \widetilde{X}_{2t}, \ldots, \widetilde{X}_{nt} \right\}_{t=1}^{T},$$

of 1-day-ahead risk factor prices. For $i = 1, \ldots, n$, each price $\widetilde{X}_{it}$ is based on the *current* value $\overline{X}_i$ of the risk factor when the VaR is measured and, under the assumption that the risk factor X_i follows a geometric process, we set

$$\widetilde{X}_{it} = \overline{X}_i \exp(r_{it}) \qquad\qquad (IV.5.32)$$

where $r_{it} = \ln(X_{it}) - \ln(X_{i,t-1})$ is the daily log return on the risk factor, in the historical sample, at time t. But under the assumption that the risk factor X_i follows an arithmetic process, we use the daily changes $x_{it} = X_{it} - X_{i,t-1}$ and simulate the risk factor prices as

$$\widetilde{X}_{it} = \overline{X}_i + x_{it}. \qquad\qquad (IV.5.33)$$

Should we use arithmetic or geometric stochastic processes to model the evolution of risk factors? Since we have a European option that is priced using the Black–Scholes–Merton formula, we should assume the underlying asset price follows a geometric Brownian motion. Thus the log return on the underlying price is a normally distributed random variable, and we should simulate prices using (IV.5.32). But what about the volatility and interest rate processes? It is not entirely clear whether these are governed by arithmetic or geometric processes in the real world. However, following our empirical results in Section II.5.3.6, I would advise that we assume the real-world processes for interest rates and volatility are also geometric. Hence, in all the case studies for this section we have used simulated interest rates and volatilities that are also based on (IV.5.32). This also has the advantage that simulated volatilities and interest rates cannot be negative.

Another reason to use log returns rather than absolute changes in risk factors is that over a long historical period there could be significant trends in the risk factors. In that case, an absolute change of 100 index points (or 100 basis points) ten years ago could have had quite a different significance compared to a similar change today.

It is also convenient to use log returns since the sum of h consecutive log returns is the h-day log return. Then, for a static VaR estimate, we use the h-day log return at time t, r_{hit} to simulate the ith risk factor price h days ahead as

---

[23] Option portfolios have volatility as a major risk factor and so their returns are unlikely to scale by the square-root-of-time rule. See Section IV.3.2.4 for a discussion of this point.
[24] See Section IV.3.2.2 for an explanation why overlapping h-day returns produces a truncation of the tail.

$$\tilde{X}_{it} = \overline{X}_i \exp(r_{hit}). \tag{IV.5.34}$$

The result of the historical simulation of the underlying risk factors will be a set of 1-day ahead or h-day ahead values for the risk factors. The time ordering implicit in these values is not important, although it *is* important to couple the simulations of the values of different risk factors, to retain the implicit correlation between them. However, the time ordering of the *returns* that are used to generate these values can be important, to adjust for volatility clustering. In that case, the simulated risk factor values are generated from the volatility-adjusted returns.

Building the P&L Distribution and Estimating VaR

In the case of our simple S&P 500 option the risk factors are just the index futures price, the option's implied volatility, and the US LIBOR rate. In static VaR, the simulated values for the risk factors are used to revalue the option at the risk horizon. If the risk horizon is h days, the maturities of the simulated futures price, implied volatility and interest rate must be reduced by h days.

By way of illustration, consider a single standard European option position, and denote the price of the option at time t by[25]

$$f_t = f(S_t, \sigma_t, r \,|\, K, T - t).$$

Suppose the VaR is estimated at time $t = 0$. Then the forward looking discounted P&L from a long position on the option in h trading days, i.e. in h^c calendar days, is

$$P\&L = \left(\exp(-r_{h^c} h^c) f_h - f_0\right) pv \tag{IV.5.35}$$

where f_0 is the current value of the option, pv is the point value for the position and r_{h^c} is the h^c-day continuously compounded discount rate. We know everything on the right-hand side of (IV.5.35) except for the option price f_h in h trading days' (i.e. in h^c calendar days') time.[26] To simulate this, we apply the Black–Scholes–Merton pricing formula to a simulated pair (S_h, σ_h) of values for the underlying price S_h and for the option's implied volatility σ_h, in h trading days' time.

Taking each vector of simulated values of the risk factors in turn, we obtain the VaR estimate as follows:[27]

- With no rebalancing (i.e. static VaR) we obtain many simulated h-day-ahead portfolio values, from which we build an empirical distribution of the h-day portfolio P&L, and discount this to today. The $100\alpha\%$ h-day VaR is minus the α quantile of this distribution.

---

[25] Here the option strike is K and its maturity date is T, the underlying price is S and its implied volatility is σ. We know that the discount rate r is such a minor risk factor that in the following we shall assume this is the same for all maturities.

[26] In our empirical examples, to avoid counting calendar days for different assumptions about the risk horizon (measured in trading days) we shall either assume the discount rate is zero or that $h^c = h$. This introduces only a very small error in the VaR calculations, since even ignoring the discount rate completely has a negligible effect on the VaR for option portfolios, as demonstrated in Example IV.5.5.

[27] Since we are only considering one-step historical simulation here, the simulated risk factor prices, and hence also the simulated portfolio P&L data, could be displayed in any order, provided only that the risk factor price series are 'shuffled' as one if the ordering is changed. That is, the changes in price, volatility and interest rate on a given day must remain linked. The reason is that the connection between price and volatility is incredibly important: an increase in volatility is far more likely to occur on a day when the price jumps than on a day when the price remains constant.

- With rebalancing to constant sensitivities (i.e. dynamic VaR) we obtain many simulated 1-day-ahead portfolio values, from which we build an empirical distribution of the daily portfolio P&L, and discount this to today. The $100\alpha\%$ 1-day VaR is minus the α quantile of this distribution. Then, to extrapolate this figure to an $100\alpha\%$ h-day VaR, we apply the square-root-of-time or some other power law scaling rule.

The next example compares the application of standard historical simulation to static and dynamic VaR estimates for a single option. Note that both approaches have errors: errors in static historical VaR arise from the use of historical overlapping samples, and errors in dynamic historical VAR arise from the use of a square-root scaling law. But these errors are unlikely to affect our decision about whether to apply static or dynamic VaR measures in the first place. This decision only depends on our assumptions about the position. If we are estimating the VaR of a non-traded position we use should static VaR, and if we are estimating the VaR of a trader's limits, or of his current position (assuming it is rebalanced to maintain constant risk factor sensitivities over the risk horizon) we should use dynamic VaR.

EXAMPLE IV.5.3: STATIC AND DYNAMIC HISTORICAL VAR FOR AN OPTION

Use standard historical simulation to estimate the 1% 10-day VaR for an unhedged position on a standard European call or put on the S&P 500 index. Estimate both

- static VaR, using 10-day overlapping returns on the risk factors, and
- dynamic VaR, scaling up the daily VaR to a 10-day horizon using the square-root-of-time rule.

Consider long and short positions on a 30-day call and a 30-day put, both with strike 1400. The VaR is estimated on 25 April 2008 when the index is at 1400 and the index volatility is at 20%. For clarity, and since this will have very little effect on the result, assume the discount rate is 0%.[28] Use the same historical scenarios on the S&P 500 index and the Vix volatility that were used in the previous example.

SOLUTION   The spreadsheet for this example generates scenarios based on the daily log returns on the S&P 500 and Vix between 3 January 1990 and 25 April 2008, as we have described above. It prices the option using each of the simulated {price, volatility} scenarios. Then it calculates the P&L as the difference between the discounted scenario price and the current price of the option. This is the P&L for a long position, and the opposite difference is the P&L for the short position. Multiplying the lower 1% quantile of the distribution of these price changes by the index point value of $250 gives the 1% 10-day VaR of the unhedged position as in Table IV.5.5.

Long positions. Since the options have only 30 days to maturity the long positions have quite a large positive gamma; the gamma effect will decrease the static VaR considerably and the application of a square-root scaling rule to 1-day VaR would underestimate this gamma

---

[28] Readers can change this in the spreadsheet, but note that we maintain some simplifying assumptions, i.e. that the changes in the relevant continuously compounded discount rate are identical to the changes in the discretely compounded 1-month discount rate and that the number of trading days in the risk horizon is equal to the number of calendar days. The errors that these assumptions introduce are very small.

Table IV.5.5   1% 10-day VaR under different rebalancing assumptions

Position	Rebalancing	Call	Put
Long	Dynamic	$10,518	$14,380
	Static	$7,112	$7,803
Short	Dynamic	$16,710	$20,407
	Static	$19,471	$18,709

effect considerably. This is why the 10-day dynamic VaR estimates for the long positions, which are based on the square-root scaling rule, are considerably larger than the static VaR estimates. However, since the simulations based on overlapping data can truncate the tails of the P&L distribution, the static VaR estimates based on overlapping data may be too low at high confidence levels (see the discussion following this example).

Why is the dynamic VaR for the long put so much larger than the dynamic VaR for the long call? The reason is the *vega effect*. The option's positive vega has the effect of offsetting the VaR for a long call, but augmenting (or at least not offsetting) the VaR for a long put, as explained in Section IV.5.2.2. The dynamic VaR is assumed to be based on a square-root scaling rule, and this could understate or overstate the vega effect, depending on the option and the risk factor characteristics. In stock index options dynamic VaR estimates tend to overstate the vega effect. This is because the daily changes in volatility have a small, negative autocorrelation and at the daily level there is a pronounced asymmetry in the index price–volatility relationship which is not present in 10-day returns (see Section IV.4.4.4). For both of these reasons, the square-root scaling rule tends overstate the vega risk of stock index options.

Short positions. We already know from the previous example that short positions on naked options are much more risky than long positions. This is why their VaR estimates in Table IV.5.5 are much larger than the VaR estimates for the long positions. The short positions have a large negative gamma, which should increase the static VaR, but in the dynamic VaR estimates the portfolio is rebalanced to keep the gamma constant over the risk horizon, so the gamma effect is diminished.

If the gamma effect were the only effect to consider we might suppose that the dynamic VaR will be *less* than the static VaR, and this is certainly the case for the short call, but this is not the case for the short put. Again, the reason lies with the vega effect, which we know from our discussion in Section IV.5.2.2 will augment the VaR for the short put position. Since dynamic VaR estimates overstate the vega effect in stock index options, the dynamic VaR estimate for the short put position is larger than the static VaR estimate.

We know from our discussion in Section IV.3.2.7 that a potential problem with using overlapping data to estimate static VaR in the historical model is that the tail behaviour of the risk factor returns can be distorted so that VaR estimates at extreme quantiles may be too low. On the other hand, the use of a square-root scaling rule for dynamic VaR estimates also introduces errors, because at least one of the risk factors (i.e. volatility) is unlikely to scale with a square-root law.[29] To illustrate these two sources of model risk, Table IV.5.6 shows the VaR estimates for the previous example, but now based on the 10% and 0.1% significance

---

[29] As demonstrated empirically in Section IV.3.2.4.

levels. Because we have a daily sample size of about 5000, there are only 500 non-overlapping 10-day P&Ls. This means that we can estimate the 10% quantile (by taking the 50th largest 10-day loss), and the 0.2% quantile is the largest loss. But we cannot measure the 0.1% quantile empirically, unless we use a statistical bootstrap, and the bootstrap merely increases the number of observations by repeating them. It introduces no new information to the data. So we only have an upper bound for the 0.1% quantile, i.e. the largest loss, which translates to a lower bound for the 0.1% VaR.

Using overlapping samples will generate about 5000 observations, but there is no new information in these data. Now it becomes possible to estimate the 0.1% quantile (as the 5th largest 10-day loss), but we would still underestimate the 0.1% quantile because the size of the 10-day losses is limited by the largest loss in the sample.

Table IV.5.6 Comparison of 10% and 0.1% 10-day VaR under different rebalancing assumptions

Position	Assumption	10%		0.1%	
		Call	Put	Call	Put
Long	$\sqrt{10}$ Scaling	$5,080	$7,216	$14,330	$19,714
	Overlapping	$4,922	$6,253	$7,793	$8,004
Short	$\sqrt{10}$ Scaling	$5,685	$7,607	$34,107	$36,027
	Overlapping	$6,094	$5,992	$34,349	$35,893

Looking at the results in Table IV.5.6, the 0.1% VaR estimates of long options exposures are far too low when based on overlapping data. This is evident from the estimates of only $7793 for the call and $8004 for the put. These 0.1% VaR estimates are not very much greater than the 10% VaR estimates! On the other hand, since we have a static position the VaR estimates based on the square-root scaling rule are too high for the long positions, and too low for the short positions, because they virtually ignore the gamma effects. They are also too high for the put relative to the call, because they overstate the vega effect, as discussed above.

In summary, there is a considerable amount of model risk in standard historical simulation when applying this methodology to measure static options VaR, even though there is no parametric model to estimate.

EXAMPLE IV.5.4: HISTORICAL VAR AND ETL OF A DELTA-HEDGED OPTION

On 25 April 2008 you sell a European put on the S&P 500 index futures with strike 1400 and maturity 30 days. The index futures price is at 1398, the market price of the option is 32, its delta is −0.4991 and its implied volatility is 19.42%. Use the historical data shown in Figure IV.5.2 to estimate the 1% 1-day VaR and ETL of the unhedged short put option position and of the delta hedged portfolio. Then compare the results with those for a long position on the put, and for both short and long positions on a call with the same strike and maturity, and the same market price as the put.[30]

---

[30] You will need to back-out the implied volatility for this call using Goal Seek or Solver, as shown in the spreadsheet. Readers can change the spreadsheet to compute the VaR of other European call or put options. Just input the strike and maturity and read off the VaR, but first follow the Goal Seek instructions to compute the correct implied volatility.

SOLUTION   Note that these options are on the futures rather than the index, although we use the index to generate scenarios for the futures price as described earlier. So we price the options on the futures using each of the {futures price, volatility, interest rate} simulations.[31] Then the unhedged P&L is calculated as the difference between the simulated option price, discounted by 1 day, and the current price of the option (i.e. 32). This is the P&L for a long position, and the opposite difference is the P&L for the short position. Multiplying the lower 1% quantile of the distribution of these price changes by the index point value of $250 gives the 1% 1-day VaR of the unhedged short put position as $6467. Clearly the VaR for naked short options position is huge, and that is why traders must hedge the options that they write.

Now consider a delta hedge that is held for a period of 1 day, offsetting the short put position by purchasing $\delta = -0.4980$ (i.e. taking a short position) on the index futures.[32] This time, the discounted price changes on the *hedged* portfolio are calculated for each of the historical scenarios. Multiplying the lower 1% quantile of the distribution of these price changes by the index point value gives the 1% 1-day VaR of the hedged short put position as $1873. This not small because we have not hedged the gamma or vega risk of the option.

For the ETL calculations we record the daily losses that exceed the 1% quantile of the daily P&L distribution.[33] Then the estimate of the daily ETL is the average of these excess losses, i.e. $8413 for the naked short put position and $2818 for the delta-hedged portfolio. These figures represent the expected loss given that the VaR is exceeded, so they provide some idea of the potential for extreme losses on options positions.

Now we use the spreadsheet to estimate the 1% 1-day VaR and ETL for the long put, and for a short and a long position on a call with the same strike and maturity, i.e. 1400 and 30 days, a market price of 32 and an implied volatility of 20.67%.[34] The results, which are displayed in Table IV.5.7, show that the long positions have much less risk than the short positions. This is because they have positive gamma. The gamma for 30-day near ATM options is relatively large, and that is why there is so much difference between the risk from going long and short these call and put options, even after delta-hedging.

Table IV.5.7   Comparison of VaR and ETL for long and short calls and puts

1% daily VaR and ETL	Position	Option	VaR	ETL
unhedged	short	put	$6467	$8413
delta-hedged			$1873	$2818
unhedged	long	put	$4605	$5513
delta-hedged			$909	$1078
unhedged	short	call	$5132	$7341
delta-hedged			$1916	$2848
unhedged	long	call	$3249	$3828
delta-hedged			$943	$1133

[31] This time, use the historical data on the 1 month US Treasury bill as a proxy for movements in the 10-day continuously compounded discount rate.

[32] Of course we cannot sell a non-integer number of futures, but we shall not consider the consequent position risk here.

[33] As before, the P&L is discounted by 1 day, although this has very little effect on the daily ETL.

[34] When you change cell B14 of the spreadsheet labelled 'VaR' to a call option, do not forget to apply Goal Seek or Solver to compute the correct implied volatility.

The historical P&L distribution has a very large excess kurtosis.[35] A long position also has a large positive skewness and a short position has a large negative skewness. The ETL increases with kurtosis in the P&L distribution but decreases with positive skewness. Hence the ETL is not very much greater than the VaR for a long position, but it is substantially greater than the VaR for a short position, particularly for the delta-hedged short positions. The long positions have an ETL that is approximately 20% greater than the VaR, whereas the delta-hedged short positions have an ETL that is about 50% greater than the VaR.

This example illustrates the huge risks taken by option traders and the clear need for accurate and active hedging. The 1% 1-day VaR of the unhedged short put is $6467, relative to a position value of $32 \times \$250 = \$7750$, and at $8413 the 1% 1-day ETL exceeds the position value. However, the delta-hedged short put has much lower VaR and ETL, and this is relative to an initial position value of $(32 + 0.4980 \times 1398) \times \$250 = \$182{,}062$.

We have already mentioned, several times, that ignoring the discount rate as a risk factor would have a negligible effect on the VaR. The next example justifies this statement empirically.

EXAMPLE IV.5.5: INTEREST RATE, PRICE AND VOLATILITY RISKS OF OPTIONS

Decompose the total historical VaR of the unhedged short put position in Example IV.5.4 into the VaR due to uncertainty in the underlying price, uncertainty in volatility and uncertainty in the discount rate. Then scale these figures up, using a square-root law, to estimate the dynamic VaR over the life of the option.

SOLUTION   From Example IV.5.4 the total 1% 1-day VaR of the unhedged short put is $6467. To disaggregate this into stand-alone components we must create three separate historical simulations of the P&L where, instead of changing all three risk factors as in the previous example, we change only one of them. Thus the *price risk* is measured by a quantile of the P&L distribution generated by changing the underlying price but keeping volatility and discount rate constant at their current levels. Similarly, the *volatility risk* is measured by a quantile of the P&L distribution generated by changing the volatility but keeping price and discount rate constant at their current levels. And the *interest rate risk* is measured by a quantile of the P&L distribution generated by changing the discount rate but keeping price and volatility constant at their current levels. The results for the 1% 1-day VaR decomposition of the unhedged short put are shown in the first column of Table IV.5.8, and in the second column we have scaled these figures up to a 30-day risk horizon, using a square-root rule.[36]

These results show that by far the most important risk factor for an option is the underlying price. The volatility risk is substantial but still, the stand-alone price risk is almost four times the stand-alone volatility risk. The only inconsequential risk is that due to uncertainty in the discount rate.

---

[35] The excess kurtosis is 5.11 for the unhedged put, 7.37 for the unhedged call, 17.51 for the hedged put and 15.88 for the hedged call. This is the same for long and short positions. For long positions the skewness is 1.08 for the unhedged put, 1.45 for the unhedged call, 2.69 for the hedged put and 2.52 for the hedged call. For short positions, multiply the skewness by −1.

[36] For simplicity, we also use 30 calendar days for the discounting.

Table IV.5.8 Disaggregation of option VaR into price, volatility and interest rate VaRs

Source of risk	1% daily VaR	1% 30-day VaR
Underling price	$5,383	$29,484
Implied volatility	$1,160	$6,354
Discount rate	$0.63	$3.05
Sum of VaRs	$6,544	$35,841

IV.5.4.2 Dynamically Hedged Option Portfolios

Typically option traders will hold portfolios that are delta–gamma–vega neutral. Of course, as the underlying risk factors change, the hedges will have to be rebalanced. Rebalancing too frequently will erode any profits from writing options because of the transactions costs. It is therefore common to rebalance positions on a daily basis, to set the delta, gamma and vega back to zero. But the trader still runs substantial risks; and these risks would not be detected in daily VaR calculations based on delta–gamma–vega portfolio mapping, since the delta, gamma and vega will always be zero when the VaR is measured.[37]

To assess such risks we consider a simple European option that is gamma and vega hedged with other options on the same underlying and then delta hedged with the underlying, as explained in Section III.3.4.6. We compute the 1-day VaR of the hedged portfolio based on exact revaluation and then, assuming the portfolio is rebalanced to be delta–gamma–vega neutral at the end of each day, the 10-day dynamic VaR is estimated as $\sqrt{10}$ times the 1-day VaR.

EXAMPLE IV.5.6: VaR AND ETL FOR A DELTA–GAMMA–VEGA HEDGED PORTFOLIO

A trader writes a standard 60-day European call on the S&P 500 index futures with strike 1400 when the current index futures is at 1398. The call has a price of 50 and an implied volatility of 22.67%. To gamma–vega hedge he buys two other S&P 500 futures options: a 30-day put with strike 1375 and a 90-day call with strike 1425. The 30-day put has price 30 and implied volatility 25.58% and the 90-day call has price 55 and implied volatility 24.38%. Using the same historical {price, volatility, interest rate} simulations that were used in Example IV.5.4, estimate the 1% 10-day VaR and ETL of the delta–gamma–vega neutral portfolio assuming it is rebalanced at the end of each day to return the delta, gamma and vega to zero. Assume the discount rate is 2.75% at all maturities up to 90 days.

SOLUTION   First, gamma–vega neutral positions are computed in the spreadsheet. Then the position delta of the gamma–vega hedged portfolio is used to determine the delta hedge position on the S&P 500 index. The resulting option positions and their risk factor sensitivities are shown in Table IV.5.9.

For gamma–vega neutrality we have a position of 0.4843 on the 30-day put and 0.5472 on the 90-day call. The resulting position in all three options has a net delta of $-0.5293 - 0.1858 + 0.2628 = -0.4523$. We assume we can buy exactly this amount of the underlying in the delta neutral hedge, so that there is no residual position risk.

---

[37] Similarly, the delta-only approximation to the VaR of the delta-hedged portfolio in Example IV.5.4 would be zero. Yet with exact re-valuation, the 1% 10-day VaR of the delta-hedged portfolio is $1,198.

Table IV.5.9   Characteristics of European options on S&P 500 futures

Characteristics	Option 1	Option 2	Option 3
Option price	50	30	55
Volatility	22.67%	25.58%	24.38%
Maturity (days)	60	30	90
Strike	1400	1375	1425
Call/put	call	put	call
Position	−1	0.4843	0.5472
Delta	−0.5293	−0.1858	0.2628
Gamma	−0.0031	0.0018	0.0013
Vega	−2.2439	0.7400	1.5040

The spreadsheet revalues each option on every historical simulation, computes the discounted total P&L on the gamma–vega neutral portfolio, and also computes the discounted P&L on the delta–gamma–vega neutral portfolio that includes the position on the S&P 500 index futures. Since we are assuming daily rebalancing to constant risk factor sensitivities, the 10-day historical VaR for the delta–gamma–vega neutral portfolio is calculated as $-\sqrt{10}$ times the lower 1% quantile of this P&L distribution, and the ETL is $\sqrt{10}$ times the average of the losses that exceed the 1% quantile of the distribution.

The VaR is not zero: the 1% 10-day VaR is $871. And the 1% 10-day ETL is $968. We conclude that even when traders rebalance daily to delta–gamma–vega neutral positions they can run significant risks. This is because we have only hedged against *small* changes in the price and volatility risk factors. A delta–gamma–vega hedged portfolio would have a much smaller risk if it were rebalanced more frequently than once per day, but then the transactions costs could erode any benefit from hedging.

Readers may verify that the result in the above example is not unusual. Changing the options in the spreadsheet leads to similar results, i.e. the dynamic VaR for a delta–gamma–vega neutral portfolio is *not* insignificantly different from zero. As already mentioned, this is because the VaR estimate is based on *exact* revaluation: of course the dynamic VaR estimate would be zero if we based it on a delta–gamma–vega mapping, because the portfolio is rebalanced daily to set the delta, gamma and vega to zero.

IV.5.4.3   Greeks Approximation

The aim of this section is to illustrate the method for computing historical VaR when options have been mapped to risk factors. For an option portfolio on a single underlying, mapped to a single volatility risk factor, a delta-gamma–vega–theta representation allows us to approximate the price of the portfolio h trading days (and h^c calendar days) ahead as

$$f_{h^c} \approx f_0 + \theta^P \Delta t + \delta^P \Delta S + \tfrac{1}{2}\gamma^P (\Delta S)^2 + v^P \Delta \sigma, \qquad (IV.5.36)$$

where f_0 is the price of the portfolio today, $\Delta t = h^c/365$, ΔS is the difference between an underlying price in h trading days' time, derived from a simulated daily log return on S, and the price today, $\Delta \sigma$ is the difference between the simulated volatility in h trading days' time and the volatility today, and θ^P, δ^P, γ^P and ν^P are the position Greeks of the portfolio. Now the approximate discounted P&L on the portfolio may be written

$$\left[\exp(-r_{h^c}h^c/365)f_h - f_0\right] \times pv$$
$$\approx \left[\exp(-r_{h^c}h^c/365)\ (\theta^P\Delta t + \delta^P\Delta S + \tfrac{1}{2}\gamma^P(\Delta S)^2 + \nu^P\Delta\sigma)\right] \times pv, \qquad \text{(IV.5.37)}$$

where pv is the point value for options on this underlying.[38]

More detailed risk factor mappings could add other Greeks, such as rho (the sensitivity to changes in interest rates) or higher order sensitivities like vanna and volga. But the minor Greeks such as rho, vanna and volga usually have little effect on the portfolio VaR, as we demonstrate in this section, so delta–gamma–vega–theta mapping is often sufficient.

When using standard historical simulation for options we are always faced with the choice between, on the one hand, estimating static VaR and using overlapping data for ΔS and $\Delta\sigma$, and, on the other hand, estimating the dynamic VaR by basing (IV.5.37) on a risk horizon of 1 day and then scaling up the result to a risk horizon of h days. The following example illustrates the effect of this decision, and also examines the accuracy of VaR estimates based on Greeks approximations.

EXAMPLE IV.5.7: HISTORICAL VAR WITH GREEKS APPROXIMATION

Estimate the 1% 1-day and 10-day VaR of long and short positions on the put option in Example IV.5.4, and for the 10-day VaR. Assume first that the position is rebalanced daily to return the risk factor sensitivities to their values at the time the VaR is estimated, and then that the position is held static. Compare the results for a long and a short position on the put, based on delta-only, delta–gamma, delta–gamma–vega, delta–gamma–vega–theta and delta–gamma–vega–theta–vanna–volga–rho approximations.

SOLUTION   In the spreadsheet for this example, the dollar Greeks are held constant and applied to the same historical {futures price, volatility, interest rate} simulations as in Example IV.5.4.[39] The results are displayed in the top half of Table IV.5.10. Note that the results based on exact revaluation were already obtained in Table IV.5.5, Example IV.5.4.

The 'delta only' VaR is imprecise because it is a linear approximation to a highly non-linear relationship. The delta only approximation behaves like a linear portfolio, and as we know from previous chapters, the VaR can be greatly affected by non-constant volatility. The put has a positive gamma and so the delta–gamma VaR for the long position is less than the VaR based on the delta only approximation. But the opposite is the case for the short put position: there were many large negative price changes in the S&P 500 futures during the historical period, and the negative gamma increases the sensitivity of the option to such moves.

The delta–gamma–vega VaR figures include the portfolio's price changes due to changes in volatility. Changes in volatility have two effects on the portfolio's VaR. One effect is that the VaR increases due to the addition of another risk factor. If this were the only effect then

---

[38] We have ignored a second term $f_0(\exp(-r_{h^c}h^c/365) - 1)$ on the right-hand side, since this is negligible unless h is very large, so it will not affect the accuracy of the Greeks approximation.

[39] For simplicity, in the static VaR calculations we assume $h^c/365 \approx h/250$ so that for the 10-day VaR, $\Delta t = 0.4$ instead of 0.3836. The theta effect is so small here that this approximation leads to inconsequential errors.

Table IV.5.10   Historical VaR with Greeks approximation

1% 1 day VaR	Long	Short
Delta only	$4,943	$4,622
Delta–gamma	$3,935	$5,504
Delta–gamma–vega	$3,941	$5,519
Delta–gamma–vega–theta	$3,941	$5,519
All Greeks	$3,941	$5,519
Exact valuation	$4,605	$6,467

1% 10 day VaR	Dynamic portfolio		Static portfolio	
	Long	Short	Long	Short
Delta only	$15,630	$14,618	$13,612	$12,719
Delta–gamma	$12,443	$17,405	$6,015	$19,392
Delta–gamma–vega	$12,462	$17,453	$6,023	$19,415
Delta–gamma–vega–theta	$12,463	$17,452	$6,024	$19,414
All Greeks	$12,463	$17,452	$6,024	$19,414
Exact valuation	$14,561	$20,451	$7,826	$17,520

VaR would increase, whatever the sign of the portfolio vega. But there is a second effect that is due to the correlation between the index price changes and the volatility changes, which is negative in this case. The net effect of adding the volatility risk factor to the delta–gamma representation is therefore indeterminate; it could increase or decrease the VaR.

It is clear from our results that once a delta–gamma–vega approximation is used, adding further Greeks has little effect on the VaR. But the most striking thing about these results is that the 1% VaR based on the Greeks approximation is considerably *less* than the VaR based on exact revaluation. Why is this difference so large? The main reason is that the historical VaR estimate is driven by some very *large* changes in the risk factors during the historical period. Specifically, there were some large price rises and volatility falls which have affected the long put, and some very large price falls and volatility rises which have affected the short put. A Greeks approximation is only accurate for *small* changes in the risk factors.

Now consider the 10-day VaR figures in the lower part of Table IV.5.10. When we assume daily rebalancing we approximate the 10-day VaR in the spreadsheet labelled 'Dynamic VaR' as the square root of 10 times the 1-day VaR. Under the no rebalancing assumption, we evaluate the 10-day VaR directly, in the spreadsheet labelled 'Static VaR', using overlapping data. The delta–gamma VaR is again less than the delta only VaR, for a long position, and greater than the delta only VaR for a short position. But now we can see that the gamma effect is *much larger* in the static VaR estimate than it is in the dynamic VaR estimate. This is because the dynamic VaR captures only a very small gamma effect, over a 1-day horizon only, and this is much smaller than the gamma effect over an h-day horizon.

This example shows that if we try to estimate VaR for a static options position or portfolio, by scaling up 1-day VaR estimates to a longer risk horizon, we will seriously underestimate the gamma effect on VaR. We would also underestimate the theta effect and distort the vega effect.[40] Instead we should compute static VaR estimates, i.e. we should estimate VaR directly from the h-day P&L distribution, without scaling up a short-term VaR estimate to a longer-term risk horizon, and use exact revaluation if possible. However, the problem with using

---

[40] The vega and theta effects are small for this particular option and risk horizon, but would not be small for long term ATM options held over long risk horizons.

standard historical simulation here is that the tails of the h-day P&L distribution become truncated, so the VaR at extreme percentiles, and the ETL, are underestimated.

The exact revaluation of complex options without analytic expressions for the price requires a significant computational effort. Hence, it is often necessary to use a Greeks approximation to compute historical VaR. But the above example highlights a major problem with the application of Greeks approximation in the estimation of historical VaR for an option portfolio. Historical scenarios on daily changes in the risk factors are not always *small* changes; indeed, it is precisely the *large* changes in the risk factors that influence the VaR estimates, especially at extreme quantiles. Hence the application of standard historical simulation to obtain VaR estimates based on Greeks approximations is prone to imprecision.

The next example shows how delta–gamma–vega approximation is applied to estimate the VaR of a large portfolio containing options on several correlated underlyings. We consider an options trading book held by a UK bank on 31 December 2006, containing standard European options on UK, US and German stocks. The risk factors are the stock index futures and their respective volatility indices. To avoid having to concatenate constant maturity futures time series over a long historical period, we again infer the changes in the futures from the changes in the spot index. Hence, we assume the basis risk is zero, which introduces a small error in the calculation, but this is a very minor source of model risk in VaR models for portfolios of options on major indices.

Figures IV.5.3 and IV.5.4 depict the historical data that will be used in the next example. They are the daily index prices and the corresponding volatility indices, from 4 January 2000 until 31 December 2006 (a total of 1666 observations on each risk factor).[41] Clearly we are estimating the VaR during a relatively tranquil period, compared with the previous examples which measured the VaR on 25 April 2008.

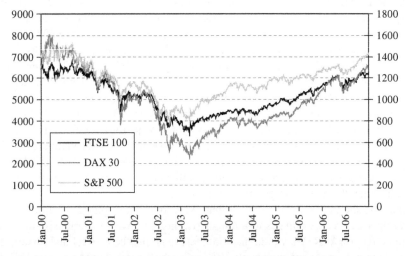

Figure IV.5.3   FTSE 100, DAX 30 and S&P 500 indices

---

[41] In Figure IV.5.3 the S&P index is measured on the right-hand scale and the FTSE 100 and DAX 30 indices are measured on the left-hand scale. All data were downloaded from Yahoo! Finance except for the Vftse index, which was calculated from option prices by my PhD student Stamatis Leontsinis.

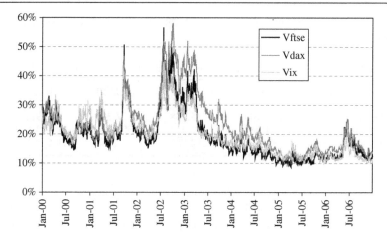

Figure IV.5.4   Vftse, Vdax and Vix volatility indices

The position delta and gamma of each sub-portfolio in UK, US and German stocks may be calculated as described in Section IV.5.3.2. But the position vega is more difficult to estimate, and we refer the interested reader to Section III.5.6 for further details. In the next example we do not compute the position Greeks, and instead we start from the delta–gamma–vega representation of each sub-portfolio.

EXAMPLE IV.5.8: HISTORICAL VAR FOR OPTIONS ON SEVERAL UNDERLYINGS

A portfolio contains various options on the FTSE 100, S&P 500 and DAX 30 futures. The portfolio has not been fully hedged and the position delta, gamma for each sub-portfolio, its position vega with respect to the relevant volatility index, and the point values of the index futures options, are shown in Table IV.5.11. The mark-to-market value of the portfolio is £1 million. Based on the data shown in Figures IV.5.3 and IV.5.4, estimate the 1% 1-day historical VaR of the portfolio on 31 December 2006. Assume that the forex rates are fixed at £/$ = 0.5 and €/$ = 0.75, and that the UK LIBOR curve is flat at 5%.[42]

Table IV.5.11   Position Greeks of large international stock option portfolio

Position Greeks	FTSE 100	S&P 500	DAX 30
Delta	−0.5	−0.2	0.7
Gamma	−0.005	−0.001	0.004
Vega	−150	−100	200
Point value	£10	$250	€5

SOLUTION   First we compute the value delta, value gamma and value vega for each sub-portfolio, expressing these in pounds sterling. Thus we multiply each position Greek by the

---

[42] So that there is no forex risk and no interest rate risk on the portfolio. Note that these fixed values can be changed by the user.

point value for each index and then by the relevant forex rate. The results are shown in Table IV.5.12.

Table IV.5.12   Value Greeks of a large international stock option portfolio

Value Greeks	FTSE	S&P 500	DAX 30	Total
Delta	−£31,104	−£35,458	£17,317	−£49,245
Gamma	−£1,934,918	−£251,447	£652,790	−£1,533,574
Vega	−£1,500	−£12,500	£750	−£13,250

Using the daily data on the equity index closing prices and their volatility indices shown, in Figures IV.5.3 and IV.5.4, we estimate VaR by taking the daily returns on the price and volatility risk factors to simulate a discounted daily P&L due to delta, delta–gamma and delta–gamma–vega approximations. The results for the 1% 1-day VaR are shown in Table IV.5.13.[43]

Table IV.5.13   Historical VaR for a large international stock option portfolio

1% 1-day VaR	
Delta-only	£1,493
Delta–gamma	£2,281
Delta–gamma–vega	£2,405

The net value gamma is large and negative, so adding the gamma effect increases the delta-only VaR considerably. In the absence of any dependence between price and volatility, the effect of adding the volatility risk factor is to increase VaR when vega is positive and to decrease it when vega is negative. In our case the net vega is negative, so adding vega risk would decrease the VaR if the price and volatility risk factors were independent. However, the price and volatility have a negative relationship, and this offsets the decrease in VaR. In fact, in our case the addition of vega risk gives a small increase in VaR.

IV.5.4.4   Historical VaR for Path-Dependent Options

The price of a path-dependent option at the risk horizon depends on the simulations of the risk factors over the risk horizon. For instance, the price of a barrier option depends on whether the underlying price has hit or crossed a barrier at any time before or at the risk horizon. This means that to assess the risk of a path-dependent product, *multi-step* historical simulation must be used, as described in Section IV.3.2.7.

In the following we shall use a look-back call for illustration. The price of a look-back call depends on the minimum of the underlying price between inception and maturity. Its pay-off is $\max(S_T - m, 0)$, where S_T is the underlying price at maturity T, and the strike m is the minimum underlying price achieved between the issue and the expiry of the option.

---

[43] In the spreadsheet readers may scale up the daily VaR estimates to longer horizons using the square-root scaling rule, bearing in mind that the theta, gamma and vega effects will be distorted if the position is in fact static. See Section IV.5.4.1, and Example IV.5.3 in particular.

Under the assumption of geometric Brownian motion with constant volatility for the dynamics of the underlying price S, the price at time t of a look-back call on a non-dividend-paying asset is given in Section III.3.9.9. The option price is

$$\exp\left(-r(T-t)\right)\left(F_t\Phi\left(d_{1t}\right) - m_t\Phi\left(d_{2t}\right) + \lambda^{-1}\left(F_t\Phi\left(-d_{1t}\right) - m_t^\lambda S_t^{1-\lambda}\Phi(-d_{3t})\right)\right), \qquad \text{(IV.5.38)}$$

where T is the expiry date of the option, $F_t = S_t\exp\left(r(T-t)\right)$, m_t is the current strike of the option, i.e. the minimum price on the underlying achieved between the time of issue and time t, r is the discount rate of maturity $T - t$,[44] $\lambda = 2r\sigma^{-2}$, σ is the volatility in the underlying price process, and

$$d_{1t} = \frac{\ln(F_t/m_t)}{\sigma\sqrt{T-t}} + \tfrac{1}{2}\sigma\sqrt{T-t}, \; d_{2t} = d_{1t} - \sigma\sqrt{T-t}, \quad \text{and} \quad d_{3t} = d_{1t} - \lambda\sigma\sqrt{T-t}.$$

EXAMPLE IV.5.9: HISTORICAL VAR FOR A PATH-DEPENDENT OPTION

Estimate the 1% 10-day historical VaR of a European look-back call on the S&P 500 index with 90 days to expiry. Suppose the current strike of the call is 1375 and that the VaR is estimated when the index price is 1400, the volatility is 20% and the 90-day US LIBOR rate is 3%. Base your calculations on the same {price, volatility, interest rate} simulations that were used in Example IV.5.4. How does the VaR for the look-back call compare with the VaR for a standard call option on the S&P 500 index with the same maturity and strike 1375? Use multi-step historical simulation on a static position in each case.

SOLUTION   The current price of the look-back call is calculated using $S = 1400$, $m = 1375$, $\sigma = 20\%$ and $r = 3\%$ in (IV.5.38), giving the current price of the call as 114.23. The option is on the S&P 500 index so we assume its point value is $250, as it is for the CME options. Hence, the current mark-to-market value of the option is $28,558.

We now use the historical simulations to price the look-back call in 10 days' time. First we calculate the strike of the look-back call as the minimum underlying price achieved between the issue of the option and 10 days forward in time, decreasing the option's maturity by 10 days when we value it. Unless the underlying price drops below 1375 over the next 10 days, this will remain at 1375. Note that we use 10 *consecutive* historical price, volatility and interest rate changes when calculating this minimum price. In this way we capture the dynamic properties of the historical scenarios, including any autocorrelated changes in prices, interest rates and volatilities.

Then the 10-day discounted P&L on the option is calculated as the point value times the difference between the discounted simulated option price and the current option price. Finally, the 1% VaR is estimated as -1 times the 1% quantile of the distribution of discounted P&L. The result is a 1% 10-day VaR of only $5249 for a long position and $17,633 for a short position.

We now compare this with the VaR of a 90-day call on the S&P 500 index, with strike equal to the current strike of the look-back call, i.e. 1375. Since the underlying is currently at 1400, the call is deep in the money (ITM) and has a current price of 74.10. In the spreadsheet for this example we use multi-step historical simulation over a 10-day risk horizon, finding that the standard European call has a 1% 10-day VaR of $10,345 for a long position and $19,071 for

---

[44] This also changes with time t but, like volatility, we assume it is constant for the derivation of the price formula.

a short position. These are greater than the corresponding VaRs for the look-back call. This is because the higher delta and the lower gamma of the standard call both augment its VaR.

The advantage of using historical scenarios to estimate the VaR of path-dependent options is that they capture the observed behaviour of the markets. Relying only on the empirical dependence between the risk factors is a clear advantage over using covariance matrices, and historical simulations also provide a natural model for autocorrelation in risk factors (in their returns and/or their squared returns) which can be an important effect to include when assessing the risks of path-dependent options. In the above example we used consecutive historical scenarios, that capture volatility clustering and autocorrelation in price and interest rate changes in an entirely natural way. This has the advantage of requiring no parametric model to capture price and volatility dynamics, but also the disadvantage that VaR at high confidence levels would be underestimated if the sample size is not sufficiently large. When VaR and ETL must be assessed at extreme quantiles and the historical sample size is not very large, then it would be better to use a parametric model such as a GARCH model for the evolution of returns over the risk horizon. That is, instead of standard historical simulation in a multi-step framework based on overlapping samples, the filtered historical simulation method that was described in Section IV.3.3.4 would be preferred.

IV.5.4.5   Case Study: Historical VaR for an Energy Options Trading Book

The case study in this section calculates the historical VaR of a portfolio of options on crude oil futures, using an exposure that represents the commodity options trading desk of a large bank, where there is at least some delta hedging with the underlying futures. In our case the risk factors will be the prices of futures with monthly maturities from 1 month to 6 months, and their ATM implied volatilities. The VaR of the trading book will be calculated on 1 August 2006 using daily closing prices from 2 January 1996 until that date, and the risk factor prices in US dollars per barrel are illustrated in Figures IV.5.5 and IV.5.6.

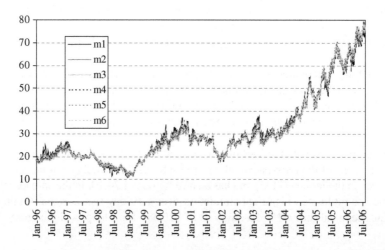

Figure IV.5.5   NYMEX WTI crude oil futures prices

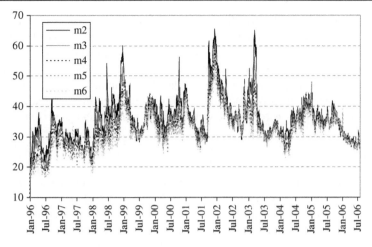

Figure IV.5.6   NYMEX WTI at-the-money volatilities

Risk Factors

Since the Iraq war in 2003 the prices of crude oil have been tremendously volatile, from around $25 per barrel at the time of the war, rising to a high of almost $150 per barrel in June 2008 then falling back to less than $100 per barrel at the time of writing. The volatility of the futures options has fluctuated within the region of 25–60%, with peaks after the terrorist attacks in the US in September 2001 and at the outbreak of the Iraq war. Interesting features of the ATM volatility series are their huge daily variations and the many spikes in volatility; in fact the 1-month ATM volatility has so many spikes that we have omitted it from the graph. These features are apparent in many energy options.

The Portfolio

We shall examine the risk taken by a trader in crude oil options of different maturities. We assume he rebalances his portfolio to keep a net delta, gamma and vega of zero, but he has permission to trade within his portfolio up to the limits shown in Table IV.5.14. These limits reflect the belief that oil prices will fall over the next few months, since the value delta up to 3 months ahead is negative. We shall assume the portfolio is rebalanced daily over the risk horizon, to return the value Greeks to their limit values. Even though the net value delta,

Table IV.5.14   Limits on value Greeks of the crude oil option portfolio

Futures	Value delta ($000)	Value gamma ($000)	Volatilities	Value vega ($000)
m1	−100	−300	ATM m1	−20
m2	−50	200	ATM m2	20
m3	−200	−700	ATM m3	−80
m4	150	300	ATM m4	10
m5	90	100	ATM m5	20
m6	110	400	ATM m6	50

gamma and vega of the portfolio are all zero, the portfolio may still run substantial risks from any non-parallel movements in the futures and volatility term structures. The futures price risk factors are very highly correlated with each other, as are the implied volatility risk factors, but they are not perfectly correlated, and so some movements will be non-parallel shifts.

To keep the analysis simple we are ignoring the cross-gamma effects, i.e. we assume the sensitivities to the second order products of returns on futures of different maturities are zero, so we have specified only a vector for the value gamma, rather than a matrix.

Historical VaR

The calculation of the historical VaR is based on a multivariate delta–gamma–vega representation with six price and six volatility risk factors. Figure IV.5.6 shows that even though the option's volatilities were lower than average at the time VaR is measured, it is quite possible that the volatilities could jump above 40% or more, over a reasonably short time horizon. Hence, we make no volatility adjustment to the portfolio P&L series.

Since we have a dynamically rebalanced portfolio, the 1% 10-day VaR is approximated as minus the lower 1% quantile of the P&L distribution, multiplied by the square root of 10.[45] The results are shown in Table IV.5.15. Whilst the gamma risk appears to be relatively small, quite a different picture might emerge if we assumed a static portfolio over a 10-day horizon. The vega risk is substantial. In commodity option portfolios the price–volatility correlation is usually positive. Hence, the addition of the volatility risk factors increases the VaR. In this case it appears to increase the VaR substantially, because the portfolio is only hedged against parallel movements in the volatility term structure, and crude oil volatility term structures often tilt or change convexity. We shall return to this case study in Section IV.5.5.8, when we explain the use of Monte Carlo simulation to estimate the VaR of the same portfolio.

Table IV.5.15 Historical VaR of the crude oil option portfolio

Delta only	$14,103
Delta–gamma	$14,547
Delta–gamma–vega	$17,940

IV.5.5   MONTE CARLO VALUE AT RISK FOR OPTION PORTFOLIOS

The main purpose of this section is to demonstrate how the repricing algorithm for an option, or an option portfolio, is applied to Monte Carlo simulations. Monte Carlo has the major advantage of generating many thousands of forward looking returns on the risk factors; there are no limitations on sample size as there are with standard historical simulation. To avoid complexity, many of our examples in this section will use an i.i.d. multivariate normal risk

---

[45] And to reduce complexity we ignore the discounting, since this has only a minor effect on the VaR over a 10-day period.

factor log returns assumption. However, very often this distributional assumption is not appropriate, and we know from the previous chapter that many other conditional and unconditional risk factor return distributions could be applied instead. We do need to build a model for risk factor return distributions that accurately represents their empirical behaviour. So another aim of this section is to quantify the impact of the risk factor returns model on the Monte Carlo VaR estimate, and to compare this source of model risk with other sources of error, such as the error induced by the risk factor mapping.

Although options are priced in the risk neutral world, where the futures price is a martingale and therefore has zero expected return, VaR is an assessment of risk in the *real* world. Therefore, we need not assume that the expected return on a futures price is a martingale, or that a spot price returns the risk free rate. In particular, we need not assume that the standard deviation of the underlying returns simulations is derived from the implied volatility of the option, since the option typically has a different maturity than the risk horizon for the VaR. It is the process volatility *over the risk horizon* that we must use in the Monte Carlo simulations for the underlying price. The implied volatility is therefore treated like any other stochastic risk factor, having its own expected return and volatility. Simulations for the underlying price and volatility must also take account of their dependence. For instance, an equity index option price and volatility might be assumed to have an asymmetric negative dependence.

This section adopts an approach that is very similar to that in the previous section, where we first explain the VaR methodology and then derive practical, general results in the context of increasingly complex but realistic examples. The CD-ROM is not large enough to contain many thousands of correlated simulations on all the risk factors for every example. Hence, I have set each workbook to have only 100 simulations. After copying the workbook for each example, readers should extend the number of simulations by filling down the last row of the simulations, and all calculations based on these, in all the spreadsheets of the workbook.[46]

IV.5.5.1   Monte Carlo VaR and ETL with Exact Revaluation

We first explain the steps involved with the computation of Monte Carlo VaR and ETL for a single-asset option assuming that the price and volatility risk factors are i.i.d. with multivariate normal distributions:

1. *State the covariance matrix of the h-day risk factor returns.* For instance, for a single option there are two main risk factors: the underlying price and its implied volatility. Their covariance matrix has three distinct elements: two h-day variances of the underlying and the implied volatility, and the covariance term, which depends on the price–volatility correlation.[47]
2. *Simulate a very large number N of uncorrelated pairs of standard normal draws.* As described in the previous chapter, we take kN random numbers, where k is the number

---

[46] For your convenience I have also switched from automatic to manual calculations. With manual calculations just press F9 to repeat the simulations.

[47] We could also include the discount rate, but this is a very minor risk factor. We shall keep the discount rate as a risk factor for our first empirical example in this section, but since the simulation error is so large, there seems no point in increasing the size and complexity of the subsequent workbooks by keeping the discount rate risk as a risk factor. Hence we shall assume this is constant from Example IV.5.10 onward.

of risk factors, so $k = 2$ in this case, transform them into independent simulations from a standard normal distribution and arrange these into columns in Excel.

3. *Use the expected returns and the Cholesky matrix to transform these columns into correlated simulations on the underlying price S_h and volatility σ_h in h trading days' time, with the targeted expected returns, volatilities and correlation.* First compute the Cholseky matrix of the h-day covariance matrix.[48] Then pre-multiply each pair of uncorrelated simulations by this Cholesky matrix. Also, in the simulated data, use the discounted expected returns on the risk factor, if these are assumed to be non-zero.[49]

4. *Apply each simulated return to the current values of the risk factors.* For instance, consider a simple option having only two risk factors, the underlying price and the implied volatility, with current values $\bar{S}$ and $\bar{\sigma}$. We shall simulate N pairs $\{S_h, \sigma_h\}$ at this stage. We often assume that the simulated returns r_{Sh} and $r_{\sigma h}$ on the underlying price and the implied volatility are log returns, so that

$$S_h = \bar{S}\exp(r_{Sh}) \quad \text{and} \quad \sigma_h = \bar{\sigma}\exp(r_{\sigma h}).$$

5. *Apply the option pricing model to each set of simulated risk factor values and hence simulate a discounted P&L distribution for the option.* For instance, with a simple European option apply the Black–Scholes–Merton formula to each pair $\{S_h, \sigma_h\}$. This gives N possible h-trading-day-ahead option prices f_h. The discounted P&L is then

$$\omega\big(\exp(-r_{h^c}h^c)f_h - f_0\big)pv,$$

where f_0 is the current value of the option, $\omega = 1$ for a long position and -1 for a short position, h^c is the number of calendar days corresponding to h trading days and r_{h^c} is the h^c-day continuously compounded discount rate. We now have N possible discounted P&L values from which we build the empirical distribution.

6. *Obtain the $100\alpha\%$ h-day VaR and ETL.* The $100\alpha\%$ h-day VaR is -1 times the lower α quantile of the distribution of discounted P&L and the $100\alpha\%$ h-day ETL is the average of all the losses that exceed $-$VaR.

The following example estimates the Monte Carlo VaR of the same European option on the S&P 500 index futures that was considered in the previous examples. In the workbook for this example the reader should follow through the calculation of each of the six steps above.[50]

EXAMPLE IV.5.10: MONTE CARLO VAR FOR A STANDARD EUROPEAN OPTION

On 25 April 2008 you sell a European put on the S&P 500 index with strike 1400 and maturity 30 days. The index futures price is at 1398, the market price of the option is 32, and its implied

---

[48] This requires the Excel add-in 'Matrix.xla'.

[49] As already mentioned, although options are priced in the risk neutral measure we assess risk in the physical or real-world measure. Hence, the drift used in the simulations should be the real-world expected return. We could assume that the underlying price returns the risk free rate, but we need not do so in the real world. Also, the implied volatility may be assumed to have an expected return of zero. But our assumption about expected returns usually makes very little difference, since market VaR is typically measured (at least initially) over short risk horizons.

[50] In the spreadsheet the uncorrelated simulations are row vectors, so we post-multiply the row vector by the transpose of the Cholesky matrix, which is equivalent to step 3.

volatility is 19.42%.[51] Assume that the expected return on the risk factors over the next 10 days is zero, except for the futures price which we expect to have the risk free rate of return.[52] Estimate the 1% 10-day Monte Carlo VaR for this static position using the following risk factor returns covariance matrices:

(a) the historical, equally weighted average covariance matrix for the price–volatility process that is estimated using the data shown in Figure IV.5.2;
(b) the option's implied volatility for the futures price volatility, an interest rate volatility of 15% and a volatility of volatility of 50%, a price–volatility correlation of −0.7, and the other risk factor correlations are zero.

How do the results compare with each other, and with the historical 1% 10-day VaR of the same option?

SOLUTION

(a) Using exactly the same data as in Example IV.5.4 allows some comparison between the historical simulation VaR and the multivariate normal Monte Carlo VaR for a simple option. Hence, we shall keep the discount rate as a risk factor, as we did in Example IV.5.4. This also serves to illustrate the Monte Carlo algorithm when there are more than two underlying risk factors, but otherwise we know from Example IV.5.5 that there is little point in assuming that the discount rate is stochastic, except perhaps for measuring VaR for very long term options over a risk horizon of many months, in currencies where interest rates are high.

So, the first step is to compute the risk factor covariance matrix using the historical data shown in Figure IV.5.2. This is calculated in the spreadsheet for that figure and the results are shown in Table IV.5.16.

Table IV.5.16 Historical volatilities and correlations for risk factors of S&P 500 option

Volatilities		
Discount rate	S&P 500	Vix
17.37%	15.90%	91.45%
Correlations		
Discount rate–S&P 500	Discount rate–Vix	S&P 500–Vix
−1.61%	1.28%	−68.33%

When simulations are based on the historical covariance matrix, the 1% 10-day VaR is about $18,000 based on $N = 10,000$ possible future values for the option. From Example IV.5.3, the 1% 10-day historical VaR of the short put based on a square-root

---

[51] To compute the VaR of other European call or put options copy the option price and volatility calculations to a different spreadsheet. Even when calculations are set to manual the simulations will be repeated when you apply Solver or Goal Seek to derive the new implied volatility. I recommend you to calculate the implied volatility in another workbook, and close any workbooks that are using Monte Carlo simulation before doing so.
[52] VaR is estimated in the real-world measure, not the risk neutral measure in which of course a futures price would be a martingale.

scaling rule is $20,407. There are two reasons why this is larger than the Monte Carlo VaR.

- The first reason is that Monte Carlo VaR assumes the risk factors have a multivariate normal distribution, whereas the risk factor returns are highly skewed and leptokurtic. The multivariate normality assumption is a significant source of model risk in this case.
- The second reason is that the historical VaR in this example uses a square-root scaling rule, which distorts the gamma and vega effects. In this case both of these effects would decrease the VaR, if they were properly accounted for.

Recall that, when the 1% 10-day historical VaR is based on overlapping data, the gamma and vega effects are not distorted, but then the distorted tails of the P&L distribution depress the historical VaR estimate. The 1% 10-day historical static VaR estimate (previously calculated in Example IV.5.3) is $18,709. This is still greater than the Monte Carlo VaR estimate, because in this example Monte Carlo VaR assumes the risk factors are i.i.d. normal.

(b) We now use the option implied data to obtain the h-day covariance matrix.[53] This gives a 1% 10-day VaR of the written put option of around $23,500 based on $N = 10,000$ possible future values for the option. This is much greater than in case (a) because we are using the implied volatility in the simulations of the major risk factor, i.e. the underlying futures prices, and this implied volatility happened to be very high at the time when the VaR was measured. However, since VaR estimates are based on a real-world risk factor return distribution, there is no particular reason why we should use the implied volatility for the process volatility in the simulations, especially since the option's maturity is not the same as the risk horizon.

Recall from Table IV.5.2 that the VaR from a long option position, call or put, was very much less than the VaR from a short position on the same option. In the workbook for the above example, change the position to 'long' instead of 'short'. Also change the option to a call with price 32, and therefore with implied volatility 20.67%. Based on the historical covariance matrix, the 1% 10-day VaR from buying the put option is about $7950 and that from buying the call is about $7300. Comparison with Table IV.5.16 shows that these results are similar to the historical VaR results based on overlapping data, but they are very far from the historical VaR estimates based on a square-root scaling rule.[54]

The main learning point from this example is that only Monte Carlo simulation can capture the proper theta, gamma and vega effects on VaR for static option portfolios, because we can estimate the h-day Monte Carlo VaR directly from a simulated h-day P&L distribution. The overriding problem with applying standard historical simulation to static option portfolios is that we need to use overlapping samples (otherwise we do not have enough data) and, as a result, the historical model will underestimate VaR at high confidence levels.

---

[53] Thus the 10-day variance of the futures price is $\sigma^2/25$ where σ is the option's implied volatility, the 10-day variance of the implied volatility is $\xi^2/25$ where ξ is the assumed volatility of volatility, the price–volatility covariance is $\varrho\sigma\xi/25$ where ϱ is the assumed price–volatility correlation, etc.

[54] In fact, the historical VAR estimates based on overlapping data are slightly less than the Monte Carlo estimates. The i.i.d. normal assumption may lead one to suppose that the Monte Carlo VaR estimates will be less than the historical VaR estimates, but the use of overlapping data truncates the tails of the historical h-day risk factor return distribution. This truncation can lead to a significant underestimation of the historical static VaR for option portfolios over long risk horizons and at very high confidence levels.

IV.5.5.2   Risk Factor Models for Simulating Options VaR

Monte Carlo simulation of risk factor returns requires assuming some parametric form for their joint distribution. In the simplest case the risk factor dynamics are assumed to be governed by an i.i.d. multivariate normal process. Multivariate Student t simulations, which still rely on a covariance matrix to capture the highly non-linear price–volatility relationship, could also be used. And, in more general Monte Carlo frameworks, the risk factor returns could have a joint distribution with different marginals and with risk factor dependency represented by a copula. Also, multi-step Monte Carlo techniques could be applied to simulate realistic dynamic features such as volatility clustering in risk factors.[55]

How important are all these 'bells and whistles' for Monte Carlo VaR models applied to option portfolios? It is an established empirical fact that most risk factor returns have highly non-normal, dynamic joint distributions – when returns are measured at a high frequency. But as the frequency of the returns diminishes, the distributions move closer to i.i.d. multivariate normality. In some markets, when risk factor returns are simulated over a 10-day horizon or longer, multivariate normality may not be such an unreasonable assumption to make.

The remainder of this section studies the importance of formulating an appropriate model for the risk factor return distribution, and the importance of theta, gamma and vega effects for different types of portfolio. Using a series of examples based on the same S&P 500 futures options studied in the previous examples of this chapter, we shall verify the following:

- It is important to capture non-normality in the distribution of risk factor returns, but only when risk factor returns have a horizon of no more than a few days.
- It is also important to capture the correct gamma and vega effects in static VaR.
- Asymmetric relationships between risk factors can be important for dynamic VaR estimates.
- Multi-step Monte Carlo VaR estimates should be based on a risk factor model with volatility clustering.

If any of the above features are lacking from the model that underpins Monte Carlo simulations, a substantial model risk will be introduced. However,

- the theta effect is important only when the static VaR is estimated over a very long risk horizon;
- it seems unimportant to capture non-linearity in the price–volatility relationship even for a daily risk horizon.

IV.5.5.3   Capturing Non-normality and Non-linearity

In this subsection we consider the effect of using a multivariate Student t distribution in Monte Carlo VaR. We also examine the effect on VaR of introducing non-linearity into the price–volatility relationship. Potentially, both of these effects will be important, even for a simple portfolio of vanilla options.

To use a multivariate Student t distribution for risk factor returns we simply use standardized Student t simulations rather standard normal simulations at step 2 of the Monte Carlo

---

[55] See Sections IV.4.3.1 and IV.4.4.1.

simulation algorithm. The risk factor returns dependency is still modelled using a correlation matrix. However, such dependency is linear and we know that price and volatility usually have an asymmetric, non-linear relationship. To capture this in the VaR estimate it is possible to derive simulations on the volatility risk factor via an estimated price–volatility model. That is, instead of using the Cholesky matrix to simulate correlated returns on two risk factors, we just take each simulated return on the underlying asset, and use an assumed or empirical non-linear relationship between price and implied volatility to infer the corresponding change in the implied volatility.

It is important to recognize that the extent of non-normality and non-linearity will depend on the frequency for the simulations (e.g. whether simulations are on daily or weekly returns). For instance, if we wish to measure dynamic VaR we should base simulations on the behaviour of the risk factor returns over a short interval such as 1 day. At this frequency the price and volatility returns could be highly non-normal and have a non-linear relationship. But if we wish to measure static VaR over a horizon of a couple of weeks or longer, the risk factor returns are likely to have distributions that are close to normality and an almost linear price–volatility relationship.

For example, consider two samples on S&P 500 index returns and the Vix between 2 January 2000 and 25 April 2008, one with daily and the other with weekly frequency.[56] The sample excess kurtosis of the S&P 500 daily log return was 2.42 and that of the S&P 500 weekly log return was 3.12. There is a highly significant leptokurtosis in *both* samples,[57] so it seems appropriate to model either daily or weekly log returns on the S&P 500 index price using a Student t distribution.[58] On the other hand, we saw in Section IV.4.4.4 that a non-linear price–volatility relationship is only a feature of these data at the daily frequency, not at the weekly frequency.

One of our aims is to investigate the importance of capturing a non-linear price–volatility relationship in the VaR estimate, so we shall keep the model as simple as possible. Based on the results in Section IV.4.4.4, in the next two examples we shall apply the relationship

$$Y_t = -4X_t + 18X_t^2 + \varepsilon_t \qquad (IV.5.39)$$

to each of the simulated log returns X_t on the S&P 500 index, and hence simulate a corresponding value for Y_t, the log return on the Vix. Also based on the results in Section IV.4.4.4, we assume the error has standard deviation 3.75% at the daily frequency, and standard deviation 7.5% at the weekly frequency. Now we can investigate the effect on VaR when we remove the non-linearity from the price–volatility relationship, by removing the quadratic term from (IV.5.39).[59]

EXAMPLE IV.5.11: NON-LINEAR, NON-NORMAL MONTE CARLO VAR

Consider the same European option positions on the S&P 500 index futures as in our previous examples. That is, the call and the put have strike 1400 and maturity 30 days on 25 April 2008. The index futures price is at 1398, the market price of both options is 32, so the put

---

[56] Data downloaded from Yahoo! Finance, symbol ^GSPC and ^VIX.
[57] The approximate standard errors for skewness and excess kurtosis are $6n^{-1/2}$ for the skewness and $24n^{-1/2}$ for the excess kurtosis, where n is the sample size.
[58] Based on a sample excess kurtosis of 2.42, the method of moments estimate of the degrees of freedom in a Student t distribution for S&P 500 daily log returns is 6.48. Similarly, the weekly return distribution has degrees of freedom parameter 5.92, for an excess kurtosis of 3.12. For simplicity, we shall assume the degree of freedom parameter is 6 for both daily and weekly log returns.
[59] For simplicity we assume the error process is normally distributed in each case.

implied volatility is 19.42% and the call implied volatility is 20.67%. Estimate the 1% daily VaR of long and short positions on the put option, and on the call option. Base your results on the non-linear model (IV.5.39) of daily log returns and then, to investigate the effect of non-linearity (i.e. an asymmetric price–volatility relationship) on the VaR estimates, drop the quadratic term from the relationship. Also, to investigate the effect of non-normality, compare the results from using price simulations from a Student t distribution with 6 degrees of freedom with those from assuming a normal distribution for daily returns on the S&P 500.

SOLUTION   In the spreadsheet labelled 'Daily P&L Simulations', we simulate 1-day-ahead futures prices using a normal distribution for the S&P 500 daily log returns. Then we use the model (IV.5.39) to derive the corresponding log return on the Vix, and hence simulate 1-day-ahead call and put implied volatilities. Then the prices of the call and the put are computed for each set of simulated risk factors, and hence the daily P&L distribution is simulated. The 1% daily VaR for a long position is estimated as -1 times the 1% quantile of the daily P&L distribution, and the 1% daily VaR for a short position is the 99% quantile of the daily P&L distribution.[60]

We then change the model (IV.5.39) to remove the quadratic term, thus assuming a symmetric linear price–volatility relationship, and proceed as before. Finally, we repeat both the above, but now we assume a Student t distribution with 6 degrees of freedom for the S&P 500 returns.[61] Table IV.5.17 displays some results, based on two different sets of 5,000 simulations.[62]

Table IV.5.17   Effect of non-linearity and non-normality on 1% daily Monte Carlo VAR

Assumptions	Position	Simulation 1		Simulation 2	
		Put	Call	Put	Call
(a)	Long	$4,450	$3,147	$4,458	$3,071
	Short	$6,461	$4,599	$6,136	$4,667
(b)	Long	$4,557	$3,232	$4,658	$3,155
	Short	$6,464	$4,626	$5,982	$4,655
(c)	Long	$5,400	$3,678	$5,444	$3,635
	Short	$8,484	$6,741	$8,354	$6,821
(d)	Long	$5,794	$3,936	$5,565	$3,918
	Short	$8,601	$6,798	$8,756	$6,451

(a) Non-linear daily model, normal S&P 500 returns
(b) Linear daily model, normal S&P 500 returns
(c) Non-linear daily model, Student t distributed S&P 500 returns
(d) Linear daily model, Student t distributed S&P 500 returns.

It is to be expected that the VaR estimates based on a normal distribution for the S&P returns are less than the corresponding VaR estimates based on a Student t distribution having 6 degrees of freedom. For a long position the VaR estimates based on a Student t distribution are about 20% greater than the normal VaR estimates, and for a short position they are

---

[60] Because the P&L for a short position is minus the P&L for a long position.

[61] To generate results for the assumption that the returns are normally distributed, just set the degrees of freedom parameter in the 'Risk Factor Simulations' spreadsheet to about 200. Remember to press F9 to recalculate, when the automatic calculation option is turned off.

[62] Of course, with only 5000 simulations there is a considerable sampling error in these results, but the workbook is already very large. Readers may like to increase the number of simulations when they have loaded the workbook on to their hard disk.

about 40% greater than the corresponding normal VaR estimates. This validates the assertion made in the previous section, i.e. that it is very important that the Monte Carlo VaR model captures any leptokurtosis in the underlying returns, particularly for positions with negative gamma.

Compared with the non-normality effect, the effect of using a non-linear price–volatility relationship for VaR estimation is insignificant. The non-linear model (IV.5.39) induces an asymmetric negative price–volatility relationship, so compared with the symmetric negative relationship in the linear model the VaR estimates based on the non-linear model should be slightly less for a long position and slightly more for a short position. Whilst the results in Table IV.5.17 do show these features, the differences between the non-linear and linear model VaR estimates are so small that they are well within the simulation error.

IV.5.5.4   Capturing Gamma, Vega and Theta Effects

It is not necessary to assume daily rebalancing with Monte Carlo VaR. Indeed, we did not make this assumption in Example IV.5.10 precisely because it does not capture the proper gamma, vega and theta effects for a static option position. Usually, by far the most important effect to capture is the delta effect, but this assumes a linear relationship between the option portfolio's P&L and that of the underlying. Introducing gamma, vega and theta effects allows one to build a better representation of the option portfolio's P&L distribution.

We already know the following:

- For standard options, the gamma effect decreases the VaR of a long position, and increases the VaR of a short position, and if the gamma is large (e.g. for short dated ATM options) this is the most important effect to capture, over any risk horizon.
- The vega effect depends on the price–volatility correlation. In equity markets, where there is a strong negative relationship between price and volatility (which we believe is also asymmetric but only at a high frequency) the main effect of vega risk is to increase the VaR for a short put position and indeed for any position with positive delta and negative vega, as explained in Section IV.5.2.2.
- The theta effect increases the VaR of a long position, and decreases the VaR of a short position, but this is only important when VaR is measured over a long risk horizon.

The next example compares these three different effects.

EXAMPLE IV.5.12: GAMMA, VEGA AND THETA EFFECTS IN SHORT TERM VAR

Continue the previous example, but this time compute the 1% 5-day VaR for a long and a short position on the call and the put. Compare your results based on the usual alternatives for the rebalancing of the position over the risk horizon, i.e. use

- (a) the daily rebalancing assumption, where the weekly dynamic VaR is the daily VaR multiplied by the square root of 5; and
- (b) the no-rebalancing assumption, where the static VaR is estimated from the P&L distribution that is derived from weekly returns on the risk factors.

In both cases assume the returns on the S&P index have a Student t distribution with 6 degrees of freedom.

SOLUTION   The results are summarized in Table IV.5.18. Comparing the results in (a) with (c), and (b) with (d), we see that it does not matter much whether we use a linear or a non-linear price–volatility relationship. In either case we find that the static VaR is considerably lower than the dynamic VaR, for a long position in either the put or the call. This observation implies that the gamma effect dominates the theta effect for a long position. For the short positions, the gamma effect also dominates the theta effect. This is obvious for the short call, since its static VaR is greater than its dynamic VaR. But the VaR for the short put is also heavily influenced by the vega effect, and with a non-linear daily model the vega effect is distorted by the square-root scaling. That is, the daily rebalancing assumption is overstating the vega effect for this position, especially when based on the non-linear model, so the short put VaR estimates in cases (a) and (c) are too high.

Table IV.5.18   Student t Monte Carlo VAR with and without daily rebalancing

Assumptions	Position	Simulation 1		Simulation 2	
		Put	Call	Put	Call
(a)	Long	$10,807	$7,569	$11,417	$7,553
	Short	$15,360	$11,852	$15,504	$12,402
(b)	Long	$7,517	$5,686	$7,618	$5,779
	Short	$15,260	$13,347	$14,878	$14,293
(c)	Long	$11,027	$7,138	$10,669	$7,169
	Short	$15,185	$12,085	$14,328	$11,782
(d)	Long	$7,598	$5,681	$7,475	$5,668
	Short	$14,718	$13,616	$13,711	$13,113

(a) Dynamic VaR: daily rebalancing over risk horizon, linear daily model,
(b) Static VaR: no rebalancing over risk horizon, linear weekly model
(c) Dynamic VaR: daily rebalancing over risk horizon, non-linear daily model
(d) Static VaR: no rebalancing over risk horizon, non-linear weekly model.

In the above example the options had a large gamma, because they were near ATM and relatively short-dated, and the theta effect was small because we considered only a very short risk horizon. Hence, the gamma effect dominated the VaR. The final example in this subsection demonstrates that the trade-off between gamma, vega and theta effects is quite different when we estimate the VaR for long dated options over a long risk horizon. Again we shall isolate the influence of each effect by comparing the VaR estimates under the assumptions of daily rebalancing over the risk horizon, where the VaR estimate virtually ignores theta and gamma effects and distorts the vega effects for static positions, and the VaR estimate under the static, no rebalancing assumption.

EXAMPLE IV.5.13: THETA EFFECTS IN LONG-TERM VAR

Consider a standard European option on the S&P 500 futures with 500 calendar days to maturity, a strike of 1400, and where both put and call implied volatilities are 20%. The futures price is currently at 1398, and the 1-year LIBOR rate is 3%. The put price is 126.062 and the call price is 124.143. Using the historical covariance matrix of Example IV.5.10, compare the 1% 250-day VaR estimates for long and short positions on the call and the put in turn, that are obtained by

(a) estimating the static VaR from the 250-day P&L distribution directly, and

(b) estimating the dynamic VaR from the daily P&L distribution and scaling this by the square root of 250.

SOLUTION   The results are computed in the spreadsheet for this example, and the VaR estimates based on one set of 10,000 simulations are displayed in Table IV.5.19. In case (a) the 1% 250-day VaR is much greater for a long position than it is for a short position. Hence, the theta effect, which increases the VaR for long positions on standard calls and puts, dominates the gamma effect, which decreases the VaR for long positions and increases the VaR for short positions on standard calls and puts. In case (b) both theta and gamma effects are minimal, because the VaR is measured over a 1-day horizon before scaling to a 250-day risk horizon. Here there is some evidence of a small gamma effect, but the main influence on the VaR is the delta effect. That is, when the VaR of an option is measured over a daily horizon and then scaled to a longer horizon, it behaves almost like the VaR of a linear position on the underlying, and this is why the estimates for case (b) are so much greater than they are for case (a).

Table IV.5.19   Long-term VaR estimates for static and dynamic portfolios

	(a) Static		(b) Dynamic	
	Put	Call	Put	Call
Long	$26,440	$14,291	$300,757	$147,188
Short	$9,537	$8,287	$389,456	$201,961

The above example illustrates that the scaling of a daily VaR for an option portfolio to a long-term VaR produces VaR estimates that are very high indeed. If the VaR relates to a position that is truly static, so there is no trading on the option portfolio over the risk horizon, the practice of scaling short-term VaR estimates up to longer-term estimates would very seriously overestimate the risk. We re-iterate that, due to data limitations, dynamic VaR estimation is usually the only alternative that is available with the standard historical VaR model. It is only with Monte Carlo simulation, or a hybrid method based on filtered historical simulation, that we can obtain realistic estimates of VaR for a static position over a long-term risk horizon.

IV.5.5.5   Path Dependency

Our next two examples investigate whether volatility clustering and autocorrelation effects in risk factor returns are important to include in the Monte Carlo simulation model. In Section IV.5.4.4, Example IV.5.9, we investigated the use of consecutive historical returns to estimate VaR for an option with path-dependent pay-off. There we noted that an advantage of using historical simulation based on h consecutive risk factor returns is that it captures, in a simple and natural way, the complex dependencies between risk factor returns, and the autoregressive behaviour in risk factor returns (and volatility clustering in particular). But it is possible that this entirely non-parametric approach may lead to underestimation of static VaR at very high confidence levels over long risk horizons, due to historical sample size limitations.

Monte Carlo simulation is not limited in sample size, and there are no problems caused by overlap between any two simulated series of consecutive returns. Our next example illustrates the effect on VaR of moving from one-step to multi-step Monte Carlo simulations over the risk horizon. We do not introduce the effect of volatility clustering and autocorrelation in the multi-step simulations until Example IV.5.15.

EXAMPLE IV.5.14: ONE-STEP VERSUS MULTI-STEP MONTE CARLO VAR

Estimate the 1% 10-day Monte Carlo VaR of a European call on the S&P 500 index with 90 days to expiry. Suppose that the current strike of the call is 1375 and that the VaR is estimated when the index price is 1400, the implied volatility is 20% and the 90-day US LIBOR rate is currently at 3%. Hence, the current market price of the call is 74.1. Estimate the VaR of both long and short positions on this option, based on a discounted 10-day P&L distribution that is obtained:

  (a) in *one step*, i.e. by applying the 10-day covariance matrix of the risk factor returns to Monte Carlo simulations of 10-day log returns;
  (b) in *multi-steps*, by applying the 1-day covariance matrix of the risk factor returns to Monte Carlo simulations of 1-day log returns, summing the 1-day log returns along a path to obtain a 10-day log return.

Base your covariance matrix on the same historical data that were used in Example IV.5.9, which is the matrix shown in Table IV.5.22. In each case use the 10-day log returns to simulate values of the risk factors in 10 days' time, hence revalue the option, and simulate a P&L by taking the difference between the discounted value of the simulated option price and the current option price.

SOLUTION   The workbook for this example is a modification of the workbook for Example IV.5.9. When Monte Carlo simulations are performed in *one* step, we obtain VaR estimates of approximately $9800 for the long call and $19,000 for the short call position. When multi-step simulations are used the Monte Carlo VaR changes only marginally, as readers can see in the spreadsheet.[63] The VaR is slightly less than when based on one step of normal simulations, and this makes sense since normal h-day log returns can be consistent with non-normal daily returns.[64] Forcing multi-step Monte Carlo to use normal daily returns could therefore understate the VaR.

The next example extends the above analysis to include volatility clustering and mean-reversion in volatility in the multi-step Monte Carlo VaR model.[65] Recall that Example IV.4.7 generated Monte Carlo simulations on a price risk factor whose volatility is modelled using an asymmetric GARCH process. This captures mean reversion and asymmetric volatility clustering in volatility, and the first of these effects is particularly important. We now implement a symmetric bivariate GARCH process to generate correlated price and volatility simulations, and subsequently we re-estimate the VaR of the option considered in the previous example.[66]

---

[63] Excel may have size problems extending all simulations in all spreadsheets so I recommend that only 5000 simulations are used in this spreadsheet. Notice that our estimates are quite close to the historical VaR estimates that were based on multi-step simulation in Example IV.5.9. Those estimates were approximately $10,300 for the long call and $19,000 for the short call position.

[64] Even when they are skewed and leptokurtic, if we sum h consecutive daily log returns we obtain an h-day log return that has an approximately normal distribution. Provided only that they are i.i.d., the central limit theorem holds, as explained in Section I.3.5.2. Normality 'kicks in' very quickly so, for example for $h = 10$, a normal approximation for the log return distributions is often appropriate even though daily log returns may be far from normal.

[65] Mean-reversion in underlying prices is often negligible, so we shall ignore this.

[66] Following Example IV.4.7, readers should find it relatively straightforward to extend Example IV.5.1.5 to an asymmetric bivariate GARCH process if required.

EXAMPLE IV.5.15: GARCH MONTE CARLO VAR FOR OPTIONS

Estimate the 1% 10-day Monte Carlo VaR of a European call on the S&P 500 index with 90 days to expiry. As in Example IV.5.14, the current strike of the call is 1375 and the VaR is estimated when the index price is 1400 and the implied volatility is 20%. However, here we assume that the 90-day US LIBOR rate is constant.[67] Estimate the VaR of both long and short positions on this option, based on a discounted 10-day P&L distribution that is obtained using multi-step Monte Carlo with a bivariate GARCH model. Assume a constant price–volatility correlation of −0.8 and use the conditional variance equation parameters shown in Table IV.5.20. Compare the result with the simulations based on i.i.d. price and implied volatility log returns, with the same unconditional volatilities as those given in the last row of the table.

Table IV.5.20   Bivariate GARCH model parameters

Parameter	Price variance	Implied volatility variance
ω	3.6E-06	5.0E-05
α	0.06	0.25
β	0.9	0.7
Unconditional volatility	15%	50%

SOLUTION   The first spreadsheet in the workbook for this example generates two sets of random numbers to use for the price and the implied volatility simulations. The second spreadsheet simulates 10-day correlated returns for price and for volatility, based first on the i.i.d. assumption and then on the GARCH volatility models. For comparison, these simulations utilize the same two sets of random numbers. The third spreadsheet prices the option and derives the 10-day discounted P&L under each of the models. The parameters and results are shown in the spreadsheet labelled 'VaR'. In this spreadsheet readers may change the size of the shock to the current price return and see the effect on the GARCH VaR. The results based on one set of 10,000 simulations are summarized in Table IV.5.21.

Table IV.5.21   Monte Carlo VaR for option based on constant volatility and GARCH

Volatility model	No shock		5% shock	
	Constant	GARCH	Constant	GARCH
VaR (long)	$10,194	$10,380	$10,225	$14,137
VaR (short)	$17,572	$18,066	$17,265	$32,186

Even without a shock to the current underlying return the GARCH VaR is marginally greater than the constant volatility VaR, as expected since we have more uncertainty in the model when volatility clusters. As the size of the shock increases so does the difference between the GARCH VaR and the constant volatility VaR. As expected, the VaR of the short call is the most affected by volatility clustering. The same comment applies for a short put option, as readers can see by changing the option type in the spreadsheet.

---

[67] This assumption helps to simplify the workbook, and it make little difference to the results because stochastic discount rates have only a very small effect on 10-day VaR.

Having discussed the importance of path-dependent behaviour in price and volatility risk factor returns, we now explain how Monte Carlo simulations are used to price path-dependent products. We shall illustrate the approach by estimating the Monte Carlo VaR of the same look-back call option that was considered in Example IV.5.9. For comparison we use a risk factor covariance matrix based on the same daily historical data as was previously used to estimate the historical VaR for this option.

EXAMPLE IV.5.16: MONTE CARLO VAR FOR A PATH-DEPENDENT OPTION

In Example IV.5.9 we estimated the historical VaR of a 90-day look-back call. The result was a 1% 10-day VaR of $5249 for a long position and $17,633 for a short position. Estimate the 1% 10-day Monte Carlo VaR of the same option under the assumption that the risk factor returns are i.i.d. and multivariate normal. Base your covariance matrix on same historical data that were used in Example IV.5.9, which is the matrix shown in Table IV.5.22.

Table IV.5.22   Risk factor covariance matrix ($\times 10^4$)

	Discount rate	S&P 500 index	Vix volatility
Discount rate	1.2067	−0.0177	0.0812
S&P 500 index	−0.0177	1.0109	−3.9729
Vix volatility	0.0812	−3.9729	33.4431

SOLUTION   The general method for evaluating VaR for a path-dependent option, and the look-back call pricing formula, are given in Section IV.5.4.4. This example is similar to Example IV.5.9, with one important difference: the underlying price, volatility and interest rates that are used to revalue the option are not taken from consecutive days in a historical data set. Instead they are obtained using correlated Monte Carlo simulations.[68] Even though simulations are only over one day, we may still include a trend in each variable in the simulations, and we shall do this to ensure that we are matching the features of the historical data as closely as possible. Hence, the average daily log return on each risk factor over the historical period is added to each simulated log return. However, readers can verify, by setting them to zero, that these trends have very little effect on the result.

Each revaluation requires the simulation of daily values for all the risk factors over the next 10 days. Only this way can we find the minimum underlying price that is used to value the look-back call 10 days ahead. There is a size limit on the number of such simulations one can perform in Excel. With 5000 simulations of price, volatility and interest rate paths, the 1% 10-day VaR for this option is approximately $6,700 if long and $11,500 if short.

Thus the Monte Carlo VaR estimate of the long position on the look-back call option is higher than the historical VaR, and the opposite is the case for a short position. This is because the historical VaR captures the empirical relationship between price and volatility, which may be non-linear and not i.i.d., whereas our Monte Carlo simulations are using a simple correlation to model their relationship. In the historical data, a long call benefits from the additional

---

[68] Here we are using correlated i.i.d. simulations simply because the workbook would become too complex if we used a bivariate GARCH process for volatility clustering, as in the previous example.

effect of a volatility increase following an underlying price fall, so the Monte Carlo VaR of a long look-back call will be greater than its historical VaR. And a short call does not benefit from the offsetting effect of a volatility decrease following an underlying price rise in the historical data, so its Monte Carlo VaR will be lower than its historical VaR.

IV.5.5.6   Option Portfolios with a Single Underlying

To assess the risk of a portfolio of options, we could value each option exactly for every simulation of the risk factors. However, for large portfolios of exotic and path dependent products on several underlyings, this takes considerable computation time, especially if we wish to decompose the VaR into stand-alone components due to the underlying price and volatility market factors. For this reason a Taylor approximation to the portfolio P&L is commonly used.

In this subsection we illustrate the direct estimation of Monte Carlo VaR, with and without a risk factor mapping based on a Taylor approximation, when all the options are on the same underlying. In this case the same simulations for the underlying price can be applied to all options, but each option will still have its own implied volatility risk factor. Without a portfolio mapping, the high correlation between the implied volatilities of different options needs to be taken into account in the VaR estimate.

The following example illustrates the direct estimation of Monte Carlo VaR, without risk factor mapping, using an extremely simple portfolio containing two standard European options.

EXAMPLE IV.5.17: MONTE CARLO VAR OF STRANGLE: EXACT REVALUATION

A speculator takes a short strangle position on S&P 500 index futures options with maturity 60 days.[69] That is, he sells two 60-day options, an ITM call and an ITM put. Suppose that the call has strike 1350 and implied volatility 25%, and that the put has strike 1450 and implied volatility 20%. The 60-day US LIBOR rate is 5%, the futures price is currently at 1400 and risk factor volatilities and correlations are shown in Table IV.5.23. Estimate the 1% 10-day VaR of the short strangle position.

Table IV.5.23   Risk factor volatilities and correlations

Volatilities		
S&P 500 futures	1350 implied volatility	1450 implied volatility
20%	60%	50%

Correlations		
	S&P 500 futures	1350 implied volatility	1450 implied volatility
S&P 500 futures	1	−0.75	−0.7
1350 implied volatility	−0.75	1	0.95
1450 implied volatility	−0.7	0.95	1

---

[69] See Section III.3.5 for a description of the strangle and other options strategies.

SOLUTION   In this example there are three major risk factors: the underlying price and two implied volatilities. Hence, the covariance and Cholesky matrices are 3×3 matrices. For each triple of simulated values for {price, 1350 implied volatility, 1450 implied volatility} we calculate the discounted P&L on the strangle position by adding the discounted P&L on the call to that of the put. Since we have a short strangle position, each P&L is estimated by taking the simulated option value from the current value of the option. All prices are, as usual, calculated using the Black–Scholes–Merton formula and the current values are 83.42 for the call and 23.67 for the put.

Based on 10,000 simulations the 1% 10-day VaR estimate for the short strangle position is about $20,000. Of course, because of its strong negative gamma, a short strangle has much greater VaR than a long strangle: the 1% 10-day VaR of the corresponding long strangle is about $4500.

When a portfolio contains many options there are a very large number of risk factors, even when all the options are on the same underlying. A portfolio with n options has $n + 1$ major risk factors – the underlying price and n different implied volatilities – excluding the minor risk factors such as discount rates and dividends. We also know that when VaR is estimated over long risk horizons it is important to include maturity effects.

To apply Monte Carlo VaR with risk factor mapping we follow steps 1–6 of the algorithm outlined in Section IV.5.5.1, but at step 5 we revalue the position using the risk factor mapping rather than the option pricing model. For instance, under a delta–gamma–vega–theta approximation the (undiscounted) price of a single option in h trading days' time is simulated as

$$f_h \approx f_0 + \theta \Delta t + \delta \Delta S + \tfrac{1}{2}\gamma(\Delta S)^2 + \nu \Delta \sigma, \qquad (IV.5.40)$$

where ΔS is the difference between the simulated underlying price (derived from a simulated h-day log return on S) and the price today, $\Delta \sigma$ is the difference between the option's implied volatility (derived from a simulated h-day log return on σ) and the volatility today, and δ, γ, ν and θ are the option's delta, gamma, vega and theta. Having revalued the portfolio approximately, we obtain an approximate discounted P&L which is, as before, given by (IV.5.37).

We can extend this to an approximation where there is more than one option in the portfolio, if all the options' implied volatilities are vega-mapped to a single reference implied volatility, σ. Then we simply use the net position delta, gamma, vega and theta in (IV.5.40). More generally, there may be several position vegas and implied volatility risk factors in the vega mapping, and correspondingly there will be several vega terms in the expression for the discounted P&L.

One of the advantages of Monte Carlo VaR is that we do not require a long data history. Multivariate normal or Student t Monte Carlo VaR only requires the risk factor returns covariance matrix and this could be estimated using daily returns over the past six months or even less. In fact, it need not be estimated from historical data at all. Nevertheless, in the next example we use the risk factor returns covariance matrix derived from the risk factor volatilities and correlations in Table IV.5.16, which are based on over 18 years of data. This is only because we want to compare the results from the next example with those obtained for the same portfolio using historical VaR, in Example IV.5.7. The portfolio is very simple: in fact we have just a single option on the S&P 500 index and we measure the Monte Carlo VaR based on different Taylor expansions for the change in portfolio value. The underlying risk factors are the S&P 500 index price, the Vix implied volatility index and the risk free interest rate of maturity equal to that of the option.

EXAMPLE IV.5.18: MONTE CARLO VAR WITH DELTA–GAMMA–VEGA MAPPING

Consider a European put on the S&P 500 index with strike 1400 and maturity 30 days. The index futures price is at 1398, the market price of the option is 32, its delta is -0.4980 and its implied volatility is 19.42%.[70] Use the covariance matrix derived from Table IV.5.16 to estimate the 1% 10-day Monte Carlo VaR and ETL of the option under the assumption that the risk factor log returns are i.i.d. with a multivariate normal distribution. Base the P&L on delta-only, delta–gamma, delta–gamma–vega and delta–gamma–vega–theta approximations and compare results with the historical VaR results for the same option, shown in Table IV.5.10.

SOLUTION   There are three risk factors, the price, the volatility and the discount rate. By contrast with historical VaR, Monte Carlo VaR only uses the covariance matrix of the returns; all the other information in the returns is disregarded. Moreover, we shall assume that the risk factors have a multivariate lognormal distribution, so we use correlated normal simulations for the log returns on the risk factors. As well as the 10-day static VaR (derived directly from the 10-day log returns, simulated using the 10-day covariance matrix) we shall simulate daily log returns using the 1-day risk factor covariance matrix, and multiply the daily VaR estimate by the square root of 10 to obtain a 10-day dynamic VaR estimate.[71]

The only difference between the VaR estimates in this example and those in Example IV.5.7 is that the correlated risk factor changes used in the Taylor expansion are generated by Monte Carlo simulation, as explained above, rather than being based on historical data. The workbook has two spreadsheets for P&L calculations, one for daily P&L and the other for h-day P&L. Table IV.5.24 displays the results based on 10,000 simulations. The P&L simulations are based on various Greeks approximations, shown in the first column of this table, and taking the appropriate quantile of the simulated P&L distributions gives the Monte Carlo VaR estimates in the columns headed (a) and (b). For comparison, in columns (c) and (d) we include the historical VaR results from Table IV.5.10.

Table IV.5.24   Comparison of Monte Carlo and historical VaR

1% 10-day VaR	Monte Carlo				Historical			
	(a) Dynamic		(b) Static		(c) Dynamic		(d) Static	
	Long	Short	Long	Short	Long	Short	Long	Short
Delta only	$12,643	$13,216	$11,998	$13,930	$15,630	$14,618	$13,612	$12,719
Delta–gamma	$10,577	$15,474	$6,067	$21,868	$12,443	$17,405	$6,015	$19,492
Delta–gamma–vega	$10,577	$15,456	$6,045	$21,853	$12,462	$17,453	$6,023	$19,415
Delta–gamma–vega–theta	$10,578	$15,455	$6,045	$21,852	$12,463	$17,452	$6,024	$19,414

---

[70] To compute the VaR of other European call or put options copy the option price and volatility calculations to a different spreadsheet. Even when calculations are set to manual, simulations will be repeated when you apply Solver or Goal Seek to derive the new implied volatility, and it will take a very long time unless you use another workbook!

[71] That is, the position is first assumed to be held static, and then assumed to be rebalanced daily to return the risk factor sensitivities to their values at the time the VaR is measured.

For reasons already explained, the gamma effect is much larger in the static VaR estimates than in the dynamic VaR estimates. Comparing the first two results in column (b), the 1% 10-day VaR of a long position on the put is virtually halved when the gamma effect is included, and the corresponding VaR for a short position is increased by approximately 50% when we include the gamma effect from a static position. Comparing columns (a) and (c), the dynamic Monte Carlo VaR estimates (i.e. those that assume rebalancing over the risk horizon) are less than the corresponding historical VaR estimates; this is because the empirical P&L distribution is heavy-tailed. Comparing columns (b) and (d), the static Monte Carlo VaR estimates can be greater than or less than the historical static VaR estimates. However, we know the historical VaR based on overlapping data in column (d) is likely to underestimate the risk of both long and short positions at high confidence levels, because the tail behaviour is distorted. Without this distortion the Monte Carlo estimates, being based on i.i.d. normal risk factors, would no doubt be less than the historical VaR estimates.

The most important feature of this example is the difference between the static and dynamic VaR results. It provides yet another illustration that, whilst this may be acceptable for linear portfolios, for option portfolios we cannot just scale up a 1-day VaR to an h-day VaR, using the square-root-of-time rule or some other power law for scaling, unless it is appropriate to assume the portfolio is rebalanced daily to keep its risk factor sensitivities constant over the risk horizon. For static positions we need to simulate h-day risk factor returns, and the only way we can do this without using overlapping data is to use Monte Carlo methods.

IV.5.5.7   Option Portfolios with Several Underlyings

The major risk factors of a portfolio containing options on n underlying assets are the asset prices $\{S_1, \ldots, S_n\}$. There are also many implied volatility risk factors that are important, and these need mapping to a reduced set of implied volatility risk factors. In the simplest form of vega mapping we would assume the implied volatilities of all the options on S_i are mapped to a single volatility risk factor σ_i, so that there are only n volatility risk factors, which we denote by $\{\sigma_1, \ldots, \sigma_n\}$.[72] Using only the price risk factors, a multivariate delta – gamma approximation of the form (IV.5.6) may be used to approximate the P&L of an option portfolio resulting from small changes in all the risk factors. As usual, we shall illustrate the method with an empirical example.

EXAMPLE IV.5.19: MONTE CARLO VAR WITH MULTIVARIATE DELTA–GAMMA MAPPING

Consider a portfolio of options on bonds and on equities with a P&L that has the delta–gamma approximation

$$P\&L \approx \begin{pmatrix} 1 & 5 \end{pmatrix} \begin{pmatrix} R_E \\ R_B \end{pmatrix} + \tfrac{1}{2} \begin{pmatrix} R_E & R_B \end{pmatrix} \begin{pmatrix} 25 & -7.5 \\ -7.5 & 125 \end{pmatrix} \begin{pmatrix} R_E \\ R_B \end{pmatrix}.$$

The units of measurement are millions of dollars. Thus the net value delta is $1 million with respect to the bond index and $5 million with respect to the equity index. The value gamma matrix is also measured in millions of dollars. Suppose that the returns on the bond and equity indices are normally distributed with volatilities of 30% and 20% and a correlation of -0.25.

---

[72] Of course, many other methods of vega mapping are possible (see Section III.5.5.2 for further details) and we adopt this simple mapping here only because our purpose is to illustrate the Monte Carlo VaR methodology, not the pros and cons of different vega mappings.

Estimate the 1% 10-day VaR of the static portfolio using Monte Carlo simulation based on a delta–gamma mapping, assuming zero discounting. How does your result compare with the Monte Carlo VaR based on a delta-only mapping?

SOLUTION   The 10-day risk factor covariance matrix has the Cholesky decomposition shown in the spreadsheet, and this is applied to simulate correlated returns on bonds and equities. Then, for each pair of simulations, the delta–gamma approximation (IV.5.6) is applied; discounting this gives the delta–gamma approximation to the portfolio's 10-day P&L; then taking the 1% quantile of this distribution gives the 1% 10-day delta–gamma VaR as -1 times this quantile. Dropping the three second order terms in the delta–gamma approximation gives the corresponding VaR estimate based on delta approximation only. Averaging results over several sets of 10,000 simulations, we obtain a 1% 10-day delta-only VaR estimate that is very close to $450,000. But when based on delta–gamma approximation, the 1% 10-day VaR estimate falls to approximately $130,000.

We can compare our results with those obtained in Example IV.5.2, where we used a Johnson SU distribution to estimate the 1% 10-day VaR of this same portfolio. We found that the delta-only VaR was $451,096, which is very close to the Monte Carlo result, but the delta–gamma VaR was $261,024. Since gamma effects give rise to a highly non-normal P&L distribution for the portfolio (as seen in Figure IV.5.1), our results show that the Johnson distribution does not capture as much of a gamma effect as the Monte Carlo approach. The VaR at extreme quantiles such as 1% is very much influenced by the tail behaviour of the P&L distribution, and it is not easy to capture this with an analytic approximation.

Finally, we illustrate the use of a *multivariate delta–gamma–vega* approximation to estimate the VaR of an option portfolio using Monte Carlo simulation. The Taylor approximation is of the form

$$\Delta P \approx \delta'_\$ \Delta \mathbf{R} + \tfrac{1}{2} \Delta \mathbf{R}' \boldsymbol{\Gamma}_\$ \Delta \mathbf{R} + \mathbf{v}'_\$ \Delta \boldsymbol{\sigma}, \qquad (IV.5.42)$$

where the risk factor sensitivities are measured in value terms, $\mathbf{R}$ is the vector of returns on the underlying assets and σ is a vector of volatility risk factors. Taking a portfolio that we have already considered (in Example IV.5.8) the last example of this chapter uses a multivariate delta–gamma–vega approximation to compare the Monte Carlo VaR with the historical VaR. We shall make the following assumptions:

- Exchange rates are constant and we ignore discounting.
- The risk factor returns have a multivariate normal distribution.
- Their covariance matrix is based on the same historical data as that used in Example IV.5.7.

EXAMPLE IV.5.20: MONTE CARLO VAR WITH MULTIVARIATE DELTA–GAMMA–VEGA MAPPING

A portfolio contains various options on the FTSE 100, S&P 500 and DAX 30 futures. The portfolio has not been hedged and the position delta, the gamma for each sub-portfolio, its position vega with respect to the relevant volatility index, and the point values of the index futures options, were shown in Table IV.5.11. The mark-to-market value of the portfolio is £1 million. Assume that the forex rates are fixed at £/$ = 0.5 and €/$ = 0.75, and that the UK

LIBOR curve is flat at 5%.[73] The volatilities and correlations of the risk factor returns, derived from the data shown in Figures IV.5.3 and IV.5.4, are given in Table IV.5.25.[74] Estimate the 10-day Monte Carlo VaR of the static portfolio.

Table IV.5.25   Risk factor volatilities and correlations

	FTSE 100	S&P 500	DAX 30	Vftse	Vix	Vdax
FTSE 100	18.35%	0.474	0.754	−0.720	−0.388	−0.630
S&P 500	0.474	18.24%	0.612	−0.383	−0.737	−0.465
DAX 30	0.754	0.612	26.43%	−0.603	−0.461	−0.727
Vftse	−0.720	−0.383	−0.603	92.80%	0.686	0.954
Vix	−0.388	−0.737	−0.461	0.686	84.90%	0.545
Vdax	−0.630	−0.465	−0.727	0.954	0.545	71.75%

SOLUTION   The workbook for this example is very similar to the workbook for Example IV.5.8, except that we have used Monte Carlo simulation instead of historical simulation to generate the 10-day returns on the price risk factors and the changes in the volatility risk factors. Table IV.5.26 compares the results, averaged over several sets of 10,000 simulations, with the historical 1% 10-day VaR results based on Example IV.5.8.[75]

Table IV.5.26   Monte Carlo versus historical VaR for a large international stock option portfolio

1% 10-day VaR	Monte Carlo static VaR	Historical dynamic VaR
Delta-only	£3,480	£4,723
Delta–gamma	£7,850	£7,213
Delta–gamma–vega	£7,590	£7,606

With only a delta approximation, the Monte Carlo VaR is smaller than the historical VaR. This is because the model assumes that risk factor returns have a multivariate normal distribution, whereas their empirical distributions are in fact highly leptokurtic. But when the gamma effects are included the Monte Carlo VaR is greater than the historical VaR. This is because the historical VaR is dynamic, so it underestimates gamma effects, and in our case the gamma effect will increase the VaR because the net value gamma of the portfolio is negative.

In general the inclusion of volatility as a second risk factor would decrease the VaR of this portfolio, because the net vega of the portfolio is negative. However, the negative price–volatility correlation offsets this decrease. With a strong negative correlation between the price and volatility risk factors, such as is apparent mainly in daily data, the VaR could increase when vega effects are added. Indeed, we see this in the historical VaR estimates. By contrast, the inclusion of vega effects marginally reduces the Monte Carlo VaR, compared with the delta–gamma approximation. Well, we already know that correlation is too crude a statistical tool for capturing the empirical characteristics of the price–volatility relationship!

---

[73] But as usual, these can be changed in the spreadsheet.
[74] In this table volatilities are along the diagonal and correlations are on the off-diagonals.
[75] The historical VaR estimates are $\sqrt{10}$ times the figures displayed in Table IV.5.13.

IV.5.5.8   Case Study: Monte Carlo VaR for an Energy Options Trading Book

In Section IV.5.4.5 we estimated the historical VaR of a portfolio of options on crude oil futures on 1 August 2006, using daily closing prices from 2 January 1996 until that date. This section calculates the Monte Carlo VaR of the same portfolio, using the same historical data to compute the risk factor model parameters. When specifying the risk factor returns model, a series of workbooks explain how we move from a basic i.i.d. multivariate normal risk factor return distribution to one that includes the features that are known to be exhibited by empirical risk factor returns.

The portfolio was characterized by its delta, gamma and vega limits, shown in Table IV.5.14. For comparison, we shall estimate both static and dynamic Monte Carlo VaR estimates, over a 10-day horizon. The dynamic VaR measures the risk if the trader stays at his limits, whereas the static VaR assumes the positions are left unmanaged for a 10-day period.

Twelve-Dimensional Multivariate Normal Distribution

Table IV.5.27 shows the correlations between daily returns on the futures (below the diagonal) and between daily changes in volatility (above the diagonal, shaded). The returns correlations are extremely high, and they decrease as the maturity gap increases, just as in any highly correlated term structure. The correlations between the implied volatility risk factor returns are lower than the correlations between the price risk factor returns, although they do increase with the options' maturities.

Table IV.5.27   Risk factor correlations

	m1	m2	m3	m4	m5	m6
m1	1.000	0.549	0.487	0.449	0.389	0.387
m2	0.962	1.000	0.889	0.820	0.751	0.708
m3	0.945	0.994	1.000	0.847	0.778	0.734
m4	0.931	0.986	0.997	1.000	0.760	0.731
m5	0.918	0.976	0.991	0.998	1.000	0.710
m6	0.906	0.966	0.983	0.994	0.999	1.000

The full 12×12 covariance matrix of price returns and volatility changes may be used to simulate values for the option portfolio; to these we apply a delta–gamma–vega mapping, and from the simulated P&L distribution we estimate the portfolio VaR. Unlike historical simulation, we are not constrained to assume the portfolio is rebalanced to constant risk factor sensitivities over the risk horizon. We may assume this, for instance if we want to estimate the VaR of the portfolio if the trader stayed at the limits shown in Table IV.5.14. Alternatively, we can examine the risk of an unmanaged 'static' portfolio, keeping the holdings constant over the risk horizon, and in that case we would simulate h-day risk factor changes to obtain a distribution for h-day P&L.

In workbook (a) the spreadsheet labelled 'Static' uses the Cholesky matrix of the h-day covariance matrix to simulate multivariate normal risk factor changes and then applies the risk factor mapping for the h-day P&L; and the spreadsheet labelled 'Dynamic' uses the same random numbers but applies the Cholesky matrix of the 1-day covariance matrix to obtain the daily P&L distribution. Then the results are shown, along with the (adjustable) holdings for the portfolio, in the sheet labelled 'VaR'. Some results for a 1% 10-day VaR based on 10,000 simulations are shown in Table IV.5.28, and the results from the historical VaR case study in Section IV.5.4.5 are also shown for comparison.

Table IV.5.28   Monte Carlo VaR of the crude oil option portfolio

1% 10-day VaR	Historical (dynamic)	Monte Carlo (dynamic)	Monte Carlo (static)
Delta only	$14,103	$12,775	$12,775
Delta–gamma	$14,547	$13,585	$15,638
Delta–gamma–vega	$17,940	$15,652	$17,263

The delta-equivalent Monte Carlo VaR is the same under the rebalancing (dynamic) or no rebalancing (static) assumptions, because the delta-only VaR assumes the portfolio is linear. The historical VaR figures in the first column may be compared with the Monte Carlo VaR estimates for a dynamic portfolio. Due to the normality assumption, the Monte Carlo model underestimates the delta-equivalent VaR, relative to the historical VaR.

The size of the gamma effect is about the same in both of the dynamic models, but much larger in the static model, for reasons we have discussed many times in this chapter. The influence of the vega effect is more difficult to predict. In this case it is large according to the historical model, but smaller in the Monte Carlo models, again because these assume multivariate normality when other distributions for volatility changes would be a better choice. The static Monte Carlo model predicts the smallest vega effect of all, but since this also has the largest gamma effect the delta–gamma–vega Monte Carlo static VaR estimate lies between the VaR estimates from the two dynamic models.

The i.i.d. multivariate normal Monte Carlo model cannot represent many important empirical characteristics of the market, and so it should be improved to allow non-normal risk factor returns. For example, the multivariate Student t, mixture or copula distributions for underlying returns would be a better choice than a multivariate normal. The risk factor returns model should also be extended to allow for volatility clustering, as we know this has an important influence on results in markets such as this.

In practice, it is not easy to use better statistical models for the risk factor returns of such large portfolios, because the price and volatility risk factors are so numerous. A typical energy options portfolio will have many different future prices as underlyings, and each underlying will have a whole surface of associated implied volatility risk factors. Hence, using advanced dynamic statistical models for risk factor return distributions in the simulations can become complex and time-consuming. How much accuracy would be lost if we applied standard techniques such as principal component analysis and vega mapping to reduce the dimension of the risk factor space? This would achieve a very effective reduction in dimensionality if the trader is trading right across the term structure, but how accurate will the results be?

Principal Component Analysis

The high correlations between crude oil futures returns indicate that little accuracy would be lost by using PCA to reduce the dimension of the price risk factor space. We now show that the VaR computations may be simplified, with very little loss of accuracy, by simulating the values for two or three principal component factors rather than the entire term structure of futures prices. Additionally, using PCA has the advantage of identifying the main sources of risk. That is, we can decompose the VaR into components corresponding to trends, tilts and convexity changes in the term structure of futures prices.

The results of applying PCA to the 10-day historical covariance matrix are obtained in workbook (b) and are displayed in Tables IV.5.29 and IV.2.30. Since the eigenvalues scale with h, the eigenvalues of the daily covariance matrix are one-tenth of the values shown in Table IV.2.29. This eigenvalue analysis shows that the first principal component alone explains over 97% of the total variation in the futures prices over the historical period. One might be tempted to represent the futures price returns using only one component, i.e. to assume the returns are perfectly correlated along the term structure. Alternatively, using two principal components in our delta–gamma representation does not assume the returns are perfectly correlated in our simulations, which is more realistic, and hardly any accuracy will be lost because the two components together explain 99.58% of the historical variation in the system. We shall report results using first one and then two components in the representation.

Table IV.5.29   Eigenvalues of 10-day historical covariance matrix for crude oil futures

Order	1	2	3	4	5	6
Eigenvalue	0.0218453	0.0005635	7.92941E-05	1.11954E-05	1.9019E-06	4.2446E-07
Variation	97.08%	2.50%	0.35%	0.05%	0.01%	0.00%

The normalized eigenvectors that generate the first two components are shown in Table IV.5.30.[76] Note that the first eigenvector, which captures the common trend in the futures term structure, is not a parallel shift.

Table IV.5.30   Normalized eigenvectors for first two eigenvalues in Table IV.5.29

w_1	w_2
0.48457	0.80597
0.44399	0.05473
0.40981	−0.14720
0.38441	−0.26294
0.36371	−0.33402
0.34651	−0.38084

The eigenvectors are used to compute the net value delta and gamma of the portfolio with respect to the first two principal components. The net value deltas are given by[77]

$$\delta_{P_1}^{\$} = \sum_{i=1}^{6} \delta_i^{\$} w_{i1} \quad \text{and} \quad \delta_{P_2}^{\$} = \sum_{i=1}^{6} \delta_i^{\$} w_{i2}, \tag{IV.5.43}$$

---

[76] We use eigenvectors that are normalized to have unit length, i.e. the sum of the squared elements of each eigenvector is one. Note that these eigenvectors are invariant under scaling the covariance matrix. Also, the diagonal matrix of eigenvalues Λ is recovered using the spectral decomposition, i.e. $\Lambda = W' \Omega W$, as demonstrated in the spreadsheet labelled 'PCA'. This is important, since these eigenvalues are the variances of the principal components in the simulations, and without such normalization the futures returns that are implicit in the simulations will not have the correct variance.

[77] This is mathematically the same as mapping deltas and gammas under price beta mapping. See Sections IV.5.2.1 and III.5.5.5 for further details.

where $\delta_i^\$$ is the value delta on the i-month futures, shown in Table IV.5.14, and w_{ij} is the ith element of the jth eigenvector shown in Table IV.5.30.

Even though the value gammas in Table IV.5.14 ignored the cross-gamma effects, so we only had a vector rather than a matrix of value gammas with respect to the futures prices, we cannot ignore cross-gamma effects in the principal component representation. The net value gammas with respect to the first two components and their cross-gamma are given by

$$\gamma_{P_1^2}^\$ = \sum_{i=1}^{6} \gamma_i^\$ w_{i1}^2, \quad \gamma_{P_2^2}^\$ = \sum_{i=1}^{6} \gamma_i^\$ w_{i2}^2 \quad \text{and} \quad \gamma_{P_1 P_2}^\$ = \sum_{i=1}^{6} \gamma_i^\$ w_{i1} w_{i2}, \tag{IV.5.44}$$

where $\gamma_i^\$$ is the value gamma on the i-month futures, shown in Table IV.5.14.

Given these formulae, we can now calculate the net value deltas and gammas corresponding to the two principal components as

$$\delta_{P_1}^\$ = -\$24,107, \quad \delta_{P_2}^\$ = -\$165,290,$$

$$\gamma_{P_1^2}^\$ = -\$42,991, \quad \gamma_{P_2^2}^\$ = -\$119,531 \quad \text{and} \quad \gamma_{P_1 P_2}^\$ = -\$165,336.$$

This shows that although the portfolio has a net value delta of zero and a net value gamma of zero, the portfolio is not immune to the most likely movements in the futures term structure. The most common movement, i.e. the common trend, is represented by the first eigenvector, and this is not a parallel shift. The large exposures to the second component, a tilt, reflects the fact that these movements, which ensure the futures prices are less than perfectly correlated, explain less than 3% of the historical movements.

The advantages of using PCA in Monte Carlo simulations are the identification of the key risks in a portfolio, the reduction in dimension of the risk factor space and the use of orthogonal risk factors. It is simple to translate the deltas and gammas with respect to the futures price changes into deltas and gammas with respect to the principal components, and it is straightforward to simulate values for two orthogonal components, with variances given by the first two eigenvalues shown in Table IV.5.29.[78] Then we just apply the delta-only or delta–gamma mapping to the principal components, with the value delta and gamma shown above, to simulate the portfolio P&L distribution.

Table IV.5.31 reports the 1% 10-day VaR based on independent normal, and then independent Student t, simulations of the principal component risk factors. For comparison, a common set of random numbers is used to generate the results, which are based first on the net delta and then on the net delta-gamma representation of the portfolio. First we assume daily rebalancing to the limit values, and so we can compare our results with the centre column of Table IV.5.28, i.e. \$12,775 for the delta-only VaR and \$13,585 for the delta–gamma VaR. Then we assume the portfolio is static, so we can compare our results with those shown in the last column of Table IV.5.28, i.e. the same delta-only VaR but \$15,638 for the delta–gamma VaR.

The first two columns of Table IV.5.31 report the 1% 10-day VaR of the portfolio when the futures prices are assumed to be perfectly correlated, and represented by the common trend component with eigenvector w_1 in Table IV.5.30. The second two columns present the same results but modified with the addition of a second component. Comparison with our earlier results shows that the delta-only VaR is substantially underestimated unless we use

---

[78] In general, we could of course use more than two principal components if this is needed for an acceptable degree of accuracy.

Table IV.5.31   Monte Carlo PC VaR for the portfolio of crude oil options

Dynamic	1 component		2 components	
Distribution	Normal	Student t	Normal	Student t
Delta only	$8,241	$9,061	$12,400	$12,881
Delta–gamma	$9,035	$10,021	$12,846	$14,051
Static	1 component		2 components	
Distribution	Normal	Student t	Normal	Student t
Delta only	$8,512	$9,533	$12,362	$13,105
Delta–gamma	$11,192	$12,894	$14,144	$16,759

both components. Only then are they capturing the essential features of dynamic and static VaR estimates. And, as expected, the use of a leptokurtic distribution for the principal components increases the VaR. The results shown in Table IV.5.31 are for 6 degrees of freedom in the Student t distribution. The further enhancement of the simulations for two principal components, for instance to include volatility clustering, is left as an exercise to the experienced reader.

Vega Mapping

We now turn to the problem of the volatility risk factors. Should we reduce the dimension of this risk factor space, and if so how? The original mapping of vega to ATM implied volatilities is already introducing a considerable model risk. What sort of additional modelling errors might be introduced by using only one or two volatility risk factors in total?

We already know that PCA on volatilities is unlikely to work as well as it does for the price risk factors, because the ATM implied volatilities are not as highly correlated as the prices. Readers could try applying PCA to the volatilities, but if we aim to reduce dimensions in this way (as we did for the price risk factors) there will be large approximation errors. So to illustrate a different type of mapping now – which could also have been applied to the price risk factors, as explained in Section III.5.5.5, though perhaps with less success than the principal component mapping – we shall use a *volatility beta mapping*, as explained in Section III.5.6.4.

An *ad hoc* choice of the 3-month volatility as the reference volatility is made. Although it may be advisable to use volatility betas relative to this reference volatility that are more risk sensitive than OLS estimates, we can quickly look at the performance of the simple volatility OLS beta estimators

$$\hat{\beta}_i = \frac{est.\text{Cov}(\Delta\sigma_i, \Delta\sigma_3)}{est.V(\Delta\sigma_3)}, \tag{IV.5.45}$$

where $\Delta\sigma_i$ denotes the i-month ATM volatility. If these perform badly relative to the historical model, it may not be worth the effort trying to refine this approach with more sensitive beta estimates. The volatility beta estimates based on the entire historical sample are shown in Table IV.5.32. The differing sizes of these betas reflects the lack of correlation in the behaviour of the implied volatilities.

Table IV.5.32   Volatility beta estimates relative to 3-month volatility

m1	m2	m3	m4	m5	m6
2.177	0.996	1.000	0.568	0.468	0.357

Given these volatility beta estimates, the net value vega of the portfolio relative to the 3-month reference volatility is given by

$$v = \sum_{i=1}^{6} v_i^{\$} \hat{\beta}_i,$$
(IV.5.46)

where $v_i^{\$}$ denotes the value vega of the portfolio relative to the i-month volatility, shown in the last column of Table IV.5.14. Workbook (c) for this case study calculates the net vega for the portfolio as $-\$70,700$.

Then we use the sample standard deviation of the 3-month implied volatility to simulate normally distributed changes in the reference volatility risk factor, and apply the vega adjustment based on these changes and the net value vega. It then proceeds in a similar fashion to workbook (a), which contains the 12-dimensional multivariate normal risk factor model, but replaces the volatility part of the model by the volatility beta mapping. The 1% 10-day VaR results are shown in Table IV.5.33.

Table IV.5.33   Influence of vega mapping on VaR for a portfolio of crude oil options

	(a)	(b)	(c)	(d)
Delta only	$12,841	$12,841	$12,841	$12,841
Delta–gamma	$13,624	$13,624	$15,775	$15,775
Delta–gamma–vega	$15,484	$14,506	$17,119	$16,412

(a) Twelve-dimensional multivariate normal i.i.d. returns, dynamic portfolio
(b) Six-dimensional multivariate normal i.i.d. price returns, vega mapping, dynamic portfolio
(c) Twelve-dimensional multivariate normal i.i.d. returns, static portfolio
(d) Six-dimensional multivariate normal i.i.d. price returns, vega mapping, static portfolio.

For both static and dynamic portfolios, the application of the vega mapping underestimates the vega effect. This is to be expected, since we have reduced the uncertainty in the model by reducing the number of volatility risk factors. It may be worth investigating whether the use of a more risk sensitive volatility beta vector would improve the accuracy of these results.

IV.5.6   SUMMARY AND CONCLUSIONS

Option portfolios range from small baskets of vanilla options on the same underlying asset to very large collections of complex products on many underlying assets. Usually option portfolios that are held by banks are managed to be delta neutral. It is the banks' business to accept risks, for instance by writing options, because they know how to hedge them. Banks need to assess the risks they are taking before and after hedging. But the numerous empirical examples in this chapter have shown that it is all too easy for risk managers to produce highly inaccurate measurements of the risks that face option traders. Even the accurate estimation of VaR for a simple basket of vanilla options on a single underlying is a difficult task that must be properly designed, as we have taken care to demonstrate in this chapter. Readers should not underestimate the very significant investment of resources necessary to implement a VaR model that is capable of producing accurate estimates for all the options positions in a large bank.

This chapter has addressed the problem of measuring the risk of option portfolios using both direct valuation and risk factor mapping. We know that risk factor mapping of any type of portfolio provides a useful method to allocate portfolio risk to different sources and to hedge these risks. And for option portfolios there is another reason to use risk factor mapping: it reduces the computation time taken for VaR calculations of complex portfolios. However, risk factor mapping of option portfolios is far less accurate than risk factor mapping of other portfolios. There are two main reasons for this. Firstly, it is based on *Taylor approximation*. But this is only accurate for small changes in the risk factors, and VaR is a loss in the lower tail of the portfolio return distribution, so large changes in risk factors are required to estimate it. Secondly, typical option portfolios have a huge number of risk factors. The underlying price and the implied volatility are the main risk factors for each individual option but, even if all the options are on the same underlying, we have a whole *volatility surface* as risk factors. Hence, we must use techniques to reduce the number of volatility risk factors, and this introduces further inaccuracies into the Taylor approximation.

Positive gamma reduces VaR and negative gamma increases VaR, relative to the delta-only VaR. We call this the *gamma effect*. To be more precise, when the net value gamma is positive the portfolio's VaR based on a delta–gamma approximation is less than its VaR based on a delta approximation, irrespective of the sign of delta. The opposite is the case when the net value gamma is negative. Similarly, adding a volatility risk factor increases VaR if the net value vega is positive, and reduces VaR if the value vega is negative. But the *vega effect* is more complex, because the net effect of adding vega risk to the mapping depends on the price–volatility correlation as well as the sign of vega. For instance, when the net position vega is positive and the price–volatility correlation is also positive (e.g. in commodity options) the delta–gamma–vega VaR will exceed the delta–gamma VaR. But when the net position vega is positive and the price–volatility correlation is negative (e.g. in equity options) there are two effects of opposite sign so the delta–gamma–vega VaR may be greater than or less than the delta–gamma VaR. Finally, since option prices generally decrease as the option approaches expiry, the maturity effect increases the risk of long positions and decreases the risk of short positions. However, this *theta effect* only has a significant influence on VaR for long-term option portfolios when risk is assessed over a risk horizon of a few weeks or more.

It is possible to approximate the VaR of an option portfolio analytically, but these approximations are not very accurate. The simplest (and least accurate) of these is the *delta–normal* VaR, which is a normal linear VaR model. Here a normal distribution for the underlying asset returns translates into a normal distribution for the delta approximation to the option portfolio's P&L. The delta–gamma approximation is not linear, so a normal distribution for the underlying asset returns does not translate into a normal distribution for the delta–gamma approximation to the option portfolio's P&L. In fact the P&L distribution resulting from the delta–gamma approximation is often bimodal, and highly positively skewed and leptokurtic. The moments of the distribution can be computed directly from the delta and gamma of the portfolio, knowing only the covariance matrix of the underlying asset returns. We showed how to fit a *Johnson distribution* to the moments and hence estimate the VaR. However, by comparing the result with the Monte Carlo VaR based on delta–gamma approximation, we find that the analytic approximation is not able to capture the tail behaviour that is so important for VaR estimation.

Most of the text in this chapter has focused on the historical VaR and Monte Carlo VaR models as applied to individual options and option portfolios. We have illustrated each point in an empirical example or case study, and the CD-ROM contains almost 30 interactive workbooks for this chapter alone. To reduce the size of the workbooks containing Monte Carlo simulations, readers will need to fill down all simulations and calculations after copying the file to the hard drive. Also, for clarity, no enhancements for advanced sampling and variance reduction have been applied. Our purpose in the Monte Carlo section of this chapter is to identify the effects that different choices of risk factor model are likely to have on our VaR estimates, rather than on the accuracy of our simulation results.

We have been very careful to state the assumptions about rebalancing that are implicit in the way we scale the VaR for an option portfolio. There are two alternatives. First, we could compute the *dynamic* VaR, i.e. the VaR of a dynamically rebalanced portfolio which is traded at the end of each day over the risk horizon, to return the risk factor sensitivities to their original values at the time the VaR is estimated. For example, this type of assumption is relevant if we wish to estimate the VaR of a portfolio that was at its trading limits. Then, if the risk factor returns are i.i.d., the same risk is faced every day during the risk horizon. In this case we can compute 1-day VaR, and scale this to an approximate h-day VaR using the square-root-of-time rule or some other power scaling rule.

The other alternative, applicable when we have a fixed position such as a single structured product, is to assume the portfolio is not traded during the risk horizon. We call this the *static VaR*. Then the correct way to estimate an h-day VaR is to use h-day risk factor returns in the simulation. We have shown, using many numerical examples, that scaling up a daily VaR estimate to a longer risk horizon would seriously distort the theta, gamma and vega effects if the portfolio is not traded during the risk horizon.

The dynamic and static VaR estimates are the *same* for a linear portfolio when the risk factor returns are i.i.d., but they are not the same for an option portfolio. For this reason, we must be very clear about what type of VaR estimate we require – static or dynamic. This choice depends on the trading environment, and on the purpose of the VaR estimation.

Standard historical simulation is suited to dynamic VaR estimation, but its application to static VaR estimation is limited. The problem with historical simulation is the sample size constraint: there are insufficient historical data to obtain accurate estimates of extreme quantiles, which is exactly what we need for VaR estimation. So if a standard historical VaR model is applied to an option portfolio we must *either* assume we have a dynamic portfolio that is rebalanced daily over the risk horizon, to keep its risk factor sensitivities constant, and therefore scale up the daily VaR using some power law; *or*, for a static portfolio, we must use overlapping h-day returns on the risk factors in the simulation. However, the use of overlapping data distorts the tail behaviour in the risk factor return distribution. For these reasons standard historical VaR is not recommended for static VaR estimation for option portfolios. The model needs to be augmented using a parametric model of volatility clustering, as in the filtered historical simulation model of Barone-Adesi et al. (1998, 1999).

For dynamic VaR estimation standard historical simulation has one distinct advantage over Monte Carlo simulation, and this is that it captures the empirical dynamic properties and non-linear dependence between risk factors in a simple and very natural fashion. There is no need to build a complex dynamic model for risk factor returns, as there is with Monte Carlo simulation. However, we know from the previous chapter that Monte Carlo simulation is flexible enough to be adapted to many multivariate distributions, and to include dynamic properties such as volatility clustering and mean reversion in risk factor returns. We have demonstrated empirically that volatility clustering in price risk factors is a very important effect to capture for accurate VaR estimates of option portfolios.

Monte Carlo VaR is also applicable to both dynamic and static portfolios, and therefore provides a means to compare the impact that our portfolio rebalancing assumption has on the VaR estimates. Static portfolios have more pronounced gamma, vega and theta effects. However, capturing these effects with a Greeks approximation to the portfolio P&L should be done with caution, since the risk factor changes over the risk horizon could be too large to be compatible with a local approximation.

This chapter has contained a sequence of progressively more sophisticated empirical examples. We have computed VaR using analytic approximations, historical simulation and Monte Carlo simulation for a standard European option, an option with path-dependent pay-off, a hedged portfolio, general portfolios of options on the same underlying asset and, finally, portfolios of options on several underlying assets. We have demonstrated that the risk of unhedged short options positions is very much greater than the risk of unhedged long options positions, and that even delta-gamma-vega hedged portfolios could have a fairly large VaR when they are not continually rebalanced. Moreover, some hedged portfolios are only hedged against certain types of movements in risk factors. For instance, the net value Greeks of our portfolio of crude oil options were all zero. But this only hedges the portfolio against *parallel* movements in the term structures of crude oil futures prices and implied volatilities, whereas non-parallel movements are actually very common. Thus a portfolio can run some very significant risks even when it appears to be fully hedged.

A certain degree of estimation risk, linked to sample size limitations, is usually unavoidable in historical VaR model. But estimation risk in Monte Carlo VaR is something that we can do our best to eliminate because simulation errors can be controlled by advanced sampling techniques. So the main source of model risk in Monte Carlo VaR stems from an inappropriate model of the risk factor returns. The chapter ends with a detailed case study that demonstrates the effect that different risk model enhancements are likely to have on the Monte Carlo VaR estimates for an energy option portfolio. The multivariate i.i.d. normal model has been used as a benchmark against which to measure the loss of accuracy induced by reducing the dimension of the underlying price and implied volatility risk factor space.

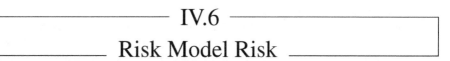

IV.6
Risk Model Risk

IV.6.1 INTRODUCTION

Portfolio risk is a measure of the uncertainty in the distribution of portfolio returns, and a *risk model* is a statistical model for generating such a distribution. A risk model actually contains three types of statistical models, for the

(i) portfolio's risk factor mapping,
(ii) multivariate distribution of risk factor returns, and
(iii) resolution method.

The choice of resolution method depends on the risk metric that we apply to the risk model. In this chapter we shall be focusing on VaR models, so the choice of resolution method is between using different analytic, historical or Monte Carlo VaR models.

The choices made in each of (i)–(iii) above are interlinked. For instance, if the risk factor mapping is a linear model of risk factor returns and these returns are assumed to be i.i.d. multivariate normal, then the resolution method for estimating VaR is analytic. This is because historical simulation uses an empirical distribution, not an i.i.d. normal one, and under the i.i.d. normal assumption there is no point in using Monte Carlo simulation because it only introduces sampling error into the exact solution, which may be obtained using an analytic formula.

Of course, the distribution of portfolio returns has an expected value, and if the risk model is also used to forecast this expected value then we could call the model a *returns model* as well. What we call the model depends on the context. For instance, fund managers normally call their model a returns model, or an *alpha model*, because the primary purpose is to provide a given level of performance. But most clients also require some limit on risk, and fund managers should take care to assess risk in the same statistical model as they assess expected returns, i.e. using their alpha model.

What about banks? Banks accept risks from their clients because they are supposed to know how to hedge them. Since the main business of banks is risk rather than returns, a risk manager in banking will call his model for generating portfolio return distributions a *risk model*. Banks account for profits and losses in their balance sheets and they use expected returns (or expected P&L) in risk adjusted performance measures. But those figures are only for accounting and capital allocation purposes. Banks often use risk models that are quite different from the models used to compute the expected returns (or P&L) on their balance sheets. More often than not their risk model assumes that all activities earn the risk free rate, even though their balance sheets and their economic capital estimates may use different figures for expected returns.

It is important to specify the expectation in the risk model. For instance, *volatility* is one, very common, risk metric that represents the extent to which the realized return can deviate from the expectation of the risk model distribution. Of course, it says nothing at all about deviations from any other expected return, and the market risk analyst must be careful to specify the expected return that this volatility relates to. Suppose the expected return is fixed by some external target. Unless the target happens to be the expected value of the risk model distribution, the risk model volatility says nothing at all about whether this target will be outperformed or underperformed. One cannot just assume the expected return is equal to the target without *changing* the risk model. Unless the model is changed to *constrain* the expected return to be the target – and this will also change the volatility in the model – the model is not appropriate for measuring risk relative to the target.[1] But this chapter is not about expected returns, and it is not until Chapter IV.8 that we shall be concerned with the interplay between risk and expected return. Here we focus on the accuracy of risk models, and we begin by putting the questions we ask about this into two categories:

1. *Model risk.* Which models should we use for the risk factor mapping, for modelling the evolution of the risk factor returns and for the resolution of the model to a single measure of risk? How do the three sub-models' statistical assumptions affect the accuracy of the risk model's risk forecasts?
2. *Estimation risk.* Given the assumptions of the risk model, how should we estimate the model parameters, and how do these estimates affect the accuracy of our risk measures?

Notice that we call the second type of model risk 'estimation risk' rather than *sampling error*. Estimation risk includes sampling error, i.e. the variation in parameter estimates due to differences in sample data. But it may also be that more than one estimation method is consistent with the risk model assumptions, and this is a different source of estimation risk. For instance, if the risk factor returns are assumed to be multivariate normal then we could apply either equally or exponentially weighted moving averages to estimate the risk factor returns covariance matrix.[2] Different estimation methods will give different parameter estimates, based on the same assumptions and given the same sample data.

To answer the questions about model risk and estimation risk above we need a methodology for testing the accuracy of a risk model. In the industry we call such a methodology a *backtest*. In academia we call it an *out-of-sample diagnostic* (or *performance*) *analysis*. Since the term 'backtest' is shorter, we shall use that term in this chapter. Several academic studies report the results of backtesting VaR models. Notably, Berkowitz and O'Brien (2002) and Berkowitz et al. (2006) suggest that the VaR models used by banks are not sufficiently risk-sensitive to generate the short-term VaR estimates they need.[3] And the results of Alexander and Sheedy (2008) suggest that risk models based on constant parameter assumptions cannot forecast short-term risk accurately, even at the portfolio level. Both volatility clustering in portfolio returns and heavy-tailed conditional return distributions are required for accurate VaR and ETL forecasts at high confidence levels and over short-term horizons.

---

[1] See Chapter II.1 for a thorough discussion of expected returns models, and their relationship with the risk metric.

[2] Or, if an asymmetric GARCH model is assumed, we could choose an E-GARCH or an A-GARCH parameterization in an asymmetric conditional multivariate normal framework.

[3] Typically, the horizons are 1 day for regulatory backtests, up to about 3 days for stress testing (or more, in illiquid markets), and 10 days for regulatory capital calculations.

The outline of this chapter is as follows. Section IV.6.2 clarifies the different sources of risk model risk and estimation risk. Section IV.6.3 derives some simple confidence intervals for VaR. Section IV.6.4 presents the core, technical part of this chapter. We first describe the general methodology for backtesting and then discuss the simple backtests required by regulators. Then we describe a more sophisticated and informative type of backtest based on the Kupiec (1995) test for coverage and the Christoffersen (1998) test for conditional coverage. Thereafter we cover backtests based on regression, which may provide a means of identifying why the VaR model fails the backtest, if it does. We describe a method for backtesting ETL due to McNeil and Frey (2000) and the application of bias statistics in the normal linear VaR framework. We also discuss backtests that examine the accuracy of the entire portfolio return distribution. As usual, Excel examples are provided to illustrate how each test is implemented, and we end the section by describing the results of some extensive backtests performed by Alexander and Sheedy (2008). Section IV.6.5 concludes.

IV.6.2   SOURCES OF RISK MODEL RISK

This section introduces the main sources of model risk and estimation risk in risk models, explaining how the two risks interact. For instance, if the risk factor returns are assumed to be multivariate normal i.i.d., in which case the model parameters are the means and the covariance matrix of these returns, then the estimation of the covariance matrix cannot be based on a GARCH model; it can only be based on a moving average model, because returns are not i.i.d. in GARCH models. So in this case estimation risk depends on the choice between three alternatives: an equally weighted covariance matrix, an exponentially weighted moving average with the same smoothing constant for all risk factors, or an orthogonal EWMA covariance matrix estimate. Further to this choice, the choice of sample data and, in the case of the EWMA matrices the smoothing constant, also influences sampling error, which is a part of estimation risk.

Sampling error in statistical models has been studied for many generations and estimated standard errors of estimators that we commonly use are well known. Almost always, in an unconditional (i.i.d.) framework, the larger the estimation sample size the greater the in-sample accuracy of the estimator. But this does not necessarily imply that we should use as large a sample as possible for VaR and ETL estimation. Apart from the fact that backtests are out-of-sample tests, we might encounter problems if the risk model is an unconditional model, because backtests are usually performed using short-term, time-varying forecasts. So there is no guarantee that larger estimation sample sizes will perform better in backtests. Indeed, the opposite is likely to be the case, because the VaR and ETL would become less risk sensitive.

In this section we shall examine the decisions that must be made at each step of the risk model design, from the models used for risk factor mapping, risk factor returns and VaR resolution to the choice of sample data and estimation methodology. We already know from previous chapters that portfolio risk may be assessed at the portfolio level, the risk factor level or even at the asset level. Each approach has its own advantages and limitations, which are summarized in Table IV.6.1. This section assumes that portfolio risk is assessed at the risk factor level, as it will be whenever the model is used for risk attribution, and we focus on the model risk that is introduced by the use of a risk factor mapping.

Table IV.6.1   Advantages and limitations of different levels of risk assessment

Level	Portfolio	Risk factor	Asset
Advantages	Simplicity; Assesses total risk directly	Allows risk attribution	Assesses total risk directly
Limitations	No risk attribution	Only assesses systematic risk; Additional model risk introduced by risk factor mapping	No risk attribution; Not practical for very large portfolios

IV.6.2.1   Risk Factor Mapping

The main focus of academic research and industry development has been on the specification of the risk factor returns model, with much less attention paid to the model risk arising from the risk factor mapping itself. However, the type of risk factor mapping that is applied, and the method and data used to compute factor sensitivity estimates, could each have a considerable impact on the VaR and ETL estimates.[4]

Effect of Vertex Choice on Interest Rate VaR

Suppose a portfolio is represented as a sequence of cash flows.[5] Given a set of vertices for the risk factor mapping, we know that we should map the cash flows to these vertices in a present value, PV01 and volatility invariant fashion. Following the method explained in Section III.5.3.4, we can do this by mapping each cash flow to three vertices. We now ask which fixed set of vertices should be chosen for the risk factor mapping. For instance, should we use vertices at monthly or 3-monthly intervals? And does this choice matter – how much does it influence the VaR estimate?

EXAMPLE IV.6.1: MODEL RISK ARISING FROM CASH-FLOW MAP

Estimate the 1% annual VaR of a cash flow with a present value of $1 million in 250 calendar days, when it is mapped in a present value, PV01 and volatility invariant fashion to three vertices, and these vertices are:[6]

(a) 8 months, 9 months and 10 months;
(b) 6 months, 9 months and 12 months.

The correlation matrix of continuously compounded discount rates at monthly maturities, and their volatilities (in basis points per annum), are shown in Table IV.6.2. In each case base your calculations on the assumption that the changes in discount rates are i.i.d. with a multivariate normal distribution.

SOLUTION   In each case we map the cash flow to the three vertices using the methodology explained in Section III.5.3.4 and illustrated in Example III.5.3. That is, first we use linear

---

[4] For instance, in an equity factor model we could use one broad market risk factor, or several fundamental factors, or statistical factors etc. Different factor models will give different VaR estimates.

[5] This includes any interest rate sensitive portfolio, and any portfolio with forward exposures to currencies, equities or commodities. But currency, equity and commodity portfolio also have a spot price as a risk factor. See Section III.5.2 if any clarification is required.

[6] Using a 30/360 day-count convention.

Table IV.6.2   Discount rate volatilities and correlations

Correlation	m6	m7	m8	m9	m10	m11	m12
m6	1	0.993	0.977	0.954	0.928	0.900	0.873
m7	0.993	1	0.995	0.981	0.963	0.941	0.918
m8	0.977	0.995	1	0.996	0.985	0.969	0.952
m9	0.954	0.981	0.996	1	0.997	0.988	0.975
m10	0.928	0.963	0.985	0.997	1	0.997	0.990
m11	0.900	0.941	0.969	0.988	0.997	1	0.998
m12	0.873	0.918	0.952	0.975	0.990	0.998	1
Volatility	33	34.5	35.75	37.25	38.75	40	41.5

interpolation on variances to estimate the volatility of the 250-day discount rate, and also calculate the covariance matrix corresponding to the volatilities and correlation. Then we apply the Excel Solver to compute the cash-flow mapping, and the result is shown in the columns headed cash-flow PV in Table IV.6.3. Next, we compute the PV01 vector of the mapped cash flow, as described in Section IV.2.3.2, and the results are shown in the columns headed PV01.[7] Finally, we use the PV01 vector to calculate the 1% annual normal linear VaR, using the usual formula (IV.2.25). The results for the 1% annual VaR are $5856.56 in case (a) and $5871.18 in case (b).

Table IV.6.3   Computing the cash-flow map and estimating PV01

	Case (a)			Case (b)	
Days	Cash-flow PV	PV01	Days	Cash-flow PV	PV01
240	$517,310	$34.49	180	$132,129	$6.61
270	$632,047	$47.40	270	$957,964	$71.85
300	−$149,357	−$12.45	360	−$90,093	−$9.01

The above example shows that the choice of vertices for the cash-flow map makes little difference to a normal linear VaR estimate, even over an annual horizon. The 1% annual VaR of a cash flow with present value $1 million is 0.5856% of the portfolio value when mapped to monthly vertices, or 0.5871% of the portfolio value when mapped to quarterly vertices. Readers can verify, using the spreadsheet for the above example, that even when interest rates are more volatile and have lower correlation than in the above example, the influence of our choice of vertices in the risk factor mapping on the interest rate VaR is minor.

The reason for this is that if the VaR is proportional to the portfolio volatility, as it is in the normal linear VaR model, the choice of the three vertices to map to should not influence the result because the VaR should be invariant under the mapping.[8] However, if we had used a VaR resolution method based on historical simulation then the difference between the two results could have been greater. Typically there are thousands of cash flows, and then the precision of the historical VaR estimate could be significantly affected by the choice of vertices for the

---

[7] Since the mapped cash flow is already in present value terms, we simply multiply the cash-flow present value by its maturity in years and then by 10^{-4}. This gives an accurate approximation to the PV01, using (IV.2.29).

[8] The small difference between the VaR estimates in this example was due to rounding errors.

cash-flow map. But this choice is far less crucial than other choices that the market risk analyst faces. For example, the choice of multivariate distribution to use for the interest rate changes, and the decision to assume they are i.i.d. or otherwise, would have a much more significant influence on the VaR estimate than the choice of vertices in the cash flow map.

Effect of Sample Size and Beta Estimation Methodology on Equity VaR

Now suppose we have spot exposures in a stock portfolio. There may be little or no flexibility regarding the choice of market risk factors. For instance, a hedge fund market risk analyst may be estimating portfolio risk in the context of a pre-defined returns model with many factors. By contrast, a market risk analyst in a large bank will probably, for the sake of parsimony, be using a single broad market index for each country. Sometimes there is a choice to be made between two or more broad market indices, but usually these indices would be highly correlated and so the choice of index is a relatively minor source of model risk. Thus, in the case of an equity portfolio held by a bank, the main sources of risk factor model risk are the sample data and the methodology that are used to estimate the market betas. The estimation of a market beta in the single index model is the subject of Section II.1.2. There we compare the ordinary least squares (OLS) and exponentially weighted moving average (EWMA) methods, illustrating the huge differences that can arise between the two estimates.[9]

Whilst fund managers are likely to base capital allocation on a returns model that uses many risk factors, with OLS estimates for risk factor betas, market risk analysts require fewer risk factors but more risk sensitive estimates for their betas. Risk managers may choose between:

- the fund manager's OLS beta estimates, which are typically based on weekly or monthly data over a sample period covering several years;
- OLS betas based on daily data over a smaller sample, under the belief that these are more risk sensitive than the fund manager's betas;[10] or
- EWMA or GARCH time-varying beta estimates.

We shall now illustrate the effect of this choice on the VaR estimate, in the context of a very simple portfolio.

EXAMPLE IV.6.2: MODEL RISK ARISING FROM EQUITY BETA ESTIMATION

On 30 May 2008, estimate the 1% 10-day systematic VaR of a position currently worth £4 million on Halifax Bank of Scotland (HBOS) PLC, using the FTSE 100 index as the market factor.[11] Compare your results when both the beta estimate and the index volatility estimate are based on:

(a) OLS estimation using weekly data since 31 December 2001;
(b) OLS estimation using weekly data since 28 December 2006

---

[9] We could also estimate betas using a bivariate GARCH model, as described in Section II.4.8.4. Typically, there is less difference between the GARCH and the EWMA beta estimates than between these and the OLS estimates.

[10] But when OLS beta estimates are rolled over time they exhibit 'ghost features' which introduce a serious bias to the estimate. The reason is that OLS assumes the returns on a financial asset are i.i.d. when they are not. So when a volatility cluster appears, the effect of this cluster does not diminish over time. Instead it persists for exactly T periods after the cluster, where T is the sample size. This is explained in detail in Section II.3.7.

[11] The price of HBOS stock on that day was £4, so 1 million shares are held. Data were downloaded from Yahoo! Finance, symbols HBOS and ^FTSE.

(c) OLS estimation using daily data since 31 December 2001;
(d) OLS estimation using daily data since 28 December 2006;
(e) EWMA estimation using weekly data with a smoothing constant of 0.95;
(f) EWMA estimation using weekly data with a smoothing constant of 0.9;
(g) EWMA estimation using daily data with a smoothing constant of 0.95;
(h) EWMA estimation using daily data with a smoothing constant of 0.9.

In each case base your calculations on the assumption that the returns on the stock and the index are i.i.d. with a bivariate normal distribution.

SOLUTION   The stock and the index prices since 31 December 2001 are shown in Figure IV.6.1.[12] The effects of the credit crunch on the stock price are very evident here: its price tumbled from a high of nearly £12 per share in January 2007 to only £4 per share by the end of May 2008. The stock returns volatility was clearly much higher at the end of the sample than it had been, on average, over the sample period, and this will be particularly reflected in the EWMA volatility estimate (h), which has a low value for the smoothing constant. The stock's index beta will currently also be much lower according this EWMA estimate because the correlation between the stock and index returns, which was fairly high during the years 2002–2006, had become very low indeed by the end of the sample.

Figure IV.6.1   HBOS stock price and FTSE 100 index

We shall estimate the VaR using the usual normal linear formula, expressing VaR as a percentage of the portfolio value. That is, the $100\alpha\%$ h-day VaR estimate is given by

$$\text{VaR}_{h,\alpha} = \Phi^{-1}(1-\alpha)\,\hat{\beta}\hat{\sigma}\sqrt{h/250}$$

---

[12] Note that the stock price, shown on the right-hand scale, is given in pence.

where $\hat{\beta}$ is the beta estimate for HBOS relative to the FTSE 100 index and $\hat{\sigma}$ is the estimate of the index volatility. In each of the cases (a)–(h) we use a different estimate for $\hat{\beta}$ and for $\hat{\sigma}$. These and the resulting 1% 10-day VaR estimates, in percentage and nominal terms, are displayed in Table IV.6.4.[13]

Table IV.6.4   OLS and EWMA beta, index volatility and VaR for HBOS stock.

	(a)	(b)	(c)	(d)	(e)	(f)	(g)	(h)
Beta	1.169	1.266	1.221	1.269	1.747	1.914	1.102	0.672
Index vol.	14.02%	14.13%	17.75%	17.18%	16.51%	16.49%	17.36%	15.11%
VaR(%)	7.63%	8.32%	10.09%	10.14%	13.42%	14.68%	8.90%	4.72%
VaR(£)	£305,127	£332,949	£403,409	£405,785	£536,851	£587,358	£356,098	£188,796

Considering the OLS estimates (a)–(d) first, we find that the betas are fairly similar whether they are based on weekly or daily data over either estimation period, but the index volatility estimates are much higher when based on daily data. As a result, the VaR estimates are greater when based on daily data. This is expected because, unless the returns are really i.i.d. as we have assumed, the volatility clustering effects are likely to be more pronounced in daily data. However, when there is volatility clustering it is not correct to scale VaR using the square-root-of-time rule. Instead we should use a GARCH model, which has a mean reversion in volatility, and the square-root-of-time rule does not apply.

For the VaR there is much less variation between the four different OLS estimates (a)–(d) than there is between the four different EWMA estimates (e)–(h). These range from 4.72% to 14.68% of the portfolio value, i.e. from £188,796 to £587,358! In this case the choice between weekly and daily data has a great effect on the VaR estimate, and so does the choice of smoothing constant in the EWMA. It is the product of the volatility and the beta that we use in the VaR so the daily data could lead to either a higher or a lower value for VaR than the weekly data.[14] In this case, it turns out that the daily data give the lower VaR estimates.

The above example illustrates some important points:

- When short-term VaR estimates are scaled to longer risk horizons using the square-root-of-time rule, a large model risk is introduced.[15] Although we should base daily VaR estimates on daily data, weekly data may provide more accurate VaR estimates over a 5-day or longer risk horizon.
- When the EWMA methodology is applied the choice of smoothing constant has a very significant effect on the VaR estimate. The problem with EWMA is that this choice is *ad hoc*.[16]

---

[13] The VaR in nominal terms is the percentage VaR estimate multiplied by the portfolio value of £4 million.

[14] Again the index volatilities are higher when based on daily data but the beta estimates are much lower. Because of the crash in the stock price just before the VaR is estimated, the lower value of 0.9 used in (h) produces the highest volatility estimate. But because of the higher index volatility and also because the daily stock returns have a lower correlation with the index returns, the daily beta estimates are much lower than those based on weekly data.

[15] See also Table IV.3.4 in Section IV.3.2.6, which shows the errors of square-root scaling under different scale exponents and over different risk horizons.

[16] And this is the reason why it is better to use a GARCH model, at least when the model is based on daily data, because the GARCH parameters may be estimated using maximum likelihood estimation. See Section II.4.2.2 for further details.

- Calculating equity VaR by mapping to major indices is fraught with difficulties. The mapping methodology (e.g. the OLS or EWMA) and the choice of parameters (e.g. estimation period, or smoothing constant) may have an enormous influence on the result. Completely counterintuitive results could be obtained, such as the result shown in column (h) above. More generally, a high risk portfolio could be uncorrelated with the market, in which case it would have a very small beta. Thus its systematic VaR could be very low indeed.

A few months later, during September 2008, HBOS became insolvent. In this light, even the largest VaR estimate in the example above would seem too conservative. However, market risk capital is not for holding against this type of loss. It is only for covering everyday losses, usually in a balanced portfolio of shares. To quantify losses that arise from stress events such as the insolvency of a major bank, stress VaR analysis should be used.

IV.6.2.2 Risk Factor or Asset Returns Model

Much of our discussion in previous chapters has concerned the specification of the risk factor or asset returns model, i.e. the way that we model the evolution of the risk factors (or assets) over the risk horizon. The analyst faces several choices here and the most important of these are now reviewed.

1. *Should we assume the returns are i.i.d. or should we capture volatility clustering and/or autocorrelation in returns?*
This choice influences both the VaR estimate itself and the way that we scale VaR over different risk horizons, if this is done. Numerous examples and case studies in the previous four chapters have discussed the impact of volatility clustering and autocorrelated returns on VaR.[17] In each case the importance of including volatility clustering effects in VaR estimates over risk horizons longer than a few days was clear. And, for a linear portfolio, we showed that even a small degree of autocorrelation in returns can have a significant impact on the scaling of short-term VaR to long-term risk horizons.

2. *Should the distribution be parametric or historical?*
At the daily frequency the historical distribution captures all the features of returns that we know to be important such as volatility clustering, skewness and leptokurtosis. It does this entirely naturally, i.e. without the complexity of fitting a parametric form. But to estimate VaR over a horizon longer than 1 day we need an h-day distribution for portfolio returns, and for reasons explained in previous chapters it is difficult to obtain an h-day *historical* distribution using overlapping data in the estimation sample. The exception is when we use filtered historical simulation (FHS), where the volatility adjusted historical distribution is augmented with a parametric dynamic model such as GARCH. An alternative to historical simulation is

---

[17] In particular, for the effect of autocorrelation on scaling parametric linear VaR, see Examples IV.2.1, IV.2.23 and the case study on credit spread VaR in Section IV.2.12. And, for the influence of volatility clustering effects on historical VaR estimates, see Example IV.3.1 and all five case studies in Section IV.3.5. These case studies deal with cash flows, a small stock portfolio, a large international stock portfolio, an international fixed income portfolio and a portfolio of crack spreads. Finally, for the effect of volatility clustering in Monte Carlo VaR estimates, see Example IV.4.6 and, for the comparison of i.i.d. versus GARCH returns on a forex portfolio, see Example IV.4.14.

to find a suitable parameterization of the conditional distributions of the risk factor returns and to model these in a dynamic framework.

The advantages and limitations of both the parametric and the empirical (historical) approaches to building a statistical model for risk factor returns have been discussed earlier in this text. In Chapter IV.3 we described the influence of this choice on VaR estimates for a linear portfolio and in Chapter IV.5 we examined option portfolios, comparing Monte Carlo with historical VaR estimates.[18] It is unlikely that the h-day risk factor return distributions based on historical data without filtering will provide VaR estimates that are as accurate as those based on appropriate parametric representations of the conditional risk factor return distributions. FHS may be more or less accurate than Student t EWMA VaR, but we cannot draw any conclusion without backtesting the performance of different models, as described later in this chapter.

3. If parametric, should the risk factor return distribution be normal, Student t, mixture or some other form (e.g. based on a copula)?
Our empirical exercises and studies have demonstrated, convincingly, that daily returns are usually neither i.i.d. nor normally distributed.[19] Typically, both daily and weekly returns exhibit skewed and leptokurtic features. When volatility clustering is included and the model has a conditional framework, as in GARCH, it is possible for unconditional distributions to be skewed and leptokurtic even when conditional distributions are normal. But when skewness and leptokurtosis in portfolio returns are very pronounced even conditional distributions should be non-normal. Hence, for a daily VaR estimate to be truly representative of the stylized empirical features mentioned above, non-normal conditional distributions should be incorporated in the risk model at this stage.

What about VaR estimates over a horizon of a month or more? If daily log returns are i.i.d. then their aggregate, monthly log return has an almost normal distribution, by the central limit theorem. And if daily log returns exhibit volatility clustering their aggregates still (eventually) converge to a normal variable, even though the central limit theorem does not apply.[20] Thus the decision about parametric form for the risk factor return distributions depends on the risk horizon. For example, whilst non-normal conditional models for risk factor return distributions are important for short-term VaR estimates, they are not especially useful for long-term VaR estimates. For long-term risk factor return distributions we may be fine using the multivariate normal i.i.d. assumption. Again, a complete answer can only be given after backtesting the models that are being considered.

4. How should the parameters of the risk factor returns model be estimated?
Even once we have fixed the distributional assumptions in parametric VaR estimates, the method used to estimate parameters can have a large impact on the VaR estimates. For

---

[18] Comparisons of parametric and historical VaR estimates for linear portfolios are discussed in Section IV.3.1 and empirical results are presented in the case studies of Sections IV.3.5.1 (for cash flows) and IV.3.5.2 (for a stock portfolio). For the comparison of historical VaR and parametric (Monte Carlo) VaR for option portfolios, see Example IV.5.18 for S&P 500 options, Example IV.5.20 for an international equity index option portfolio, and the case studies in Sections IV.5.4.5 and IV.5.5.8 for an energy option portfolio.
[19] Numerous exercises and case studies in Chapter IV.2 have addressed this question, by examining the VaR for a linear portfolio under different parametric assumptions. We also asked a similar question in the context of Monte Carlo VaR models in Chapter IV.4. Normal, Student t, and normal or Student t mixture i.i.d. VaR estimates for a linear portfolio are compared in Examples IV.2.19, IV.2.21 and IV.2.22. The case study of Section IV.2.12 also compares the effect of different parametric assumptions on credit spread VaR. Finally, the comparison of i.i.d. normal, Student t and copula-based Monte Carlo VaR estimates is presented in Examples IV.4.8–IV.4.11.
[20] See Alexander et al. (2008) for the proof.

instance, the RiskMetrics™ VaR estimates given in Example IV.2.26 are all based on the same i.i.d. normal assumption for risk factor returns, with an *ad hoc* value chosen for the smoothing constant. But the estimated VaR can differ enormously, depending on the sample data and the methodology used to estimate the risk factor returns model parameters. On changing the assumptions made here, a VaR or ETL estimate could very easily be doubled or halved! And we have seen that if the estimates are based on historical data, the sample size used to estimate the model parameters has a very significant impact on the VaR estimate. So, as well as back-testing the risk factor returns model, we also have to backtest the sample size, and/or anything else which determines the values that are chosen for the model parameters.

In summary, the four previous chapters have informed readers about the consequences of their decisions about the choices outlined above. Using numerous empirical examples and case studies to illustrate each choice, it has been possible to draw some general conclusions. For convenience, these conclusions are summarized below.

- If returns are autocorrelated, this affects the way that we scale the VaR estimate to longer horizons. Positive autocorrelation increases the VaR, and negative autocorrelation decreases the VaR.
- Incorporating volatility clustering makes the VaR estimate more risk sensitive. It will increase the VaR estimate if the market is currently more volatile than usual, and decrease the VaR estimate if the market is currently less volatile than usual.
- Parametric models for returns may produce VaR estimates that are less than or greater than the VaR estimates based on empirical return distributions. Often the empirical VaR estimates are greater than normal VaR estimates based on the same historical data, but this depends on the estimation sample and on the confidence level at which VaR is estimated.
- When the functional form of parametric distribution has leptokurtosis and negative skew-ness, the VaR at high confidence levels will be greater than the normal VaR. However, the opposite is the case at lower confidence levels.
- The data and methodology that are applied to estimate the parameters of the risk factor mapping and the returns model parameters can have a huge effect on the VaR estimate. However, it is not easy to know *a priori* how this choice will affect a particular VaR estimate.

When building a VaR model a market risk analyst enters a labyrinth where the path resulting from each choice leads to further choices, and each path branches into several paths. The outcome from each path is difficult to predict and outcomes resulting from quite different paths could be similar, or very different indeed. Given the myriad decisions facing the market risk analyst about the risk factor or asset return distributional assumptions, and given that the choices made play such an important role in the estimation of VaR and ETL, it is helpful to offer some guidance.

First, an analyst should choose distributional assumptions, including the assumptions about parameter values, that reflect his *beliefs* about the evolution of risk factor returns over the risk horizon. These assumptions need not be unique; indeed, the analyst may hold a distribution of beliefs over several different scenarios. In particular, these assumptions need not be based on the empirical distributions observed in the past, unless historical simulation is used to resolve the model. But it is sensible to base assumptions for short-term VaR estimates on current market conditions. For instance, at the time of writing, in the wake of the credit crisis, it is hardly feasible that equity markets and credit spreads will return to their previous levels of volatility within a short risk horizon. So the parameter estimates for *short-term* VaR estimation should take the current market conditions into account, even when subjective values are used rather than estimating model parameters from historical data.

Secondly, the analyst should build his model on sound principles, based on all the information that he believes is relevant to the evolution of the risk factors over the risk horizon. Nevertheless, building a model that – in the analyst's view – properly represents the returns process is not necessarily the same thing as building an *accurate* model. So the third point of guidance is to recognize that by far the most important aspect of building a risk model is the *backtesting* of this model.

The main purpose of this chapter is to explain how to perform backtests. Backtests need to be run using several alternative model assumptions. These assumptions concern the evolution of risk factor return distributions and the estimation of factor model parameters. The backtest results will tell the analyst how accurate the VaR and ETL estimates are for each of the models he is considering, using out-of-sample performance analysis that embodies the way that the model is actually used.

The model construction is based on many decisions, as we have explained above. And each choice facing the analyst should be backtested. Thus an analyst must invest much thought, time and effort into comparing how different model specifications perform in out-of-sample diagnostic tests. Backtests should be based on an estimation sample that is rolled over a long historical period. Additionally, the backtest data may include hypothetical scenarios that are designed to evaluate model performance during stressful markets.

IV.6.2.3   VaR Resolution Method

If historical VaR estimates at extreme quantiles are required there are several ways in which semi-parametric or parametric methods can be applied to fit the lower tails of the empirical portfolio returns or P&L distribution.[21] Or, if we require historical VaR estimates over a risk horizon longer than a few days, then filtering the evolution of returns over the risk horizon has a very significant impact on the VaR estimates. And if Monte Carlo VaR estimation is used, there are several advanced sampling and variance reduction techniques that could be applied to reduce the sampling error.[22]

The only way to decide which VaR resolution method best suits the positions that the analyst must consider is to invest considerable time and effort in backtesting different approaches. Such research is likely to take months or years, but it is one of the most interesting parts of the analyst's job. Given the turmoil that has hit many markets during the year preceding the publication of this book, senior managers may be predisposed to allocate resources in this direction. Distributions that are approximated using Cornish–Fisher expansion may offer significant improvement on backtesting results for a standard historical VaR model. Adding filtering to simulate 3-day risk factor returns may have little impact on the quality of the 3-day backtest results. We do not know how much value is added by refining the VaR resolution method unless we do the backtests. However, sophisticated resolution methods may be less important to senior management than applying other types of refinements to enterprise-wide

---

[21] These are described in Section IV.3.4.
[22] See Section IV.4.2.2 and IV.4.2.3 for further details.

risk models. The implementation of an enterprise-wide VaR model that is capable of netting the risks of a large corporation is a huge undertaking, and *aggregation risk* in enterprise-wide risk estimates is by far the most important aspect of enterprise-wide risk model risk.[23] Indeed, a market risk analyst may be well advised to accept a simple kernel fit and a simple EWMA filtering if he is using historical VaR, so that he can focus resources on the major challenge of aggregating different market risks across the firm.

IV.6.2.4   Scaling

Market risk analysts are also faced with a decision regarding the holding period of the VaR and ETL estimates. Should we estimate VaR and ETL directly over every risk horizon that is applied? The alternative is to estimate them over a short risk horizon and then scale them up, somehow, to obtain the VaR and ETL over a longer risk horizon. But how should this scaling be done? The answer depends on the type of portfolio (whether linear, or containing options) and the resolution method.

In the normal linear VaR model it is straightforward to implement either of these alternatives. In fact, if the risk factor returns are multivariate normal and i.i.d. and the expected excess return is zero, scaling will produce *identical* results to estimation directly over an h-day horizon. This is because we can scale either the covariance matrix or the final VaR estimate using the square-root-of-time rule. The exception is when the portfolio is not assumed to return the risk free rate. In that case, VaR does not scale with the square root of time, even when returns are i.i.d., and we should estimate the normal linear VaR directly over the risk horizon. And when the portfolio is assumed to return the risk free rate, as is usually the case in banks, but the portfolio returns are positively (negatively) autocorrelated, we should scale up short-term VaR to be greater than (less then) the VaR that is implied by a square-root scaling rule.

In the historical VaR model without filtering, the use of overlapping data truncates the tail of the portfolio return distribution, so that ETL (and VaR at extreme quantiles) can be seriously underestimated. So unless we add some parametric filtering for modelling dynamic portfolio returns over the h-day horizon we are initially forced to estimate VaR and ETL at the daily level. As explained in Section IV.3.2, it may be possible to uncover a *power law scaling rule*, to extend the daily VaR to longer horizons, but this can only be applied to linear portfolios, or to estimate the dynamic VaR of option portfolios.[24] If there is no power law or if it is not the square root of time, using a square-root-of-time rule can lead to a very serious error in long-term VaR estimates.

In the Monte Carlo VaR model we can either estimate VaR directly over the risk horizon or, under certain assumptions, scale up a short-term VaR estimate to a longer horizon. If the risk factor returns are multivariate normal i.i.d. the two approaches only give the same result for a linear portfolio.[25] For option portfolios the two approaches to estimating long-term VaR yield different results. The approach that is used will depend on the portfolio's valuation (i.e. Taylor approximation versus full valuation) and the rebalancing assumption for the portfolio over the risk horizon.[26]

---

[23] See Section IV.8.3.3 for further details.

[24] Dynamic VaR is based on the assumption that the portfolio is rebalanced daily to keep its risk factor sensitivities constant.

[25] But in this case it is more accurate to use an analytic formula, if available.

[26] If Taylor approximation is used, do not overlook the huge model risk that is introduced by using h-day changes in risk factors, when even daily changes can be too large for low-order Taylor approximations to be accurate. See Section IV.5.2.4 for further details.

IV.6.3   ESTIMATION RISK

Even in the context of a single risk factor returns model and a single VaR resolution method, VaR estimates can vary enormously according to our choice of sample data and our choice of estimation methodology. For example, the resolution method may be a standard historical simulation, in which case the risk factor return distribution will be a simulated empirical distribution, but VaR estimates can be very sensitive to the sample size, i.e. the number of historical simulations used. In fact, the case study in Section IV.3.3.1 showed that the sample size is a much more important determinant of the VaR estimate than the resolution method.

For another example, under the normal i.i.d. assumption for returns, a risk factor covariance matrix might be estimated using an equally weighted average of the previous T daily returns, the estimation sample size T being chosen fairly arbitrarily. Or we may use an exponentially weighted moving average with some *ad hoc* value for the smoothing constant λ. In both these cases we can estimate the standard error of the estimator.[27] It is useful to extend these standard errors to an approximate standard error for a VaR estimate. These standard errors could indicate, for example, whether there is a statistically significant difference between two different VaR estimates. Alternatively, they can be used to obtain an approximate confidence interval for a VaR estimate. That is what we do in this section: we derive approximate confidence intervals for VaR estimates, based on both analytic and simulation VaR resolution methods.

IV.6.3.1   Distribution of VaR Estimators in Parametric Linear Models

If the portfolio is expected to return the risk free rate, the VaR estimate in the normal or Student t linear model behaves like volatility. For a fixed significance level α and a fixed risk horizon of h days, the $100\alpha\%$ h-day VaR estimate is a constant times the portfolio volatility. If this volatility is estimated using an equally weighted average of squared returns based on a sample of size T, or if it is estimated using EWMA with a given λ, we can derive the confidence interval for VaR from the known confidence interval for volatility, as described below.

Normally Distributed Portfolio Returns

The assumption that portfolio returns are i.i.d. normal leads to the formula

$$\text{VaR}_{h,\alpha} = \Phi^{-1}(1 - \alpha)\,\hat{\sigma}\sqrt{h} \tag{IV.6.1}$$

where $\hat{\sigma}$ is the estimated standard deviation of the portfolio's daily returns. For simplicity, we assume the portfolio is expected to return the risk free rate.

Since the quantile $\Phi^{-1}(1 - \alpha)$ of the standard normal distribution and the square root of the holding period $\sqrt{h}$ are both constant, we may use the standard error of the standard deviation estimator to derive a standard error for the VaR estimate. In Section II.3.5.3 it is proved that the standard error of the equally weighted standard deviation estimator $\hat{\sigma}$, when it is based on a sample of size T, is approximated by

$$est.s.e.(\hat{\sigma}) \approx \frac{\hat{\sigma}}{\sqrt{2T}}. \tag{IV.6.2}$$

---

[27] This is described in Section II.3.5.3 and II.3.8.5.

Hence, in this case the standard error of the VaR estimator at the portfolio level is approximately equal to

$$est.s.e.\left(\mathrm{VaR}_{h,\alpha}\right) \approx \Phi^{-1}(1-\alpha)\,\hat{\sigma}\sqrt{\frac{h}{2T}} = \frac{\mathrm{VaR}_{h,\alpha}}{\sqrt{2T}}. \qquad\qquad \text{(IV.6.3)}$$

In Section II.3.8.5 it is proved that the standard error of the EWMA standard deviation estimator $\hat{\sigma}$, when it is based on a smoothing constant λ, is approximated by

$$est.s.e.\left(\hat{\sigma}\right) \approx \hat{\sigma}\sqrt{\frac{1-\lambda}{2\,(1+\lambda)}} \qquad\qquad \text{(IV.6.4)}$$

Hence, the standard error of the VaR estimator at the portfolio level is approximately equal to

$$est.s.e.\left(\mathrm{VaR}_{h,\alpha}\right) \approx \Phi^{-1}\,(1-\alpha)\,\hat{\sigma}\sqrt{\frac{h\,(1-\lambda)}{2\,(1+\lambda)}} = \mathrm{VaR}_{h,\alpha}\sqrt{\frac{1-\lambda}{2\,(1+\lambda)}}. \qquad \text{(IV.6.5)}$$

EXAMPLE IV.6.3: CONFIDENCE INTERVALS FOR NORMAL LINEAR VaR

Portfolio returns are assumed to be i.i.d. and normally distributed. When the portfolio volatility is estimated as 20%, estimate the $100\alpha\%$ h-day normal linear VaR and its approximate standard error for different values of α and h,

(a) an equally weighted model with a sample size 100, and
(b) EWMA with a smoothing constant of 0.94.

How do your results change for different sample sizes in (a) and for different smoothing constants in (b)?

SOLUTION   The VaR estimates based on (IV.6.1) and their standard errors based first on (IV.6.3) with $T = 100$, and then on (IV.6.5) with $\lambda = 0.94$, are calculated in the spreadsheet for different values of α and h, and the results are displayed in Table IV.6.5. The VaR estimates and their standard errors increase with both the risk horizon and the confidence level. For our choice of parameters, i.e. $T = 100$ and $\lambda = 0.94$, the EWMA VaR estimates are less precise than the equally weighted estimates, since their standard errors are always greater.

How do these standard errors behave as the sample size changes in the equally weighted model, or as the smoothing constant changes in the EWMA model? Figure IV.6.2 depicts the 1% 10-day normal linear VaR estimate (by the horizontal black line at 9.31%) and two-standard-error bounds, based on the equally weighted estimate (IV.6.3) for different values of T. Figure IV.6.3 depicts the same VaR estimate of 9.31% and two-standard-error bounds based on the EWMA estimate (IV.6.5) for different values of λ. Both graphs are based on the assumption that returns are i.i.d. and the portfolio volatility is 20%. The standard errors decrease as the sample size increases in the equally weighted model, and decrease as the smoothing constant increases in the EWMA model.

The equally weighted variance estimate is a sum of i.i.d. variables,[28] so by the central limit theorem its distribution converges to a normal distribution. But the VaR estimate behaves

---

[28] Since the returns are assumed to be i.i.d., so are their squares.

Table IV.6.5   Normal linear VaR estimates and approximate standard errors

h				α	
		0.10%	1%	5%	10%
1	VaR	**3.91%**	**2.94%**	**2.08%**	**1.62%**
	s.e.($T=100$)	0.28%	0.21%	0.15%	0.11%
	s.e.($\lambda=0.94$)	0.49%	0.37%	0.26%	0.20%
3	VaR	**6.77%**	**5.10%**	**3.60%**	**2.81%**
	s.e.($T=100$)	0.48%	0.36%	0.25%	0.20%
	s.e.($\lambda=0.94$)	0.84%	0.63%	0.45%	0.35%
5	VaR	**8.74%**	**6.58%**	**4.65%**	**3.62%**
	s.e.($T=100$)	0.62%	0.47%	0.33%	0.26%
	s.e.($\lambda=0.94$)	1.09%	0.82%	0.58%	0.45%
10	VaR	**12.36%**	**9.31%**	**6.58%**	**5.13%**
	s.e.($T=100$)	0.87%	0.66%	0.47%	0.36%
	s.e.($\lambda=0.94$)	1.54%	1.16%	0.82%	0.64%
25	VaR	**19.54%**	**14.71%**	**10.40%**	**8.11%**
	s.e.($T=100$)	1.38%	1.04%	0.74%	0.57%
	s.e.($\lambda=0.94$)	2.43%	1.83%	1.29%	1.01%
100	VaR	**39.09%**	**29.43%**	**20.81%**	**16.21%**
	s.e.($T=100$)	2.76%	2.08%	1.47%	1.15%
	s.e.($\lambda=0.94$)	4.86%	3.66%	2.59%	2.02%
250	VaR	**61.80%**	**46.53%**	**32.90%**	**25.63%**
	s.e.($T=100$)	4.37%	3.29%	2.33%	1.81%
	s.e.($\lambda=0.94$)	7.69%	5.79%	4.09%	3.19%

Note: Estimates are based on a sample size of 100 and a normal population with mean zero and volatility 20%.

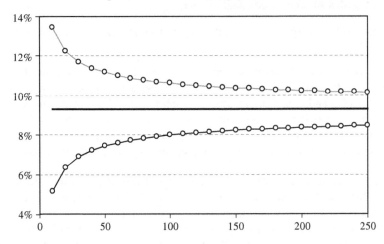

Figure IV.6.2   1% 10-day VaR with two-standard-error bounds versus sample size

like the square root of the variance.[29] In fact, the standard errors shown in these figures are approximated using Taylor expansion, as in Section II.3.5.3, without knowing the functional form of the volatility estimator.

---

[29] The distribution of the volatility estimator is not the square root of the distribution of the variance estimator, so we cannot just use the square root of the standard errors of the variance estimator as the standard errors of the volatility estimator.

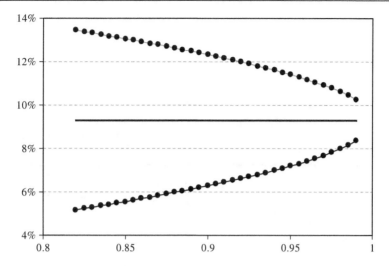

Figure IV.6.3   1% 10-day VaR with two-standard-error bounds versus EWMA λ

Student t Distributed Portfolio Returns

From our discussion in Section IV.2.8.2 we know that the one-period VaR estimate based on an assumed i.i.d. Student t distribution for portfolio returns, with ν degrees of freedom, is

$$\text{Student } t \text{ VaR}_{\alpha,\nu} = \sqrt{\nu^{-1}(\nu - 2)}\, t_\nu^{-1}(1 - \alpha)\sigma, \qquad (\text{IV.6.6})$$

where σ is the standard deviation of the portfolio's daily returns and the portfolio is expected to return the risk free rate. When h is relatively small the errors from square-root scaling on a Student t distribution are not too large, so a very approximate formula for the $100\alpha\%$ h-day VaR,[30] as a proportion of the portfolio value, is

$$\text{Student } t \text{ VaR}_{h,\alpha,\nu} = \sqrt{\nu^{-1}(\nu - 2)h}\, t_\nu^{-1}(1 - \alpha)\sigma. \qquad (\text{IV.6.7})$$

When h is more than about 10 days (or more, if ν is relatively small) the normal linear VaR formula should be applied, because the sum of h i.i.d. Student t distributed returns will have an approximately normal distribution, by the central limit theorem.

In the linear VaR model the leptokurtosis of a Student t distribution usually increases the 1% VaR estimate and its estimated standard errors, relative to a normal distribution assumption. Figure IV.6.4 compares the 1% 10-day VaR estimate, and the two-standard-error bounds, based on normal returns and based on Student t returns with 6 degrees of freedom.[31] As in the previous figures the sample size is shown on the horizontal axis, and we suppose that the portfolio volatility is 20%, but this – and the degrees of freedom and other parameters – can be changed in the spreadsheet. As expected, the confidence intervals become wider under the Student t assumption, but the main effect of the leptokurtosis that is introduced by the Student t

---

[30] Approximate because the Student t distribution is not stable.
[31] Here if we assume that the degrees of freedom parameter is imposed rather than estimated from the portfolio returns. When the degrees of freedom parameter is estimated from the portfolio returns, another sampling error is introduced, so the confidence interval becomes even wider.

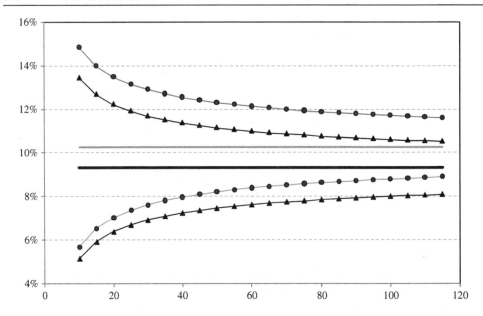

Figure IV.6.4   1% 10-day VaR with two-standard-error bounds – Student *t* versus normal

distribution is to increase the 1% VaR estimate itself, from 9.31% 10.26%. This is depicted by the horizontal grey line in the figure, and the two-standard-error bounds on the student *t* VaR are depicted by the lines with circle markers.

When linear VaR estimates are based on a multivariate elliptical (i.e. normal or Student *t*) i.i.d. model for risk factor returns, estimation risk arises from the covariance matrix estimator which, as we know from Chapter II.3, can be equally weighted or exponentially weighted. In the case of equities, another important source of estimation risk arises from the model used to estimate the factor betas. The risk factor return distribution parameters, and the factor betas are not necessarily based on the same model, or even on the same sample. And even when they are, it is quite complex to estimate the standard error of a quadratic form: the VaR estimator is a non-linear estimator and so its variance does not obey simple rules.

IV.6.3.2   Distribution of VaR Estimators in Simulation Models

Rather than derive an approximate formula for the multivariate elliptical linear VaR estimates, we might consider using an approximate standard error for a quantile estimator directly, as explained below. But these standard errors are much less precise than those considered in the previous subsection. That is because those derived from the variance estimator, whilst still approximate, utilize the normality (or Student *t*) assumption for the portfolio returns, whilst the standard errors for quantile estimators use no information about the return distribution (other than that it be continuous) and – so that we can derive a relatively simple form for the standard error of a quantile estimator – they employ a very crude assumption that the density is constant in the relevant region of the tail.

When VaR estimation is based on historical or Monte Carlo simulation, sampling error can be a major cause of estimation risk. Even in the standard historical model (i.e. the model with no parametric or semi-parametric volatility adjustment or filtering of returns) sampling error can introduce considerable uncertainty into the VaR estimate. Sampling error is usually much easier to control in the Monte Carlo VaR model but, unlike standard historical simulation, the Monte Carlo approach is also prone to estimation risk stemming from inaccuracy in parameter estimates.

For instance, using a normal i.i.d. model for portfolio returns in Monte Carlo VaR, we have a sampling variation which depends on the number of Monte Carlo simulations, and we also have a standard error of the VaR estimate arising from the volatility estimator, as described in the previous subsection. Variance reduction techniques – and using a very large number of simulations – can reduce sampling variation substantially, so the parameter estimation risk and the more general model risk arising from the choice of parametric form tend to dominate the standard error of the Monte Carlo VaR estimate. Quite the opposite is the case for the standard historical simulation VaR model. Here there are no parameters to estimate so the historical sample size has everything to do with the efficiency of the quantile estimator.

As a proportion of the portfolio value, $\text{VaR}_{h,\alpha}$ is -1 times the α quantile of an h-day portfolio return distribution. So standard errors for historical VaR may be derived from an approximate distribution for the estimator of an α quantile, based on a random sample size T.

Let us denote the α quantile estimator based on a random sample size T by $q(T, \alpha)$. First we derive the distribution of the number of observations less than the α quantile, denoted $X(T, \alpha)$. Then we translate this into a distribution for $p(T, \alpha) = T^{-1}X(T, \alpha)$, the proportion of returns less than the α quantile. Finally. we derive the distribution of $q(T, \alpha) = F^{-1}\big(p(T, \alpha)\big)$, where F denotes the distribution function of the portfolio returns, using an approximation.

Since the sample is random, $X(T, \alpha)$ has a binomial distribution with parameters T and α. Hence, its expectation and variance are $T\alpha$ and $T\alpha(1 - \alpha)$, respectively.[32] But as $T \to \infty$ and when α is fixed, a special case of the central limit theorem tells us that the binomial distribution converges to a normal distribution,

$$\frac{X(T, \alpha) - T\alpha}{\sqrt{T\alpha(1 - \alpha)}} \to N(0, 1).$$

Dividing both the numerator and the denominator of this statistic by T, we have

$$\frac{p(T, \alpha) - \alpha}{\sqrt{T^{-1}\alpha(1 - \alpha)}} \to N(0, 1). \tag{IV.6.8}$$

We have already used this result to derive approximate confidence intervals for quantiles, and a numerical example to demonstrate this is given in Section II.8.4.1. But here we want to derive an approximate standard error for the quantile in large samples. So, on noting that $p(T, \alpha) = F\big(q(T, \alpha)\big)$, we first write (IV.6.8) as

$$F\big(q(T, \alpha)\big) \overset{asy}{\sim} N\big(\alpha, T^{-1}\alpha(1 - \alpha)\big). \tag{IV.6.9}$$

Following Kendall (1940), we now assume that F is approximately linear 'in the material range of the sampling distribution'. That is, we use the local approximation

$$F\big(q(T, \alpha)\big) \approx q(T, \alpha)f\big(q(T, \alpha)\big)$$

---

[32] See Section I.3.3.1.

where $f(q(T, \alpha))$ is the density function at $q(T, \alpha)$. In other words, the density function is assumed to be flat in the region of the tail that we are considering. Substituting this in (IV.6.9) gives an approximate distribution for $q(T, \alpha)$ as

$$q(T, \alpha) \overset{asy}{\sim} N\left(f(q(T, \alpha))^{-1} \alpha, f(q(T, \alpha))^{-2} T^{-1}\alpha(1 - \alpha)\right). \tag{IV.6.10}$$

In particular, an approximate standard error for the quantile estimator $q(T, \alpha)$ is given by

$$s.e.(q(T, \alpha)) \approx f(q(T, \alpha))^{-1} \sqrt{T^{-1}\alpha(1 - \alpha)}. \tag{IV.6.11}$$

Since the $100\alpha\%$ VaR is $-q(T, \alpha)$, it has the same standard error as $q(T, \alpha)$.

The formula just derived requires knowledge of the portfolio return distribution, and in particular of its density function f. Then it may be applied to estimate approximate standard errors for historical VaR estimates. However, these standard errors are based on a very strong assumption about the shape of the tail of the distribution, i.e. that it is locally flat. So the standard errors (IV.6.11) are very approximate indeed. To demonstrate this, the following example compares standard errors that are estimated using (IV.6.11) with those based on (IV.6.3) in the case where the density function in (IV.6.11) is known to be normal.

EXAMPLE IV.6.4: CONFIDENCE INTERVALS FOR QUANTILES

Given a random sample of size 1000 from a normal distribution with known mean zero and volatility 20%, derive the approximate standard errors (IV.6.11) for $100\alpha\%$ h-day VaR, for different values of α and h. How does the result change with the random sample size? Compare these standard errors with the estimated standard errors (IV.6.3) that are based on sampling error in equally weighted volatility estimators.

SOLUTION   When the distribution is known to be normal with mean zero and volatility σ, the quantile estimate $q(T, \alpha)$ is given by the Excel function NORMINV($\alpha, 0, \sigma$), and this is independent of the sample size T. The first factor on the right-hand side of (IV.6.11), i.e. $f(q(T, \alpha))^{-1}$, is given by the Excel function

$$= 1/\text{NORMDIST(NORMINV}(1 - \alpha, 0, \sigma), 0, \sigma, \text{false})),$$

and the dependence of the estimated standard error on sample size only enters through the second factor $\sqrt{T^{-1}\alpha(1 - \alpha)}$ in (IV.6.11).

In the spreadsheet we compute (IV.6.11) for different values of α and h and with a sample size of 1000. Results are summarized in Table IV.6.6, which is similar to Table IV.6.5 except that, for comparison with the quantile-based standard errors, the sample size for the equally weighted volatility-based standard errors is 1000 rather than 100. As a result, the estimated standard errors based on σ are much smaller than those in Table IV.6.5.

Figure IV.6.5 depicts the estimated standard error of the 1% 10-day VaR estimate based on (a) the equally weighted volatility estimator for σ and (b) the quantile estimator. As in the example above, we assume the population is normal with mean zero and volatility 20%, so the VaR estimate is 9.31% of the portfolio value. The figure shows the effect that sample size has on the standard error of the VaR estimate. For small samples, the precision of the

Table IV.6.6   VaR standard errors based on volatility and based on quantile

h		α			
		0.10%	1%	5%	10%
1	**VaR**	**3.91%**	**2.94%**	**2.08%**	**1.62%**
	s.e.(based on σ)	0.09%	0.07%	0.05%	0.04%
	s.e.(based on quantile)	0.38%	0.15%	0.08%	0.07%
3	**VaR**	**6.77%**	**5.10%**	**3.60%**	**2.81%**
	s.e.(based on σ)	0.15%	0.11%	0.08%	0.06%
	s.e.(based on quantile)	0.65%	0.26%	0.15%	0.12%
5	**VaR**	**8.74%**	**6.58%**	**4.65%**	**3.62%**
	s.e.(based on σ)	0.20%	0.15%	0.10%	0.08%
	s.e.(based on quantile)	0.84%	0.33%	0.19%	0.15%
10	**VaR**	**12.36%**	**9.31%**	**6.58%**	**5.13%**
	s.e.(based on σ)	0.28%	0.21%	0.15%	0.11%
	s.e.(based on quantile)	1.19%	0.47%	0.27%	0.22%
25	**VaR**	**19.54%**	**14.71%**	**10.40%**	**8.11%**
	s.e.(based on σ)	0.44%	0.33%	0.23%	0.18%
	s.e.(based on quantile)	1.88%	0.75%	0.42%	0.34%
100	**VaR**	**39.09%**	**29.43%**	**20.81%**	**16.21%**
	s.e.(based on σ)	0.87%	0.66%	0.47%	0.36%
	s.e.(based on quantile)	3.75%	1.49%	0.85%	0.68%
250	**VaR**	**61.80%**	**46.53%**	**32.90%**	**25.63%**
	s.e.(based on σ)	1.38%	1.04%	0.74%	0.57%
	s.e.(based on quantile)	5.94%	2.36%	1.34%	1.08%

Note: Estimates are based on a sample size 1000 and a normal population with mean zero and volatility 20%.

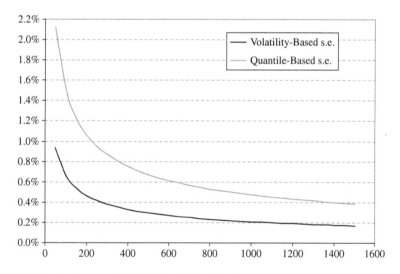

Figure IV.6.5   Standard errors of 1% 10-day VaR estimate
Note: This graph assumes portfolio returns are normal with volatility of 20%.

quantile estimates is very low. For every sample size, the quantile-based standard error is approximately twice the size of the volatility-based standard errors.[33]

IV.6.4   MODEL VALIDATION

This section presents a series of increasingly complex approaches to VaR model validation through out-of-sample forecast evaluation techniques that are commonly termed *backtests*. Failure of a backtest indicates VaR model misspecification and/or large estimation errors, and regression-based backtests may also help diagnose the cause of a model failure.

IV.6.4.1   Backtesting Methodology

A backtest takes a fixed portfolio, which we shall call the *candidate portfolio*, and uses this portfolio to assess the accuracy of a VaR model. The term 'candidate portfolio' is used to denote a portfolio that represents a typical exposure to the underlying risk factors. If the portfolio is expressed in terms of holdings in certain assets or instruments, we assume the weights or the holdings are fixed for the entire backtest.[34] More usual is to express the portfolio in terms of a risk factor mapping, in which case – for a dynamic VaR estimate – we assume the risk factor sensitivities are constant throughout the backtest.

The result of a backtest depends on the portfolio composition, as well as on the evolution of the risk factors and the assumptions made about risk factor return distributions when building the model. Thus, it is possible for the same VaR model to pass a backtest for portfolio A, but fail a backtest for portfolio B, even when the portfolios have identical underlying risk factors.

We should perform a backtest using a very long period of historical data on the asset or risk factor values. Otherwise the test will lack the power to reject inaccurate VaR models. And because we need to base the test on a very large non-overlapping sample, backtests are usually performed at the daily frequency. So in the following we shall assume we have a large sample of daily returns on all the relevant risk factors. The entire data period will often encompass many years. For instance, more than 10 years of daily data are needed to backtest ETL, as described later in this section. The longer the backtest period, the more powerful the results will be.

First, assuming the VaR estimate will be based on historical data,[35] we fix an *estimation period* which defines the sample used to estimate the VaR model parameters. We tend to use much shorter estimation periods for parametric linear VaR models and Monte Carlo VaR models than we do for historical simulation VaR models. And in the parametric models, the estimation period also tends to increase with the risk horizon. This is because smaller samples yield VaR estimates that are more *risk sensitive*, i.e. that respond more to changes in the current market conditions.

Then we employ a *rolling window* approach as follows. The *estimation sample* is rolled over almost the entire data period, keeping the estimation period constant, starting at the beginning

---

[33] This depends on the significance level of the VaR but not on the sample size. For a 1% VaR estimate, the quantile-based standard error is 2.28 times as large as the volatility-based standard error; but for a 0.1% VaR, this multiple increases to 4.3.

[34] If it is a long-only (or short-only) portfolio, we could keep either the portfolio weights or the portfolio holdings constant; otherwise we keep the holdings constant. Note that keeping the weights constant assumes dynamic rebalancing over the risk horizon (i.e. dynamic VaR) whereas keeping the holdings constant produces a static VaR estimate.

[35] This is always the case for the historical simulation model. It may also be the case for parametric linear and Monte Carlo VaR models, where historical data are used to estimate the parameters of the risk factor returns distribution.

of the data period. We fix the length of the risk horizon, and the test sample starts at the end of the estimation sample. If the risk horizon is h days, we roll the estimation and test periods forward h days, and we keep rolling the estimation and test samples over the entire data period until the test sample ends on the last day of our data period. In this way, we do not use *overlapping data* in the test sample.

Figure IV.6.6 illustrates the rolling window approach: the bold line at the bottom indicates the whole sample covering the entire historical data period. The estimation and test samples are shown in black and grey, respectively; during the backtest these are rolled progressively, h days at a time, until the entire sample is exhausted.

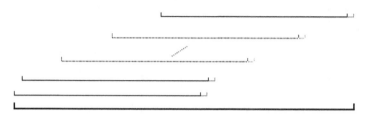

Figure IV.6.6   Rolling windows with estimation and test samples

For example, consider a sample with 10,000 daily observations where the estimation sample size is 1000 days and the risk horizon is 10 days. The backtest proceeds as follows. Use the estimation sample to estimate the 10-day VaR on the 1000th day, at the required confidence level. This is the VaR for the 10-day return from the 1000th to the 1010th observation. Then, assuming the VaR is expressed as a percentage of the portfolio value, we observe the *realized return* over this 10-day test period, and record both the VaR and the realized return.[36] Then we roll the window forward 10 days and repeat the above, until the end of the entire sample. The result of this procedure will be two time series covering the sample from the 1010th until the 10,000th observation, i.e. covering all the consecutive rolling test periods. One series is the 10-day VaR and the other is (what econometricians call) the 10-day 'realized' return or P&L on the portfolio. The backtest is based on these two series.

Figure IV.6.7 depicts two such series that will form the basis of most of the backtests that are illustrated in this section.[37] The backtest sample, which is constructed from all the consecutive test periods, is from January 2000 until December 2007. For simplicity there will be 2000 observations in many of the backtests, and we shall base the tests on the 1% daily VaR. So we expect the VaR to be exceeded 20 times (in other words, the expected number of exceedances is 20). *Exceedances* occur when the portfolio loses more than the VaR that was predicted at the start of the risk horizon.[38] We have depicted the series -1 times the VaR prediction in the figure so that the exceedances are obvious when the grey P&L line crosses the black VaR line; for instance, an exceedance already occurs on the very first day of the backtest sample.

---

[36] Here we are using the term 'realized return' in the econometric rather than the accountancy sense. However, if the VaR is expressed in value terms, so we need to observe the P&L over this 10-day test period, to say we record the 'realized P&L' is rather confusing. For clarification, see Section IV.6.4.2, where we emphasize the distinction between *realized* P&L and *unrealized* P&L. An econometrician does not make this distinction, and in fact realized return or P&L for an econometrician is hypothetical, *unrealized* return or P&L for an accountant!

[37] In the spreadsheet for this figure readers will see that the VaR is for a $100 per point position on the S&P 500 index, and the estimate is based on the normal linear model using 250 daily log returns to estimate the standard deviation.

[38] Other terms used instead of 'exceedance' are 'violation' and 'hit'.

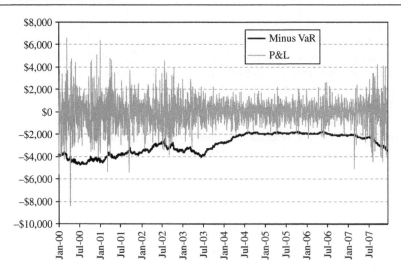

Figure IV.6.7   1% daily VaR and daily P&L

In total the VaR is exceed 33 times, not 20 times, in this figure. By changing the parameters in the spreadsheet readers will see that the 5% daily VaR is exceeded 105 times instead of 100 times.[39] It appears that our VaR estimates may be too low because a higher VaR would give fewer exceedances. How can we use this information to construct a statistical test of the hypothesis that the VaR estimates provide accurate forecasts?

Most backtests on daily VaR are based on the assumption that the daily returns or P&L are generated by an i.i.d. *Bernoulli process*. A Bernoulli variable may take only two values, which could be labelled 1 and 0, or 'success' and 'failure'. In our context, we would call 'success' an exceedance of the VaR by the return or P&L, and further assign this the value 1. Thus we may define an *indicator function* $I_{\alpha,t}$ on the time series of daily returns or P&L relative to the $100\alpha\%$ daily VaR by

$$I_{\alpha,t+1} = \begin{cases} 1, & \text{if } Y_{t+1} < -\text{VaR}_{1,\alpha,t}, \\ 0, & \text{otherwise.} \end{cases} \tag{IV.6.12}$$

Here Y_{t+1} is the 'realized' daily return or P&L on the portfolio from time t, when the VaR estimate is made, to time $t+1$.[40]

If the VaR model is accurate and $\{I_{\alpha,t}\}$ follows an i.i.d. Bernoulli process, the probability of 'success' at any time t is α. Thus the expected number of successes in a test sample with n observations is $n\alpha$. Denote the number of successes by the random variable $X_{n,\alpha}$. From Section I.3.3.1 we know that our assumptions imply that $X_{n,\alpha}$ has a binomial distribution with parameters n and α. Thus

$$E(X_{n,\alpha}) = n\alpha, \tag{IV.6.13}$$

---

[39] We keep the number of observations in the backtests constant at 2000, whatever the risk horizon, so for a 1% VaR the expected number of exceedances is always 20, but for a 5% VaR we expect 100 exceedances.
[40] If VaR is expressed in value terms our series $\{Y_t\}$ is a series of P&L, and if VaR is expressed as a percentage of portfolio value our series $\{Y_t\}$ is a series of portfolio returns.

and the variance is

$$V(X_{n,\alpha}) = n\alpha(1 - \alpha). \qquad (IV.6.14)$$

The standard error of the estimate, $\sqrt{n\alpha(1 - \alpha)}$, provides a measure of uncertainty around the expected value. Due to sampling error we are unlikely to obtain exactly the expected number of exceedances in a backtest; instead we should consider a confidence interval around the expected value within which it is very likely that the observed number of exceedances will fall. When n is very large the distribution of $X_{n,\alpha}$ is approximately normal, so a two-sided 95% confidence interval for $X_{n,\alpha}$ under the null hypothesis that the VaR model is accurate is approximately

$$\left(n\alpha - 1.96\sqrt{n\alpha(1 - \alpha)}, n\alpha + 1.96\sqrt{n\alpha(1 - \alpha)}\right). \qquad (IV.6.15)$$

For instance, if $n = 2000$ and $\alpha = 1\%$ the standard error is $\sqrt{20 \times 0.99} = 4.4497$. So, based on (IV.6.15), a 95% confidence interval for the number of exceedances is approximately (11.28, 28.72). The observed value of 33 exceedances for the 1% daily VaR in Figure IV.6.7 lies outside this interval, so obtaining such a value is likely to lead to a rejection of the null hypothesis, but this depends on the particular backtest that we employ. The rest of this section describes different backtest statistics, most of which are based on the exceedances that have been described above.

IV.6.4.2   Guidelines for Backtesting from Banking Regulators

Section IV.8.2.4 describes the use of VaR models for estimating regulatory market risk capital and, in particular, the use of a *multiplier* to convert VaR estimates into the minimum market risk capital requirement. Banking supervisors will only allow internal models to be used for regulatory capital calculation if they provide satisfactory results in backtests. The 1996 Amendment to the 1988 Basel Accord contains a detailed description of the backtests that supervisors will review and models that fail them will either be disallowed for use in regulatory capital calculations, or be subject to the highest multiplier value of 4.

Regulators recommend a very simple type of backtest, which is based on a 1% daily VaR estimate and which covers a period of only 250 days. Hence, the expected number of exceedances is 2.5 and the standard error of the number of exceedances, i.e. the square root of (IV.6.14), is $\sqrt{2.5 \times 0.99} = 1.5732$. Regulators wish to guard against VaR models whose estimates are too low. Since they are very conservative they will only consider that models having 4 exceptions or less as sufficiently accurate. These so-called *green zone* models have a multiplier of 3. If there are between 5 and 9 exceptions, the model is *yellow zone*, which means it is admissible for regulatory capital calculations but the multiplier is increased as shown in Table IV.6.7. A *red zone* model means there are 10 or more exceptions. Then the multiplier takes its maximum of value 4, or the VaR model is disallowed.

When regulatory capital is calculated using an internal VaR model it is based on 1% 10-day VaR. So why do regulators ask for backtests of daily VaR? It would be difficult to perform a backtest on 250 non-overlapping 10-day returns, since the data would need to span at least 10 years for the backtest to have sufficient accuracy. Is it possible to derive a simple table such as Table IV.6.7 using *overlapping data* in certain backtests, i.e. to roll the estimation and test periods forward by only one day even when the risk horizon is longer than one day? Then we could not use our standard assumption that exceedances follow an *i.i.d. Bernoulli*

Table IV.6.7   Basel zones for VaR models

Number of exceedances	Multiplier for capital calculation
4 or less	3
5	3.4
6	3.5
7	3.65
8	3.75
9	3.85
10 or more	4

process. Exceedances would be positively autocorrelated (for instance, one extremely large daily loss would impact on ten consecutive 10-day returns) and so, whilst the expected number of exceedances would remain unchanged from (IV.6.13), the variance would no longer be equal to (IV.6.14). In fact, it would be much greater than (IV.6.14) because the exceedances are positively autocorrelated, so the confidence interval (IV.6.15) would become considerably wider and the backtest would have even lower power that it does already.

Nevertheless, in practice 10-day VaR estimates *are* based on overlapping samples, since we estimate 1% 10-day VaR every day. So we have allowed readers to use most of the spreadsheets for this chapter to examine the pattern of exceedances based on overlapping data. Daily clustering of exceptional losses that exceed the VaR is much more likely when both the VaR estimate and the P&L are based on a 10-day risk horizon. By examining series such as these 10-day returns based on overlapping samples, banks could gauge the likelihood that their minimum regulatory capital may be exceeded on every day during one week, for instance. Formal backtests are difficult to derive theoretically for overlapping estimation samples, but at least banks would be examining the 10-day VaR estimates that they actually use for their risk capital calculations.

Most regulators allow banks to base regulatory capital on daily VaR estimates and then scale these estimates up using a square-root-of-time rule. But this rule is only valid for linear portfolios with i.i.d. normally distributed returns, and since most portfolios have non-normally distributed returns that are not i.i.d., the use of square-root scaling is a very common source of model risk. If regulators changed the number exceedances in green, yellow and red zones to correspond to autocorrelated 10-day VaR estimates, resulting from overlapping estimation samples, then banks would have the incentive to increase the accuracy of 10-day VaR estimates by scaling their daily VaR appropriately, or by estimating 10-day VaR directly without scaling up the daily VaR at all. Another feature of regulatory backtests that is not easy to understand is why they require only 250 days in the backtest. With such a small sample the power of the test to reject a false hypothesis is very low indeed. So, all in all, it is highly likely that an inaccurate VaR model will pass the regulatory backtest.

VaR estimates are based on one of two theoretical assumptions about trading on the portfolio. Either the portfolio is assumed to be rebalanced over the risk horizon to keep its asset weights or risk factor sensitivities constant, or it is assumed that the portfolio is held static so that no trading takes place and the holdings are constant. The assumption made here influences the VaR estimate for option portfolios over risk horizons longer than 1 day. But both assumptions lack realism. In practice, portfolios are actively managed at the trader's discretion, and the actual or *realized P&L* on the portfolio is not equal to the hypothetical, *unrealized P&L*, i.e. the P&L on which the VaR estimate is based. In accountancy terminology the unrealized P&L is the mark-to-market P&L, whereas the realized P&L includes all the P&L from intraday trading and is based on prices that are actually traded. Realized P&L may also include fee income, any use of the bank's reserves and funding costs. With these additional items we call it *actual P&L* and without these it is called *cleaned P&L*. To avoid confusion, we shall call the hypothetical, unrealized P&L the *theoretical P&L*.

Many banking regulators (for instance, in the UK) require two types of backtests, both of which are based on the simple methodology described above. Their tests must be based on both realized (actual or cleaned) P&L and on theoretical P&L. Backtests based on theoretical P&L are testing the VaR model assumptions. However, those based on realized 1-day P&L are not testing how the model will perform in practice, as a means of estimating regulatory capital, unless the scaling of 1-day VaR to 10-day VaR is accurate.

IV.6.4.3 Coverage Tests

Unconditional coverage tests, introduced by Kupiec (1995), are also based on the number of exceedances, i.e. the number of times the portfolio loses more than the previous day's VaR estimate in the backtest. They may be regarded as a more sophisticated and flexible version of the banking regulators' backtesting rules described above. The idea was both formalized and generalized by Christoffersen (1998) to include tests on the *independence of exceedances* (i.e. whether exceedances come in clusters) and *conditional coverage* tests (which combine unconditional coverage and independence into one test). Section II.8.4.2 described these tests in the context of any model for forecasting either or both tails, or indeed any interval of a distribution. In this subsection we discuss their application to VaR models, which specifically forecast the lower tail of a portfolio returns or P&L distribution.

An unconditional coverage test is a test of the null hypothesis that the indicator function (IV.6.12), which is assumed to follow an i.i.d. Bernoulli process, has a constant 'success' probability equal to the significance level of the VaR, α. The test statistic is a likelihood ratio statistic given by (II.8.17) and repeated here for convenience. It is

$$LR_{\mathrm{uc}} = \frac{\pi_{\exp}^{n_1} \left(1 - \pi_{\exp}\right)^{n_0}}{\pi_{\mathrm{obs}}^{n_1} \left(1 - \pi_{\mathrm{obs}}\right)^{n_0}}, \tag{IV.6.16}$$

where $\pi_{\exp}$ is the expected *proportion* of exceedances, π_{obs} is the observed proportion of exceedances, n_1 is the observed *number* of exceedances and $n_0 = n - n_1$ where n is the sample size of the backtest. So n_0 is the number of returns with indicator 0 (we can call these returns the 'good' returns). Note that $\pi_{\exp} = \alpha$ and $\pi_{\mathrm{obs}} = n_1/n$. The asymptotic distribution of $-2 \ln LR_{\mathrm{uc}}$ is chi-squared with one degree of freedom.

EXAMPLE IV.6.5: UNCONDITIONAL COVERAGE TEST

Perform an unconditional coverage test on the 1% daily VaR for a $100 per point position on the S&P 500 index, where the backtest is based on 2000 observations from January 2000 to December 2007, as in Figure IV.6.7.

SOLUTION   We have 33 exceedances based on sample of size 2000. Hence

$$n = 2000, n_0 = 1967, n_1 = 33, \pi_{\exp} = 0.01, \text{ and } \pi_{\mathrm{obs}} = 33/2000 = 0.0165. \tag{IV.6.17}$$

It is better to compute the log of the likelihood ratio statistic directly, rather than computing (IV.6.16) and afterwards taking the log, because in this way the rounding errors are reduced. Hence, we use the parameter values (IV.6.17) to calculate

$$\ln(LR_{uc}) = n_1 \ln(\pi_{exp}) + n_0 \ln(1 - \pi_{exp}) - n_1 \ln(\pi_{obs}) - n_0 \ln(1 - \pi_{obs}),$$

obtaining the value -3.5684. Hence $-2\ln LR_{uc} = 7.1367$. The 1% critical value of a chi-squared distribution with one degree of freedom is 6.6349. So we reject, at the 1% significance level, the null hypothesis that the VaR model is accurate in the sense that the total number of exceedances is close to the expected number.

Using the spreadsheet for Example IV.6.5 we can plot the indicator function (IV.6.12) for the case $\alpha = 1\%$ and $h = 1$. This is shown in Figure IV.6.8. It is clear from this figure that the exceedances come in clusters. There are no exceedances at all in 2003 and 2004, but plenty during 2007. In fact, during the last six months of the backtest there are 12 exceedances, shown in the inset to the figure, although the expected number is less than 2.

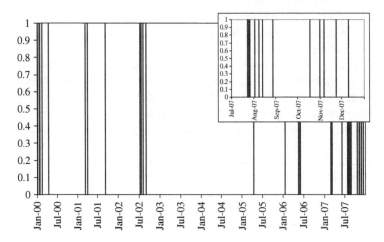

Figure IV.6.8   Indicator of exceedances

Clustering of exceedances indicates that the VaR model is not sufficiently responsive to changing market circumstances. In the case in point, the last six months of the backtest marked the beginning of the credit crisis. But the normal linear VaR estimates here were based on an equally weighted average of the last 250 squared log returns, so this model does not account for the volatility clustering that we know is prevalent in many markets. Even if the model passes the unconditional coverage test, i.e. when the observed number of exceedances is near the expected number, we could still reject the VaR model if the exceedances are not independent.

A test for independence of exceedances is based on the formalization of the notion that when exceedances are not independent the probability of an exceedance tomorrow, given there has been an exceedance today, is no longer equal to α. As before, let n_1 be the observed number of exceedances and $n_0 = n - n_1$ be the number of 'good' returns. Further, define n_{ij} to be the number of returns with indicator value i followed by indicator value j, i.e. n_{00} is the number of times a good return is followed by another good return, n_{01} the number of times a good return is followed by an exceedance, n_{10} the number of times an exceedance is followed by a good return, and n_{11} the number of times an exceedance is followed by another exceedance. So $n_1 = n_{11} + n_{01}$ and $n_0 = n_{10} + n_{00}$. Also let

$$\pi_{01} = \frac{n_{01}}{n_{00} + n_{01}} \quad \text{and} \quad \pi_{11} = \frac{n_{11}}{n_{10} + n_{11}}, \tag{IV.6.18}$$

i.e. π_{01} is the proportion of exceedances, given that the last return was a 'good' return, and π_{11} is the proportion of exceedances, given that the last return was an exceedance. Now we can state the independence test statistic, derived by Christoffersen (1998), as

$$LR_{ind} = \frac{\pi_{obs}^{n_1} (1 - \pi_{obs})^{n_0}}{\pi_{01}^{n_{01}} (1 - \pi_{01})^{n_{00}} \pi_{11}^{n_{11}} (1 - \pi_{11})^{n_{10}}}. \tag{IV.6.19}$$

The asymptotic distribution of $-2 \ln LR_{ind}$ is chi-squared with one degree of freedom.

EXAMPLE IV.6.6: INDEPENDENCE TEST

Perform the independence test for the data of the previous example.

SOLUTION   In addition to the results in (IV.6.17) we have only two sets of two consecutive exceedances. The rest are isolated, if only separated by a few days in many cases, as is evident from Figure IV.6.8. Hence,

$$n_{11} = 2, n_{00} = 1936, n_{01} = n_{10} = 31.$$

Using these values in (IV.6.18) and in (IV.6.19) gives $\ln(LR_{ind}) = -1.2134$, so $-2 \ln LR_{uc} = 2.4268$. The 10% critical value of a chi-squared distribution with one degree of freedom is 2.7055. Hence, we cannot even reject the null hypothesis that the exceedances are independent at 10%.

Why is the independence test unable to detect the clustering in exceedances that is clearly evident from Figure IV.6.8? The problem is that in the above example we often have a day (or two or three) with no exceedance coming between two exceedances, and the Christoffersen independence test only works if exceedances are actually consecutive. That is because the test is based on a first order Markov chain only, and to detect the type of clustering we have in this example it would have to be extended to a higher order Markov chain, to allow more than first order dependence.

   A combined test, for both unconditional coverage and independence, is the *conditional coverage* statistic given by

$$LR_{cc} = \frac{\pi_{exp}^{n_1} (1 - \pi_{exp})^{n_0}}{\pi_{01}^{n_{01}} (1 - \pi_{01})^{n_{00}} \pi_{11}^{n_{11}} (1 - \pi_{11})^{n_{10}}}. \tag{IV.6.20}$$

The asymptotic distribution of $-2 \ln LR_{cc}$ is chi-squared with two degrees of freedom. On comparing the three test statistics it is clear that $LR_{cc} = LR_{uc} \times LR_{ind}$, i.e.

$$-2 \ln LR_{cc} = -2 \ln LR_{uc} - 2 \ln LR_{ind}.$$

For instance, in the above examples we have

$$-2 \ln LR_{cc} = 6.6349 + 2.4268 = 9.0617.$$

The 5% critical value of the chi-squared distribution with 2 degrees of freedom is 5.9915 and the 1% critical value is 9.2103. Hence we reject the null hypothesis at 5% but not (quite) at 1%.

IV.6.4.4 Backtests Based on Regression

In our empirical examples of the previous subsection, where we were backtesting a normal linear VaR model for a simple position on the S&P 500 index, the results suggested that the clustering of exceedances could be linked to market volatility. This would be the case when a VaR model is not accounting adequately for the volatility clustering in a portfolio's returns. Indeed, such a link is clear from Figure IV.6.9, which shows the indicator of exceedances alongside the Vix (the S&P 500 implied volatility index) over the same period as the backtest. Exceedances are more common when there is a large daily change in the implied volatility, especially when volatility jumps upward after a long period of low volatility. This observation explains why we have so many exceedances during the recent credit crisis, and provides an understanding of how to improve the VaR model. This observation also suggests a backtest based on a regression model that takes the indicator function as the dependent variable and, in this case, the daily change in the Vix as the explanatory variable.

If past information can be used to predict exceedances, the VaR model is not utilizing all the information available in the market. More generally, if we believe that the VaR model is misspecified because it is not utilizing information linked to *lagged* values of one or more variables, which we summarize in the vector $\mathbf{x} = (X_1, \ldots, X_k)$, then a backtest could be based on a regression model of the form

$$I_t = \beta_0 + \beta_1 X_{1,t-1} + \ldots + \beta_k X_{k,t-1} + \varepsilon_t. \tag{IV.6.21}$$

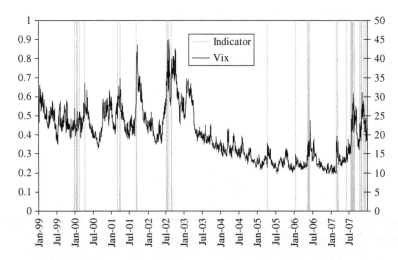

Figure IV.6.9 Relation between exceedances and implied volatility

Taking the conditional expectation of this yields

$$P(I_t = 1 \,|\, \mathbf{x}_{t-1}) = \beta_0 + \beta_1 X_{1,t-1} + \ldots + \beta_k X_{k,t-1}, \qquad (IV.6.22)$$

since

$$E(I_t \,|\, \mathbf{x}_{t-1}) = 1 \times P(I_t = 1 \,|\, \mathbf{x}_{t-1}) + 0 \times P(I_t = 0 \,|\, \mathbf{x}_{t-1}) = P(I_t = 1 \,|\, \mathbf{x}_{t-1}). \qquad (IV.6.23)$$

But if the model is well specified, then $P(I_t = 1 \,|\, \mathbf{x}_{t-1}) = \alpha$. Hence, the backtest is based on the null hypothesis

$$H_0 : \beta_0 = \alpha, \quad \beta_1 = \ldots = \beta_k = 0. \qquad (IV.6.24)$$

This can be tested by estimating the parameters using OLS, and then using one of the hypothesis tests described in Section I.4.4.8.

We now illustrate this approach to backtesting using a standard F test of the composite hypothesis (IV.6.24), based on the statistic (I.4.48), repeated here for convenience:

$$\frac{p^{-1}(RSS_R - RSS_U)}{v^{-1}RSS_U} \sim F_{p,v}, \qquad (IV.6.25)$$

where p is the number of restrictions and v is the sample size less the number of variables in the regression including the constant. The regression model is estimated twice, first with no restrictions, giving the *unrestricted* residual sum of squares RSS_U, and then after imposing the restrictions in the null hypothesis, to obtain the *restricted* residual sum of squares RSS_R.

EXAMPLE IV.6.7: REGRESSION-BASED BACKTEST

For our S&P 500 normal linear model for 1% daily VaR, implement a backtest using the statistic (IV.6.25) and based on a model of the form

$$I_t = \beta_0 + \beta_1 \Delta \mathrm{Vix}_{t-1} + \varepsilon_t. \qquad (IV.6.26)$$

SOLUTION   In the spreadsheet for this example we first estimate (IV.6.26) using OLS, giving $RSS_U = 32.4317$. Then we take the sum of the squared deviations of the indicator function from α, where α is set to 1% in this case, giving $RSS_R = 32.5409$. We have $p = 2$ and $v = 1998$, and substituting these values into (IV.6.25) gives a value for the F statistic of 3.3637. The 5% critical value for the F distribution is 3.0002 and the 1% critical value is 4.6158. So we reject the null hypothesis

$$H_0 : \beta_0 = \alpha, \quad \beta_1 = 0, \qquad (IV.6.27)$$

at 5%, but only just.

However, the rejection of the null in this case is because $\beta_0 \neq \alpha$ and not because $\beta_1 \neq 0$. We can verify this using a simple t test for the two hypotheses $H_0 : \beta_0 = \alpha$ and $H_0 : \beta_1 = 0$ separately.[41] For $H_0 : \beta_0 = \alpha$ versus $H_1 : \beta_0 \neq \alpha$ we obtain a t ratio of 2.2817, whereas the 5% critical value is 1.9612 and the 1% critical value is 2.5783. So we can reject the null hypothesis

---

[41] See Section I.4.2.5 for further details.

at 5% but not at 1%. But for $H_0 : \beta_1 = 0$ versus the two-sided alternative, we obtain a t ratio of only 1.2109, so we cannot even reject this hypothesis at 10%.[42]

Given the features observed in Figure IV.6.9, why does the regression model indicate no significant relationship between the exceedances and the lagged changes in the Vix? Because the large increases in the Vix index are recorded on the actual day that the VaR is exceeded, not on the day before. In fact, the contemporaneous correlation between the indicator variable and daily changes in the Vix is approximately 0.4, and a regression model (IV.6.26) with *current* changes in the Vix instead of lagged changes indicates a very strong relationship between the two variables. The t statistic for $H_0 : \beta_1 = 0$ versus the two-sided alternative gives a t ratio of 19.2358, so we can reject this hypothesis at the very highest significance level.

Note that the regression-based backtest must be based on *lagged* values of explanatory variables, because the test is derived by taking the conditional expectation of the indicator assuming the values of the explanatory variables are known. So the fact that current changes in Vix can explain the exceedances is of no value for the backtest in the above example. However, this observation *does* help to identify the cause of the failure of the backtest, and it helps to determine ways in which the model could be improved. In our example above it may well be that accounting for volatility clustering will improve the model's VaR forecasts. The next example investigates this possibility.

EXAMPLE IV.6.8: COVERAGE TESTS WITH VOLATILITY CLUSTERING

Repeat the coverage tests on the 1% daily VaR for the $100 per point position on the S&P 500 index, this time replacing the equally weighted volatility estimate by the RiskMetrics™ daily volatility estimate.

SOLUTION   The RiskMetrics™ daily volatility estimate is an EWMA estimate with a smoothing constant of 0.94.[43] For the S&P 500 index and for the period of the backtest, this is shown in Figure IV.6.10. The spreadsheet for this example repeats the unconditional coverage test, the independence test and the conditional coverage test as before, but now using 1% daily VaR estimates based on the normal linear model with the RiskMetrics™ EWMA volatility. The VaR estimates in the earlier examples used an equally weighted volatility based on the past 250 daily returns, and there were 33 exceedances of the VaR, with two consecutive pairs. The unconditional coverage statistic was 7.1367 and we rejected the null hypothesis of a well-specified model at 1%. With the RiskMetrics™ EWMA volatility there are now only 30 exceedances, so the unconditional coverage statistic takes a lower value of 4.3785; as a result we can only reject the null at 5%.

Moreover, the independence test is irrelevant because there are no consecutive exceedances. However, the exceedances are still clustered. Readers will be able to see from the spreadsheet that there are no exceedances at all between April 2002 and April 2004 and that, again, exceedances are clustered around periods of high volatility. We conclude that the RiskMetrics™ daily VaR estimates can improve the forecasting properties of basic VaR models, but the methodology may still be too simple to properly capture volatility clustering.[44]

---

[42] The 10% critical value is 1.6456.

[43] See Section II.3.8 for an introduction to EWMA and Section II.3.8.3 for a description of RiskMetrics.

[44] Also, the EWMA methodology may be disallowed by regulators, for reasons that will be explained in Section IV.8.2.3.

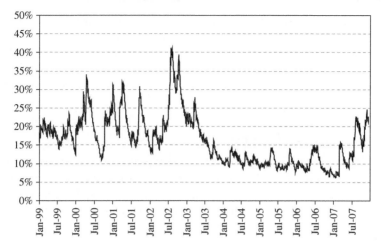

Figure IV.6.10   RiskMetrics™ daily volatility of S&P 500 index

In fact, there is a considerable academic literature that examines coverage tests and other backtests on different types of VaR models and the consensus of this applied research is that non-normal GARCH models are much better than other parametric models (such as EWMA) for forecasting volatility and VaR.[45]

Table IV.6.8 sets out the coverage test results for backtesting the RiskMetrics™ daily VaR for our position on the S&P 500, for different values of the VaR significance level α. Below the table we display the relevant critical values for the test statistics shown in the last three rows of the main table. The results indicate that the model becomes less accurate as α decreases, i.e. as we try to forecast VaR at higher confidence levels. The failure of the unconditional coverage tests for high confidence levels indicates that a normal distribution does not capture the tail behaviour of the S&P 500 returns adequately. A possible improvement, which is left to the reader to investigate, is the use of a leptokurtic (and possibly also skewed) conditional distribution to generate the VaR estimates.

Table IV.6.8   Coverage tests on RiskMetrics™ VaR of S&P 500 index

α	0.1%	1%	5%
Expected no. of exceedances	2	20	100
Observed no. of exceedances	8	30	107
No. of consecutive exceedances	0	0	9
Unconditional coverage	10.1987	4.3785	0.5048
Independence	0	0	1.8136
Conditional coverage	10.1987	4.3785	2.3184

Chi-squared critical values:

Degrees of freedom	1%	5%	10%
1	6.63	3.84	2.71
2	9.21	5.99	4.61

---

[45] For instance, see Berkowitz and O'Brien (2002), Berkowitz et al. (2006) and Alexander and Sheedy (2008)

Another feature of the RiskMetrics™ daily VaR estimates is that they never fail the independence test, even though visual examination of the exceedances shows that they are clustered, and related to the index volatility. In general, there are too few exceedances during tranquil markets when volatility is low, and too many when volatility is high. Also, we find that although two exceedances are not consecutive they are often separated by only one or two days.[46]

IV.6.4.5   Backtesting ETL Forecasts

Section IV.1.8.2 defines the *expected tail loss* as the expected loss given that the loss exceeds the VaR. There, and in Section IV.2.11 where we derived some analytic formulae for ETL in the context of an i.i.d. risk model, the notation we used expressed the expectation as conditional on the loss exceeding the VaR, but it was not conditional on time. However, we need to use a slightly more elaborate notation now that we are concerned with backtesting. We must consider the VaR and ETL that are estimated at time t and are used to forecast the tail of the distribution of the return from time t to time $t + 1$. So in this subsection we use the following notation for the $100\alpha\%$ daily ETL, measured at time t, and used to forecast returns 1 day ahead:

$$\mathrm{ETL}_{1,\alpha,t} = -E_t(Y_{t+1} | Y_{t+1} < -\mathrm{VaR}_{1,\alpha,t}), \tag{IV.6.28}$$

where $\mathrm{VaR}_{1,\alpha,t}$ is the $100\alpha\%$ daily VaR that is estimated at time t. If Y_{t+1} denotes the realized daily return on the portfolio from time t to time $t + 1$, both the VaR and the ETL are expressed as a proportion of the portfolio's value; if Y_{t+1} denotes the theoretical daily P&L on the portfolio from time t to time $t + 1$, both the VaR and the ETL are expressed in value terms.

McNeil and Frey (2000) develop a methodology for backtesting ETL that is based on a time series of *standardized exceedance residuals*, defined as

$$\varepsilon_{t+1} = \begin{cases} \dfrac{-Y_{t+1} - \mathrm{ETL}_{1,\alpha,t}}{\hat{\sigma}_t}, & \text{if } Y_{t+1} < -\mathrm{VaR}_{1,\alpha,t}, \\ 0, & \text{otherwise.} \end{cases} \tag{IV.6.29}$$

Here, as in the next subsection, $\hat{\sigma}_t$ is the forecast of the standard deviation of the daily return (or P&L) from time t to time $t + 1$, so $\hat{\sigma}_t$ is the 1-day forecast that is made at time t.

The test is based on the observation that, if the process dynamics are correct and ETL is an unbiased estimate of the expectation in the tail below the VaR, the standardized exceedance residuals should behave as a sample from an i.i.d. zero mean process. The null hypothesis is that ε_t has zero mean, against the alternative that the mean is positive, since it is a positive mean that suggests that the ETL is too low, and underestimation of the ETL is what we want to guard against. So the test statistic is

$$t = \frac{\bar{\varepsilon}}{est.s.e.\,(\bar{\varepsilon})}, \tag{IV.6.30}$$

---

[46] Readers can see from the indicator function in the spreadsheet that runs of 5 or more exceedances of 10-day VaR estimates are found around the time of the September 2001 terrorist attack on the World Trade Center, in May 2006 and again February 2007. During these periods the minimum regulatory capital based on the RiskMetrics VaR model would have been exceeded on every day during one week. Recall that whilst readers will see coverage test results for risk horizons longer than 1 day in these spreadsheets, the coverage tests are not valid because the assumption that exceedances are i.i.d. cannot be justified.

here denoted t because it looks like a standard t ratio, where $\bar{\varepsilon}$ denotes the sample mean of the standardized exceedance residuals. But (IV.6.30) does not have a standard distribution. Instead, we must estimate its distribution using a *bootstrap* simulation such as that described in Section II.8.2.3.

A sample size problem arises, because we only use the observations corresponding to exceedances in the test, simply throwing away the rest of the original sample. For instance, if we are backtesting a 1% 1-day ETL using an original sample size for the backtest of 5000 daily observations, we expect to have only 50 data points on which to calculate (IV.6.30). To alleviate this problem, at least somewhat, in the following example we use daily data on the S&P 500 from 3 January 1950 until 31 December 2007. So the original sample has 14,470 observations and our backtest sample has 14,220 observations. Thus the ETL backtest should be based on approximately 150 observations.[47]

EXAMPLE IV.6.9: BACKTESTING ETL

Find the standardized exceedance residuals (SER) for the normal linear VaR models of the S&P 500 position considered in this section, using (a) the RiskMetrics™ regulatory model, which is based on an equally weighted variance estimate based on 250 days, and (b) the RiskMetrics™ daily model, which is based on the EWMA variance with a smoothing constant of 0.94. Hence, calculate the statistic (IV.6.30) and comment on the results.

SOLUTION   The ETL is calculated using the formula derived in Section IV.2.11.1. Note that in the time series for ε_t we only use those dates for which the VaR is exceeded, and the other observations are simply excluded. The expected number of exceedances is 142.2 in both cases. However, there are 248 exceedances in case (a) and 270 exceedances in case (b). Clearly the models are underestimating VaR.

Table IV.6.9 summarizes the results, including the values of the ETL backtest t statistic (IV.6.30). Do not be fooled by the low values of the test statistic in this table, because although (IV.6.30) looks like a t statistic its critical values are much lower than the usual critical values of the Student t distribution. Indeed, if we had used the bootstrap to simulate the critical values (which we do not in this example, since it is too onerous in Excel without using VBA) we would almost certainly find that the null hypothesis would be rejected at a very high significance level in both cases.

Examination of the exceedance residuals shows that there are many small positive and negative residuals and a few very large positive ones. That is, the observed loss is usually a little more or less than the ETL, but occasionally very much larger. This is evident from Figures IV.6.11 and IV.6.12, which plot the standardized exceedance residuals for each case.

IV.6.4.6   Bias Statistics for Normal Linear VaR

In the normal linear VaR model the VaR is proportional to the standard deviation of the portfolio return. Hence, we can assess the accuracy of the VaR model by assessing the accuracy of the standard deviation or variance forecast. Let Y_{t+1} denote the daily return on the portfolio that is realized from time t to time $t + 1$. Denote by $\hat{\sigma}_t$ the forecast, made at time t, of the

---

[47] The spreadsheet is so large that this example has its own workbook.

Table IV.6.9   Exceedances and t ratio on standardized exceedance residuals

	(a)	(b)
No. of exceedances	248	270
Mean SER	0.5029	0.4096
StDev SER	1.2357	1.2352
t	0.4070	0.3316

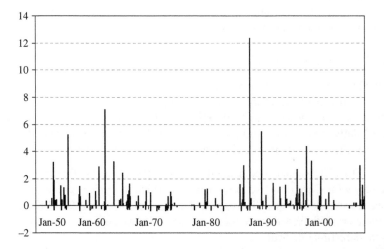

Figure IV.6.11   Standardized exceedance residuals from RiskMetrics™ regulatory VaR

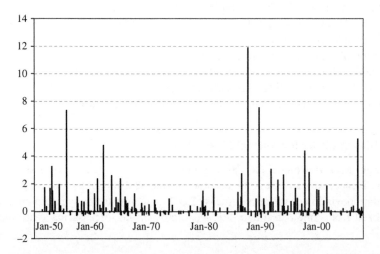

Figure IV.6.12   Standardized exceedance residuals from RiskMetrics™ daily VaR

standard deviation of the daily return from time t to time $t + 1$. Then the *standardized return* at time $t + 1$ is defined as

$$Z_{t+1} = \hat{\sigma}_t^{-1} Y_{t+1}. \tag{IV.6.31}$$

Thus, if the returns are i.i.d. with standard deviation σ and the risk model forecasts σ accurately, then the standard deviation of the time series $\{Z_t\}$ should be unity.

Following Connor (2000), we define the *bias statistic, b*, to be the standard deviation of $\{Z_t\}$. So the null hypothesis that the risk model forecasts σ (and hence also the normal linear VaR) accurately is

$$H_0 : b = 1. \tag{IV.6.32}$$

The alternative can be two-sided or one-sided. For instance, the alternative hypothesis

$$H_1 : b > 1 \tag{IV.6.33}$$

corresponds to the case where the model is under-predicting the normal linear VaR, which is usually the hypothesis of interest.

Returns are assumed to be i.i.d. and normally distributed in the normal linear VaR model. So in this case we can base the test statistic for (IV.6.32) on the assumption that $\{Z_t\}$ is an i.i.d. standard normal series. Then, when the backtest is based on a sample of size T, the estimated standard error of b is approximately equal to $(2T)^{-1/2}$, as shown in Section II.3.5.3. However, b is not normally distributed so we cannot base the test on a sort of t ratio such as $\sqrt{2T}(\hat{b} - 1)$, where $\hat{b}$ denotes the estimated standard deviation of $\{Z_t\}$ over the backtest sample. This is because this ratio does not have a standard distribution such as the Student t.

In fact, we only know that if we assume the portfolio returns series is an i.i.d. normal process then $T b^2 \sim \chi_T^2$. The mean and variance of a chi-squared distribution with T degrees of freedom are T and $2T$, respectively. Hence, by the central limit theorem,

$$\frac{Tb^2 - T}{\sqrt{2T}} \overset{asy}{\sim} N(0, 1).$$

In other words, when the backtest sample size is very large,

$$b^2 \overset{approx.}{\sim} N\left(1, \frac{2}{T}\right). \tag{IV.6.34}$$

From this, using the same type of Taylor expansion argument that was used in Section II.3.5.3 to derive the standard error of a volatility estimator from the standard error of a variance estimator, we can derive a normal approximation for the distribution of the bias statistic that is valid only for large backtest sample sizes, and on i.i.d. normal portfolio returns:

$$b \overset{approx.}{\sim} N\left(1, \frac{1}{2T}\right). \tag{IV.6.35}$$

Very approximate confidence intervals for the bias statistic can therefore be based on normal standard error bounds. For instance, an approximate 95% confidence interval for b when T is large is

$$\left(1 - 1.96/\sqrt{2T}, 1 + 1.96/\sqrt{2T}\right). \tag{IV.6.36}$$

If we obtain a value $\hat{b}$ that lies above this interval the model may be under-predicting VaR, and if $\hat{b}$ lies below this interval it could indicate that the model over-predicts VaR.

EXAMPLE IV.6.10: BIAS TEST ON NORMAL LINEAR VAR

Find an approximate 95% confidence interval for the bias of each of the two volatility estimators that have been used in this section. That is, using (a) the RiskMetrics™ regulatory VaR model and (b) the RiskMetrics™ daily VaR model. Use a 1-day risk horizon and base your results on the sample of S&P 500 prices from 4 January 1999 to 31 December 2007.

SOLUTION   Rather than restricting the backtest sample size to 2000, which was convenient when discussing coverage statistics, now we shall use the maximum number of observations in the backtest, i.e. 2011. With $T = 2011$ we have $\sqrt{2T} = \sqrt{4022} = 63.4192$. Hence the approximate 95% confidence interval (IV.6.36) is

$$(1 - 1.96/63.4192, 1 + 1.96/63.4192) = (0.9691, 1.0309).$$

For each case, the spreadsheet computes the standardized returns and their standard deviation, which is the bias statistic $\hat{b}$. We obtain a value of 1.0364 for the equally weighted estimator (a) and a value of 1.0515 for the EWMA estimator (b). Thus our conclusion should be that, if the assumptions of the test are valid, then both of the RiskMetrics™ volatility estimators underestimate S&P 500 volatility and hence will also underestimate the VaR, for every value of the significance level α. Moreover, it appears from this result that the EWMA VaR estimator is the more biased of the two.

These conclusions agree with those drawn from the coverage tests, where there were too many exceedances, indicating that the VaR was underestimated rather than overestimated. However, readers are urged to exercise extreme caution when using bias statistics. If returns are *not* generated by a normal i.i.d. process, as assumed for the bias statistics, the results are not valid. In fact, it makes no sense at all to use the bias statistic in this setting. Therefore, before considering the use of a bias statistic, analysts should test their sample of portfolio returns for normality and for i.i.d. behaviour, as explained in Chapter I.4.[48]

IV.6.4.7   Distribution Forecasts

A VaR estimate is just one quantile of an entire distribution that is forecast over an h-day risk horizon. Hence, an assessment of the accuracy of the entire distribution, instead of just one of its quantiles, is a more extensive test of the risk model. In this subsection we ask: what is the probability of obtaining *any* of the out-of-sample returns resulting from the backtest,

---

[48] A simple way to test for independence is to test for *autocorrelation* in the returns, and also for autocorrelation in the squared returns and higher powers of returns. These tests are described in Section I.4.5.3. If one of these tests is rejected (and often squared returns are found to be autocorrelated, due to volatility clustering) then the returns cannot be independent. However, acceptance of these tests does not imply independence. Similarly, rejecting a test for *heteroscedasticity* (see Section I.4.5.4) does not imply the distributions are identical. Finally, see Section I.4.3.5 for the *Jarque–Bera* normality test.

according to our risk model? In other words, we assess the quality of the entire distribution forecast, rather than focusing exclusively on the tails.

Let us denote the forecasted distribution function by F_t. The subscript t is there to remind us that the forecast of the forward-looking h-day return or P&L is made at time t. Set

$$p_{ht} = F_t(Y_{t+h}),\qquad\text{(IV.6.37)}$$

where Y_{t+h} denotes the realized return or P&L on the portfolio between time t and time $t+h$ in the backtest. Assuming that the backtest is based on non-overlapping data, our null hypothesis is

$$H_0 : p_{ht} \sim i.i.d. \; U[0,1]\qquad\text{(IV.6.38)}$$

where $U[0, 1]$ denotes the standard uniform distribution.[49] In other words, our null hypothesis is that the probabilities p_{ht} should be a sequence of random numbers. Put another way, our risk model should not be able to predict the probability of the realized return.

Why does testing the hypothesis (IV.6.38) constitute a backtest? Suppose our risk model systematically underestimates the tail risk. Then there will be more realized returns in the tail than are predicted by the model. As a result, the backtest will generate too many values for p_{ht} that are near 0 or near 1. Likewise too many values will lie near the centre also, due to the higher peak of a leptokurtic density. In other words, the empirical density of the return probabilities would have a 'W' shape instead of being flat, as it should be according to the standard uniform distribution.

A test of (IV.6.38) is therefore a test on the proximity of our empirical distribution to a theoretical distribution, which in our case is standard uniform. However, tests on the standard uniform distribution are not as straightforward as tests on the standard normal distribution, so we transform p_{ht} to a variable that has a standard normal distribution under the null hypothesis. To do this, we set

$$Z_{ht} = \Phi^{-1}\left(p_{ht}\right),\qquad\text{(IV.6.39)}$$

where Φ denotes the standard normal distribution function. The null hypothesis may now be written

$$H_0 : Z_{ht} \sim i.i.d. \; N(0,1)\qquad\text{(IV.6.40)}$$

and a very simple alternative is

$$H_1 : Z_{ht} \sim i.i.d. \; N\left(\mu_h, \sigma_h^2\right), \quad \mu_h \neq 0, \sigma_h \neq 1.\qquad\text{(IV.6.41)}$$

A parametric test statistic may now be based on a likelihood ratio statistic of the form

$$-2\ln LR = -2\ln\left(\frac{L_0}{L_1}\right) \sim \chi_2^2,$$

where the likelihood function under the null hypothesis, L_0 is the product of the standard normal density functions based on the realized returns, and the likelihood function under the alternative hypothesis, L_1 is the product of the normal density functions with mean μ_h and

---

[49] See Section I.3.3.3.

standard deviation σ_h based on the realized returns. If the backtest sample size is T then, using the log likelihood of the normal distribution,[50] it can be shown that

$$-2\ln LR = \sum_{t=1}^{T} z_{ht}^2 - \sum_{t=1}^{T} \left(\frac{z_{ht} - \hat{\mu}_h}{\hat{\sigma}_h}\right)^2 - T\ln\hat{\sigma}_h^2, \tag{IV.6.42}$$

where $\hat{\mu}_h$ and $\hat{\sigma}_h$ denote the sample mean and standard deviation of Z_{ht}.

EXAMPLE IV.6.11: LIKELIHOOD RATIO BACKTEST OF NORMAL RISK MODELS

Perform a likelihood ratio test on the normal linear risk model using each of the two volatility estimators that have been used in this section, i.e. (a) the RiskMetrics™ regulatory VaR model and using (b) the RiskMetrics™ daily VaR model. Use a daily risk horizon and base your results on the sample of S&P 500 prices from 4 January 1999 to 31 December 2007.

SOLUTION   For each risk model we first compute the time series Z_{1t}, in this example denoted just Z_t for convenience, using (IV.6.37) and (IV.6.39). The backtest sample size is $T = 2011$ and the sample means and standard deviations of these series are given in the spreadsheet. They are summarized in the first two rows of Table IV.6.10. The third row shows the value of the test statistic (IV.6.42) in each case, which should be compared with the critical value of a chi-squared variable with 2 degrees of freedom. The 5% critical value is 5.9915 and the 1% critical value is 9.2103. Hence, we do not reject the null hypothesis at 5% in case (a) but we reject the null hypothesis at 1% in case (b).

This leads to the conclusion that the RiskMetrics™ regulatory model provides better 1-day-ahead distributions for portfolio returns than the RiskMetrics™ EWMA daily model, which is again rather counterintuitive. However, the inadequacy of both risk models for the S&P 500 is clearly evident from a histogram of the probabilities p_{1t}, which is shown in Figure IV.6.13 for each of the models. We see that, rather than being flat, both histograms have the 'W' shape one would expect if the normal risk model were systematically underestimating the tails and the centre.

We can conclude that the use of an i.i.d. alternative, as in this example, is too simple. Instead we could consider a more complex, non-i.i.d. alternative. In the next example we consider an alternative where the variance in the alternative hypothesis (IV.6.41) is time-varying.[51]

Table IV.6.10   Results of likelihood ratio test

	(a)	(b)
Mean	0.0066	−0.0024
Stdev	1.0364	1.0504
$-2\ln LR$	5.2691	9.9668

---

[50] See Example I.3.16.
[51] An alternative with a time-varying mean is considered by Christoffersen (2003, pp. 192–193).

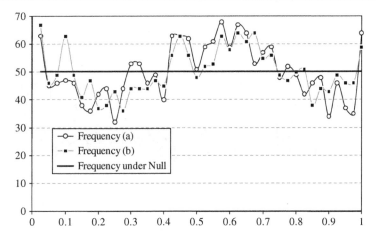

Figure IV.6.13   Empirical frequencies of the return probabilities

EXAMPLE IV.6.12: A DYNAMIC DISTRIBUTION BACKTEST

Repeat the likelihood ratio test for the two risk models of the previous example, but in this case use an alternative hypothesis of the form

$$H_1 : Z_t \sim N\left(\mu, \sigma_t^2\right), \quad \mu \neq 0. \tag{IV.6.43}$$

Base the time-varying variance in the alternative hypothesis on a simple EWMA model with smoothing constant 0.94 in both case (a) and case (b).

SOLUTION   With this alternative the value of the test statistic (IV.6.42) changes considerably. In fact we now obtain values for $-2\ln LR$ that far exceed the critical values. They are 480.37 in case (a) and 248.87 in case (b). With the time-varying volatility alternative we always reject the null at the very highest confidence level, for any reasonable choice of the EWMA smoothing constant. As the smoothing constant increases from 0.94 to 1 we converge to the result for the i.i.d. alternative that was obtained in the previous example.

Figure IV.6.14 shows the EWMA standard deviation of the realized return probabilities under each of the risk models, when the smoothing constant is 0.94.[52] It is clear from this figure that neither VaR model is accurate, because the realized return probabilities show signs of non-i.i.d. behaviour.

IV.6.4.8   Some Backtesting Results

Alexander and Sheedy (2008) provide extensive backtests of simple linear exposures to different currency pairs, using eight risk models that are popular in the industry. Our backtesting methodology is designed for VaR models that are used for stress testing, so the paper assesses

---

[52] This is still rather simplistic, because of course the test results will depend on this *ad hoc* choice. In fact, the reader can change the smoothing constant value in cell R2 and see the effect on the test statistic. A better alternative would use a GARCH model. Then the GARCH model parameters would be estimated optimally in the usual way (see Section II.4.2.2) and the degrees of freedom for the test statistic would increase by the number of parameters in the GARCH model.

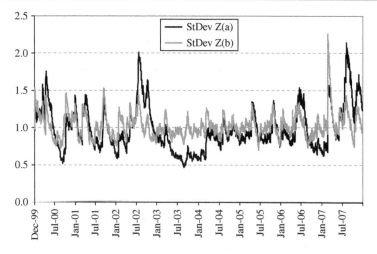

Figure IV.6.14   EWMA standard deviation of the realized return probabilities

the accuracy of extreme quantile forecasts over short risk horizons. The results provide strong support for VaR models with both volatility clustering and non-normal conditional distributions for portfolio returns.

The models that are tested specify the following distributions for the portfolio returns:

(a) unconditional normal;
(b) unconditional Student t;
(c) historical, using the Epanechnikov kernel for smoothing the distribution;[53]
(d) unconditional mixture of two normal distributions;[54]
(e) symmetric normal GARCH;
(f) symmetric Student t GARCH;
(g) filtered historical simulation, with symmetric GARCH;
(h) normal mixture with volatility clustering.

Models (e)–(h) are the extension of the first four models to include volatility clustering. To extend models (a) and (b) we use a symmetric GARCH process with innovations drawn from the specified distribution in each case. To extend the standard historical simulation (c) to its filtered counterpart (g) we standardize the returns with a filtering based on the symmetric GARCH process and simulate using the methodology described in Section IV.3.3.4. For the normal mixture with volatility clustering the historical returns are standardized, as in case (g), but a mixture of two normal distributions is fitted to the standardized returns.

The eight risk models were applied to long and short positions on three currency pairs: the British pound in terms of US dollars (GBP/USD), the US dollar in terms of Japanese yen (USD/JPY) and the Australian dollar in terms of US dollars (AUD/USD). A range of possible estimation sample sizes of between 250 and 2000 daily log returns were used for each model. Approximately 6000 estimates of VaR and ETL were obtained for a 1-day horizon, and around 2000 non-overlapping estimates of VaR and ETL for a 3-day horizon. We considered

---

[53] See Section IV.3.4.1.
[54] This is fitted using the *EM algorithm* – see Section I.5.4.3.

confidence levels of 99%, 99.5% and 99.9%. Each time the VaR and ETL were estimated they were based on revised estimates using the most recent estimation window.

Then the coverage tests that are described in Section IV.6.4.3, and the ETL tests described in Section IV.6.4.5, were applied. Our results confirmed that large estimation sample sizes (say, 2000 days) performed better than small estimation sample sizes (say, 250 days), especially for historical simulation and also for all four of the volatility clustering models. Our results for the normal and normal GARCH models showed that the assumption of normality cannot be justified, particularly when estimating ETL. Including volatility clustering using the GARCH process improved the performance of the normal linear VaR model, but even then the ETL consistently understated the true potential for losses beyond the VaR. Our ETL results for the normal mixture model were also disappointing, even with volatility clustering. However, the Student t GARCH model produced ETL test results that were the best of all the risk models considered in our study. In fact, our results indicated that the Student t GARCH model may even be too conservative, since no exceedances were recorded at all for two of the portfolios.

For each portfolio and at each significance level the two top performing models were the Student t GARCH model and the historical simulation with GARCH filtering. This suggested that the distribution of major currency returns could be adequately described by a single heavy-tailed distribution, in combination with a GARCH model. In other words, occasional large shocks are observed from time to time, which are then followed by further large price movements, which is consistent with volatility clustering. Very often we found that if we did not adjust for volatility clustering the model failed the independence test, i.e. the P&L would exceed the VaR on several days in succession. We also concluded that it is important to capture non-normality in the conditional return distributions, at least for portfolios of these major currencies.

IV.6.5 SUMMARY AND CONCLUSIONS

This chapter deals with the accuracy of risk models: the sources of risk model risk and the methods for testing risk model accuracy. Building a risk model, and specifically a VaR model, actually involves three distinct types of statistical analysis: firstly, we need the specification and estimation of a factor model for mapping the portfolio to its risk factors; secondly, we need a design for modelling the evolution of the risk factors, including the methods for estimating parameters if the risk factor returns model contains parametric elements; and thirdly, we need a method for resolving the model, either analytically or using some type of historical or Monte Carlo simulation.

The market risk analyst faces numerous decisions concerning the theoretical specifications of the factor model for portfolio mapping and the risk factor returns model. These decisions focus on the choice of sample data and statistical methods used to estimate the model parameters. The choices made about the theoretical model specification affect the *model risk*, and the parameter estimation data and methods affect the *estimation risk*.

We have shown that the factor model risk, i.e. the model risk associated with the portfolio mapping, is relatively small for interest rate sensitive portfolios that are mapped as cash flows, but it is relatively large for stock portfolios. And, for any type of portfolio, the model risk arising from the specification of the risk factor returns model is huge. The analyst needs to make many choices here: the returns might be assumed to be i.i.d. or otherwise; the distribution could be parametric or empirical; and if parametric, the analyst must choose between several possible functional forms. It is not very realistic to assume risk factor returns are i.i.d., and this assumption can induce very large errors in VaR estimates. For instance, the VaR could be seriously underestimated if the risk factor returns were positively correlated, especially over a long risk horizon.

For short-term risk horizons the most important effect to include in the risk factor returns model is *volatility clustering*. This makes the VaR estimate more risk sensitive, increasing the VaR if the market is currently more volatile than usual, and decreasing the VaR estimate if the market is currently less volatile than usual. There is a considerable body of empirical research which demonstrates that volatility clustering also makes short-term VaR and ETL estimates more accurate.

Next the analyst must choose between an empirical and a parametric model for the evolution of risk factor returns – or a combination of the two. There is little doubt that using the empirical distribution without any adjustment for volatility clustering, as in standard historical simulation, produces VaR estimates that are quite inaccurate. Accuracy is increased considerably if one augments the empirical distribution with parametric volatility clustering behaviour – as in the filtered historical simulation model. Empirical studies have shown that it is also important to allow for *non-normal* conditional distributions in a parametric risk factor model specification. Otherwise both VaR and ETL can be underestimated, especially at high confidence levels and over short-term risk horizons.

As the risk horizon increases to several months or more, it becomes less important to include volatility clustering and non-normal effects. Over long horizons an important source of model risk stems from the *inappropriate scaling* of short-term VaR estimates to represent VaR over long horizons. Often analysts simply measure market VaR at the daily horizon and scale up this estimate to longer risk horizons using a square-root scaling law. But this law is only applicable if all exposures are linear and all risk factors are i.i.d. and normally distributed. Since these conditions are rarely met in practice, the model risk for long-term VaR and ETL estimates that are scaled up in this fashion is huge. Moreover, it is very difficult to test the accuracy of these estimates, since most backtesting methodologies are designed for use with daily or weekly historical data and can therefore only test the accuracy of short-term VaR and ETL.

Estimation risk stems from two decisions: about the sample data and about the methodology applied to estimate the model parameters. There is some evidence that – assuming the model accounts properly for volatility clustering – larger samples lead to more accurate short-term VaR and ETL estimates. This is because a large part of estimation risk is *sampling error*. By considering the sampling error of a volatility estimator, and then of a quantile estimator, we have derived confidence intervals for VaR. Those based on the standard error of the volatility estimator are much tighter than those for quantile estimators, but they are only valid in the parametric linear VaR model with elliptical i.i.d. risk factor returns.

By far the most important aspect of building a risk model is the *backtesting* of this model. So the main, technical focus of this chapter was to present a variety of statistical tests that can be used to backtest VaR or ETL. After explaining the general backtesting methodology underpinning these tests, we presented a critical discussion of the Basel recommendations for backtesting. Then we presented empirical examples of the various backtests that we have described, on a normal linear VaR model applied to a simple position on the S&P 500 index. The index volatility was estimated using two different methods: one in which variance is set to an equally weighted average of the past 250 squared returns (the RiskMetrics™ regulatory model); and another with a exponentially weighted moving average variance based on a smoothing constant of 0.94 (the RiskMetrics™ daily EWMA model). These two models were backtested using unconditional coverage, independence and conditional coverage criteria, using regression-based backtests and using backtests for ETL. We also examined the bias statistics for these VaR models, and discussed various means of evaluating the entire distribution that is forecast by the risk model, rather than merely focusing on the lower tail.

All the empirical examples on backtesting in this chapter were performed at the portfolio level. So we have not illustrated one of the most important sources of model risk, i.e. *aggregation risk*. This is the risk arising from the inappropriate aggregation of component risks into a total risk. Aggregation risk affects the accuracy of VaR and ETL at every level of the organization. It stems from the use of an inaccurate correlation matrix (or, indeed, the inappropriate use of correlation as a dependency metric) and from the application of simple rules to aggregate VaR and ETL estimates from different lines of business to a total risk estimate for the entire firm. The implementation of an enterprise-wide risk model that is capable of netting the risks of a large organization accurately is a huge undertaking, and aggregation risk in enterprise-wide risk management is much the most important aspect of enterprise-wide risk model risk. The plethora of parametric and non-parametric models for the evolution of risk factor returns may seem confusing but, in the final analysis, a market risk analyst would be well advised to accept a simple but 'good enough' fit for the VaR models applied to different types of portfolios so that he can focus resources on the major challenge of aggregating different market risks across the entire firm. We shall discuss this is more detail in Section IV.8.3.3.

IV.7
Scenario Analysis and Stress Testing

IV.7.1 INTRODUCTION

Previous chapters have focused on VaR estimates that are based on historical asset or risk factor returns. Believing these data capture the market circumstances that are assumed to prevail over the risk horizon, we then obtain a distribution of the returns (or P&L) on a portfolio and estimate the VaR and ETL at the required confidence level over the risk horizon. Whilst such a belief may seem fairly tenuous over risk horizons that are longer than a few months, experience proves that in the absence of a shock, such as the terrorist attacks on the US in 2001, market behaviour and characteristics are unlikely to alter completely over a risk horizon of a few days or weeks. It is therefore reasonable to base short-term VaR and ETL estimation on historical data, provided it is adjusted to reflect current market conditions, but as the risk horizon increases the case for using other beliefs than 'history will repeat itself' becomes stronger.

A main focus of this chapter is to describe the application of a particular type of belief, which is called a *stress scenario*, to risk models. Stress testing is a risk management tool for quantifying the size of potential losses under stress events, and for quantifying the scenarios under which such losses might occur. A traditional definition of a *stress event* is an exceptional but *credible* event in the market to which the portfolio is exposed. Then, in a stress test one subjects the risk factor returns to *shocks*, i.e. extreme but *plausible* movements in risk factors.

But how can we define the terms 'credible' or 'plausible', or similar terms such as 'reasonable', 'rational', 'realistic' etc., except in terms of probabilities? People tend to use such verbal descriptors because it is more difficult to phrase beliefs in terms of probability distributions. One of the main aims of this chapter is to help risk analysts to develop the mathematical framework for scenario analysis, and in particular the means to represent beliefs as probability distributions rather than using vague linguistic terminology. We shall, of course, be covering the traditional approach to stress testing in which stress scenarios are usually based on a *worst case loss*. However, the concept of a worst case loss is not only imprecise, it is mathematically meaningless. Indeed, there is no such thing as a 'worst case' loss other than losing the entire value of the investment.[1] In summary, to attempt to derive a 'worst case' loss resulting from a 'realistic' scenario is to apply a mathematically meaningless quantity to an imprecise construction. So, rather than waste much time on this, after describing the traditional approaches we introduce mathematically meaningful frameworks for stress testing, with illustrative examples that are supported by simple Excel spreadsheets.

Scenario analysis and stress testing actually pre-date VaR modelling. The first commercial application of stress testing was by the Chicago Mercantile Exchange (CME) during the

---

[1] Or, for a short position, losing so much that the firm becomes insolvent.

1980s. The CME requires margins of 3–4 times what could be lost in a single day, as do most futures exchanges. In the early 1980s these margins were contract-specific and so some contracts such as calendar spreads (which trade a long and a short futures, with different maturities, on the same underlying) had zero margins. In 1988 the CME adopted the *Standard Portfolio Analysis of Risk®* (SPAN)[2] system in which daily margin requirements are based on a set of standard stress scenarios including not only parallel shift but also tilts in the yield curve.[3] This system has since been adopted by many exchanges.

The purpose of this chapter is to explain how risk models may be applied to scenario data and how the analyst can formalize his beliefs about the behaviour of the market over a risk horizon in a mathematically coherent framework. A complete formalization of beliefs provides a multivariate distribution of risk factor returns, to which one can apply the mapping of any portfolio and hence derive a scenario-based returns (or P&L) distribution for the portfolio over the risk horizon. The main applications of this scenario-based distribution are the same as the usual applications of return or P&L distributions that are based on historical data, i.e. to risk assessment and optimal portfolio selection.

We shall distinguish between *single case scenarios* that provide just one value for the vector of risk factor returns, as in the SPAN system, and *distribution scenarios* that prescribe an entire multivariate distribution of risk factor returns. We shall also distinguish between *historical scenarios* and *hypothetical scenarios*. A single hypothetical parallel shift of 100 basis points on a yield curve is an example of a single case hypothetical scenario. It aims to provide an 'extreme but plausible' value for the vector of risk factor returns, and the analyst can use the portfolio mapping to derive a 'worst case' loss resulting from this scenario. But he cannot assign a probability to this loss. A simple example of a hypothetical distribution scenario is that changes in yields are perfectly correlated and normally distributed, and they all have mean 100 basis points and standard deviation 50 basis points.[4] Distribution scenarios provide a mathematically coherent framework for scenario analysis and stress testing. That is, because they specify an entire multivariate distribution rather than just a single vector of risk factor changes, probabilities may be assigned to different levels of loss.

Given the tremendous number of historical and hypothetical scenarios that are possible, the analyst needs to have some tool that restricts the number of scenarios that are explored. Often he will perform a preliminary *sensitivity analysis* that examines the *loss profile* of a portfolio as a function of possible values for all of its risk factors. This helps him to distinguish between the main *risk drivers* and the minor risk factors for his portfolio, so he can focus his scenarios on movements in the factors that are most likely to affect his portfolio adversely. It may be the case, especially in option portfolios that have highly non-linear loss profiles, that it is a small movement rather than a large movement in a major risk factor that incurs the largest losses.

The outline of this chapter is as follows. Section IV.7.2 provides a classification of the scenarios that we usually consider in market risk analysis. We also comment on the process of constructing hypothetical scenarios that are consistent with the views of the analyst and of senior management. Section IV.7.3 explains how to apply distribution scenarios in a risk model

---

[2] See http://www.cme.com/span/ for details.
[3] A parallel shift in a yield curve will leave the value of a one-for-one calendar spread unchanged, but a tilt in the yield curve affect its value. For example, if the short rate increases but the long rate decreases, then a spread position that is long the short-maturity futures and short the long-maturity futures will increase in value.
[4] Or, the correlations could be less than one and the standard deviation could be different for yields of different maturities, as indeed could the mean. Neither is it necessary to assume changes in yields have a multivariate normal distribution: for instance, a multivariate Student t distribution, a normal mixture distribution or a general distribution based on a copula may be preferred.

framework, to derive a scenario VaR and ETL. We consider a number of increasingly complex scenarios that are based on both parametric and non-parametric return distributions and take care to distinguish between the different use of information in scenario VaR and Bayesian VaR.

Section IV.7.4 introduces the traditional approach to stress testing portfolios, in which a 'worst case' loss is derived by applying the portfolio mapping to a set of possible stress scenarios, taking the maximum loss over all scenarios considered. We review the Basel Committee's recommendations for stress testing and provide an overview of the traditional approach based on worst case scenarios.

Section IV.7.5 presents a coherent framework for stress testing, illustrated with many empirical examples. We begin by focusing on stressed covariance matrices and how they are used in the three broad types of VaR models, including historical simulation, to derive stressed VaR and ETL estimates. Then we explain how to derive hypothetical stressed covariance matrices, ensuring that they are positive semi-definite. Section IV.7.5.3, on the use of *principal component analysis* in stress tests, highlights their facility to reduce the complexity of the stress test at the same time as focusing attention on the types of market movements that are most likely to occur. Section IV.7.5.4 describes how to estimate *liquidity-adjusted* VaR, differentiating between *exogenous* and *endogenous* liquidity effects. We end this chapter by explaining how to incorporate volatility clustering effects, which can have a significant impact on stress VaR and ETL when the position is held for several days.

IV.7.2   SCENARIOS ON FINANCIAL RISK FACTORS

Historical data on financial assets and market risk factors are relatively easy to obtain, compared with credit risk factors (e.g. default intensities) and especially compared with operational risk factors (e.g. the loss associated with low probability events such as major internal fraud). Market risk analysts can usually obtain many years of daily historical data for their analysis, but this is not always the case. For instance, when estimating the equity risk of a portfolio containing unlisted stocks or the credit spread risk of a portfolio of junk bonds, a market risk analyst typically has little or no historical data at his disposal. Nevertheless, so much of the documented analysis of market risk is based on historical data, that analysts may not know how to proceed when they have little or no 'hard' data available. By contrast, operational risk analysts are used to having virtually no history of experienced large losses in their firm. As a result operational risk analysts have developed methods based on their own *personal views* – in other words, based on *hypothetical* scenarios on risk factors.

Market risk analysis has developed in an environment where, typically, a wealth of historical data on market risk factor returns is available. For this reason risk analysts tend to rely on historical data for quantifying market risks far more than they do for operational risks, or even for credit risks. But there is a real danger in such reliance because excessive losses due to market risk factors are often incurred as a result of a scenario that is not captured by the historical data set. For instance, the Russian bond default in 1998, the bursting of the technology bubble in 2000, the credit crunch in 2007 and the banking crisis in 2008 all induced behaviour in risk factor returns that had no historical precedent at the time they occurred.

In my opinion the quantity of historical data that is commonly available for market risk analysis has hampered the progress of this subject. Market risk managers may be lulled into a false sense of security, believing that the availability of historical data increases the accuracy of their risk estimates. But risk is a *forward looking* measure of uncertainty, and it may be based on *any* distribution for risk factor returns, not only a historical one. In this text we have, until now, been estimating the parameters of these distributions using purely historical data. But this is in itself a subjective view – i.e. that history will repeat itself! So now we extend our analysis to encompass other subjective views, which could be entirely personal to the risk analyst and need not have any foundation in historical events at all.

At the time of writing the majority of financial institutions apply very simple stress tests and scenarios, using only the portfolio mapping part of the risk model to derive 'worst case' losses without associating any probability with these losses. The aim of this section is to help market risk analysts to think 'out of the box'; to use their entire risk model – not just the portfolio mapping – to report on the extent of losses that could be incurred when the unexpected happens; and to do all of this within a mathematically coherent framework.

IV.7.2.1   Broad Categorization of Scenarios

We shall categorize scenarios on the risk factors of a given portfolio using two dimensions: first, the *type* of changes that we consider in risk factors; and second, the *data* that are used to derive these changes. Within the first dimension we consider two separate cases:

- *Single case scenarios*. These scenarios are for a single vector of the risk factor returns, such as a shift of a given magnitude in a yield curve, or a single value for the return on each major stock index. With a single case scenario we can apply the risk factor mapping model to the scenario and hence obtain a single profit or loss for our portfolio resulting from the scenario. Single case scenarios include the *worst case scenarios* that are applied in the traditional approach to stress testing, the *base case scenarios* that are used in decision analysis to capture the event that current market conditions continue to prevail over the risk horizon, and any scenario between these two extremes.
- *Distribution scenarios*. In a distribution scenario our beliefs are encapsulated by a continuous, multivariate distribution of risk factor returns. Applying the risk factor mapping model to such a scenario yields an entire distribution of portfolio returns or P&L. Thus, a distribution scenario allows the estimation of a *scenario* VaR and ETL of our portfolio.[5] We shall also be extending simple distribution scenarios to *compound distribution scenarios*, where our beliefs are encapsulated by a discrete distribution over scenario distributions.

Regarding the data that are used, we also consider two separate cases:

- *Historical scenarios*. These concern a repeat of a historical event such as the global equity crash of 1987 or the banking crisis of 2008. By saving the market data from this period we can apply them to the current portfolio mapping or, better, to the entire risk model since this allows us to derive a coherent scenario analysis for our portfolio.
- *Hypothetical scenarios*. These can involve any changes in any risk factors and they need not have any historical precedent. For instance, a single case scenario when the vector of risk factor returns is a term structure of AA credit spreads could be that the curve shifts upwards by 50 basis points at all maturities.

---

[5] Given a distribution of portfolio returns or P&L we can of course obtain any quantile of this distribution and hence estimate the VaR and/or corresponding ETL.

Hence, there are four broad scenario categories that institutions could consider and these are summarized, along with simple illustrative examples for the iTraxx credit spread index, in Table IV.7.1.

Table IV.7.1   Scenario categorization, with illustration using the iTraxx index

Data	Type of risk factor change	
	Single Case	Distribution
Historical	An upward jump in the index of 50 bps over a 1-month horizon.*	A normal distribution for daily changes in the index with a mean of −1.236 bps and a standard deviation of 9.011 bps.**
Hypothetical	A downward jump in the index of 100 bps over a 10-day period.	A normal distribution for weekly changes in the index with a mean of −10 bps and a standard deviation of 50 bps.

* The index was at 91 bps on 15 February, and by 13 March it had risen to a historical high of 141 bps.
** This is the high volatility component of a mixture of two normal distributions that was fitted to the iTraxx daily changes using data from June 2004 to March 2008. See the case study in Section IV.2.12.

IV.7.2.2 Historical Scenarios

Both single case and distribution scenarios can be based on historical events. By storing the market data that were recorded at the time of a specific event, we could apply either a worst case scenario (e.g. based on the total drawdown that was experienced on major risk factors over a specified time horizon) or a distribution scenario (based on an experienced distribution of risk factor returns over a specified time horizon).

Common examples of historical scenarios include: the 1987 global equity crash; the 1992 European Exchange Rate Mechanism crisis; the 1994 and 2003 bond market sell-offs; the 1997 Asian property crisis; the 1998 Russian debt default and the ensuing falls in equities induced by the threat of insolvency of the Long Term Capital Management hedge fund; the burst of the technology stock bubble that started in 2000 and lasted several years; the terrorist attacks on the US in 2001; the credit crunch of 2007 and the banking crisis of 2008. The following example illustrates how historical data from one of these crisis periods can be used to formulate both a worst case scenario and a distribution scenario.

EXAMPLE IV.7.1: HISTORICAL WORST CASE AND DISTRIBUTION SCENARIOS

Use historical data on daily closing prices of the FTSE 100 index during the period of the 1987 global equity crash to estimate the worst case daily return and worst case monthly return corresponding to this scenario. Also estimate the first four sample moments of daily returns over this period and hence estimate the $100\alpha\%$ daily VaR for a linear exposure to the FTSE index, comparing the results obtained for $\alpha = 0.1$, 0.01 and 0.001 using a Cornish–Fisher expansion with those based on a normal distribution assumption.

SOLUTION   Daily closing prices on the FTSE index were downloaded from Yahoo! Finance for the period from 13 October to 20 November 1987.[6] The maximum loss over 1 day, which

---

[6] The symbol is ^FTSE.

occurred between 19 and 20 October, was 12.22% of the portfolio value, and over the entire data period the loss on a linear exposure to the index was 30.5%. Both these figures could be used as worst case scenarios but over different time horizons, i.e. 1 day and 30 days. For instance, if we have an exposure of £10 million to the FTSE index, then the worst case daily loss according to this scenario is approximately £1.222 million and the worst case monthly loss is approximately £3.05 million.

For the distribution scenario we need to estimate the sample moments of daily returns. The results are: mean $= -1.21\%$, standard deviation $= 3.94\%$, skewness $= -0.3202$ and excess kurtosis $= 1.6139$. The distribution scenario allows us to compute the VaR of a linear exposure to the FTSE index, with different degrees of confidence, conditional on the occurrence of this historical scenario. Using the same calculations as were used in Example IV.3.4 to estimate the daily VaR based on a Cornish–Fisher expansion, we obtain the results shown in the column headed 'CF VaR' in Table IV.7.2. The last column shows the normal VaR estimates that assume the skewness and excess kurtosis are both zero. Due to the strong negative skewness and positive excess kurtosis in the sample, the CF VaR is greater than the normal VaR and the difference between the CF VaR and the normal VaR increases as we move to higher confidence levels.

Table IV.7.2   VaR estimates based on historical scenarios

α	Confidence	CF VaR	Normal VaR
0.1	90%	6.0%	5.0%
0.01	99%	12.6%	9.2%
0.001	99.9%	20.4%	12.2%

We might conclude from this example that if there was a repeat of the global stock market crash of 1987 starting tomorrow and if we did nothing to hedge our position for 24 hours, we could be 90% confident that we would not lose more than 6.0% of the portfolio's value and 99% confident that we would not lose more than 12.6% of the portfolio's value over a 24-hour period.[7] It is a very simple example, but it already demonstrates how distribution scenarios can provide more information than worst case loss scenarios, because we can associate a *probability* with each given level of loss.

IV.7.2.3   Hypothetical Scenarios

The advantage of using historical scenarios is that they are certainly credible, having actually been experienced in the past. The limitation is that they are restricted to losses that have actually occurred. Hence, most institutions also apply hypothetical scenarios in their risk analysis. To give the reader a sense of the hypothetical single case scenarios that financial institutions may be using, the following worst case scenarios were recommended by the Derivatives Policy Group in 1995:[8]

---

[7] Notice that a normal assumption would lead to a much more conservative conclusion.

[8] The Derivatives Policy Group was comprised of principals representing CS First Boston, Goldman Sachs, Morgan Stanley, Merrill Lynch, Salomon Brothers, and Lehman Brothers. It was organized to respond to public policy issues raised by the over-the-counter derivatives activities of unregulated broker-dealers and futures commission merchants, including the need to gain information on the risk profile of professional intermediaries and the quality of their internal controls.

- a parallel shift in a yield curve of ±100 basis points;
- a linear tilt in a yield curve of ±25 basis points;[9]
- a parallel change in credit spreads of ±20 basis points;
- a stock index return of ±10%;
- a return of ±6% on a major currency pair, or of ±20% for a minor currency against another currency;
- a relative change in volatility of ±20%.

If the portfolio has a non-linear pay-off it is quite possible that the maximum loss will not occur at one of the extremes, such as a stock index return of +10% (for a short position) or −10% (for a long position). Hence, more recently regulators of financial institutions require them to run scenarios that are specific to their portfolios individual characteristics. Further details on the new regulations for stress testing in banking institutions are given in Section IV.7.4.1.

Hypothetical scenarios such as those defined above may be applied individually or simultaneously. If simultaneously, they may or may not respect the codependence between risk factors. For instance, no such dependency is respected in the *factor push* stress testing methodology that is described in Section IV.7.4.3. On the other hand, the analyst may feel that the simultaneous scenario of a 10% fall in a stock index and a 20% relative fall in its volatility is so improbable that it will not be considered.

More complex single case hypothetical scenarios can be designed that respect a sequence of events on the different risk factors of a portfolio that, in the analyst's view, is plausible. For example, suppose that a US bank announces that it must write off $20 billion of tier one capital due to defaults on loans and credit derivatives. Here is an example of a single case scenario encompassing the behaviour of US credit spreads, US money market rates, dollar exchange rates, global equity prices and stock volatility over the week following this announcement:

- US credit spreads in the US banking sector increase by 80 basis points.
- Other credit spreads on investment grade US companies increase by between 50 and 200 basis points, depending on their credit rating.[10]
- To compensate for higher spreads, the Federal Reserve cuts base rates by 25 basis points. As a result money market rates decrease by between 25 and 50 basis points, depending on maturity.[11]
- Funds flow out of the dollar into other major currencies, against which the dollar depreciates by 5%.
- The Dow Jones and S&P 500 stock indices fall 10% on fears about the US economy, and some other major stock markets that are highly correlated with the US markets follow suit.
- The volatility of US stocks (and of other highly correlated stock markets) increases by 20%, relative to its value before the announcement.

---

[9] That is, the shortest rate moves up (or down) by 25 bps and the longest rate moves down (or up) by 25 bps, and the movements in other rates are determined by linear interpolation.

[10] For instance, AA spreads increase by 50 basis points and B-rated spreads increase by 200 basis points.

[11] For example, 50 basis points for overnight rates and 25 basis points for the annual rate.

This way the analyst can think through the repercussions of his hypothetical event on the behaviour of all the relevant risk factors. It is also possible to associate a time scale with the risk factor changes, as we have done above. However, what we cannot do with single case scenarios is associate a *probability* with the sequence of events. For this we need to construct a distribution scenario.

We now explain how to design a mathematically coherent hypothetical distribution scenario for a vector of risk factors of the portfolio. First we state the steps to be followed and then we provide an illustrative example.

1. State the hypothetical *scenario event* in as much detail as possible. For instance, the scenario event could be that Georgia joins NATO, Russia invades Georgia and NATO troops defend Georgia.
2. Identify the *risk drivers*. Often there will be a single risk factor that drives the scenario, for instance a fall in the S&P 500 index or rises in the values of the US dollar and gold.
3. Specify *conditional scenarios* on the main risk driver. That is, specify a distribution that represents your beliefs about the possible values of the main risk driver resulting from the scenario event. Note that the conditional scenarios can be a set of distributions, each referring to a different *time horizon*. For instance, when specifying conditional scenarios on the government yield curve in Singapore, conditional on an unpegging of their currency from the US dollar, the analyst may specify the distribution of interest rate changes over the next week, the next month, the next three months and so on.
4. Conditional on each possible value for the main risk driver, specify scenarios on other risk factors of the portfolio. For instance, suppose the scenario event is that, as a result of the credit crisis, a major US bank becomes insolvent. Given the nervousness in the market at the time of writing, credit spreads on AA bonds could rise to 150 basis points within a month.[12] Conditional on this, what could happen to the secondary drivers, i.e. interest rates and equities prices? Perhaps it is more likely that the government will bring down interest rates than raise them, and it is also more likely that equity prices would fall. So, conditional on a 150 basis points rise in AA spreads over the next month we have a distribution of interest rate changes and another distribution of equity returns over the next month. These distributions refer to the same time horizon as the change in the main risk driver that they are conditional upon.

EXAMPLE IV.7.2: HYPOTHETICAL DISTRIBUTION SCENARIO: BANK INSOLVENCY

One of the major US banks announces that it must write off $10 billion of tier one capital due to defaults on loans and credit derivatives. Formulate your hypothetical distribution for credit spreads and US interest rates.

SOLUTION   The main risk driver of this scenario is a credit spread index for the banking sector in the US. Figure IV.7.1 depicts my personal view about the possible changes in this index over the next week.[13]

Now, conditional on each of the possible changes in the credit spread index I must formulate a view on the possible weekly change in interest rates. Figures IV.7.2 and IV.7.3 depict two distributions for interest rate changes, each conditional on a different level for the credit spread.

---

[12] They almost reached this level at the beginning of the credit crisis and so it is plausible that they could do so again.
[13] This is a Student t distribution with 6 degrees of freedom, a mean of 40 bps and a standard deviation of 15 bps.

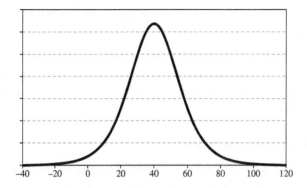

Figure IV.7.1   A personal view on credit spread change during the week after a major banking crisis

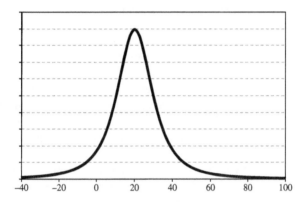

Figure IV.7.2   Distribution of interest rate changes conditional on a 20 basis point fall in the credit spread

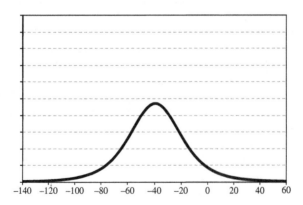

Figure IV.7.3   Distribution of interest rate changes conditional on a 40 basis point rise in the credit spread

My view assumes that there is a negative correlation between interest rates and credit spread changes, and that my uncertainty surrounding interest rate changes is directly proportional to the absolute change in spread. For instance, conditional on the credit spread increasing by 40 basis points, my beliefs about the interest rate are captured by the distribution shown in Figure IV.7.3, which has a lower mean and a higher standard deviation (i.e. more uncertainty) than my subjective distribution conditional on the spread decreasing by 20 basis points, which is shown in Figure IV.7.2.

IV.7.2.4   Distribution Scenario Design

The encoding of subjective beliefs into probability distributions has been studied by many cognitive psychologists and by the Stanford Research Institute (SRI) in particular.[14] A number of cognitive biases are known to be present, one of which is that most people have a tendency to be overconfident about uncertain outcomes.

For instance, consider the following experiment that was conducted by SRI researchers during the 1970s. A subject is asked to estimate a quantity which is known but about which they personally are uncertain.[15] Ask the subject first to state a value they believe is the most likely value for this quantity: this is the median. Then ask them to state an interval within which they are sufficiently sure the quantity lies – sufficiently sure to place a double-or-nothing bet on being correct. This is the interquartile range. Then, by associating ranges with other bets, elicit responses for 90%, 95% and 99% confidence intervals for the value of the quantity in question. Finally, reveal the true value, and mark the quantile where it lies in the subject's distribution. Repeat this for a large number of different uncertain quantities and for a large number of different subjects. If the subjects were encoding their beliefs accurately we should find that 10% of the marks fall outside the subject's 90% confidence intervals, 5% fall outside the 95% intervals and 1% fall outside the 99% confidence intervals. However, the empirical results from SRI established that these intervals were far too narrow. For instance, approximately 15% of marks fell outside the 99% confidence intervals.

This type of bias is particularly relevant for analysts who wish to encode a senior manager's beliefs into a quantifiable scenario distribution that is to be used for stress testing, since the effect of the bias is to reduce the probability in the tails. In other words, people have the tendency to assign a lower probability to a stress scenario than they should. Spetzler and Staël von Holstein (1977) describe a general methodology for encoding a subject's probability distribution about an uncertain quantity using a series of simple questions. The methodology is designed to deal with a variety of cognitive biases, such as the tendency towards overconfidence that most subjects exhibit in their responses. Armed with such a methodology, how could it then be applied to formulate distribution scenarios for stress testing?

The first distribution to encode should relate to the main risk driver of the scenario, such as changes in the credit spread or the oil price. Then encode the distributions for related risk factors conditional on different values for the main risk driver. For instance, conditional on the BBB-rated credit spread increasing by 100 basis points or more, encode the subjective distribution of the change in the base interest rate. Let X denote the change in the credit spread and Y denote the change in the interest rate, both in basis points. From the first encoding we obtain $P(X \geq 100)$ and from the second we obtain $P(Y \leq y \mid X \geq 100)$ for different values of y,

---

[14] Interested readers are recommended the excellent paper by Spetzler and Staël von Holstein (1977).
[15] Such as the height of Nelson's Column in Trafalgar Square, London.

e.g. for $y = -50$. Then the joint probability of credit spreads increasing by 100 basis points or more and the interest rate decreasing by 50 basis points or more is $P(Y \leq -50$ and $X \geq 100) = P(Y \leq -50 | X \geq 100)P(X \geq 100)$.

The sequential encoding of conditional distributions aims to assign a probability to any vector of risk factor returns, and to a vector corresponding to extreme returns in particular. Then, substituting this vector into the portfolio mapping, we obtain a worst case loss with a specified subjective probability. However, the method described above is very subjective, and depends heavily on the analyst's ability to encode complex beliefs into quantifiable distributions. There are more tangible ways in which one can associate a probability with a loss that is incurred under a stress scenario, some of which are described in the next section.

IV.7.3 SCENARIO VALUE AT RISK AND EXPECTED TAIL LOSS

In this section we describe how to apply VaR models to either historical or hypothetical distribution scenarios, focusing on the latter case. We begin by considering the simplest, normally distributed scenarios for risk factors and then explain how these scenarios have a natural extension to a *compound distribution scenario* using the normal mixture framework. Then we explain how to derive scenario VaR and ETL using a more general non-parametric framework for compound distribution scenarios. Finally, we describe how 'hard' data based on the historical evolution of risk factors may be combined with 'soft' data based on the analyst's personal views in a *Bayesian* VaR analysis.

IV.7.3.1 Normal Distribution Scenarios

The normal linear VaR formula (IV.2.5) depends on two parameters of the portfolio's h-day discounted return distribution, its expected value μ_h and its standard deviation σ_h, which until now have been estimated from historical data on the portfolio returns.[16] It is important to note that the standard deviation represents the uncertainty about the expected value, i.e. the dispersion of the discounted return distribution about its centre. It does not represent uncertainty about any other value. Thus, to apply the formula (IV.2.5) to a scenario VaR estimate, the analyst should express his views about the discounted expected return on the portfolio using his point forecast of the discounted expectation and his uncertainty about this forecast, in the form of a standard deviation.

We now present some numerical examples that show how to estimate a normal distribution scenario VaR and ETL based on increasingly complex, but plausible scenarios.

EXAMPLE IV.7.3: SCENARIO BASED VAR FOR UNLISTED SECURITIES

You hold a large stake in an unlisted company. Based on analysts' forecasts you believe that over the next month the asset value will grow by 2% in excess of the risk free rate. But you are fairly uncertain about this forecast: in fact, you think there is a 25% chance that it will in fact grow by 3% less than the risk free rate. Using a normal distribution scenario, estimate the

---

[16] When the risk horizon h is small we usually assume the expected value is zero, i.e. that the portfolio is expected to return the discount rate. It is only when the risk horizon exceeds several months that the discounted expectation has a significant effect on the VaR estimate.

10% 1-month scenario VaR and ETL, expressing both as a percentage of your investment in the company.

SOLUTION   Suppose X denotes the return on the company's asset value over the next month. Your discounted expected return over 1 month is 2% and we can express your uncertainty forecast as

$$P(X < -0.03) = 0.25.$$

Applying the standard normal transformation gives

$$P\left(Z < \frac{-0.03 - 0.02}{\sigma}\right) = 0.25, \quad Z = \frac{X - 0.02}{\sigma},$$

where Z is a standard normal variable. Thus

$$\frac{-0.05}{\sigma} = \Phi^{-1}(0.25) = -0.6745 \quad \Rightarrow \sigma = \frac{0.05}{0.6745} = 7.413\%.$$

We now apply the normal linear VaR formula to obtain the VaR estimate

$$\Phi^{-1}(0.9) \times 0.07413 - 0.02 = 7.5\%.$$

The 10% 1-month normal scenario VaR estimate is 7.5%, so we are 90% sure that you will lose no more than 7.5% of your investment over the next month.
   Next, applying the formula (IV.2.84) for the normal ETL, we obtain

$$0.1^{-1} \varphi\left(\Phi^{-1}(0.1)\right) \times 0.07413 - 0.2 = 11.01\%.$$

Thus, if you do lose more than 7.5% of your investment you should expect to lose about 11% of your money over the next month.

EXAMPLE IV.7.4: SCENARIO INTEREST RATE AND CREDIT SPREAD VAR

A bank has an exposure of $0.25 billion to 5-year BBB-rated interest rates in the US. The interest rate is currently 6.5%. Over the next 3 months you expect that BBB-rated 5-year credit spreads will increase by 50 basis points and that 5-year LIBOR rates will fall by 75 basis points. You express your uncertainty about these expected values using a bivariate normal distribution scenario with the following parameters:

   5-year LIBOR volatility $= 100\,\text{bps}$
   5-year spread volatility $= 125\,\text{bps}$
   LIBOR–spread correlation $= -0.25$.

Estimate the 0.1% scenario VaR over the next 3 months that is due to changes in interest rates and credit spreads.

SOLUTION   We shall use the normal linear VaR formula (IV.2.14), i.e.

$$\text{VaR}_{h,\alpha} = \Phi^{-1}(1-\alpha)\sqrt{\boldsymbol{\theta}'\boldsymbol{\Omega}_h\boldsymbol{\theta}} - \boldsymbol{\theta}'\boldsymbol{\mu}_h, \tag{IV.7.1}$$

where $\boldsymbol{\theta}$ denotes the 2×1 vector of the exposure's PV01 to LIBOR rates and credit spreads and $\boldsymbol{\Omega}_h$ and $\boldsymbol{\mu}_h$ are defined below, for a risk horizon of 3 months. Using the approximation (IV.2.27), we obtain the PV01 of a \$5 billion exposure at 5 years over a 3-month risk horizon when the interest rate is 6.5% as

$$\text{PV01} \approx \$5 \times 10^9 \times 0.25 \times (1.065)^{-6} \times 10^{-4} \approx \$85,667.$$

Thus the sensitivity vector to LIBOR and credit spread changes is $\boldsymbol{\theta}' = (85,667 \quad 85,667)'$. The expected changes in LIBOR and spread over the next 3 months are summarized in the vector

$$\boldsymbol{\mu}_{3\text{mths}} = \begin{pmatrix} -75 \\ 50 \end{pmatrix}.$$

The covariance matrix that expresses your uncertainty about this expectation is[17]

$$\boldsymbol{\Omega}_{3\text{mths}} = \frac{1}{4}\begin{pmatrix} 100^2 & -0.25 \times 100 \times 125 \\ -0.25 \times 100 \times 125 & 125^2 \end{pmatrix} = \begin{pmatrix} 2500 & -781.25 \\ -781.25 & 3906.25 \end{pmatrix}.$$

Now substituting these values into the VaR formula with $\alpha = 0.001$ gives the 0.1% 3-month VaR as \$20,566,112. This is 8.23% of the exposure. Thus, according to our scenario we are 99.9% confident that the bank will not lose more than 8.23% of the exposure due to changes in credit spreads and interest rates over the next 3 months.

EXAMPLE IV.7.5: SCENARIO BASED VAR FOR COMMODITY FUTURES

An oil company produces 10 million barrels of crude oil per month. Figure IV.7.4 depicts, by the black line, the current term structure of crude oil prices for the 1- to 12-month futures contracts. The dotted line in the figure shows the company's expectation for the term structure of futures prices one week from now. The current prices and the expected changes in the prices are given in Table IV.7.3.

Suppose the company's uncertainty about the percentage returns at each maturity is represented by a standard deviation equal to the absolute value of the expected percentage return. For instance, the standard deviation of the 1-month futures is

$$\left| \frac{-2}{110} \right| = 1.82\%.$$

We also assume the correlation between the returns on i-month futures and j-month futures is $0.96^{|i-j|}$.

---

[17] Note that the factor of $\frac{1}{4}$ here expresses the fact that we have a 3-month covariance matrix, not an annual one.

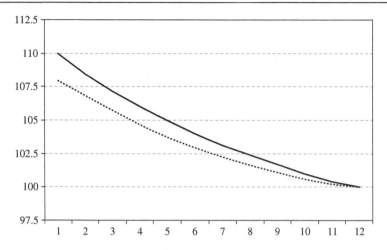

Figure IV.7.4   Term structure of crude oil futures now and in one week

Table IV.7.3   Prices for crude oil futures ($/barrel)

Maturity (months)	1	2	3	4	5	6	7	8	9	10	11	12
Current price	110	108.5	107.2	106	105	104	103.1	102.4	101.7	101	100.4	100
Expected change	−2	−1.67	−1.5	−1.34	−1.17	−1	−0.81	−0.67	−0.52	−0.35	−0.16	0

Table IV.7.4   Expected weekly returns, standard deviations and correlations

$\sigma_5 = -\mu_5$		1	2	3	4	5	6	7	8	9	10	11	12
1.82%	1	1.000	0.960	0.922	0.885	0.849	0.815	0.783	0.751	0.721	0.693	0.665	0.638
1.54%	2	0.960	1.000	0.960	0.922	0.885	0.849	0.815	0.783	0.751	0.721	0.693	0.665
1.40%	3	0.922	0.960	1.000	0.960	0.922	0.885	0.849	0.815	0.783	0.751	0.721	0.693
1.26%	4	0.885	0.922	0.960	1.000	0.960	0.922	0.885	0.849	0.815	0.783	0.751	0.721
1.11%	5	0.849	0.885	0.922	0.960	1.000	0.960	0.922	0.885	0.849	0.815	0.783	0.751
0.96%	6	0.815	0.849	0.885	0.922	0.960	1.000	0.960	0.922	0.885	0.849	0.815	0.783
0.79%	7	0.783	0.815	0.849	0.885	0.922	0.960	1.000	0.960	0.922	0.885	0.849	0.815
0.65%	8	0.751	0.783	0.815	0.849	0.885	0.922	0.960	1.000	0.960	0.922	0.885	0.849
0.51%	9	0.721	0.751	0.783	0.815	0.849	0.885	0.922	0.960	1.000	0.960	0.922	0.885
0.35%	10	0.693	0.721	0.751	0.783	0.815	0.849	0.885	0.922	0.960	1.000	0.960	0.922
0.16%	11	0.665	0.693	0.721	0.751	0.783	0.815	0.849	0.885	0.922	0.960	1.000	0.960
0.00%	12	0.638	0.665	0.693	0.721	0.751	0.783	0.815	0.849	0.885	0.922	0.960	1.000

The first column of Table IV.7.4 shows the assumed vector of standard deviations of the returns over the next week (which is set equal to the absolute value of the expected return) at different maturities. The rest of the table displays their assumed correlation matrix. Based on these hypothetical data, use a multivariate normal distribution scenario to estimate the 1% 10-day scenario VaR of this exposure (ignoring discounting, for simplicity). What is the difference between this result and the result based on a scenario where the expected futures price change is zero for all maturities, but where the uncertainty is still specified by Table IV.7.4?

SOLUTION   The expected weekly return μ_5 is given by -1 times the first column of Table IV.7.4 and the weekly covariance matrix Ω_5 is obtained using the usual matrix product **DCD** where **D** is the diagonal matrix of weekly standard deviations given in the first column of Table IV.7.4. Here **C** is the correlation matrix shown in the remaining part of the table. The weekly covariance matrix is computed in the spreadsheet for this example. Since Table IV.7.4 refers to weekly returns, for a 10-day VaR we multiply both the expected weekly return and the weekly covariance matrix by 2.

Now we apply formula (IV.7.1) where θ denotes the vector of the nominal exposures to each futures contract, which is calculated by multiplying the current price of each futures contract by 10 million, this being the number of barrels produced each month. In the spreadsheet we calculate the VaR with and without the expected return term, obtaining a 1% 10-day VaR of $347 million when we ignore the expected loss in revenues, and $607 million including the expected loss in revenues.

A couple of comments are required about the practical aspects of the above example. First, we have ignored the oil company's production costs. If they are significantly less than the current price of oil then they will be making a large profit, and do not need to hold any capital against expected losses, or against their uncertainty about expected losses. Second, even when production costs are large and profits are jeopardized by an expected price fall, most large corporations employ *historical accounting*, not mark-to-market accounting, for their production. So their corporate treasury will not necessarily use VaR as a risk metric.[18]

IV.7.3.2   Compound Distribution Scenario VaR

Compound distribution scenarios lend themselves to situations where the analyst believes there is more than one possible distribution scenario for the evolution of his portfolio value, and when he has a subjective estimate of the probability of each distribution scenario. In this subsection we illustrate a simple compound distribution scenario based on a normal mixture distribution. A mixture of two normal distributions can be used to represent beliefs about a market crash, when the probability of a crash during the risk horizon is specified. Two numerical examples illustrate the application to credible scenarios on equities and credit spreads. Then we define a general theoretical framework in which the component distributions in the scenario are not constrained to be normal.

The application of normal mixture scenarios to long-term VaR has more mathematical (as well as economic and financial) meaning than the blind extrapolation of short term market risks to very long horizons, based on totally unjustified statistical assumptions. We should question the standard practice of estimating VaR over a short risk horizon and then scaling the estimate to a longer horizon under the assumption that the portfolio returns are i.i.d. The i.i.d. assumption is seldom justified, and it introduces a considerable model risk in long-term VaR estimates. In this section we demonstrate how the analyst could use his knowledge of financial markets and economic policy to formulate a subjective view on the long-term return distribution, and hence obtain an appropriate VaR estimate, in the normal mixture framework.

---

[18] The historical and mark-to-market accounting frameworks are explained, briefly, in Section IV.8.2.2.

EXAMPLE IV.7.6: SCENARIO VaR WITH A SMALL PROBABILITY OF A MARKET CRASH

A portfolio has shown a steady positive return in excess of the risk free rate of 3% per annum with a volatility of 25%. The portfolio manager believes there is a small chance, say 1 in 100, that the market will crash during the next 10 days, in which case he believes that the expected portfolio excess return over a 10-day period will be -10% with an annual volatility around this of 100%. What is the $100\alpha\%$ 10-day normal mixture VaR and how does it compare with the VaR under the assumption of that no crash can possibly occur? Compute the answer as a percentage of the portfolio value, and for $\alpha = 0.05, 0.01, 0.005$ and 0.001.

SOLUTION   To answer this we use the implicit formula for the mixture VaR that is derived in Section IV.2.9.2 with two 2-component normal densities and where:

π is the probability of regime 1 (i.e. 0.01),
$\mu_{1,10}$ is the 10-day excess return in regime 1 (i.e. -0.1),
$\sigma_{1,10}$ is the 10-day excess return standard deviation in regime 1 (i.e. 0.2),
$\mu_{2,10}$ is the 10-day excess return in regime 2 (i.e. $0.03/25 = 0.0012$), and
$\sigma_{2,10}$ is the 10-day standard deviation in regime 2 (i.e. $0.25/\sqrt{25} = 0.05$)

Using the Excel spreadsheet for this example with Solver (or Goal Seek) applied each time we change the significance level, we obtain the normal mixture VaR figures in the first row of Table IV.7.5.

Table IV.7.5   Normal mixture VaR versus normal VaR

Significance level	10%	5%	1%	0.5%	0.1%
Normal mixture VaR	6.43%	8.35%	12.57%	15.26%	35.64%
Normal VaR 1	6.97%	8.95%	12.67%	14.03%	16.84%
Normal VaR 2	6.29%	8.10%	11.51%	12.76%	15.33%

The two set of figures corresponding to normal VaR, shown in the last two rows of Table IV.7.5, are calculated using a single value for the discounted returns standard deviation and expected value over the holding period. The 'normal VaR 2' figures are computed using the second (i.e. 'ordinary market circumstances') distribution of excess returns. That is, we ignore the possibility of a market crash in the 'ordinary' normal VaR and use the expected value of 0.0012 and standard deviation of 0.05. For the 'normal VaR 1' figures shown in the table we apply the normal linear VaR using a density that has the same mean and standard deviation as the normal mixture density. By (IV.2.73) the standard deviation is the square root of

$$\pi\left(\sigma_{1,10}^2 + \mu_{1,10}^2\right) + (1-\pi)\left(\sigma_{2,10}^2 + \mu_{2,10}^2\right) - \left(\pi\mu_{1,10} + (1-\pi)\mu_{2,10}\right)^2,$$

and the mean is $\pi\mu_{1,10} + (1-\pi)\mu_{2,10}$. These adjust the 'ordinary' market mean and standard deviation to take account of the possibility of a crash, but after this the VaR is computed using a normal assumption for portfolio returns.

From the results in Table IV.7.5 it is clear that ignoring the possibility of a crash can seriously underestimate the VaR at high confidence levels. The normal mixture VaR estimates are based on a distribution with extremely high excess kurtosis, because the probability of a market crash is very small. Hence it is only at the very high confidence of 99.5% and 99.8% that the normal mixture scenario VaR exceeds the normal VaR estimates. Even if one were always to assume a normal distribution, comparing the normal VaR 2 results (which exclude the manager's beliefs about the crash entirely) with the normal VaR 1 results, the latter is larger especially at the high confidence levels.

Readers may use the spreadsheet for the above example to compute the scenario VaR during periods of intense volatility, such as October 2008, when the analyst's view on the crash probability may be considerably greater than 1% and, if the market recovers, the expected daily excess return could be considerably greater than 0.12%.

To demonstrate how flexible normal mixture scenario VaR is, the next example considers the case where a risk analyst estimates the annual VaR of a 5-year BBB-rated bond at the 99.9% confidence level. The VaR estimate is based on his personal beliefs about the possible values of the bond's credit spread one year from now, which are summarized in a distribution that is derived from a mixture of three normal distributions with different means and variances. The density function for this distribution is shown in Figure IV.7.5.[19]

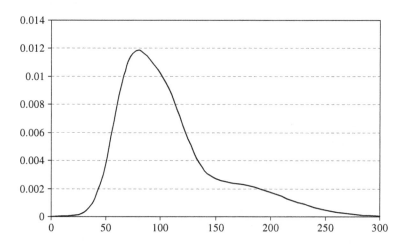

Figure IV.7.5 Personal view on credit spread of bond, one year from now

EXAMPLE IV.7.7: CREDIT SPREAD NORMAL MIXTURE SCENARIO VAR

You have invested several million dollars in a 5-year BBB-rated zero coupon bond. The PV01 of your exposure at 5 years is $1000 and the current credit spread on this bond is 100 basis points. You believe that, 1 year from now, there are only three possibilities. The bond will either be upgraded to an A rating, downgraded to a BB rating, or remain in the same credit rating, and your subjective probabilities for the occurrence of these three scenarios are 0.3, 0.3 and 0.4, respectively. Your beliefs about the change in the credit spread, in basis points

---

[19] Readers may change the parameters of the normal mixture distribution in the spreadsheet until they are satisfied that the distribution represents their own beliefs about the credit spread on a BBB-rated bond in 1 year's time. Since mixtures with three normal components are very flexible, a great variety of shapes may be obtained.

and over an annual horizon, are summarized in Table IV.7.6. Assuming that your uncertainty about each of the three component scenarios is captured by a normal distribution, the resulting mixture distribution is depicted in Figure IV.7.5. Use this personal view to estimate the 0.1% annual VaR and ETL for your exposure to this bond.

Table IV.7.6   Analyst's beliefs about credit spreads

	Downgrade	Upgrade	Rating unchanged
Probability	0.3	0.3	0.4
Expected change in spread	60	-30	0
Volatility of change in spread	50	15	20

SOLUTION   In the spreadsheet for this example we use the Solver to back out the VaR from the normal mixture VaR formula derived in Section IV.2.9.2 with three component normal densities. The result is an estimate of 0.1% annual VaR equal to $78,942. The reader may change the personal view and/or the VaR parameters and recalculate the VaR, but note that a suitable starting value in cell B10 is sometimes needed for Solver to converge.

Compound distribution scenarios that involve Student t distributions can be dealt with in the simple framework illustrated by the two previous examples, simply by replacing one or more of the normal components in the mixture VaR formula (IV.2.72) by Student t distributions with specified degrees of freedom.[20]

We now explain a general simulation method for simulating scenario VaR and ETL using component distribution scenarios that need not be Student t or normally distributed. Suppose beliefs are captured by a compound distribution scenario, similar to the normal mixture scenarios described in the examples above, but now we allow the distribution function for each scenario to be any distribution we like. For instance, one or more components could be non-parametric distributions based on empirical observations on risk-factor returns drawn from different historical periods. Or we could use one or more empirical distribution components plus one or more parametric distribution components with parameters that are assigned subjectively according to our views about the return distribution in the case that this scenario pertains. We also require a subjective estimate for the mixing law of the compound distribution, i.e. a probability vector whose components correspond to our subjective probability assigned to each scenario.[21]

For simplicity we shall henceforth assume that there are only two components in the compound distribution scenario, since the extension to more than two (but still a finite number of) components is straightforward to extrapolate from this description. Thus we represent the mixing law by a vector $(\pi, 1 - \pi)$ with $0 < \pi < 1$, and we denote the two component distribution functions $G(x)$ and $H(x)$ where x is the return on our portfolio.[22] The compound scenario is represented by the distribution

$$F(x) = \pi G(x) + (1 - \pi)H(x). \tag{IV.7.2}$$

---

[20] See the numerical examples provided in Section IV.2.9.4 for further illustration.
[21] For example, in Example IV.7.7 the probability vector representing the mixing law was (0.3, 0.3, 0.4).
[22] More generally, we could replace x by a vector of risk factor returns $\mathbf{x}$, and use multivariate distribution functions for $G(\mathbf{x})$ and $H(\mathbf{x})$. Then at the second simulation stage we must apply a multivariate method – see Section IV.4.4.1 for further details.

The VaR and ETL corresponding to this scenario are then estimated using the following two-step simulation algorithm:

1. Draw a random number u from a standard uniform distribution: if $u < \pi$ then select the distribution $G(x)$, otherwise select $H(x)$.
2. Simulate a return from the selected distribution using the standard (historical or Monte Carlo) approach.
3. Return to step 1 and repeat thousands of times to obtain an empirical, simulated return distribution.

This way we simulate from the compound return distribution (IV.7.2) that represents our beliefs, and thereafter we can estimate the VaR and ETL from the simulated return distribution in the usual manner.

IV.7.3.3 Bayesian VaR

The classical or 'frequentist' approach to statistics focuses on the question: what is the probability of the data, given the model parameters? This probability is measured by the likelihood function of the data, which is introduced in Section I.3.6.1. The functional form and the parameters of the distribution are assumed to be fixed, although unknown, but the point to emphasize is that classical statisticians assume that at any point in time there is *one true value* for each model parameter. Hence, they only make probabilistic statements about the likelihood of the sample data, *given* that the assumed distribution is the true distribution.

Bayesian statistics, on the other hand, focuses on our uncertainty about model parameters.[23] There may be a true value for each parameter at any point in time, but we shall never know for sure what it is. Bayesians represent the possibilities for true values of a parameter by a probability distribution. In this way probabilistic statements can be made about model parameters, thus turning the classical question around, to ask: what is the probability of the parameters, given the data?

The Bayesian process of statistical estimation is one of continuously revising and refining our subjective beliefs about the state of the world as more data become available. It can be considered as an extension of, rather than an alternative to, classical inference: indeed, some of the best classical estimators may be regarded as restricted forms of Bayesian estimator.[24] Bayesian estimators are based on a combination of prior beliefs and sample information. The idea is to express uncertainty about the true value of a model parameter with a *prior distribution* on the parameter that describes one's beliefs about this true value. Beliefs, i.e. personal views, can be entirely subjective, but more 'objective' information may be added to these prior beliefs when it becomes available, in the form of the likelihood of an observed sample of data. The likelihood function is used to update the prior distribution to a *posterior distribution* using *Bayes' rule*.

---

[23] The Bayesian approach is named after Rev. Thomas Bayes, whose 'Essay Towards Solving a Problem in the Doctrine of Chances' was published posthumously in the *Philosophical Transactions of the Royal Society of London* in 1764.

[24] Bayesian estimates of parameters are usually based on an assumed *loss function* (e.g. a quadratic loss function) and it is only for certain types of loss function that we recover the classical estimates as a special case of Bayesian estimates. For instance, the maximum likelihood estimator of a parameter is a Bayesian estimator with a *non-informative prior* (i.e. the prior distribution is uniform) and a *zero–one loss function* (i.e. the loss is zero if the estimator has no error, and one for any other value). Thus the maximum likelihood estimator – the jewel in the crown or classical statistics – is the most basic of all Bayesian estimators, because it is based on no prior information and a very crude loss function.

Bayes' rule, the cornerstone of Bayesian analysis, is based on the *theorem of conditional probability* which is described in Section I.3.2.2. There we stated Bayes' rule for two probabilistic events A and B as

$$P(A|B) = \frac{P(B|A)P(A)}{P(B)}. \tag{IV.7.3}$$

When Bayes' rule is applied to distributions about model parameters we let A be the parameters and B be the data, and Bayes' rule is usually written as[25]

$$P(\text{parameters}|\text{data}) = kP(\text{data}|\text{parameters})P(\text{parameters}).$$

We identify $P(\text{parameters})$ with the *prior density*, often based entirely on a subjective view about the possible values for each parameter, and $P(\text{data}|\text{parameters})$ with the *sample likelihood* which, for Bayesian VaR analysis, will usually be based on historical data. Then $P(\text{parameters}|\text{data})$ is the *posterior density* on possible parameter values, which takes account of the extra information we have obtained by observing the sample data.

Hence Bayes' rule may be written[26]

$$\text{Posterior density} \propto \text{Likelihood} \times \text{Prior density}. \tag{IV.7.4}$$

Note that the posterior will be normal if both the likelihood and the prior are normal, because the product of two normal density functions is another normal density function. In fact, if the sample distribution is $N(\mu_1, \sigma_1^2)$ and the prior distribution is $N(\mu_2, \sigma_2^2)$ then the posterior distribution is $N(\mu, \sigma^2)$ with

$$\mu = \left(\frac{\sigma^2}{\sigma_1^2}\right)\mu_1 + \left(\frac{\sigma^2}{\sigma_2^2}\right)\mu_2,$$

$$\sigma^2 = \left(\left(\frac{1}{\sigma_1^2}\right) + \left(\frac{1}{\sigma_2^2}\right)\right)^{-1}. \tag{IV.7.5}$$

To prove this, write the product of the two normal density functions as

$$C_1 \exp\left(-\frac{1}{2}\left[\left(\frac{x - \mu_1}{\sigma_1}\right)^2 + \left(\frac{x - \mu_2}{\sigma_2}\right)^2\right]\right),$$

where C_1 is a constant (i.e. it does not depend on x). Now, after some algebra it may be shown that the term in square brackets above may be written in the form

$$\left[\frac{x - \mu}{\sigma}\right]^2 + C_2,$$

with μ and σ given by (IV.7.5) and where C_2 is another constant. We can ignore the constants, because we will normalize the posterior density after multiplying the two density functions representing the likelihood and the prior, as explained above.

---

[25] The unconditional probability of the data $P(B)$ is regarded as a scaling constant, k, whose value is set to ensure that the distribution on the left-hand side is normalized (so that its sum or integral is one).

[26] The symbol $\propto$ denotes 'is proportional to'.

When formulating prior distribution scenarios one should always use a prior that reflects all the information, views and opinions that one has *a priori* – no more, no less. This is crucial for rational descriptions and decision making. Note that if there is no prior information, then the prior beliefs are that all possible values of parameters are equally likely. In this case the prior distribution is just the uniform distribution. Then the posterior density is just the same as the sample likelihood, so the Bayesian VaR and ETL estimates will be identical to the standard VaR and ETL estimates.

EXAMPLE IV.7.8: COMPARISON OF BAYESIAN VAR AND SCENARIO VAR

Consider two ways of forming a personal view about the portfolio's annual return distribution:

(a) Analyst A believes that there is a 1 in 10 chance that some major political event will occur during the next year, in which case the portfolio's expected return over the next year will be −10%, with a volatility of 30%.

(b) Analyst B has the prior belief, in the absence of any historical information on the portfolio's performance, that the portfolio will return −10% over the next year, with a volatility of 30%.

Now both analysts observe some 'objective' sample data on the portfolio's returns. These have mean zero and volatility 20%. Assuming both the objective data and the personal views have distributions that are normal, combine the beliefs with the objective data to estimate the 5% and the 1% annual VaR expressing the result as a percentage of the portfolio value.

SOLUTION   The difference between case (a) and case (b) is subtle. In case (a), which corresponds to a normal mixture scenario, we have more information about the probability with which each scenario will occur than we do in case (b), which represents the Bayesian view. The view of analyst A is that there is a 90% chance that the objective sample represents the return distribution and a 10% chance that some adverse political event will occur. But this information is not used for the Bayesian view. That is, case (a) uses a weighted sum of normal densities, which is not another normal density, but case (b) takes the *product* of the densities, which is another normal density. We now describe the distribution of returns in each case and estimate the VaR.

Analyst A

The analyst's view is represented by a normal mixture distribution with parameters

$$\pi = 0.9, \quad \mu_1 = 0, \quad \sigma_1 = 20\%, \quad \mu_2 = -10\%, \quad \sigma_2 = 30\%.$$

This is depicted by the grey curve in Figure IV.7.6. Using Solver to back out the VaR in the usual way, we obtain: 5% VaR = 36.37%, 1% VaR = 54.27%.

Analyst B

We find the posterior density by multiplying together two normal density functions: the likelihood has mean zero and standard deviation 0.2 and the prior has mean −0.1 and standard deviation 0.3. Hence, by (IV.7.5) the posterior distribution is a normal distribution with

$$\sigma = \left(\left(\frac{1}{0.2^2} \right) + \left(\frac{1}{0.3^2} \right) \right)^{-1/2} = 16.64\%,$$

$$\mu = \left(\frac{\sigma^2}{0.2^2} \right) \times 0 - \left(\frac{\sigma^2}{0.3^2} \right) \times 0.1 = -3.08\%.$$

Using these in the normal linear VaR gives the result: 5% VaR = 30.45%, 1% VaR = 41.79%.

The Bayesian posterior density corresponding to analyst B is depicted by the normal black curve in Figure IV.7.6.[27] Notice that the normal mixture scenario corresponding to analyst A has a heavier lower tail than the Bayesian posterior distribution, so the normal mixture scenario VaR at high confidence levels could be much greater than the Bayesian VaR.

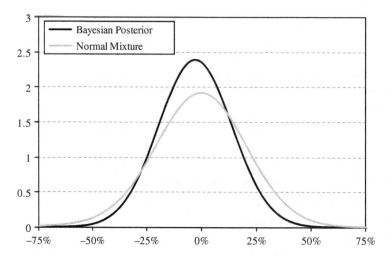

Figure IV.7.6   Comparison of normal posterior with normal mixture

IV.7.4   INTRODUCTION TO STRESS TESTING

Since the 1990s regulators of financial institutions have been encouraging risk managers to look beyond the standard risk metrics such as volatility and VaR, and to think for themselves about circumstances that could generate extreme losses. Mechanically reapplying the same risk metric to the same risk model each day, where the only difference is that the portfolio sensitivities and the corresponding data for the risk factors have been updated, is like playing the same score on a pianola, day after day.[28]

If estimating VaR is like playing a pianola then stress testing is like performing on a concert grand. Over the course of the last decade the design, structure and implementation of risk models have all evolved considerably, and what was state-of-the-art 10 years ago now seems

---

[27] Notice that the posterior distribution has a volatility that is *less* than both the historical and the prior's volatility. This will always be the case when the likelihood and the prior are both normal. The rationale that justifies this result is that additional information should reduce one's uncertainty. However, when the likelihood and prior are not both normal, the uncertainty in the posterior distribution need not be less than in both the likelihood and the prior.

[28] A pianola is a mechanical piano (see www.pianola.org).

simplistic in the extreme. Today, in most major financial institutions, advances in theoretical financial risk analysis, computational power and database design have combined to produce sophisticated models for measuring market risk. Regulators lay down few prescriptive rules for stress testing, leaving analysts a fairly free choice of what to 'play' on their risk model. But all too often they only play some variation on *Chopsticks*.[29]

If the risk analysts are musicians then the senior managers and board members that are responsible for the overall solvency of the firm are the conductors. It is the task of the most senior members of the firm to define the stress scenarios that are used, and to formulate dynamic contingency plans under each scenario, just as it is the conductor's task to direct the musicians in the orchestra. At the time of writing the majority of conductors are directing some version of *Chopsticks* where the score (not that *Chopsticks* really requires a score) is a 'worst case' scenario (not that this actually means anything).

The challenge facing the profession today is that many senior managers and board members are unaware how to direct analysts to produce meaningful results. With the new professional standards that we have been setting since the 1990s, risk analysts should now be sufficiently well trained; it is the senior managers who all too often fail to understand the risk model properly. Yet, to assess risks in a coherent mathematical framework, they must learn to conduct a score that is a little more complex than *Chopsticks*.

Well, one can take analogies only so far, so – although I could easily continue because I feel in need of some light relief, having worked so long on these books – let me now summarize my views and close by focusing on an important learning point. After nearly two decades of rapid development, market risk management systems and the analysts that work with them have evolved to an extent that *meaningful* stress tests can be performed. But in order to do this, analysts must first ask senior managers the right questions, and senior managers must learn to understand these questions. 'What is the worst case scenario' is not the right sort of question, because an analyst cannot apply his risk model to such a scenario; he can only apply the portfolio mapping. And, in this case, the result is meaningless because there is no *probability* associated with a 'worst case' loss. Instead the analyst needs to design a simple set of questions that aim to encode the senior manager's beliefs about changes in major risk factors into a *distribution* scenario. Given this distribution the analyst can use his entire risk model – not only the portfolio mapping – to apply meaningful and coherent stress tests corresponding to each such scenario.

IV.7.4.1   Regulatory Guidelines

The internal calculations for market risk capital are based on 1% 10-day VaR estimates that are derived using historical data, but these calculations cannot reveal the extreme losses that could be incurred in unexpected exceptional circumstances. Since the end of 1997, financial institutions using internal VaR models to assess capital adequacy have been required to implement stress testing. The 1996 Market Risk Amendment to the 1988 Basel Accord specified that a bank wishing to use an internal model for market risk capital must have in place a rigorous and comprehensive stress testing program designed to identify events or influences that could have a significant impact on the bank's capitalization. Stress scenarios need to cover a

---

[29] *Chopsticks* is the name given to extremely simple piano pieces that can be played with two fingers, acting like chopsticks (see http://en.wikipedia.org/wiki/Chopsticks_(music)).

range of factors that can create extraordinary losses in trading positions. The results of stress tests should be routinely communicated to senior management, and periodically to directors.

Consequently, for the past 10 years banks have been considering low probability events on all major risk factors – without assigning any numerical value for this probability – and from these events they have been deriving extreme scenarios for the risk factors that, when input to a portfolio mapping, produce a so-called 'worst case' loss. Regulators require that banks do this for both linear and non-linear exposures and that they provide a qualitative as well as a quantitative analysis in their stress testing reports to supervisors. The quantitative report describes 'plausible' stress scenarios that could have a significant impact on their particular exposures in numerical terms, and evaluates the total loss incurred by the bank under such scenarios. The qualitative report evaluates the bank's capacity to absorb losses of this magnitude and identifies the bank's strategy for reducing risk and conserving capital under a stress scenario.

More recently regulators have emphasized the importance of stress test results for determining capital adequacy in banks, by requiring that a bank's minimum regulatory capital for market risk covers the losses that are quantified in stress tests. Specifically, the Basel II Accord, which was adopted in the EU countries in January 2007 and in the US in January 2008,[30] states that 'A bank must ensure that it has sufficient capital to meet the minimum capital requirements set out in the Market Risk Amendment *and* to cover the results of its stress testing required by that amendment.' Moreover, in addition to the stress tests recommended in the Basel I Amendment, banks must consider stress tests relating to a number of specific scenarios, including illiquidity,[31] concentrated positions, gapping of prices,[32] one-way markets and default events.

The results of stress tests help regulators to assess the capital adequacy of a particular institution, and in particular they are supposed to give regulators an idea – however crude – of the likelihood of insolvency over some future time horizon.[33] Banking supervisors will want to see:

- a document describing the stress testing methodologies used;
- the results of a portfolio sensitivity analysis that aims to identify the key risk factors for each of the major lines of business;[34] and
- full details of the largest losses that were recorded during the reporting period – how they were incurred and whether the loss exceeded the VaR estimate at the time of the loss.

The main effect of the Basel II Accord on market risk capital is that supervisors can impose an additional capital charge under Pillar 2 if they deem it appropriate.[35] Hence, if they are concerned that the bank has insufficient capital to cover its stress testing results, the regulatory risk capital requirement could be increased.

---

[30] Simple methods only: However, advanced credit and operational risk models were adopted in the UK in January 2008.

[31] They specifically mention deep out-of-the-money options positions. Also the exogenous and endogenous aspects of liquidity should be considered. See Section IV.7.5.4 for further details.

[32] That is, a very large difference between yesterday's closing price and today's opening price.

[33] In fact most credit rating agencies such as Standard and Poor's, Moody's and Fitch also require firms to provide stress testing results that support their claims about capital adequacy.

[34] This analysis should be designed around the bank's current trading positions and also take account of current market circumstances. For instance, at the time of writing, volatile oil prices and credit spreads are the two main risk drivers that could be affecting the solvency of a bank.

[35] The three 'pillars' of the new Basel Accord are: Pillar 1, *capital requirements*; Pillar 2, *enhanced supervision*; and Pillar 3, *public disclosure and market discipline* (see Section IV.8.2.3 for further details).

IV.7.4.2 Systemic Risk

Systemic risk is the risk that the insolvency of a few large firms spreads throughout the sector, and possibly into other sectors of the economy. Local regulators can gain some idea of the extent to which mass insolvency could affect their sector of the global banking system by aggregating the stress test results, usually based on standard stress scenarios, over all banks under their supervision.

The three main factors that contribute to systemic risk are the similarities of risk assessment and risk management procedures, collateral shortages and illiquid markets. We discuss each of these in turn.

The regulations governing financial institutions actually encourage institutions to assess and manage risk in a similar fashion. Under Pillar 3 of the new Accord banks must declare the methods used to assess risks and their Pillar 1 regulatory capital requirements. The public disclosure of risk capital based on a standard methodology (i.e. usually a VaR model) coupled with the rapid dissemination of information that is facilitated by technological advances (e.g. via electronic trading platforms) can precipitate a sequence of rapid responses to an adverse event that culminates in institutions displaying *herd behaviour*, where traders have virtually simultaneous, similar responses. Market participants attempt to 'beat the herd' by trading first, shocks are augmented because short term volatility increases, and a one-way market may ensue.

Many financial institutions hold sufficient collateral to cover only 'normal' contingencies and long term average liquidity demands. But a stress event can create a collateral shortage that is contagious. Suppose counterparty A defaults on counterparty B because it lacks collateral. Counterparty B must absorb a large fraction of the loss and, as a result, may now have difficulty meeting its own obligations, so it may default on counterparty C, and so the contagion spreads.

A market's liquidity is reflected by the size of the bid–ask spread (exogenous liquidity) and the market depth (i.e. the ability to do large trades with little price effect, which is an endogenous form of liquidity). In the event of a crisis, exogenous illiquidity can spill over from one market to another, because an increase in one market's bid–ask spread can increase demand in another market. For instance, traders may be using a market for hedging because it is the cheapest of several alternative markets to trade in, but if spreads widen in that market then traders will seek to use another market for hedging. A sudden increase in demand in this second market could then decrease its liquidity; in other words, a reduction in liquidity in one market may affect liquidity in other markets.

IV.7.4.3 Stress Tests Based on Worst Case Loss

A 'worst case' loss purports to quantify the tails of the distribution of losses beyond the threshold (typically 99%) used in VaR analysis. It is derived from a set of simplistic extreme scenarios on the risk factor returns. Each extreme scenario is a vector of risk factor returns and the worst case loss is the maximum loss that is recorded over all the identified scenarios. But since a worst case loss is not based on a distribution of risk factor returns the result is a loss to which we cannot assign a probability, so the output is impossible to interpret in any meaningful way. Nevertheless, this approach to stress testing remains popular at the time of writing, mainly because it is easy to understand and cheap to implement. To derive a 'worst case' loss one only has to substitute some extreme value for each risk factor return in the portfolio mapping, and the portfolio mapping is the only part of the risk model that is used.

The application of worst case scenarios to stress tests may be based on hypothetical or historical events. A common hypothetical event is a *six sigma event*, meaning a loss that is at least six standard deviations from the expectation of a distribution.[36] Simply put, if the historical (or hypothetical) P&L standard deviation is $\hat{\sigma}$ dollars, then the worst case loss is $6\hat{\sigma}$ dollars. More generally, suppose we are stress-testing a portfolio that has k risk factors whose returns are denoted $X_1, \ldots, X_k$ and whose P&L is denoted $f(X_1, \ldots, X_k)$. Given an estimated or hypothesized value for the means $\hat{\mu}_i$ and the standard deviations $\hat{\sigma}_i$, $i = 1, \ldots, k$, the six sigma loss is defined as $f(\hat{\mu}_1 \pm 6\hat{\sigma}_1, \ldots, \hat{\mu}_k \pm 6\hat{\sigma}_k)$, where the $+$ or $-$ is chosen independently for each risk factor in order to maximize the loss.

This is an example of the *factor push* methodology for stress testing, in which each risk factor is 'pushed' by a certain amount, in a direction that will incur the greatest loss, without respecting any assumption about the risk factor correlations. More generally, a factor push method generates a P&L of the form

$$f(\hat{\mu}_1 + a_1\hat{\sigma}_1, \ldots, \hat{\mu}_k + a_k\hat{\sigma}_k)$$

where the integers $a_1, \ldots, a_k$ can be positive or negative. This method is commonly used by traders for assessing the risks of their own positions, but since it takes no account of risk factor correlations the factor push methodology has limited application to firm-wide solvency assessment.

EXAMPLE IV.7.9: A FACTOR PUSH STRESS TEST

A UK bank has invested £5 million in a US equity index. Assuming the $/£ exchange rate is currently 2, with a volatility of 10%, and the equity risk factor volatility is 25%, find the six sigma daily return in each risk factor and hence estimate the worst case loss to the UK investor over a daily horizon.

SOLUTION   The daily standard deviation of the forex rate is $\hat{\sigma}_1 = 0.1/\sqrt{250} = 0.00632$ and that of the equity index is $\hat{\sigma}_2 = 0.25/\sqrt{250} = 0.01581$. The six sigma daily return is six times these, i.e. 3.79% for the forex rate, 9.49% for the equity index.[37] The original value of the position, based on a forex rate of 2, is $10 million. With a positively stressed equity return of 9.49% the new position value is $10 \times \exp(0.0949) = \$10,995,141$, and with a positively stressed forex return the new exchange rate is $2 \times \exp(0.0379) = 2.077$. Hence the stressed value of the new position is $\$10,995,141/2.077 = £5,292,861$. So, under this scenario, the position would make profit of £292,861.

Table IV.7.7   Six sigma losses

Sign on forex return	1	−1	1	−1
Sign on equity return	1	1	−1	−1
Stressed value	£5,292,861	£5,710,197	£4,378,132	£4,723,343
P&L	£292,861	£710,197	–£621,868	–£276,657

---

[36] The six sigma methodology was originally developed as a set of practices designed to improve manufacturing processes and eliminate defects. See http://en.wikipedia.org/wiki/Six_Sigma for more information.

[37] Note that the latter is the dollar return, not the return in pounds sterling, and we assume that all returns are log returns.

The P&L corresponding to the four possible directions of the changes in the two risk factor returns is displayed in the last row of Table IV.7.7. From this it is clear that the worst case loss of £621,868 occurs when the exchange rate appreciates and the equity index falls.

The factor push approach does not respect correlations between risk factors and, although these may indeed change during stressful periods, there are some correlations that must always be respected if the market is to be arbitrage free. For instance, it is impossible for interest rates along a yield curve to move independently by any amount and in any direction without creating arbitrage opportunities using calendar spreads.

A more sophisticated method for estimating worst case loss, developed by Studer and Lüthi (1997), uses a *trust region* in risk factor returns space to derive a worst case loss that respects correlations between risk factors. Denote the risk factor covariance matrix by $\boldsymbol{\Omega}$ and the risk factor returns vector by $\mathbf{x} = (X_1, \ldots, X_k)'$. If the risk factor returns have a multivariate normal distribution then the regions defined by $\mathbf{x}'\boldsymbol{\Omega}^{-1}\mathbf{x} = c$ for some constant c are concentric ellipsoids. For instance, if $k = 2$ then the ellipsoid curves are ordinary two-dimensional ellipses. They correspond to the level sets of the bivariate normal density function. By requiring $\mathbf{x}'\boldsymbol{\Omega}^{-1}\mathbf{x} \le c$ for some constant c, we are therefore requiring that the risk factor returns lie in a confidence region that is determined by c. This region is called a 'trust' region because the smaller the value of c the smaller the possible range for risk factors returns about their expected value, and therefore the more likely they are to occur.

The matrix $\boldsymbol{\Omega}$ may be specified according to historical returns behaviour, or by a stressed covariance matrix such as those described in Section IV.7.5. Either way we can derive a constrained maximum loss as the solution to the following optimization problem:

$$\min_{\mathbf{x}} f(\mathbf{x}) \quad \text{such that } \mathbf{x}'\boldsymbol{\Omega}^{-1}\mathbf{x} \le c, \tag{IV.7.6}$$

where $f(\mathbf{x})$ is the P&L for the portfolio, according to the portfolio mapping f.

EXAMPLE IV.7.10: WORST CASE LOSS IN SPECIFIED TRUST REGION

A UK bank holds £5 million in S&P 500 futures and £5 million in FTSE 100 futures and the $/£ exchange rate is 2. The two equity indices each have a volatility of 25% and the forex rate has a volatility of 10%. The correlation between the forex rate and S&P 500 dollar returns is 0.25, the correlation between the forex rate and the FTSE 100 index is −0.15, and the correlation between the local currency returns on the equity indices is 0.5. Use these data to set up the optimization problem (IV.7.6) for trust levels $c = 0.05$, 0.1 and 0.25, each time recording the vector of optimally stressed risk factor returns and the corresponding worst case loss on the portfolio.

SOLUTION   The optimization problem is set up in the spreadsheet for this example, using the Solver settings shown there. Readers are free to change the covariance matrix and/or the trust level, but must remember to reapply Solver each time. The results are summarized in Table IV.7.8. The first three rows show the optimized returns on each of the risk factors and the last row shows the worst case loss under these risk factor returns. As c increases the optimized vector of risk factor returns may be less likely to occur. In other words, as the worst

Table IV.7.8   Results of worst case loss optimization

c	0.05	0.1	0.25
USD/GBP return	−0.382%	−0.540%	−0.855%
FTSE100 return	4.969%	7.029%	11.116%
S&P 500 return	4.460%	6.305%	9.967%
Worst case loss	£502,768	£718,359	£1,159,302

case loss shown in the table increases from £502,768 to £1,159,302 it may also become less likely under a multivariate normal distribution for the returns.[38]

IV.7.5   A COHERENT FRAMEWORK FOR STRESS TESTING

The most straightforward method of encoding stress scenarios for distributions of risk factor returns is to assume that the functional form of the risk factor return distributions remains the same in stressful markets.[39] For instance, if the risk factor returns have a multivariate Student t distribution with 8 degrees of freedom in 'normal' market circumstances, then we assume that they still have a multivariate Student t distribution with 8 degrees of freedom during stressful periods; the only change is to the mean and covariance parameters of this distribution.

This section will illustrate the use of a *stressed* covariance matrix to calculate VaR and ETL corresponding to stressful scenarios.[40] This way, a stress test is derived from the entire risk model, not only the portfolio mapping, and so we can quote the result of a stress test as a probabilistic statement. Note that we should stress not only the covariance matrix but also the expected risk factor returns in the stress test. The vector of expected returns can contain many extreme values that impact the portfolio with substantial losses, so accounting for the expected return could have a significant effect on the stressed VaR and ETL even over a very short time horizon.

One of the methods that regulators recommend for constructing stressed covariance matrices is to 'make up' a hypothetical covariance matrix. But in so doing there is no guarantee that the matrix will in fact represent a covariance matrix, because when correlations are altered in an arbitrary fashion the matrix need not be positive semi-definite. We discuss this problem in Section IV.7.5.2, and explain how to find the 'nearest' covariance matrix to the one that is specified in our hypothetical example. Section IV.7.5.3 addresses the problem of dimension in the context of stress testing. Stress tests commonly involve changing a very large number of risk factors, many of which are often highly correlated. We already know how to use principal component analysis to reduce the dimension of the risk factor space, and this subsection illustrates the application of stress tests to principal components of a large number of correlated risk factors. Section IV.7.5.4 explains how to model liquidity effects in stress tests, distinguishing between *exogenous* effects where illiquidity is reflected in an increase in the bid–ask spread, and *endogenous* effects which include the impact of the quantity traded on the mid price

---

[38] It is also possible – though complex – to associate a probability with a worst case loss that is derived using this method by computing the value of the multivariate normal distribution function at $\mathbf{x}$, when $\mathbf{x}'\Omega^{-1}\mathbf{x} = c$. See Studer and Lüthi (1997).

[39] However, Berkowitz (1999) has argued that the distribution of an asset or risk factor during periods of market stress is very different from its usual distribution.

[40] The Basel Committee recommends the use of both hypothetical stressed covariance matrices, and those derived from historical crisis periods.

in the market. We explain how to model the gradual liquidation of a position – or the gradual hedging – over a period of several days, and how to incorporate this into a *liquidity-adjusted* estimate in the stressed VaR calculation. Finally, we discuss volatility clustering, which has a significant influence on VaR and ETL even in 'normal' market circumstances. In stressful markets this effect becomes even more pronounced, as we demonstrate in Section IV.7.5.5.

IV.7.5.1 VaR Based on Stressed Covariance Matrices

The 1996 Amendment to the Basel Accord recommended that banking regulators require stress tests to be performed using stressed risk factor covariance matrices. Such matrices could be obtained using historical data on daily risk factor returns from a crisis period in the past. The crisis period should cover the period where there is a concentration of extreme returns. For instance, the next example computes a simple covariance matrix for the FTSE 100 and S&P 500 indices using data from around the period of the global stock market crash.

EXAMPLE IV.7.11: COVARIANCE MATRIX FROM GLOBAL EQUITY CRASH OF 1987

Use daily prices on the FTSE 100 and S&P 500 indices from just before and after the global stock market crash in October 1987 to derive a historical covariance matrix for these two risk factors. Use this matrix, and the other sample moments from the same period, to estimate the 0.1% daily equity VaR of a portfolio with equal amounts invested in the two indices, and discuss your results.

SOLUTION   Data from 13 October to 20 November 1987 were downloaded from Yahoo! Finance.[41] Figure IV.7.7 shows that the FTSE index fell on most of the days from 13 October until 10 November.[42] Based on the 20 observations from 13 October to 10 November, the sample moments are displayed in Table IV.7.9.

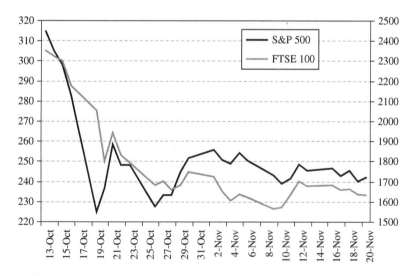

Figure IV.7.7   S&P 500 and FTSE 100 indices during global crash of 1987

---

[41] Codes ^FTSE and ^GSPC. Note that the closing prices are not contemporaneous, as the UK market closes 4.5 hours before the US market, and hence the correlation is likely to be underestimated.
[42] The S&P index is on the left-hand scale and the FTSE 100 index is on the right-hand scale.

Table IV.7.9 Sample moments of S&P 500 and FTSE 100 index returns during global crash period

	FTSE 100	S&P 500
Daily mean	−1.90%	−1.18%
Annualized mean	−474%	−294%
Daily std. dev.	4.28%	6.03%
Volatility	68%	95%
Skewness	−0.05	−1.56
Excess kurtosis	1.43	5.00
Correlation		0.47

The covariance matrix based on these data, expressed in annual terms, is

$$\begin{pmatrix} 0.68 & 0 \\ 0 & 0.95 \end{pmatrix} \begin{pmatrix} 1 & 0.47 \\ 0.47 & 1 \end{pmatrix} \begin{pmatrix} 0.68 & 0 \\ 0 & 0.95 \end{pmatrix} = \begin{pmatrix} 0.46 & 0.30 \\ 0.30 & 0.91 \end{pmatrix}.$$

It is clear from the high negative sample skewness and positive sample excess kurtosis that a normal distribution assumption is not appropriate. We shall consider instead the Student t VaR formula (IV.2.63), using the negative mean returns to pick up the negative skewness. First, just for comparison, we shall use the above matrix in the normal linear formula.

The portfolio weights vector is $(0.5 \quad 0.5)'$ and the mean return vector is $(−0.0190 \ − 0.0118)'$.[43] Thus the 0.1% daily normal equity VaR, expressed as a percentage of the portfolio value, is

$$\Phi^{-1}(0.999)\sqrt{(0.5 \quad 0.5)\begin{pmatrix} 0.46 & 0.30 \\ 0.30 & 0.91 \end{pmatrix}\begin{pmatrix} 0.5 \\ 0.5 \end{pmatrix}} - (0.5 \quad 0.5)\begin{pmatrix} -0.0190 \\ -0.0118 \end{pmatrix} = 15.27\%.$$

Note that ignoring the mean adjustment gives a result that is only 13.73% of the portfolio value, so the adjustment is important even over a 1-day horizon.

Now we use a simple method of moments to estimate the degrees of freedom for a Student t distribution of each return. Using (IV.2.60), we can set $\nu = 6\hat{\varkappa}^{-1} + 4$ where $\hat{\varkappa}$ is the sample excess kurtosis. Solving this gives a degrees of freedom parameter of 8.2 for the FTSE 100 index and 5.2 for the S&P 500 index. We could then use a normal copula for the multivariate return distribution, but this would require simulation, and to keep this illustration simple we prefer a closed-form VaR formula. We therefore use (IV.2.63) where ν is the average of the two degrees of freedom, i.e. 6.7.[44]

Based on this approximation, the 0.1% daily Student t equity VaR, expressed as a percentage of the portfolio value, is estimated as

---

[43] We can ignore discounting with no real loss of accuracy since the risk horizon is only 1 day.
[44] This is, of course, a crude approximation. But then the functional form we have chosen is fairly arbitrary anyway, since the Student t distribution is symmetric. On the plus side, (IV.2.63) is just as easy to compute as the normal linear VaR, and at least it is a more accurate reflection of the data than a normal distribution.

$$t_v^{-1}(0.999)\sqrt{\frac{4.7}{6.7}} \times \sqrt{\begin{pmatrix} 0.5 & 0.5 \end{pmatrix} \begin{pmatrix} 0.46 & 0.30 \\ 0.30 & 0.91 \end{pmatrix} \begin{pmatrix} 0.5 \\ 0.5 \end{pmatrix}} - \begin{pmatrix} 0.5 & 0.5 \end{pmatrix} \begin{pmatrix} -0.0190 \\ -0.0118 \end{pmatrix} = 20.92\%.$$

This time ignoring the mean adjustment gives a result of 19.38%. Either way, our VaR estimate at the 99.9% confidence level would be very seriously underestimated if we ignored the leptokurtosis in returns during market crises and tried to estimate a stressed VaR based on a normal distribution. Still, we have not accounted properly for the strong negative skewness in equity returns at the time of a crash – this could be captured using a Cornish–Fisher approximation or a normal mixture VaR formula – but these extensions are left to the interested reader.

Normal or Student t Monte Carlo VaR models are also based on a covariance matrix, so using a stressed covariance matrix with these models produces a stressed VaR estimate – and these are applicable to *non*-linear portfolios. We may also use a stressed covariance matrix to estimate historical VaR. Using an idea that was introduced by Duffie and Pan (1997), we can change the covariance structure of the historical data on risk factor returns to reflect the covariances during the crisis period. The idea is simply an extension of the volatility adjustment of historical returns, already described in the case study of Section IV.3.5.2.

Suppose there are k risk factors and T observations on each factor in the historical sample. Denote the $T \times k$ matrix of historical risk factor returns by $\mathbf{R}$, denote their covariance matrix by $\mathbf{V}$ and denote the Cholesky matrix of $\mathbf{V}$ by $\mathbf{Q}$. So

$$V(\mathbf{R}) = \mathbf{V} = \mathbf{QQ}'.$$

Now take a stressed covariance matrix for these risk factor returns, denote this by $\mathbf{V}^*$ and denote the Cholesky matrix of $\mathbf{V}^*$ by $\mathbf{Q}^*$. So

$$\mathbf{V}^* = \mathbf{Q}^*\mathbf{Q}^{*\prime}.$$

Now set $\mathbf{R}^* = \mathbf{R}(\mathbf{Q}^*\mathbf{Q}^{-1})'$. Then

$$\begin{aligned} V(\mathbf{R}^*) &= V\left(\mathbf{R}(\mathbf{Q}^*\mathbf{Q}^{-1})'\right) = \mathbf{Q}^*\mathbf{Q}^{-1}V(\mathbf{R})\mathbf{Q}'^{-1}\mathbf{Q}^{*\prime} \\ &= \mathbf{Q}^*\mathbf{Q}^{-1}\mathbf{QQ}'\mathbf{Q}'^{-1}\mathbf{Q}^{*\prime} = \mathbf{Q}^*\mathbf{Q}^{*\prime} = \mathbf{V}^*. \end{aligned} \qquad \text{(IV.7.7)}$$

Thus $\mathbf{R}^*$ is a stress-adjusted set of historical returns, i.e. returns that are adjusted to have the stressed covariance matrix $\mathbf{V}^*$.

After adjusting the historical returns as above, i.e. so that their covariance structure is that of the stressed market throughout, we apply the portfolio mapping to the standard historical simulation model to derive a stressed portfolio return distribution. Then we estimate the stressed historical VaR as an extreme quantile of this distribution.

EXAMPLE IV.7.12: STRESSED HISTORICAL VAR

Use daily historical returns on the FTSE 100 and S&P 500 indices from 3 January 1996 to 21 April 2008 to estimate the 0.1% daily historical equity VaR for a portfolio with equal amounts invested in the two indices, where the returns are adjusted to have the stressed covariance matrix that was derived in the previous example.

SOLUTION   The spreadsheet first derives the covariance matrix based on daily returns over the whole historical period. This is

$$\mathbf{V} = \begin{pmatrix} 1.277 & 0.591 \\ 0.591 & 1.272 \end{pmatrix} \times 10^{-4}.$$

For the stressed covariance matrix use the daily covariance matrix from the 1987 stock market crash, derived in the previous example, i.e.

$$\mathbf{V}^* = \begin{pmatrix} 18.351 & 12.116 \\ 12.116 & 36.372 \end{pmatrix} \times 10^{-4}.$$

Clearly both volatilities and the correlation are far higher during the period of the global stock market crash in 1987. Now we adjust the historical returns using a transformation that is based on historical and stressed Cholesky matrices, which are

$$\mathbf{Q} = \begin{pmatrix} 1.130 & 0 \\ 0.523 & 0.999 \end{pmatrix} \times 10^{-2} \quad \text{and} \quad \mathbf{Q}^* = \begin{pmatrix} 4.294 & 0 \\ 2.828 & 5.327 \end{pmatrix} \times 10^{-2}.$$

The transformation matrix is given by

$$\mathbf{Q}^*\mathbf{Q}^{-1} = \begin{pmatrix} 3.7911 & 0 \\ 0.0363 & 5.3297 \end{pmatrix},$$

and post-multiplying the transpose of this matrix by the returns gives the stress-adjusted returns. The historical stressed equity VaR is minus the 0.1% quantile of this return distribution, which is calculated in the spreadsheet as 19.63% of the portfolio value. This should be compared with the ordinary historical 0.1% daily equity VaR on 21 April 2008, which is just 4.32%.

IV.7.5.2   Generating Hypothetical Covariance Matrices

Stressed covariance matrices may also be based on hypothetical scenarios for the risk factor volatilities and correlations. In fact, the Basel Committee recommended this in their stress testing guidelines of the 1996 Market Risk Amendment. For instance, we could assume that the volatility of a risk factor is five times the current level of volatility. Provided volatilities are positive, the stressed covariance matrix will be positive semi-definite if and only if its associated correlation matrix is positive semi-definite.[45] Risk factor correlations tend to be augmented during crisis periods, so we could likewise assume that a risk factor correlation increases by 50% of its current level. However, although we are free to change volatilities to any positive quantity that we like, we are not free to change correlations. In doing so we could be specifying a matrix which is not positive semi-definite and which therefore cannot, in fact, be a correlation matrix.

Nevertheless risk analysts and portfolio analysts find it very useful to 'make up' correlation matrices to represent their own personal views on the market behaviour over the risk or

---

[45] For the proof of this see Section I.2.4.3.

investment horizon. So we need to check hypothetical 'correlation' matrices to test whether they are positive semi-definite.[46] If not, we need to transform a matrix into another matrix that is positive semi-definite and that is, in some sense, as 'close' as possible to the hypothesized matrix.

There are several measures of 'closeness' that can be applied to two matrices. Any such measure is defined using a *matrix norm*, which is a generalization of the concept of 'length' for a vector.[47] Perhaps the most popular matrix norm is the *Frobenius norm* which, for a real matrix $\mathbf{A}$, is defined as

$$\| \mathbf{A} \| = \sqrt{\mathrm{tr}(\mathbf{A}'\mathbf{A})}, \qquad (\mathrm{IV.7.8})$$

where 'tr' denotes the trace operator (i.e. the sum of the diagonal elements of a square matrix). For our purposes we have two square symmetric matrices, $\mathbf{C}$ and $\tilde{\mathbf{C}}$ where $\mathbf{C}$ is the hypothesized matrix (and which we suppose is not a correlation matrix because it is not positive semi-definite) and $\tilde{\mathbf{C}}$ is the closest correlation matrix to $\mathbf{C}$. In other words, $\tilde{\mathbf{C}}$ is a symmetric, positive semi-definite matrix such that the matrix

$$\mathbf{A} = \mathbf{C} - \tilde{\mathbf{C}}$$

has the smallest possible matrix norm. Moreover, both $\mathbf{C}$ and $\tilde{\mathbf{C}}$ must have 1s along the diagonal, and off-diagonal elements that are less than or equal to 1 in absolute value.

To find $\tilde{\mathbf{C}}$ we have to perform an optimization. This takes the form of minimizing (IV.7.8) or some other matrix norm, with $\mathbf{A} = \mathbf{C} - \tilde{\mathbf{C}}$, and subject to the constraints that $\mathbf{A}$ has zero diagonal elements and $\tilde{\mathbf{C}}$ has off-diagonal elements that are less than or equal to 1 in absolute value.

EXAMPLE IV.7.13: FINDING THE 'NEAREST' CORRELATION MATRIX

Suppose an analyst hypothesizes that the returns on four risk factors have the 'correlation' matrix

$$\mathbf{C} = \begin{pmatrix} 1 & 0.8 & -0.4 & -0.2 \\ 0.8 & 1 & -0.3 & 0.5 \\ -0.4 & -0.3 & 1 & 0.5 \\ -0.2 & 0.5 & 0.5 & 1 \end{pmatrix}.$$

Show that this is not in fact a correlation matrix, because it is not positive semi-definite. Then use the Frobenius norm to find the nearest correlation matrix to the hypothesized matrix.

SOLUTION First we use the determinant test for positive definiteness described in Section I.2.2.8. That is, we find the matrices of the successive principal minors, i.e. of the 2×2 and 3×3 matrices with diagonal elements along the main diagonal, and the determinant of the matrix itself. These are 0.36, 0.302 and -0.1284. Not all of these are non-negative, so the matrix is not positive semi-definite.

Next we apply Solver to find the nearest positive semi-definite matrix, subject to the constraints on the elements described above. We shall impose a non-trivial lower bound for the determinant test on the result; otherwise the optimization is likely to return a matrix that has

---

[46] We can check a matrix for positive semi-definiteness either by finding its eigenvalues and checking that none of these are negative, or by checking that all its principal minors have positive or zero determinant. See Sections I.2.2.8 and I.2.3.7.
[47] See http://en.wikipedia.org/wiki/Matrix_norm.

a zero determinant, so it will only be positive semi-definite. In this example we have required that all principal minors be greater than or equal to 0.01.[48] The result of the optimization is the positive definite matrix

$$\tilde{C} = \begin{pmatrix} 1 & 0.7539 & -0.4146 & -0.1661 \\ 0.7539 & 1 & -0.2795 & 0.4541 \\ -0.4146 & -0.2795 & 1 & 0.4842 \\ -0.1661 & 0.4541 & 0.4842 & 1 \end{pmatrix}.$$

IV.7.5.3   Stress Tests Based on Principal Component Analysis

Regulators recommend that portfolios be stress-tested for parallel and tilt movements in term structures. For instance, the Derivatives Policy Group recommended that yield curves be subject to a parallel shift of 100 basis points in either direction, and also to a linear tilt of 25 basis points. In the light of the recent credit crisis, their recommendation that credit spreads be subject to a parallel shift of 20 basis points along the maturity curve may seem rather too mild to be classed as a stress scenario. This is so often the case – after the event!

The problem with simple scenarios such as parallel shifts is not so much the magnitude of the shock – after all, it is simple to make this as large we like – but whether in fact parallel shifts and linear tilts in a term structure of interest rates are truly capturing the weak spots of the portfolio. Indeed, portfolios may be hedged against parallel movements,[49] and in this case stress tests against parallel moves in interest rates of all maturities will not produce extreme losses for a 'worst case' scenario.

Here again we have an example where the term 'worst case' loss is totally inappropriate. Not only because 'worst case' is a logical misnomer whenever it is used, but because by far the most common type of movement in a highly correlated yield curve is the movement captured by the first principal component. Typically this is *not* a parallel shift, and because it is the most commonly occurring type of movement (given the historical data used in the analysis) it is *this* movement that a trader should really be hedging against.[50] If the portfolio has only been hedged against a parallel shift, stress testing with a parallel shift will not produce an extreme loss; but stressing the first principal component could produce a significant loss. In short, principal component analysis is not only a very useful tool for hedging, it is an ideal method for generating more realistic 'shocked' term structures than parallel shifts and linear tilts.

Principal component analysis also reduces the complexity of a stress test. Typically a three-component representation is all that we need to capture about 99% of the historical variation of yield curves, or credit spread curves, or term structures of futures or forwards, or even volatilities of different maturities. Hence, there is a large dimension reduction and this greatly simplifies the stress test. Principal component analysis produces a small number of new, uncorrelated risk factors. Because they are uncorrelated there is no need to consider their dependency in the stress test. Thus, instead of stress-testing the simultaneous, correlated movements of, say, 60 correlated risk factors we can stress test separately the movements of 3 uncorrelated ones! That is, each stress test can be performed by shocking just *one* of

---

[48] Without this, the resulting matrix has determinant 2.75×10^{-8}.

[49] For instance, bond portfolios are commonly 'immunized' against parallel movements – see Section III.1.5.6 for further details.

[50] For details on how to do this, see Section II.2.4.4.

these components to an extreme value, such as a six standard deviation move, in either direction. Or, we could change all the components simultaneously, by different positive or negative amounts.

In Section II.2.4.6 we presented an empirical example of a stress test of a UK bond portfolio that was based on principal component analysis. The first component corresponded to a roughly parallel shift in interest rates longer than 18 months' maturity, but with considerably less movement in the money market rates. The intuition that this type of movement is the most commonly occurring type of variation in UK interest rates rests on the observation that short rates are tied to monetary policy targets, and were less variable than long rates over the historical period considered.

In this example the portfolio incurred the worst loss, amongst all the scenarios considered, when the first principal component experienced a six sigma downward movement, but not all linear portfolios will experience worst case losses as a result of a large movement in the first principal component (i.e. a roughly parallel shift). It depends on the hedging strategy for the portfolio, as demonstrated by the following example.

EXAMPLE IV.7.14: PRINCIPAL COMPONENT STRESS TESTS

Consider the bond portfolio in Example IV.2.9. In that example we derived a three principal component factor model representation for the P&L of this portfolio, i.e.

$$P\&L = £428P_1 - £2795P_2 + £1041P_3.$$

We know from Table IV.2.9 that this representation captures over 99% of the historical variation in the portfolio. The standard deviations of the first three principal components were calculated in that example as:

$$\sigma_1 = \sqrt{856.82} = 29.27, \quad \sigma_2 = \sqrt{45.30} = 6.73, \quad \text{and} \quad \sigma_3 = \sqrt{9.15} = 3.02.$$

Find the maximum loss incurred from uncorrelated six sigma adverse changes in each of the principal components separately.[51]

SOLUTION   Denote by β_i the portfolio's sensitivity to the ith component so, for example, $\beta_1 = £428$. Set $P_i = -6\beta_i\sigma_i$ for $i = 1$, 2 and 3 separately, and hence obtain the worst case loss corresponding to a six sigma change in each component. The results are a loss of £75,169 for the six sigma move in the first component, £112,871 for the second component and £18,894 for the third component. Thus the portfolio is more exposed to an unusual tilt in the curve than it is to a shift or a change in convexity.

However, our results in Example IV.2.9 showed that movements in the first component accounted for over 93% of the historical variation in the yield curve, whereas the second component only accounted for about 5% of the movements. In this example the loss incurred through an extreme change in the first principal component is less than the loss resulting from an extreme change in the second component, but the first type of loss is far more likely to occur, if we assume the historical data to be representative of the future.

---

[51] Note that the first component is not a parallel shift, as we can see from Figure IV.2.3.

To summarize, the use of principal component analysis for worst case loss calculations provides:

- a reduction in the complexity of stress tests through the use of a few, uncorrelated risk factors that can be stressed separately;
- stress tests against the scenarios that are most likely to occur, according to historical experience; and
- an indication of the relative likelihood, according to historical experience, of the losses that we compute.

IV.7.5.4   Modelling Liquidity Risk

There are two types of liquidity risk:

- *Market liquidity risk* is the risk associated with an inability to perform market transactions at the current mark-to-market value. Market liquidity is commonly measured by an exogenous factor, i.e. the relative size of the *bid–ask spread*, and by an endogenous factor, i.e. *market impact*. Market impact relates to *market depth*, i.e. the ability to trade a substantial amount without seriously impacting the mid price.
- *Funding liquidity risk* refers to the inability to raise funds or collateral to meet obligations.

Funding illiquidity is a prime risk driver of default risk, but not of market risk. Hence this section focuses only on market liquidity risk, and in particular on methods that incorporate exogenous and endogenous illiquidity effects into stressed VaR calculations.

Standard VaR analysis assumes that all trades are at the mid market price. It ignores the increase in the bid–ask spread and the reduction in market depth that so often occurs at the time of a stress event. However, traders attempting to close out or hedge large positions in stressful market conditions may find that they cannot transact efficiently, resulting in exposure to adverse market conditions for longer periods and additional losses resulting from wider spreads.

Liquidity varies between markets and over time, as illustrated by Borio (2000), and in many markets it decreases as market volatility increases, as observed by Bangia et al. (2002). These authors also propose a methodology for estimating a *liquidity-adjusted* VaR that captures exogenous liquidity effects via an 'add-on' to the changes in mid price that we usually model in a stress test, where the size of the add-on depends on the size of the bid–ask spread. They assume that extreme market events are perfectly correlated with extreme liquidity events because this simplifies the analysis considerably, and it is also fairly realistic.

Define the relative bid–ask spread by

$$S = \frac{P_A - P_B}{P_M}, \qquad (IV.7.9)$$

where P_A, P_B and P_M are the ask, bid and mid prices respectively, and $P_M = \frac{1}{2}(P_A + P_B)$. We assume that S is a random variable and thence define the cost of exogenous liquidity, $C_{\alpha,t}$ at the α quantile at time t by

$$C_{\alpha,t} = \frac{1}{2} x_{1-\alpha,t} P_{M,t}, \qquad (IV.7.10)$$

where $P_{M,t}$ denotes the current mid price and $x_{1-\alpha,t}$ denotes the $1 - \alpha$ quantile of the spread distribution. The motivation for this definition is that standard VaR calculations assume transactions are at the mid price, but on average we expect the ask price to be $\frac{1}{2}\mu_S$ above this price, and the bid price to be $\frac{1}{2}\mu_S$ below it, where μ_S denotes the expected value of the spread. The definition (IV.7.10) thus adjusts the transaction price to be at the $1 - \alpha$ quantile of the spread distribution, where α corresponds to the quantile of the VaR estimate. Then the liquidity-adjusted $100\alpha\%$ VaR (or ETL) is the standard VaR (or ETL) plus the cost of exogenous liquidity. The next example illustrates the calculation under the assumption that the spread is lognormally distributed.

EXAMPLE IV.7.15: STRESSED VAR WITH EXOGENOUS ILLIQUIDITY

Suppose an investor has equal amounts invested in FTSE 100 and S&P 500 index futures. Assume that spreads are perfectly correlated in these markets and that in each market the relative bid–ask spread is lognormally distributed. Suppose that historical observations on the relative spread during stressful markets indicate that the mean and standard deviation of the spread in each market are given by[52]

$$\mu_{S\&P} = 0.0123\%, \quad \sigma_{S\&P} = 0.0162\%, \quad \mu_{FTSE} = 0.0203\% \quad \text{and} \quad \sigma_{FTSE} = 0.0267\%.$$

Estimate the cost of liquidity for this position at the 99.9% confidence level, and compare your result with the historical stressed VaR that was estimated in Example IV.7.12.

SOLUTION   In the spreadsheet for this example we apply the Excel LOGINV function to estimate the 99.9% quantile of the lognormal spread distribution for each pair of mean and standard deviation parameters. The result is 0.1645% for the S&P 500 and 0.2713% for the FTSE 100 index. Since our position has equal amounts invested in each futures market, the cost of liquidity expressed as a percentage of the portfolio mid price is

$$\frac{1}{4}(0.1645 + 0.2713)\% = 0.109\%.$$

This is negligible compared with the 0.1% stressed VaR of the portfolio, which was estimated to be 19.64% of the portfolio value in Example IV.7.12.

The above example demonstrates that this type of exogenous liquidity adjustment to stressed VaR is of negligible importance in the world's main futures markets. Bangia et al. (2002) also report that no significant liquidity adjustment is necessary for major currency markets. Readers are free to change the parameters used in the previous example to reflect the behaviour of bid–ask spreads in less liquid markets.

There are two drawbacks to the methodology just described. First, it takes no account of endogenous liquidity, i.e. the relationship between the price that is realized and the size or quantity of the transaction relative to the normal lot size in the market. Secondly, it is not

---

[52] These values are very small, reflecting the fact that FTSE 100 and S&P 500 futures are major markets that tend to remain highly liquid even in stressful circumstances. Note that the parameters of a lognormal distribution are the mean and standard deviation of the corresponding normal distribution, i.e. the mean and standard deviation of the log spread in this case. The figures here for the spread mean and standard deviation are actually derived from choosing suitable values for the mean and standard deviation of the log spread. See (I.3.40) and (I.3.41) for the formulae used in the spreadsheet to relate the mean and standard deviation of the log spread to the corresponding parameters for the spread.

easy to assess the appropriate value of the quantile of a spread distribution in stressful market conditions because, typically, only a few empirical observations are available.

Angelidis et al. (2004) suggest a method that accounts for the market impact of trades that are larger than normal. For instance, for quantities in excess of the normal market lot size N we could assume a linear or quadratic increasing function for the expected size of the spread as a function of the quantity transacted. Specifically, we could assume that the expected value of the relative spread μ_S is related to the quantity q that is traded as

$$
\mu_S = \begin{cases} \overline{S}, & \text{if } q \leq N, \\ \overline{S} + g(q - N), & \text{if } q > N. \end{cases} \tag{IV.7.11}
$$

Here g denotes some increasing linear or quadratic function such that $g(0) = 0$. For instance, if g is linear then

$$
g(x) = k(x), \quad k > 0. \tag{IV.7.12}
$$

Estimation of the value of k could be based on dealers' quotations during a crisis in the past, or on the subjective judgement of experienced traders.

EXAMPLE IV.7.16: STRESSED VAR WITH ENDOGENOUS LIQUIDITY

An illiquid stock has a bid–ask spread that is assumed to follow a lognormal distribution. The mean relative spread is 0.4% and its standard deviation is 0.2%. Find the cost of liquidity adjustment that should be made to the VaR at the 99.9% confidence level. Now assume the normal lot size is 1000 and that we need to make a transaction of 50,000 shares. Assume the quantity impact on the mean relative spread is given by (IV.7.11) where g is given by (IV.7.12) with $k = 10^{-7}$. Find a revised estimate of the cost-of-liquidity adjustment to be made to the VaR.

SOLUTION   In the spreadsheet we use Solver to back out the appropriate mean and standard deviation of the log spread, since these are the parameters used in the Excel LOGINV function. Thereafter the first case is a straightforward repeat of the calculations used in the previous example, and we obtain a cost-of-liquidity adjustment of 0.2684% to the 99.9% VaR, expressed as a percentage of the investment value.

The second part of the calculation assumes the mean relative spread is only 0.4% when 1000 shares are transacted. Since we are trading 50 times this amount, we use the function (IV.7.12) with $k = 10^{-7}$ and $q - N = 49,000$ to obtain an adjustment to the mean spread of 0.49%. Hence, with this quantity adjustment the new mean relative spread is 0.89%. Leaving the standard deviation unchanged and repeating the calculation gives a cost-of-liquidity adjustment of 0.7276% of the portfolio value.

It is clear from the above examples that spread adjustment has a relatively small impact on the stressed VaR, except in highly illiquid markets. However, spread size is not the most important variable that is adversely affected by the quantity traded; the main liquidity effect arises from movements in the mid price itself as it comes under pressure in a one-way market. For instance, in liquid stock markets the daily average trading volume (DATV) is approximately 0.5% of the market capitalization of the stock. So to effect a sale of, say, 1% of the market cap the dealer will divide the order into normal size lots and execute each order over a period of time.[53] But if he does this too quickly, for example over the course of only one day, there comes a point when a downward price pressure is exerted on the mid price. Thus both bid and ask prices could trend upward during a buyers market, or downward during a seller's market.

It may be necessary to introduce gradual liquidation of a period over several days. For example, one might assume that a large position is divided into three parts, each a multiple of the standard lot size Q, and then traded on successive days. Then, denoting the quantity traded on day t by q_t, the mid-price at time t may be adjusted by assuming a linear price impact relationship of the form

$$P_M(q_t) = \tilde{P}_M \times \left(1 + \omega k(q_t - Q)\right), \qquad \text{(IV.7.13)}$$

where $\tilde{P}_M$ is the mid price just before the trade occurs, $\omega = +1$ for a purchase order and $\omega = -1$ for a sell order, and the constant k is set relative to the standard lot size, for instance using the judgement of experienced traders. Setting $k = c/Q$ for some constant c, and setting $q_t = m_t Q$, rearrangement of (IV.7.13) gives an alternative expression for the price impact relationship as

$$\frac{P_M(q_t) - \tilde{P}_M}{\tilde{P}_M} = \omega\, c(m_t - 1), \qquad \text{(IV.7.14)}$$

where the left-hand side is the percentage return due to the price impact of the trade. To account for the price impact effect, the absolute value of this return should be added to the VaR that is estimated without accounting for the quantity impact, assuming the VaR is expressed as a percentage of the portfolio value.

EXAMPLE IV.7.17: ADJUSTING VAR FOR PRICE-QUANTITY IMPACT

Suppose daily log returns, based on the mid price of an illiquid asset, are i.i.d. and normally distributed with volatility 30%. We have to sell 50% of the DATV, which itself is equal to 1000 standard lots. Assume the quantity impact on the mid price is given by (IV.7.14) with $c = 5 \times 10^{-5}$. Calculate the price impact of the quantity traded when it is traded on one day, and when it is traded in parcels of 100 times the standard lot size on each of five successive days. In each case show how we should adjust the 1% VaR to account for the expected price depreciation resulting from the unusual size of our position. Is it better to liquidate the position immediately, or to spread the liquidation uniformly over 5 days? How does your conclusion change if the quantity impact coefficient increases to $c = 2 \times 10^{-4}$?

SOLUTION   We must sell 500 standard lots, and with $c = 5 \times 10^{-5}$ and $\omega = -1$ the price impact on the return (IV.7.14) is

$$\frac{P_M(q_t) - \tilde{P}_M}{\tilde{P}_M} = -5 \times 10^{-5}\,(500 - 1) = -2.495\%,$$

assuming the sale is made on one day. The 1% daily VaR is given by the usual normal linear VaR formula, so if we ignore the price-quantity impact we have

$$1\%\ \text{VaR} = \Phi^{-1}(0.99) \times 0.3/\sqrt{250} = 4.414\%.$$

---

[53] The normal lot size is 100 for US stocks and 1000 for UK stocks, since the price per share of US stocks tends to be higher than it is in the UK. Normal lot sizes for currencies are usually in units of $1000. Transactions at multiples of $1000 usually have smaller spreads than transactions at intermediate amounts.

Adding the absolute value of the return created by the price-quantity impact, the total 1% VaR, including the price-quantity impact, is 6.909%.

Now consider the case where we divide the sale into five lots of 100, traded over five successive days. Although the price impact is less on each day, the position remains open for 5 days instead of 1, and so we must compute a 5-day VaR instead of a 1-day VaR. On each day the price-quantity impact induces a negative return of only

$$-5 \times 10^{-5}(100 - 1) = 0.495\%$$

instead of 2.495%, but we must account for the gradual stepping down of the exposure over the five successive days.

On the first day we have 1% daily VaR of 4.414% and an add-on for the price impact of 100 lot sizes traded of 0.495%, so the total daily VaR is 4.909%. On the second day the 1% daily VaR is $(4/5) \times 4.414\% = 3.531\%$ and the add-on for the price impact is $(4/5) \times 0.495\% = 0.396\%$ so the total daily VaR on the second day is 3.927%. On the third, fourth and fifth day we continue to step down the exposure uniformly, until on the last day the 1% daily VaR is $(1/5) \times 4.414\% = 0.883\%$ and the add-on for the price impact is $(1/5) \times 0.495\% = 0.099\%$, so the total daily VaR on the last day is only 0.982% of the original value of our position.

To find the total VaR we need to aggregate the daily VaRs obtained above in accordance with our risk model. Since this assumes the returns are normal and i.i.d., returns are additive. So the total price-quantity impact is just the sum of the add-ons due to the negative returns given by the price-impact function. The VaR in this model is a constant multiple of volatility, but it is variance not volatility that is additive in our risk model. So to find the total VaR, unadjusted for the price impact, we take the square root of the sum of the squared daily VaRs. The results are set out in Table IV.7.10, where the aggregates in the last row are obtained as the square root of the sum of the squares for the unadjusted VaR, and as a simple sum for the add-ons that account for the price quantity impact. Thus the total 1% VaR, including the price-quantity impact, which is now measured over a 5-day horizon, is $6.547\% + 1.485\% = 8.032\%$. Since this is greater than 6.909%, we conclude that the quantity impact is low enough for it to be preferable to liquidate the position immediately.

Table IV.7.10   Adjusting VaR for uniform liquidation

	Unadjusted VaR	Add-on
1	4.414%	0.495%
2	3.531%	0.396%
3	2.648%	0.297%
4	1.766%	0.198%
5	0.883%	0.099%
Aggregate	6.547%	1.485%

Readers may change the constant c in the spreadsheet to alter the cost of liquidation, and will see that when the price impact of large trades is great, it pays to liquidate more slowly. For instance, if we change cell B5 to $c = 2 \times 10^{-4}$ the price-quantity impact is very significant. If the entire job is executed in one day the effect on the return is −9.98% and so the daily VaR corresponding to immediate liquidation jumps up to 14.394%. However, gradual liquidation over a 5-day period yields a total 5-day VaR of 12.487%, so in this case it pays to liquidate the position more slowly.

IV.7.5.5   Incorporating Volatility Clustering

In the previous subsection the model of gradual liquidation assumed the returns were normal and i.i.d. This assumption led to a simple analysis but it is not very realistic. In this subsection we explain how to incorporate volatility clustering into stressed VaR calculations when the exposure is hedged or liquidated gradually, over a horizon of several days. The importance of volatility clustering effects for stressed VaR calculations cannot be understated. For example, in an extensive empirical analysis of VaR-based stress tests in which many different frameworks for estimating VaR are compared, Alexander and Sheedy (2008) show that it is only the risk models that incorporate volatility clustering that are able to provide accurate predictions of VaR at extreme quantiles in stressful currency markets.

Here we shall illustrate the methodology in the framework of two VaR models: the filtered historical simulation (FHS) model that was introduced in Section IV.3.3.4 and the Monte Carlo VaR model with volatility clustering, introduced in Section IV.4.3.2. Both frameworks utilize a simple volatility clustering model for the conditional return distribution, and this effect is incorporated into our VaR calculations. An illustration of the FHS approach was given in Example IV.3.2, and applications of volatility clustering models to multi-step Monte Carlo were provided in Examples IV.4.6 and IV.4.7.

In Example IV.3.2 we estimated 10-day VaR at various quantiles and performed a simple scenario analysis based on shocking the current volatility. But for a stress test based on FHS we should shock both the current volatility and the current return. For example, we might assume that both are shocked to six times their normal value, and that the return is negative for a long exposure or positive for a short exposure. The following example extends Example IV.3.2 in this manner.

EXAMPLE IV.7.18: USING FHS FOR STRESS TESTING

The asymmetric GARCH model with parameters given in Table IV.3.5 is the model for S&P 500 returns that was estimated in Example IV.3.1. Use this model to estimate the 0.1% 10-day VaR following a shock to the daily return of -10% and a simultaneous shock to volatility, so that it is 60% in annual terms. Apply the FHS approach, bootstrapping the sample of returns that was used to estimate the GARCH model, and assume the exposure is liquidated uniformly over a 10-day period.

SOLUTION   The spreadsheet for this example is an adaptation of the FHS spreadsheet for Example IV.3.2. We use the same asymmetric GARCH model as in that spreadsheet and the only differences are that (a) we now use shocked values for the returns and volatility, and (b) we *step down* the exposure so that the total return is a weighted sum of the returns over the next 10 days.[54]

The shock to the daily return is -10% and the shock to the daily standard deviation is $0.6/\sqrt{250} = 3.79\%$. Based on 10,000 simulations we obtain a 0.1% 10-day stressed VaR of approximately 35% of the portfolio value.[55] This more than double the 0.1% VaR estimate in Example IV.3.2, which was computed under 'normal' market circumstances.

---

[54] The formula used in cell AH2 accounts for uniform liquidation over a 10-day period.

[55] As usual, readers should extend the number of simulations by filling down, after copying the spreadsheet from the CD-ROM to their hard disk. But due to the limitations of Excel we are not able to simulate very many 10-day returns for the empirical distribution that forms the basis of our stressed VaR estimation; that is why our results are based on only 5000 simulations.

Finally we illustrate the use of multi-step Monte Carlo to incorporate volatility clustering into stress tests. In fact, Example IV.4.7 already performed a simple stress test by shocking the daily return to be ±10%. We used the example to show that, because the GARCH model is asymmetric, the losses following a negative shock to the return are greater than those following a positive shock.[56] In the next example we shock the current volatility as well as the current return.

EXAMPLE IV.7.19: USING GARCH WITH MONTE CARLO FOR STRESS TESTING

Use the asymmetric GARCH model of the previous example to estimate the $100\alpha\%$ 10-day VaR following a shock to the daily return of -10% and a simultaneous shock to volatility, so that it is currently 60% per annum. Again assume the exposure is liquidated uniformly over a 10-day period, but this time apply conditional normal Monte Carlo simulation for the returns.

SOLUTION   We use $\alpha = 0.001$, 0.01, 0.05 and 0.1 in the spreadsheet and the results are calculated based on 10,000 simulations. One set of simulations gives the results shown in Table IV.7.11. Notice that the 0.1% 10-day stressed VaR is 32.49%, which is less than that of the previous example, even though both examples use the same GARCH model. This is because here we have used standard normal simulations for the returns rather than bootstrapping them from an empirical and leptokurtic return distribution.

Table IV.7.11   Stressed VaR at different confidence levels based on Monte Carlo GARCH

α	0.001	0.01	0.05	0.1
VaR	32.49%	23.20%	15.71%	11.90%

IV.7.6 SUMMARY AND CONCLUSIONS

Historical data on major market risk factors are usually easily available. As a result, market risk analysts have developed a tendency to rely on these data when forecasting the market risk of a portfolio, even over a long risk horizon. In doing so the analyst is implicitly adopting a subjective view that history will repeat itself. However, when the risk horizon is more than a few days, there is much to be said for using an alternative subjective view that is not necessarily tied rigidly to historical experience. In my view there is far too much reliance on historical data when computing VaR, and analysts should develop the confidence to use their own personal views as well. In any case, this becomes essential when there are little or no historical data available. Any critics of the subjective nature of the methodology we have proposed in this chapter should bear in mind that, so far, each new financial crisis entails events, and precipitates market behaviour, for which we have no historical precedent.

Scenarios can be categorized by the type of data that are used to construct them, and by the mathematical quantity that the scenario concerns. The data can be based on either *historical* experience or *hypothetical* views. The mathematical quantity in the scenario can be a single

---

[56] This depends on the sign of the asymmetric coefficient λ, which was positive in this case. But if λ were negative then the losses following a positive shock to the return would be greater than those following a negative shock.

vector of risk factor returns (as it is in 'worst case' scenarios) or one or more parameters of the risk factor return distribution (as it is in the covariance matrices that regulators recommended for use in stress testing). One may also apply empirical risk factor return distribution scenarios, without specifying a parametric form, such as those that were experienced during stress events in the past. When a scenario is on a single vector of risk factor returns, we apply the portfolio mapping to derive the portfolio's P&L associated with the scenario, and we ignore the rest of the risk model. It is only when scenarios concern the *distribution* of risk factor returns that we can use the risk model in the stress test, and it is only when we use the risk model that can we associate a *probability* with the resulting P&L.

Financial institutions and regulators regard stress testing as an essential complement to the VaR and ETL calculations that are based on 'normal' market circumstances. There is no single standard approach to stress testing, and the methodology that is chosen often depends on the context in which the results will be used. But stress testing, as it is practised by many institutions today, is an art without a proper mathematical foundation. Stress scenarios are chosen to result in a so-called 'worst case' loss, but there is nothing to guarantee that the loss that is calculated will not be exceeded, and no statement of the probability that this loss will occur.

The main focus of this chapter has been to develop a coherent framework for stress testing, in the context of the risk model that is used for standard VaR and ETL calculations. Personal views of the analysts may be used to forecast the market VaR of a portfolio in both 'ordinary' and stressful market conditions. We have focused on some empirical examples that incorporate the use of scenarios for portfolio returns over a long horizon, and have contrasted the differing ways that subjective information is used in *scenario VaR* and in *Bayesian VaR*. We have described the impact of scenarios for returns on stressed VaR. We have also shown how to obtain the correlation matrix that is 'closest' to a hypothesized matrix that cannot be a correlation matrix because it is not positive semi-definite. We have advocated the use of *principal component analysis* for stress testing on a highly correlated set of risk factors such as a yield curve, or credit spreads of different maturities. We have also explained how to adjust VaR and ETL by adding on a *cost of liquidity* adjustment that accounts for *exogenous* liquidity effects on the bid–ask spread in illiquid markets, and *endogenous* liquidity effects on the price impact of trading quantities that are large, relative to the DATV. The cost of endogenous liquidity effects is usually much greater than the cost of exogenous effects, except in highly illiquid markets, and we have demonstrated how a trader's liquidation or hedging strategy can be tailored to the size of the liquidation costs. The chapter ends with a description of the use of both FHS and standard Monte Carlo simulation to incorporate *volatility clustering* effects into a stress test, when positions are liquidated or hedged only gradually over a period of several days, so as to minimize the liquidity costs.

IV.8
Capital Allocation

IV.8.1 INTRODUCTION

The senior management and board of directors of a financial institution have an important role, which is to ensure that capitalization is sufficient to cover the risks that are being taken. Their duty is to the shareholders and, in banking, also to the regulators. Thus, a major task facing the risk manager in a bank or financial firm is to assess the level of risk relative to the capitalization, at various activity levels and within each line of business. Also, the value of the firm is reflected by its credit rating, which is linked to the probability of default over a long time horizon. Thus, good risk management should encompass a rigorous stress testing programme that is designed to increase the probability that the firm remains solvent over this time horizon.

The solvency of banks is particularly important for the stability of the financial system. Governments, central banks and the Basel Committee have a strong interest in systemic risk, where insolvency in one sector of an economy can lead to a national – if not global – economic crisis. Thus the global recession following the stock market crash of 1987 prompted a revision of banking regulations and, in the mid 1990s, new minimum requirements for the regulatory risk capital owned by banks were imposed on all banks in the G10 countries, and these were later adopted by most of the developed countries in the world.

The computation of regulatory capital for various activities in each line of business is an important task for the risk managers in a bank. But, unlike economic capital, when estimating the legal minimum level of capitalization required for the bank as security against its market risk exposures, the manager is not free to use the risk models, risk metrics and data that he deems most appropriate. He may even use no risk model at all, and merely apply the standardized rules that are set by the regulators. Alternatively, he could use an internal risk model to estimate risk capital, provided it is validated by the regulator and provided that the risk management structure in the bank satisfies certain qualitative criteria. However, the internal model must conform to some fairly strict quantitative criteria. In most countries it can be one of two broad types, either a scenario model or a VaR model;[1] and regulatory capital is based on an aggregate *maximum loss* if the scenario model is used or the 1% 10-day VaR if the value-at-risk approach is used.

By contrast, the computation of economic capital can be based on *any* internal risk model, any risk metric and any data. The only proviso is that the methodology is acceptable to the board of directors. An economic capital model could be based on any assumptions about risk factor evolution over the risk horizon and the data that are used could be purely historical,

---

[1] Most major banks would adopt a VaR model, but some regulators allow scenario models to be used by smaller banks.

purely hypothetical (e.g. as in hypothetical stressed VaR) or a combination of the two. The risk manager is also free to recommend whatever risk metric or metrics he believes to be appropriate, and apply these to the economic capital model. In fact, for economic capital estimation many large banks use ETL rather than VaR, and they may also use at least some data from historical or hypothetical market crises.

At the elemental level, economic capital does not need to correspond to real capital. It is a risk measure, such as VaR or ETL, at a fairly high confidence level and assessed over a fairly long horizon. The confidence level $1 - \alpha$ and risk horizon h are linked to the solvency condition, whereby the total economic capital for the firm as a whole can be interpreted as the minimum level of capitalization required so that the probability of insolvency over a risk horizon h is no greater than α. But capital reserves do not have to match economic capital in the same way that they must match minimum regulatory capital. In fact, many institutions carry a much higher level of capital than they need to justify their credit rating, as a signal of confidence to their investors and their counterparties.

In a large organization it is usual to assess risks first at a fairly elemental level, then progressively aggregate positions into larger and larger portfolios. This is because different individuals assess market risks for different reasons. Starting at the most granular level, each trader is concerned with the accurate assessment of the risk of every instrument in his book, the risk of portfolios of similar instruments and, finally, the risk of the book as a whole. Both he and the head of the desk should be monitoring these risks, and limits will be placed on the total risks that each trader can take. The head of desk will be monitoring portfolios consisting of each single book, up to a portfolio that contains all the instruments in all his trading books. Then the risk manager at the head of the business unit has the job of ensuring that the market risks taken by the head of each desk in the business unit remains within reasonable limits, as he monitors the total market risk taken by the unit as a whole. Finally, the global head of market risk examines the market risks of each business unit and the total market risk at the company or group level, and reports these to the board of directors. Thus a 'portfolio' can be anything from a single instrument to all the positions in the entire firm.

In other words, we first assess the risk of individual instruments, then of portfolios of similar instruments, and then we aggregate the risks in a (hopefully) intelligent manner to obtain the risk for progressively larger and larger portfolios containing different aggregate positions. At some stage, often at the business unit level, the total market risk is aggregated with the total credit risk and the total operational risk, to produce a combined estimate for the total risk of the business unit. Finally, the business unit risks are aggregated to obtain a firm-wide estimate of risk against which the total capitalization of the firm may be assessed. This so-called 'bottom-up' approach is the most common risk assessment paradigm.

By contrast, the process of economic capital allocation takes a 'top-down' approach. Having assessed the total, firm-wide risk and made a judgement on the required level of total economic capital for the firm, this capital is then assigned to different business units, and to different activities within each unit. Finally, economic capital is assigned to the desk level and possibly even to the level of the trader. The greater the economic capital assigned, the greater the risks that can be taken, and the freer the desk or trader becomes. Hence, the increase or withdrawal of an economic capital allowance becomes a useful tool whereby senior managers can control different activities in the organization. Nowadays most large organizations have a management structure that is driven by economic capital, because it is a tool that allows the risks of all the different activities in the firm to be compared on a standard scale, and because it can be aggregated for the purpose of 'bottom-up' firm-wide risk capital estimation and disaggregated for 'top-down' capital allocation, in a mathematically coherent framework.

One of the major disadvantages of the 'bottom-up' approach to risk assessment is that most risk analysts use a simple dependency metric, i.e. correlation, for the aggregation of risks, as if all dependencies were linear and normal. *Aggregation risk* is the model risk that arises through inappropriate assumptions on risk factor dependencies when assessing portfolio risk, and this is the major source of *model risk* in firm-wide risk capital assessment. The 'bottom-up' paradigm also assumes that we know the current value of all our positions precisely. Yet only a limited number of positions can be marked to market. These include the liquid exchange traded contracts and some over-the-counter (OTC) contracts, if quoted by the brokers. Many other positions will need to be valued by *marking to model*, and this introduces a *pricing* model risk, as opposed to *risk* model risk, that can be very significant indeed.

The remainder of this chapter is structured as follows. Section IV.8.2 deals with the estimation of the minimum market risk capital requirements for banks. Here we describe the Basel regulations, which were broadly defined in the 1996 Market Risk Amendment and later refined with the new Basel II Accord; we summarize the differences between the accounting frameworks that are used in the banking and trading books (typically, market risks are only assessed on the trading book); we describe the regulatory framework for estimating minimum capital requirements for market risks, using both internal models and the standardized rules that the Basel Committee recommends for adoption into national regulations; and then we describe the 'add-ons' to the general market risk capital charge that account for *specific risks*, and the *incremental risk charge* that the Basel Committee has recently recommended for banks that use internal models with specific risk recognition.

Section IV.8.3 introduces economic capital: the methods used to assess it and the optimal allocation of economic capital as a risk management tool. We show that the aggregate economic capital for a firm, defined as the minimum level of capitalization that the firm should aim for in order to achieve a high probability of remaining solvent over some future time horizon, is a risk metric which corresponds to a quantile, like VaR. But, unlike regulatory capital for banks, firms are free to choose whatever metric they like for economic capital, provided it is acceptable to shareholders. The risk-adjusted performance of each activity in the firm may be assessed by combining forecasts of expected profits and losses with a measure of economic capital for this activity. Finally, we show how to achieve an efficient allocation of economic capital to different activities, by optimizing the firm-wide risk-adjusted performance, focusing on the maximization of risk adjusted return on capital (RAROC) which is one of the performance measures that is most commonly applied in the industry today.

IV.8.2   MINIMUM MARKET RISK CAPITAL REQUIREMENTS FOR BANKS

This section focuses on the 1996 Market Risk Amendment to the 1988 Basel Accord, and the modifications to market risk capital requirements under the new Basel II Accord. Section IV.8.2.1 describes the history of the Basel Committee and its regulatory initiatives; Section IV.8.2.2 defines the banking and trading books and provides an overview of the accountancy frameworks used in each; Section IV.8.2.3 describes the regulatory framework for controlling market risk in the banking system, which is based on three 'pillars' of regulation. Thereafter we focus on the Pillar 1 capital charge, explaining how the general, specific and incremental market risk charges are calculated using an internal model, or using a set of standardized rules defined by the Basel Committee.

IV.8.2.1 Basel Accords

In 1974 the central bank governors of the G10 countries created a forum to debate and coordinate best practices for risk management and banking supervision. The *Bank for International Settlements* (BIS), located in Basel, offered its premises and facilities for meetings and a permanent secretariat, hence the name *Basel Committee on Banking Supervision* (BCBS or 'the Committee').[2] The Committee now has about 30 workgroups and task forces addressing various issues affecting banks and their supervisors, focusing on broad standards and statements of best practice. The recommendations put forward in the two Basel Accords are now almost universally adopted into national legislation. However, whilst the Committee has great influence, it has no legal power.

The defining initiative of the Committee was the 1988 Basel Accord which was implemented in the G10 countries in 1992. Prior to this, banking supervisors were content with requiring disclosure of exposures (mostly foreign exchange and interest rate) and setting some limits on concentrations of risks (large exposure limits, and country risks). Adequacy of capital was a topic of discussion between supervisors and banks, but there were no strict requirements. The main contribution of the 1988 Basel Accord was to set core principles for adequate supervision and minimum capital standards. At the same time, regulatory convergence and coordination were sought across countries as well as between banking and securities' businesses.

For the first time, the 1998 Basel Accord set quantitative minimum capital requirements for banks based on the level of credit risk in their assets. The Accord, and its subsequent 1996 Amendment for Market Risk in the Trading Book,[3] has been progressively adopted into legal regulations by over 100 countries, so that the Accord has now become the global standard for evaluating banking risk. An important initiative in the 1996 Amendment was a long technical appendix that responded to the industry calls for the use of internal models, rather than standardized rules, to assess market risk capital.

Extensive revisions to the assessment of credit risks and the introduction of a capital charge to cover operational risks were the main features of the new Basel II Accord in 2005.[4] Developments in credit derivatives and the rapid growth in the markets for credit default swaps and collateralized debt obligations in particular, meant that sophisticated credit mitigation techniques were no longer recognized efficiently under the old Accord. And because of the increasing complexity of financial markets there was greater need for transparency of accounts and risk disclosures. But, in contrast to the 1996 Amendment, the initiative for a new Accord was driven by regulators, not by the industry. Industry consultation on Basel II took almost 6 years and many contentions remain even now, after its implementation in major countries.

The primary objectives of the old accord were safety and market stability. In addition to maintaining these prime objectives, the Basel II Accord aims to harmonize banking regulations among countries and to foster better risk management in an evolutionary approach, starting with simple rules for all banks but providing incentives in the form of reduced capital

---

[2] See the Bank's website, www.bis.org for further details about the BIS and the BCBS. In particular, for more detailed information on the structure and activities of the BCBS, see http://www.bis.org/bcbs/
[3] See BCBS (1996). This was implemented in the G10 countries in January 1998.
[4] See BCBS (2005). A compilation of this paper and some key previous publications by the Basel Committee may also be found in BCBS (2006).

requirements for banks with more sophisticated risk management. The new regulations should not affect global capital requirements, but they do introduce greater risk discrimination, and this will lead to a redistribution of capital among financial firms.

The market risk capital requirements under Basel II are largely unchanged from the 1996 Amendment, except for the definition of the trading book as positions in financial instruments and commodities held either with trading intent or to hedge other elements of the trading book.[5] And now, under the new Accord, exceptional market risks should be monitored in the banking book. For example, the Basel Committee have recommended that interest rate exposure be stress-tested by assuming a 200 basis point parallel shift in the zero coupon curve. However, any additional capital charges for market risks in the banking book are left to the discretion of national supervisors.

IV.8.2.2   Banking and Trading Book Accounting

In the current spectrum of accounting standards, banks currently apply these forms of accounting:

- In *historical* (also called *accrual* or *cost*) accounting, cash flows are recorded as they occur, and assets are held at cost. This form of accounting does not reflect the current value of a business. Therefore, for prudence, it is accompanied by a 'reserves and provisioning' policy that is designed to cover future potential losses, in which provisions (but not reserves) are limited, to avoid manipulation of profit and tax avoidance.
- *Fair value* accounting is reserved for positions that have a visible value in a liquid market (positions that can be *marked to market*) or that have a value which can be objectively and accurately estimated (positions that can be *marked to model*).

Cost accounting is easier to understand than fair value accounting, being based on observed cash flows rather than complex marking-to-model calculations. And there is less subjectivity in cost accounting than there is in fair value accounting. The only subjective elements of the cost accounting framework are in the reserves and provisions that are made. Since these reserves and provisions are to cover expected losses, not worst case losses, the accent of cost accounting will be on a conservative valuation of assets and liabilities, based on their historical cost. But cost accounting is backward looking, so it is not an appropriate starting point for the evaluation of risk. It does not assess *variations* in economic value about its fair (i.e. expected) value. In fact, it does not even assess the fair economic value of a business.

In fair value accounting the accent is on 'true and fair' assessment of asset values, although the interpretation of these concepts is somewhat subjective.[6] As a result, fair value accounting is more subjective than cost accounting. At the same time, being based on market (or model) prices of financial instruments, it is also less consistent across different countries and businesses (e.g. banks, securities firms and insurance companies) than cost accounting. However, it is *forward looking*, since market prices provide a signal about traders' expectations. The disadvantages of fair value accounting are that it can be complex, costly and unreliable. For

---

[5] Trading intent may be evidenced by a clearly documented trading strategy that is approved by senior management, and/or by clearly defined policies and procedures for the active management of the position.
[6] The Financial Accounting Standards Board in the US defines fair value as 'the amount at which an asset could be bought or sold in a current transaction between willing parties, that is, other than being forced into liquidation'. Therefore, the assessment of fair value is straightforward if quoted market prices exist. If they do not, the instrument can be marked to model, but not without introducing pricing model risk.

instance, it would be very difficult to reach a consensus on the expected losses due to counterparty default in illiquid markets. Nevertheless, it is in fair value rather than cost accounting that we find the appropriate foundation for risk evaluation.

The *trading book* contains on and off balance sheet positions that are held with the intent of deriving short term profits. This implies that they are liquid enough to be closed down rapidly and can be easily valued by marking to market. Derivative instruments such as futures, swaps and options are *off balance sheet* instruments that are marked in the trading book. The *banking book* contains all transactions that cannot be valued easily or are held for the long term with no trading intent. They are usually accounted for on an accrual basis with adequate reserves and provisions for potential losses, but marking to market is permitted where safe. Thus the distinction between the two books is based on an accounting issue, i.e. that of valuing liquid versus illiquid assets. Banks normally use fair value accounting in the trading book and cost accounting for most of the positions in the banking book.

Reporting standards for basic accounts (or supplementary risk disclosures) play a critical role in risk evaluation and capital allocation. These are essential for the evaluation of performance, the disclosure of risks and the enforcement of market as well as supervisory discipline. Accounting standards need to be global, to facilitate comparisons across nations and businesses. International accounting standards also save costs and facilitate access to international capital markets. However, despite the extensive work that has been carried out by the International Accounting Standards Committee (IASC) since its creation in 1974, progress is slow because of differences in national traditions and legal systems.

Like the BCBS, the standards developed by the IASC have no legal power until accepted and enacted by national authorities. In 2000 the Securities and Exchange Commission (SEC) in the US adopted the FAS 133 standards in which derivatives are recorded in the trading book at fair value.[7] Since January 2005 the EU has required quoted companies to produce accounts according to the much more comprehensive IAS 39 standards.[8]

IV.8.2.3   Regulatory Framework for Market Risk

The Basel II Accord reaffirmed the three pillars of regulation that were defined in the first Accord:

- Pillar 1 – *minimum capital standards*. This sets the minimum level of eligible capital that banks must hold as insurance against risk.
- Pillar 2 – *supervisory review*. This sets out the recommendations for inspection and the reporting requirements for banks.
- Pillar 3 – *public disclosure and market discipline*. This aims to support the supervisor by enhancing market scrutiny by competitors, clients and shareholders.

The three pillars are seen as equally important. They are also complementary. For example, the flexibility to use internal models for calculating risk capital in Pillar 1 means greater responsibility for the supervisor to inspect and approve these models under Pillar 2.

---

[7] Financial Accounting Standards (FAS) Board Statement No. 133, Accounting for Derivative Instruments and Hedging Activities. Available from www.fasb.org/derivatives.

[8] International Accounting Standards 39: Financial Instruments: Recognition and Measurement.

The central concept in the Pillar 1 capital requirement is a solvency ratio, called the *Cooke ratio*, which is defined as the ratio of eligible capital to the total capital charge, both of which are defined below. The *minimum solvency ratio* is the minimum value for the Cooke ratio that is set by the national regulator, and for well-managed banks with at least an A credit rating it is at least 8%. National supervisors are entitled to set higher ratios for poor-quality or less well-managed banks, and to set different minimum solvency ratios for the trading and banking books within a bank.

The numerator in the solvency ratio, *eligible capital*, consists of three tiers, defined in decreasing order of reliability for capital reserves:

- Tier 1 (*core capital*) consists of paid up share capital plus audited retained P&L on investing this capital;
- Tier 2 (*supplementary capital*) consists of undisclosed reserves, revaluation reserves, general provisions, hybrid instruments and subordinated debt with maturity at issue of at least 5 years;
- Tier 3 (*sub-supplementary capital*) consists of subordinated debt with maturity at issue of 2–5 years.[9]

For eligibility under Tier 2 or Tier 3 capital, instruments must be free from any restrictive covenants on their tradability, or they must be able to be hedged completely. Tier 2 capital must also be less than Tier 1 capital.

The denominator in the solvency ratio, the *risk weighted assets*, is the sum of risk measures for market, credit and operational risks. The *market risk capital charge* (MRC) applies to all on and off balance sheet positions in a trading book.[10] The MRC is defined as the sum of a general risk charge (GRC), plus a *specific risk charge* (SRC) or an *incremental risk charge* (IRC):

$$MRC = GRC + \{SRC \ or \ IRC\}. \tag{IV.8.1}$$

The specific or incremental risk components of the MRC may be applied to both equity and interest rate exposures under the Basel recommendations, but they do not apply to commodities or currencies.

Subject to certain qualitative requirements on its risk management procedures and quantitative requirements on the structure of the risk model, set out below, banks may use an internal risk model to estimate the MRC.[11] The qualitative criteria that must be satisfied for use of an internal model to assess MRC include:

- *independence* between risk control and business trading, with risk managers reporting directly to the senior management of the bank;
- a regular *backtesting* programme, as well as initial and ongoing validation of the internal model;
- *involvement* of the board of directors and senior management in the risk control process, to which they must be committed;
- *use tests* whereby the internal model is closely integrated into daily risk management, including its use in conjunction with trading and exposure limits;

---

[9] Tier 3 capital is not counted in the assessment of the credit risk capital requirement.

[10] The risk measure for market risk is 12.5 times the market risk capital charge evaluated directly. Market risks for non-traded positions in a banking book are largely ignored, except possibly as a small additional charge under Pillar 2.

[11] These criteria are stated in more detail in BCBS (2005).

- a routine and rigorous programme for *stress testing*, with results being regularly reviewed by senior management, and dynamic contingency plans must be in place;
- *documentation* for the technical framework of the risk model, and for internal policies, controls and procedures for operating the model;
- the regular internal *auditing* of the risk model, to assess the above.

Regulators pay particular attention to the possibility of large losses, that is, to the negative tail of a return distribution. Consequently, they focus on VaR to determine the minimum level of regulatory capital. The quantitative criteria recommended by the Basel Committee for the use of internal models are as follows:

- The 1% 10-day VaR must be estimated on a daily basis. For linear portfolios this may be computed as $\sqrt{10}$ times the 1% 1-day VaR.
- The historical sample must be at least 1 year (or, for banks that use a weighting scheme or other methods, the weighted average time lag of the individual observations must be at least 6 months). Also data must be updated at least every 3 months or when there has been a sharp change in prices.[12]
- No particular type of model is prescribed. So banks are free to use models based, for example, on covariance matrices, historical simulations, or Monte Carlo simulations. Discretion may be exercised to recognize empirical correlations within and across broad risk categories, including implied volatilities in each risk factor category, provided that the supervisory authority is satisfied that a bank's system for measuring correlations is 'sound and implemented with integrity'.
- Models must capture the risks associated with option portfolios accurately using a 10-day price shock, corresponding to static rather than dynamic options VaR;[13] they must also capture option portfolios' non-linear price characteristics (i.e. *gamma risk*) and the volatility of underlying rates or prices (i.e. *vega risk*).[14]

IV.8.2.4   Internal Models

For banks that use an internal VaR model to estimate the MRC the general risk charge is calculated as k times the average of the 1% 10-day VaR over last 60 days, or yesterday's VaR on the current portfolio, if this is greater:

$$\text{GRC}_t = \max\left(\frac{k}{60} \sum_{i=1}^{60} \text{VaR}_{10,0.01,t-i}, \text{VaR}_{10,0.01,t-1} \right).$$ (IV.8.2)

The multiplier k takes a value between 3 and 4 depending on the model's backtesting results. If backtests reveal statistical inaccuracies in the VaR estimates, k takes a higher value or the VaR model may be disallowed.[15]

---

[12] Supervisors may also require a bank to use a shorter historical period if this is justified by a significant upsurge in price volatility.

[13] For evaluating market risks of option portfolios banks are ultimately expected to move towards the application of a full 10-day price change. But in the interim, they may adjust their capital measure through other methods, e.g. via periodic simulations or by stress testing.

[14] Banks with relatively large and/or complex option portfolios should measure the volatilities of options positions broken down by different maturities. This requires a form of vega bucketing or, preferably, volatility beta mapping, as described in Section III.5.6.

[15] See Section IV.6.4.2 for further details on the way that supervisors set the value for k. If the model is disallowed the MRC must be calculated using the standardized rules.

It is easy to show that a multiplier of between 3 and 4 produces a much higher (i.e. far more conservative) risk measure than a 99.9% annual VaR. For example, even when k takes its lowest value 3 and the returns are normal and i.i.d., we have

$$3 \times 1\% \ 10\text{-day VaR} = 3 \times 2.32635\sigma = 6.979\sigma.$$

Hence, the GRC is approximately 7σ away from the expected portfolio return. The probability of a return that is less than this, in a 10-day period during which the portfolio is static, can be found using standard normal tables: it is approximately 1.5×10^{-12}. Hence, it is extremely unlikely that the GRC would be exceeded over a 10-day horizon.

But what about exceeding the GRC over an annual horizon – how likely is this? We should *not* just extrapolate the GRC to an annual horizon using the square-root-of-time rule, i.e. by multiplying it by $\sqrt{25} = 5$, because the portfolio is likely to be rebalanced, except in cases of extreme illiquidity. If the portfolio is rebalanced every 10 days then it is reasonable to assume the 10-day returns are i.i.d., and in this case the probability of not exceeding $3 \times 1\%$ 10-day VaR over an annual horizon is $\left(1 - 1.5 \times 10^{-12}\right)^{25}$. So the probability of exceeding a level of loss that is set at $3 \times 1\%$ 10-day VaR, over 250 days, is

$$1 - \left(1 - 1.5 \times 10^{-12}\right)^{25} = 3.7 \times 10^{-11}.$$

Clearly, this is much more stringent than using a 99.9% confidence level over a 250-day horizon.

In a steady market the GRC will be dominated by k times the average VaR and, as we have just demonstrated, it is unlikely that losses would exceed the capital requirement in this case. The averaging process also smooths out sharp variations in MRC and reduces the procyclical tendency for capital requirements. However, if there is a sharp increase in the bank's aggregated market risk, the average VaR term in (IV.8.2) is replaced by yesterday's VaR, that is, the VaR estimate does not increase enough when the portfolio make a large loss. This increases the risk sensitivity of the MRC. Problems will arise, however, if the risk model that is used to estimate VaR is insufficiently risk-sensitive, that is, the VaR estimate does not increase enough when the portfolio make a large loss. This is one reason why regulators require the VaR model to pass certain quantitative backtesting requirements.

EXAMPLE IV.8.1: CALCULATING GRC FOR A LONG-ONLY POSITION USING VAR

In Example II.1.2 we considered a portfolio of two US stocks, American Express (AXP) and Cisco (CSCO) in the S&P 100 index. Using daily data from 3 January 2000 to 31 December 2007, we estimated the stock's betas and the specific volatility of the portfolio. Estimate the GRC for the same portfolio, which is continually rebalanced to have 60% invested in American Express and the rest in Cisco. Assume the GRC multiplier $k = 3$ and use the normal linear model based on 250 daily returns to estimate the portfolio beta and the 1% 10-day VaR.

SOLUTION   We estimate the 1% 10-day VaR using the normal linear VaR formula

$$\text{VaR}_{10,0.01,t} = \sqrt{10} \times \Phi^{-1}(0.99) \times \beta_t \times \sigma_t,$$

where β_t and σ_t are the portfolio beta and the standard deviation of the S&P 100 index returns respectively, both based on equal weighting over the last 250 observations. Then we apply the GRC formula (IV.8.2). This result of rolling this calculation over the sample period is the series shown by the black line in Figure IV.8.1, measured on the left-hand scale. The S&P 100 index volatility is also shown on the left-hand scale and the pro-cyclical tendency of the GRC, to move with the market volatility, is clear.

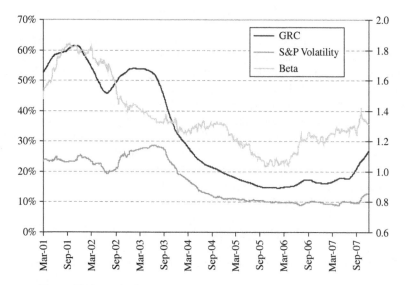

Figure IV.8.1   GRC for the US stock portfolio and S&P 100 volatility

The portfolio beta, shown on the right-hand scale, is always greater than 1. Hence, this is a 'high risk' portfolio, and this explains why the GRC is so large. Around 50% of the portfolio value would need to be held as the general risk capital charge in the early part of the period, but during 2004–2006 it reduced to less than 20% of the portfolio value. It rose again at the end of the data period due to the credit crunch, which had a serious impact on US stock market volatility.

In some jurisdictions banks may be allowed to use another approach to compute the GRC using an internal model.[16] This is the *scenario analysis* approach to estimating GRC, in which exposures in each division of the trading book are subjected to hypothetical changes to major risk factors, as if the position has a risk factor sensitivity of 1.[17] The extent of the hypothetical change depends on the type of risk factors. For instance, equity indices are subjected to a maximum of ±8% changes in price and ±25% relative changes in volatility.[18] Within these limits a two-dimensional 'grid' of possible price and volatility changes is drawn, and the P&L of the book as a whole is calculated at several points within this grid. The aim is to quantify the maximum loss that could be made and, for non-linear exposures, the maximum loss may occur at an interior point, not necessarily at one of the extremes. For each type of risk and within each geographical zone, the maximum loss is recorded for each book, and these losses are

---

[16] For example, the Financial Services Authority in the UK may allow scenario-based internal models to be used by some banks.

[17] In this approach, and in the standardized rules approach, a capital charge is assessed, initially, for each part of the trading book (e.g. UK equities, US bonds, currencies and gold, etc.).

[18] The scenario method is basically an extension of the standardized rules that are described in the next subsection, since the maximum changes for the risk factors as well as the duration or maturity banding of interest rate exposures are defined in a similar way.

then summed over all books covering different risk types and geographical zones, to produce the market GRC for the bank. Small 'boutique' banks that have just a few large exposures may find that this approach produces lower GRC estimates than would be obtained under the standardized rules, and which may be easier to estimate than VaR-based GRC.

IV.8.2.5   Standardized Rules

An alternative to using internal models to estimate capital requirements is to apply a 'building block' approach, in which separate charges for equity, currency, commodity and interest rate exposures are estimated and then summed across the four categories of risk.[19] In the standardized approach the MRC is based on instrument-specific rules. For equity exposures the GRC is 8% of the exposure (long or short, with netting allowed within a book) summed over all books. Then there is an additional *specific risk charge* (SRC) for equity risk because, in the risk factor mapping of a stock portfolio's returns, idiosyncratic risk could be significant. This risk cannot be overlooked, except when all equity books contain large, well-diversified portfolios. The SRC for equities is calculated, *without* netting long and short exposures in the same book, as a percentage of nominal exposure. The SRC is 8%, unless the portfolio is both liquid and well diversified, in which case the charge is 4%. Then the SRC is summed over all books to obtain the total SRC for equity risk.

The SRC add-on may apply to internal models as well as the standardized rules. Banks using internal VaR models to calculate the GRC for equities may already be capturing specific risk when the only significant risks are those due to the risk factors that they are using in the risk model. If a bank's internal model has gained *specific risk model recognition* (i.e. if the bank can convince the supervisor that the model is capturing specific risk adequately), then it is exempt from the SRC. Otherwise it must add on the SRC that is calculated according to these standardized rules.

For example, the GRC for the portfolio in Example IV.8.1, when based on the standardized rules, is 8% of the portfolio value. To this we must add a *specific risk charge* of 8%, because the portfolio is not well diversified. So, the MRC under the standardized rules will be 16% of the portfolio value. But the internal model produced a GRC of more than 16% throughout the data period considered. Moreover, it is unlikely that this model would gain specific risk recognition, so the bank would still need to add on an SRC of 8%.[20] Hence, the use of an internal model in this simple example would lead to a much higher VaR estimate than the application of the standardized rules.

The standardized rules for currencies and gold require the nominal amount (or net present value) of the net position in each foreign currency and in gold to be converted at spot rates into the reporting currency. The overall net open position is measured by aggregating the sum of the net short positions or the sum of the net long positions in currencies, whichever is the greater; plus the net position (long or short) in gold, regardless of sign. Then the GRC is 8% of the overall net open position. There is no specific risk charge for currencies and gold, so MRC ≡ GRC.

---

[19] Gold is included in currency risk, not commodity risk.
[20] It is difficult to obtain specific risk recognition with such a simple model and such a small portfolio. Indeed, in the spreadsheet for Example IV.8.1 we also calculate the GRC based on the portfolio returns – i.e. without using a portfolio mapping – and find that it is considerably greater than the GRC based on the portfolio beta mapping, especially during the early part of the sample.

The standardized rules for interest rates are more complex.[21] For general interest rate risk due to discount curve movements, exposures within each currency are banded into duration or maturity bands. The bands are then grouped into three zones, according to the duration or maturity of the band. In each band the exposures (long and short) are weighted by a series of factors that depend on the zone.[22] Then 'vertical and horizontal disallowances' are calculated. First, we net long and short exposures within each band and find the matched amount and an excess amount. The excesses are then matched within the zone, giving a second matched amount, the *vertical disallowance*, and an excess. These excesses are matched across different zones, giving the *horizontal disallowance*, and a final net unmatched amount. Thus the GRC is the sum of these components:[23]

(i) a small percentage of the matched positions in each zone;
(ii) a larger percentage of matched positions across different zones;
(iii) the net (long or short) position in the whole trading book.

Separate maturity ladders are used for each currency and capital charges are calculated for each currency separately, and then summed with no offsetting between positions of opposite sign, to obtain the total GRC for interest rate risk.

The reason for an additional specific charge for interest rate risk is that a single discount curve for the risk factors of an interest rate sensitive portfolio ignores the risk due to changes in credit spreads. The SRC for interest rate exposures depends on the credit rating of the issuer. For example, the SRC for a government security varies from 0% (for a government with at least an AA– rating) to 12% (for a government with a rating below B–). Banks using internal VaR models to calculate the GRC may already be using credit spread curves as risk factors, in which case the model may have gained specific risk recognition, and then it is exempt from the SRC. Otherwise it must add on the SRC that is calculated according to the standardized rules. Full details are given in BCBS (2005).

The standardized approach for commodity risk entails a *maturity ladder* with position matching that is similar to that used for interest rate exposures. The percentages used to calculate the GRC depend on maturity, except when a simplified method is used. In the simplified method the GRC for *directional risk* is 15% of the net position, long or short, in each commodity. Added to this is an additional capital charge equivalent to 3% of the bank's gross position (i.e. long plus short) in that particular commodity, to cover *basis risk*. There is no specific risk charge for commodities, so MRC ≡ GRC.

IV.8.2.6 Incremental Risk Charge

After the credit crunch that began in 2007 a new requirement for banks using internal models, for holding capital against default risk, was proposed by the Committee, and this is *incremental* to any default risk already captured. Regulators are concerned that the VaR framework ignores important differences in the underlying liquidity of trading book positions, and that it may not fully reflect large but infrequent daily losses, or losses that occur as a result of large cumulative price movements over periods of several weeks or months. Also, following the Committee's

---

[21] Readers are referred to BCBS (1996) or its amended version, BCBS (2005), for complete details and numerical examples.
[22] And on coupon, if the maturity band approach is used.
[23] An additional charge is required for positions in options, where appropriate.

recommendations, many banks are using VaR models with equal weighting of about 250 days of historical data. Now the Committee is concerned that this approach yields insufficient capital to be held against trading positions following periods of relative calm in financial markets.

In July 2008 the Basel Committee introduced an incremental risk charge, which applies to default risk in the trading book, in response to the increasing credit risk exposure in banks' trading books where the illiquidity of certain products is not reflected in standard VaR estimates.[24] The IRC represents an estimate of the trading book's overall exposure to systematic and specific default, credit migration, credit spread and equity price risks over a 1-year horizon at a 99.9% confidence level, taking into account the liquidity horizons of positions.[25]

Current proposals are that the IRC must capture all material risks affecting prices of IRC covered positions that are attributable to IRC market risk factors, *irrespective* of whether they are already incorporated into a bank's 1% 10-day VaR estimate. For example, the IRC would capture price risks associated with movements in broad indices of stock prices and market credit spreads even though typically such price risks are already captured in a bank's VaR calculations.[26]

The Committee expects banks to develop their own models for calculating the IRC, and broad guidelines for these models are provided in BCBS (2008). Note that banks are now required to meet these guidelines in order to receive specific risk model recognition. For portfolios or products for which banks have already received specific risk model recognition under the 1996 Market Risk Amendment, banks are required to implement the IRC in January 2010. For banks without specific risk model recognition, and in particular for banks that apply the standardized rules, the current rules for calculating capital charges remain unchanged.

The guidelines set out in BCBS (2008) require that banks pay particular attention to the appropriate *liquidity horizon* in their IRC models. This represents the time required to sell the position or to hedge all risks related to the IRC market factors in a stressful market. The minimum liquidity horizon has a floor equal to:

- 1 month for equities traded on a recognized exchange, and for exposures to broad equity market indices, and benchmark interest rate spreads traded in liquid markets;
- 1 year for re-securitizations; and
- 3 months for all other IRC covered positions.

Alternatively, if this is greater, the liquidity horizon is set to be consistent with the bank's actual experience. Thus, the size of the IRC will depend very much on the liquidity of the exposure.

We now discuss how large the IRC might be for a specific, highly liquid portfolio. Most banks actively hedge their portfolios and so Example IV.8.1, which was used to demonstrate the methods that may be used to calculate MRC, is not very realistic in practice. The next example is also very simple, but it is more relevant than the previous one because we examine a liquid, hedged portfolio. If the portfolio is exactly hedged all the time, and the bank has

---

[24] This encompasses all positions subject to the 1996 Market Risk Amendment, regardless of their perceived liquidity, except those positions whose valuations depend solely on commodity prices, foreign exchange rates, or the term structure of default-free interest rates. So it includes debt securities, equities, securitizations of commercial and consumer products, structured credit products as well as derivatives on such instruments. Full details are given in BCBS (2008).

[25] This is similar to the credit and operational risk capital charges.

[26] A bank's IRC model should normally incorporate credit default and migration risks for positions subject to credit risk and, by January 2010, must incorporate all remaining price risks for credit positions (that are unrelated to defaults or credit migrations) as well as all price risks for equity positions. At the time of writing the Committee has not determined whether to allow a bank's IRC to be adjusted for double-counting of risks that are already included in the 10-day VaR capital calculation.

specific risk model recognition, then the internal models-based GRC should be zero, and the MRC will simply be equal to the IRC. However, we shall assume that the hedge is rebalanced only once per day, so the portfolio's daily P&L is non-zero. Also, we shall assume there is a *position risk* in the hedged portfolio which depends on the size of the exposure.[27]

Normally, banks are not allowed to buy each other's shares, because this would allow them to increase their capitalization without using any capital. Two banks could merely swap shares, without any money changing hands. However, small amounts of another bank's shares may be held for market making purposes, when a bank's brokerage business needs to fulfil the orders from its clients, and so forth.

EXAMPLE IV.8.2: COMPARISON OF INTERNAL AND STANDARDIZED MRC FOR A HEDGED POSITION

A bank holds 10,000 shares in Barclays and each day it rebalances the short position in Lloyds TSB shares needed to match, as closely as possible, the value of the Barclays shares. It can only trade Lloyds TSB shares in units of 100. What is the MRC associated with this hedged portfolio, according to the standardized rules and based on an internal model?

SOLUTION   We shall use daily data from 3 January 2005 until 14 November 2008 to answer this question.[28] Over this period, the prices (in pence) of the two shares are shown in Figure IV.8.2. The effect of the banking crisis in 2008 is clear, as both share prices tumbled from about £5 per share to less than £2 per share, even though these banks were cash-rich retail banks that fared much better than many other banks during the crisis.

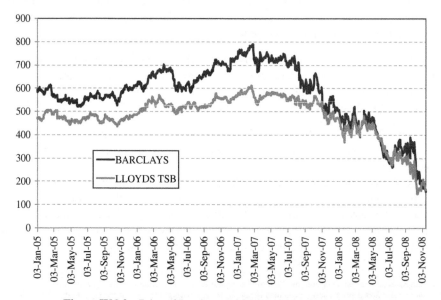

Figure IV.8.2   Price of Barclays and Lloyds TSB shares (in pence)

---

[27] Position risk arises when it is not possible to take a position with size equal to the size of an optimal contract. For instance, it is not possible to buy or sell a non-integer number of shares.
[28] Data downloaded from Yahoo! Finance, codes BARC.L and LLOY.L.

The hedge is rebalanced once each day, and we shall ignore transactions costs. So the market risk on the hedged portfolio arises from the daily P&L, as the previous day's portfolio is marked to market before rebalancing. There is also a small position risk, since we can only trade shares in units of 100. The standard deviation of the hedged portfolio's P&L determines the VaR.

Each day we use the past 250 observations on daily P&L to calculate its standard deviation. Then the normal linear VaR is calculated by applying the usual formula and we use (IV.8.2) to estimate the GRC. The standardized rules require holding 8% of the hedged portfolio value for the GRC plus 8% of the gross exposure (long and short, no netting) for the SRC. Hence the SRC is the main component of the standardized rules-based MRC (as can be seen by comparing the size of the figures in columns N and P in the spreadsheet). Rolling the calculation of capital charges daily over the entire sample gives the black line labelled GRC (Internal) and the grey line labelled MRC (Standardized) in Figure IV.8.3.

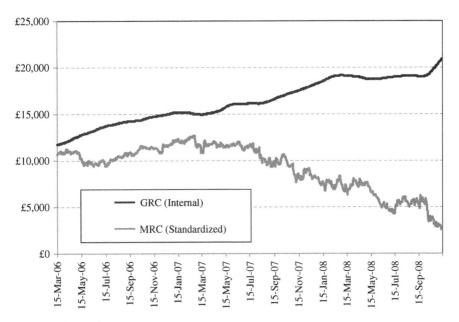

Figure IV.8.3 Internal GRC and standardized MRC for hedged portfolio

If the internal model does not have specific risk recognition, then the specific risk charge would be added to the internal model-based GRC to obtain the MRC. And if it does have specific risk recognition, then the Basel Committee are now recommending that a new, incremental risk charge should be added to the internal model-based GRC to obtain the MRC. Either way, the use of an internal VaR model will lead to a charge that is far greater than it would be under the standardized rules. As can be seen in Figure IV.8.3, the GRC (internal) is already greater than the standardized rules-based MRC. In fact, although the two were fairly close at the beginning of the sample, by November 2008 the GRC (internal) was about 8 times large than the MRC (standardized).

The Basel Committee have proposed the IRC because they believe that internal models with specific risk recognition could induce a bank to hold relatively little risk capital against hedged portfolios. However, the above example demonstrates that the capital charges based on internal models may be substantially greater than those based on the standardized rules, for hedged portfolios as well as for unhedged portfolios. Therefore, if the proposed IRC is adopted into national regulations, then some banks may have the incentive to revert to the standardized rules for calculating MRC, if they are allowed to do so.

IV.8.3   ECONOMIC CAPITAL ALLOCATION

Innovation and progress in financial risk management have been driven by the regulators but led by the industry, and risk professionals in the industry have always questioned the methods that regulators propose for estimating regulatory risk capital. The standardized rules approach is extremely crude and imprecise, and even the internal models that most large banks use for calculating regulatory risk capital are based on questionable assumptions. For example, using a square-root scaling rule for assessing VaR of linear exposures assumes that daily returns on portfolios are normal and i.i.d., but we know this is very unlikely from observing historical samples. Another very imprecise practice is to adopt a value for the GRC multiplier that depends on only a single year of backtesting results. Moreover, it is extremely unlikely that the GRC will be exceeded over a 1-year horizon.[29] And there are many other ways in which the regulatory rules are being questioned by industry practitioners.

Financial firms are bound by fewer modelling constraints when they assess their internal risk capital, i.e. their *economic capital* (EC). There may be an external demand, from rating agencies, who use EC as one indicator of the firm's solvency, and it is not uncommon for a rating agency to place some requirements on a firm's economic capital measurement methodology. An internal constraint is that senior managers should adopt an EC measurement approach that is in line with shareholders' personal views.[30] Other than this, financial firms are free to use any methodology they wish to arrive at a figure that they choose to label the 'economic capital' associated with an activity; the only provisions being that it is acceptable to the shareholders and the rating agencies used by the firm.

IV.8.3.1   Measurement of Economic Capital

Economic capital is the name that is usually given to a particular risk metric, estimated according to internal methods. The aggregate EC for the entire firm, which is derived by accounting for the firm's diversification of activities, reflects the desirable level of capital the firm would like to hold for insurance against its risks. However, the components of EC that are allocated to individual activities need not refer to real capital at all. Real capital should add up, but EC is a risk metric and its aggregation should account for the correlation between different components.

Definitions of economic capital vary across firms; EC estimates are generally based on a quantification of extreme losses, and although the assessment methods are free from regulatory constraints, they tend to ape the Basel methodology. Thus, whereas some firms base EC on stress testing alone, others use risk metrics such as VaR or ETL at extreme quantiles, or a mixture of VaR and 'worst case' losses.

---

[29] Even when $k = 3$ the probability of exceeding the GRC over 1 year is less than 10^{-10}. See our comments in Section IV.8.2.4.

[30] For instance, if stress scenarios are used to determine economic capital then these scenarios should confirm to shareholder's beliefs.

We now use a simple, stylized framework to show that aggregate EC corresponds to a minimum level of capitalization for a firm, defining the firm's capitalization as its *net asset value*, i.e. the asset value minus the value of all the liabilities of the firm. The firm's aggregate EC can be thought of as the *current* net asset value such that there is a high probability that the asset value remains positive for one year. In other words, the EC is the current net asset value which guarantees (at some confidence level) that the firm remains technically solvent over a one year horizon.

Having defined the basic framework, we now introduce some notation. The current value of the firm's assets is known and denoted by A_0, and the annual return on assets R_A is uncertain. Hence, 1 year from now, the asset value is $A_T = A_0(1 + R_A)$ and the α quantile of the asset value distribution is $A_{T,\alpha} = A_0(1 + R_{A,\alpha})$, where $R_{A,\alpha}$ denotes the α quantile of the asset return distribution. The current liabilities, or debt is denoted D_0 and we assume there is a constant annual rate of debt financing, R_D. Hence, the value of the debt, including the financing cost, 1 year from now is $D_T = D_0(1 + R_D)$.

To find the minimum level of capitalization we ask what is the minimum level of debt, D_0^*, such that the probability that the firm is insolvent 1 year from now is very small. More precisely:

Find $D_T^* = D_0^*(1 + R_D)$ such that $P(A_T < D_T^*) = \alpha$ and where α is small.[31]

The important observation here is that, by definition,

$$D_T^* = A_{T,\alpha}.$$ (IV.8.3)

Then, since $A_{T,\alpha} = A_0(1 + R_{A,\alpha})$,

$$D_0^*(1 + R_D) = A_0(1 + R_{A,\alpha}).$$

In other words, if the current level of debt is no greater than

$$D_0^* = A_0(1 + R_{A,\alpha})(1 + R_D)^{-1},$$

then the capitalization is at least

$$A_0 - D_0^* = A_0(1 - (1 + R_{A,\alpha})(1 + R_D)^{-1}),$$ (IV.8.4)

and consequently there is a high probability, of $1 - \alpha$, that the firm remains solvent by the end of the year.

Expression (IV.8.4) defines the EC as the minimum level of capital that must be assigned to the firm to meet the solvency condition, i.e.

$$EC = A_0 - D_0^*.$$ (IV.8.5)

---

[31] Since α is the probability of default over 1 year, firms set α according to their target credit rating. For instance, for a AAA rated firm a typical value for α would be 0.03%.

We now observe that

$$E(A_T) = A_0(1 + E(R_A)) \text{ and } A_{T,\alpha} = D_T^* = D_0^*(1 + R_D).$$

Hence, with definition (IV.8.5), EC is the present value of $E(A_T) - A_{T,\alpha}$, where the expected asset value, $E(A_T)$ is discounted at rate $E(R_A)$ and the value of the debt $A_{T,\alpha}$ is discounted at rate R_D. This shows that EC, defined as the minimum requirement of real capital, or net asset value, for the firm to remain solvent over a period of time, is a risk metric. EC is the present value of the difference between the expected asset value 1 year from now and the α quantile of the future asset value distribution, $A_{T,\alpha}$. The expectation refers to the *assets* of the firm, and the α quantile $A_{T,\alpha}$ represents the *liabilities* side of the firm's balance sheet: it corresponds to the maximum level of liabilities so that the probability of insolvency in one year is no greater than $1 - \alpha$. Note that, when discounting the EC risk metric to present value terms, the assets and liabilities in the definition of EC are discounted at different rates.

Figure IV.8.4 depicts the relationship between EC, the expected asset value and the maximum value of the liabilities such that the firm remains solvent with probability $1 - \alpha$ after one year. The grey curve represents the asset value distribution 1 year from now, and the EC is the distance between the current asset value, A_0 and the maximum present value of the liabilities, D_0^*.

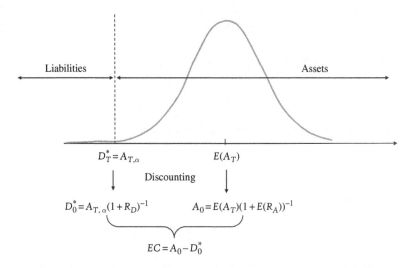

Figure IV.8.4 Relationship between economic capital and capitalization

EXAMPLE IV.8.3: MRC AND ECONOMIC CAPITAL

A firm has a current asset value of £50 million and the annual return on assets is normally distributed with mean 5%, and volatility 10%. The total liabilities of the firm are £40 million and debt is financed at a rate of 3% per annum. Find the probability that the firm becomes insolvent 1 year from now. How low should the firm's current liabilities be to ensure there is no more than 1 chance in 1000 that the firm becomes insolvent at the end of the year? Derive the EC corresponding to this level of liabilities.

SOLUTION   Since the expected asset return is 5% the expected asset value in 1 year is

$$E(A_T) = \text{£}50\text{m} \times 1.05 = \text{£}52.5\text{m}.$$

And, since the standard deviation of the asset return is 10%, the standard deviation of A_T is

$$SD(A_T) = \text{£}50\text{m} \times 0.1 = \text{£}5\text{m}.$$

The value of the liabilities in 1 year is

$$D_T = \text{£}40\text{m} \times 1.03 = \text{£}41.2\text{m}.$$

Since A_T is normally distributed, we can use Excel to look up the probability that $A_T < D_T$ using the NORMSDIST function.[32] That is, we find

$$P(X < 41.2) \text{ given that } X \sim N(52.5, 25).$$

In other words, applying the standard normal transformation, we seek

$$P\left(Z < \frac{41.2 - 52.5}{5}\right) = P(Z < -2.26) \text{ where } Z \sim N(0, 1).$$

The result is NORMSDIST$(-2.26) = 1.19\%$. This is the probability that the firm goes bankrupt by the end of the year.

Now we compute the EC in two equivalent ways. First, we use the Excel Solver to find the value of the current debt that would lead to a probability of bankruptcy of only 0.1%. The Solver settings are shown in the spreadsheet, and the result is £35,969,746. With this level of debt the firm's net asset value would be £14,030,254 and this is the minimum level of capitalization required to ensure the solvency condition, i.e. the EC.

Secondly, we calculate the EC (in non-discounted terms first of all) as the difference between the expected asset value and the 0.1% quantile of the asset value distribution. That is,

$$\text{non-discounted } EC = \text{£}52,500,000 - \text{£}37,048,838 = \text{£}15,451,162.$$

Then we discount each term using the appropriate rate, i.e. using the return on assets for the expected return and using the debt financing rate for the quantile, since the quantile is the value of the debt 1 year from now, by definition. Hence,

$$EC = \text{£}52,500,000 \times 1.05^{-1} - \text{£}37,048,838 \times 1.03^{-1} = \text{£}14,030,254$$

as before.

---

[32] In fact, in the spreadsheet we use the NORMDIST function, so we do not need to apply the standard normal transformation.

Many firms base EC measures on risk metrics such as VaR or ETL at extreme quantiles, although they are free to choose whatever metric they like (unlike regulatory capital for banks). The most important criteria for an EC measurement approach are that it:

(i) refers to an appropriate risk horizon,
(ii) is based on coherent mathematical assumptions, and
(iii) utilizes intelligent risk aggregation methods.

A minimal requirement for aggregating risks is that they are based on a common horizon. EC is often defined with reference to risks over a 1-year risk horizon and with reference to a quantile that is consistent with the target credit rating of the firm. For instance, the quantile could be 0.03% for an AA-rated firm, or 0.10% for an A-rated firm. Whilst credit and operational risks are often assessed over a 1-year horizon, market risks are typically assessed over a much shorter term. Thus, to aggregate market risks with credit and operational risks, market risk measures will need extending to a longer risk horizon.

In contrast to credit and operational risks, market risks are typically highly liquid, so it makes no sense to extend a daily VaR to a 1-year horizon using a scaling rule such as the square root of time over the full 250-day period. In adverse market circumstances most exposures can be hedged or closed out easily, typically within a period of no more than a few weeks, and the scaling horizon should refer only to the time period during which there is an exposure. For instance, a gradual stepping down of the exposure could be made, at a rate that depends on the liquidity in the market.[33]

Another important criterion is that the EC model be based on coherent mathematical assumptions. Unfortunately, many models fall far short on this criterion. EC models tend to focus on measuring the risks that are relatively easy to quantify, ignoring the risks that are difficult to measure. Furthermore, totally different mathematical assumptions and accounting frameworks are applied to measure market, credit and operational risks. Because of this it is impossible to aggregate the three main risk types in a proper mathematical framework. Even within a given risk type – and we are concerned here with market risk – the bottom-up approach to EC measurement tends to apply a single figure such as VaR at an early stage in the aggregation, forgetting about the underlying distribution of which the VaR is the quantile. Distribution aggregation is relatively straightforward, given some assumptions on the dependency between risks; but if we forget about the distributions and simply summarize the risk with a single figure such as VaR, then it is not at all straightforward to aggregate risk estimates in a mathematically coherent way.

The 'intelligent aggregation' criterion is extremely important because EC measurement is usually approached within the 'bottom-up' paradigm. That is, a detailed model of individual positions or activities is applied at the portfolio level, and then for a particular activity, and then for an entire line of business, and so on. At each stage the EC measure is progressively aggregated into EC measures for larger and larger portfolios, until we arrive at an EC measure for the entire firm. Simply summing the component risk capital estimates ignores the diversification of the firm's activities and will lead to a gross overestimate of the total EC. The aggregation of market, credit and operational EC (which can be done at any level, from a single portfolio to the entire firm) also needs to be performed in an intelligent manner, taking account of diversification effects and avoiding double-counting of risks.

---

[33] Then a scaled market VaR could be set, for example, following the liquidity adjusted VaR framework that was introduced in Section IV.7.5.4.

IV.8.3.2 Banking Applications of Economic Capital

However it is measured, EC is primarily a tool for *risk budgeting*. That is, its main purpose is to set a *limit* on the risks that can be taken by each of the risky activities in a firm, by placing an upper limit on the EC itself or by increasing the *cost of risk capital* and allowing the line managers to determine their own maximum EC. Decisions about risk budgeting are typically based on the maximization of a *risk adjusted performance measure* (RAPM). EC is commonly used as the denominator in a RAPM, and in this case the optimal allocation of risk capital to cover various risky activities can be determined by maximizing the value of this RAPM. That is what we mean by *economic capital allocation*, and we shall describe this process in more detail below.

A bank (normally) has easy access to funding; essentially, it only requires capital as a buffer against risk. The risk management structure in most major banks is *economic capital driven* because they use risk capital, as measured by EC, rather than real capital as the prime risk management tool. This is because many of the higher-risk activities within a bank – and derivatives trading in particular – do not require a significant amount of real capital for funding their activities, because they are highly leveraged. But, precisely because they are highly leveraged, there is considerable uncertainty about the returns on these activities, so they *do* need a significant amount of risk capital. Hence, in the process of risk budgeting, funding costs may be negligible, but we can still associate a cost of *risk* capital with every activity.

Rating agencies assess the credit quality of debt issues, usually with maturities of several years, and by extrapolation they assess the long term credit-worthiness of firms. The capitalization of a bank is one of the many important factors that will affect their credit rating. Banks wish to hold sufficient EC because they care about their credit rating: it gives an important signal to their customers, and their debt holders. The main customers in a retail or commercial bank are the depositors and mortgage holders, and for an investment bank the customers include the counterparties to OTC transactions. All these customers must have confidence in the solvency of the bank. Indeed, without this confidence the bank could fail.

Here is a recent example where lack of counterparty and investor confidence precipitated the bankruptcy of a UK retail bank, Northern Rock, whose prime business was mortgage lending. To finance its loans the bank borrowed short term funds in the inter-bank market and then periodically securitized its mortgages to repay its borrowings. With the onset of the banking crisis in 2008, credit spreads soared and the higher costs in the inter-bank loan market led to considerable uncertainty about the credit quality of all counterparties. Northern Rock in particular found it difficult to secure short-term funds in the inter-bank market because, like several other retail banks in the UK, it depended very heavily on securitization – issuing mortgage backed securities (MBS) and collateralized debt obligations (CDO) – rather than funding through depositors. When the MBS and CDO markets dried up Northern Rock found it could not raise funds, either on the inter-bank market (where LIBOR rates had jumped to more than 200 basis points above base rates) or by securitizing its mortgages. Since no private banks would deal with Northern Rock, they sought help from the Bank of England. This request became public knowledge, and signalled a crisis to the bank's depositors who then withdrew their funds. Due to European regulations on subsidization the Bank of England could not provide special loan facilities. Currently an administrator has been appointed by the government and Northern Rock has effectively been nationalized.

IV.8.3.3   Aggregation Risk

Since the components of risk capital that are assigned to different activities need not refer to real capital, risk capital need not be aggregated by simply summing its components. Indeed, this ignores the effects of diversifying into activities whose returns are not perfectly correlated. *Aggregation risk* is a form of risk model risk that stems from the aggregation of component risk capital into a total risk capital measure. It refers, in particular, to an inappropriate assumption about the dependencies between two or more risks when aggregating risk capital.

A very basic example of aggregation risk arises in an assessment of portfolio volatility, when we assume an incorrect value for the correlation between the returns on the constituent assets. More generally, whenever we make an inappropriate assumption about dependencies between the different components of total risk, we have aggregation risk. Aggregation risk can be huge; indeed, it is likely to be by far the most important source of model risk in any firm-wide risk assessment system. We now provide some simple but illustrative examples that support this assertion.

EXAMPLE IV.8.4: AGGREGATION OF ECONOMIC CAPITAL

A firm measures EC for market risk using a 4-week VaR at the 99.9% confidence level.[34] The firm undertakes two different activities, labelled A and B, with $25 million dollars invested in each activity. Suppose that the joint distribution of the returns to the two activities, in excess of financing costs at the risk free rate, is a bivariate normal distribution, with volatilities 25% and 40% and with correlation 0.2. Suppose also that the annual expected excess return is 5% for activity A and 10% for activity B. Estimate the EC for each activity. Now aggregate these EC estimates according to the risk model. How different would your result be if you simply added the two EC estimates?

SOLUTION   The mathematical problem is conceptually identical to the risk aggregation problems in a multivariate normal setting that we considered in Chapter IV.2. There are small differences due to the time horizon and the use of non-zero excess returns in the EC estimates, which are also based on VaR estimates at a very low quantile. But the general framework for the solution is identical to that used in previous examples.[35]

The EC estimates are obtained using the normal linear VaR formula with a mean adjustment, due to the non-zero expected excess returns on these activities. That is, if X denotes the returns over the risk horizon of the EC estimate,

$$X \sim N(\mu, \sigma^2) \Rightarrow EC = \text{VaR}_\alpha = \Phi^{-1}(1 - \alpha)\sigma - \mu. \qquad (\text{IV.8.6})$$

In our example, we have set $\alpha = 0.1\%$ and a risk horizon of 4 weeks. Hence, for activity A,

$$EC_A = 0.5 \times \left(\Phi^{-1}(0.999) \times 0.25 \times \sqrt{\frac{4}{52}} - \frac{0.05 \times 4}{52} \right) = 10.52\%,$$

---

[34] This is consistent with the 99.9% confidence level that the Basel Committee have adopted as standard, and is also consistent with a 1-year horizon if we assume that 1 month is enough time to liquidate or hedge any positions in any adverse circumstances.
[35] For instance, see Example IV.2.14 which refers to the aggregation of equity risk with forex risk in the normal linear VaR model.

and for activity B,

$$EC_B = 0.5 \times \left(\Phi^{-1}(0.999) \times 0.4 \times \sqrt{\frac{4}{52}} - \frac{0.1 \times 4}{52} \right) = 16.76\%.$$

Note that the initial multiplication by 0.5 arises because we have expressed the resulting EC as a percentage of the total sum invested in the two activities, i.e. as a percentage of the firm value.

To estimate the aggregate EC for the firm as a whole we find the weighted sum of the returns to the two activities and use the correlation between the returns to derive the overall volatility of the firm's returns. Thus in (IV.8.6) we use the values

$$\mu = 0.5 \times 0.05 + 0.5 \times 0.1 = 7.5\%$$

and

$$\sigma = \sqrt{0.5^2 \times 0.25^2 + 0.5^2 \times 0.4^2 + 2 \times 0.2 \times 0.5 \times 0.5 \times 0.25 \times 0.4} = 25.62\%.$$

Hence,

$$\text{Aggregate } EC = \Phi^{-1}(0.999) \times 0.2562 \times \sqrt{\frac{4}{52} - \frac{0.075 \times 4}{52}} = 21.38\%.$$

The results for each activity and for the firm as a whole are summarized in Table IV.8.1. Here we express the EC first as a percentage of the firm value of $50 million, and then in nominal terms.

Table IV.8.1   Aggregation of economic capital

EC_A	10.52%	$5,260,573
EC_B	16.76%	$8,378,455
$EC_A + EC_B$	27.28%	$13,639,027
Aggregate EC	21.38%	$10,689,561

The risk capital that is allocated to cover the risks of both activities is 21.38% of the total sum invested, i.e. $10,689,561. Of the £50 million invested 10.52%, i.e. $5,260,573, is required to cover the risks of activity A and 16.76%, i.e. $8,378,455, is required to cover the risks of activity B. Since the correlation is less than 1 the aggregate EC is less than the sum of the two EC estimates. Because of the diversification effect from spreading the investment equally over two different activities, we can hold considerably less risk capital than 27.28%, i.e. $13,639,027, and still cover both the risks.

Correlation is a very important determinant of the aggregate EC: the lower the correlation, the lower the aggregate EC. During stressful markets equity volatilities and correlations tend to increase. The assumed correlation has no effect on the individual EC estimates, but it has a significant effect on the aggregate EC, and it is this effect that we associate with aggregation risk. We now continue the previous example by supposing the correlation between returns of the two activities is different from 0.2, and then we compare the aggregate EC obtained using different correlations. This illustrates the extent to which our assumption about correlation affects the EC allocated to the two activities.

EXAMPLE IV.8.5: SIMPLE ILLUSTRATION OF AGGREGATION RISK

Suppose that the correlation between returns of the two activities in Example IV.8.4 is 0.6 rather than 0.2. By how much does the aggregate EC in that example underestimate the total EC that should be allocated to the two activities?

SOLUTION   By changing the value for the correlation in cell B8 of the spreadsheet to 0.6 we estimate an aggregate EC of 24.5% of the total sum invested, i.e. \$12,251,314. This is 14.6% greater than the aggregate EC estimate derived under the assumption that the returns on the activities have a correlation of 0.2.

Figure IV.8.5 illustrates how the aggregate EC estimate depends on the assumed value for the correlation, keeping the volatilities and expected excess returns of the two activities fixed. The assumed value for the correlation is shown on the horizontal axis, and the resulting aggregate EC estimate is depicted by the grey curve, expressed on the vertical axis as a proportion of the total capital invested in the two activities. The straight lines show the individual EC estimates and their sum, which do not depend on correlation.

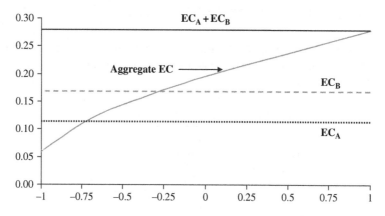

Figure IV.8.5   Effect of correlation on aggregate EC

The figure shows how important correlation is for determining the aggregate EC. The diversification that arises from investing in two activities increases as their correlation decreases, and so the aggregate EC decreases. At the two extremes we would have to allocate 27.28% of our capital to cover both risks if the returns on the two activities were perfectly correlated, compared with only 5.85% of our capital if the returns were perfectly negatively correlated.

IV.8.3.4   Risk Adjusted Performance Measures

A business may be considered as a collection of investments in risky activities, with a common set of constraints and funded from a common pool of resources. Not all risks are undesirable.

Some risks are expected to be well rewarded because they have substantial diversification properties that can reduce the overall risk of the business. Efficient EC management does not necessarily reduce all risks; its aim is to achieve the best *mix* of business activities. But what do we mean by 'best'? And how certain are we that this 'best mix' of activities will be achieved? These are the questions that we try to answer with the theory of optimal capital allocation.

A standard objective for optimal capital allocation is to achieve the best *risk adjusted performance* or the best *reward to risk ratio*. To define 'performance' or 'rewards' we require a comprehensive description of the good and the bad consequences of an allocation; typically there are many attributes to consider, such as profit, reputation, agreements with competitors and so forth, and the consequences are realized over a period of time. In this general framework the *risk* associated with an allocation refers to our uncertainty about the results, and which is the 'best' allocation depends on a criterion that associates some performance measure with each probability distribution of results. To simplify this problem, we assume that all the results of an investment are represented by the distribution of its return, and that an investor always prefers a larger return to a smaller one. That is, the return scale satisfies what economists call the *principle of non-satiation*, i.e. 'the more the better'. This still leaves a wide choice, and there is no 'best' choice of performance measure, only choices more or less well suited to a decision situation.[36]

In general a *risk adjusted performance measure* (RAPM) is a ratio of expected reward to a risk measure. It is designed to choose the best mix of risky activities under restrictive circumstances, such as when a risk free asset is available, or to judge the relative attractiveness of various risky activities.[37] But a RAPM cannot indicate how *much* should be invested in the best portfolio of risky activities; in general it can only be used to *rank* various activities. RAPMs have been designed to suit different risk types (e.g. those with symmetric, skewed, or heavy tailed return distributions) and to suit different contexts (e.g. total, systematic, or specific risks). Given the limitations of the ordinary Sharpe ratio and in view of the non-normal characteristics of many financial return distributions, many RAPMs have been designed in an *ad hoc* manner to focus only on downside risks.[38]

The RAPMs that are commonly applied in the context of optimal EC allocation, are commonly based on the risk measures VaR or ETL. The inputs to the firm's RAPM (i.e. expected returns, risks and correlations) are forecasts, and so they cannot be predicted with certainty. Past performance may give a useful indication of future performance in a stable environment, but may be unreliable if the allocation of resources is changed dramatically or if circumstances (e.g. competition, technology, regulation) evolve.

A simple example is the *return on risk adjusted capital* (RORAC), usually defined as the ratio of the expected net profit of an activity to the EC associated with that activity. When EC is defined as a percentage of the investment,

---

[36] Nevertheless, some of the performance measures described in Chapter I.6 are difficult to justify theoretically because they cannot be linked directly to a utility function, or because the implied utility function has strange characteristics.

[37] For instance, in Section I.6.5 we introduced the concept of the *Sharpe ratio*, which is a RAPM that is linked to the capital asset pricing model (CAPM) and which is relevant when there is the possibility of unlimited risk free lending and borrowing. It is defined as the ratio of the expected return in excess of the risk free rate to the standard deviation of the return distribution. Thus, when an investor uses the Sharpe ratio, his preferences are entirely determined by the knowledge of the expected return and the standard deviation of the return. However, even the standard Sharpe ratio, along with other RAPMs that are derived in the CAPM framework, does not satisfy the basic axiom of *weak stochastic dominance*. Yet no rational investor would prefer a investment that is weakly stochastically dominated by another.

[38] These include the *Sortino ratio* and the *kappa* and *omega* indices that were introduced in Section I.6.5.6.

$$\text{RORAC} = \frac{E(R)}{EC},$$ (IV.8.7)

where $E(R)$ is the expected return on an activity in excess of funding and operating costs and after tax. Alternatively, as in the example below, when EC is defined in nominal terms,

$$\text{RORAC} = \frac{E(\text{P\&L})}{EC},$$ (IV.8.8)

where $E(\text{P\&L})$ is the expected profit (or loss) after accounting for funding and operating costs and after tax.

EXAMPLE IV.8.6: CALCULATING RORAC

A firm has an asset value of £130 million with expected return of 5%, and a debt value of £98 million with cost of debt of 3%. It pays a tax on net profits of 40% and its total EC over a 1-year horizon is £15 million. Calculate the firm's RORAC.

SOLUTION   The expected profit on the firm's assets less the funding cost is $130 \times 0.05 - 98 \times 0.03 = $ £3.56 million. After paying 40% tax on this, the expected after-tax profit is £2.136 million. The RORAC is the expected after-tax profit per unit of risk:

$$\text{RORAC} = 2.136/15 = 14.24\%.$$

EXAMPLE IV.8.7: AGGREGATING RORAC

Calculate the RORAC for each of the activities defined in Example IV.8.4, and the total RORAC on the two activities. Assume that funding is available at the risk free rate and there is a 40% tax on profits. As in Example IV.8.4, assume the EC is based on a 4-week VaR at a 99.9% confidence level, and derive the aggregate RORAC as a function of the correlation between the returns on the two activities.

SOLUTION   Half of the firm's capital is invested in each activity, and the EC estimates that were derived in Example IV.8.4 were expressed as a percentage of the firm's total capitalization. So that the expected excess return that appears in the numerator of the RORAC is the excess return on the total capital, we multiply the expected excess return on each activity by 0.5. Hence, the RORAC for activity A, whose expected excess return is 5%, is

$$\text{RORAC}_A = \frac{0.05 \times 0.5 \times 0.6}{0.1052} = 14.26\%,$$

and similarly, since activity B has expected excess return 10%,

$$\text{RORAC}_B = \frac{0.10 \times 0.5 \times 0.6}{0.1676} = 17.90\%.$$

The total expected excess return after tax is

$$(0.05 \times 0.5 + 0.1 \times 0.5) \times 0.6 = 4.5\%,$$

which is independent of the correlation between the two activities. But the aggregate volatility, and hence also the aggregate EC and the aggregate RORAC, depends on the correlation, i.e. it depends on the diversification that the firm achieves with its mix of activities.

Table IV.8.2 displays the aggregate volatility, EC and RORAC for correlation values between −0.5 and +0.5. The EC increases with the volatility of the net returns which itself increases as diversification effects decrease. Hence, as correlation increases, diversification effects decrease and the aggregate EC increases. Since the numerator of the RORAC is unaffected by correlation, the RORAC increases as the aggregate EC decreases, i.e. as the correlation decreases.

Table IV.8.2   Aggregate RORAC as a function of correlation

	Correlation				
	−0.5	−0.25	0	0.25	0.5
Aggregate volatility	17.50%	20.77%	23.58%	26.10%	28.39%
Aggregate EC	14.65%	17.80%	20.21%	22.37%	24.34%
Aggregate RORAC	30.71%	25.28%	22.26%	20.12%	18.49%

Risk adjusted performance measurement began in the late 1970s when Bankers Trust, prompted by the growing role of trading and the development of new financial instruments, introduced the *risk adjusted return on capital* (RAROC) as its preferred performance metric. This metric has now been adopted by many major banks (e.g. Deutsche Bank, ING and CIBC) and insurance companies (e.g. Swiss Re) to price and rank the profitability of deals, for EC allocation and even for compensation schemes.

A general definition of RAROC is the ratio of risk adjusted expected net income after tax to EC. But, just as there are numerous ways to define EC, so there are numerous ways to define risk adjusted expected net income. Many banking activities – trading in derivatives in particular – require very little real capital for their operation. However, they do require risk capital to insure against potential losses. Hence, a simple risk adjustment to expected net income after tax is to subtract the *cost of risk capital* that is allocated to that activity. For instance, we could define[39]

$$RAROC = \frac{E(P\&L) - k \times EC}{EC},$$ (IV.8.9)

where k is some multiplier, called the cost of capital coefficient.

Equation (IV.8.9) may be applied to obtain an aggregate RAROC for the entire firm, and it may be applied to individual activities or mixes of activities in the firm. At the level of the firm, the EC term in (IV.8.9) is the aggregate EC of the firm and, as shown in Section IV.8.3.1,

---

[39] The precise definition of RAROC is determined by senior managers in consultation with the shareholders and the board. Although RAROC is the most common RAPM used in banking, numerous other performance metrics are used in the financial industry. Some of these are defined relative to assets rather than capital, for instance Matten (2000) lists return on assets (ROA), risk adjusted return on assets (RAROA) and return on risk adjusted assets (RORAA).The ROA and a related performance metric, the return on accounting capital (ROC), are not often used because they ignore the relative risk of different activities; RORAA, like RORAC, applies a risk adjustment to the denominator only; only RAROC and its related measure, RORAA, apply an risk adjustment to both the numerator and the denominator of the RAPM.

this should be greater than or equal to the minimum level of capitalization for the firm required to meet the solvency condition. When aggregate EC is equal to the minimum level of capitalization for the firm, the cost of capital coefficient k is equal to the real funding cost for the firm. For instance, we might assume that k is the risk free rate plus some margin.

In general, it is not optimal for a firm to favour or reward activities with the largest RAROC. It is the *incremental* contribution of an activity to total EC that is important. Assigning different values for k, the cost of capital coefficient, to different activities is just an artifice, to achieve the maximum global RAROC without forcing each business line to consider its incremental contribution to global risk.

When we apply the RAROC formula to an individual activity, such as a trading desk in a bank, then the EC term in (IV.8.9) need not refer to real capital at all. In this case, the cost of capital coefficient k is set by senior management. In general, the value of k for each activity should increase with the total demand for capital within the firm, relative to the total capitalization of the firm. If the total demand for real or risk capital is high relative to the capitalization of the firm, the cost of capital coefficient k would increase for all activities. But if senior managers wish to reward an activity – perhaps because it is particularly well managed or because it provides a good source of diversification – they may encourage it to grow by reducing its cost of capital. The ability to assign *different* values for the cost of capital coefficient to different activities is a management tool that can be used to alter the mix of activities in the firm over a period of time.

We also need to distinguish between funded and unfunded activities. In funded activities, such as trading securities, real capital is allocated to the activity in addition to economic (risk) capital. Then the financing cost of the real capital should be included in the expected P&L before accounting for tax. Alternatively, if funded activities are not operating as separate budgetary units, in which case no financing costs are accounted for in the expected P&L, the adjustment term in the numerator of (IV.8.9) could be set at some multiple k of the total capital, i.e. the funding capital plus the risk capital, that is allocated to the activity.

We illustrate the application of (IV.8.9) by continuing the previous example, to estimate the firm's aggregate RAROC as a function of both the correlation between the activities and the cost of capital coefficient k, which is assumed to take values between 0 and 25%. The results are shown in Table IV.8.3. Like the firm's RORAC, the total RAROC decreases as the opportunity for diversification in the firm's mix of activities decreases (i.e. as the returns correlation of the activities increases). But now, the cost of risk capital also affects the performance measure. As the cost of capital increases, the RAROC declines. When the cost of capital is high and there is low diversification in the firm's activities, the RAROC even becomes negative.

Table IV.8.3 Effect of cost of capital and correlation on aggregate RAROC

k	Correlation				
	−0.5	−0.25	0	0.25	0.5
0	30.71%	25.28%	22.26%	20.12%	18.49%
5%	25.71%	20.28%	17.26%	15.12%	13.49%
10%	20.71%	15.28%	12.26%	10.12%	8.49%
15%	15.71%	10.28%	7.26%	5.12%	3.49%
20%	10.71%	5.28%	2.26%	0.12%	−1.51%
25%	5.71%	0.28%	−2.74%	−4.88%	−6.51%

The next example distinguishes between two types of activities in an investment bank: a highly leveraged activity that requires no real capital for financing (other than operating costs), even though the notional size of the business is huge; and a funded activity that requires funding of the full notional size. In each case the expected P&L term in the numerator of RAROC is the expected revenue from the activity, less expected losses, less any funding and operating costs, and this total is adjusted to be after tax.

EXAMPLE IV.8.8: COMPARING RAROC FOR SWAPS AND BONDS

A UK bank has an interest rate swaps desk with a notional size of £100 billion. The profit margin built into each deal is 3 basis points, the annual operating costs are 1 basis point and the EC is 5 basis points. The same bank has a corporate bond desk that buys bonds and finances these transactions through loans from depositors, loans on the inter-bank market and securitization of low grade bonds. The notional size of the bond portfolio is £10 billion, the expected revenue from the portfolio over the next year is 10%, the expected losses due to defaults are 3%, the financing cost is 6%, the operating cost is 10 basis points and the EC allocated to this portfolio is 3% of the notional. Assuming that the bank pays a profits tax of 30% and charges each desk a 15% cost of risk capital, calculate the RAROC for each desk, before and after tax.

SOLUTION   For the swaps desk we have:

Profit margin	£30 million
Operating costs	£10 million
Net expected profit	£20 million
Economic capital	£50 million

So before tax,

$$\text{RAROC} = \frac{20 - 0.15 \times 50}{50} = 25\%,$$

and after tax,

$$\text{RAROC} = \frac{0.70 \times 20 - 0.15 \times 50}{50} = 13\%.$$

For the bond desk we have:

Expected revenue	£1 billion
Expected losses due to default:	£300 million
Financing costs	£600 million
Operating costs	£10 million
Net expected profit	£90 million
Economic capital	£300 million

So before tax,

$$\text{RAROC} = \frac{90 - 0.15 \times 300}{300} = 15\%,$$

and after tax,

$$\text{RAROC} = \frac{0.70 \times 90 - 0.15 \times 300}{300} = 6\%.$$

In this example the results are actually independent of the notional size of each business, because the expected profits, losses, costs and tax are all defined as proportional to size. The reason why we have set up this example to include a figure for the notional size of each business is that we shall be using this example in the next subsection to illustrate how the bank may prefer to alter the relative size of each business, to optimize the aggregate RAROC.

IV.8.3.5   Optimal Allocation of Economic Capital

Since the portfolio theory of Markowitz (1959) modern finance theory has attempted to explain the balance between risks and returns in securities markets. In Chapter I.6 we explained how this balance affects the optimal allocation of scarce resources to risky investments, taking account of portfolio diversification effects through the correlation of the returns on different investments. There we adopted the perspective of a global asset manager who evaluates the performance of different portfolios of a set of risky assets, and hence decides how to allocate his capital in an optimal manner, according to his utility function. But, as noted in Section I.6.1, another main application of optimal capital allocation theory is to the allocation of EC in a financial institution. This is the perspective that we adopt in the present section.

In fund management investors are free to select assets according to their expected returns, volatilities and correlations. A risk free asset is usually available, at least for investment. An optimal investment strategy can therefore be designed in three steps:[40]

1. Construct the opportunity set of all investment opportunities and determine its efficient frontier in risk–return space.
2. Determine the tangency portfolio which yields the maximum Sharpe ratio, or by maximizing another RAPM that is consistent with the CAPM.
3. Construct the optimal portfolio as the combination of the tangency portfolio and the risk free asset that maximizes expected utility, or the certain equivalent of the portfolio.

An optimal EC allocation strategy follows a similar design, since it is based on a very similar mathematical framework. In business, shareholders switch their investments to maximize some RAPM, such as RAROC. Hence, senior managers should adopt a similar objective. A critical element in the consistent application of a RAPM is that one should compare bundles of business units, or activity mixtures, to investigate the ideal mix for the firm. Thus, the optimum notional capital allocation to a business unit depends on its correlation with other business units as well as on its own profile of risk and return. This is a problem equivalent to the selection of an optimal portfolio of securities, but with additional constraints. The three steps to follow in an optimal capital allocation strategy are as follows:

1. Assess the EC of all activities, for instance within each line of business.
2. Aggregate the EC across activities, taking into account their dependencies.

---

[40] See Section I.6.3 for further details.

3. Change the capital allocated to different activities, or the cost of risk capital charged to the activity, to maximize the RAPM, taking account of any risk capital constraints.

In the last step, after solving the allocation problem for the complete business, subject to a constraint on the total EC, one can either budget EC or set a cost for EC for each business unit. In the latter case the internal costs for risk capital will depend on correlations between businesses.

EXAMPLE IV.8.9: MAXIMIZING RAROC FOR OPTIMAL CAPITAL ALLOCATION

Suppose a firm measures EC for market risk using a 4-week VaR at the 99.9% confidence level, and that the firm has $1 billion to invest in two diversified activities, A and B. Assume the joint distribution of the two returns in excess of the risk free rate is a bivariate normal distribution, having volatilities 30% and 50% and correlation −0.25. The expected excess annual return is 5% for activity A and 12% for activity B and there is no tax. The firm charges a cost of capital of 10% to each activity, and the overall cost of economic capital is 6%. First, assuming that equal amounts are invested in each activity, calculate the RAROC for each activity and the aggregate RAROC. Now find the optimal allocations to the two activities that will maximize the aggregate RAROC.

SOLUTION   When exactly half the capital is invested in each activity we have, using (IV.8.6) with $\alpha = 0.1\%$ and a risk horizon of 4 weeks,

$$EC_A = 0.5 \times \left(\Phi^{-1}(0.999) \times 0.30 \times \sqrt{\frac{4}{52}} - \frac{0.05 \times 4}{52} \right) = 12.66\%.$$

Hence, for activity A,

$$RAROC_A = \frac{0.05 \times 0.5 - 0.1 \times 0.1266}{0.1266} = 9.74\%.$$

And, for activity B,

$$EC_B = 0.5 \times \left(\Phi^{-1}(0.999) \times 0.50 \times \sqrt{\frac{4}{52}} - \frac{0.12 \times 4}{52} \right) = 20.97\%,$$

and

$$RAROC_B = \frac{0.12 \times 0.5 - 0.1 \times 0.2097}{0.2097} = 18.62\%.$$

The multiplication by 0.5 arises because we have expressed the result as a percentage of the total sum invested in the two activities.

To estimate the aggregate EC we use (IV.8.6) with the values

$$\mu = 0.5 \times 0.05 + 0.5 \times 0.12 = 8.5\%$$

and

$$\sigma = \sqrt{0.5^2 \times 0.3^2 + 0.5^2 \times 0.5^2 + 2 \times 0.2 \times 0.5 \times 0.5 \times 0.3 \times 0.5} = 25.74\%.$$

Hence,

$$\text{Aggregate } EC = \Phi^{-1}(0.999) \times 0.2574 \times \sqrt{\frac{4}{52} - \frac{0.085 \times 4}{52}} = 21.41\%$$

and

$$\text{Aggregate } RAROC = \frac{0.085 - 0.06 \times 0.2141}{0.2141} = 33.71\%.$$

In nominal terms, we have an aggregate risk capital of 21.41% of $1 billion, i.e. $214,065,036. The component risks are 12.66% of $1 billion, i.e. $126,638,358, for activity A and 20.97% of $1 billion, i.e. $209,653,674, for activity B.

We now ask whether we could change the proportions invested in each activity to increase the aggregate RAROC. The optimization problem is set up in the spreadsheet, using the Solver, and we find that we could increase the aggregate RAROC to 34.33% if we invested $572,872,462 in activity A and $427,127,538 in activity B, instead of investing of $0.5 billion in each activity. With this optimal mix of activities we would increase the allocation of EC for activity A to $145,095,256 and decrease the EC allocation to activity B to $179,097,715. We would also have a lower aggregated EC: it is reduced from $214,065,036 to $198,108,377.

The final example illustrates how to implement a constraint on the optimal allocation of EC where the aggregate EC must be equal to a bank's minimum regulatory capital.

EXAMPLE IV.8.10: CONSTRAINED ECONOMIC CAPITAL ALLOCATION

Consider again the interest rate swaps and corporate bond desks of a UK bank in Example IV.8.8. Calculate the:

  (i) aggregate EC when the two desks have a returns correlation of 0.5, assuming that equal amounts are invested in each activity;
  (ii) aggregate RAROC when the bank pays a 6% cost for financing, and the cost of overall EC is also 6%;
  (iii) optimal EC allocation to the two desks when the aggregate EC is equal to minimum regulatory capital covering these activities, and this is £80 billion.

SOLUTION   Using our results from Example IV.8.8, on the swaps desk we have an expected net return after tax of £14 million, with an EC of £50 million, and on the corporate bond desk an expected net return after tax of £63 million, with an EC of £300 million.

(i) The aggregate EC is calculated using the formula

$$EC = \sqrt{EC_1^2 + EC_2^2 + 2\varrho EC_1 EC_2}, \tag{IV.8.10}$$

where EC_1 and EC_2 are the EC of each desk and ϱ is the returns correlation. Using the results from Example IV.8.8, we have

$$EC = \sqrt{50^2 + 300^2 + 50 \times 300} = \pounds 327,871,926.$$

(ii) The aggregate RAROC is thus

$$\text{RAROC} = \frac{77,000,000 - 0.06 \times 327,871,926}{327,871,926} = 17.48\%$$

(iii) The above results may be seen in the spreadsheet by changing cell C3 to 100 and cell G3 to 10. The constrained optimum aggregate RAROC is found by changing the notional size of each desk to maximize the RAROC, subject to the constraint that the aggregate EC is £80 million. The EC of the bond desk alone is £300 million, which far exceeds the minimum risk capital required. Hence a constrained optimization of RAROC will reduce the size of the corporate bond trading desk quite substantially. Using the Solver, just as we did in the previous example, but now adding the EC constraint, we find that we should increase the notional on the swaps desk to £128,102,523,043 and decrease the notional on the corporate bond desk from £10 billion to only £854,016,820. The new EC allocations are now £64,051,262 for the swaps desk and just £25,620,505 for the bond desk and, taking account of the correlation between the two activities, the aggregate EC is exactly £80 million. With these new allocations, the overall RAROC of the two desks would be increased to 23.14% and the bank would be holding no more than the minimum risk capital required by the regulators.

In the above examples the firm implements the optimum RAROC by changing the allocation of EC to each activity. Alternatively, a firm could adjust the cost of capital rather than change the EC allocation and let the line managers determine their own EC subject to a lower limit on the RAROC of their business. This allows more freedom for the internal risk management in each activity.

Optimal capital allocation may recommend a very significant change in EC allocations, especially when subject to minimum regulatory capital constraints. But it is difficult to alter the business mix rapidly. Instead, hedging could be considered as an intermediate step. We also need to understand how the performance of an activity and its correlation with others will change with a significant redistribution of the sizes of various activities. In reality we may only know the marginal change in profitability for a relatively small change in size, and have very little idea about the effect of scale on correlations. For all these reasons the determination of an optimal EC allocation in practice is an iterative process giving, at each step, only a direction for improvement rather than leading in one step to a realistic optimum.

IV.8.4   SUMMARY AND CONCLUSIONS

This chapter has described how regulators, senior managers and the board of directors may use VaR, ETL and/or stress scenarios to estimate the minimum level of a firm's capitalization that ensures a high probability of solvency over a fixed time horizon. Regulators have required a minimum level of capitalization for banks to cover market risks since the 1990s. Consequently, developments in the assessment of risk capital have been driven by banking regulators, who themselves have been led by the Basel Committee. However, more than a decade before minimum regulatory risk capital requirements were enforced, the banking system had already adopted a framework for risk management that is based on the optimization of an enterprise-wide *risk adjusted performance metric*. Nowadays virtually all the major banks have risk management systems that are driven by an allocation of internal risk capital – called *economic capital* – which is based on an optimization of risk adjusted performance. In this way, over a period of time, senior managers and the board of directors may alter the preferred mix of business units within the bank.

The minimum requirements for market risk capital that are prescribed by regulators are based on a *minimum solvency ratio*, i.e. a minimum value for the Cooke ratio of eligible capital to a minimum risk capital requirement. There are strict rules for the methods used to assess the minimum risk capital requirement. For capital covering market risks a bank can either adopt the *standardized rules* approach, which prescribes rather onerous capital requirements, at least for hedged positions, or an *internal models* approach where minimum market risk capital is usually assessed using a 1% 10-day VaR measure, aggregated over all the lines of business in the bank. But risk capital does not add up like real capital. Indeed, the whole point is to account for the less-than-perfect correlation between activities so that the aggregate risk capital is less than the sum of the components.

In addition to a *general risk* capital charge, the Basel Committee has recently recommended that banks which use internal models that have specific risk recognition, so that they are exempt from the *specific risk* charges in the standardized rules, should increase their risk capital charge by adding an *incremental risk charge* to cover equity and credit spread risk. At the time of writing the incremental risk charge has not yet been adopted in national regulations: it is a recent innovation of the Basel Committee, suggested in response to the credit crisis that began in 2007, more than a year after the new Basel Accord. However, a capital charge that is calculated using internal models is likely to favour banks that are better able to net their exposures. Hence the current rules for internal models and the proposed incremental risk charge may favour the large banks that are dominating the industry. In view of the greater systemic risk posed by failures of very large banks, a better alternative may be to require capital charges to be directly proportional to the bank's size.

A financial institution is free to use any method it wishes for the assessment of EC, provided it is acceptable to the shareholders and, if the firm's issues have credit ratings, the rating agencies. The aggregate EC for the entire firm reflects the desirable level of capital the firm would like to hold for insurance against its risks. It is important for the firm to hold a level of EC that is sufficient to justify its credit rating. And achieving a satisfactory level of total capitalization is particularly important for banks, since inadequate capitalization can adversely affect the confidence of both investors and counterparties, as was the case during the banking crisis in October 2008.

When EC is allocated to different activities within the firm, it need not refer to real capital at all; it merely corresponds to a risk metric. Many activities such as derivatives trading do not require much real capital for funding their activities, because they are very highly leveraged, but they do require a capital buffer to cover their risks. Hence *risk budgeting* is a process of economic capital allocation rather than the allocation of real capital to fund different activities.

Shareholders switch their investments to maximize a risk adjusted performance measure, so senior managers should do likewise. The most prevalent risk adjusted performance measure that is used in financial risk management today is the *risk adjusted return on capital* (RAROC). This is the ratio of risk adjusted expected net income after tax to EC. Since EC appears in the denominator of RAROC, the maximization of aggregate RAROC (or a similar risk adjusted performance metric) for the entire firm or for various mixes of business activities allows managers to set limits on the EC, and therefore also limit the risks that can be taken at every level of the firm. In this way, senior managers and the board of directors use EC allocation to influence the mix of business activities undertaken by the firm.

But it is difficult to forecast EC, since it typically depends on the volatilities and correlations of business activities over a long time horizon. It is also difficult to forecast future net income, which appears in the numerator of the risk adjusted performance metric. Moreover, when the aggregate risk adjusted performance metric for a bank is maximized subject to the constraint that it is greater than or equal to the bank's minimum regulatory capital, the preferred mix of business activities may require a very significant change in the size of some operations. Thus, economic capital allocation in practice is a process that takes time, in which only gradual steps towards improving risk adjusted performance should be taken at any point.

References

Alexander, C. and Barbosa, A. (2007) Effectiveness of minimum variance hedging. *Journal of Portfolio Management* 33, 46–59.

Alexander, C. and Sheedy, E. (2008) Developing a stress testing framework based on market risk models. *Journal of Banking and Finance* 32(10), 2220–2236.

Alexander, C., Lazar, E. and Stanescu, S. (2008) Analytic moments for conditional and aggregated GARCH variances and returns. ICMA Discussion Papers in Finance DP2008–08.

Alexander, C., Lazar, E. and Stanescu, S. (2009) Analytic approximations to VaR in a GARCH framework. ICMA Discussion Papers in Finance.

Angelidis, T., Benos, A. and Degiannakis, S. (2004) The use of GARCH models in VaR estimation. *Statistical Methodology* 1, 105–128.

Aragones, J., Blanco, C. and Dowd, K. (2001) Incorporating stress tests into market risk modeling. *Derivatives Quarterly* 7(3), 44–49.

Artzner, P., Delbaen, F., Eber, J. and Heath, D. (1999) Coherent measures of risk. *Mathematical Finance* 9, 203–228.

Bangia, A., Diebold, F.X., Schuermann, T. and Stroughair, J.D. (2002) Modeling liquidity risk, with implications for traditional market risk measurement and management. In S. Figlewski and R.M. Levich (eds), *Risk Management: The State of the Art*. Kluwer Academic, Boston.

Barone-Adesi, G., Bourgoin, F. and Giannopoulos, K. (1998) Don't look back. *Risk* 11, 100–103.

Barone-Adesi, G., Giannopoulos, K. and Vosper, L. (1999) VaR without correlations for nonlinear portfolios. *Journal of Futures Markets* 19, 583–602.

Basel Committee on Banking Supervision (1996) Amendment to the capital accord to incorporate market risks. Available from http://www.bis.org (accessed August 2008).

Basel Committee on Banking Supervision (2005) Amendment to the capital accord to incorporate market risks (Updated). Available from http://www.bis.org (accessed August 2008).

Basel Committee on Banking Supervision (2006) International convergence of capital measurement and capital standards: A revised framework (Comprehensive version). Available from http://www.bis.org (accessed August 2008).

Basel Committee on Banking Supervision (2008) Guidelines for computing capital for incremental risk in the trading book. Available from http://www.bis.org (accessed August 2008).

Berkowitz, J. (1999) A coherent framework for stress-testing. *Journal of Risk* 2(2), 1–11.

Berkowitz, J. and O'Brien, J. (2002) How accurate are value-at-risk models at commercial banks? *Journal of Finance* 57, 1093–1111.

Berkowitz, J., Christoffersen, P. and Pelletier, D. (2006) Evaluating VaR models with desk-level data. Working paper, McGill University.

Borio, C. (2000) Market liquidity and stress: selected issues and policy implications. *BIS Quarterly Review*, 38–51.

Boudoukh, J., Richardson, M. and Whitelaw, R. (1998) The best of both worlds. *Risk* 11(5), 64–67.

Butler, C. (1999) *Mastering Value at Risk: A Step-by-Step Guide to Understanding and Applying VaR*. Financial Times Pitman, London.

Butler, J.S. and Schachter, B. (1998) Estimating VaR with a precision measure by combining kernel estimation with historical simulation. *Review of Derivatives Research* 1, 371–390.

Chen, S. and Tang, C. (2005) Nonparametric inference of value-at-risk for dependent financial returns. *Journal of Financial Econometrics* 3, 227–255.

Christoffersen, P. (1998) Evaluating interval forecasts. *International Economic Review* 39, 841–862.

Christoffersen, P. (2003) *Elements of Financial Risk Management*. Academic Press, Boston.

Committee on the Global Financial System (2005) Stress testing at major financial institutions: survey results and practice. CGFS Publications No. 24. Available from http://www.bis.org/publ/cgfs24.htm (accessed August 2008).

Connor, G. (2000) Robust confidence intervals for the bias test of risk forecasts. Technical report, MSCI Barra.

Cornish, E.A. and Fisher, R.A. (1937) Moments and cumulants in the specification of distributions. *Review of the International Statistical Institute* 5, 307–320.

Danielsson, J. (2007) *The Value-at-Risk Reference: Key Issues in the Implementation of Market Risk*. Risk Publications, London.

Derivatives Policy Group (1995) Framework for voluntary oversight: the OTC derivatives activities of securities firm affiliates to promote confidence and stability in financial markets. http://riskinstitute.ch/137790.htm (accessed August 2008).

Dowd, K. (2005) *Measuring Market Risk*, 2nd edition. John Wiley & Sons, Ltd, Chichester.

Duffie, D. and Pan, J. (1997) An overview of value at risk. *Journal of Derivatives*, Spring, 7–49. Reprinted (2001) in G. Constantinides and A.G. Malliaris (eds), *Options Markets*. Edward Elgar, Cheltenham.

Garman, M. (1996) Improving on VaR. *Risk*, 9(5), 61–63

Gencay, R. and Selcuk, F. (2004) Extreme value theory and VaR: Relative performance in emerging markets. *International Journal of Forecasting* 20, 287–303.

Giot, P. and Laurent, S. (2003) Value-at-risk for long and short trading positions. *Journal of Applied Econometrics* 18, 641–664.

Glasserman, P. (2004) *Monte Carlo Methods in Financial Engineering*. Springer-Verlag, New York.

Glasserman, P., Heidelberger, P. and Shahabuddin, P. (2000) Variance reduction techniques for estimating value-at-risk. *Management Science* 46, 1349–1364.

Holton, G. (2003) *Value-at-Risk: Theory and Practice*. Academic Press, Amsterdam.

Huisman, R., Koedijk, K.G. and Pownall, R.A.J. (1998) VaR-x: Fat tails in financial risk management. *Journal of Risk* 1(1), 47–61.

Hull, J. and White, A. (1998) Incorporating volatility updating into the historical simulation method for value-at-risk. *Journal of Risk* 1(1), 5–19.

Johnson, N.L. (1954) Systems of frequency curves derived from the first law of Laplace. *Trabajos de Estadística* 5, 283–291.

Jorion, P. (2006) *Value-at-Risk*, 3rd edition. McGraw-Hill, New York.

Kendall, M.G. (1940) Note on the distribution of quantiles for large samples. *Supplement to the Journal of the Royal Statistical Society* 7(1), 83–85.

Kupiec, P. (1995) Techniques for verifying the accuracy of risk measurement models. *Journal of Derivatives* 2, 173–184.

Longin, F. (2000) From value at risk to stress testing: The extreme value approach. *Journal of Banking and Finance* 24, 1097–1130.

Longin, F. (2005) The choice of the distribution of asset returns: How extreme value theory can help. *Journal of Banking and Finance* 29, 1017–1035.

Markowitz, H. (1959) *Portfolio Selection*. John Wiley & Sons, Inc., New York.

Matten, C. (2000) *Managing Bank Capital: Capital Allocation and Performance Measurement*, 2nd edition. John Wiley & Sons, Ltd, Chichester.

McNeil, A. and R. Frey (2000) Estimation of tail-related risk measures for heteroscedastic financial time series: An extreme value approach. *Journal of Empirical Finance* 7, 271–300.

McNeil, A., Frey, R. and Embrechts, P. (2005) *Quantitative Risk Management*. Princeton University Press, Princeton, NJ.

Mina, J. and A. Ulmer (1999) Delta-gamma four ways. RiskMetrics Working Paper. http://www.riskmetrics.com/publications/working_papers.html (accessed August 2008).

Mittnik, S. and Paolella, M. (2000) Conditional density and value-at-risk prediction of Asian currency exchange rates. *Journal of Forecasting* 19, 313–333.

Patton, A. (2008) Copula-based models for financial time series. In T.G. Andersen, R.A. Davis, J.-P. Kreiss and T. Mikosch (eds), *Handbook of Financial Time Series*. Springer-Verlag, Berlin.

Perignon, C. and Smith, D. (2006) The level and quality of value-at-risk disclosure by commercial banks. Working paper, Simon Fraser University, Vancouver.

Pritsker, M. (2006) The hidden dangers of historical simulation. *Journal of Banking and Finance* 30, 561–582.

Sharpe, W.F. (1994) The Sharpe ratio. *Journal of Portfolio Management* 21, 49–59.

Sheather, S. and Marron, J.S. (1990) Kernel quantile estimators. *Journal of the American Statistical Association* 85, 410–416.

Silverman, B.W. (1986) *Density Estimation for Statistics and Data Analysis*. Chapman & Hall, London.

So, M. and Yu, P. (2006) Empirical analysis of GARCH models in value at risk estimation. *International Financial Markets, Institutions & Money* 16, 180–197.

Spetzler, C. and Staël von Holstein, C.-A. (1977) Probability encoding in decision analysis. In R. Howard and J.E. Matheson (eds), *Readings in Decision Analysis*, 2nd edition. Stanford Research Institute, Menlo Park, CA.

Studer, G. and Lüthi, H.-J. (1997) Quadratic maximum loss for risk measurement of portfolios. Risklab report. http://citeseerx.ist.psu.edu/viewdoc/summary?doi=10.1.1.17.2585 (accessed August 2008).

Szegö, G. (ed.) (2004) *Risk Measures for the 21st Century*. John Wiley & Sons, Ltd, Chichester.

Tuenter, H. (2001) An algorithm to determine the parameters of SU curves in the Johnson system of probability distributions by moment matching. *Journal of Statistical Computation and Simulation* 70(4), 325–347.

Venter, J. and de Jongh, P. (2002) Risk estimation using the normal inverse Gaussian distribution. *Journal of Risk* 4(2), 1–24.

Index